www.wadsworth.com

www.wadsworth.com is the World Wide Web site for Thomson Wadsworth and is your direct source to dozens of online resources.

At *www.wadsworth.com* you can find out about supplements, demonstration software, and student resources. You can also send e-mail to many of our authors and preview new publications and exciting new technologies.

www.wadsworth.com
Changing the way the world learns®

Psychopathology

A Competency-Based Treatment Model for Social Workers

SUSAN W. GRAY
Barry University,
Ellen Whiteside McDonnell School of Social Work

with

MARILYN R. ZIDE
Barry University,
Ellen Whiteside McDonnell School of Social Work

THOMSON

BROOKS/COLE

Australia • Canada • Mexico • Singapore • Spain
United Kingdom • United States

Psychopathology: A Competency-Based Treatment Model for Social Workers, First Edition
Susan W. Gray with Marilyn R. Zide

Editor: Lisa Gebo
Assistant Editor: Alma Dea Michelena
Editorial Assistant: Sheila Walsh
Technology Project Manager: Barry Connolly
Marketing Manager: Caroline Concilla
Marketing Assistant: Rebecca Weisman
Advertising Project Manager: Tami Strang
Signing Representative: Miguel Ortiz
Project Manager, Editorial Production: Lori Johnson
Art Director: Vernon Boes

Print Buyer: Judy Inouye
Permissions Editor: Stephanie Lee
Production Service: Matrix Productions
Copy Editor: Janet Tilden
Illustrator: Interactive Composition Corporation
Cover Designer: Denise Davidson, Simple Design
Cover Image: © Rubberball Productions
Cover Printer: Transcontinental Printing/Louiseville
Compositor: Interactive Composition Corporation
Printer: Transcontinental Printing/Louiseville

Printed in Canada
1 2 3 4 5 6 7 09 08 07 06 05

For more information about our products, contact us at:
Thomson Learning Academic Resource Center
1-800-423-0563
For permission to use material from this text or product, submit a request online at **http://www.thomsonrights.com.**
Any additional questions about permissions can be submitted by e-mail to **thomsonrights@thomson.com.**

Library of Congress Control Number: 2005922092

ISBN 0-534-54210-7

Thomson Higher Education
10 Davis Drive
Belmont, CA 94002-3098
USA

Asia (including India)
Thomson Learning
5 Shenton Way
#01-01 UIC Building
Singapore 068808

Australia/New Zealand
Thomson Learning Australia
102 Dodds Street
Southbank, Victoria 3006
Australia

Canada
Thomson Nelson
1120 Birchmount Road
Toronto, Ontario M1K 5G4
Canada

UK/Europe/Middle East/Africa
Thomson Learning
High Holborn House
50/51 Bedford Row
London WC1R 4LR
United Kingdom

Latin America
Thomson Learning
Seneca, 53
Colonia Polanco
11560 Mexico
D.F. Mexico

Spain (including Portugal)
Thomson Paraninfo
Calle Magallanes, 25
28015 Madrid, Spain

To my beloved husband,
Kenneth E. Gray, JD,
. . . once again.

Foreword

Social workers struggle daily to help people suffering from schizophrenia, depression and other mood difficulties, cognitive disorders primarily associated with aging, anxieties and phobias, eating difficulties, and various addictions. People not only have to manage these conditions, but also have to deal with the social constructions and stigma associated with them. Mental illness and psychopathology conjure up a sense of hopelessness and pessimism. People are set apart from others. Their problems often feel intractable because they can be chronic and persistent, or sometimes, acute and unexpected. Family, community, and organizational supports cushion the associated pain and suffering. However, when supports and resources are nonexistent or tenuous, people with these life conditions are at risk of social, emotional, and cognitive deterioration.

Psychopathology: A Competency-Based Treatment Model for Social Workers provides knowledge about diagnostic entities as well as guidelines for professional interventions. Each diagnostic category is explained and illustrated in an informative and precise manner. This provides social workers with a rich resource. To Professor Gray's credit, she does not settle for a DSM-IV book. She goes much further by integrating "doing" with "knowing." While each chapter contains information about a diagnostic category, it also includes a section on competency-based interventions in which she reviews and illustrates relevant practice approaches. The integration of professional knowledge and professional action represents a unique contribution to the literature and distinguishes this book from other texts dealing with mental disorders. The book provides social workers with methods to help clients to live with mental illness and more effectively deal with the associated life stressors.

Professor Gray views mental illness through theoretical lenses that attempt to move away from treating a "disease" to capturing people's unique experiences with mental illness. Her message is clear: a person is much more than her or his diagnosis. She focuses on people's strengths and uniqueness and their struggles with mental illness. Her message is one of hope and optimism. Her work will impress you. Professor Gray deserves our praise and appreciation.

Alex Gitterman
Professor of Social Work
University of Connecticut School of Social Work

Contents

Chapter 2

Counseling and Social Work Theories and Methods Supporting Competency-Based Practice   34

Chapter 4

Schizophrenia and Other Psychotic Disorders   119

Chapter 5

Mood Disorders   153

Chapter 6

Anxiety Disorders   179

Chapter 9

Eating Disorders   267

In Memoriam

This book is dedicated to the memory of Marilyn R. Zide, Ph.D., Associate Professor of Social Work, co-author of our first book, *Psychopathology: A Competency-Based Assessment Model for Social Workers*, who died July 3, 2003. She was a dedicated teacher, untiring scholar, and a professor of social work besides being a great wife, mother, and grandmother. Most importantly, she was also my colleague and friend of twenty years. A graduate of Barry University's undergraduate, graduate, and doctoral programs, she was proud to have been a part of the faculty where she joined the Ellen Whiteside School of Social Work in 1994.

Before starting her career in education, Marilyn worked in Miami-Dade and Broward counties in social work, including the Henderson Mental Health Clinic in Broward where she supervised the youth clinic. Marilyn's vita reflects an extensive list of publications and presentations on local, state, national, and international levels. Before her death, she had published or presented almost 90 papers. She had a wide range of professional interests, and her scholarly accomplishments were impressive.

Marilyn was also active in our professional community. She was a visible leader through her membership in the National Association of Social Workers and the Association for the Advancement of Social Work with Groups. Marilyn had also become involved with the Council on Social Work Education as a well-received Annual Program Meeting participant.

Throughout her academic career, Marilyn was committed to helping others and gained a reputation of excellence. She was the ideal colleague, with a penchant for hard work, humor, and superb skill. Marilyn would come up with interesting ideas, write, organize, and present at professional conferences and workshops with excellent competence. Her energy was exceeded only by her pursuit of knowledge, wisdom, and integrity. She was known among her colleagues as a particularly able, dedicated, and loved instructor—one of those teachers whom students hold in high acclaim.

Knowing how closely we worked together, many have shared with me their experiences and memories of Marilyn. Those who had been fortunate to be in her classroom comment on her remarkable teaching skills, applauding Marilyn's well-organized approach to the material and her sincere interest in their progress. She loved teaching, and her favorite course was psychopathology. One student characterized Marilyn as someone who "always made you feel special." Added another, "She worked really hard to make sure you understood. You know, one of those teachers who goes out of her way for you." They saw Marilyn not only as a source of information but also as a role model for the profession. Despite undergoing a rigorous course of treatment for cancer in the last year of her life, she rarely missed a class. Marilyn never complained and seemed more concerned about others. Teaching and her commitment to students always came first.

It's hard to think about how you want to be remembered, but one's greatest epitaph, I believe, is that he or she has touched the life of another. Marilyn touched the lives of so many. It was not unusual to pass by her office and find a student sitting with her. It was easy to notice her compassion for their anxiety, the astuteness of her questions, her respect and thoughtful feedback about their work. Those who have been fortunate to have Marilyn as their teacher came out of her classes feeling extremely knowledgeable about our profession and well prepared for practice. Having given so much of herself, I'm confident a little part of her is then carried forward. The world is a better place for her having been here. She will be greatly missed.

I shared this dedication with Marilyn's husband, Nelson R. Zide, MD, who wanted readers to know that Marilyn's passion was to be a part of this book but "she just gave out too soon." The genesis of this book is the intellectual product of two people: my dear colleague Marilyn and myself.

Susan W. Gray, Ph.D., Ed.D.
Professor of Social Work
Barry University

About the Author

Susan W. Gray has been a member of the faculty at Barry University, Ellen Whiteside McDonnell School of Social Work since 1980. She earned her baccalaureate from Caldwell College for Women, her master's degree from Rutgers–the State University, a doctorate in education from Nova Southeastern University, and a doctorate in social work from Barry University. She is a full professor, teaching graduate courses in the Human Behavior in the Social Environment and the Methods of Direct Practice sequences. She also teaches an elective course on Crisis Intervention and a course in social work education in the university's doctoral program. Dr. Gray is a licensed clinical social worker and brings to Barry a diverse clinical practice background. Before joining the faculty she worked for many years as a clinical social worker and supervisor in the fields of health and mental health. Dr. Gray is active in the professional community, and her service includes work with a community mental health center, hospice, nursing association, senior citizens foundation, marine institute, the Florida Keys Area Health Education Center, and the American Cancer Society. Her publications reflect her wide interests, including clinical supervision, professional regulation and licensure, rural practice, bereavement groups, intergenerational family assessment tools, the brief solution-focused model of practice, methods of classroom teaching, and aspects of cultural diversity. Recognized as an engaging and informative speaker, she has presented numerous papers and workshops on the local, state, national, and international levels.

Preface

Social workers comprise the largest group of direct service mental health professionals in the United States (Miller, 2002; Newhill & Korr, 2004; O'Neill, 1999). Historically, social work was carried out in "traditional settings" such as outpatient community mental health centers, nonprofit counseling agencies, state or local governmental organizations, and private hospitals and clinics. Practice included a variety of helping venues consisting of casework, group work, group therapy, individual and/or family counseling, and community organization services (Hepworth, Rooney, & Larsen, 2002; Sheafor & Horejsi, 2003; Okun, 2002). In recent years, the profession has become more diversified and the scope of practice has expanded. Today's social workers are employed in every area of mental health practice, including rehabilitation centers, private practice, the court system, hospitals, schools, inpatient psychiatric facilities, and advocacy programs providing linkages to services, monitoring, and education (Bentley, 2002; Maguire, 2002).

Social work has a century-old tradition of being at the forefront of consumer advocacy, and this role is as important today as it ever has been. Today's practitioners are challenged to reconfigure the helping relationship; explore client strengths, coping skills, and resilience; and discover untapped "potentials" (Gitterman, 2001; Greene, 2002; Saleebey, 2002; Walsh, 2000). Moreover, our clients have a right to receive services in a manner consistent with prevailing best practices and in accordance with ethical standards (NASW, 1996).

The advent of managed care during the early 1980s brought about profound changes in social work practice. Many mental health care providers believe managed care has become overly reliant on providing only low-cost and quick results regardless of client concerns or needs. Treatment issues connected to efficiency and cost-containment are viewed with mixed emotions, and the effects and implications reverberate throughout the practice nexus. Economic concerns and the exigencies of managed care raise new clinical dilemmas, intensify diversity-related challenges, and influence core practice activities including how mental health problems are articulated, interventions are selected, and services are provided.

As David Austin so eloquently stated,

The most dramatic changes in the institutional structure for human services for the immediate future are occurring in the provision of health care and mental health care services through 'managed care' systems—that is, through the commercialization of health and mental health services. Nonprofit organizations are competing with 'for-profit' organizations for participation in health care/mental health care networks that may be put together by insurance companies, mega health care/hospital corporations like Columbia HCA, large employers, existing nonprofit health care providers, or by individual entrepreneurial professionals, including social workers (1997, p. 400).

This book is about what social workers actually do to help clients solve problems and enhance social functioning. The intent is to help the social work practitioner respond to the ever-increasing demands found in clinical social work practice in the field of mental health. Social workers have been exposed to a wide variety of practice theories found in the professional literature and taught in social work educational programs. This text is meant to support the historical traditions of social work practice while meeting the current challenges facing our profession.

Over the past decade, mental disorders have increasingly been attributed to diseases in the brain (Miller, 2002). However, this perspective does not explain why some persons respond to treatment better than others do. This book asserts that the etiology, structure, and course of one's struggle with a mental disorder affect treatment outcomes. Each person's experience with mental illness is unique and includes the multiple interactions of biological, psychological, social, and cultural dimensions along with the effects of a diagnosis. This perspective supports the conceptualization of competency-based treatment that provides an integrated framework for working with individuals and their families struggling with mental illness. The competency-based approach moves away from treating "disease" and toward individualizing a person's encounter with mental illness. This book breaks new ground as one of the first new-generation psychopathology textbooks offering an integrative and multi-dimensional social work practice framework. By focusing on a client's capacities, strengths, and resources rather than pathology, the author hopes the reader will "hear" a message of hope rather than despair regarding the impact of mental illness on an individual and his or her family.

Now a bit about how the book is organized. The first chapter describes the basic principles supporting the competency-based treatment model. This perspective focuses on the interface among the client's personal, interpersonal, community, and environmental systems while placing an equal emphasis on discovering strengths, enhancing coping skills, and fostering resilience. Competency-based treatment provides a strengths-based lens for practice in the field of mental health and thus is not driven by any one particular theoretical orientation. This book rests on a systematic integrative approach to treatment drawn from numerous counseling theories and methods extant to social work practice. It assumes clients have the capacity to reorganize their lives with appropriate resources and supports. The content is organized around the biopsychosocial framework anchored in ecological systems theory, and presents competency-based treatment interventions targeting individuals, families, communities, and the larger social systems. This text is meant to complement a previous book by the same authors, *Psychopathology: A Competency-Based Assessment Model for Social Workers* (Zide & Gray, 2001), which focused on the assessment process. The current text provides an integrative context for helping clients find ways to resolve the real-life problems of living with mental illness.

The competency-based model guides the practitioner in exploring the client's problems, attempting to understand the client's worldview, and considering what to do next with that information. Chapter 2 provides an overview of the major counseling theories supporting competency-based treatment, including crisis intervention, solution-focused therapy, cognitive-behavioral therapy, psychosocial therapy, psychoeducation, and methods of family and group work practice. The author's choices are predicated on current clinical practice supported by the professional literature, empirical research, and the philosophical underpinnings of social work. Each theoretical orientation is introduced with a brief historical overview, followed by a description of the major tenets and principles of practice, and the discussion concludes with an overview of advantages and disadvantages. The intent is to provide a conceptual map to identify key practice principles aimed toward bringing about opportunities for client change. Since psychotropic medication is an often used adjutant to counseling, Chapter 2 also provides an overview of the biological therapies that are available.

Subsequent chapters are organized around merging the *Diagnostic and Statistical Manual* (American Psychiatric Association, 2000) or DSM classification of mental disorders with the competency-based treatment model. The social work profession is divided concerning the usefulness of the DSM. Despite its well-documented limitations and the challenges inherent to its application by social work practitioners, the DSM remains enormously popular and continues to provide the accepted language for mental disorders used by mental health professionals, insurance companies, and the pharmaceutical industry (Kirk & Kutchins, 1994; Kutchins & Kirk, 1995, 1997; Lacasse & Gomory, 2003). It is hoped the competency-based model balances the tensions inherent in the DSM's focus on deficits and pathology by taking into account a parallel consideration of resilience and protective factors found in the client's life. You will notice an absence of any discussion of the disorders of childhood. This decision allowed for a more extensive discussion of each major adult disorder.

Chapters 3 through 11 begin with an introduction to a specific DSM diagnostic category, followed by a summary of signs and symptoms, moving on to a discussion of the relevant current literature on the major treatment interventions specific to that mental disorder. At the risk of providing too much information, interventions commonly used for a particular diagnosis are covered to further support the integrative approach that is central to competency-based treatment. Included in the discussion is a summary of various risks associated with the disorder. Case vignettes are provided to illustrate how competency-based practice guides the practitioner in selecting treatment strategies. Through the use of dialogue between client and practitioner, the many ways that real people respond to life's challenges are emphasized. The case illustrations are intended to represent the challenges that social workers typically encounter in contemporary professional practice. These vignettes are based on real-life issues drawn from the author's experiences as a practitioner, supervisor, and educator, and give attention to prevailing social work practices. In these vignettes just as in real life, mistakes are made, and these errors are explored as a part of the discussion. The cases presented here were drawn from the first book. The major difference in the current text is that it advances treatment considerations that go beyond a competency-based assessment.

Each case vignette brings to the foreground a particular aspect of competency-based treatment. For example, the influence of culture is highlighted for the practitioner working with Jean Redhorse Osceola, a First Nations person who struggles with depersonalization disorder. The social worker must decide between using mainstream versus indigenous helping strategies. In another instance, the importance of self-awareness and using supervision is underscored for the practitioner whose client diagnosed with malingering disorder abruptly ends the interview and storms out of her office. A discussion follows each case vignette to operationalize competency-based treatment and describe the treatment approaches selected.

For each case, a chart outlines the risks, protective factors, and buffers found in the client's life. This visual summary is intended to help the reader to integrate the intervention theories supporting the competency-based model and to begin to think critically about treatment centering on client strengths and resilience. As in the first book, a section entitled "Practitioner Reflections" is included at the end of each chapter to help the practitioner consider the full range of the client's experiences living with mental illness. Some of the exercises highlight ethical dilemmas a social worker is likely to encounter in practice. It is hoped this perspective will increase the practitioner's accountability, improve the quality of care provided, and foster more effective participation in the contemporary managed care environment. An appendix delineating the DSM-IV-TR classification system can be accessed at the Book Companion Site at **http://www.wadsworth.com/social_work_d.** There, you can download the file to view online or to print. Simply type the book's ISBN into the Search field at the upper left corner of your screen and click on "Student Book Companion Site."

This textbook has been written by a social worker for social workers who are in different stages of professional development. The challenge was to help the reader bring together knowledge of psychopathology with treatment interventions in a way that is useful and understandable. The book is intended to be a major text for courses in psychopathology, human behavior in the social environment, or methods of direct practice as well as elective courses in graduate and undergraduate social work programs. It addresses the issue of what a social worker needs to know and be able to do to provide individualized clinical services to individuals and their families struggling with mental illness, one of the most vulnerable and at-risk populations we serve. As a corollary, the practitioner will be able to work more effectively with other interdisciplinary professionals in a collaborative manner. I hope this book will also be a useful reference for professionals in other disciplines, such as mental health counselors and family therapists. It is written for both clinical professionals and students alike. It is intended to be a practical reference text that readers will use over and over as they encounter clients who meet diagnostic criteria found in the DSM. Each chapter can stand on its own as well as serve as an integrated part of the entire text. The book is written in a style that is meant to be highly readable and user friendly. The content goes beyond describing a diagnosis and helps the reader advance his or her understanding of the treatment implications.

The major objective in writing this book has been to convey the importance of focusing on how each individual copes with a mental illness rather than dehumanizing clients and pathologizing their experiences. By taking this perspective, the practitioner is attentive to the client's worldview of mental illness and develops an appreciation for the factors that shape each person's experiences.

ACKNOWLEDGMENTS

A book of this scope and magnitude cannot be written solely through hard work and the tenacious commitment to an idea. The task was made all the more difficult by the untimely death of my co-author. Many people offered their support and encouragement from behind the scenes, and I would like to take this opportunity to thank them for their invaluable help. The genesis for this book emerged from my long practice history, classroom teaching, and the challenges associated with teaching content about psychopathology, a topic often associated with a deficit perspective and the medical model of treatment. Students struggled with trying to maintain the profession's values and apply social work ethics and ideals, while at the same time balancing the tensions associated with a client's diagnosis. The first book introduced a competency-based method of assessing mental illness, and this book advances the discussion to include competency-based treatment. Many books have been written about treatment, but the inspiration for this book was to provide a social work orientation to practice intended to convey a message of hope rather than despair regarding the impact of mental illness on individuals and their families.

I wish to thank Lisa Gebo, Social Work Executive Editor, for her support and encouragement. The entire team working with her was equally outstanding, beginning with the delightful Alma Dea Michelena, Assistant Editor for the Helping Professions. While Lisa kept me on her radar screen, it was Alma Dea who was consistently available and answered questions that I had not even thought to ask. I am appreciative to be working with them again and also with Caroline Concilla, Marketing Manager, and her Marketing Assistant, Rebecca Weisman, who offered many useful suggestions. Tami Strang, Senior Marketing Communications Manager, also contributed to marketing efforts. I would like to thank Megan Hansen, Associate Project Manager, Editorial Production, for coordinating the work of the unique cover design developed by Denise Davidson of Simple Design, which nicely complements the cover of the first book. During the production process, Lori Johnson ably served as Project Manager, keeping everyone on task. I appreciate the contributions of Merrill Peterson, Production Coordinator, of Matrix Productions, Inc., who made the editorial process go smoothly. A special note of recognition goes to Janet Tilden, Copy Editor, who added many constructive comments and suggestions.

I would once again like to acknowledge my Dean, Stephen M. Holloway, and Associate Dean, Debra McPhee, who continue to foster an organizational climate in which endeavors like this one can be completed. I extend a heartfelt thank you to all of my students who shared the classroom with me. They asked the hard questions, brought the tough cases, and continually reminded me of the triumphs and challenges of our social work profession. I am especially grateful for the research support of graduate social work students Christine Flury and Caesar Corzo. I also appreciate the efforts of another of my graduate students, Leroy Kerr, who somehow managed to fix up my old laptop computer so I could work on the book almost anywhere.

I appreciate the thoughtful comments and useful suggestions made by the reviewers who took time away from their own busy schedules to read the manuscript. I am indebted to Carlton Munson of the University of Maryland at Baltimore, Vikki Vandiver of Portland State University, Glenn Rohrer of East Carolina University, Maria Carroll of Delaware State University, A. Suzanne Boyd of the University of North Carolina at Charlotte, Catherine Hawkins of Southwest Missouri State University, and Janis Feldman of the University of Texas–Pan American.

Last, but certainly not least, I am grateful to my husband for his continuing patience, love, and support throughout the writing of this book. There were many times when we would skip meals, eat out, or have lunch at 3 or 4 in the afternoon because I "just need another minute to finish this thought." His faith in me is really special!

References

American Psychiatric Association. (2000). *Diagnostic and statistical manual of mental disorders: Text revision DSM-IV-TR* (4th ed.). Washington, DC: American Psychiatric Association.

Austin, D. (1997). The profession of social work: In the second century. In M. Reisch & E. D. Gambrill (Eds.), *Social work in the twenty-first century* (pp. 396–407). Thousand Oaks, CA: Pine Forge Press.

Bentley, K. J. (Ed.) (2002). *Social work practice in mental health: Contemporary roles, tasks, and techniques.* Pacific Grove, CA: Brooks/Cole.

Gitterman, A. (Ed.). (2001). *Handbook of social work practice with vulnerable and resilient populations* (2nd ed.). New York: Columbia University Press.

Greene, R. R. (2002). *Resiliency: An integrated approach to practice, policy, and research.* Washington DC: NASW Press.

Hepworth, D. H., Rooney, R. H., & Larsen, J. (2002). *Direct social work practice: Theory and skills* (6th ed.). Pacific Grove, CA: Brooks/Cole.

Kirk, S. A., & Kutchins, H. (1994). The myth of the reliability of DSM. *Journal of Mind and Behavior, 15,* 1–2.

Kutchins, H., & Kirk, S. A. (1995). Should DSM be the basis for teaching social work practice in mental health? No! *Journal of Social Work Education, 31,* 159–165.

Kutchins, H., & Kirk, S. A. (1997). *Making us crazy: DSM: The psychiatric bible and the creation of mental disorders.* New York: Free Press.

Lacasse, J. R., & Gomory, T. (2003). Is graduate social work education promoting a critical approach to mental health practice? *Journal of Social Work Education, 39*(3), 383–408.

Maguire, L. (2002). *Clinical social work: Beyond generalist practice with individuals, groups, and families.* Pacific Grove, CA: Brooks/Cole.

Miller, J. (2002). Social workers as diagnosticians. In K. J. Bentley (Ed.), *Social work practice in mental health: Contemporary roles, tasks and techniques* (pp. 43–72). Pacific Grove, CA: Brooks/Cole.

National Association of Social Workers. (1996). *Code of ethics.* Washington, DC: NASW.

Newhill, C. E., & Korr, W. S. (2004). Practice with people with severe mental illness: Rewards, challenges, burdens. *Health and Social Work, 29*(4), 297–305.

O'Neill, J. V. (1999, June). Profession dominates in mental health. *NASW News, 44*(6), 1 & 8.

Okun, B. F. (2002). *Effective helping: Interviewing and counseling techniques.* Pacific Grove, CA: Brooks/Cole.

Saleebey, D. (2002). *The strengths perspective in social work practice* (3rd ed.). Boston: Allyn & Bacon.

Sheafor, B. W., & Horejsi, C. R. (2003). *Techniques and guidelines for social work practice* (6th ed.). Boston: Allyn & Bacon.

Walsh, J. (2000). *Clinical case management with persons having mental illness: A relationship-based perspective.* Pacific Grove, CA: Brooks/Cole.

Zide, M. R., & Gray, S. W. (2001). *Psychopathology: A competency-based assessment model for social workers.* Pacific Grove, CA: Brooks/Cole.

AN INTRODUCTION TO THE COMPETENCY-BASED TREATMENT MODEL

This chapter introduces a framework for competency-based practice that addresses contemporary demands within the mental health field. People who live with mental illness, particularly those with severe and persistent symptoms, are often set apart from others. Even the term "mental illness" implies that people are likely to be dangerous to themselves and/or to others (Szasz, 2003). The nature of the mental disability and the stigma associated with having a mental illness profoundly affect this population of clients. As noted by Segal, Silverman, and Temkin (1993), "Each person must have a diagnosis in order to receive services. The individual's behavior, feelings, and attitudes become interpreted as this diagnosis, which then becomes a form of social identity" (Gutierrez, Parsons, and Cox, 1998, p. 90). Manning (1998) cautions the practitioner against interpreting a client's behavior, feelings, and attitudes in terms of a diagnosis rather than seeing the whole person.

The competency-based model for practice presented in this text focuses on the uniqueness of each person with an emphasis on strengths, resilience, coping capacities, and those environmental influences that affect patterns of relating and behaving. It assumes clients have the capacity to reorganize their lives as long as they have appropriate resources and supports. This approach focuses on helping clients find ways to resolve the real-life problems of living with mental illness. The residual effects of mental illness may include poverty, a lack of belonging within the family, community, or society, and inadequate medical, social, and psychosocial care. Competency-based practice attempts to understand the phenomenological presentation of self that has developed not only over time but also through interpersonal influences. In addition, the multiple effects of family, community, and cultural values are strongly considered (Zide & Gray, 2001).

THE NEED FOR COMPETENCY-BASED PRACTICE

An estimated 22.1 percent of Americans ages 18 and older, or about 1 in 5 adults, have experienced some form of a diagnosable mental disorder in a given year (National Institute of Mental Health, 2001), and social workers are the major providers of mental health services (Stromwall, 2002). Additionally, 4 of the 10 leading causes of disability in the United States are mental disorders: major depression, bipolar disorder, schizophrenia, and obsessive-compulsive disorder (National Institute of Mental Health, 2001). As the population ages, depression, suicide, and dementia are predicted to increase. The social worker's role in the mental health care field is also expected to expand (Substance Abuse and Mental Health Services Administration, 1999; Vourlekis, Edinburg & Knee, 1998). Bentley and Taylor (2002) observe that mental health is the largest field of practice in social work. Among members of the National Association of Social Workers (NASW), 33 percent identify mental health as their primary area of practice (Ginsberg, 1995).

In recent years, some of the more traditional ways social workers have looked at clients have been changing, especially when planning treatment based on presenting symptoms. The *Diagnostic and Statistical Manual* (DSM) classification system is commonly used to meet requirements for assessing mental illness and third-party payments. The author recognizes that using the DSM format has been a long-standing and controversial assessment tool in social work practice (Kirk & Kutchins, 1992, 1994; Kirk, Siporin, & Kutchins, 1989; Kutchins & Kirk, 1987). Despite some of its drawbacks, the manual continues to serve as the standard for evaluation and diagnosis of people with mental illness. The competency-based framework described in this text is intended to affirm and support an orientation to social work practice that centers on client strengths while balancing the limitations attributed to the DSM classification system.

The profession's growing emphasis on promoting social and economic justice coupled with its historic focus on individuals and their environments have served as the impetus to consider a broader perspective toward offering help to clients (Robbins, Chatterjee, & Canda, 1998, 1999). The clinical practitioner tries to understand the factors that put certain populations at a disadvantage or at-risk and how clients' backgrounds and characteristics may be related to their present problems. The revised National Association of Social Workers (NASW) Code of Ethics strikingly references social justice for all members of society (Swenson, 1998). Specifically, the Code of Ethics says that all professional social work practitioners should strive to

- Eliminate personal and institutional discrimination;
- Ensure access to needed resources and opportunities for all;
- Expand options and opportunities for everyone, but especially for those individuals who are disadvantaged or disenfranchised;
- Respect cultural diversity in society;
- Advocate for changes that improve social conditions and promote social justice;
- Encourage participation in the democratic process;
- Encourage people to develop their own voice.

In sum, practitioners must effectively engage in building a social environment compatible with human needs. This objective reflects the profession's commitment to promote social justice and encompasses issues of diversity, oppression, and populations at risk, such as persons with mental illness. Building on client strengths

(Jongsma & Peterson, 1995; Saleebey, 1994, 1996, 1997, 2001) is central to competency-based practice and is a good fit with the values of social justice. For example, gender biases may result in more women being diagnosed with mood disorders than men (Walker, 1994) and too frequently prescribed anti-depressive medication (Fellin, 1996). Rather than succumb to the tendency to "split" the client's intrapersonal world from interpersonal and environmental influences, the competency-based framework serves as a way of making connections among these domains in the client's life.

Organized around a biopsychosocial framework and anchored in ecological systems theory, the competency-based approach to treatment begins with a multidimensional assessment (Zide & Gray, 2001). In conducting the assessment, the practitioner considers the potential influence of biophysical, intrapersonal capacities and resources, interpersonal relationships, and social or environmental factors in the client's life (Table 1.1) and begins to develop interventions that target individual, family, community, and larger social systems.

TABLE **1.1**   **THE CLIENT'S CURRENT LIFE SITUATION**

I. Intrapersonal Issues

Cognitive Functioning

What is the client's perception of the problem?

Is there evidence of the client's capacity to solve problems?

Is there evidence of rational versus irrational thoughts?

Emotional Functioning

Describe the client's affect.

Is there evidence of appropriate versus inappropriate affect?

Has the client been under stress or recently experienced pressure that has been difficult to manage?

Behavioral Functioning

What is the client's physical appearance?

Mannerisms?

Disabilities?

Physiologic Functioning

Has the client been seen medically during the past year?

If so, what are the results?

Has the client had any recent illness or surgery?

Is there any evidence of drug or/and alcohol usage?

Any medications taken?

Describe diet, caffeine use, and so forth.

(continued)

TABLE 1.1   *CONTINUED*

Mental Status

Note:

Disturbances in appearance, dress, or posture.

Disturbance in thoughts, such as hallucinations or delusions.

Disturbances in level of awareness, such as memory, attention.

Disturbances in emotional tone such as deviations in affect, or a discrepancy between the client's verbal report of mood/affect and what the practitioner observes.

Degree to which client seems aware of the nature of the problem and the need for treatment.

Client Roles and Role Performance

What roles does the client perform, such as wife, mother?

Are the client's issues related to role performance?

Are the client's issues related to role satisfaction or dissatisfaction?

Has the client had any serious problems with their children, their marriage, or other close relationships?

Developmental Considerations

Trace the birth, developmental history (including the mother's pregnancy), developmental milestones, or illness.

Sexual, marital, and family history (such as domestic violence, abuse).

Is there a legal history?

What has family life been like when the client was growing up?

Does the client recall any specific events while growing up, such as a parent dying or divorcing when the client was young?

II. Interpersonal Family Issues

What is each family member's perspective of the problem(s)?

Marital Status

What is the client's sexual, dating, or marital history?

What is the quality of the client's intimate relationships?

What year (or years) did the client marry?
    If married more than once, how many times?

Family Structure

What is the quality of the client's family interactions?

Describe the family system: composition; structure; boundaries; cohesion; flexibility; rules; family alliances; family power; negotiation; family decision-making; problem solving; and family communication patterns.

Has there been any recent serious illness or death in the client's family?

How does the client describe his or her parents?

(continued)

III. Interpersonal—Work or School

Occupation or Grade in School

Satisfaction with Work/School

Are there indicators of successful achievement in this setting?

Are there issues related to grades, or pay, or to promotions?

Describe the client's relationships with colleagues/peers.

Do(es) the presenting problem(s) occur in this setting also?
   If so, how does the client get along with peers, teachers, boss or other authority figures?

What is the academic/work history?

Is the client having any problems with money or with their job?

Is the client seriously in debt?

IV. Interpersonal—Peers

Who are the client's friends, and what is the quality of these relationships?

Is the client satisfied with their friends/peers?

Reprinted with permission from *Psychopathology: A Competency-Based Assessment Model for Social Workers* by Zide/Gray (Belmont, CA: Wadsworth, 2001), p. 14.

Using the competency-based treatment model, the practitioner works directly with clients, includes the family or other personal sources of support whenever possible, and pays attention to community resources. Interpersonal relations and social life can add to or shape the experiences of the person struggling with mental illness. The competency-based framework is sensitive to diversity (such as gender, sexual orientation, age, religion and/or social class) and how ethnic and cultural experiences within the prevailing social environment may influence those who are coping with mental illness. The practitioner considers the meanings projected onto the mentally ill person by the surrounding society. This is particularly important if the person with a mental illness is degraded and stigmatized. Understanding a person's cultural identity and the manifestations of his or her mental illness adds another dimension to the assessment. Thus, a competency-based perspective focuses on the whole person as well as environmental influences (Table 1.2).

Competency-based practice accentuates a person's strengths, resources, and capabilities. Clients are viewed as being able to influence their environment as well as being influenced by it. For example, persons who are living with the psychiatric diagnosis of schizophrenia often experience a distorted sense of self, isolation, and withdrawal from their social environment. These symptoms may be exacerbated by relationship problems and difficulty with normal life functions such as keeping a job or going to school. Anchored in a strengths perspective, the competency-based model explores the risks in a client's life while paying equal attention to resilience and buffering factors. Returning to the example of the problems associated with schizophrenia, the competency-based perspective calls upon the social work practitioner not only to identify but also to capitalize on the person's strengths and

TABLE 1.2 **THE CLIENT'S CONTEXT AND SOCIAL SUPPORT NETWORKS**

Clarify the environmental characteristics that influence the coping and adaptive patterns of the client:

What environmental resources does the client have?
   How adequate are the client's material circumstances—housing, transportation, food?
   What does the client know about community resources and how to use them?

What actual or potential supports are available in the environment?
   Does the client have access to family or peer supports or support from agencies in the neighborhood that are not being used?

What are the risks and vulnerabilities in the client system?

What blocks, obstacles, or/and deficits interfere with the client's life processes and adaptive strivings?

What is the "goodness of fit" between the client system and the environment?

Ethnic/cultural considerations:

What is the client's ethnic or cultural group?

What is the degree of acculturation?

Is there evidence of prejudice or discrimination by others toward the client?

To what extent is there isolation from (or participation in) extra-familial groups and associations, such as ethnic or cultural groups?

What is the client's perception of how ethnic/cultural group identification has helped or not helped?

How do sociocultural factors interfere with the client's functioning (such as racism, sexism, and cultural values)?

Can the client draw from the resources of his or her culture or ethnic group?

Reprinted with permission from *Psychopathology: A Competency-Based Assessment Model for Social Workers* by Zide/Gray (Belmont, CA: Wadsworth, 2001), p. 15.

to reinforce external supports. Thus, the social worker may look at how the person has tried to cope with a diagnosis as well as explore the nature and availability of family and/or professional supports and concrete resources (including self-help programs).

IMPORTANCE OF THE WORKING RELATIONSHIP

Beginning with Perlman's (1957, 1970, 1979) formulation of the problem-solving model for social casework, most current approaches to practice include some version of her conceptualization of practice. While there are various configurations of the phases of problem solving (see, for example, Compton, Galaway, & Cournoyer, 2005; Gambrill, 1983, 1997; Gitterman, 2001; Hepworth, Rooney & Larsen, 2002; Hollis, 1970; Johnson & Yanca, 2001; Kirst-Ashman & Hull, 2002; Miley, O'Melia & DuBois, 2001; Sheafor, Horejsi, & Horejsi, 2000; Shulman, 1999; Smalley, 1967;

Zastrow, 1999), all include the establishment of a working alliance; that is, a collaboration between the practitioner and the client(s) that makes it possible for them to work purposefully together. Notes Gutierrez (as cited in Miley, O'Melia, & DuBois, 2001), the process of collaboration around what works in the client's life involves

> basing the helping relationship on collaboration, trust, and shared power; accepting the client's definition of the problem; identifying and building on the client's strengths; actively involving the client in the change process; (and) experiencing a sense of personal power within the helping relationship (p. 120).

This focus on client empowerment is embedded in the competency-based model for practice.

When working with people who have a history of psychiatric disorders and in whom symptoms may worsen over time or in response to stress, it is essential to understand their life experiences with mental illness while simultaneously developing a productive helping relationship. For the client living with severe impairment, his or her symptoms may interfere with the practitioner's attempts to identify strengths. However, the competency-based model accentuates the importance of acknowledging people's abilities instead of emphasizing deficits. The social worker conveys respect for the individual as a fellow human being rather than focusing solely on the person's mental illness. While it is important to understand the attributes of the diagnostic categories of mental illness set forth in the *Diagnostic and Statistical Manual*, the practitioner pays equal attention to the unique features of each individual, his or her current concerns or distress, and ways of coping with disadvantage. All too often, persons with mental illness have internalized social stigma, formed low expectations of themselves, and experienced dehumanizing clinical practices. The challenge for every practitioner is to find ways to support the person's recovery and the empowerment process. It becomes important to listen attentively to the voices of clients who should be actively involved in the helping relationship (Boehm & Staples, 2002). Competency-based practice explores the full range of the individual's current functioning rather than simply paying attention to deficits.

An integral part of the competency-based model is the social worker's self-awareness (Caplan & Thomas, 2001; Jacobson & Christensen, 1996; Jenkins, 1993). This means that the practitioner does not disconnect himself or herself from the negative thoughts or feelings that may be evoked while trying to build a relationship with a client during the interview. Rather, one tries to focus on an emotional level or "stay in the moment" while simultaneously reflecting on what is happening in the particular situation. Social workers practicing with clients who consistently challenge the relationship may be at a higher risk of compassion fatigue (Figley, 1995, 2002). Listening to the client's story with compassion and empathy while putting aside their vexing or annoying behaviors can place additional stress on the practitioner and may lead to inappropriate or inconsistent interventions. Instead of taking a client's behaviors personally, the practitioner must attempt to stay centered and instead consider what is actually transpiring in the session (despite feelings of irritation with the client). The practitioner's self-reflection moves beyond the actual exchange to include considering what the client might be trying to say beneath the overt content of the message. This means that the practitioner resists the choice to react precipitously, but rather tolerates some degree of discomfort and contemplates the implications of her or his actions.

Listening to the client's story may stir up feelings in the social worker. The practitioner's personal feelings and reactions to the client, also known as countertransference, should be regarded as an important and viable part of the helping relationship. Countertransference issues, if left unaddressed, can potentially influence treatment strategies and the practitioner might not even be aware of the way therapeutic decisions are made (Bradley, 2003; Kanter, 1995). Notes Walsh (2000), the social worker's values cannot be kept out of professional practice, and self-awareness includes acknowledging and working through personal reactions. Practitioners' feelings about clients are communicated verbally or nonverbally and can potentially limit the relationship or move it forward. Insight and self-reflection help practitioners to be aware of the multiple factors that may affect their work.

Building on an empowerment and strengths perspective, the therapeutic relationship becomes a conversation that encourages clients to define and ascribe meaning to their own life situation. This shared experience validates the client's self-perceptions and world view. Instead of playing the role of the "expert," the practitioner honors clients' expertise and knowledge of their own life circumstances (Berg, 1994; Berg & Miller, 1992; de Shazer, 1991; Lipchik, 1994; Miller, de Shazer, Berg, & Hopwood, 1993). To maintain this perspective, therapeutic approaches such as cognitive behavioral practice theory that place the practitioner in the role of "expert" must be adapted to make the helping relationship more collaborative and egalitarian. The qualities embedded in the working relationship found in competency-based treatment are characterized by collaboration, support, and empathy. The client and practitioner work together as partners. Clients are not seen solely by their problems and/or plight but rather as competent persons who bring strengths and resources to be utilized in order to improve their own quality of life and the environment in which they live. Whenever possible, authoritarian relationships should be avoided and a focus on professional expertise demystified. Instead of directing the client to do something, the practitioner offers suggestions, helps the client think about options, and support for what seems to be the most effective strategy. This does not mean that the practitioner accepts without question those client attitudes, behaviors, or decisions that could be characterized as abusive or exploitative. Instead, the practitioner initiates a dialogue and then invites the client to think critically about the internal and external aspects of a problem or issue. In this way, the helping relationship sets the stage for clients to participate constructively while inviting them to assume responsibility for their actions. The practitioner's focus is on instilling hope, maintaining a positive outlook, and helping to empower the client. Saleebey (1997) notes,

> Clients want to know that you actually care about them, that how they fare makes a difference to you, that you will listen to them, that you will respect them no matter what their history, and that you believe that they can build something of value with the resources within and around them. But

most of all, clients want to know that you believe that they can surmount adversity and begin the climb toward transformation and growth (p. 12).

He identifies five principles that underlie the guiding assumptions of the competency-based model for practice:

- Every group, family, individual, and community has strengths.
- Clients often experience crisis, illness, trauma, and/or abuse. While they may cause the client to struggle, these same events may also be opportunities for growth.
- Practitioners must assume they do not know the limits of their clients' capacity for change and growth. Group, community, and individual aspirations are taken seriously.
- The helping relationship is characterized by collaboration.
- The practitioner assumes that every aspect of the client's environment contains resources.

CLIENT STRENGTHS AND THE COMPETENCY-BASED TREATMENT MODEL

Using a resilience lens fundamentally shifts our perspective by enabling the social worker to recognize, affirm, and build upon client strengths. The practitioner's emphasis moves toward exploring ways of turning adversity into opportunities for growth. The competency-based treatment model provides a conceptual map to identify practice theories and principles aimed at bringing out the best in each client. Instead of focusing on where the client has failed, attention can be directed toward creating opportunities to succeed.

The competency-based framework encompasses a wide range of practice approaches. In Chapter 2 we will explore the major theoretical perspectives that support competency-based treatment. Because of the focus on the client's social context, a synopsis of family and group work methods is also provided. It was difficult to decide which practice theories and methods to include in this book as a part of competency-based practice. The chosen approaches are widely used in current practice, supported in the empirical literature, and reflective of the philosophical underpinnings of the social work profession. This discussion will not address every type of client circumstance one may encounter in practice, but instead should provide a starting point for considering intervention strategies that illustrate the parameters of "best practices." As with all of our clients, the practitioner is expected to use sound judgment grounded in the ethical values of the profession (Swenson, 1998). Using appropriate indicators to measure client successes and paying attention to the relevant research information about specific intervention techniques are integral to competency-based treatment planning. The theoretical perspectives described in Chapter 2 are intended to help the practitioner determine what is achievable and address the biophysical and intrapersonal aspects of a client's behavior as well as the interpersonal and environmental factors that influence it. Ideally, the reader will be able to discern how the competency-based model provides a structure to evaluate the relevance of multiple theoretical frameworks and to select specific interventions that fit each client's unique situation. The integrative use of many different practice theories and techniques helps to guide the practitioner to create more opportunities for each client to be in charge of his or her own change process.

Each theoretical perspective should be adapted to the unique life circumstances and perspectives of our clients. As the social work profession looks to the future, practitioners will continue to face critical choices about what comprises the essential knowledge and skills for effective clinical practice. Increasingly clients are presenting themselves with more complex and difficult life situations that cannot be addressed by only one approach. No single theory guides the activities of all or even most social workers (Walsh, 2000), and therefore a variety of approaches must be considered.

RECENT CHANGES IN THE MENTAL HEALTH CARE FIELD

Practitioners confront a number of ethical issues and challenges in working with mental health clients. Schamess and Lightburn (1998) express the concern that social work values and the well-being of clients may be compromised by recent developments. The Federal privacy and compliance standards regarding clients' confidential mental health information along with shifts in funding introduced by managed care initiatives have been altering the way social work is practiced. For example, since April 14, 2003, health care providers and insurers have been required to comply with the Health Insurance Portability and Accountability Act of 1996 (HIPAA). This legislative act set national standards for the protection of health information as applied to health plans, health care clearinghouses, and health care providers who conduct transactions electronically. For the first time, a foundation of federal protections was established to protect health-related information. Computerized databases are commonly used to transmit information, but reliance on this kind of technology can jeopardize confidentiality (Rock & Congress, 1999). Despite protective legislation, breaches of confidentiality can be expected to happen in electronic media. Cooper and Lesser (2005) caution social workers to use additional means to safeguard information that is potentially life-threatening. Confidentiality is challenged in other ways. Practitioners are required to submit documentation to managed care companies that includes the client's symptoms, his or her diagnosis, the length of time needed to obtain results, and specific details about treatment. The process of authorizing treatment is often cumbersome and can entail extensive paperwork and numerous telephone calls. While the practitioner may obtain a release of information from the client to share this highly personal data with the managed care organization, the managed care group may not treat client information with the same caution.

Clients' rights under behavioral managed care systems are another growing source of concern to practitioners (Sands, 2001). Corcoran (1997) notes that some managed care contracts contain nondisclosure clauses, sometimes referred to as gag orders, that require the practitioner to conceal some aspects of the managed care group's influence with the client. This restriction conflicts with the social worker's obligation under the Code of Ethics to provide services based on client self-determination and informed consent (NASW, 1997).

In addition, a case coordinator from a managed care company may dictate the length of treatment and what kind of help the client can receive under company policy, thus threatening professional autonomy. The practitioner's relationship with his or her client now includes a third party, the managed care company (Cooper & Lesser, 2005). The company can overrule the practitioner's recommendations, suggest another provider or terminate treatment altogether (Sands, 2001). The advent of managed care is changing definitions of what constitutes the appropriate manner of treatment of someone's illness and who should make care-related decisions.

As a consequence of this paradigm shift, the profession is now grappling with increasingly complex issues (Corey, Corey, & Callahan, 2003; Lowenberg, Dolgoff, & Harrington, 2000; Reamer, 1998, 1999, 2000, 2001; Witkin, 2000) and concerns unique to mental health practice that create additional uncertainties for social workers (Lowenberg, Dolgoff, & Harrington, 2000). For instance, the practitioner may need to work within multiple-client systems and negotiate between often-conflicting interests. The case of Zelda "Jean" Pfohl (Chapter 3) illustrates these opposing perspectives. On one side, the family struggles with the decision to place their mother who is diagnosed with Alzheimer's dementia into a nursing home. On the other side, staff members at the nursing home express apprehension about the patient's adjustment to the facility. The family's struggle with the decision to place their mother into long-term care is quite different from the uneasiness expressed by the nursing staff about the patient's adjustment. Another challenge for the practitioner is the need to be attentive to issues of competing values, as illustrated in the case of Rudy Rosen, a gentleman with schizophrenia paranoid type (Chapter 4). The issue revolves around preserving Rudy's self-determination while finding ways to protect him during those times when his paranoid symptoms prevail. A further challenge is that some situations present a certain degree of ambiguity; that is, there may be times when it is difficult to make a decision about the degree of danger a client's particular symptoms may pose. For example the practitioner may have to decide whether to hospitalize someone struggling with suicidal ideation, a common complication associated with major depression (Zide & Gray, 2001).

Guidelines for Ethical Practice

Over the past twenty years social workers have designed ethical guidelines and promoted professional standards in response to the changing nature of practice and shifting boundaries of the profession. As mentioned earlier, the National Association of Social Workers has developed a professional code of ethics designed to provide guidelines for the practitioner. This code is intended to address issues related to professional conduct and comportment, and to outline responsibilities to clients, colleagues, the profession of social work, and society. Notes Reamer (2002),

> Most ethical issues in the profession are routine and relatively straightforward. For example, social workers know that ordinarily they must obtain clients' consent before releasing confidential information, respect clients' rights to self-determination, and obey the law (p. 65).

Situations that are more complex or ambiguous challenge the practitioner's skill to implement ethical decisions effectively. Ethical issues have always been central to guiding the practitioner's conduct (Gibelman & Schervish, 1997; Jayaratne, Croxton, & Mattison, 1997; Linzer, 1999; Marsh, 2000, 2003; Reisch & Gorin, 2001), and the literature advances several decision-making protocols for the more difficult situations one may encounter (Congress, 1998; Lowenberg & Dolgoff, 1996; Reamer, 1999). Most include several steps to guide the practitioner's systematic evaluation of a potential ethical dilemma. These guidelines do not dictate a single course of action but instead provide a means of evaluating and deciding among competing options. Reamer (2002) outlines the following blueprint aimed at helping the practitioner to arrive at sound decisions:

- Identify all ethical issues including professional social work values and duties that conflict.
- Identify individuals, groups, and organizations most likely to be affected by the potential ethical decision.
- Identify all possible courses of action (including an assessment of all possible risks and benefits) and the participants involved in each potential action.
- Examine the reasons in favor of and in opposition to each possible course of action (considering relevant ethical theories, principles and guidelines; codes of ethics and legal principles; practice theory and principles; personal values).
- Consult with colleagues and appropriate experts (for example, supervisors, agency administrators, attorneys, ethics committees, institutional review boards).
- Make the decision and document the decision-making process.
- Monitor, evaluate, and document the decision.

Making ethical decisions requires the practitioner to distinguish between competing choices. To practice competently, social workers must become familiar with ethical and professional issues involved in social work practice, state licensing and regulatory statutes, agency policies, and the profession's Code of Ethics. When ethical dilemmas are inherent in the case illustrations presented in this book, they will be highlighted in the treatment discussion or in the section entitled "practitioner reflections."

Issues involving privileged communication, confidentiality, and funding have become particularly important in the current era of managed care and health maintenance organizations (Swenson, 1997). The following discussion provides a backdrop for understanding the practice challenges presented by managed care.

Effects of Managed Care on the Field of Mental Health

Since the early 1980s, social work practice and human service organizations have been increasingly affected by the prevalence of managed care. For example, agency budgets have become leaner, and new skills compatible with managed care models are now required (Berkman, 1996; Davis & Meier, 2001; Edinburg & Cottler, 1995; Fletcher, 1999; Jacobson, 1998; Kadushin, 1996; Leahy, 1997; Mitchell, 1998; Perloff, 1998; Veeder & Peebles-Wilkins, 2000; Wernet, 1999). Health care costs in the United States had risen rapidly during the 1970s, and managed care was seen as a means of structuring, financing, and administering health services to deliver care that would be cost-effective, efficient, and of high quality. Despite the advent and growth of managed care, however, the costs of providing mental health and substance abuse services have continued to skyrocket. From 1987 to 1991, for example, the average cost per employee increased 86 percent (Employee Benefit Research Institute, 1995). When insurance payers began demanding reduced costs for mental health and substance abuse services, managed care organizations began to delegate the provision of these services to managed behavioral health care organizations.

The 1990s witnessed rapid growth within the managed care industry. In 1992, an estimated 44 percent of Americans with health insurance had their mental health benefits managed by specialty programs. By 1995, approximately 60 percent of people in the United States were enrolled in some form of managed health care plan (Health Insurance Association of America, 1996). Two short years later, estimates regarding enrollment in managed behavioral health organizations (MBHO) and health maintenance organizations (HMOs) reported approximately 75 percent or 168.5 million Americans eligible for health insurance (Wineburgh, 1998). By the end of 1997, 85 percent of Americans belonged to some type of managed health care plan (Winslow, 1998). Karger and Stoesz (2002) observe that under aggressive managed care plans, many found their mental health services rationed or eliminated entirely. These cutbacks set in motion advocacy efforts on behalf of legislation to extend mental health coverage.

The Mental Health Parity Act of 1996 (which took effect in 1998), states that employers that have more than 50 employees and are providing any mental health coverage must include mental health benefits comparable to health benefits. Unfortunately, this legislation had some loopholes. Although 86 percent of employers reported compliance with the legislation, most had changed employee benefits so that mental health benefits were more restrictive (General Accounting Office, 2000). The 1996 parity law was due to expire in 2001, and there was an attempt to replace this legislation with a Mental Health Equitable Treatment Act (DiNitto & Cummins, 2005). However, the proposed legislation was defeated and the 1996 law extended. Advocacy for full parity for mental health and substance abuse services continues as individual states enact parity legislation for the first time and others expand coverage on existing state statutes (DiNitto & Cummins, 2005). As of 2001, 34 states had parity legislation (National Alliance for the Mentally Ill, 2001). On a federal level, several parity bills have been introduced in Washington, DC, to ensure that insurance providers cover mental health and substance disorders to the same extent as physical illnesses (Library of Congress, 2004). Along the same lines, the DSM Task Force for the current edition of the manual pointed out that in treating mental disorders, the practitioner must consider both the mental and the physical aspects of a person's life. In particular, it

> should not be taken to imply that there is any fundamental distinction between mental disorders and general medical conditions, that mental disorders are unrelated to physical or biological factors or processes, or that general medical conditions are unrelated to behavioral or psychosocial factors or processes (American Psychiatric Association, 2000, p. xxxc).

In addition, practitioners in the field of mental health care have begun to recognize the importance of biological knowledge, and in particular the need to understand psychopharmacology (Bentley, 2002; Bentley & Walsh, 1998, 2001).

The national managed care figures continue to grow. The data for 2003 indicate that 86 percent of Americans (184.7 million) are enrolled in managed health care plans (InterStudy, 2003). Managed care dictates that service providers must move rapidly from assessing the client's problem to formulating and implementing the treatment plan. The goal, according to the managed care industry, is to expedite the treatment process by identifying and then changing a client's problems as quickly and economically as possible (Weissman, Myers, & Ross, 1986). Managed care regulates service delivery by implementing a system of provider payment arrangements and promoting the integration of relevant services. The managed care industry aims to assure that services provided are both high in quality and cost-efficient. However, the notion that mental health services might be "manageable" has been called into question for several reasons. Mental illness and substance abuse problems encountered today are often more complex than in the past. Socioeconomic stigma is associated with mental illness, and success and/or outcome criteria are sometimes unclear (Wineburgh, 1998).

Most managed care programs are based on the medical model where the focus is primarily on the elimination or treatment of symptoms. Rose and Moore (1995) posit that managed care should be referred to as "managed competition." Therapy is no longer seen as an opportunity to "just talk" about thoughts, ideas, or emotions until the client feels better (Jongsma & Peterson, 1995; O'Neill, 2000). As noted by Sands (2001),

> Interactions with clients need to be considered in the context of their behavioral health insurance, the agency, available services and the best interests of clients. Mental health agencies are funded by multiple sources, public and private, including sponsors of supportive services. With so many parties involved, it is a challenge for social workers to maintain a focus on clients and their empowerment (p. 11).

Certainly, it would be ideal if every agency or social welfare organization were to offer services fostering client change through a well-crafted treatment plan that clearly stipulates individualized goals and objectives that are measurable and intended to help set milestones to chart client progress. Case management represents a shift away from therapy for severe or long-term problems and toward management and stabilization.

Case management approaches require practitioners to develop specific skills and expertise (Moseley & Deweaver, 1998). According to Woodside and McClam (1998), case management has evolved into an essential service provided by social workers in a wide variety of settings. Practitioners who function as "case managers" link clients to needed resources as well as coordinate and monitor services, and this approach can incorporate the holistic person-situation orientation embedded in the competency-based model. The case manager coordinates social and professional supports, including concrete resources. An extended community network can strengthen external supports and capitalize on a client's internal strengths (Pescosolido, Wright, & Sullivan, 1995; Walsh, 2000). This broad system of care reinforces both the professional or formal helping networks as well as the informal systems of care found in the client's family and community systems. The goal is to help clients get the most out of life and maximize the benefits they receive from available resources.

In summary, managed care introduces both opportunities and challenges for the practitioner (Riffe & Kondrat, 1997). Notes Cress (2001), managed care has propelled social work practice to move toward community-based work, prevention of hospitalization, and a focus on wellness, and created a need for different kinds of acute care services. Practitioners must approach these situations with an understanding of all of the systems involved in a client's life (Gibelman, 2002). Managed care has brought private-sector services within the reach of many marginalized clients who would otherwise have been limited to clinic services with long waiting lists. Cooper and Lesser (2005) posit that this change has introduced greater equity within the health care arena. Managed care represents a system that stresses cost-effectiveness and preventive, brief, solution-focused interventions. Practitioners are challenged to carefully document their work and empirically study the effectiveness of their services. These requirements add another level of accountability to clients, agencies, and funding and regulatory sources (Rock, 2001). Social workers have always had a professional obligation under the Code of Ethics to ensure the dignity and worth of clients, ensure self-determination and informed consent, and maintain the confidentiality of the client-worker relationship while ensuring the client's safety. The relatively new systems of service delivery under managed care support the need for competency-based practice that emphasizes cultivation of strengths and formation of a partnership between the practitioner and clients served.

CHARACTERISTICS OF COMPETENCY-BASED PRACTICE

Competency-based treatment provides a framework for the integrated use of specific interventions. The aim is to help the clinical practitioner carry out a multidimensional assessment of the various domains in a client's life while formulating a plan of intervention. More than twenty years ago, Eileen Gambrill (1983) described the following key elements of competency-based practice:

- Practice outcomes are important to clients and significant others involved in their environment;
- The practitioner works collaboratively with clients (and their families);
- Treatment planning is concerned with generalizing change to other aspects of the client's life;
- The selection of assessment and intervention procedures is based on research literature;
- The client's successes are carefully tracked;
- Client assets are emphasized rather than focusing on pathology;
- The assessment process is based on observation and systematic exploration rather than unsupported inference;
- The discriminating use of intervention procedures considers the client's goals and life circumstances;
- The practitioner considers ethical issues and legal constraints;
- Attention is paid to individual and situational differences; and
- The client's competencies and values are integral to treatment.

This framework incorporates the social work profession's hundred-plus years of a historic mission that includes a focus on social and economic justice, enduring values, and ethical conduct. It underscores the importance of looking at environmental factors to better understand the client's situation and maintains a sense of realistic optimism about possibilities for change.

Throughout this book, detailed case examples illustrate how to engage clients (and their families) who are struggling with mental illness and working toward change. The author hopes to present a realistic picture of practice, and therefore some examples include the practitioner's mistakes while others have outcomes that are less than ideal. The author acknowledges that the struggle to deal with one's own mistakes persists throughout one's professional life. The cases are intended to encompass a variety of clinically relevant practice situations including the use of supervision. The process of offering help involves many factors and consists of a wide range of preventative, supportive, and therapeutic strategies. Competency-based treatment defines clinical practice to include change efforts aimed at influencing the intrapersonal and interpersonal aspects of a client's life, and advocating for disadvantaged and disenfranchised groups by engaging in social action, along with social policy reform (Jongsma & Peterson, 1995). In addition to implementing therapeutic techniques that focus on internal change, the social worker must be able to work with organizations within the community to provide an effective network of services.

It is important to realize that community institutions can be a useful resource as well as a cause of problems for clients. To illustrate, a colleague recounted an incident regarding one of her former clients. "James" was a 28-year-old African-American male who had been diagnosed 10 years previously with undifferentiated schizophrenia. James had been taking his anti-psychotic medication on a regular basis and seemed to be doing very well. He was able to move out of his parents' home and into in an assisted living facility (ALF). Six months after moving into the ALF, this young man converted to the Islamic faith and changed his name to Ibraham. When the holy month of Ramadan began, Ibraham refused to take his medication during daylight hours. The rules of his new faith required him to abstain from food or drink between 4 a.m. and 8 p.m. Ibraham was willing to take his medication, but only during the late evening or early morning hours. The agency monitoring his care believed this was not in Ibraham's (James') best interest and involuntarily admitted him to an inpatient psychiatric facility. Once admitted, he was forced to take his medication during daylight hours. Rather than being supportive in this instance, the agency became a source of problems for the client. What the agency failed to recognize was the importance of the client's religious customs and their positive effects on his life (Singleton, 2002).

Considerations of community work and policy development are not emphasized in this book's discussion of clinical practice. Instead, the focus is on illustrating the practitioner's adaptation of treatment theories, principles, and skills centering on capabilities and aspirations, clients' coping techniques, expectations, and perceptions of what is going on in various areas of their lives. However, community and policy practices are not totally ignored. For example, the case illustration of Jean Redhorse Osceola (Chapter 8), a client who is a First Nations person struggling with depersonalization disorder, includes the practitioner's recognition of the importance of advocating within the school system for a better understanding of indigenous persons. Developing an in-service training program targeting bias and misunderstanding becomes an integral part of the practitioner's treatment plan.

Throughout the book, we look at specialized techniques that are helpful for specific psychiatric disorders. For example, Chapter 11 discusses motivational enhancement as another way of working with persons with substance-related disorders. At the risk of providing too much information, it is hoped this discussion serves to expand the range of interventions to further support the integrated approach fundamental to competency-based practice. Each chapter is organized around a specific mental illness, and case vignettes are included to illustrate competency-based practice. For a more detailed discussion of the major disorders found in each vignette, the reader is referred to *Psychopathology: A Competency-Based Assessment Model for Social Workers* by Zide and Gray (2001). There are many books that focus specifically on children's mental health, and the author does not wish to duplicate these efforts. For more information, the reader is directed to: *Childhood Disorders: Diagnostic Desk Reference* by Fletcher-Janzen and Reynolds (2003); *Understanding Child Behavior Disorders* (4th ed.) by Gelfand and Drew (2003); and *Treatment of Childhood Disorders* (2nd ed.) by Mash and Barkley (1998).

The *Diagnostic and Statistical Manual* serves as the standard to describe and classify mental disorders. The competency-based treatment framework operationalizes the process of classifying the information found in the DSM and shifts the practitioner's focus to looking for strengths and resources in the person and his or her related social systems that can be developed and supported. A brief overview of the DSM follows.

THE ROLE OF THE DIAGNOSTIC AND STATISTICAL MANUAL

Use of the *Diagnostic and Statistical Manual of Mental Disorders* (DSM) to identify specific conditions involves making an assessment on a multiaxial system that uses five distinct levels, each referring to a different domain of personality and behavioral information:

- Axis I refers to clinical disorders and other conditions that may be a focus of clinical attention (including V codes). If there is more than one Axis I disorder, the practitioner lists each individually in order of primary severity.
- Axis II denotes personality disorders and mental retardation. This axis is used to note various aspects of personality functioning and the presence of maladaptive personality features. For example, the practitioner may note the person's characteristic coping style, which might include defense mechanisms of splitting, projection, or denial. Any diagnosis of mental retardation must be made prior to the age of 18.
- Axis III, general medical conditions, includes all general medical diseases or conditions that may be clinically relevant to the mental disorders reported on Axis I and Axis II.
- Axis IV, psychosocial and environmental problems, calls attention to relevant psychosocial and environmental issues.
- Axis V, or the Global Assessment of Functioning (GAF) Scale, is used to assess the individual's overall psychological, occupational, and social functioning.

The *Diagnostic and Statistical Manual of Mental Disorders* poses challenges and dilemmas to practitioners in the mental health field. The newly released DSM-IV-TR (American Psychiatric Association, 2000) includes 100 additional pages of text focusing on the increased enumeration of criteria and specifiers. Kutchins and Kirk (1997) suggest that the DSM format fails to provide convincing evidence for both the reliability and validity of diagnostic criteria. Wakefield (1992) observes that the DSM provides insufficient and hard-to-operationalize conceptualizations of mental disorders. Wolin and Wolin (1993) further caution that the ever-widening definition of disorders now allows for a person's "bad habits" or annoying traits to be categorized as "mental disorders." Tavris (1992) suggests that the DSM has a history of developing diagnostic categories that are unfavorable to women and to members of some racial groups. Another limitation found in the DSM is the tendency to label clients rather than attempt to understand them as unique persons within a particular social context.

In keeping with a medical model, the DSM stresses treatment first while the alleviation of the client's problems in living receives secondary attention. Unfortunately, this focus "involves assessing and treating pathology. Indeed one could argue that this is part of what we are paid to do, as every insurance company requests a DSM-IV diagnosis of what is 'wrong' with our client" (O'Gorman, 2000, p. 15). In the social work realm the attention is reversed; that is, the client's problems in living are addressed first and treatment comes after an assessment is made (Karls & Wandrei, 1992). From this perspective, clients who come into treatment realize that while they may struggle with a particular diagnosis they also have resources they can draw upon and abilities they can use. This shift provides a positive starting point from which people can search for solutions to the issues that are troubling them.

Despite its noted weaknesses and the challenges inherent to social work practice, the DSM continues to be enormously popular. It has become recognized as the accepted diagnostic language of the mental health professions, insurance companies, and the pharmaceutical industry (Kutchins & Kirk, 1997). The DSM represents an evolving social norm and cultural dynamic of "progressive infirmity" (Saleebey, 2001, p. 183). As a result, practitioners must learn to balance some of the contradictions found in the DSM together with a treatment framework emphasizing strengths found in the individual and his or her family, community, and culture (McQuaide, 1999). Karls and Wandrei (1992), Lutz and Flory (1993), and Bentley (2002), note some advantages to using the DSM:

- The DSM can be a useful tool to help the practitioner organize observations and information about one (or more) aspect of the client's life.
- This system of categorization provides a common language among mental health practitioners to communicate about client status.
- Assessment can be more efficient.
- The ability to identify a client's problems reduces anxiety for the client.
- Identifying the problem helps the client to have some control over it and the ability to become empowered over the problem.

Depending on how it is used, the DSM can help or disempower clients. The competency-based assessment framework advanced by Zide and Gray (2001) underscores the notion that a person is not summed up by a diagnosis but rather is a unique individual who also struggles with a mental illness. While it is essential to clarify the meaning of the diagnosis, social workers must also be familiar with the attributes of DSM diagnoses. The diagnostic categories found in the DSM refer to empirical events. As such, knowing about the specific circumstances in the client's life is necessary to fully understand each individual and be able to intervene in a way that is appropriate for the client's real-life circumstances. Once the practitioner starts to individualize patterns of mental illness outlined in the DSM, effective treatment approaches can be more effectively considered. The competency-based model for practice helps to guide the creation of a treatment plan that makes sense of clients' problems, attempts to understand their world view, and considers what to do next with that information. Competency-based treatment offers a systematic approach that synthesizes biological, psychological, ecological, and social perspectives. The DSM format helps to organize psychosocial data so that practitioners can use a competency-based model to begin to put the pieces of the "puzzle" together.

COMPONENTS OF THE COMPETENCY-BASED TREATMENT MODEL

The competency-based treatment model uses a biopsychosocial framework together with elements of systems theory, an ecological perspective, and a strengths perspective.

- The biopsychosocial framework validates the potential importance of biogenetic, psychosocial, social, and environmental factors in understanding human behavior.
- Systems theory promotes an understanding of the interconnectedness of different aspects of the client's life.
- The ecological perspective draws attention to clients' multiple interactions with their surroundings.
- The strengths perspective shifts the focus from individual pathology and problem-solving to clients' potential for growth.

At the heart of this conceptualization is an emphasis on understanding how each person is affected by mental illness and then choosing practice strategies that will foster resilience. A brief overview of the components of the competency-based treatment model follows.

The Biopsychosocial Framework

George Engel (1977, 1980, 1997) is considered the leading proponent of the biopsychosocial framework. According to Engel, the biological component addresses relationships among normal biology, disease processes, and genetic influences, making a connection with each person's biological functioning. The psychological component addresses those factors that include thoughts, feelings, perceptions, motivation, and reactions to illness. The social component examines cultural, environmental, and familial influences. According to Bandura (1969, 1977), reciprocal interactions are assumed between people's behavior and their environments. Understanding how clients function at all levels helps provide a more complete clinical picture; one which highlights competencies that may be built upon. It is essential to discern clients' medical status, individual psychology, and sociocultural factors affecting their behavior.

The biopsychosocial framework supports the competency-based model in several important ways. First, its emphasis on understanding the client's present functioning and its relationship to past events underscores the need to fully understand each client's distinctive history. Second, this model relies on conducting a thorough assessment and prioritizing problems. Third, it pays attention to the multiple systems that affect the client, including biological, psychological, social, and cultural aspects. A fourth supportive factor is its focus on positive behaviors and events rather than an emphasis on deficits. Finally, the biopsychosocial framework supports the competency-based model by focusing on the relationship between behavior and surrounding events—that is, those events that can either elicit or maintain problematic behaviors. Applying this model emphasizes the importance of examining all aspects of client difficulties while at the same time looking for client strengths.

Concepts from Systems Theory

Systems theory provides a conceptual framework for the person-in-environment perspective commonly recognized throughout the social work profession. Ludwig von Bertalanffy (1968) developed systems theory during the 1940s and 1950s. This approach brought an understanding of interconnectedness of the various relationships within a person's life. From the beginning, systems theory postulated that the behavior of any living system was not fixed by its initial conditions. Instead, Bertalanffy suggested that all social sciences could be integrated by using systems as a unit of analysis; that is, the biological system and the personality system as well as the social system. Systems theory helped organize the practitioner's understanding of human development. The theory does not attempt to explain human behavior but asserts that it should be viewed in the context of distinct systems such as the biological, psychological, and social. These three major systems found in the client's life, when merged with the DSM multi-axial classification system, provide an individualized way of looking at the client, the client's social context, and the treatment process. By drawing upon these perspectives, it is hoped that the practitioner will obtain a fuller picture of what helps clients to function effectively and a better understanding of their individual experiences with mental disorders.

Systems theory clarifies the person-situation gestalt by conceptualizing the client's world. It moves away from a linear explanation of cause-and-effect to appreciate the complex interactions between the individual and all aspects of the biopsychosocial system. Systems theory helps the social work practitioner pay attention to complex interactions between the client and his or her environment. The competency-based model for treatment considers clients' capacities, motivations, and environmental factors as components of their interactions with their social environments.

Contributions from the Ecological Perspective

The ecological perspective provides a way to look at people within their own context. Germain (1973) introduced the "ecological metaphor" as a way to expand the focus of social work practice by emphasizing the interaction between people and their environments. The ecological perspective primarily focuses on human ecology, or the way human beings and their environments accommodate to each other (Germain, 1991; Germain & Gitterman, 1995). This interaction is considered dynamic; that is, the "goodness of fit" between individuals and their surroundings is achieved through mutual interaction, negotiation, and compromise. A key strength of the ecological perspective is that it draws attention to each person's unique history and also considers the complexity of the human experience. The practitioner looks at those transactions that either promote or inhibit growth and development. This perspective helps the practitioner work collaboratively with clients to mobilize strengths and coping skills, locate resources, and explore opportunities within the client's environment that may pave the way for the client to achieve success rather than remaining powerless or disenfranchised.

Lehmann and Coady (2001) identify several concepts that inform the ecological perspective:

- "All people or groups of people in a system share a reciprocal influence on one another" (p. 71).
- "In systems, causes are considered to be circular rather than linear" (p. 71).
- "Systems possess structure, consisting of predictable patterns of behavior and boundaries" (p. 71).
- "Boundaries are qualitatively different, in that the type and amount of information they restrict vary" (p. 72).
- "Along with a degree of structure, which lends them predictability, the complexity of systems lends them the opposite quality" (p. 72).

In sum, the ecological perspective complements systems thinking and adds another important dimension to practice; that is, the "goodness of fit" or the adequacy of the many relationships that link clients to their social and physical environments (Germain & Gitterman, 1995; Meyer, 1993a). The ecological perspective views individuals as moving through a series of life transitions that require environmental supports and coping skills. These supports can be categorized into four types (Gitterman, 2001; Lehmann & Coady, 2001): (1) concrete, instrumental supports characterized by the services and material goods used to cope with life demands; (2) information support or the knowledge and skills that help people to cope with life's demands; (3) emotional supports provided through relationships distinguished by understanding and safety; (4) affiliational (or appraisal) support that evolves when one has access to meaningful social roles and is validated as competent. These supports provide the essential ingredients for dealing with life transitions and stressors.

The Partnership between Strengths, Empowerment, and Resiliency

The strengths perspective has been used with a variety of populations and presenting problems (Rapp, 1998; Saleebey, 1992, 1997; Tice & Perkins, 1996) and this discussion will focus on its appropriateness to the field of mental health. Although persons with mental illness face numerous challenges, the strengths perspective assumes they also possess skills and competence to draw upon in times of stress. Each person is viewed as having a wide range of life experiences, personality characteristics beyond the diagnosis, and roles that contribute to a sense of identity (Saleebey, 1997; Weick, 1983; Weick & Chamberlain, 1997). In other words, people who seek help for their problems are more than just their "problem." The strengths perspective attempts to understand clients in terms of competence and abilities and involves looking at how people manage to survive. Through an exploration of presenting concerns, the social worker seeks to clarify the client's competence (see Table 1.3).

TABLE 1.3 **THE NATURE OF THE PRESENTING PROBLEM**

Identify the reason for referral:

What made the client seek help now and not before?

How has the client sought to solve the problem previously including other therapy (and with what results)?

What is the client's ability to identify and define problems; or to discuss probable causative factors?

Describe the events leading to referral or other factors precipitating the referral.

Identify the contributing conditions and components of the problem:

History

When did the problem first occur?

Is this a long-standing unresolved problem, or a recent one?

Duration

How long has the problem been going on?

Frequency

How often does the problem occur?

Magnitude

What is the intensity of the problem?

Antecedents

What happens immediately before the problem occurs?

Consequences

What happens immediately after the problem occurs?

Clarify the client's competence:

What are the unique capacities, skills, attitudes, motivations, strengths, and potentialities of the client?

What are the particular areas of coping strengths?

What are indicators of resilience in the person?

Which areas of competence need to be reinforced or supported?

Which life experiences may be mobilized to stimulate or support the process of change?

What client resources are available for solving the problem?

How does the client relate to the worker and demonstrate the ability to use help?

What is the social worker's perception of the problem? How much agreement is there between the worker and the client concerning these problems?

Are there other difficulties associated with (or in addition to) the problem?

Reprinted with permission from *Psychopathology: A Competency-Based Assessment Model for Social Workers* by Zide/Gray (Belmont, CA: Wadsworth, 2001), p. 13.

Knowledge about ways of managing one's life in the face of adversity is useful in planning treatment and draws upon the client's resourcefulness and perseverance. The presenting problem shifts to being an opportunity to affirm the client's capabilities rather than to focus on "what is wrong." Clients are encouraged to define and ascribe meaning to their own situations (Walsh, 1996, 1998). This provides opportunities for the practitioner to validate clients' own expertise and understanding about their situation.

One of the major foci of the strengths perspective is the therapeutic relationship, which is built upon collaboration and partnership. The relationship begins when clients share their definition of the situation, the desired outcomes, and ideas about how to pursue therapeutic goals. For clients to become empowered, they must be able to attribute change, at least in part, to their own actions. It is the client's vision for his or her life that helps establish the direction for working with the practitioner. There may be times when clients do not have the "answers" about what might relieve their current distress. For example, a client who is struggling with major depression may need to obtain immediate relief from suicidal ideation. Once these emergent issues have been resolved, the strengths perspective presumes that clients do have some vision of what they want their lives to look like. The emphasis on collaboration means the social worker does not assume total responsibility for making things better. Instead, social supports such as family members, friends, and community agencies become partners in the ongoing intervention process.

The empowerment tradition in social work expands the practitioner's relationship with clients and offers an overarching perspective for thinking about any form of oppression. Thirty years ago, Solomon (1976) observed that empowerment practice can help a person realize her or his own ability to overcome personal or environmental obstacles. Empowerment involves helping stigmatized and vulnerable groups or individuals such as the mentally ill to increase and exercise interpersonal skills or community influence. In today's practice arena, oppression continues to affect our clients but empowerment practices can help them to develop a more positive sense of self, gain more knowledge about social and political environments, obtain resources and strategies that promote competence, and be supported in making meaning of their experiences (Dietz, 2000; Lee, 2001; Walsh, 1996, 1998). As such, empowerment is both a process and a goal. Empowerment occurs when people feel a sense of mastery and competence in managing their many social environments.

Although there is no universally accepted definition of empowerment, there is general agreement in the literature about the role of the practitioner as a nondirective and enabling facilitator (Boehm & Staples, 2002). As Lee (2001) posits, "people empower themselves; social workers should assist" (p. 60). Empowering practice, as defined by Rose (1990), is "a process of dialogue through which the client is continuously supported to produce the range of possibilities that she/he sees appropriate to her/his needs" (p. 49). Pinderhughes (1989) calls attention to the dynamics of power, a concept central to empowerment, and looks to the working relationship with clients as a way to foster "achieving reasonable control over one's destiny, learning to cope constructively with debilitating forces in society, and acquiring the competence to initiate change at the individual and systems levels" (Ibid., p. 136). Overcoming a sense of powerlessness is facilitated by the practitioner sharing power with clients by offering choices about ways of helping and goals. The idea is to form a working partnership with clients.

The central principles of empowerment encompass the personal, interpersonal, and community aspects of a client's life (Bartle et al., 2002; Cook et al., 1996; Gutierrez, GlenMaye, & DeLois, 1995; Kruger, 2000; Lee, 2001; Rappaport, 1987; Robbins et al., 1998, 1999; Staples, 1999). At the personal or intrapersonal level, empowerment encourages clients to actively manage their psychiatric symptoms, make choices about the development and implementation of their treatment, and develop a positive sense of self. At the interpersonal level, empowerment can be seen when a client develops social support systems or networks. At the community level, empowerment consists of participation in employment programs or collective actions to advocate for rights, improve programs, and influence governmental decisions (Kruger, 2000; Stromwall & Hurdle, 2003). Empowerment shifts clients' participation in the helping relationship from passively receiving services to actively making decisions affecting their own lives and collaborating within their social networks. Hepworth, Rooney, and Larsen (2002) underscore the importance of supporting the dignity and worth of the individual, paying attention to their "lived experience" or personal story about disempowering experiences, and tapping into energies for change. Instead of being the all-knowing expert, the practitioner actively involves clients in the helping process (Gutierrez, 1990; Gutierrez et al., 1998). The working relationship is based on mutuality and facilitating a two-way process that identifies choices and options (Deegan, 1992; Fox, 1984; Pinderhughes, 1989, 1995; Staples, 1999).

The practitioner, the client, other professionals, and lay people (including family members and others) collaborate to access resources, learn skills, and practice behaviors to improve the client's situation. The practitioner also uses environmental modification and advocacy. For example, persons with severe mental illness are often negatively labeled according to their symptoms. As a result, they experience difficulty accessing needed resources. Together, practitioners and clients challenge these negative stereotypes and present a more complete picture of the person rather than just a diagnostic "label."

According to Early and GlenMaye (2000), a "fundamental assumption of the strengths perspective is the idea that human beings are resilient" (p. 120). Emphasizing the client's resilience brings a renewed sense of hope, and this requires the practitioner to assume that clients are motivated to overcome hardship. The practitioner supports the client's belief that, with help, they can choose their own path to recovery. Resilience can be thought about as a dynamic response to multiple biological, psychological, social, and other environmental influences in a client's life (Fraser, Richman, & Galinski, 1999). Resilience consists of the internal strengths a person draws on in times of stress while protective factors represent those resources that facilitate resilience. In other words, people often survive and thrive despite the risk factors for various types of problems and situations. For example, a survivor of the World Trade Center terrorist attacks on September 11, 2001, may be struggling with the effects of post-traumatic stress disorder (e.g., flashbacks, recurrent and waking nightmares, hyper-vigilance, and autonomic responses) but may have also gained a more positive outlook and a deeper appreciation for the meaning of life and survival. During this difficult time a person may turn to family, friends, and/or other social networks for support. Resilience comes into play as individuals maintain health and wellness in the face of challenges over time.

Resilience therefore is characterized as one's ability to survive, rebound, or overcome a variety of life experiences that include adversity, stress, and deprivation (Garmezy, 1993; Hirayama & Hirayama, 1998; Kirby & Fraser, 1997). Resilience combines the interaction of both risk and protective factors (Barnard, 1994; Benard, 1997; Norman, 2000). Risk factors are stressful life events or other adverse environmental conditions that increase the individual's vulnerability, while "protective factors refer to influences that modify, ameliorate, or alter a person's response to some environmental hazard that predisposes to a maladaptive outcome" (Rutter, 1985, p. 600). Additionally, protective factors buffer, moderate, and protect a person against risk factors. These protective factors can include interpersonal relationships and the social context or support networks in the client's life. Within the strengths perspective, each person is viewed as having the potential to recover, adapt, and rebound from adversity.

People inevitably will face some form of adversity or major problem in their lives. A common response to adversity is to become overwhelmed and simply not function very well. However, some individuals are able to tap into strengths and assets that help them to quickly rebound (Gitterman, 2001; Saleebey, 1996; Saleebey, 1997). These persons, regardless of their specific problems, socioeconomic levels, ethnic or racial backgrounds, seem more competent, stable, and generally have a more positive outlook on life, appear more flexible and adaptive to changing life conditions, and are more successful in mastering developmental tasks. While there is no single strategy for helping people rebound from adversity (McCubbin, McCubbin, & Thompson, 1993; Hawley & de Hann, 1996), social workers are paying increasing attention to those factors contributing to such resilience (Greene, 2002). Notes Walsh (1995, 1996, 1998), identifying and helping people fortify those processes helps empower clients to withstand and rebound from difficult life conditions. The sense of being able to survive in the face of adversity, to be able to overcome misfortune and weather hardship seems to strengthen the individual's overall functioning. The strengths perspective and resilience share four major tenets: (1) the primary resources for change can be found in the clients themselves; (2) experience is a source of strength; (3) every environment has resources; and (4) strengths can be enhanced.

Competency-based practice is imbedded in the strengths perspective and views the interactional processes in a client's life through a resiliency lens. Treatment goals place less emphasis on viewing people as "sick" or "dysfunctional" and focus more on identifying strengths. The practitioner attempts to ascertain how persons who are dealing with adversity manage to survive and regenerate. The assumption is that all people possess strengths and resources, and the job of the practitioner is to look for those factors. This focus emphasizes strengths building and client empowerment. Resilience operationalizes the strengths perspective and sends a message of hope rather than despair regarding the impact of mental illness on an individual and his or her family.

MERGING THE DSM, RESILIENCE, AND THE COMPETENCY-BASED MODEL OF TREATMENT

The DSM–IV–TR does not support a specific theoretical orientation, and the diagnostic categories are supported by field investigations of specific factors. The classifications of mental disorders have evolved and changed over the past 50 years. According to the American Psychiatric Association (2000), genetics, biology, use of substances/alcohol, stress, and physical and psychological assaults are generally recognized as the causes of mental illness. Whatever the origins of the person's diagnosis, "it must currently be considered a manifestation of a behavioral, psychological, or biological dysfunction in the individual" (American Psychiatric Association, 2000, p. xxi). In other words, the conceptualization of a specific diagnosis suggests that it reflects the accumulation of risk and the interaction among risks rather than risk factors operating in isolation.

The competency-based model for practice balances the DSM focus on pathology by including a parallel assessment of resilience and protective factors found in the client's life. In this way, the practitioner explores how people become maladaptive and also fosters those mechanisms that foster resilience (Cowan, Cowan, & Schulz, 1996; Walsh, 1996, 1998). This paradigm considers the focus on risks but also looks for those areas that may buffer the harmful effects of various life conditions and circumstances. The competency-based treatment model identifies and capitalizes on the client's internal strengths and reinforces external supports. The assumption is that both risk and protective factors are found throughout one's life. The practitioner begins with an assessment across the life cycle to set the stage for prevention and/or intervention efforts. Typically, practitioners do not see clients when they are at their best and instead intervene in times of crisis. Looking for strengths in the face of the disruptive symptoms of mental illness is no easy task. One must look beyond these behaviors and join with the client to identify and capitalize on strengths. Genetic and biological factors can be considered as risks or protective factors. For example, genetics play a major role in the development of Bipolar Disorder or Schizophrenia. Conversely, higher than average intelligence (genetically inherited) can be considered a protective factor (Radke-Yarrow & Sherman, 1990) because these individuals can quickly grasp the complexities of a particular situation and engage in more creative forms of problem resolution.

According to Ryff, Singer, Love, and Essex (1998), there are three categories of protective factors (Table 1.4). The first category is psychological and refers to how individuals cope with and react to the events and challenges facing them. The second category is social or relational and includes family, peers, and other social supports. The third category of protective factors is sociological or environmental and is classified as social buffers.

TABLE 1.4	PROTECTIVE FACTORS AND BUFFERS IN A CLIENT'S LIFE
Client Domain	**Protective Factors and Buffers**
Psychological factors	Temperament
	Attachment
	Early coping skills
	Parenting experiences
	Belief in one's self-efficacy
	Flexible
	Adaptive
	Range of problem-solving skills
	Spirituality
	Sense of humor
	Self-esteem
	Feeling competent
	Sense of belonging
	Feeling useful, valuable
	Sense of potency
	Optimism
	Compensatory strengths
Social or relational factors	Family characterized as psychologically healthy, communicative, stable, and supportive
	Adaptive family belief systems, organizational patterns, and communication processes
	Performs well in academic and/or vocational settings
	Positive, supportive peer and/or intimate partner relationships
Sociological or environmental buffers	Network of community relationships
	Available and appropriate professional resources and knowledge about how to access help
	Adequate environmental resources (such as housing, transportation, food)
	Supportive ethnic/cultural belief system and values

Psychological Protective Factors

Early in life, temperament, attachment, early coping skills, and parenting experiences (for example, nurturance, consistency, and positive bonding) can be assessed as psychological protective factors. Intrapersonal ways of coping include a sense of self-efficacy (Aro, 1994; Rutter, 1987; Valentine & Feinauer, 1993), flexibility and adaptability (Wagnild & Young, 1993), problem-solving skills, spirituality (Valentine & Feinauer, 1993), a sense of humor (Broden, 1994), liking oneself, and strong self-esteem (Rutter, 1987; Valentine & Feinauer, 1993; Wagnild & Young, 1993). Callahan & Turnbull (2001) note, however, that "the true meaning of self-esteem in the building of resilience is controversial" (p. 177). They define self-esteem on the basis of succeeding at tasks, facing and overcoming challenges, and actual achievement. According to Smith and Carlson (1997), self-esteem is also influenced by the quality of positive interactions over time.

Sagor (1993, 2002) examined the experiences of children who continued to struggle and persevere despite the numerous obstacles and challenges before them. He found that these youngsters possessed the following personal character-istics: feeling competent; a sense of belonging; feeling useful and valuable; a sense of potency described as the belief that they have the power to change what hap-pens in their lives; and an optimistic attitude.

Von Bulow and Braiman (2001) note that becoming an articulate advocate for personal issues in a way that can help others is another valuable coping mecha-nism. The National Alliance for the Mentally Ill (NAMI) has become a powerful voice for consumers and their families on behalf of those struggling with mental illness. NAMI has been effective in teaching its members how to advocate for themselves and has become a resource for family members and professionals (Lefley, 1996). Working together through advocacy groups to fight against the stigma of mental illness and to create opportunities and services helps to raise self-esteem (Deegan, 1992). In a similar vein, developing compensatory strengths serves as a protective factor. People struggling with a mental disorder often feel defeated and view themselves as failures. Encouraging clients to use their abilities in an area where they can do well can build their confidence and self-esteem.

Social or Relational Factors

Social or relational protective factors are found in families characterized as psy-chologically healthy, communicative, stable, and supportive (Conrad, 1998; Liem, James, O'Toole, & Boudewyn, 1997). Several family processes have been identified that foster resilience and promote the development of strategies to turn adversity into true opportunities for growth. Froma Walsh (1996, 1998) developed a con-ceptual framework consisting of three domains of family functioning that foster healthy individual functioning. Her first domain consists of belief systems or the meaning a family attributes to adversity, maintaining a positive outlook, spirituality, and transcendence, such as the ability to envision new possibilities. The second do-main represents organizational patterns or the ways families are structured to carry out essential tasks. Aspects in this domain include capacity to change, flexibility, connectedness or the extent members invest themselves in one another, and social and economic resources. The third domain consists of communication processes or the family's ability to express and respond to the needs and concerns of its mem-bers and to negotiate system change to meet new demands. In particular,

> Families must also be inventive to weather and rebound from adversity. A well-functioning family draws on a wide variety of inspirations to solve its problems, including past experience, family myths and stories, creative fantasy, and new and untried solutions (Walsh, 1998, pp. 73–74).

Peer relationships begin to gain a greater importance during the early school years and are heightened during adolescence. During this phase of development, relationships extend beyond the nuclear family and begin to include intimate partners, presenting new opportunities for positive or negative changes. As the person moves into adulthood, a developmental stage characterized by the challenges of establishing a family and career, there is an increasing aggregation of risk requiring greater protection to offset those risks. The ability to perform in academic or vocational settings and to deal appropriately in social situations gains increasing importance in adult life.

Sociological or Environmental Buffers

Ecological variables such as poverty or harsh community circumstances exert a continuous influence on the client's struggles with mental illness. External support and environmental resources can act as buffers. For example, social support is important to persons with schizophrenia, a disorder characterized by withdrawal and isolation. A network of good interpersonal relationships that provide emotional support and monitor the person's illness can protect against or buffer risk factors (Aro, 1994; Valentine & Feinauer, 1993). Professional resources extend the system of care and provide additional supports for people coping with mental illness (Lukens, 2001).

The literature on adapting the concept of resilience in mental illness has assumed increasing importance in recent years. The earlier work of Rutter (1985, 1987, 1988) and others recommends that the practitioner pay attention to protective factors in the client's life, as there is evidence they improve outcomes. Further, there is reason to believe that protective factors interact with risk factors to mediate negative outcomes (Rutter & Casaer, 1991; Zimmerman & Arunkumar, 1994). Fostering resilience requires a mind-set that assumes clients are motivated to overcome hardship. In sum, client strengths can be seen and understood as a repertoire of responses protecting against risks together with the ability to use various coping mechanisms in different situations. Resilience is a dynamic process that comes into play as individuals face naturally occurring challenges over time. The central idea of tapping into resilience is to rekindle hope concerning the impact of mental illness (Greene & Livingston, 2002).

The practitioner draws from different treatment theories appropriate for each client's struggle with mental illness and related challenges. For example, psychopharmacology can be used to relieve targeted symptoms and comorbid disorders. The setting of service also plays a role; for example, hospitalization may be indicated in those instances when the person poses an imminent risk to self or others or there is deterioration in medical status. The competency-based model guides the selection of specific techniques of intervention and suggests that the practitioner choose the least restrictive level of intervention, such as partial hospitalization and/or residential treatment settings.

SUMMARY

This chapter provided an overview of the competency-based model for treatment and a description of the major elements of the model. The advantages of looking for client "strengths" without discounting the diagnostic classification system found in the DSM were elaborated. It is not unusual to find that prior to seeking professional attention, clients have tried to deal with their psychological suffering on their own or with the help of friends or family. When those efforts have failed, they seek out professional assistance. The competency-based treatment model provides a guideline on how to proceed and operationalizes the process of summarizing, prioritizing, and classifying the information found in the DSM. At the same time, the practitioner focuses on supporting client strengths and resilience while looking for resources that can be developed and supported.

Goldstein and Noonan (1999) note, "This proliferation of social work practice models has expanded the repertoire of helping approaches but also has led to fragmentation and polarization" (p. 33). As part of the integrated approach, the competency-based treatment model provides a framework for an integrative use of practice theories and techniques. Rather than simply matching procedures to specific problems, competency-based treatment helps the practitioner develop a comprehensive understanding of client struggles with mental illness and ultimately select interventions that fit with this in-depth understanding. Self-awareness and acknowledgment of cultural values are essential to effective counseling. In addition, some settings may fit well with certain practice theories. For example, many agencies set a limit on the number of sessions offered and thus the practice theories oriented toward longer-term interventions would be inappropriate. The reader is encouraged to be open to investigating different practice theories.

Chapter 2 reviews the advantages and limitations of the practice theories commonly used when working with persons with major mental illness. Subsequent chapters provide an overview of specific practice approaches considered useful for a particular disorder. As previously noted, no single perspective can address the full range of client needs or problems; however, competency-based treatment provides an orientation to treatment that draws on recent developments in the field while respecting the profession's practice wisdom and rich casework traditions. It is based on interventions identified by the practitioner and understood by the client and his or her family. Another characteristic of competency-based treatment is the identifiable connection between the client's definition of the presenting problem and skills for dealing with change. Further, competency-based treatment assumes that the practitioner *and* the client can implement the intervention with reasonable effort. In sum, the competency-based model for practice assumes that clients are able to reorganize their lives as long as they have appropriate family, community, societal, and environmental supports and resources. This paradigm shift provides a message of hope rather than despair regarding the impact of mental illness on the individual and his or her family.

Practitioner Reflections

1. Discuss the following ideas with a colleague, a group of colleagues, and/or your supervisor:
   - To what extent is competency-based treatment relevant to all populations, communities, or practice issues you encounter? As a part of this discussion, can you identify some populations or communities for whom this approach to treatment would be inappropriate?
   - How can competency-based treatment be applied to your social work agency (and also to other settings with which you are familiar)?

2. Reflect back on a particularly difficult situation in your own life. Identify those resources you were able to draw upon to move through this life event. Compare these resources to the resilience and buffering factors discussed in this chapter. As a corollary, interview a family member or friend about how they dealt with a particularly difficult situation and identify the resources and buffers drawn upon to move through this event.

3. Identify a client from your current (or past) practice experience. As you review the client's life history and struggles, what factors might you tap into to foster resilience? Include in your discussion:
   - How does the client see his or her strengths?
   - Does the client's self-perceptions of strengths agree with your assessment?
   - Taking a proactive stance, what do you think is needed in this client's current situation to prevent problems and prepare for future challenges? Be sure to identify potential or actual barriers to accessing needed resources.

4. Select one of your clients (past or current) and develop a genogram to visualize the client's network of relationships. As you review the client's family system, note patterns of alliance, conflict, and cutoff. Shifting your focus to strengths, examine the family as a potential source of resilience and identify existing and potential resources offered by extended kin and social networks. You might want to repeat this activity by drawing an ecomap.

5. The social work profession gives primacy to the interests of clients and the Code of Ethics addresses self-determination. Imagine for a moment that you are working with someone who is struggling with a diagnosis of schizophrenia and is also homeless. Identify the rights *and* needs of that individual. As part of your consideration, reflect on what factors may influence the client's ability to take care of him- or herself, consider the client's right to stay where he or she wishes even if it means living on the streets, and identify factors that may affect the client's recognition of the need for mental health treatment.

6. Take a piece of paper and fold it in half. Label one side of the paper "risks and vulnerabilities" and label the other side "protective factors and buffers." Interview a colleague about one of her or his cases. Inquire about the client's psychosocial history, current concerns and life circumstances (or conditions),

attempts at coping with the presenting problem, and interventions. As you listen, record the risks and vulnerabilities and protective factors and buffers in the client's "story." Once you have finished making these lists,

- Discuss which side of the paper has the longest list and why;
- Brainstorm together to determine if additional protective factors and buffers can be identified; and
- Discuss how the protective factors and buffers in the client's life can be used in treatment.

Counseling and Social Work Theories and Methods Supporting Competency-Based Practice

Working in myriad settings and agencies, today's social work practitioner is called upon to provide a wide variety of services to clients while also striving for community and social change. Practice is becoming increasingly complex, and the skilled practitioner usually must become familiar with several counseling theories and techniques to be able to intervene effectively with clients and communities. Some techniques are particularly useful in a managed care context with its emphasis on brief, time-limited treatment (Gibelman, 2002) and others have an established history in the profession. To anchor the integrative approach around which the competency-based treatment model is organized, this chapter provides an overview of the most widely used interventions for working with individuals living with mental illness. This overview is intended to provide a cognitive map to guide the social work practitioner through the various life circumstances or events experienced by a client whose life is dominated by mental illness. This discussion sets the stage for the practitioner's critical thinking when building a treatment plan that promotes the client's full range of competence. The goal is to recognize the difficulties in a client's life while reaching beyond these problems to tap into strengths and resources.

The chapter highlights information and skills that a social worker will need in order to provide individualized clinical services to persons struggling with mental illness—some of the most vulnerable and at-risk populations we serve (Summers, 2003). A person who is diagnosed with a mental illness must cope with complicated life conditions that have social, genetic, biochemical, and/or physiological bases. These concerns may be characterized as chronic and persistent, transient or episodic, or acute and unexpected. Often clients and their family members must confront desperate and stressful life circumstances without much forethought or careful planning. For example, in the case of Zelda "Jean" Pfohl (refer to Chapter 3 describing cognitive disorders), Jean's husband, Harry, struggles with placing his wife in a nursing home. Jean's diagnosis of Alzheimer's disease interferes with her ability to participate in the placement decision, and Harry's actions are complicated by his feelings of guilt because he and Jean had promised "never to place the other in a nursing home, no matter what." Jean is finally placed after she wanders off one night, creating a crisis for the entire family.

The author recognizes that social workers have been exposed to a wide variety of practice theories throughout their careers. In fact, during the early 1980s Corsini (1981) identified 250 different forms of psychotherapy, and fifteen years later the total had grown to more than 400 (Corsini & Wedding, 1995, 2000). It is practically impossible for social workers to have a working knowledge of all of the specialized interventions available. The practice orientations described in this chapter reflect the current literature and the profession's heightened concern for providing clinical services to those struggling with mental illness. The models presented support competency-based treatment as well as concomitant emphases on recognition of culture and diversity, creation of a collaborative relationship, and attention to the personal, interpersonal, and environmental systems in a client's life. There are no simple guidelines for matching practice theories to a client's struggles, because each individual (and his or her family) makes sense of the dominant issues and concerns differently. However, competency-based treatment does provide a framework for the practitioner to integrate a range of theoretical approaches in order to understand and respond to the client's distinctive experiences. This serves to highlight the stance or posture the practitioner takes in relation to working with this vulnerable and at-risk population. As the practitioner engages in open conversations with the client (and his or her family), the therapeutic relationship develops as a collaborative effort in which relationships are strengthened, motivation is reinforced, and everyone's contributions are fostered. Ultimately, the practitioner conveys a message of hope rather than despair regarding the impact of mental illness on the individual and his or her family.

The counseling theories and techniques reviewed in this chapter include crisis intervention, solution-focused therapy, cognitive-behavioral therapy, and psychosocial therapy. The discussion begins with an introduction to each practice perspective followed by the relevant historical background, major tenets, salient principles of practice, and advantages and disadvantages. Also reviewed are psychoeducation and practice methods for family and group work that help the practitioner to identify and promote other ways of supporting the client's social context.

Included in this chapter and those that follow are discussions of the current literature on the specialized treatment approaches considered particularly helpful for a specific diagnosis. By opening up the practitioner's thinking about the selection of treatment modalities for certain disorders, we hope to strengthen the integrative approach characteristic of the competency-based model. For example, Chapter 10 addresses the personality disorders and includes an overview of dialectical behavior therapy.

It is not unusual for social workers to work with clients who are taking psychotropic medications, and it is helpful to understand the impact of these medications. The mental health field continues to alternate between viewing mental disorders as brain diseases to be treated medically and as emotional problems to be addressed through social and psychological interventions. Since the 1960s, research has underscored the biological components of mental illness, and there is growing evidence that some disorders have a genetic component or involve a biochemical or neurological abnormality (Bradley, 2003; Gabbard & Kay, 2001). As well, economic and social forces are advancing the use of biological treatments for mental disorders (Bentley, 2003; Wade & Tavris, 2003; Walsh & Bentley, 2002). As a consequence, the practitioner is called upon to critically address the benefits of medication and to integrate this perspective into a truly biopsychosocial framework. The author recognizes that the utility, safety, and efficacy of psychiatric medications have been debated in the literature (Andreasen & Black, 2001; Austrian, 2000; Bentley & Walsh, 2001; Breggin & Cohen, 1999; Cohen, 2002, 2003; Glenmullen, 2000; Healy, 2002). However, biological explanations and related treatments have become increasingly important in today's practice arena (Luhrmann, 2000). To encourage the practitioner's critical thinking when psychiatric medications are used as a part of treatment, this chapter begins with an overview of the biological therapies. The specific medications commonly prescribed for a particular disorder are also detailed in the following chapters where appropriate; for example, Chapter 4 addresses schizophrenia and other psychotic disorders and describes the antipsychotic medications commonly prescribed for persons with this diagnosis. A medication is referred to by its generic name followed by the major trade name in parentheses.

BIOLOGICAL THERAPIES

Social workers spend a considerable amount of time with their clients—more than physicians or other members of the treatment team—and therefore play key consultative roles in assessing and monitoring medication effects (Bradley, 2003; Slavin, 2004; Walsh, 2000). They are closer to their clients and engage them on levels beyond medical concerns. Fundamental knowledge of the various chemical processes associated with medications is essential for those who work with clients taking these drugs. Thus it is helpful for the practitioner to understand the medications used in the treatment of mental disorders. This knowledge can help the practitioner discern the nature and significance of changes in physical and/or mental status, comprehend the rationale for dosage, distinguish among different means of administration, and more effectively collaborate with clients and others involved in their care.

Appropriate use of psychopharmacologic agents is intended to prevent the risk of relapse, avoid re-hospitalization, and avert adverse side effects. The wide disparity among symptom presentation, as well as clients' varying responsiveness to medication, frequently complicates a clear-cut pharmacological approach. The scope of this discussion is not to provide an in-depth course on neuroanatomy, molecular biology, or pharmacology but to describe how and why certain drugs affect people who have certain mental disorders.

Historical Background

To better understand the place of the biological therapies in the treatment of persons with mental disorders, it is helpful to look at the past. This section reviews some of the salient historical forces that have contributed to today's practice climate in the mental health field. For a more detailed overview, the reader is referred to *A History of Psychiatry: From the Era of the Asylum to the Age of Prozac* by Shorter (1997) or *Healing the Mind: A History of Psychiatry from Antiquity to the Present* by Stone (1997).

In Colonial America, those suffering from mental illnesses were referred to as "lunatics," a term derived from the root word "lunar" referring to the influence of the moon. It was believed that insanity was caused by a full moon when a baby was born or by the baby sleeping under the light of a full moon. Lunatics were thought to be possessed by the devil and were usually removed from society and locked away. Persons were grouped into two primary categories: mania and melancholy. Treatment centered on the concept of catharsis, which involved attempts to catalyze crisis or expel crisis from the individual. Procedures involved submerging a person in an ice bath until he or she lost consciousness, inducing vomiting, and causing the person to bleed. These procedures usually resulted in death or the need for lifelong care.

In 1751, Pennsylvania Hospital in Philadelphia was established as the first hospital to provide services for the mentally ill. Within the field of mental health practice, this was known as the era of "moral treatment." Treatment approaches considered the environment to play a central role, and interventions were structured so that persons could stabilize their uncontrolled thoughts and emotions. Institutionalized patients were treated as normally as possible in settings where typical social interactions were promoted and encouraged (Taubes, 1998). Work programs and recreational activities were devised to occupy patients. The science of phrenology was introduced in which the shape of the skull was studied to explain illnesses and arrive at a diagnosis.

During the mid-1800s, American psychiatrist John P. Grey championed the position that insanity was due to physical causes (Bockoven, 1963). Mental illness was thought to be caused by brain pathology and considered incurable (Barlow & Durand, 2005). Unfortunately, the use of humane treatment approaches for the mentally ill began to decline during the second half of the nineteenth century. The population of the United States grew rapidly and public institutions soon became overcrowded. Moral treatment gave way to pressures to manage patients and control their unruly behavior. Dorothea Dix called for reform and led the efforts to improve treatment of the "insane" (Kreisler & Lieberman, 1986; Marshall, 1973). She was effective in advocating for more humane care and inspired the construction of numerous new institutions. However, overcrowded and understaffed hospital conditions created ongoing demand for custodial management of patients. The population in public asylums had also changed and now included large numbers of alcoholics, violent persons, and immigrants who were said to have not adapted to the benign regime of moral treatment. With a population that was now more difficult to manage, methods of restraint were used and custodial care soon became the norm (Caplan, 1969; Rothman, 1971).

Ultimately, the mentally ill were seen as genetically defective and inferior people who were unfit for survival (Sands, 2001). Institutions, commonly referred to as asylums, became warehouses for poor people and social rejects. In the latter part of the nineteenth century medications began to be used to control aggressive behavior. The generic sedative chloral hydrate was the most popular drug, despite its potentially dangerous side effect of respiratory system paralysis. These early uses of drugs introduced questions about appropriate treatment. As noted by Bentley and Walsh (2001), "The concept of medication as restraint fostered suspicion in many social workers and other professionals through the twentieth century" (p. 10). By the end of the nineteenth century, hospitalization, such as it was, continued to be the only available course of treatment for people with mental illness.

The first two decades of the twentieth century were characterized as the progressive era in the United States. Psychological perspectives on mental illness began to re-emerge as the country began to look at the impact of social class and economic conditions on individual well being. During this time Clifford Beers published an autobiographical account of the abusive and punitive treatment he had received when he was hospitalized for delusions, suicide, depression, and mania (Sands, 2001). His book, *A Mind That Found Itself: An Autobiography* (1980), was widely read and contributed to the beginning of the "mental hygiene movement." He vividly described being restrained for days at a time, leaving him helpless and in pain. Along with reforms in the care of the mentally ill, prevention efforts also became a part of the movement (Caplan, 1969). An early supporter of the mental hygiene movement was Adolf Meyer, a neurologist and psychiatrist who envisioned the development of a comprehensive, community-based mental hygiene system (Sands, 2001). Social work reformer Julia Lathrop worked with Dr. Meyer when both were employed at an Illinois state hospital. She also advocated on behalf of the mentally ill, eventually founding the National Committee for Mental Hygiene (Costin, 1986).

During the first decade of the twentieth century social workers held positions in hospitals treating the mentally ill, and Adolf Meyer's wife was said to have been one of the first such workers (Sands, 2001). Rest, baths, and hydrotherapy along with nonspecific sedative drugs such as barbiturates, bromides, and chloral hydrate were the primary treatments through the 1940s. Between 1900 and 1950, the physical interventions of shock therapy and the lobotomy (a surgical procedure in which certain nerve tracts in the frontal lobe area of the brain were severed in an attempt to reduce a person's tension and psychotic symptoms) were developed. The lobotomy was considered a delicate procedure that could be performed quickly and easily to ameliorate a patient's symptoms. By today's standards the surgery could be considered barbaric. It involved several quick shocks to the patient's head to induce sedation. Next, one of the patient's eyelids would be rolled back and the physician would insert a device about two-thirds the size of a pencil through the upper eyelid into the head. Guided by markings, the device would be tapped with a hammer into the frontal lobe of the brain. After the appropriate depth was achieved, the physician would manipulate the device back and forth in a sweeping motion within the patient's head. Because the lobotomy appeared to effectively alter the mental health of patients, it was widely used in the nation's asylums. However, the procedure became increasingly controversial after it was linked to numerous complications and deaths.

The second half of the twentieth century saw dramatic changes in treatment practices. During the 1950s the first effective drugs for severe psychotic disorders were systematically developed and the therapeutic effects of the drug chlor-promazine (Thorazine) were reported (Bentley & Walsh, 2001). Ten years later, researchers discovered a series of drugs forming the major classifications that continue to be used today in the treatment of mental illness. Beginning in the 1960s, state and federal public policies further changed approaches to treatment. Most notable was the move to deinstitutionalize mental patients. Advances in drug treatment, together with passage of the Comprehensive Mental Health Bill in 1964 and the Medicare and Medicaid Acts in 1966 led to diminished use of existing mental health hospitals. The practices of involuntary commitment, cruel or nonexistent treatment, and methods of controlling patients were investigated (Cooper, 1967; Laing, 1967; Scheff, 1966; Szasz, 2001). To protect patients' human rights, individualized treatments were emphasized (Sands, 2001). Individuals who had been institutionalized were now able to function in society with adequate outpatient care. Some have argued that deinstitutionalization was made possible by psychotropic medication (Brill, 1980), and it is clear that medications became a natural part of life for many with serious mental illness and a necessary support to live in the community (Gelman, 1999). Outpatient services, day and night hospitalization, diagnostic services, and aftercare programs were introduced. Community mental health centers, private hospitals, and general hospitals with psychiatric wings increased and the more restrictive long-term care provided in state mental institutions diminished throughout the late 1960s and early 1970s. The use of medications had become prevalent and produced new forms of therapeutic and management relationships (Longhofer, Floersch, & Jenkins, 2003). During the last decades of the twentieth century, managed mental health care was introduced as a cost-effective means to provide employees with health care benefits, and the private sector began to take a more active role in managing costs.

In summary, there have been many changes in the treatment of persons with mental illness over the years. The evolution of medications as treatment resources poses ongoing challenges for practitioners in the twenty-first century. The introduction of psychotropic medications seems to have created sharp distinctions between the medical approach to treatment and social and community interventions. It would seem that today's practitioner is called upon to critically evaluate these divergent perspectives in order to integrate them into the biopsychosocial framework that is fundamental to the social work profession.

Tenets of Biological Therapies

The psychotropic medications are divided into various "classes" or groups. Sources used to develop the following discussion include Austrian (2000); Bentley and Walsh (2001); Dziegielewski (2002); Kaplan and Sadock (1998); and Walsh and Bentley (2002). The main classes of drugs used to treat mental and emotional disorders are described below.

Antipsychotic Drugs Sometimes referred to as *neuroleptics*, these medications are used in treating schizophrenia and other psychoses. The antipsychotic medications can reduce the positive symptoms of schizophrenia, including agitation, delusions, and hallucinations, and can shorten schizophrenic episodes. They offer little relief and in some cases may even worsen negative symptoms such as emotional flatness, isolation, concentration, or confused thoughts. The newer or second-generation drugs do not seem to cause the same levels of side effects found with the earlier drugs, including extrapyramidal effects (such as akathisia or extreme internal restlessness and muscle discomfort; dystonias or involuntary movements of the tongue, jaw, or entire body; and parkinsonian effects) and anticholinergic effects (such as dry mouth, blurred vision, constipation, and urinary hesitancy that can result from the suppressive action of certain antipsychotic and antidepressant medications on the action of acetylcholine in the brain and peripheral nervous system). As well, these second-generation drugs may reduce some negative symptoms.

Antidepressant Drugs   These drugs are used primarily in treating aggression, anxiety, phobias, and obsessive-compulsive disorder. The types include monoamine oxidase inhibitors (MAOIs), the cyclic drugs (so named for their chemical structure or rings), and the newest category of selective serotonin reuptake inhibitors (SSRIs). There are also a number of "atypical" antidepressant drugs that do not fit into the aforementioned categories because of their unique chemical make-up.

Mood Stabilizing Drugs   This is a special category of drug, called lithium (Lithium Carbonate), found helpful for people who struggle with bipolar disorder. A person's blood levels must be carefully monitored while taking lithium because too little medication will not provide a therapeutic effect and too much is toxic and can even be fatal. Certain antiseizure medications can also act as mood stabilizers, including valproate (Depakote) and carbamazepine (Tegretol).

Anti-Anxiety Drugs   This category is also commonly referred to as tranquilizers, and the benzodiazepines comprise the largest class of anti-anxiety drugs. They were primarily developed for treatment of mild anxiety and are designed for short-term use. Long-term use can contribute to problems with withdrawal and tolerance (a condition in which the person needs larger and larger doses to achieve the same results).

Herbs and Stimulants   Herbs, often referred to as botanicals, are used for medicinal purposes. They may come from the stems, leaves, roots, and flowers of various plants. Herbal remedies and other dietary supplements are currently exempt from regulation by the Food and Drug Administration (FDA), and specific brands may vary in quality and in the amount of active ingredient they contain.

Each class of medications has a distinct chemical structure that acts on different chemicals in the brain. The following discussion provides a brief overview of how these drugs work.

Principles of Practice

The primary functions of the nervous system are to gather and process information, produce responses to stimuli, and coordinate the workings of different cells (Preston & Johnson, 2001; Walsh & Bentley, 2002). The central nervous system (which includes the brain and spinal cord) receives, processes, interprets, and stores information and sends messages to the muscles, glands, and organs. Neurons are the basic units of the nervous system. The nervous system comes to life with chemical couriers such as the neurotransmitters. The brain directs and controls behavior by the transmission of messages across neurons in the brain through a complicated process of electrical and chemical reactions (Stuart & Laraia, 2001; Wade & Tavris, 2003). These messages are forwarded by means of chemicals called neurotransmitters (formed in the cell body of the neuron by the interaction of specific enzymes and amino acids).

Neurons do not directly touch each other but are separated by a very minute space called the synaptic cleft; that is, the place where the axon terminal of one neuron nearly touches a dendrite or the cell body of another neuron. The entire site, including the axon terminal (or the presynaptic neuron), the cleft, and the covering membrane of the receiving dendrite or cell (postsynaptic neuron) is called a synapse. When a neural impulse reaches the axon terminal's tip, it must get its message across the synaptic cleft to another cell. At this point, synaptic vesicles (or tiny sacs in the tip of the axon terminal) open and release a few thousand molecules of a chemical substance called a neurotransmitter. Figure 2.1, adapted from Barlow and Durand (2005), Sands (2001), and Wade and Tavris (2003), illustrates this process.

At this point, one of three things happens to the neurotransmitter: (1) it binds to a specific site on the postsynaptic cell membrane of the next neuron; (2) some of the neurotransmitter is reabsorbed into the presynaptic cell to be stored until the next release of transmitter; (3) some of the neurotransmitter is broken down and metabolized by enzymes such as monoamine oxidase or acholinesterase.

Through their effects on specific nerve circuits, neurotransmitters can affect behavior that is demonstrated by mood, emotion, and/or psychomotor activity. Some of the better-understood neurotransmitters and their known or suspected effects are listed below:

- *Serotonin* affects neurons involved in sleep, appetite, sensory perception, temperature regulation, pain suppression, and mood.
- *Dopamine* affects neurons involved in voluntary movement, learning, memory, and emotion.
- *Acetylcholine* affects neurons involved in muscle action, cognitive functioning, memory, and emotion.
- *Norepinephrine* affects neurons involved in increased heart rate and the slowing of intestinal activity during stress, and neurons involved in learning, memory, dreaming, waking from sleep, and emotion.
- *GABA* (gamma-amino butyric acid) functions as the major inhibitory neurotransmitter in the brain (Wade & Tavris, 2003).

Abnormal levels of neurotransmitters have been implicated in several disorders, including Alzheimer's disease, psychosis, anxiety, and depression (Brems, 2000; Stuart & Laraia, 2001). For example, people with Alzheimer's disease lose brain cells responsible for producing acetylcholine, and this loss may help account for their memory problems. Psychosis is thought to involve excessive dopamine and serotonin neurotransmission. Low levels of serotonin and norepinephrine

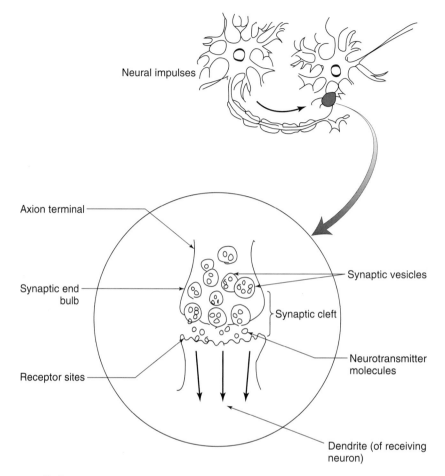

FIGURE **2.1**

TRANSMISSION OF MESSAGES ACROSS NEURONS IN THE BRAIN

have been associated with severe depression. Anxiety is believed to involve a dysregulation of GABA and other transmitters.

Unquestionably, drugs have helped people reduce the sadness, despair, confusion, and anxiety associated with various diagnostic categories. Thanks to these medications, many persons struggling with severe and debilitating behaviors have been able to respond to psychotherapy and function productively. Despite the increasing popularity of medication, however, a few words of caution are in order. It is helpful for the practitioner to think critically about the biological therapies. According to Paul and Elder (2002), critical thinking means stepping outside of the dominant perspective and examining ideas in a logical and ethical fashion. Biological therapies are not perfect, and we need to weigh their drawbacks against the benefits they can produce.

Advantages and Disadvantages of Biological Therapies

Advantages   Biological therapy has been seen as a safe and effective treatment for many disorders. For instance, antidepressant drugs are reported to be 60 to 70 percent effective in the treatment of mood disorders (Bentley & Walsh, 2001; Dziegielewski, 2001). They have enabled some persons struggling with severe depression to function and participate actively in counseling (Andreasen & Black, 2001; Moncrieff, 2001). Others have gained relief from panic attacks or the debilitating behaviors associated with obsessive-compulsive disorder or schizophrenia. According to Hales and Hales (1995), the newer psychiatric medications are correcting chemical imbalances in the brain and have fewer side effects than the earlier drugs.

Critically assessing the role of medication in treatment and integrating these ideas with the client's beliefs about health and illness gives us an opportunity to become more aware of our own beliefs about what helps people. It also makes it possible to become more sensitive to the client's experience with mental illness. For example, how does the fragmented, confusing, chaotic experience of the client with schizophrenia influence her or his perceptions of antipsychotic medications (Bradley, 2003)? Consciously reflecting on these multiple dynamics sets the stage for a deeper understanding of the client, the diagnosis, and the relevance of biological interventions.

As a parallel, the practitioner can also focus on his or her own countertransference reactions (those conscious or unconscious emotional reactions to a client experienced by the practitioner) (Rubin, 2001). Bradley (2003) suggests looking at how one considers a referral for medication for those clients characterized as "hard to treat"—for example, someone who is grandiose, belligerent, sexually provocative, elated, or sad and depressed. This level of self-reflection can foster a greater appreciation for the client's capacities and strengthen the helping relationship in a way that is not possible if we distance ourselves from uncomfortable feelings by focusing on medication.

Disadvantages   After six decades of outlawing direct-to-consumer advertising of prescription drugs, in 1997 the U.S. Food and Drug Administration (FDA) began allowing pharmaceutical companies to advertise directly to consumers, a practice prohibited in other countries such as Canada (Cohen, 2003; Littrell, 2003). The marketing campaigns we all now commonly see on television of drugs such as Paxil, Prozac, Zyban, or Zoloft indicate that these prescribed medications can now be sought after on the basis of consumer preferences. The individuals featured in those advertisements look attractive and healthy, leading the public to believe that one can look and act just like them by taking the medication featured in the ads.

Gosden and Beder (2001) suggest that the pharmaceutical industry, one of the most profitable industries in the United States, is setting the agenda in mental health. Drug companies are spending fortunes to study and market highly profitable products (Fortune, 2000). Once the FDA approves a drug, it can be prescribed for other conditions and to populations other than those on which it was originally tested. Wade and Tavris (2003) note that when the patent for Prozac expired, it was renamed Sarafem and marketed to women for "premenstrual dysphoric disorder." Researchers who are examining the effectiveness of various medications can fall prey to the influence of money and power (Healy, 2002; Safer, 2002; Schulman et al., 2002). For instance, some have financial ties to the pharmaceutical industry and obtain lucrative consulting fees or funding for studies, stock investment opportunities, and patents (Angell, 2000; Bodenheimer, 2000). Social work professor David Cohen (2002, 2003), an ardent critic of psychiatric medication, cautions the practitioner to consider the industry's economic interest in promoting the biological therapies.

Ross and Pam (1995) observe that improvements in symptomatology are not always supported by sound neuroscience research. Instead, effectiveness seems to be ascertained through a process of trial and error. If one medication does not work, another medication (or combination) is tried to determine the most effective regimen. Another challenge with medication is to find the therapeutic window or the amount that is enough but not too much. This trial-and-error process is complicated by the fact that the same dose may be metabolized differently in men and women, and in members of different age and/or ethnic groups (Lin, Poland, & Chien, 1990; Morley & Hall, 2004; Willie, Rieker, Kramer, & Brown, 1995). For instance, African Americans diagnosed with depression or bipolar disorder seem to require lower doses of tricyclic antidepressants and lithium than other ethnic groups (Strickland, Lin, Fu, Anderson, & Zheng, 1995; Strickland et al., 1991). Fava (2003) questions whether antidepressants may in fact worsen depression. After reviewing decades of clinical literature and recent neurobiological findings, he has concluded that long-term treatment with antidepressants has had poor outcomes. He goes on to suggest that people may develop a tolerance and resistance to antidepressants independent of symptom severity (a phenomenon known as fading). Others view medication as a powerful form of social control, or worse yet, as dangerous neurotoxins with no clear benefit (Breggin, 1997; Breggin & Cohen, 1999).

Another disadvantage to the biological therapies is the unpleasant side effects, which cause half to two-thirds of people to stop taking their medication (Glenmullen, 2000; Torrey, 1995). Some antipsychotic drugs are known to have dangerous or even fatal consequences when taken for many years. For example, approximately one-fourth of all adults and one-third of elderly persons taking antipsychotics develop tardive dyskinesia (hand tremors and other involuntary muscle movements) (Saltz et al., 1991). Less is known about the long-term effects of taking antidepressants (Glenmullen, 2000).

Despite the disagreement about safety and efficacy, biological therapy continues to be widely used. Yet it is not uncommon for the social worker in mental health settings to encounter clients who do not take their medication regularly. This can create potential ethical issues surrounding adherence since there is a fine line between coercing versus encouraging a person to take their psychotropic medication. Walsh (as cited in Slavin, 2004) observes, "It is better to think in terms of risk factors for nonadherence and protective factors for adherence" (p. 4). Risk factors may include, for example, the adverse side effects, forgetfulness, a history of substance abuse, or an aftercare setting that could be characterized as cold, unfriendly, and unsupportive. Protective factors include acknowledgment that one has an illness, adequate education about potential side effects, and financial resources to afford the medication.

Whatever one's perspective on the effects of medications on mental illness, the author hopes this basic overview of a very complex process will provide a rudimentary understanding of the psychotropic medications. The following section shifts the discussion to an overview of crisis intervention.

CRISIS INTERVENTION

Many people experience times in their life when they become severely distraught by a problem or situation and feel unable to manage what has happened. The defining characteristic of people in crisis is disequilibrium, a state in which people may feel overwhelmed, confused, upset, or disorganized and may lack the ability to make rational decisions (Myer & James, 2005). Therefore, it is essential for the practitioner to distinguish a person in crisis from someone who is simply feeling stressed. According to Dattilio & Freeman (1994), "The term *crisis* generally evokes an image of any one of a number of very negative life events" (p. 1). Kaplan and Sadock (1998) posit that a crisis is the individual's response to hazardous events, experienced as a "painful state." Some practitioners consider the crisis to be an emergency situation wherein clients are dangerous to themselves or others; for example, they may be unable to feed, clothe, or care for themselves. Others believe that clients who ask to be seen immediately are likely to be experiencing a crisis situation. On the other hand, if clients believe their problem can wait 48 hours, then perhaps they may be simply "stressed."

Regardless of which definition of *crisis* is used, practitioners generally agree that crisis intervention focuses on responding to a wide range of phenomena that affect the biopsychosocial functioning of the client, family, or group and create a serious state of disequilibrium (Parad & Parad, 1990, 1999). Crisis intervention is an approach that is limited by the parameters of the client's current presenting problem. Whatever fuels a crisis is not simply defined by a particular situation or set of circumstances, but rather by the person's perception of the event and his or her ability (or inability) to effectively cope with those circumstances.

Crisis intervention views the emotional disturbance as a two-fold process: first, the stressful situation, and second, the underlying emotional dispositions that come to the surface during this crisis situation (Zastrow, 1999). Persons living with mental illness encounter many situations for which crisis intervention strategies are considered very appropriate, such as episodes of depression, suicidal ideation, or lack of medication adherence. Crisis intervention focuses on relieving the acute symptoms experienced while at the same time promoting adaptation and the ability to cope (Eaton & Roberts, 2002; James & Gilliand, 2005). According to Parad and Parad (1999), the practitioner considers three areas: (1) What is most worrisome to the client? (2) Why is the client currently seeking help? (3) How can assistance most effectively be provided? The first two areas focus on the client's presenting problem and his or her perception of the crisis event. The third area explores the client's ideas about how the practitioner might be helpful. The practitioner provides information and education, while the client becomes better informed about what is happening to him or her and able to consider different options and resources.

Historical Background

The origin of crisis intervention can be traced to Eric Lindemann and his colleagues at Massachusetts General Hospital. They played an important role following the devastating loss of 493 lives in Boston's Coconut Grove nightclub fire on November 28, 1942. This disaster is considered the worst single-building fire in United States history. Lindemann and his associates immediately began helping those who survived the fire, as well as those who lost family members and friends. After working with these survivors and bereaved persons, Lindemann (1944) theorized that people deal with grieving and loss as a series of stages through which they must progress if they are to accept and resolve loss. His seminal work laid the groundwork for what is now called crisis intervention. Several years later, Lindemann and his associates were instrumental in establishing Boston's Wellesley Human Service, one of the country's first community mental health agencies, which earned a reputation for providing short-term preventative therapy.

Sociologist Reuben Hill (1949) furthered the systems perspective supporting Lindemann's work. Hill began examining war-induced family stress, separation, and reunion during and after World War II. Hill proposed the ABCX framework for working with families in crisis. He posited that when "A" (the event) interacted with "B" (the family's crisis-meeting resources) and "C" (the definition each family member attributed to the event), it produced "X" (the crisis). He suggested that determinants "B" and "C" lie within the realm of the family itself, and should be seen in terms of the family's resources and values (Ell, 1995). Hill's work helped explain and predict dysfunctional family behavior and family breakdown (McCubbin & McCubbin, 1992).

Tyhurst (1958) described the reactions of "healthy" individuals experiencing severe stress. His work advocated prompt intervention soon after the exposure to a traumatic event in order to bring about a positive outcome. Crisis intervention views the client as extremely resilient and able to survive even under the most catastrophic life conditions, threats, and traumas. Selye's (1956) work described an "alarm reaction"; that is, change in one part of an individual causes disequilibrium among all parts. How a person struggles to regain a sense of balance, known as "homeostasis," provides insight into how she or he will cope with change. Selye further refined the concept of the precipitating event by noting that people can become exhausted by repeated attempts to overcome "the threat."

Psychiatrist Gerald Caplan (1964) suggested the three most important factors sustaining an individual's mental health were the state of the ego, the stage of maturity, and the quality of life. Caplan postulated that assessing the individual's ego state should be based on three areas: (1) the capacity to withstand both stress and anxiety in order to maintain equilibrium; (2) the degree of reality recognized and faced in problem solving; and (3) the range of effective coping mechanisms used. Caplan (1964) suggested that crisis occurs

> when a person faces an obstacle to important life goals that is, for a time, insurmountable through the utilization of customary methods of problem solving. A period of disorganization ensues, a period of upset, during which many abortive attempts at solutions are made (p. 8).

Caplan further believed that individuals should be seen as constantly living in a state of emotional equilibrium with the goal of always returning to (or maintaining) that state. According to Caplan, the "crisis" occurs when conventional problem-solving techniques cannot be used and the individual's balance or equilibrium is upset. The person must either solve the problem or not, and in either case a new state of equilibrium develops.

During the late 1960s and the 1970s, social worker Howard Parad (1971) further refined crisis theory. The concept of crisis intervention emphasized not only immediate responses to an emergency situation, but included longer-term support aimed at preventing future problems. Slaiku (1990) defined crisis as "a temporary state of upset and disorganization, characterized chiefly by an individual's inability to cope with a particular situation using customary methods of problem-solving, and by the potential for a radically positive or negative outcome" (p. 15). In sum, crisis intervention aims at resolving the immediate crisis and restoring individuals to their previous level of functioning (Aguilera, 1998).

Tenets of Crisis Intervention

Crisis intervention techniques are borrowed from other approaches. Key strategies include behavioral rehearsal or role-playing, support, confrontation, and active listening. Whitaker's (1974) classic work summarizes crisis counseling as follows:

> Requisite worker skills include the ability to function effectively in an emotionally tense atmosphere and to give support and direction while at the same time helping the client to develop autonomous coping skills. Crisis intervention generally progresses in the following manner: (1) an attempt is made to alleviate the disabling tension through ventilation and the creation of a climate of trust and hope. (2) Next the worker attempts to understand the dynamics of the event that precipitated the crisis. (3) The worker gives his (or her) impression and understanding of the crisis and checks out these perceptions with the client. (4) Client and worker attempt to determine specific remedial measures that can be taken to restore equilibrium. (5) New methods of coping may be introduced. (6) Finally, termination occurs—often after a predetermined number of interviews—when the agreed-upon goals have been realized (p. 212).

Clients who struggle with mental illness (and/or their families) may experience a number of circumstances and stressful events encountered by people without a DSM diagnosis, such as physical illness, the loss of a loved one, divorce, major life transitions, homelessness, moving to a new location, getting married, having a child, or experiencing a natural or man-made disaster (Dattilio & Freeman, 1994;

James & Gilliand, 2005). The major goal of crisis intervention is to help the client regain psychological equilibrium as quickly as possible. Greenstone & Leviton (2002) suggest seven steps for successful intervention: the practitioner must act immediately, take control, listen, access the situation, decide how to handle the situation, make a referral (if needed), and follow up.

Okun (1997) identifies six core components of crisis intervention:

- Focus on specific and time-limited treatment goals to help the client reduce the "tension" and learn adaptive problem solving.
- Clarify and accurately assess the source of stress and the meaning the client attributes to the stressor.
- Foster the client's adaptive problem-solving mechanisms aimed at helping to return to pre-morbid functioning.
- Identify the client's cognitive perceptions, confronting denial and distortions, and provide emotional support.
- Use existing client relationship networks and/or develop new ones to provide additional avenues of support and help to implement effective coping strategies.
- Reduce the client's need for future services (p. 235).

Principles of Practice

There are many ways to intervene in a crisis situation. The following intervention sequence is based on ideas from Aguilera (1998), Okun (1997), and Wells and Giannetti (1993).

STAGE ONE: FORMING THE RELATIONSHIP AND SETTING THE STAGE FOR CHANGE

Step One: Entry.
- Assess cognitive, affective, and behavioral reactions to crisis incident(s) and explore what the incident(s) mean to the client.
- Explore significant relationship systems, such as family, employment, friends, and community supports.
- Provide ongoing opportunities to express and/or ventilate feelings.

Step Two: Clarifying the presenting problem.
- Examine major environmental variables, including the "how," "when," or "where" associated with the presenting problem.
- Determine strengths or weaknesses in the client's situation.
- Ascertain the events leading up to the crisis, paying particular attention to the past 24 hours.
- Determine the reason the client requires help at this time.
- Evaluate problem-solving and coping strategies used in dealing with this crisis or similar life events.
- Determine the phase of crisis: for example, whether the client is disorganized and/or overwhelmed by the crisis or moving toward recovery of a "steady state."
- Assess the severity of the crisis, such as the client's potential danger to self or others.

Step Three: Contracting the helping relationship.
- Help the client gain an intellectual understanding of the crisis event.
- Reduce the tension that immobilizes the client.
- Begin setting goals for the "work."

Step Four: In-depth exploration of crisis situation and reactions.
- Explore the extent to which the crisis has disrupted the client's life.
- Examine the effects of this disruption on others in the client's environment.
- Find alternative ways of coping.
- Reinforce adaptive coping.

Step Five: Discuss goals and objectives for treatment.
- Restate problem focus.
- Set time limits.
- Introduce new supports into the client's world, if needed.
- Establish "responsibilities"—for example, what practitioner can and cannot do to help.

STAGE TWO: STRATEGIES

Step 1: Achieve mutual acceptance of defined goals and objectives.
- Both the client and the practitioner have a clear understanding of what needs to happen.
- Both the client and the practitioner agree on the "next steps."

Step 2: Plan strategies.
- Consider utilization of support groups and other types of resources.

Step 3: Carry out strategies (including, but not limited to, the following).
- Information and advocacy
- Facilitation of linkages with natural support systems, including family members and friends
- Referral to appropriate resources
- Concrete assistance
- Assertiveness training
- Modeling, coaching, and behavioral rehearsal
- Contracting
- Cognitive restructuring
- Ventilation
- Decision making
- Systematic desensitization
- Gestalt experiments

Step 4: Evaluate strategies.
- Establish procedures to measure goals.

Step 5: Terminate the intervention.
- Set realistic plans for the immediate future.
- Reiterate the client's accurate appraisal of crisis event and confirm the appropriate management of feelings.

- Ensure the client's willingness to seek and accept help from others when appropriate.
- Discuss anticipatory planning of future crisis events.

Step 6: Follow up with the client.
- Determine whether the crisis resolution endured.

The practitioner focuses on the client's presenting problem and perceptions regarding the crisis-induced concern, and then decides upon the actual method of intervention. The goal is to return clients to their previous level of functioning, address potentially self-destructive behaviors, and avoid a future recurrence. Typically, crisis strategies aim at helping the client cushion the stressful event by providing emotional and environmental supports while helping clients to strengthen coping skills during the active crisis period (Parad & Parad, 1999; Scaturo, 2002).

Crisis intervention is brief in nature and provides rapid assistance during a time when clients are emotionally distressed. Community supports and resources are most helpful during the active crisis state and include a range of services such as incarceration (Fox, 1999), mental health facilities, halfway housing, runaway shelters (Zide & Cherry, 1992), emergency foster care, hospitalization, domestic battery shelters (Corcoran, Stephenson, Perryman, & Allen, 2001), social networks involving children, adolescents, and families (Fanolis 2001; Tyson, 1999), homemaking or respite care services, trauma care (Miller, 2001), or legal aid services (Parad & Parad, 1990, 1999). The practitioner may also refer clients to self-help resources such as 12-step programs (for example, Alcoholics Anonymous) or bereavement groups (Gray, Zide, & Wilker, 2000).

Advantages and Disadvantages of Crisis Intervention

Advantages   Crisis intervention techniques help people strengthen their resources and identify, affirm, and potentially reinforce ways of turning adversity into strength and growth. A crisis can present both threat and opportunity (Aguilera, 1998), and prior success in coping with stressful events often fosters resilience (Rutter, 1987; Smith & Carlson, 1997; Walsh, 1996; Blagys 2002). Notes Walsh (1998), successful mastery can "attest to the human potential to emerge from a shattering experience scarred yet strengthened" (p. 9). More significantly, people can come to believe their efforts and actions can yield success. In other words, learned helplessness can be unlearned through experiences of mastery as clients begin to acknowledge their efforts and actions as being successful.

Social work practitioners have progressively become more attracted to crisis intervention as an effective method of delivering rapid services for clients experiencing acute problems (Keitel & Kopala, 2000), interpersonal stress (Corsini & Wedding, 2000), life cycle or other transitional changes (Zastrow, 1999), and natural or man-made disasters (Keane, 1998). This approach relies on the structured use of time limits; understanding client dynamics within a systems perspective; use of the family life-style concept, with attention to its values, roles, and communication patterns; appreciation of the intervening problem-solving used by families to cope with crisis events; and the relevance of the need-response pattern as a way of measuring the success of these coping efforts (Currie, 2002; Greenstone & Leviton, 2002; Parad & Parad, 1990, 1999).

Crisis intervention aims at helping the client achieve a "homeostatic balance" and is considered an effective way to help those who struggle with mental illness (Roberts & Dziegielewski, 1995). Services are offered through a variety of social work agencies in both traditional and nontraditional settings (Zastrow, 1999; Parad & Parad, 1990, 1999), as well as multidisciplinary settings including public social services, community mental health centers, hospital emergency rooms, "hotlines," and mobile crisis units. Crisis intervention helps to limit long waiting lists, avoids complex intake screening, encourages an open door policy, uses telephone follow-up interviews, and avoids transferring clients to other agencies for longer-term treatment.

Disadvantages   Ell (1995) suggests that not enough attention has been paid to comparative outcome studies for different types of crisis techniques. Little is known about how well crisis intervention practice works with culturally diverse populations. In addition, diverse community settings such as churches, mutual help groups, and senior centers have been found to be effective buffers to life stresses, but the ways in which crises are precipitated, mediated, or exacerbated by social systems or by the absence of adequate community service systems is less clearly understood.

Another counseling perspective supporting competency-based practice is the solution-focused therapy model.

SOLUTION-FOCUSED THERAPY

Despite efforts to incorporate a strengths-based or empowerment perspective in mental health practice, the pathology-oriented medical model continues to be the dominant perspective (Gingerich & Wabeke, 2001). Solution-focused therapy, by contrast, is a post-modern approach that shifts the treatment perspective away from a deficit-based orientation. Each client experience is seen as individualized, and the use of general, predetermined meanings and contents is rejected. Organized around constructivist theory, this approach emphasizes the client's frame of reference (or view of reality) and explores the "fit" between the client and relevant aspects of his or her environment. Constructivism provides a rationale for respecting the preeminence of the client's world-view and emphasizes the client's own idiosyncratic meaning system as the impetus for therapy.

Solution-focused therapy is extremely versatile and has been successfully adapted to a variety of different populations and life conditions, circumstances and events, including nursing home placement (Sidell, 1997), alcohol abuse (Berg & Reuss, 1997; Reuss, 1997), incarcerated criminals (Lindforss & Magnusson, 1997), bereavement (Wilker, Gray, & Zide, 1998; Gray, Zide, & Wilker, 1998, 2000; Webb, 1999; Zide & Gray, 1999), sexual abuse (Kruczek & Vitanza, 1999; O'Hanlon &

Bertolino, 1998a), discharge planning (Nickerson, 1995); mandated clients (Osborn, 1999), anxiety disorders (Araoz & Carrese, 1996), chronic mental illness (Booker & Blymer, 1994; Rowan & O'Hanlon, 1999; Webster, Vaughn, & Martinez, 1994), school problems (Durrant, 1995; Teall, 2000), difficult adolescents (Selekman, 1993; Summers, 2003), in-patient psychiatric care (Kok & Leskela, 1996; Osborn, 1999), weight loss (Dolan, 1997); homeless mothers (Lindsey, 2000), homeless substance abusers (Berg & Hopwood, 1991), immigrant health issues (Aambo, 1997), child protection/custody (Barsky, 1995; Berg & Kelly, 2000), domestic violence (Lee, Greene, & Rheinscheld, 1999), client emotions (Kiser, Piercy, & Lipchik, 1993; Miller, Hubble, & Duncan, 1996), intergenerational family issues (O'Hanlon & O'Hanlon, 2002; Zide & Gray, 2000), single-session adolescent groups (Littrell, Malia, & Vanderwood, 1995), and supervision (Gray & Zide, 1998; Lowe & Guy, 1996; Triantafillou, 1997; Wetchler, 1990).

Historical Background

Solution-focused brief therapy (SFBT) is a strengths-based approach developed at the Brief Family Therapy Center in Milwaukee, Wisconsin. Pioneers of this approach include Steve de Shazer (1982, 1985, 1988, 1990, 1991, 1994), Insoo Kim Berg (Berg & Miller, 1992; Berg, 1994; Berg & de Jong, 1996), and others (Adams, Piercy, & Jurich, 1991; Miller, Hubble, & Duncan, 1996; Nichols & Schwartz, 1995; Rowan & O'Hanlon, 1999; Walter & Peller, 1992). Many of the adaptations of brief therapy used today originated within the early family therapy movement, primarily from the strategic approaches that evolved during the late 1950s and early 1960s. It was during this period that Milton Erickson introduced several important concepts that influenced the advancement of this approach (Horne, 2000). Erickson used the client's own cognitive processes and applied them to problematic situations in ways that helped change behaviors (Cade & O'Hanlon, 1993; Rowan & O'Hanlon, 1999). He emphasized interactional skills aimed at helping the client develop better ways of dealing with relationships, and his therapeutic interventions were oriented toward the future. He believed the client's history or problem formulation was irrelevant to the work of change. Erickson employed symbolic and metaphorical communication, and he emphasized results achieved rather than how long the client was in treatment (Fanger, 1995).

During the late 1970s de Shazer adapted many elements of Erickson's work and by the early 1980s a distinctive approach had emerged that focused on solution development (de Shazer, 1985, 1990), currently referred to as solution-focused brief therapy. The task of treatment shifts to solution formulation instead of focusing on the "problem" (Berg & de Jong, 1996; de Jong, 2002; de Jong & Berg, 1998, 2002). Solution-focused therapy focuses on the client's strengths and resources rather than on problems, deficiencies, or pathology (de Jong & Berg, 1997, 1998, 2002). This approach moves away from other traditionally held forms of therapy in several notable ways. First, because the solution-focused approach is designed to be brief, the practitioner plays a more active role in shifting the focus of work as quickly as possible from problems to solutions (Prochaska & Norcross, 1999; Quick, 1998; Redpath & Harker, 1999; Sharry, Madden, & Darmody, 2003; Teall,

2000) while guiding the client to explore strengths and work toward solutions. Second, the client is considered to be in charge and is viewed as the "expert" regarding which goals to construct. A third difference from other forms of therapy revolves around perspectives about how clients change. Solution-focused therapy is concerned with helping clients co-construct their own "solutions" by exploring the future despite the fact that the future has not yet occurred. This perspective assumes people have inherent resources to change and are able to construct their own solutions. "Smart questioning techniques" aim to help the client think about behavioral changes that emphasize solutions. This focus on "smart questioning" distinguishes solution-focused therapy from other approaches. Using these smart questions helps the practitioner to move the client beyond a sense of failure they may have experienced through repeated attempts at trying to "solve the problem" and shift the focus to negotiating goals and possibilities, determining the direction of change, and providing future-oriented questions (Berg, 1994). Using the "miracle question" helps the client visualize future solutions; "scaling questions" identify ways to measure success, client motivation, and/or the ability to prioritize "next steps"; and "exceptions" and "coping" questions provide a blueprint for identifying times when the problem is either not a problem or less important (see Berg & de Jong, 1996; Cade & O'Hanlon, 1993; de Jong & Berg, 1997, 2002; Gray, Zide, & Wilker, 2000).

Compared with other therapy approaches (see Carter & McGoldrick, 1989, 2005; Goldenberg & Goldenberg, 1991, 1997, 2000; Kerr & Bowen, 1988; McGoldrick & Gerson, 1985; McGoldrick, Gerson, & Shellenberger, 1999; Nichols & Schwartz, 1995), solution-focused treatment views the process of change as being "inevitable and constantly happening" (Zide & Gray, 2000, p. 5). The solution-focused perspective posits that it is much easier to construct solutions than to remain stuck on "problems." The practitioner does not concentrate on client dysfunction, pathology, or problem saturation, but rather pays attention to what the client may already be doing to solve problems. This focus helps set the stage for supporting positive changes that may have already begun (Gray, Zide, & Wilker, 2000). The practitioner begins to ascertain when "exceptions" to the client's complaints occur, depathologizes the problem, and generates workable goals. Goals are defined as those salient to the client's worldview, and they are spelled out in specific and understandable language.

Tenets of Solution-Focused Therapy

The core therapeutic task of solution-focused therapy is helping the client to imagine how things might be better and to identify what might be necessary to achieve that end. O'Hanlon (1990) asserts that solution-focused therapy supports two important objectives: to "change the viewing" and "change the doing" of the problem. In "changing the viewing," the practitioner helps the client reframe the problem as a challenge or opportunity for growth. In this way, the client begins to learn new ways to relate, care for, or interact with others. In helping to "change the doing," the practitioner strives to motivate the client to change his or her behavioral actions and interactions. This change takes place through structured activities that invite the client to experience problematic situations in new, and ideally more satisfying, ways (Horne, 2000; Teall, 2000).

According to de Shazer (1991), "Goals are depictions of what will be present" (p. 112). The criteria for constructing well-defined goals are outlined below (also see, for example, Berg & Miller, 1992; Berg & de Jong, 1996; de Jong & Berg, 1997, 1998, 2002; de Shazer, 1994; Miller, Hubble, & Duncan, 1996; and Walter & Peller, 1992).

- *Positive*—The focus should be on what the client can change. The practitioner might explore for positive goals by asking, for example, "What will you be doing instead (of maintaining the problem)?"
- *Process*—A key focus is how will the client change; for example, "How will you change what you are currently doing?" or "What are some of your alternatives?"
- *Present*—The client understands that change occurs "in the now" and the focus of work is for today, not tomorrow; for example, "When you leave my office today, what will you be doing differently or saying differently to yourself?"
- *Practical*—The focus is on what is reachable; for example, "How attainable is your goal?"
- *Be as specific as possible*—Ask the client to be specific in identifying what to change; for example, "What specific steps will you take to accomplish your goal?"
- *Client control*—Help the client understand that he or she is in control of finding solutions and making changes; for example, "What will you be doing differently to make things better?"
- *Client language*—Avoid using unwieldy theoretical terminology; instead, use the client's own words and symbols.

The collaborative relationship between the practitioner and the client is seen as being the "start" of something rather than the "end" of something. Solution-focused therapy identifies levels and degrees of motivation (Berg & Miller, 1992; de Jong & Berg, 1997, 1998, 2002; de Shazer, 1991; Walter & Peller, 1992) by identifying three types of clients: the "customer," the "visitor," and the "complainant" (de Shazer, 1988, p. 87). The "customer" type of client can identify the problem, come up with solutions, and see himself or herself as part of the solution. This type of client is considered highly cooperative and willing to change. The second type of client is the "visitor." This client is able to identify problems and solutions but does not visualize himself or herself as part of the solution. These clients are usually mandated into treatment or initiate counseling at the request of others (and might be considered "resistant" or noncompliant). The third type of client encountered in solution-focused therapy is the "complainant." This client will discuss his or her problems but is unable to formulate solutions, much less see how to be part of the solution. Clients in this category are involved in multi-problem situations and are not motivated to change disruptive patterns.

Solution-focused therapy assumes that change is occurring all the time and asserts that when clients make changes they need to move away from "problems talk" and shift to "solutions talk." "For a client to learn to be the person he or she wants to be is quite different (and often less time-consuming) than learning why the client is the way he or she is" (Zastrow, 1999, p. 394). Practitioners enter into and understand the world in which the client operates (de Jong & Miller, 1995; Harper & Lantz, 1996). They assume the client wants to change, is doing his or her best to make change happen, and has the capacity to envision changes in order to make them happen. Furthermore, solution-focused practice assumes that the solution, or at least part of it, is probably already happening, and shifts the therapeutic conversation to explore "exceptions" or times in the client's life when the problem does not occur (Fish, 1996; Gingerich & Wabeke, 2001).

de Shazer (1988) identifies three assumptions that support the philosophy of solution-focused practice and promote successful goal attainment:

- *If it ain't broke, don't fix it.* The practitioner should not delve into problems the client does not present, no matter how obvious or glaring the problem may seem.
- *Once you know what works, do more of it.* The practitioner should help the client continue to engage in newly discovered successful behaviors.
- *If it doesn't work, don't do the same thing again; do something different.* The practitioner and the client should avoid repeating unsuccessful outcomes and should continue to search for solutions elsewhere.

de Shazer (1985, 1988, 1994) suggests the following strategies for constructing solutions:

- *Goal focus*—Therapy begins with a focus on setting client goals that can construct a better future.
- *Present orientation*—Treatment centers on the present rather than problems stemming from the past. Asking the client "How can I be of help to you today" sounds very different from "How long have you had this problem?"
- *Problem focus*—Clients tend to be socialized around talking about problems and what brings them into treatment. The practitioner gently begins to shift the conversation toward finding solutions; for example, "You've had this problem for the past five years, and what needs to happen for you to move away from this?"
- *Solution focus*—When moving toward "solutions," the practitioner begins to explore what has worked; for example, "What will you be doing differently when you no longer experience the problem?"
- *Exception focus*—The practitioner looks for times when the client doesn't have a problem with the problem, asking, for example, "Are there times when the problem does not occur? What did you do differently?"

Principles of Practice

Several principles distinguish solution-focused treatment from other approaches: pre-session change, exceptions, coping, scaling, and the "miracle question."

Pre-Session Change The solution-focused practitioner inquires about pre-session changes, coping, and times when exceptions occur; helps the client to become more specific about finding solutions; understands the client's current status; and takes into account the client's worldview (Berg & Miller, 1992; de Jong & Berg, 1997, 1998, 2002; Gingerich & Eisengart, 2000; Miller, Hubble, & Duncan, 1996; Zide & Gray, 2000). The purpose of asking the client about pre-session change is to pay attention to what happened in the client's life after making the appointment but before the first session occurred (Redpath & Harker, 1999; Weiner-Davis, 1987). By exploring what steps the client has already taken independently, the practitioner and client can better determine what was helpful and begin resolving "the problem" (Fraser, 1995).

Exceptions Solution-focused treatment makes a point of looking for "exceptions," or those times when anticipated problems did not occur, or when the client did not have a problem with the problem. Exploring the client's definition of "the problem" and learning how he or she has struggled becomes more important than how the problem originated. Discovering when exceptions occurs draws on the client's strengths, provides a clear vision for goals, and instills hope by affirming that change is within reach. The primary task is helping clients reinforce their goals, repeat positive exceptions, and build on what is already being done.

Coping By inquiring how the client copes with difficulties, the practitioner challenges the client's beliefs that change is hopeless while carefully looking for any small positive changes that may already be occurring. If change is not readily apparent, the practitioner asks the client, "What would you like to see happen?" No matter how minor a change may seem, even the smallest step toward change helps create a path toward building more successful measures. In this way, both the client and the practitioner begin to emphasize building solutions and shift their attention away from "the problem." Coping questions seek to amplify what the client actually does to accomplish these "non-problem" times (Berg & de Jong, 1996; de Jong & Berg, 1998, 2002; Gingerich, de Shazer, & Weiner-Davis, 1988). The practitioner strives to convey that no matter whatever happened before, the client is surviving the current difficulty and is managing to avoid making things worse.

Scaling Questions involving scaling can be used to specify treatment goals, investigate the client's readiness and motivation for change, evaluate commitment to relationships, explore future steps, and/or highlight progress already made (Berg & Miller, 1992; Cade & O'Hanlon, 1993; de Jong & Berg, 1998, 2002; de Shazer, 1985, 1988, 1991, 1994). Scaling can also be used to acknowledge the client's hard work and to assess pre-session changes, self-esteem, self-confidence, hopefulness, and perceptions about what others may think of the situation. An example of a scaling question used to explore future steps could be:

> On a scale of one to ten, with the number one being the most difficult and chaotic . . . sort of how you felt when you first started seeing me here at the agency . . . and the number ten being when everything is going well, where would you say you are right now?

Scaling questions emphasize that change is a continuous process that can be controlled by the client. Interestingly, encouraging people to talk about where they want to be, rather than focusing on their problems, often makes them feel better. Clients are helped to take ownership of, and responsibility for, their own treatment and for evaluating the change process.

The Miracle Question   The miracle question shifts the client's conversation toward identifying the specific first steps they took in trying to resolve their problems (Berg, 1994). The practitioner asks the client to put aside any current difficulties and instead "imagine a miracle happens and the problem that brought you here is solved" (Berg & Miller, 1992, p. 78). This strategy accomplishes two important things. First, it creates an image of what the client's life would be like when the identified problem is solved. Second, the client can visualize what a different life might look like in the future. The practitioner listens carefully to responses to the miracle question, looking for change strategies that are realistic, detailed, and achievable within the context of the client's life.

Advantages and Disadvantages of Solution-Focused Therapy

Advantages   Solution-focused therapy assumes clients already have the skills needed to address their problems and are capable of change (de Jong, 2002). This approach emphasizes finding possible solutions to the problem rather than specifically solving it. Little or no emphasis is placed on recognizing or understanding the origin or reason for the presenting problem, because change can occur without this information (O'Hanlon & Weiner-Davis, 1989; Stalker, Levene, & Coady, 1999). The practitioner takes a "solution stance" by listening to the client's story, clarifying rather than confronting, and cooperating with the client's efforts to solve problems rather than trying to pathologize or label the client as resistant. Client resiliency (in finding their own solutions) is considered most important. Fanger (1995) notes, "Learning to be the person you want to be is quite different—and often less time consuming—than learning why you are the way you are" (p. 88).

Because solution-focused therapy is designed to be brief, the practitioner plays a more active role by shifting the focus as quickly as possible away from discussing the client's presenting problems to formulating solutions. The role of the practitioner is to patiently guide the client toward exploring strengths and ultimately constructing solutions. The therapeutic conversation revolves around co-constructing what brought the client into treatment while at the same time preparing the groundwork for making changes. Focusing on "what's possible" facilitates opportunities for clients to take charge of their own change process. Clients are regarded as "the experts" on what goals they want to construct, and the role of the solution-focused practitioner is to assist clients to produce successful solutions (de Jong, 2002; Prochaska & Norcross, 1999; Teall, 2000). Thinking about treatment in terms of successfully developing solutions in reaction to the client's complaints is a major strength of solution-focused therapy (Rowan & O'Hanlon, 1999). Problems presented are viewed positively, and the emphasis is on identifying patterns of change that may be successful. As small changes are achieved, the client becomes empowered to elicit larger ones (O'Hanlon & Weiner-Davis, 1989; Walter & Peller, 1992). LeCroy (1999) cautions that while solution-focused therapy may seem "simple," it is not necessarily easy to use.

Solution-focused practice is consistent with the competency-based model in which clients are seen as competent and resourceful. Both perspectives emphasize strengths and view the therapeutic relationship as a co-collaboration. Because of its brief, future-oriented, and goal-directed focus, solution-focused therapy is compatible with managed behavioral health care settings (Franklin & Jordan, 1999).

Disadvantages   In this age of accountability, it is important for practitioners to remain mindful of the empirical support for the therapeutic approaches they employ and use only interventions that have been proven effective. The professional literature contains many anecdotal reports of the usefulness of solution-focused brief therapy. Unfortunately, these reports do not provide strong evidence of the efficacy of this approach, either by themselves or when compared with other known intervention methods (Gingerich & Eisengart, 2000; Gingerich & Wabeke, 2001). One major disadvantage of solution-focused treatment is the fact that only a small number of published studies empirically validate the effectiveness of this approach (Beyebach, Morejon, Palenzuela, & Rodriguez-Arias, 1996; La Fountain & Garner, 1996; Seagram, 1997; Stalker, Levene, & Coady, 1999; Triantafillou, 1997). Scientific evidence from larger, controlled clinical trials or even single-system research designs is needed to demonstrate the effectiveness of solution-focused treatment (Araoz & Carrese, 1996). Outcome research is needed to develop a more solid empirical base for using solution-focused treatment (Beyebach et al., 1996; Gingerich & Wabeke, 2001).

Cognitive-Behavioral Therapy

Approaches such as crisis intervention, solution-focused brief therapy, family therapy, and psychosocial treatment have evolved from direct clinical practice, whereas behavioral approaches were developed in psychological laboratories. Behavioral approaches arose from the inability to measure and evaluate the outcomes of psychoanalysis and determine its role in the helping process. The reasoning suggested if the practitioner could not "see" the client's problem, then it could not be quantified. Cognitive-behavioral therapy underscores only those behaviors that can be evaluated (Okun, 1997).

Cognitive-behavioral therapy focuses on changing clients' thoughts or cognitive patterns in order to influence their behavior and emotional state. This approach unites behavioral strategies with cognitive processes to bring about behavioral and cognitive change. The focus is on relationships between the client's thinking and behavior.

Historical Background

The theoretical underpinnings of cognitive-behavioral therapy are derived from three main sources: *the phenomenological approach to psychology, structural theory,* and *cognitive psychology.* The phenomenological approach can be found in Immanuel Kant's (1798) discussion of the conscious subjective experience. The individual's view of self and his or her personal world are central to behavior. These concepts have been explored in the writings of Alfred Adler (1936), Karen Horney (1950), and Harry Stack Sullivan (1953). Structural theory appreciates the development and role of the individual's knowledge of self and the world. If the self-concept is distorted or rigid, the individual is considered unable to assimilate life experiences effectively and thus becomes vulnerable to emotional distress or maladjustment. George Kelly's (1955) work influenced contemporary developments in cognitive psychology by emphasizing the role of an individual's beliefs in bringing about behavioral change.

Cognitive therapy began in the early 1960s as the result of Aaron Beck's work with people who were considered depressed (1963, 1964, 1967). Beck attempted to validate Freud's earlier concepts about depression being caused by "turning anger on the self." Beck was unable to substantiate Freud's work and instead found clients worked through their anger with waking thoughts or dreams. Arnold (1960), Mahoney (1974), Bandura (1977), Meichenbaum (1977), Mahoney and Arnkoff (1978), and Lazarus (1984) made other major contributions to the advancement of cognitive therapy.

The formative years of behavior therapy saw the development of various approaches, including stimulus-response, behavior modification, and social learning. Today, these behavior therapies have been integrated with cognitive approaches to create cognitive-behavioral therapy (Okun, 1997). Albert Ellis' (1962) work proved to be a major catalyst toward furthering cognitive behavior therapies. Ellis rejected his previous analytic training and replaced it with actively listening and talking with his clients. Ellis believed individuals consciously adopted explanations for their behavior, and he viewed a client's underlying assumptions as targets for intervention (Beck & Weishaar, 1995).

The cognitive-behavioral approach is very effective in treating a broad range of mental health disorders and related behavioral problems, including substance-related problems (Haddock, Barrowclough, & Tarrier, 2002; Shorley, 1994); chronic pain (Currie, 2002); obsessive compulsive disorder (Whittal & McLean, 2002); posttraumatic stress disorder (Foa, Rothbaum, Riggs, & Murdock, 1991; Dancu & Foa, 1992); eating disorders (Garner, 1994; Garner & Friedman, 1994; Pendleton, Goodrick, & Reeves, 2002; Wilson, Agras, Kraemer, Fairburn, & Walsh, 2002); anxiety disorders (Dattilio & Kendall, 1994; Glazer, 2002; Schmidt, Wollaway-Bickel, & Trakowski, 2002; Thyer & Birsinger, 1994); personality disorders (Mohan, 2002); body dysmorphic disorder (Veale, 2002); suicide and/or depression (Ablon, 2002; Grant & Casey, 2000; Hollon & Haman, 2002; Pidlubny, 2002; Reinecke, 1994); violence (Fox, 1999); sexual abuse (Deblinger, 1992); sex offenders (Duehn, 1994); divorce (Granvold, 1994); psychosis (Fowler, Garety, & Kuipers, 1998; Haddock et al., 1999; Norman & Townsend, 1999); marital distress (Granvold & Jordan, 1994); childhood and adolescence issues (Lesure-Lester, 2002; Lumpkin, Silverman, & Markham, 2002; Stallard, 2002); and family therapy (Munson, 1994).

Tenets of Cognitive-Behavioral Therapy

Cognitive therapy shares many similarities with other forms of behavior therapy. At one end of the behavioral spectrum is applied behavioral analysis, an approach that ignores "internal events" such as the ways in which clients interpret information or form inferences. At the other end of the behavioral spectrum lies cognitive mediating; this includes a variety of cognitive-behavioral approaches that put varying degrees of emphasis on the cognitive process. Both cognitive and behavioral therapy share common features that include a focus on presenting concerns, a full understanding of the client's problem, and identification of situations in which the problem occurs and the aftermath of the problem. Cognitions, like behaviors, can be modified when new learning is fostered. In contrast to the behavioral approaches based on simple conditioning paradigms, cognitive therapy sees the client as an active participant in the change process (Beck & Weishaar, 1995).

Techniques used in cognitive-behavioral treatment are designed to shift information processing to a more functional position and to modify faulty beliefs. The cognitively oriented techniques focus on the client's misinterpretations and provide a mechanism for testing them, exploring their logical (or illogical) basis, and then correcting them. Additionally, the client's mental imagery is used as a pictorial representation of "cognitive distortions." The client's basic beliefs are explored in a somewhat similar method and tested for their accuracy and adaptive value. When clients discover that some of their beliefs are inaccurate, they are encouraged to try out a different set of beliefs and then determine if the latter are more accurate and functional (Beck & Weishaar, 1995). Specific techniques include creating a dysfunctional thought record, thought catching, and activity scheduling. [Granvold's (1994) *Cognitive and Behavioral Treatment: Methods and Applications* provides a more detailed discussion of cognitive-behavioral approaches.]

Cognitive-behavioral therapy is highly structured and short-term, usually lasting no longer than 12 to 18 weeks. The practitioner is actively engaged in collaboration with the client in exploring the client's own behavior, stated thoughts, emotions, and goals. The work focuses on building linkages among the client's symptoms, conscious beliefs, and current experiences (Beck & Weishaar, 1995). The ultimate goal is to help the client replace his or her maladaptive beliefs with more accurate beliefs through the application of logic versus dysfunctional thoughts or ideas. Also important is distinguishing who the principal figures are in the client's life and whether the treatment goals represent some type of attempt to compensate for a deficiency or feelings of inferiority. This shift to normal cognitive processing is accomplished by using behavioral experiments in order to test the client's dysfunctional beliefs and/or distorted interpretations. Ultimately the client must take responsibility for his or her behavior and not blame past issues for present behaviors. The practitioner continually challenges the client's cognitive errors, providing feedback to gradually restore more adaptive functioning. Change is achieved by expanding the client's view of self, others, and the world. This model focuses on strengths rather than pathology.

Principles of Practice

The practitioner begins by establishing a trusting alliance characterized by working with the client to look for evidence to support or refute beliefs about the presenting problem. The practitioner attempts to foster trust by displaying empathy and conveying a true sense of hope. Direct confrontations or challenges to the client's beliefs that can threaten or disrupt rapport must be avoided. By fostering an atmosphere of experimentation, the practitioner invites clients to look for evidence supporting their beliefs while searching for alternative explanations.

During the initial phase of treatment, the practitioner conducts a comprehensive assessment of the client's problems; for example, clients may be asked to evaluate the degree of conviction associated with each of their beliefs. The least firmly held beliefs should initially be targeted for intervention. This is done to increase the probability of success and also foster the client's trust and confidence in the therapeutic process. The practitioner provides information to the client, such as an explanation of how stress may exacerbate symptoms. Positive behaviors and perceptions are reinforced. The need for additional interventions such as hospitalization or medication must be carefully evaluated. This initial phase concludes with the establishment of a "contract" and assignment of a homework task. Assignment of homework conveys at the outset that the client will be an active participant in the therapy process.

Three concepts fundamental to phase two of cognitive therapy are *collaborative empiricism, Socratic dialogue,* and *guided discovery* (Kelly, 1955). Collaborative empiricism views the client as a "practical scientist"; in other words, one who lives by interpreting stimuli but has been temporarily thwarted by malfunctions in the information gathering and integrating apparatus. Socratic dialogue distinguishes the therapeutic conversation. This technique involves asking questions in a way that helps clients look at their assumptions objectively and nondefensively, gaining new learning and forming conclusions about what is actually happening. To better understand the client's perspective, the practitioner listens carefully to the client's responses. The concept of guided discovery is directed toward uncovering what threads or patterns run through the client's present misperceptions and beliefs and then linking them to similar past experiences. The focus is to improve the client's reality testing (Beck & Weishaar, 1995).

To foster a Socratic dialogue and promote client observations, practitioners may initially ask a client questions like these:

"As you see it, what problem(s) brings you here?"
"Is there anything you do to or have done to prevent your problem (or what, if anything seems to work)?"
"What happened to lead you to seek help at this time?"
"What has been going on in your life over the past few weeks?"
"Can you provide a specific example of how your problem presents itself?"

"Can you think back to the last time your problem occurred?"
- "What was going on at that time?"
- "How did you feel?"
- "What were you thinking at the time?"
- "How did you know you were experiencing the problem?"
- "What sorts of things made it better/or worse?"
- "Who else is involved?"

"With everything going on in your life right now, could you rate how serious this problem is for you?"

"Who is most concerned by your problem?"

"How does this problem prevent you from doing the things you would like to do?"

"Have you ever had similar feelings (and thoughts) about other situations (and in what ways are they similar)?" (If the answer is yes, then inquire what the client makes of these similarities.)

During phase two, the practitioner may also assign homework intended to help clients uncover and/or examine their thoughts and subsequently change their behaviors. The homework assignments are completed between therapy sessions and brought in to serve as a foundation for discussion. These homework assignments may consist of real-life "experiments"; for example, the client will try out a new response to a situation. Another useful technique is known as cognitive rehearsal (or role play) whereby the client is asked, in session, to imagine himself or herself in a difficult situation. The practitioner then carefully guides the client through the process of successfully dealing with the predicament. The client takes an active role through practicing or rehearsing to prepare for times when the particular situation may happen in real life. The practitioner also models appropriate behaviors or responses to the client's experiences. Education is often provided during this phase of treatment and is expanded to include teaching adaptive strategies such as relaxation techniques, social skills, or conflict resolution.

In phase three, the practitioner's main focus is on the application and reinforcement of basic and intermediate coping skills. One useful technique includes asking clients to keep a detailed daily journal recounting their thoughts, feelings, and/or actions when certain situations take place. The goal is helping clients to become aware of any maladaptive thoughts they may have and at the same time show some behavioral consequences that might occur. Alternatively, the journal may also be used to reinforce positive behaviors.

Two main strategies are employed in cognitive-behavioral treatment. The first is issuing a "verbal challenge" in which the practitioner begins to sow a seed of doubt in the client's mind by questioning evidence for client beliefs and by pointing out and discussing any discrepancies in the person's account. Once the possibility of doubt is introduced to the client, the practitioner can begin offering alternative explanations to account for "the evidence" while encouraging the client to reconsider certain beliefs. The second strategy builds on the first by engaging clients in "behavioral experiments" or "planned reality testing" to evaluate the evidence for their beliefs and then encouraging them to look for alternative explanations.

The last phase of treatment, or termination, focuses on integration of newly learned skills and resumption of normal activities. The therapeutic discussion focuses on helping clients to understand any vulnerabilities, find new ways to cope, and develop proactive methods to avoid relapse.

Advantages and Disadvantages of Cognitive-Behavioral Therapy

Advantages   Cognitive-behavioral therapy is well suited to exploring the impact of cognitive deficits for persons with a variety of mental disorders. For instance, some clients may experience problems because they do not foresee delayed or longer-term negative consequences while other clients may have trouble concentrating, thinking, or recalling important information. Cognitive deficits produce perceptual errors as well as faulty interpretations. Unfortunately, inadequate cognitive processing also interferes with how a person copes with interpersonal problem solving (Corsini & Wedding, 1995, 2000). These difficulties are particularly noted in persons struggling with affective and mood disorders, anxiety or panic disorders (including agoraphobia), post-traumatic stress disorders, eating disorders, and substance-related disorders.

Cognitive-behavioral therapy supports the competency-based model with its emphasis on client strengths and resilience (Power & Holmes, 2002). As Walsh (1998) explains, "Beliefs tend to modify what we look for, what we recognize, how we interpret, and how we respond to these interpretations" (p. 160). This approach provides the practitioner with a variety of strategies to help challenge a client's self-limiting assumptions. If left unchallenged, cognitive distortion reinforces a self-perpetuating cycle of self-blame, feelings of inferiority, and internalized oppression. The collaborative relationship between the client and practitioner promotes the equal partnership characterizing the competency-based model for treatment.

Disadvantages   There are some limitations to the broad use of cognitive-behavioral therapy for persons living with mental illness. Reliance on cognitive processes is not helpful for persons who are severely psychotic or cognitively impaired, as in the case of someone with late-stage dementia, Alzheimer's type. Jacobson and Christensen (1996) suggest a number of limitations that may occur when a practitioner puts too much reliance on reinforcement, extinguishing behaviors, or modeling. Future research involving cognitive intervention methods is needed (Persons, 1997) as it would add further insight about which strategies are most effective.

PSYCHOSOCIAL THERAPY

In many respects social work practice embodies a psychosocial or "person-in-environment" perspective. Whether the target of service is an individual or the family, societal problems or social change, social workers have traditionally paid attention to the alleviation of suffering and enhancement of the human condition.

What has become known as psychosocial therapy grew out of earlier efforts of caseworkers to support the well-being of individuals and families by helping them to restore social functioning, strengthen coping capacities, negotiate problems in living, and improve interpersonal relationships in the face of adversity (Borden, 2000; Woods & Hollis, 2000).

Psychosocial therapy centers on treating clients in relationship to their social environments. A major goal is helping to restore, maintain, and enhance client functioning by mobilizing strengths, supporting coping capacities, modifying dysfunctional behavioral patterns, and forming linkages to important resources (Goldstein, 1995). Psychosocial therapy recognizes the interplay among biological factors, internal psychological and/or emotional processes, and external social and physical conditions. The practitioner strives to address client problems that have arisen from disequilibrium between clients and their environment. This approach is built on a client-practitioner partnership based on promoting mutual understanding of the client's problems (and their origins), goals, and motivations, and providing an atmosphere in which interventions can be planned (Woods & Hollis, 2000). Treatment is not directed toward pathology or dysfunction per se; rather, it addresses aspects of the client's life that are most accessible and amenable to change. The practitioner-client relationship is central to the success of treatment and is considered one of its most influential tools in this approach. The practitioner maintains objectivity and demonstrates warmth, concern, acceptance, genuineness, empathy, respect for the importance of self-direction, and realistic optimism about client change.

Historical Background

Mary Richmond, one of the founders of social work, helped set the stage for modern casework theory and practice. Richmond's first book, entitled *Friendly Visiting among the Poor: A Handbook for Charity Workers* was published in 1899. Richmond postulated that "good deeds," "good intentions," and "friendly visiting" were simply not enough when working with people in need of help. Richmond suggested that social relations along with the person's environment, including past and present life experiences, were the major influences shaping the personality. She was convinced that external factors needed to be addressed in order to promote a better adjustment between individuals and their surroundings. Based on her experiences working in children's agencies, medical and hospital settings, and the field of family practice, Richmond promoted the value of differential diagnosis and treatment. Her later work, *Social Diagnosis* (1917), emphasized the need to thoroughly study the client's immediate social environment along with present and past experiences to develop an accurate understanding of each case.

According to Richmond (1917), "Case records often show a well-made investigation and a plan formulated and carried out, but with no discoverable connections between them" (p. 348). Her dual focus on people and their environment marked the beginning of the person-in-situation orientation of psychosocial practice. Richmond defined ways to intervene in the client's environment, locate resources, and cooperate with all possible sources of assistance and influence (Woods & Hollis, 2000).

The decade following the publication of *Social Diagnosis* was one in which the new "scientific practice" flourished and was subsequently introduced into schools of social work. In reaction to this movement, Virginia Robinson in her book (1930), *A Changing Psychology in Social Casework,* noted, "These various and often conflicting viewpoints are frequently used indiscriminately, and nowhere has there been any attempt by a caseworker to organize or originate any psychological principles of interpretation" (p. 81).

For more than thirty years, Mary Richmond (1917, 1922, 1930) examined theories about practice and tried to respond to concerns or questions raised by the growing number of social workers. During the early thirties social casework shifted its focus from a "technical school" orientation toward a scientific base of practice. From the late 1930s through the mid-1950s Freudian psychology was widely accepted by caseworkers as the most useful approach for understanding personality. Several attempts were made during the late 1950s to bridge the gaps between the different approaches to casework, and Helen Harris Perlman's (1957) "problem-solving" approach, which borrowed heavily from Freudian psychology, evolved from that effort. In 1964, Florence Hollis published her seminal work, *Casework: A Psychosocial Therapy* (Woods & Hollis, 2000). Hollis emphasized a diagnostic-differential approach incorporating concern for the client's social and psychological aspects of life. Her book became a benchmark for the basic principles and theoretical framework of psychosocial casework. Later editions of her book demonstrated how the psychosocial framework easily integrated various ideas, many of which have held up over time. Today the psychosocial approach has expanded far beyond the diagnostic-differential approach on which it was originally based (Turner, 2002).

Currently, psychosocial treatment pays special attention to the unique experiences, characteristics, strengths, and coping strategies of women, members of cultural and racial minority groups, and often oppressed groups such as gay and lesbian persons. This approach incorporates many of the principles found in other interventions developed specifically for working with these populations (see, for example, Chamberlin, 1997; Cowger, 1997; Gutierrez, DeLois, & GlenMaye, 1995a, 1995b; Mondros & Wilson, 1994; Rapp, 1998; Saleebey, 1997).

According to Goldstein (1995), the practitioner must incorporate diverse theories of human behavior and the social environment in order to fully understand clients, their situations, levels of functioning, and the effects of oppression and social deprivation (see, for example, Ainsworth, 1973; Barnard & Corrales, 1979; von Bertalanffy, 1968a; Bowlby, 1969, 1973; Bronfenbrenner, 1989; Davis, 1986; Finklestein, 1987; Humphries & Stern, 1988; Kernberg, 1984; Kohut, 1977; Lee, 1996; Mahler, 1968; Mahler, Pine, & Bergman, 1975; Satir, 1967; Silverstein, 1994; and Sussal, 1992). The psychosocial approach asserts that people of all ages have the capacity to learn, grow, adapt, and to some degree modify their social and physical environment (Woods & Hollis, 2000). When people are engaged in empathic human relationships, whether with a social worker or loved ones, untapped strength and resilience are often released. Today the psychosocial approach has been extended to include almost every conceivable type of client situation, including people living with AIDS (Dane & Miller, 1992), substance abusers (Straussner, 1993), victims of rape and physical assault (Abarbanel & Richman, 1990), abused children (Brekke,

1990), adult survivors of sexual abuse (Courtois, 1990), homeless people (Belcher & Ephross, 1989), and persons with chronic mental illness (Harris & Bergman, 1986).

Tenets of Psychosocial Therapy

The diagnostic assessment is a fundamental aspect of psychosocial therapy (Meyer, 1993). It considers the client's perception of needs and difficulties, state of mind, level of awareness, cultural background, gender, sexual orientation, and personality characteristics (Goldstein, 1995). To capture the person-in-situation gestalt, the psychosocial approach has incorporated many concepts from general systems theory and the ecological perspective (Woods & Hollis, 2000).

Psychosocial therapy draws on four psychodynamic frameworks to understand personality in depth and the coping capacities that clients bring to their life transitions: Freudian theory, ego psychology, object relations theory, and self-psychology. The author recognizes that the relevance of psychodynamic ideas for contemporary clinical practice in the mental health field has been debated (Kirk & Einbinder, 1994). However, these concepts call attention to the subtle aspects of the client-practitioner relationship and are thus included here. Psychosocial therapy also addresses the impact on people of organizational structures and processes as well as the community context (Goldstein, 1995).

Principles of Practice

Psychosocial therapy underscores two important social work standards. The first is acceptance, described as an attitude of warmth and goodwill. The second is respect for the client's right to be self-directive: to make choices and conduct the direction of his or her own life (Goldstein, 1995). Similar to the competency-based model for practice, psychosocial therapy recognizes the client as being competent in his or her own right and having the ability to assume self-responsibility.

Six major principles are used to further mutually determined goals (Woods and Hollis, 2000). They revolve around building rapport; offering suggestions; helping clients discharge pent-up feelings; gathering information; and encouraging reflective consideration of clients' present circumstances, patterns of behavior, and the influence of early life experiences on present attitudes, beliefs, and actions. The major principles of psychosocial therapy can be summarized as follows:

- *Sustainment*—Verbal and nonverbal communication demonstrates the practitioner's interest, acceptance, empathy, understanding, reassurance, and encouragement. Support is conveyed through questions that provide assurance and encouragement.
- *Direct influence*—The practitioner offers suggestions or advice to the client and/or family. While it is preferable for clients to arrive at their own decisions, psychosocial therapy includes the opportunity for the practitioner to offer more direction if indicated.
- *Exploration, description, and ventilation*—Clients are encouraged to express their feelings and to talk about problems. As a result of this conversation, clients may experience feelings of relief.

- *Person-situation reflection*—This form of reflection is directed toward helping the client to look at issues that concern others, the client's outside world, health, consequences of one's behavior, interactions between self and others, self-evaluation, and the practitioner-client relationship. The focus on "reflection" fosters the client's insight into the nature of his or her behavior. At the same time, the client becomes more aware of perceptions, thoughts, and feelings associated with the current situation and interactions with others.
- *Pattern dynamic reflection*—The practitioner helps the client to identify patterns of thinking and feeling to derive greater insight about participation in certain events.
- *Developmental reflection*—This technique involves assisting the client to reflect on early life and family-of-origin experiences that may contribute to his or her current personality and functioning. The goal is to help the client gain new insight into the ways in which early life experiences may influence current behavior (Woods and Hollis, 2000).

The first three principles of psychosocial therapy (sustainment, direct influence, and ventilation) are intended to help the client feel less isolated and overwhelmed; diminish feelings of anxiety, guilt, depression, or anger; make problems more manageable; move toward appropriate action; and instill hope, motivation, self-confidence, and acceptance. The last three principles (person-situation, pattern-dynamic, and developmental reflection) help increase the client's awareness of maladaptive or irrational behaviors that cause them anxiety.

Advantages and Disadvantages of Psychosocial Therapy

Advantages Psychosocial therapy is easily adapted to a broad range of mental health problems and can be used in conjunction with case management activities, discharge planning, and linkages to community and social resources, as well as supporting the client's functioning (Summers 2001, 2003). It is appropriate for short- or long-term treatment and aims at helping clients to deal with the complexities of everyday life. Psychosocial therapy works well with diverse, oppressed, and economically disadvantaged populations. According to Turner (2002),

> psychosocial therapy is an approach to the practice of social work that builds its interventions on a broad understanding of individuals, dyads, families, and groups, as well as the systemic influence of society and its resources or lack of them. The goal is to assist persons to achieve the highest level of which they are capable through an understanding of their past, their present, and their potential. It is a theory that reflects the century-old commitment of social work. Although for many it seems old-fashioned, psychosocial therapy will continue to be the essence of contemporary social work practice. (p. 111)

Disadvantages One of the strengths of psychosocial therapy is its versatility, yet this characteristic has also made it difficult to precisely delimit its knowledge base and present a fully integrated view of its theoretical underpinnings. Continuing efforts also are needed to articulate how this approach applies to problems found in today's practice arena. Consequently, it is more accurate to describe the psychosocial approach as a perspective that guides practice, rather than a distinct orientation to practice (Goldstein, 1995). Finally, while psychosocial therapy seeks to strengthen individuals by helping them deal with current dilemmas, it pays scant attention to the social and economic injustices found within the client's community context.

PSYCHOEDUCATION

Over the last two decades, a wide range of psychoeducational approaches have been developed to address the needs of persons living with mental health issues (Falloon & Liberman, 1983a, 1983b; Miller & Mason, 1998; Pomeroy, Kiam, & Green, 2000; Simon, McNeil, Franklin, & Cooperman, 1991; Strom-Gottfried, 2002). An early study by Garson (1986) surveyed members of the California National Alliance for the Mentally Ill (NAMI). Garson's findings suggested that families who had a relative with a psychiatric diagnosis were very interested in learning how to cope with and manage the potentially disabling effects of mental illness. Garson's findings were later substantiated by the National Alliance for the Mentally Ill (NAMI, 1999).

Some psychoeducational approaches may include a component of treatment or therapy while others are strictly educational in design; hence the term "psychoeducation" (Hatfield, 1990; Lam, 1991; Lukens & Thorning, 1998). Psychoeducation has not been consistently defined (Lukens & Thorning, 1998). However, it is generally characterized as those interventions conducted for the purpose of educating and providing support to clients and families (Miller, 2001).

Psychoeducation assumes a variety of formats and is most frequently conducted in combination with family and/or group work methods (Bogart & Solomon, 2000; Craighead, Milkowitz, & Frank, 2002; Cummings, 1996; Dixon, McFarlane, Hornby, & Murray, 1999; McFarlane, 1994; McFarlane, Lukens, Link, & Zuccato, 1995; Miklowitz, Richards, George, Suddath, & Wendel, 2000; Solomon, 1996; Solomon, Draine, Mannion, & Cohen, 1997; Torres-Rivera, 1999; Walsh, 2000). These interventions have been shown to benefit families by providing support to a family member living with mental illness (Franklin & Streeter, 1992; Lefley, 1987, 1996; Mannion, Mueser, & Solomon, 1994; Milstein & Argiles, 1992). Psychoeducation can provide additional knowledge beyond the traditional family therapy and biomedical interventions generally available in mental health settings (Garrett & Rice, 1998; Jordan, Barrett, Vandiver, & Lewellen, 1999). Psychoeducation can also be combined with psychosocial, cognitive, and behavioral techniques (McFarlane et al., 1995). Intervention may focus on the individual living with mental illness and may include family sessions or a multiple-family-group approach (Dixon, Adams, & Lucksted, 2000; Fristad, Gavazzi, & Soldano, 1999; Goldstein, 1996; Lundwall, 1996; McFarlane, 1997, 2000; Solomon, 1996).

Historical Background

From its earliest inception, the social work profession has placed a strong emphasis on education as an important way to help empower and enable clients become independent and self-sufficient (Germain & Gitterman, 1996). Training, teaching, and education have always been considered a central tenet of social work practice (Ackerson & Harrison, 2000; Chamberlin, 1997; Cohen, 1998; Gutierrez, DeLois, & GlenMaye, 1995a, 1995b; Lee, 1996; Rapp, 1998; Saleebey, 1997).

Tenets of Psychoeducation

If asked, most people would say they have a basic understanding of what a psychiatric disorder is. It is far more difficult, however, to grasp the real struggles and challenges of someone living with mental illness. Along with information, psychoeducation provides educational supports, social skills training, family educational interventions, and social and community supports.

- *Educational supports* provide specific information to individuals and/or their family members; for example, a person diagnosed with bipolar disorder would probably receive information about symptoms, course of the disease, medications, and strategies for coping with mood fluctuations.
- *Social skills training* addresses topics such as interviewing for a job and how to manage independent living and day-to-day tasks—for example, grocery shopping, using public transportation, balancing a checkbook, and making friends.
- *Family educational interventions* are aimed at helping to improve communication, resolve conflicts, and deal with family problems.
- *Social support* is intended to offer opportunities to offset some of the isolating effects of mental illness and encourage participation in group activities. Within the context of sharing common interests and experiences, clients become involved with other supportive individuals and groups.
- *Community supports* include a wide range of settings, such as aftercare agencies, homeless shelters, respite care, church or synagogue groups. Community supports are designed to offer supportive help to families and/or individuals; for example, a husband struggling with his wife's progressively debilitating Alzheimer's disorder may join a caregivers' support group that meets at a nearby community center.

In sum, psychoeducation provides a straightforward way of sharing information about mental illness and its management.

Principles of Practice

Depending on the intervention format, educational material might be covered in one or two sessions, all-day workshops, or a series of sessions over several months (McFarlane et al., 1995; Sharf, 2001; Thorning & Lukens, 1999). Garson (1986), Hatfield (1990), Mermier (1993) and others (Hatfield & Lefley, 1993) have identified basic information that mentally ill people and their families want to know. The most frequently mentioned topics are listed below:

- Signs and symptoms of mental illness, medications, and impact on day-to-day functioning.
- How to cope with crisis situations.
- Ways of dealing with particular behaviors, including aggression, suicide, and substance abuse.
- Techniques for reducing anxiety.
- What to expect from service providers.
- How the family can get a member who has been diagnosed with a mental illness into treatment centers, including hospitalization and outpatient treatment.
- Ways to access available interventions (including self-help).
- Realistic expectations.
- How to maintain positive relationships.
- How to manage the stigma of mental illness.
- Long-range planning, including the pros and cons of a relative with mental illness living at home, choices for living outside the home, and approaches that motivate the affected relative to change.

In sum, psychoeducation focuses on providing information to help people and their families understand and cope with mental illness (Lam, 1991; Mueser & Gingerich, 1994; Smith & Birchwood, 1987). The practitioner educates clients and their families or significant others about topics related to mental illness.

Advantages and Disadvantages of Psychoeducation

Advantages   A distinct advantage of psychoeducation is that it lends itself to brief interventions and can easily be combined with family and group methods as well as with other therapies. The emphasis on brief techniques is compatible with today's managed care environment (Gibelman, 2002; Hutchins, 1996; Riffe & Kondrat, 1997; Strom-Gottfried, 1997). Psychoeducational programs can utilize a variety of family assessment tools and techniques. For example, the eco-map or genogram can be incorporated with various educationally focused techniques such as role-playing or behavioral rehearsal. Multiple-family groups can provide education, offer social support, and enhance problem-solving abilities. Psychoeducation supports the competency-based treatment model, as persons with mental illness are considered viable, active, and empowered learners. Psychoeducation does not delve into pathology, and instead focuses on ways to understand and cope with mental illness (Jordan et al., 1999).

Psychoeducation empowers individuals by providing them with knowledge about mental illness and offering strategies to reduce stress and anxiety. Families are seen as competent to learn, able to benefit from information provided, capable of participating in the client's treatment, and able to function as allies in the treatment process (Jordan et al., 1999). Psychoeducation not only provides information but also supports clients and their families.

Disadvantages While psychoeducation has been empirically validated as effective, there continues to be a lack of research focusing on its use with ethnically and culturally diverse clients and families (Biegel, Song, & Milligan, 1995; Jordan & Franklin, 1995; Jordan et al., 1999). Simon and colleagues (1991) propose that some psychoeducational programs maintain too much of a focus on "family blaming." They suggest that future studies explore psychoeducation's positive influence on clients and their families.

METHODS OF FAMILY PRACTICE

Most psychiatric disorders affect the family as well as the individual. It is not uncommon for individuals to rely on family members for support, housing, or caretaking. This section shifts the emphasis from treating the individual who is diagnosed with a mental illness to include family members as part of treatment (Janzen & Harris, 1997).

Family patterns are diverse and can take a variety of forms. The definition of a "family" may include not only heterosexual married couples with children but also childless married couples, gay and lesbian families (with or without children), single-parent households, grandparents raising their grandchildren, blended families, and unmarried couples.

A distinction is made between family therapy and a family systems approach. The former is often questioned by social workers (Aronson, 1996; Franklin & Jordan, 1999) as being too narrow in its psychotherapeutic approach. Because the sociopolitical environment cannot be separated from the contexts in which social workers provide help, family systems approaches pay attention to the social policies affecting families. This section is not meant to serve as a theoretical treatise on family therapy. It does, however, provide an overview of the dynamics and principles of family systems work and those concepts considered most compatible with the competency-based model for practice. (For an in-depth discussion of various family therapy approaches, see Becvar & Becvar, 1996; Bowen, 1978; Carter & McGoldrick, 1989, 2005; Franklin & Jordan, 1999; Goldenberg & Goldenberg, 2000; Hartman, 1995; Horne, 2000; Janzen & Harris, 1997; Nichols & Schwartz, 1995; Satir, 1967; Walsh, Walsh, & McGraw, 1996).

Historical Background

The practice of working with the entire family can trace its beginnings to the Vienna-born physician, Sigmund Freud, whose work focused on uncovering and mitigating symptomatic behavior seen in patients he considered "neurotic." While Freud recognized the importance of family influence on a person, he did not believe including a patient's family in treatment would be helpful. Almost ten years later, Alfred Adler moved beyond Freud's teachings and began emphasizing the importance of family context for understanding neurotic behavior. During the 1920s, Harry Stack Sullivan adopted what he identified as an "interpersonal view" based on his experiences with hospitalized patients who had schizophrenia. Although Sullivan did not work directly with families, he speculated on the important role they played in the person's illness and recovery. Don Jackson, Murray Bowen, and Frieda Fromm-Reichmann all trained under Sullivan and expanded his work by refining the understanding of dysfunctional family interactive patterns.

Bateson, Jackson, Haley, and Weakland (1963) speculated that *double-bind* communication patterns within a family might account for the onset of schizophrenia in one of its members. Although current views about the origins and etiology of schizophrenia emphasize a genetic predisposition exacerbated by environmental stresses, Bateson (1991) and his associates deserve special credit for their landmark position hypothesizing that schizophrenia was somehow affected by interpersonal factors such as a poor family communication system. Building on Bateson's work, Lidz and his colleagues (1957) suggested that individuals with schizophrenia might not have received proper nurturance as children.

Nathan Ackerman, who focused primarily on the study of schizophrenia in the 1950s, saw the value of considering the entire family as a unit in assessing and treating dysfunction. In his landmark book, *The Psychodynamics of Family Life* (1958), Ackerman argued that no one family member could be understood apart from other family members. Salvador Minuchin and his associates (1967) developed a number of brief, action-oriented therapeutic procedures. Many other theorists contributed to the evolution of family therapy as a distinct method of practice (see, for example, Boszormenji-Nagi, 1987; Boszormenji-Nagi & Framo, 1965; Bowen, 1960, 1978; Charny, 1966; Duhl & Duhl, 1981; Feldman, 1985, 1992; Framo, 1970; Goldenberg & Goldenberg, 1991, 1996, 1997, 2000; Haley, 1976; Jordan & Franklin, 1995; Norcross & Goldfried, 1992; Pinsof, 1983, 1995; Sander, 1979; Satir, 1972; Satir & Baldwin, 1983; Satir, Banmen, Gerber, & Gomori, 1991; and Whitaker & Bumberry, 1988).

Horne and Passmore (1991) have identified as many as 17 different approaches to family treatment. Theorists have attempted to distinguish areas of overlap and similarities, as well as areas of difference and uniqueness (Kolevson & Green, 1985; Nichols, 1984). Currently there appear to be seven overarching theoretical approaches of family therapy: *object relations family therapy* (Framo, 1970; Scharff & Scharff, 1987, 2002); *experiential family therapy* (Connel, Bumberry, & Mitten, 1999; Greenberg & Johnson, 1988; Keith, 2000; Napier & Whitaker, 1978; Satir, 1967, 1972; Snow, 2002; Whitaker, 1965; Whitaker & Bumberry, 1988); *transgenerational family therapy* (Bowen, 1978; Boszormenyi-Nagi, 1987); *structural family therapy* (Aponte, 1992, 1994, 2002; Aponte & DiCesare, 2000, 2002; Aponte & VanDeusen, 1981; Lebow, 1997; Minuchin, 1974; Minuchin, Montalvo, Guerney, Rosman, & Schumer, 1967, 1978; Minuchin & Fishman, 1981; Santisteban, Coatsworth, & Perez-Vidal, 1997); *strategic family therapy* (Watzlawick, Beavin-Barelas, & Jackson, 1967; Boscolo, Cecchin, Hoffman, & Penn, 1987; Carlson & Kjos, 1998; Carlson, 2002; Corey & Bitter, 2001; Haley, 1976, 1987; Selvini-Palazzoli, Boscolo, Cecchin, & Prata, 1978, 1980; Watzlawick, Weakland, & Fisch, 1974); *cognitive-behavioral family therapy* (Beck

& Weishaar, 1995); and *social constructionist family therapy* (Berg, 1994; Berg & de Jong, 1996; Berg & Kelly, 2000; Bertolino & O'Hanlon, 2001; de Shazer, 1982, 1985, 1988, 1991, 1994; Gergen, 1985; O'Hanlon, 1996; O'Hanlon & Bertolino, 1998a, 1998b; O'Hanlon & O'Hanlon, 2002; White, 1995; Zide & Gray, 2000).

Social Work and the Family Systems Approach to Practice

Although family treatment as a method of practice was formally introduced in the 1950s, some of the underlying ideas and observations supporting this process appeared in social work literature as early as the beginning of the twentieth century. The early foundations of social work practice were firmly rooted within a family perspective. Mary Richmond (1917, 1922, 1930) noted the importance of the family and its pivotal role in providing the psychological foundation for identity development and growth. She believed in the importance of knowing the main "drift" of the family's life as a key to understanding what might be troubling to family members. She emphasized the importance of understanding each family's history in delivering casework services. Richmond notes, "The next stage in development is to bring the client and those to whom he is socially related together . . . and then to observe the relationship in being, instead of merely gathering a report of it secondhand" (Richmond, 1922, p. 138). Her perspectives about involving family members in formulating change were visionary, especially when one considers that her views were formulated during a time when psychoanalytic theory and individual treatment formed the prevailing base of social work practice (Janzen & Harris, 1997).

Ludwig von Bertalanffy's (1968a) seminal work on general systems theory helped advance the family perspective. General systems theory posits that symptoms exhibited in one family member signal family dysfunction rather than individual psychopathology. The fledgling movement toward a family systems approach can be seen throughout social work literature published during the mid-twentieth century. For instance, Frances Scherz (1953) suggested that a single individual "could not be adequately understood or helped in isolation from persons with whom he had close emotional ties" (p. 343). Siporin (1956) recognized the importance of role theory and small group theory, and was among the first to characterize the family as a "social system." Robert Gomberg (1958) identified the limitations implicit in relying exclusively on a single person's psychology for understanding human problems and stressed the need to include the family. Gomberg (1958) recognized "the nature of family equilibrium, social roles, and role expectations characteristic between husband and wife, parent and child, siblings, and within the family group as a whole" (p. 75). Sanford Sherman (1959) coined the term "joint interviewing" and noted, "Sometimes the best treatment for the individual is treatment for his family" (p. 22). Grace Coyle (1962) believed the family could be likened to the group process wherein members had specific roles and responsibilities in achieving goals. Changes in the ways the family interacted would ultimately produce changes in the way the individual family member related to others. The eco-systems perspective (Meyer, 1993) shifted the emphasis from the individual to family group treatment.

The concept of engaging families as a part of practice expands the intrapersonal focus of social work and encourages the practitioner to consider the social, cultural, and environmental factors in a client's life. Selection of salient family therapy theories and techniques for inclusion in this chapter has been guided by looking through the "lens" of the competency-based model. Needless to say, family therapy has wide gaps, and the principles of practice vary in their levels of abstraction and inclusiveness. Nevertheless, it is clear that psychiatric disorders affect the family as well as the individual. The constructs that follow represent a "best effort" to incorporate key concepts from competency-based practice and various family therapies.

Tenets of Family Therapy

According to Janzen and Harris (1997), good clinical practice does not ignore the individual or the family context. Buckley (1967) suggests that a family system involves a "complex of elements or components directly or indirectly related in a causal network such that each component is related to at least some other parts in a more or less stable way within a particular period of time" (p. 41). By adopting a family focus, the practitioner pays simultaneous and specific attention to the family's structure, including how it arranges, organizes and maintains itself, its process, how families evolve, adapt or change over time (Goldenberg & Goldenberg, 2000).

Aside from the theoretical concepts derived from the various perspectives delineated above, certain assumptions and values apply when engaging families as an integral part of practice and thus merit the label of tenets:

- *Context*—When working with family systems (either one individual or the whole family) the practitioner expands the intrapersonal focus to consider the context of problematic behavior in planning and carrying out clinical interventions.
- *System*—The family is an ongoing and dynamic system. The practitioner's role is to help the family carve out adaptive and flexible rules that account for changing conditions.
- *Relationship*—To establish and maintain a productive relationship with clients and their families, the practitioner must relate sensitively and empathetically with the client system.
- *Interventions*—The practitioner effects change through direct and indirect therapeutic activities.
- *System change*—The practitioner's role is not to "change" or "fix" clients; rather, the work should revolve around placing the responsibility for change within the client system. The practitioner serves as a facilitator maintaining a genuine relationship and respect for the client and his or her family.
- *Motivation*—The practitioner creates a supportive environment that fosters motivation; client change is not likely to happen if the client remains unmotivated.
- *Competence*—The practitioner looks for strengths, resources, coping skills, and resilience within the family system.

- *Diversity*—The practitioner considers the influence of gender, age, sexual identity/orientation, religion, culture, ethnicity, socioeconomic status, and political affiliation.

Principles of Practice

Our focus in this section is on how the social work practitioner can be helpful working with family systems. Given the wide range of life circumstances and events experienced by persons living with mental illness, it should not come as a surprise that the family may also experience a similar amount of stress. In some instances families do not know what to do or how to stop the "aberrant behavior." In other situations, they feel powerless in the face of overwhelming mental health issues. In order to cope, family members often use a variety of means to deal with their stressful situation (Fox, 1992). The case illustration of Zelda "Jean" Pfohl (discussed in Chapter 3) describes one family's response to placing a relative in a nursing home due to Alzheimer's disease. Although relationships were strained by the situation, the family was able to talk with the social worker about the decision to place Jean and how it had affected each of them. This family dealt with their situation by tapping into community resources, such as the social worker and nursing home care. They were able to work together to confront the stresses around institutionalizing a family member, and they ultimately gained a greater appreciation for each other. At some point all families will encounter problems, but how a family confronts and manages a disruptive experience distinguishes "healthy" families from those with dysfunctional coping patterns.

The field of family therapy is complex, and techniques vary tremendously from one approach to another. However, certain practice principles have been identified as reflecting the values of social work practice with families (Maguire, 2002). They include reframing or relabeling; questioning; examining interactional sequences; providing directives; and respecting physical cues.

- *Reframing or relabeling*—The practitioner redefines problems and interprets them differently to help families find new and constructive ways of interacting with each other. The situation might not change, but the meaning associated with it changes and ultimately facilitates new actions and/or consequences. The practitioner helps the family to gain insight into patterned interactions, de-pathologize problems, and reduce strong emotions associated with "labels" (Lauer & Lauer, 2002). The practitioner reframes and ascribes positive connotations instead of unsupportive implications; for example, "isolation" might be redefined as "loneliness." Stories and metaphors can also be used to explain symptoms and present a different perspective.
- *Questioning*—Through targeted questioning, the family is encouraged to think about and/or examine their dynamics realistically. The technique of circular questions (Boscolo, Cecchin, Hoffman, & Penn, 1987; Hanna & Brown, 1995; Selvini-Palazzoli et al., 1980; Woods & Hollis, 2000) focuses on interactions and behavioral exchanges within the family rather than symptoms. Circular questions include relational and interaction pattern

questions; future-oriented questions; comparison and ranking questions; and before-and-after questions. Circular questioning may in itself trigger major changes in the thinking of each family member as each hears of the others' perceptions of the same event. The focus is on changing specific behaviors rather than discussing feelings or interpretations. Another questioning technique involves situating questions (Madsen, 1999). Situating helps the practitioner make his or her work more accountable to the family. It refers to identifying the intentions that guide the question; for example, the practitioner might ask, "Would you be interested in knowing why I'm asking this question?" or "I'm thinking about asking about the earlier days of your marriage; how would that work for you?"

- *Examining interactional sequences*—All families develop ways of perceiving, interpreting, and interacting with their social world. Interactions and patterns of relating develop with very little conscious awareness. The practitioner focuses on specific behaviors to help family members become aware of these interactional sequences (Reiss, 1981). This practice principle assumes problems will persist only if they are maintained by behaviors of the client or those with whom the client interacts (Watzlawick, Weakland, & Fisch, 1974). By altering the behaviors that keep problems in place, the patterns of interaction and influence contributing to family dysfunction will be resolved (or vanish entirely) (Hanna & Brown, 1995). The family is encouraged to look at how they interact—for example, who speaks to other family members, who listens, who interrupts, and what are the alliances between family members. By becoming consciously aware of interactional sequences, the family is encouraged to become more objective about their behaviors without blaming or assigning pathology.

- *Providing directives*—Anchored in strategic family therapy, directives are seen as assignments. They can be accomplished within or outside the session and consist of tasks, homework, or instructions (Haley, 1976). Clients are encouraged to behave differently, and change involves a shift in the balance and structure of the family wherein one member gives up something to another member.

- *Respecting physical cues*—All behavior is communication at some level (Bateson, 1991). With regard to physical cues, the practitioner pays attention to seven physical actions: eye contact, greetings, breathing, sitting, positioning, diversions, and voice modulation (Maguire, 2002). This technique underscores the importance of being attentive to the influence of culture. For example, families of Haitian descent may find it disrespectful to look directly at someone they consider an authority figure, such as a social worker, teacher, or physician. This avoidance of direct *eye contact* should not be misinterpreted as low self-esteem, resistance, or reluctance to work with the practitioner. In the same vein, when initially *greeting* a family and setting the tone for a session, it is important to respect the "machismo" attributed to males in Hispanic families and show deference (even if the practitioner personally feels such patterns are sexist and offensive). The technique of *breathing* involves mirroring the pace of a client's breathing.

Sitting consists of the practitioner emulating a client's posture; for example, if the client sits at the edge of a chair, the practitioner will assume a similar stance. *Positioning* suggests that the practitioner note (and possibly comment on) where each family member sits during the session. *Diversions* refer to what members do to take the focus away from the problem. In the author's experience working with a family, whenever the wife would try to introduce the topic of her husband's drug abuse, their five-year-old daughter would (predictably) jump off her mother's lap, find a paper clip on the office floor, and crawl toward the nearest electrical socket. The child's behavior very effectively diverted the conversation away from the topic of substance abuse. *Voice modulation* requires the practitioner to model communication. For example, using a calm voice can be particularly effective for families who are loud, argumentative, and who shout at one another.

Another perspective regarding physical cues suggests that the practitioner pay attention to nonverbal communication occurring in families. Satir regards discrepancies between verbal and nonverbal cues in families as "incongruent communication" (Satir et al., 1991, p. 32). For example, a family member struggling with major depression may comment, "I feel really great today," while looking tired and sad. When communication is incongruent, these messages can put members in a bind, making them unable to ascertain whether or not to respond (Janzen & Harris, 1997). The practitioner focuses on clarifying messages (verbal and nonverbal) exchanged among family members (including distortions and unexplored assumptions), which then become "grist for treatment" (Woods & Hollis, 2000). Relationships and interactions depend not only on *what* family members communicate, but also on *how* the message is sent.

It should be clear from the overview presented in this section that there are many variations of conceptualizing family problems, approaches to family work, the individual living in the family, and the principles guiding family systems practice. In later chapters and case vignettes we will explore the ways in which competency-based practice draws from the practice principles previously highlighted. A competency-based approach favors individual growth, promotes overall family well-being, and puts a high priority on targeting solutions to the client's presenting problem. Competency-based treatment is oriented more toward changing behavior and relationships than on providing interpretations of mental illness or describing "symptoms." Additionally, the cooperative relationship characterizing competency-based practice extends to family members. The practitioner attempts to collaborate with family members, develop solutions, and plan the next steps needed for change to take place. While history and past relationships with extended family are significant and useful in developing our understanding, the competency-based model focuses more on present relationships.

Advantages and Disadvantages of Family Practice

Advantages   Family therapy and clinical services are normally provided through private practice and the more traditional public social agencies; however, the trend is toward educationally focused, brief, solution-oriented practice (Berg, 1994; Berg & de Jong, 1996; Berg & Kelly, 2000; Corcoran & Vandiver, 1996; Gray, Zide, & Wilker, 2000; Strom-Gottfried, 1997; Zide & Gray, 2000). With the emergence of managed care and its emphasis on a symptom-based medical model, the structure of practice has moved in the direction of requiring measurable behavioral goals (Corcoran & Vandiver, 1996; Custer, Kahn, & Wildsmith, 1999; Hoyt, 1995). The family systems approach encourages a broad view of the client's problem situation and includes family and social influences as a part of setting treatment goals. Analogous to the competency-based model, this perspective encourages the practitioner to move beyond a symptom-based orientation to include relational, cultural, and social factors as an integral part of goal setting and treatment planning.

Working with the family as a group provides the practitioner with opportunities to directly observe family dynamics and interactions. In family sessions, the practitioner has the chance to see and hear each member's perspective. The temptation to take sides or become "biased" is also diminished. From the very first session, families are expected to communicate. This establishes a norm of open, honest communication in which family members hear, listen to, interact with, and respond to one another. Families are less likely to act out too aggressively in the presence of a "stranger" such as the practitioner. In this way, seeing the family together establishes an environment in which people behave in a more socially acceptable manner. Certainly families have their differences, but the pressure to at least appear appropriate with one another can be exerted by the practitioner's attempts to involve the family in treatment.

Disadvantages   Under what circumstances is working with the entire family contraindicated? In some situations it may already be too late or too difficult to establish and/or maintain a productive working relationship. Some members may be unavailable or simply refuse to attend sessions. Resistance may be so strong that it interferes with the practitioner's efforts to change destructive patterns. In some instances, members may be aware of the practitioner's attempts to initiate change and may divert their energy into figuring out what the practitioner is trying to do to them. Anything the practitioner tries may only heighten the members' defenses. Sometimes one disturbed or seriously mentally ill member may dominate the family with harmful, destructive motives or behavior. In other cases, the individual may be so violent or abusive that working with the family becomes impossible. Some members may face retribution, including physical violence, between family sessions.

METHODS OF GROUP WORK PRACTICE

In 1954 Helen Phillips published her seminal paper in *The Group* journal. She underscored the objective responsibility in social work groups by asking, "What is group work skill?" Phillips proposed that all definitions of social work with groups should affirm the "dual aim for the development of individuals and development of the group as a whole toward social usefulness" (p. 3). She stated that the social worker's objectives doing group work should be:

- To help members of the group to value their real selves and discover, use, and develop their strengths through their group association so they find a more responsible and satisfying relation to other group members, the worker, agency, and community.
- To help the group as a whole develop social interests and activities that will contribute to movement toward a more democratic society (p. 3).

It is not an easy endeavor when people come together with the goal of accomplishing a task. Each member brings to the group their own past, present, and future. Each individual has a unique set of dynamics, support systems, values, and ways of coping with stresses and strains found in their environment (Stevenson & Wright, 1999; Wilson & Stevens, 1999).

The interactions of group members offer possibilities for change and growth, while the practitioner's main focus is to provide support and manage behavior (Gitterman, 2001a; Woodstock, 2001). Group practice encompasses a broad spectrum of approaches, including cognitive-behavioral, single-session, interpersonal, supportive, multi-family groups, structured, limit setting, telephone and computer groups, self-help groups, and family therapy (Ebenstein, 1998; Gladstone & Reynolds, 1997; Joyce, Duncan, Duncan, Kipnes, & Piper, 1996; Kaslyn, 1999; MacKenzie, 1996; Meezan, O'Keefe, & Zariani, 1997; Ronel, 1998; Schopler, Galinsky, & Abell, 1997). In sum, today's group work practice comprises many populations, practice settings, practitioners' roles, and practice approaches.

Group interventions for persons with mental illness have existed in various formats for many years (Budman et al., 1996; Cummings, Long, Peterson-Hazan, & Harrison, 1998; Hall, Schlesinger, & Dineen, 1997; Gendron, Poitras, Dastoor, & Perodeau, 1996; Heller, Roccoforte, Hsieth, Cook, & Pickett, 1997; Hewitt, 1996; Martichuski, Knight, Karlin, & Bell, 1997; Miller & Mason, 1998; Rutan & Rice, 1999; Walsh, 2000; Yellow Horse Brave Heart, 1998). These groups tend to focus on practical issues in relationships, day-to-day challenges, social functioning, and problems coping with mental health symptoms. The group itself, with its multiple helping relationships, becomes the primary source of change. This section traces the history of group work, outlines the basic elements of group process, and presents key concepts and techniques found in several important group approaches.

Historical Background

As a part of the social reform movement of the late nineteenth century, group work practice first began in the settlement houses. Witnessing the terrible living conditions that existed among the poor and immigrant populations greatly distressed social workers and other community workers of this period. Many immigrant families had made their way to the United States hoping to find a new life. Instead, they were overworked, crowded into horrible living conditions, and generally were separated from the surrounding society because of differences in culture and language.

In the late 1890s Jane Addams founded Hull House in Chicago to specifically serve people experiencing housing problems, poor sanitation, and high crime rates. In 1911, Hull House established one of the first playgrounds for children supervised by trained kindergarten teachers and police officers. Some of the most notable police officers included Theodore Roosevelt, Luther Gulick, and Jacob Riis.

Group work advanced during the early twentieth century with the formation of educational and recreational activities organizations including the Boy and Girl Scouts, 4-H clubs, Young Men's and Young Women's Christian Associations (YMCA/YWCA), Jewish centers, Campfire Girls, and community centers. Men and women who took jobs working with the YMCA and YWCA were called "Y workers"; those working for settlement houses were known as "settlement workers"; and those who worked on playgrounds were "recreation workers." These groups were generally started by a small cohort of concerned citizens who usually focused on serving a particular group of children. Eventually these groups evolved into national and international organizations. Some organizations stressed the development of honor, loyalty, physical fitness, social and racial consciousness, and love of country, class, party, or sect. The primary goals for other groups were young people's intellectual development or increased appreciation of art, nature, and aesthetics. The organization's aims were often expressed in generalizations such as character building, development of personality, good citizenship, and control over nature.

By the 1930s, the settlement movement, the recreation movement, and the adult-education movement were well established in the United States. By 1955, group work was recognized by the National Association of Social Workers and group methods were finding their place in the profession. In 1906, the New York School of Philanthropy began offering a course of study that prepared students for positions in social settlements. By 1913 the school offered a full course of study for playground recreational work. Group work's linkage to social work was reinforced by the growing number of schools offering courses on group work for students interested in working in this field of practice.

A number of distinctive characteristics differentiated group work in its early development from the more dominant method of social casework (Pernell, 1986). Group work practice emphasized:

- working with group members versus individual clients;
- doing *with* versus doing *for;*
- doing versus talking about doing;
- acting as primary agents in the helping process versus the worker acting alone as the primary change agent;
- focusing on personal and social development versus remedial and rehabilitative efforts;
- promoting health and strength versus remedying sickness and breakdown.

By the early 1940s World War II influenced a growing number of mental health clinics and hospitals who began using groups as part of their services for returning veterans and military personnel. During the same time, several residential treatment centers were established to work with "troubled youths." A number of summer camps experimented with group work methods as a way of helping "disturbed children." Increasingly, the term "social" was appended to the term "group work," suggesting identification with the profession of social work.

While there is no single orientation for successfully working with groups, a number of approaches have evolved, each with roots embedded in group work's history. As a social work method of practice, group work is considered a specific strategy for working collaboratively with individuals, organizations, and communities. This orientation of collaboration and broad practice perspective is congruent with the competency-based model. Most practitioners are involved in some form of working with support groups, treatment groups, advocacy groups, or recreational groups. Social workers are often called to serve as leaders or members of various agency groups, such as multidisciplinary teams, task forces, and committees. Additionally, social workers may be asked to consult with community action groups or advocacy groups. Theories, skills, and values important to group practice cut across all areas of social work. Group work can be characterized by its breadth, which spans a range of populations, settings, and practice approaches.

Tenets of Group Work

Group work includes two basic categories: treatment and task groups (Toseland & Rivas, 1984). Treatment groups focus on education, growth, remediation, and socialization. The most common types of treatment groups are therapy, counseling, encounter and sensitivity, self-help, and support groups (Zastrow, 1999). Therapy groups are widely used for relationship difficulties and the emotional problems associated with mental illness (Yalom, 1995). Counseling groups are usually more short term in duration and educationally focused (Henry, 1992). Encounter and sensitivity groups, popular in the 1960s and 1970s, help members gain new insights about themselves. Self-help groups deal with common problems or political issues. Members come together as peers and provide mutual support (Oren, Carella, & Helma, 1996; Sandstrom, 1996). Examples of self-help groups are Alcoholics Anonymous (AA) or Families of Adult Mentally Ill (FAMI). Support groups are also characterized by an element of self-help but are often led by social workers or other counseling professionals. Members come together to share their experiences, offer suggestions, and provide support. Task groups are usually convened to accomplish a specific purpose and include committees, administrative groups, treatment conferences, and social action groups.

There are several basic factors to consider when starting a treatment group. The practitioner's tasks include:

- Deciding to establish a therapy group;
- Determining the setting and size of the group;
- Establishing the frequency and length of group sessions;
- Choosing the group venue (open versus closed format);
- Formulating group policy;
- Setting appropriate goals for the group.

Schwartz (1971, 1974) describes five major tasks that the worker addresses in the group situation:

- Searching out the common ground between clients' perceptions of their own need and the aspects of environmental demands with which clients are faced;
- Detecting and challenging the obstacles that obscure the common ground and frustrate the efforts of clients to identify their own needs and the needs of "significant others";
- Contributing ideas, facts, and/or value concepts that are not available to clients as they attempt to cope with problems;
- "Lending a vision" to clients;
- Defining the requirements and limits of the problem-solving situation in which clients and the worker interact.

Groups evolve over time and go through predictable stages of development regardless of the type of group or style of leadership (Corey, 2000, 2001; Gladding, 1995; Yalom, 1995). The stages are not perfectly linear, and groups may move forward and backward in the process. Garland, Jones, and Kilodney (1965) provide the most commonly used depiction of the stages of group development. Based on their work with children, they identified five stages:

- *Preaffiliation* or approach/avoidance, when members are polite and ambivalent about membership;
- *Power and control*, when members test the leader, establish rank, and may exclude some members or drop out of the group;
- *Intimacy*, when members grow in their acceptance of the group;
- *Differentiation*, when members form strong, supportive, or caring relationships that allow for individual differences;
- *Separation*, when members reflect on what has happened, summarize the work, and move toward termination.

Tuckman and Jensen (1977) provide another conceptualization of the group process. In the first stage, described as *forming*, group members are polite and tentative with each other and initial sessions are filled with silences. During the second stage, *storming*, hostility develops among members, ideas may be criticized, and leadership is tested. The third stage is characterized by *norming*, where members develop rules or norms of behavior and build consensus. *Performing*, the fourth stage, occurs when members work together cooperatively. During the last stage, *adjourning*, members begin to separate from one another, often sharing feelings of regret.

Principles of Practice

The practitioner's role as group leader is not just to help people adjust, but instead to free them from their past, from social pressures, from self-defeating behaviors, and from factors within their environment that prevent them from coping as fully functioning persons. Sometimes groups do not prosper because of a lack of careful thought and planning during the conception stage. The practitioner needs to address some of the more practical implications of the group's structure, including who will be included in the group, where and when the group will meet, how to prepare members, and who will establish goals for the group. Planning a successful group cannot be left to chance. The group leader considers the following questions:

- What is the primary focus of the group? Is it education? Mutual sharing? Behavioral change?
- What is the purpose of the group? What does the group leader hope to achieve?
- What population is to be served by the group? Are there any unmet needs of the group?
- Will the group have one or two leaders?
- How will members be selected?
- What number of group members is best in order for the group to achieve its goals/purpose?
- How will members be prepared for the group?
- Will the group be open-ended or closed-ended? What is the duration of the group (for example, 6 weeks, 12 weeks)?
- What issues/topics will be addressed in the group?
- What ground rules (if any) need to be established for the group at the outset?
- Is there agency sanction?
- What are the physical arrangements? What environment will afford members privacy and comfort?
- What will be the group worker's role?

The group leader performs several tasks in order to facilitate the group process. One task is to ensure member involvement and interaction. The practitioner helps members feel comfortable and begin relating to one another, and intervenes when needed to make sure that no one dominates the session. Another task is to set the tone for the group and model preferred behaviors. Each person needs to feel welcomed and respected. The practitioner shows openness and a non-judgmental attitude. As the group develops, the practitioner may be the target of anger and must model non-defensiveness and a willingness to invite conversation about the "conflict." Another task involves confronting unproductive behaviors such as hostility, anger, or resistance. Finally, the group leader needs to be prepared to start each session by eliciting the ideas, interests, or concerns of the members. Discussion needs to stay focused and on track. As the session draws to a close, the practitioner summarizes the group's discussion, shares insights, and encourages the group to deal with specific issues in the next session, as appropriate.

Advantages and Disadvantages of Group Work Practice

Advantages   One of the main reasons for group work's popularity is its proven effectiveness. Groups create a unique social system with properties distinct from those found in dyadic counseling. The communication that occurs between group members and the group leader generates a whole series of actions and reactions. The leader helps to ensure an impartial view of the members and thereby promotes a balanced treatment of their problems. Through group participation, members enhance the meaningfulness of their life experiences and expand their range of behavior choices.

The group environment provides opportunities for members to try out different adaptive patterns of behavior. The group setting is a place where members explore styles of relating to others, learn effective social skills, discuss perceptions with one another, and receive feedback on how they are perceived. Groups offer a supportive environment in which clients learn how to cope with the problems associated with mental illness by observing others with similar concerns, gain feedback and/or insights from other members, and practice new skills both within the group setting and in everyday interactions outside the group (Corey, 2000, 2001).

Disadvantages   Sometimes a practitioner may have very little exposure to the theory and techniques of group work and may be thrust into the role of group leader without adequate preparation or training (Corey, 2000, 2001). It is important for group workers to be aware of and monitor their strengths and weaknesses and the effects these may have on group members. Certain member behaviors, such as sporadic attendance or trying to force others to speak, may challenge the practitioner. It is helpful to seek consultation and/or supervision regarding concerns that may interfere with effective functioning as a group leader. Unfortunately, supervisors may not keep abreast of consultation practices or principles of group theory and process, thus limiting their effectiveness (Jacobs, Masson, & Harvill, 2002).

The major ethical issues and dilemmas that frequently arise in groups include confidentiality, self-determination, and conflict of interest (Congress & Lynn, 1997). There are no easy answers to ethical questions, and practitioners need to be aware of practice guidelines such as the *Standards for Social Work Practice with Groups* (Association for the Advancement of Social Work With Groups, 1999) in order to effectively address these issues. It is also important for the practitioner to be cognizant of how sociopolitical contexts may influence group work practice. Any group has within itself the talent or unrealized capacity of moving its members to engage in social action activities (Breton, 1995) and the practitioner needs to have the ability to exercise institutional intervention skills on behalf of the group.

Within the social work profession, one's worldview, beliefs, and values strongly affect one's practice and comfort with groups (Kurland & Salmon, 1999). The practitioner must not be tied down to a particular approach to group facilitation and recognize that helping styles may be culture-bound (Kelsey, 1998). Practitioners can be vulnerable to their own limitations, and it is important to distinguish the competencies and expertise necessary for working with group members who are different from them in terms of race, ethnicity, culture, gender, sexual orientation, abilities, religion, spirituality, and socioeconomic status.

SUMMARY

Since many people with serious mental illness are receiving some form of medication (Bentley, 2003), the chapter began with an explanation of biological therapies to help the practitioner gain an awareness of the role of psychotropic medications in treatment. Next was a synopsis of the major counseling theories and methods supporting competency-based treatment with persons living with mental illness, their families and significant others. The various practice theories and methods have developed techniques through research and practice experience, and there is some overlap between them. The primary therapeutic techniques associated with each approach are summarized in Table 2.1 so that further comparisons can be made.

While there are numerous practice theories, the focus of this overview was to provide a foundation to support the integrative approach around which the competency-based model is organized. Most practitioners borrow principles, concepts, and techniques from a variety of different theoretical viewpoints and ultimately develop into an integrated approach, as no single theoretical approach is considered appropriate for all client problems. However, the competency-based treatment model requires the practitioner to strive to be consistent and comprehensive when integrating counseling theories into his or her practice. This framework encourages the practitioner to purposefully select counseling theories suitable for each client and also to strive to understand why certain viewpoints hold more appeal than others.

The counseling theories and techniques reviewed in this chapter were crisis intervention, solution-focused therapy, cognitive-behavioral therapy, and psychosocial therapy. Following a brief introduction, the history, major tenets, salient principles of practice, and advantages and disadvantages of each theory were outlined. This selection is not meant to diminish the importance of other approaches to treatment, nor is it intended to be the "final word" on practice. As a matter of fact, subsequent chapters provide an overview of additional therapies. However, the intent of the various approaches elaborated here is to set the stage for the practitioner's critical thinking when building a treatment plan that promotes the client's full range of competence.

Over the past 25 years, families have demanded greater participation in the care of their mentally ill loved ones and have fought to dispel stigmatizing attitudes toward mental illness. Recognizing this development, psychoeducation, with its emphasis on educating persons with mental illness and their family members, was included in this chapter. Methods of family and group work practice were covered to expand the practitioner's consideration of ways to work within the client's social context.

The following websites may be of interest to readers:

www.culturalorientation.net

The United States Refugee Program helps refugees to resettle in the United States. As part of this preparation, cultural orientation (CO) training is provided to

TABLE 2.1	SUMMARY OF THE PRIMARY THERAPEUTIC TECHNIQUES ASSOCIATED WITH EACH PRACTICE THEORY AND METHOD

Crisis Intervention

- Relationship formation
- Clarification (of the presenting problem)
- Exploration
- Ventilation
- Contracting
- Planning goals and treatment objectives
- Providing information and advocacy
- Facilitating linkages with support systems
- Making referrals
- Assertiveness training
- Modeling
- Coaching
- Behavioral rehearsal or role play
- Cognitive restructuring
- Decision making
- Systematic desensitization
- Gestalt experiments

Solution-Focused Therapy

- Pre-session change questions
- Exception finding
- Coping questions
- Scaling
- Miracle question

Cognitive-Behavioral Therapy

- Challenging conviction(s) associated with beliefs
- Providing information/education
- Reinforcing positive behaviors/perceptions
- Assigning homework
- Collaborative empiricism
- Socratic dialogue
- Guided discovery
- Real-life "experiments"
- Modeling
- Cognitive rehearsal
- Relaxation techniques
- Social skills
- Conflict resolution
- Journaling

Psychosocial Therapy

- Sustainment
- Direct influence
- Exploration, description, ventilation
- Person-situation reflection
- Pattern dynamic reflection
- Developmental reflection

(continued)

Psychoeducation

- Education and information
- Formats:
    One session
    Workshop
    Seminar series
    Combined with other methods (individual, family, group)

Family Practice

- Reframing or relabeling
- Questioning
- Examining interactional sequences
- Providing directives
- Respecting physical cues

Group Work Practice

- Establishing group focus
- Defining group purpose
- Identifying population to be served
- Selecting members
- Defining number of group members
- Preparing members for the group
- Setting time frame (open or closed-ended)
- Selecting topics/issues
- Establishing ground rules
- Obtaining agency sanction
- Establishing physical arrangements
- Group leader's role:
    Help members feel comfortable.
    Ensure member involvement and interaction.
    Set the tone for the group.
    Model preferred behaviors.
    Show openness and a non-judgmental attitude.
    Invite conversation about "conflict."
    Confront non-productive member behaviors.
    Keep discussion focused and on track.
    Summarize group discussion.
    Share insights and encourage members to deal with issues.

refugees. This website was established to create linkages between overseas providers of CO and domestic resettlement programs. Helpful links are provided on this website for the following topics:

- Culture profile—refugee country and cultural information;
- Best practices—cultural orientation activities;
- Frequently asked questions—questions refugees ask;
- Resources—links to refugee-related websites.

www.brieftherapy.org

The Brief Therapy Practice organization was founded in 1989 in Great Britain to develop solution-focused therapy ideas within the British context. This website provides information about brief therapy practice, research, courses, conferences, and practice notes, to list a few.

www.needymeds.com

A social worker (Libby Overly) and a family physician (Richard Sagall) run this website. It lists more than 1,200 medications and more than 240 patient assistance programs offering free or low-cost medications to economically disadvantaged persons. Unfortunately the economic guidelines are stringent, but one can determine eligibility by entering the name of the medication or the pharmaceutical company that produces it.

www.helpingpatients.org

This website is run by the pharmaceutical industry–sponsored organization Pharmaceutical Research and Manufacturers of America. It offers additional resources for those in need of financial assistance obtaining medications. It asks for more specific information than the "NeedyMeds" website to determine eligibility.

www.rxassist.org

Run by the Robert Wood Johnson Foundation, this website offers links to patient assistance programs and state medication discount programs for elderly, low-income, and disabled persons. It also provides information on drug-discount cards.

PRACTITIONER REFLECTIONS

1. Reflecting on your practice experiences, create a psychoeducational program for families with a member who struggles with mental illness.
   - Include a list of topics that you believe group members would want to see addressed.
   - Be prepared to present your "proposal" to your agency or supervisor. Include the specific steps you would consider to start up the program.

   As an alternative, create the same psychoeducational format for persons with mental illness. Are the proposed topics the same or different? Explain.
2. Develop a list of the challenges encountered by someone living with mental illness; be as complete as you can.
   - Reflect on what would you do to be helpful to that person.
   - Which one of these "challenges" will be the hardest for you to handle? Why?
   - Talk with colleagues and/or your supervisor about this listing and ask which "challenge" would be the most troublesome for them. Can they add to your listing?
   - Which "challenge" would make it difficult for you to develop a collaborative therapeutic relationship? What would you do to foster collaboration?
3. Reflecting on the counseling theories and techniques described in this chapter, identify those you have found helpful in your work with clients who

struggle with mental illness. Identify the theories and techniques helpful for working with family members of a person struggling with mental illness.

4. Interview a professional who works with persons (and/or family members) with mental illness. Ask the practitioner to identify what counseling theories and related techniques he or she considers most helpful.

   - How does this list compare with the theories and techniques reviewed in this chapter?
   - How does it compare with your response to question 3?

5. Reflect on a client you have worked with who is struggling with mental illness. Role-play a situation in which you, the practitioner, attempt to help this individual to talk about his or her reactions to the pressures (or stresses) associated with having a diagnosis. This activity is intended to increase your understanding of the interplay between mental illness and life circumstances and/or events related to a particular diagnosis.

   - Will you plan to work with the individual, the whole family, with different groupings of family members, or/and with significant others in the client's life?
   - Will you consider group work practice, and if so, what kind of group would be of benefit?
   - Discuss how the competency-based treatment model guides the selection of specific techniques from the counseling theories and/or practice methods presented in this chapter.

6. Interview three to four individuals asking them about their personal and professional experiences with drugs of all kinds. Based on the information you have gathered, assess attitudes and the knowledge people have about drugs as an aspect of our social environment.

COGNITIVE DISORDERS, INCLUDING DELIRIUM AND DEMENTIA

Of all the psychiatric disorders noted in the *Diagnostic and Statistical Manual* (American Psychiatric Association, 2000), only late-life dementias are associated with aging. Of these, the Alzheimer's type is the most common (Hooyman and Kiyak, 1996). In the twenty-first century, people are living longer than ever before and enjoying better physical health as well as declining rates of chronic illness. In contrast to the normal aging process, this chapter will pay particular attention to three classes of cognitive disorders that are more likely to be found in older people than other segments of the population: delirium, dementia, and amnestic disorders (amnesia).

Faster than any other age group in our society, the number of older persons is growing. One in five Americans will be 65 years of age or older by the year 2050 (Richardson, 2002). Those aged 85 and over are showing the most rapid increase. This population of the "oldest old" is at highest risk for dementing illnesses such as Alzheimer's disease (AD); for example, individuals between the ages of 65 and 74 have a 1 in 25 chance of having AD, while those 85 years of age and older have a 1 in 2 chance of developing the disorder (National Institutes of Health, 1992). It is estimated that up to 4 million people in the United States and 20 million world-wide currently suffer from dementia, and the prevalence (the number of people with the disease at any given time) doubles for every 5 years over the age of 65. It is estimated that almost 400,000 new cases will occur each year and that this number will increase significantly as the overall population ages (Brookmeyer, Gray, & Kawas, 1998).

According to the latest U.S. Census, growth of the aging population will accelerate rapidly beginning in 2010, when the first wave of baby boomers reach age 65. In 1980 approximately 25.7 million persons aged 65 and older made up about 10 percent of the total population of the United States. By the year 2050 the size of this group will have multiplied to over 70 million people or approximately 22.9 percent of the total population (Atchley, 1994). This trend is not only evident in the United States but worldwide. As more people are living longer, the number of people affected by diseases of aging, including Alzheimer's disease, will continue to increase. Specific groups of elders are also increasing, particularly women and ethnic minorities (Dunkle & Norgard, 1995; Kart & Kinney, 2001; Richardson, 2002; Rosen & Zlotnik, 2001; Torres-Gil & Moga, 2001). While the lives of older persons show significant gains overall, a large portion of our older population experience hardship, particularly the "oldest old," women, and ethnic minorities. These population groups are more likely to encounter physical, social, and economic difficulties. Over the next several decades, it is anticipated that the number of older persons who require the intensive services of institutions such as nursing homes and hospitals will increase.

Reactions to medications and certain medical disorders can precipitate psychiatric conditions. At the same time, psychiatric conditions can influence physical health. Older persons have specific health care needs, and their unique biopsychosocial characteristics influence the presentation, evaluation, and management of cognitive disorders. The integrated approach characterizing competency-based treatment addresses the multifaceted problems confronting older persons and provides a framework for the social work practitioner to address all areas of the client's life, including intrapersonal (or personal), interpersonal (or social), and environmental domains.

UNDERSTANDING THE COGNITIVE DISORDERS

A comprehensive evaluation is necessary for diagnosing cognitive disorders and planning competency-based treatment. Each client should be treated as a unique person who also happens to be struggling with a mental illness. This focus on uniqueness opens up possibilities to explore the client's experiences with the diagnosis within a family, social, cultural, and environmental context. A thorough psychosocial history (including a mental status exam) helps the practitioner to discern all of the factors contributing to the person's life condition and circumstances. When working with someone struggling with a cognitive disorder, it is often helpful for the practitioner to obtain additional information from the family or others who know the individual. For example, observing the client's interactions with significant others in the context of a family interview not only provides additional insights about the presenting problem but also helps the practitioner to tap into existing resources and supports. The mental status examination should be especially detailed when there is any evidence or high risk of cognitive dysfunction. Eisendrath and Lichtmacher (2001) suggest that the mental examination address the following features:

- *Appearance*—It is helpful to note any unusual modes of dress, use of makeup, and so forth.
- *Activity and behavior*—Carefully evaluate the person's gait, gestures, and coordination of bodily movements.
- *Affect*—Appraise the outward manifestation of emotions such as depression, anger, elation, fear, resentment, or lack of emotional response.

- *Mood*—Listen carefully to the person's report of feelings and observe emotional manifestations.
- *Speech*—Assess the coherence, spontaneity, articulation, hesitancy in answering, and duration of response of the person's speech patterns.
- *Content of thought*—This includes associations, preoccupations, obsessions, depersonalization, delusions, hallucinations, paranoid ideation, anger, fear, or unusual experiences and suicidal ideation.
- *Thought process*—This includes loose associations, flight of ideas, thought blocking, tangentiality, circumstantiality, perseveration, and racing thought(s).
- *Cognition*—Evaluate the following aspects of a person's cognition:
  - (a) Orientation to person, place, time, and circumstances
  - (b) Remote and recent memory and recall
  - (c) Digit retention (six forward is normal) or calculation of serial sevens or threes
  - (d) General fund of knowledge, such as presidents, naming states in the United States, distances, events
  - (e) Abstracting ability, which can be tested using common proverbs or analogies and differences (for example, asking, "How are a lie and a mistake the same, and how are they different?")
  - (f) Ability to identify by naming, reading, and writing specified test names and objects
  - (g) Ideomotor function, which combines understanding and the ability to perform a task (for example, asking the person "Show me how to throw a ball")
  - (h) Ability to reproduce geometric constructions (for example, drawing a parallelogram or intersecting squares)
  - (i) Right-left differentiation
- *Judgment regarding commonsense problems*—This may include asking about what to do when one runs out of medicine.
- *Insight into the nature and extent of the current difficulty* and its ramifications in the person's daily life.

The practitioner may consult with other professionals such as a psychologist, psychiatrist, or a physician with expertise in both psychiatry and neurology in order to help differentiate psychologically oriented problems from organic ones. Examples of commonly used objective tests for the diagnosis of organicity include the Bender Gestalt, the Wechsler Memory Scale, and intelligence tests such as the Wechsler Adult Intelligence Scale–Revised (WAIS–R). Intelligence tests help to quantify the intellectual deterioration that has occurred. Brain imaging techniques for detecting structural abnormalities in the person who presents with nondefinitive history and examination, such as computed tomography (CT) or magnetic resonance imaging (MRI), have become standard methods in psychiatric diagnosis. The MRI is a much more sensitive tool and particularly helpful when evaluating small-vessel ischemic injury. One disadvantage is that some persons cannot tolerate confinement within the MRI machine. In Alzheimer's disease, the

MRI may appear "normal" but more frequently reveals diffuse cerebral atrophy. Electroencephalography is particularly helpful for diagnosing seizure disorders and differentiating delirium from depression or dementia.

Delirium

Delirium is one of the first mental disorders to be described in history and over time has been known by many different names, including acute confusional state, toxic psychosis, acute brain syndrome, and metabolic encephalopathy (Zide & Gray, 2001). Delirium is frequently found in older patients hospitalized for acute illness or postoperative care and can be considered both a common and serious complication of acute illness. Affecting more than one-third of all hospitalized persons 65 or over, delirium is often misdiagnosed or unrecognized by caregivers. Delirium occurs in up to 40 percent of patients admitted to intensive care units. The incidence of postoperative delirium following general surgery is 5 to 10 percent, with consistently high rates following hip fracture repair and, to a lesser extent, after cardiac and transplant surgery, and after abdominal aortic aneurysm repair (O'Keeffe, 1999). Brennan (1999) observes that patients are often slow to recover their previous level of functioning. There is growing evidence that the cognitive impairment of delirium is not entirely reversible in all patients, and it is possible that delirium represents a time of significant risk for the progression of underlying dementia.

Delirium develops as an acute episode lasting anywhere from several hours to a number of days. It is characterized by a disturbance of consciousness, and symptoms tend to fluctuate during the course of the day (APA, 2000). Typically a person will experience relatively lucid periods in the morning with a maximum disturbance at night (APA, 2000; Zide & Gray, 2001). Etiology is related to a general medical condition or substance intoxication or withdrawal, with supportive evidence from the person's history, physical examination, and/or laboratory findings. The most common causes are drugs, various systemic disorders, and primary central nervous system disorders such as infections, head trauma, neoplasms, and cerebrovascular disorders.

Disturbed consciousness and impaired ability to attend to one's environment are central features of delirium. The individual's confused state is often associated with delusions (or fleeting delusions), hallucinations, and bizarre behavior. Delusions are common and often persecutory in nature. Perceptual misidentifications and visual hallucinations are particularly likely to occur at night in a phenomenon known as sundowning, but there are few studies to support how to manage these behaviors (McGaffigan & Bliwise, 1997). The author recalls one experience working in a hospital when a patient was being transferred from one floor to another at the end of the day. Once inside the elevator, the patient looked around and with a cheerful smile remarked what a delightful cruise ship this was! Affect is variable, often characterized by fear and anxiety. The person's behavior can vary greatly, ranging from agitation, excitement, and combativeness to apathy and lethargy. The individual is highly distractible and unable to focus or sustain attention. Often, questions need to be repeated. Short-term memory and orientation to time are almost always impaired. Speech patterns are rambling or illogical and incoherent. The individual may also seem to be depressed, tearful, or anxious. The evaluation and management of delirium is considered a medical emergency (Brennan, 1999).

Dementia

In 1906, German neuropathologist Dr. Alois Alzheimer became intrigued with the signs and symptoms exhibited by one of his patients, "Augusta D." Dr. Alzheimer noted that the patient exhibited angry outbursts, fits of paranoia, and often patted the faces of others (apparently mistaking them for her own). At the time of her death at age 55 she had spent many of the last years of her life in a mental institution. On post-mortem examination, Dr. Alzheimer microscopically analyzed a segment of her brain tissue and made a startling discovery. Her brain tissue contained what he described as "plaques and stringy tangles," thus indicating the specific distinguishing "twin markers" for making a diagnosis of the disease which eventually bore the doctor's name.

Dementia is characterized by multiple cognitive deficits that include impairment in memory (APA, 2000). The term *dementia* does not imply a specific cause or pathologic process, as more than 55 illnesses (some non-progressive) can cause dementia (Mayeux, Foster, Rossor, & Whitehouse, 1993; Roses, Saunders, Charness, & Rubinstein, 1996). Not all cases of dementia, broadly defined as a progressive or permanent decline in intellectual functioning, are caused by Alzheimer's disease. There are many conditions that are mistakenly diagnosed as dementia but in fact only mimic the symptoms of dementia, including Pick's disease, Creutzfeldt-Jakob disease, Parkinson's disease, delirium, drug overdose, vitamin deficiencies, dehydration, depression, anemias, or viral infections. With proper medical attention, most of these conditions are reversible, whereas Alzheimer's disease is not reversible.

Senility (another name for dementia) was once accepted by society as part of normal aging, and little was done medically to alleviate the symptoms. Today we have a greater understanding of the severity, impact, and causes of dementia. All forms of dementia, of which Alzheimer's type is the most common, involve some impairment of the person's memory, thinking, reasoning, and language. Personality changes and abnormal behavior can also occur as dementia progresses, disrupting the individual's daily activities significantly (and the lives of others close to them). About 10 percent of dementia sufferers are victims of a series of small strokes called transient ischemic attacks (TIAs), in which certain areas of the brain tissue deteriorate. Long-standing hypertension or the narrowing of heart arteries increases the risk of this type of dementia.

An individual with suspected dementia requires a thorough evaluation to exclude the presence of infrequent but reversible conditions. Making this diagnosis can be tricky because people with dementia are often uncommunicative and may be unable to answer questions posed to them or to provide a reliable history. Nevertheless, making an accurate diagnosis is an important first step because it helps practitioners to know what to expect or what intervention might be useful to reduce further problems.

Alzheimer's Disease

Although the risk of a person developing Alzheimer's disease increases with age, it is not part of the normal aging process. In most individuals with Alzheimer's disease, symptoms appear after the age of 60. The earliest symptoms characteristically include recent loss of memory, later compounded by faulty judgment and changes in personality. Progressive disorientation with respect to time and place is universal. The typical course of Alzheimer's disease is characterized by a progressive decline, but some people experience periods of mild plateaus. The average individual lives 8 to 10 years after diagnosis, although the range varies considerably and includes survival for up to 20 years.

Dementia is a complex clinical condition that includes neurological, cognitive, affective, psychiatric, and behavioral problems (Parnetti, 2000). People in the earliest stages think less clearly and tend to become confused and bewildered. Later in the disease progression they forget how to perform simple tasks, such as how to correctly dress or feed themselves. Over time, people progressively lose the ability to function on their own and eventually become entirely dependent on others for daily care and support. Ultimately they are reduced to being bedridden, incontinent, and vulnerable to developing other illnesses and opportunistic infections. From the perspective of loved ones, dementia has been referred to as "the longest good-bye" (Zide & Gray, 2001, p. 34).

One hundred years after Dr. Alzheimer's discovery, scientists and researchers continue to debate which of the two brain lesions associated with Alzheimer's disease is more important. Is it the plaques littering the empty spaces between nerve cells or the stringy tangles that erupt from within? Others grapple with not limiting this disorder to which of these markers is more important but rather coming to terms with whatever it is that produces both abnormalities. Currently, researchers are analyzing genetic factors and looking for clues regarding which protein structures hasten the disease process, what mechanisms cause the disease, and how the disease unfolds. Up to this point, no one has been able to definitively explain what actually causes Alzheimer's disease. What is known is there are two types of Alzheimer's disease: familial Alzheimer's disease (FAD) which follows certain inheritance patterns (Strittmatter et al., 1993), and sporadic Alzheimer's disease, in which no obvious inheritance patterns are evident.

Manifestations of Alzheimer's include problems with orientation, short or fluctuating attention span, loss of recent memory and recall, impaired judgment, emotional instability, lack of initiative, impaired impulse control, inability to reason through problems, depression (worse in mild to moderate types), confabulation, constrictions of intellectual functions, visual and auditory hallucinations, and delusions (Eisendrath & Lichtmacher, 2001). Alzheimer's disease advances progressively from mild forgetfulness to a severe loss in mental and physical functioning. Additionally, individuals display one or more other cognitive disturbances, including aphasia (difficulty with language), apraxia (impaired motor functioning), agnosia (failure to recognize common objects), or difficulty performing activities that include planning, coordinating, sequencing, or abstracting information. These cognitive impairments also have a serious negative impact on social and occupational functioning and represent a significant decline from previous abilities.

The Three Stages of Alzheimer's Disease

The characteristic cognitive feature of Alzheimer's disease is progressive memory impairment, predominantly loss of short-term memory. The ability to focus attention and recall remote events may be subtly impaired at first and always worsens with time. Progressive disorientation with respect to time and place is universal (Geldmacher & Whitehouse, 1996). Social workers may come into contact with clients who are described as being "confused," "bewildered," "baffled," or "senile." No two individuals with Alzheimer's will exhibit exactly the same symptoms, and among the three stages, some overlap will occur. It is important to be able to recognize each stage.

Stage I: Mild (lasts from two to four years)
- Increased forgetfulness that interferes with the ability to hold a job or perform household chores (for example, cutting the grass or cooking meals)
- Inability to recall names for simple things like milk, bread, or eggs
- Difficulty remembering what numbers mean
- Loss of interest in initiating favorite hobbies (such as playing cards or gardening)
- Decreased judgment that leads to accidents or injuries

Stage II: Moderate (from two to eight years)
- Lack of recognition of close family members and friends
- Wandering away from home and not knowing how to return
- Increased confusion, anxiety, and personality changes
- Inability to perform common daily tasks such as dressing oneself or feeding oneself
- Delusions (sometimes hallucinations)
- Difficulty sleeping during nighttime hours; agitation

Stage III: Severe (from one to three years)
- Inability to remember anything (including spouse, children, grandchildren)
- Inability to process new information
- Loss of the capacity to use or understand words (although people in this stage may continue to respond to touch, smiles, music, or eye contact)
- Bladder and/or bowel incontinence
- Difficulty eating food or swallowing liquids (food must be pureed or liquified)
- Inability to sit independently

Amnestic Disorder

This disorder is not frequently encountered by the practitioner but is included in the chapter discussion because of its potential impact on the individual. One of the most famous patients with amnestic disorder was "H. M.," who underwent bilateral medical temporal lobe resection to treat his severe epilepsy (Milner, 1959; Milner, Corkin, & Teuber, 1968). After the surgery, he experienced difficulty recalling some events of the past and had an even more severe inability to make new memories.

H. M. was said to have described his condition as feeling like he was continuously waking from a dream.

Amnestic syndrome is characterized by a severe loss of memory, and this is the most outstanding symptom noted (APA, 2000; Zide & Gray, 2001). People with amnestic disorder experience difficulty recalling certain kinds of memories. They are aware of memory impairment (which differentiates it from delirium) and have not experienced any significant loss of other intellectual abilities (differentiating it from dementia). When there is more than one amnestic syndrome, the differences among them revolve around what individuals can and cannot remember. The most common amnestic disorder is Korsakoff's syndrome, which is associated with chronic alcohol use and characterized by confabulation with severe short- and long-term memory impairments. Immediate memory may be fairly well preserved. Impaired abstraction and perseveration are also commonly observed in people with Korsakoff's syndrome (alcohol amnestic disorder).

OVERVIEW OF MAJOR INTERVENTIONS

Treatment of Delirium

Delirium is a common and serious complication of acute illness in older patients (O'Keeffe, 1999). The management of delirium is multifaceted, but the first step in treatment is to precisely diagnose the syndrome and assess contributors while concurrently providing supportive measures to prevent harm and minimize further distress. It may also be helpful to identify persons at high risk of delirium before it develops so preventive measures can be taken.

Delirium is common in hospitalized older persons and at the time of admission, between 10 and 22 percent are considered delirious (O'Keeffe, 1999). Social workers employed in hospital settings frequently provide outreach services, so it is helpful to consider the effects of hospitalization on this diagnosis. Inouye and Charpentier (1996) have identified several factors that contribute to the development of delirium after a person is admitted to the hospital: use of physical restraints, weight loss, addition of more than three drugs, bladder catheterization, and any iatrogenic event in the hospital. Other common causes of delirium found in hospital patients include chest or urinary tract infections, hypoxia due to cardiac or respiratory disease, medication toxicity, dehydration and electrolyte disturbance, and stroke (Moore & O'Keeffe, 1999; O'Keeffe, 1999). Delirium is also found in older patients who have had hip surgery (Edlund, Lundstrom, Lundstrom, Hedqvist, & Gustafson, 1999; Jagmin, 1998).

Taking a complete psychosocial history from a relative or caregiver about when the client's cognitive (and behavioral) disturbance first began and how it may have changed can help the practitioner to distinguish between chronic cognitive impairment and delirium (Wahlund & Bjorlin, 1999). Older persons are vulnerable to prolonged hospital stays, functional decline during hospitalization, complications such as pressure sores, falls, infections, urinary incontinence, and poor nutrition. These factors are more common in persons with delirium and may prolong or exacerbate the delirium (Elie et al., 1998; Francis, 1997; Murray & Levkoff, 1993; Schor & Levkoff, 1992). Delirium is a true medical emergency that can be initially mistaken for other conditions such as dementia or functional psychosis, making crisis treatment the intervention of choice (Murphy, 2000).

Biological Therapies

When prescribing medications for older persons, it is helpful to note that they are more prone to experiencing toxic effects. Aging is associated with liver changes that decrease oxidative mechanisms, lowered serum albumin that provides binding sites, and/or a decline in kidney function, any of which increases drug half-life. For delirium, pharmacological therapy may be considered but is not necessary for all patients. Each individual may have a very different clinical profile indicating a need to particularize treatment strategies. The determination of biological interventions will depend on the specific features of the person's condition, the underlying etiology of the delirium, and any associated comorbid conditions. Antipsychotic medications are often the treatment of choice. Butyrophenones, particularly haloperidol (Haldol) and droperidol (Inapsine), are considered the safest and most effective antipsychotics for delirium. Droperidol is associated with greater sedation and hypotensive effects and haloperidol is usually considered adequate for older patients. Haloperidol has fewer active metabolites, limited anticholinergic effects, fewer sedative and hypotensive effects, and can be administered by different routes. Recently, there has been increased use of risperidone (Risperdal) (Sipahimalani & Masand, 1997; Ravona-Springer, Dolberg, Hirschmann, & Grunhaus, 1998). Benzodiazepines are the treatment of choice for withdrawal states, particularly those associated with seizures or withdrawal from alcohol or sedatives. They are also a useful adjunctive treatment for patients who cannot tolerate antipsychotic drugs. Cholinergics such as physostigmine (Antilirium) may be useful in delirium known to be caused specifically by anticholinergic medications. However, the therapeutic effect is short-lived and there are serious side effects. Palliative treatment with opiates may be needed for patients with delirium for whom pain is an aggravating factor. Persons who are hallucinating can experience considerable distress. Physical restraints are sometimes used to prevent people from harming themselves but can be inhumane for those who are already distressed and may be potentially dangerous in agitated patients. Whenever possible, other means should be used, such as having someone sit with the individual.

Environmental and Supportive Interventions

For persons struggling with delirium, supportive measures may involve providing them with their glasses and hearing aid (if worn) to minimize sensory deprivation. It is also helpful if family members can remain with their loved one to explain medical procedures, particularly if the procedures will be painful or unpleasant. Both the patient and his or her family may benefit from reassurance and education about delirium; that is, the situation is usually temporary and the symptoms are part of a medical condition. The practitioner may encourage the family to bring in familiar objects from home such as photographs. For the person whose decision-making impairs the ability to give informed consent about medical care, the practitioner may involve family members, obtain a court-appointed guardian, or facilitate an immediate hearing with a judge. Many patients are discharged before their symptoms of delirium are fully resolved, and the practitioner is active in developing a discharge plan aimed at reducing the factors that may exacerbate delirium, reorient the person, and provide needed services.

Treatment of Dementia—Alzheimer's Disease

In the past 100 years, institutions providing care to people with Alzheimer's disease have changed from state mental hospitals, county almshouses, and a smattering of private boarding homes to an industry of more than 16,000 mostly privately owned nursing homes (Jarrett, Rockwood, & Mallery, 1995; Brookmeyer et al., 1998). Dementia is a complex clinical condition that involves cognitive, personality, and behavioral changes. From the outset, the therapeutic approach should be a comprehensive plan considering both pharmacological and psychosocial interventions. Complete recovery is impossible and the practitioner's goal is to help the person with Alzheimer's and his or her family manage the chronic, progressive, and disabling symptoms of the disease. The deterioration of functional abilities of daily living has a major impact on the quality of life and, as will be seen in the case of Zelda "Jean" Pfohl, is a critical predictor for institutionalization.

The most immediate need is to help control the symptoms of cognitive loss and problem behaviors such as verbal and physical aggression, agitation, wandering, depression, sleep disturbances, and delusions. Delusions may affect up to 50 percent of individuals diagnosed with Alzheimer's disease. Paranoid delusions seem to be the most common and often lead to accusations of theft, marital infidelity, and persecution. Visual hallucinations occur in approximately 25 percent of persons with Alzheimer's disease; they frequently describe seeing their deceased parents, siblings, mysterious intruders, or menacing animals. Psychoeducation for the person and his or her family, coupled with support and reassurance, are particularly helpful.

Language impairment is another important sign of Alzheimer's disease (Hebert, Wilson, Gilley, Beckett, & Scherr, 2000) and often manifested first as difficulty in finding words in spontaneous speech. As the disease progresses, language use is often described as vague and characterized by increased use of automatic phrases and clichés. This level of language is often adequate for superficial conversations found in most social settings; for example, it's easy for a person to say "how nice this is" when commenting about the food at a holiday gathering without going into details about the ingredients or recipe. However, communication patterns eventually become disrupted and typically cause problems in the caregiving relationship (Ripich, Vertes, Whitehouse, & Fulton, 1991). Anomia (impaired naming ability, especially for parts of objects) is frequently a prominent symptom, and complex deficits in visual and spatial abilities can also be seen; for example, the person may be unable to recognize familiar faces and may mistake shrubs in the backyard for people (Geldmacher & Whitehouse, 1996). The practitioner may engage the person struggling with the early stages of Alzheimer's disease in a life review. As the disease progresses, describing photographs of familiar family members may provide a concrete way to help orient the person and offer reassurance.

People with Alzheimer's disease eventually become unable to drive a car, carry out activities of daily living, dress themselves, use eating utensils, balance a checkbook, or manage personal financial affairs. They are normally incapable of performing complex yet once familiar tasks such as preparing meals and managing their personal hygiene. Family members may become central in assuming the caregiving role at this time.

Family Interventions   Amid ongoing changes in agencies and funding for services, social work practitioners are continually challenged to find better ways to help clients, families, and caregivers cope with the devastating decline in mental and physical abilities and the problem behaviors that accompany Alzheimer's disease. An important social work role is to help support and sustain those who care for persons suffering from Alzheimer's. Research indicates that families may benefit from a combination of traditional psychosocial counseling and psychoeducational interventions (Mittelman, Ferris, & Shulman, 1995, 1996). Mittelman and his colleagues conducted a longitudinal study of nursing home residents diagnosed with Alzheimer's disease (and their families) and found positive benefits from a combination of support group participation, individual and family counseling, and ad hoc consultations for the primary caregiver. The researchers also found that caregiving families experience a great deal of stress that is "normative" to the situation. These are not "troubled" families but people coping with a difficult life transition.

Biological Interventions   The etiology of Alzheimer's disease is complex, and therefore treatment strategies rely on generalized pathological findings. Cholinesterase inhibitors address a generalized deficit of central nervous system (CNS) acetylcholine and are the first class of agents specifically approved for the treatment of Alzheimer's. Although cholinesterase inhibitors are not curative for Alzheimer's disease, clinical evidence indicates that these drugs can significantly delay the progress of cognitive impairment and represent a useful treatment for the symptoms of Alzheimer's disease in older people (VanDen Berg, Kazmi, & Jann, 2000).

Treatment of Amnestic Disorder

Amnestic disorder can be reversible, as in the case of drugs, or irreversible, as with a memory deficit caused by permanent brain damage. Drug-induced reversible amnestic syndromes can be treated by eliminating the offending medication. There is no treatment for permanent brain damage, although rehabilitation may be helpful for those persons with milder syndromes; for example, teaching patients to use visual mnemonics may be beneficial for those who still have the ability to retrieve visual images. New information about the brain and memory is continually emerging, but the treatment of amnestic disorders remains in its infancy.

RISKS ASSOCIATED WITH COGNITIVE DISORDERS

Intrapersonal Risks

Age It is an alarming thought, but by the time each of us reaches our sixty-fifth birthday, we have more than a 5 percent chance of being afflicted with Alzheimer's disease. The risk increases to 20 percent after the age of 80 (Warner, 2001). Because of the worldwide aging phenomenon in both developed and developing countries, dementia has growing implications for public health.

Alzheimer's disease is the most common type of dementia among people age 65 and older and represents a major health problem in the United States because of its enormous impact on individuals, families, the health care system, and society as a whole. As the "graying" population grows older, social work practitioners will increasingly face the challenges of finding ways to assist both individuals and families in dealing with dementia (Beck, 1998). It is estimated that by 2030, older adults (65+) will comprise 22 percent of the population, double the number of older people today (Kennedy, 2000). This explosion of elders who will be living longer requires greater understanding of the illnesses common to this age group. There are also a number of risk factors for persons diagnosed with delirium, including advanced age, an existing diagnosis of dementia, impaired functional status, chronic comorbidities and medications, and the severity of the acute illness or surgery (Flacker & Marcantonio, 1998).

Heredity Researchers and scientists still do not know why Alzheimer's disease occurs. A consistent association with Alzheimer's disease is advancing age and a family history of dementia. Although age and heredity are two proven risk factors, the current thinking suggests dementia may be caused by a combination of factors.

Gender As noted earlier, the number and proportion of very old persons within the general population in the United States is increasing. The segment growing most rapidly is those over age 75, and particularly women (U.S. Bureau of the Census, 1996) who continue to live longer than men. Dunkle and Norgard (1995) reported that among those over the age of 85, there were 39 men for every 100 women. The risk of developing Alzheimer's disease increases with advancing age. As a parallel, the incidence of Alzheimer's disease is significantly higher for women than men, possibly reflecting their longer life span.

Interpersonal Risks

The burdens of caregiving have been divided into two aspects: objective and subjective (Biegel, 1995; McCallion et al., 2002). Objective burden is considered to be the actual time and effort spent caring for another, including the specific time involved, tasks performed, chronic fatigue and related changes in physical health, or financial resources expended (Cox, 1996). Subjective burden refers to perceptions, feelings, and attitudes associated with the tasks of caregiving. The subjective burdens tend to be the most difficult for caregivers to handle. Spouse caregivers are particularly vulnerable to the strain and tension of caring for their loved one with dementia and often experience feelings of guilt, grief, anger, frustration, and depression (Gaugler, Leitsch, Zarit, & Pearlin, 2000; Kosloski, Young, & Montgomery, 1999; Whitlatch, Feinberg, & Stevens, 1999).

Relationships among family members change when a relative develops dementia, thereby adding to their stress (Gutheil & Tepper, 1997; Severson, Smith, & Tangalos, 1994). Personality changes associated with Alzheimer's range from progressive compliance or passivity to marked hostility and aggression, often developing before the actual cognitive impairment. Many of the non-cognitive or behavioral symptoms are important, but how these changes may stress the caregiver is often overlooked. It is the caretaker who must deal with the individual's increased stubbornness, diminished initiative, decreased emotional expression, and greater suspiciousness. Having to respond to the agitated behavior associated with a diagnosis of dementia can physically and emotionally challenge the caregiver. In addition, secondary stressors such as marital stress or relationship changes may be introduced.

The average age of the care recipient is 77 years, while the typical caregiver is a married woman in her late 40s. Note Zarit and Edwards (1996), the decision to place a family member in a formal institution is a critical event. As will be seen in the case discussion of Zelda "Jean" Pfohl, the placement usually occurs following a crisis and the family often does not have the opportunity to acknowledge and deal with the feelings associated with this decision. The accumulation of stressors over time may further debilitate family members' abilities to care for their aging relatives.

Community and Environmental Risks

Ageism   Historically, older persons have been viewed as a social class that personifies and embodies social problems. While the older population is heterogeneous, special populations may include those persons stressed by life events and life circumstances especially associated with aging, such as illness, the loss of a life partner, institutionalization, decreased income, and an increasingly common social phenomenon of grandmothers raising grandchildren (Berman-Rossi, 2001). The capacity to cope with change is influenced by a lifetime of experiences, but in our society, aging is seen as a stage of life characterized by deterioration and uselessness (Laws, 1995). While there is no evidence to support the belief that memory impairment is normative to the aging process (Kaplan & Sadock, 1998), ageist assumptions portray our elders as "forgetful" or "old codgers," "curmudgeons," "doddering," or simply "senile" (Zide & Gray, 2001). These beliefs seem to be commonly accepted within the dominant culture of the United States as well as within many minority communities (Kane, 2000). Our society seems more preoccupied with looking young and staying healthy than with growing old gracefully. Individuals struggling with Alzheimer's disease experience symptoms that may be categorized as neurological, cognitive, affective, behavioral, and psychological. As symptoms escalate and become more progressive, the person is at increased risk of being institutionalized, or at the very least in danger of losing all of his or her autonomy or self-support. Family members find themselves adapting to a person who often seems like a total stranger (Beck, 1998). In turn, family caregivers experience isolation, anxiety, depression, and increased physical illnesses (Lawton, Van Haitsma, & Klapper, 1996).

Access to needed services such as transportation or health care can also be problematic for older persons. With advanced age, people may no longer be able to drive or use public transportation. Some older persons distrust formal services and are unaccustomed to presenting their problems to someone outside of the family, such as a professional social worker (Richardson, 2002). They may be more comfortable talking about a physical illness than with sharing feelings of loneliness, anxiety, fear, or depression.

Older people may experience a sense of disengagement and a lack of intimacy as their children grow up and move away from home (Eisendrath & Lichtmacher, 2001). Friends have died and neighborhoods may have changed, further isolating older people from the community. Retired from work and living on a fixed income, they may experience additional financial strain with the advent of illness and related medical expenses. The process of aging is often poorly accepted in our society, which places a high value on a youthful appearance. It may be difficult for some people to accept the changes associated with aging. In sum, older people may be characterized as a vulnerable population stressed by life events and life circumstances associated with the aging process.

Cultural Factors The proportion of older people in our society has been increasing in recent years, and the growth of specific cultural groups of elders has also accelerated. One of the fastest-growing cohorts can be found within the African American community, which has a higher percentage of persons over the age of 65 than any other minority group (Lewis & Ausberry, 1996). Some studies indicate that African Americans may have a higher overall risk for Alzheimer's disease (Fillenbaum, Heyman, Huber, & Woodbury, 1998; Tang, Stern, Marder, Bell, & Gurland, 1998). Also, the presence of dementia, particularly vascular dementia, seems to be a result of the prevalence of hypertension in this group (Johnson & Gant, 1996; Kumanyika, 1997; Yeo, Gallagher-Thompson, & Lieberman, 1996). Members of the African American community tend to be reluctant to seek outside services, either because they are unaware of what is available or the services are located at a great distance from where they live (Ballard, Nash, Raiford, & Harrell, 1993).

There is great diversity among the group identified as Asian Pacific Islander Americans, which comprises Cambodian Americans, Chinese Americans, Filipino Americans, Hawaiians, Hmong Americans, Japanese Americans, Korean Americans, Samoans, Vietnamese Americans, persons from the Pacific Islands and other Asian groups (Ho, 1987). Although memory impairment may be viewed as a normal part of the aging process by these groups (Braun, Takamura, Forman, Sasaki, & Meininger, 1995), the psychiatric symptoms often associated with dementia are likely to bring shame and stigma to the family (Elliott, Di Minno, Lam, & Tu, 1996; Phillips, 1993).

Similarly, Henderson (1996) notes that Cuban and Puerto Rican caregivers view the psychiatric symptoms connected to Alzheimer's disease and other types of dementia, such as delusions, hallucinations, ruminations, paranoia, and labile emotions, as a source of shame and stigma for the family. This sense of family embarrassment and shame extends to Mexican American persons as well (Gallagher-Thompson, Talamantes, Ramirez, & Valverde, 1996). Members of this group may also perceive dementia as the will of God.

While the course of dementia varies (Kaplan & Sadock, 1998), cultural influences highlight the importance of the practitioner being attentive to the many factors that can influence a person's eventual risk of developing Alzheimer's disease. Aside from racial or ethnic diversity, differences in access to health care, socioeconomic status, and education may play a role (Shaw & Krause, 2001). Even the ways in which diagnostic tests which measure language, memory, and cognitive function are constructed and applied may cause people to be inappropriately diagnosed with Alzheimer's disease (Hebert et al., 2000).

CASE ILLUSTRATION: ZELDA "JEAN" PFOHL

The case of Zelda "Jean" Pfohl was first discussed by Zide and Gray in Psychopathology: A Competency-Based Assessment Model for Social Workers *(2001). Jean was a 76-year-old woman who had been married for almost 56 years to her husband, Harry. The couple's problems began when Jean was diagnosed with Alzheimer's dementia of late onset. Their difficulties centered on the family's adjustment to Harry's decision to place Jean in a nursing home. Competency-based treatment highlights strengths and developing a working partnership with clients. This case illustration shows how the social worker assessed the risks and protective factors in Jean's life and engaged in co-collaboration with the family around planning treatment. After Harry abruptly left a support group session at the nursing home, the practitioner reached out to the entire family system.*

"You people, you people!" shouted Harry Pfohl. "You talk about them as if they were dead . . . but not my Jean! She's alive, very much alive!" He then jumped up and abruptly left the group session. The social worker, Alison Linea, sat there stunned and thought to herself, "This is not the Mr. Pfohl I first encountered when he admitted his wife to the nursing home."

Alison flashed back to the first time they had met. Sitting quietly in the home's formal parlor away from the activity of the residents and staff, Mr. Pfohl appeared visibly upset. Throughout the admission interview he struggled to hold back tears as he recounted the events leading up to his decision to place Jean in the nursing home.

Mr. Pfohl shared, "You know, I'm still not so sure about putting Jean in here." He went on to say that they had promised each other that they would never put the other one in a nursing home "no matter how bad things got." They had made a promise to each other to share their golden years together. During the early years of their retirement things had been great. They would sit around the pool, go to the movies, go out to dinner, or play cards each weekend with friends at the condo. Each spring the Pfohls went to the baseball training games. They knew all the players, and Harry even taught Jean how to keep score. Once, remembered Mr. Pfohl, they caught a fly ball. "We gave it to our youngest grandson, Kenny."

Ms. Linea asked about events leading up to the decision to place his wife, and Mr. Pfohl responded, "I guess I knew for a long time that things weren't going right, but I kept hoping it would get better. Times just got worse when Jean started to forget where she left her purse, and then she would leave the stove on. She was such a good cook, but then Jean would get something started in the kitchen and the next thing I knew a pot would be burned to a crisp! You know, it was more than just forgetting. It was almost like she forgot the idea of what was involved with cooking in the first place. At first I would say, 'Jean, this is your favorite pot for spaghetti, remember?' She could remember if you prompted her. Five or six years ago, I didn't think too much of it, but then as time went on it just got worse. Eventually she would just look at a pot and not even seem to know what it was for. Once she almost set the whole kitchen on fire. It was not just her memory; Jean's behavior also started to change. She was always so easygoing and had a great personality. That's what attracted me to her in the first place! Then, at times she would be 'as placid as a lamb' and at others she would become agitated and lash out."

It had been particularly trying when Harry was trying to bathe or dress her. When Jean did try to dress herself she would put her clothes on backwards or inside out or sometimes just sit naked until Harry dressed her. "She was always so proud of how she looked, and she was a 'looker,' but no more," recalled Harry. On several occasions Jean would open the front door of their condo and simply wander away. "You know how people gossip in those condos," added Harry. Friends started to drift away, and the Pfohls became increasingly isolated.

Harry sounded lonesome for Jean's companionship. He noted that after almost 56 years of marriage, Jean no longer recognized Harry and "babbles nonsense." Jean had also become increasingly unsteady on her feet and had fallen several times. Harry recounted the difficulty of caring for Jean when she had a full cast on her arm. He started using a wheelchair because it was easier than letting Jean walk.

Jean had become increasingly restless and didn't sleep well at night. As a result, Mr. Pfohl hired someone to help out at home. "I'll always remember her name. It was Mary Washington. Oh, she was such a nice woman. She would come in six days a week and cook meals for us, bathe Jean, and provide 24-hour care. For me, it was 'peace of mind' just to have Mary around. Jean had always spoiled me, and I never knew how to cook, let alone where things are in the kitchen."

Then one of Mary's relatives got sick and she could no longer come in and help Harry and Jean. Harry described his struggles caring for Jean on his own. Most often, Jean didn't recognize Harry. He was exhausted just dressing and feeding her. It would take almost the entire morning just to get her "presentable." Jean was usually the most agitated at night, and watching over her left Harry with little sleep. He tried all sorts of things to keep her in bed, but to no avail. "The most depressing part was changing her diapers," recalled Harry.

Although they had two children living nearby, Harry didn't ask them for help caring for Jean. "I don't want to bother them. They're so busy, you know," he stated. Harry's oldest, Nancy Conig, was divorced but reported to be doing very well. She had three grown children and had recently earned a master's degree in teaching. Harry spoke of her accomplishments with pride. Harry and Jean's son, Jerry, was a physician who had married his high school sweetheart. They had three children and were also doing well. Harry added, "The kids bring food and meals over, but how much can I expect of them? They have their own lives to live. I don't want to be a bother to them."

After the nurse's aide had left, Harry had begun thinking that the best thing would be to put Jean into a nursing home. He went on, "Well, actually the last straw was the night Jean managed to get out of the apartment while I was asleep. I never heard her leave. I'm sure I had the double locks on the door. I even bought one of those gizmos you see on TV that sounds an alarm if the door opens. I would pin little bells on her nightgown, too." (He looked a little embarrassed at this point.) "Nothing worked! I'm sure one of the neighbors must have recognized Jean wandering by the pool. That's how the police knew to bring Jean home to me! She could have fallen in! I got scared. When do I sleep?"

The social worker's attention returned to the group. Harry's uneasy departure evoked feelings of loss for the members, and the conversation shifted to how hard it was to cope when a loved one had Alzheimer's. One member said, "You keep hoping they're going to get better. It's easy to ignore the little things when you love somebody. You figure it's just 'forgetfulness.' At first some days were better than others, but it just broke my heart when my own mother didn't recognize me anymore. It's like they're there one day and somehow gone the next." The group members shared their own experiences with the crises brought on by the disorder. "Yeah, it's like the longest good-bye," added another.

The support group session drew to a close, and Alison Linea began thinking about her appointment with Harry Pfohl and his children scheduled for the next day. She was glad that she had earlier made plans to see them. Since Jean's admission to the nursing home, Alison had noticed that the family would faithfully visit Jean every day but the visits had become shorter and shorter, and then there was the tension with the nurses. Each time the family left, someone had a complaint about Jean's care. In their own way, Nancy and Jerry seemed to be struggling with their mother's admission to the home, too. Alison wondered if it was just her imagination, but somehow Mr. Pfohl looked much smaller. He seemed to have lost some weight, had huge circles under his eyes, walked more slowly, and was a bit more hunched over. He looked so very alone and defeated. It was like he had not only lost his best friend but he had also lost the hope of finding her again. Ms. Linea made a mental note to evaluate for the possibility that Mr. Pfohl might be experiencing depression after his long ordeal caring for Jean on his own. Her personality changes associated with Alzheimer's disease seemed so devastating for Harry.

The next day, Mr. Pfohl, his daughter, son, and daughter-in-law came in for their scheduled appointment with the social worker. Ms. Linea had visited with Jean earlier that day. She wanted to get to know her client a little better, so she observed the morning routine and spoke with staff about how Jean was adjusting. Ms. Linea noticed that Jean seemed to relate especially well to two nurse's aides, so she consulted with the director of nurses to ensure that these staff members were routinely assigned to care for Jean.

Ms. Linea then touched base with the aides and shared details about the significance of the personal items the family had brought in from home. For instance, Harry would give Jean a purse of loose coins to keep in her pocket. The jingle of this loose change, explained Ms. Linea, seemed reassuring to Jean. Ms. Linea and the nurse's aides chatted for awhile about Jean's adjustment to the nursing home, and Ms. Linea was impressed by their calm, relaxed demeanor and sincere interest in Jean. The aides made every effort to respond positively to Jean's appropriate actions and were careful not to reinforce obstreperous behavior. The staff seemed to understand and accept Jean's limitations, knowing the sometimes unruly behavior represented a nondirective response to frustration and the inability to function. Although Jean's cognitive awareness was limited, Ms. Linea had the impression that the aides' soothing voices and reassuring mannerisms were comforting. She noted that both aides had been working on the same unit for several years and seemed to enjoy their work. She made a mental note to be sure to commend them to their supervisor.

Finally, Ms. Linea spent some time alone with Jean. Conversation was limited, so Ms. Linea focused on describing the family members in the pictures in Jean's room. Jean's mood seemed to brighten with this dialogue.

After everyone was settled in her office, Ms. Linea started the interview by describing her role in the nursing home and inquiring how things had gone during their visit with Jean. Resolutely, Jean's daughter, Nancy Conig, responded, "Mom looks just fine!"

Harry sat in the corner adjusting his hearing aid as a small whining noise came from his ear. "Dad!" Nancy said sharply, with a note of exasperation in her voice. "Pay attention to the nice lady and stop fiddling with that thing!"

"What? What?" uttered Harry.

"Look, Dad, pay attention to the nice lady and we'll all go for ice cream afterwards," said Nancy.

"Ahhhh! Ice cream. That would be nice," said Harry.

"See! He hears only when he wants to hear," Nancy said. Alison noticed that Harry's son, Jerry, sat off to the side holding his wife Diane's hand. He looked as if he felt helpless.

Ms. Linea recalled that her goal for the interview was to encourage the family to talk about Jean's admission to the home and explore their adjustment to this change in their lives. She recognized that the family was facing a challenge dealing with Jean's illness and wondered how each family member perceived the need to place Jean in the nursing home. Harry had been struggling for a long time caring for his wife, and Ms. Linea remembered the Pfohls' lifelong pact to stay together "no matter what." Surely this memory weighed heavily on Harry's adjustment to placing Jean in the home, reflected Ms. Linea. In her experience, many families did not plan ahead for a nursing home placement, and it was usually a crisis that brought them to make the decision. For Harry, recalled Ms. Linea, the combination of the loss of the temporary help at home, Jean's increasingly unmanageable behavior, and his own physical exhaustion had ultimately forced him to make the decision that he needed to place his wife in a safer environment. However, this also meant that he was betraying their long-held promise to stay together.

Since Jean's admission, Harry and his children had seemed to find fault with her care on every visit. A frequent complaint was that her food was served cold or looked unappetizing. Another was that the roommate would eat from Mrs. Pfohl's tray. The family also complained when they could not find Jean in her room. They seemed uncomfortable interacting with other residents in the home as they went searching for her. Jean often gravitated to the day room where there was usually a lot going on. Her mental deterioration was even more obvious to the family when they could see the other residents involved in crafts or card games while Jean just sat off to the side with a contented but blank look on her face.

Focusing on strengths, Ms. Linea reframed the family's criticism about Jean's care to discomfort about having to institutionalize Jean. She wondered if the family's underlying belief was that no one else could really care for Jean as well as they could. She also began to wonder how this family had resolved prior challenges. Ms. Linea began, "Give me an idea of the most recent episode you have been dealing with that will give me an illustration of the kind of problem we need to work on. Walk me through it so I can feel like I have been there step-by-step: who was there, what were people doing, and what happened."

Nancy was the first to respond. She described a "typical" call from her father after a visit with Jean at the nursing home. As she spoke, Harry sat nervously fiddling with his hearing aid while a slight high-pitched whine came from the device. Talking over the noise, Nancy sighed, "I feel like I can never do enough. It all falls to me. My brother" (she looked toward Jerry) "is really just too busy with his medical practice. I understand. He does what he can. As a matter of fact, he was really helpful when Mom was in the hospital. He made sure she had the best of care."

Ms. Linea further inquired, "I understand that your father calls you after each visit with your mother. What happens next?" Nancy looked thoughtful for a moment and then replied, "I know I should be there for Dad. I just listen, or try to listen, but it's so hard. You know, I work all day, and when I come home I'm tired. I really don't feel like talking to anyone. One or the other of the kids usually stops by and wants to talk with me. My youngest son just left the house, and he really wants my advice on something or other. Silly things, like how do you make macaroni and cheese? I kind of like it, though. Makes me feel that I'm still important to him somehow. Then, in the middle of this, Dad calls!"

"What? What?" asked Harry, with his hearing aid still whining. He fumbled with it in his ear, took it out, put it back in, and took it out again. Harry clumsily handled the battery, and seemed to carefully examine the device with great interest.

"Nothing ever seems right!" Nancy went on, ignoring her father's behavior. "Dad is so sad, and there is really nothing I can do to change Mom's condition. Somehow Dad manages to call just at the worst time of my day, and I know that I need to pay attention to him, too. Sometimes I just feel like hanging up, but on the other hand I don't want to cause more hurt for him."

Ms. Linea asked, "How do you feel about it?"

Tears began to roll down Nancy's cheeks, and she said, "I feel awful. I can never do enough."

Suddenly Harry blurted, "It'll be okay. I know. I know your Mother will be okay."

Nancy took her father's hand and turned to her brother and his wife. "Thank you, Jerry, for your help. I know this hasn't been easy on you and your family, either."

Jerry responded, "Yeah, I know. But since Mom has been here I feel like there is less and less that I can really do. I can solve almost any problem at work, but this . . . ? Dad looks to you for Mom's day-to-day care. He always did, you know?"

Nancy explained, "Jerry paid for most of the bills for the nurse's aide for Mom, but it really is my job to make sure that everything gets done right."

Her brother, Jerry, looked down but seemed grateful for his sister's acknowledgment of his efforts.

Nancy continued, "When we were growing up, Jerry was always the smart one, and I somehow felt in his shadow. I was more interested in boys than the books at school. Mom always said I had 'special talents.' I used to think she said that just so I wouldn't feel so bad. I guess I have learned through all this stuff going on with Mom right now that I really am the 'strong one,' and we each have something special to give back. Jerry, I didn't know you felt so bad about all this, too. I guess we've come a lot closer since Mom came here to the home."

Ms. Linea waited a moment and then interjected, "Let's generate a list of problems you have recently been struggling with and then discuss what specific concern you would like to start with first."

She acknowledged the family's difficulties around placing Jean and said that she did not want to overwhelm them right now with too many things to do. Her impression of the family's problem-solving style at this point was that members seemed to draw together in a time of crisis and were struggling to make some meaning of recent events. They seemed to respect and genuinely care for each other, and really listened when one another spoke. Ms. Linea wondered if Harry's difficulties with the hearing aid served as a distraction from the feelings of guilt associated with having to institutionalize Jean, who seemed so much a part of everyone's life.

During this interview, it seemed to Ms. Linea that this may have been the first time that the Pfohls had shared their own individual struggles with their mother's progressive symptoms of Alzheimer's disease and the decision to place her in the nursing home. Ms. Linea had the impression that this was a close-knit family prior to Mrs. Pfohl's placement, but she planned to further explore relationships in the future to rule out any potential unresolved issues that may be influencing Jean's adjustment to the home.

Each member contributed to the list of problems: Nancy was interested in finding some ways to manage her stress; Jerry wanted to know how to make sure the staff would be informed of his mother's living will; Jerry's wife Diane wanted to know what to say during a visit, especially if no other family members were there with her (Jean's attention span had deteriorated to the extent that she was not able to carry on a conversation); and Harry wanted to know how to make Jean "comfortable."

At this point, Ms. Linea's goal was to open up possibilities for the family. She asked, "How can we begin to see which of these make more sense than others to pursue? Let's review the list for the benefits and disadvantages of each and then begin to narrow down where to start first. I've written down the entire list and we can refer to it in the future to discuss progress at a later point in time." Her purpose was to encourage the entire family's involvement in problem solving and to normalize their feelings about admitting Jean into the nursing home. Overall, she felt the family had established rapport with her, and their work together seemed energized as they brainstormed ways to move through the concerns about Jean. Ms. Linea also thought about other resources that might be helpful to this family, such as self-help groups, literature, or websites providing information about Alzheimer's disease.

OPERATIONALIZING COMPETENCY-BASED TREATMENT

During the interview, Ms. Linea reaches out to the Pfohls and involves them as much as possible in Jean's adjustment to the nursing home. Jean's symptoms of Alzheimer's disease are expected to progressively deteriorate. How the family defines and gives meaning to their struggles with Jean's diagnosis sets the tone for the helping relationship. Adopting cognitive-behavioral strategies, Ms. Linea began the work by brainstorming a list of problems, thus setting the stage for a collaborative alliance with the family. Though not highlighted in the vignette, there seemed to be an unspoken agreement among family members that Jean had deteriorated and placement in a safer environment was an unwelcome but necessary step in her care. Exploring the benefits and disadvantages associated with each problem increased their sense of choice and counteracted feelings of helplessness and guilt. The starting point was based on what the family saw as the problem that they needed to deal with first.

Ms. Linea's efforts were directed toward the social and family problems confronting Jean's husband and children, the primary caretakers. Identifying risks and protective factors, as well as community resources or buffers and how they can be utilized in Jean's care, is a central focus of competency-based treatment. This process provides the organizing framework for the practitioner's understanding of the present and anticipated challenges associated with the diagnosis of Alzheimer's disease and assists in the development of intervention strategies. Table 3.1 illustrates the risks, protective factors, and buffers in Jean's life.

TABLE 3.1   RISKS, PROTECTIVE FACTORS, AND BUFFERS IN ZELDA "JEAN" PFOHL'S LIFE

	Risk Factors	Protective Factors and Buffers
Intrapersonal	Alzheimer's disease, late onset	Amiable, pleasant, and easygoing personality prior to Alzheimer's diagnosis
	Personality and memory changes; occasional agitation, increasing restlessness, inability to do self care	Positive relationship with spouse/children
	Recently admitted to nursing home after a crisis	Responds to behavioral interventions (i.e., conversations revolving around reminiscence)
	Health history	Adjusting to nursing home placement
	• Broken arm	
	• Falls easily	
	• Unsteady on her feet	
	• Not sleeping well at night	
Interpersonal	Spouse	Married 56 years
	• Lives alone	Supportive family
	• Dependent on Jean	Children
	• Left support group	• Live nearby
	• Unsure about decision to place Jean (feelings of guilt, anger, loneliness, possible depression)	• Visit Jean daily
	• Health concerns (insufficient sleep, weight loss, exhaustion from caring for Jean)	• Involved in Jean's care
	• Caregiver burden/stress	Family
	Family	• Close-knit, mutually respectful of each other
	• Conflicted feelings about institutionalizing Jean	• Success with prior challenges caring for Jean
	• Strained relationships	• Attempting to "make meaning" of Jean's placement
	• Each face a different challenge about Jean's care	
	• Daughter struggling with caring for both parents	
Social and Environmental	Isolation from neighbors and long-time friends	Services available and accessible (i.e., home care, nursing home)
	Harry is struggling with guilt about not keeping Jean at home	Prior active social life in community
	Family has multiple complaints about quality of nursing home care	Financially stable
		Son also helping with finances
		Family receptive to social work intervention
		Spouse had some involvement in support group

Working with Jean Individually

In addition to assisting Jean's family members, Ms. Linea worked on Jean's behalf. Ms. Linea paid attention to Jean's medical status, the specific stage of the Alzheimer's disease, and related changes in her level of functioning. Because Jean had become less cognizant of her surroundings, Ms. Linea became the client's "voice" and assumed the role of mediator and advocate in the nursing home. In particular, Ms. Linea looked for patterns in Jean's behavior, such as the occasions when she was disruptive and the circumstances in which the disruptive behavior occurred. Ms. Linea consulted with staff to identify possible "triggers" for Jean's fear and to discuss ways to respond. Behavioral modification techniques and environmental manipulation were found to be useful for disturbances such as aggression and agitation. Ms. Linea worked with the nursing home staff and collaborated with the family to bring in transitional objects from home, such as family photos, aimed at providing sensory stimulation. In this case, Jean seemed comforted by the family pictures placed in her room. Staff reinforced Jean's positive behaviors and were careful not to reinforce obstreperous behavior.

Since patients in a nursing home receive around-the-clock care, there is a constant change of caretakers. This turnover further challenges someone with Alzheimer's. Noticing that Jean related better to two staff members than to others, Ms. Linea consulted with the director of nurses to modify staff assignments. The same aides were routinely assigned to Jean's care, thus reducing the stress of having to adjust to a different caretaker every change of shift. Ms. Linea also invited the family's input around Jean's habits and explored how Jean's preferences might be adapted to the nursing home routine. Jean seemed calmed by keeping a small purse of loose coins in her pocket. Effort was made to make Jean's life as routine and familiar as possible. Ms. Linea focused her attention on creating an environment in which the reassurance of touch, voice, and human presence could be provided (Epple, 2002).

Family Intervention

Carol Swenson (2004) chronicles her experiences caring for her mother-in-law who was diagnosed with Alzheimer's disease. She comments, "If encroaching dementia is nothing else, it is dis-ordering" (Swenson, 2004, p. 458). The relationship between Jean and her family has changed and will never be the same again. The nature of Alzheimer's disease prevented Jean from continuing to fulfill the family roles she has held in the past (Epple, 2002).

Ms. Linea reached out to the family to learn more about their problems and concerns. At the time of Jean's admission to the nursing home, her husband Harry seemed drained by the demands of caring for his wife. He had struggled for years to deal with her progressively deteriorating condition. A survey conducted by the National Family Caregivers Association (1997) found that 80 percent of the caregiving was done at home and 61 percent of the caregivers reported feelings of depression and isolation related to their caregiving responsibilities. In Jean's situation, Harry had hired a nurse's aide rather than "burden" his children who lived nearby. The survey goes on to note that 76 percent of respondents noted a major difficulty was not having consistent help from family and friends. When help is available, it is often unpredictable and insufficient. When the nurse's aide left because of family problems of her own, Harry felt his only recourse was to place his wife in a nursing home. This meant that Harry would have to break a lifelong pact with his wife to "stay together" in their advanced years "no matter what." Jean's personality changes associated with her Alzheimer's were perhaps the most devastating challenges for Harry. Their sociable lifestyle in the retirement community had turned into one of isolation.

Ms. Linea inquired into how the family had been coping and listened for the family's capacity to master adversity in various caregiving situations. Walsh (1998) underscores the importance of making meaning of adversity. Through their conversation with the social worker, the Pfohls were able to recognize how much closer they had become since Jean's admission to the nursing home. Each seemed to recognize the others' unique contributions to the family; for instance, Jean's daughter Nancy attended to Jean's day-to-day care while her son Jerry ensured that his mother's medical needs were met.

Competency-based treatment encompasses a helping relationship characterized by mutual collaboration, and Ms. Linea drew upon cognitive behavioral strategies in asking the family to generate a list of problems. This exercise set the groundwork for the family to guide the direction of the work. While remaining mindful of the family's conflicted feelings about Jean's nursing home placement, Ms. Linea focused on opening up "possibilities" rather than dwelling on problems. Together, the social worker and the family reviewed the advantages and disadvantages of addressing each listed problem in order to set priorities. In this way, feelings associated with placement were normalized and the family collaborated with the practitioner around the work ahead. Keeping the list and periodically reviewing progress provides a concrete way to measure and document change.

Group Work Intervention

Group work is becoming more common, but it can sometimes present special issues for the practitioner (Brennan, Downes, & Nadler, 1996; Ebenstein, 1998; McCallion & Toseland, 1995). In this case discussion, Ms. Linea was initially surprised by Mr. Pfohl's abrupt departure from the group. Based on his tearful demeanor around his wife's admission to the nursing home, the social worker originally thought Mr. Pfohl could benefit from the facility's support group. After getting to know the family better and learning about their struggles institutionalizing Jean, the practitioner better understood their feelings, especially the guilt associated with this decision. Thompson and Gallagher-Thompson (1996) report that caregiver support groups have been found to be effective in providing peer support but not as useful for helping people deal with highly personal and painful negative emotions such as guilt or anger. Kelly (1999) notes that persons experiencing a vulnerable life condition or circumstance will bring different issues and behaviors to mutual aid groups. This individuality underscores the importance of particularizing group practice to the needs of different populations. The practitioner begins by carefully recruiting group members around a particular issue such as the decision to institutionalize a loved one, then allows sufficient time for the beginning phase, sets realistic goals, and deals with factors related to group membership—for example, group membership may depend on the level of burden and the amount of informal support available to the caregiver. For the Pfohls, the children tried to regularly visit Jean in the nursing home and to offer support to their father, Harry. While this created some degree of strain and tension among the extended family members, the children provided a level of support to Harry that would normally be found in a group setting.

Recent studies indicate that in most cases groups can be highly beneficial to family caregivers and help prevent or alleviate the problems associated with caregiving (Bourgeois, Schulz, & Burgio, 1996; Gruetzner, 1997; McCallion & Toseland, 1995; Toseland & McCallion, 1997). Groups help members to identify, develop, and use resources. The rationale for using groups is related to creating a forum for airing the problems faced by members and then mobilizing the supportive and therapeutic forces that operate in groups. In mutual aid support groups, a sense of psychological closeness is provided through the exchange of shared problems and concerns. The group members offer each other information, coping strategies, and community resources. Mutual aid is provided, and group identity is based on a common life situation. Most groups mix education, discussion, and social activities centering on mutual sharing and mutual help. Other groups are psychoeducationally oriented or focus on problem-solving and coping skills.

Environmental Interventions: Institutional Care and Nursing Home Placement

When Harry could no longer care for Jean at home, nursing home placement became a safe alternative for her care. To Harry, it symbolized his inability to cope with the demands of caregiving and underscored the fact that he was not fulfilling his promise to keep his wife at home "no matter what." People struggling with Alzheimer's usually come to the attention of the practitioner as the result of a crisis. When Jean slipped out of the house alone one night despite the elaborate precautions Harry had taken, he reluctantly came to the conclusion that he could no longer care for his wife alone. Placement became the only option, but the Pfohls had no time to prepare for and accept the move. The process was rushed, and the family struggled with this life transition. These tensions had become evident in the Pfohls' criticisms of the nursing home; for example, the family complained that Jean's food arrived cold, her roommate ate from her tray, or Jean couldn't be found in her room when the family came to visit.

Ms. Linea was patient and supportive during this time and focused on helping Harry and his family better understand the situation. Ms. Linea also educated staff about the underlying meaning of these "complaints"; for example, it was not so much a matter of Jean's food looking unappetizing but that the Pfohls were having a difficult time relinquishing Jean's care to the nursing home.

Although this possibility is not illustrated in the vignette about Jean Pfohl, it is important for the practitioner to be attentive to the potential for abuse, particularly with someone like Jean whose cognitive abilities are compromised and can be expected to diminish. People with Alzheimer's seem to enjoy relatively good physical health in the early stages, but as their behavior continues to deteriorate and approaches a vegetative state, the practitioner may consider arranging additional resources such as hospice care.

Conclusion

The case of Zelda "Jean" Pfohl explores how the practitioner can use competency-based treatment to tap into the protective factors and buffers found in the multiple dimensions of a client's life and reduce the risks associated with the devastating changes of a diagnosis of Alzheimer's disease. On the intrapersonal dimension, Jean experienced multiple deficits in her functioning. On the dimension of interpersonal relationships, Harry struggled with his grief over the loss of his wife as he had known her. At the same time, his children's concerns and anxieties increased. Cognitive-behavioral strategies designed to enhance naturally occurring protective factors formed the basis for the practitioner's interventions on these multiple levels. In particular, Ms. Linea was attentive to Jean's adjustment to the home, consulted with the staff around Jean's care, and engaged the family as equal partners in problem solving around the struggles with placement. The protective factors in this family included good communication skills, mutual respect, positive parent-child relationships (despite the strain of the current situation), and flexibility.

The level of care needed for persons struggling with Alzheimer's disease increases over time. Although the Pfohls had some reduction in the objective burdens of caregiving when Jean was placed in the nursing home, the subjective emotional demands continued. Her husband Harry had been the primary caregiver, but as he became more exhausted, his daughter Nancy assumed more of the caregiving responsibilities. As noted by Toseland, Smith, and McCallion (2001), the responsibility for the care of a frail, aging family member is rarely shared equally by all family members. The stresses of caring for his wife put Harry at risk for increased emotional distress, isolation, and altered relationships with his children. The case discussion underscores the importance of understanding the context of the client's struggles. The risks associated with Jean's diagnosis of Alzheimer's extended beyond Harry to encompass the entire family system. The Pfohls could not be characterized as a "troubled" family requiring intensive family therapy. Instead, they were struggling to deal with the stresses of a life transition associated with placing Jean in a nursing home. According to Gaugler et al. (2000), it is not uncommon for family members to face a variety of challenges when placing a cognitively impaired relative in a nursing home. The social support systems in this family mitigated some of the difficulties encountered when caring for Jean and guided the family's decisions about her care.

Competency-based treatment moderates the effects of risks, enhances the family's ability to adapt and cope with the stressors associated with the diagnosis of Alzheimer's disease, keeps the practitioner's focus on client resources, and guides the selection of interventions. In this case example, the chosen interventions were drawn primarily from a cognitive-behavioral orientation. In sum, a range of intervention strategies attentive to the multiple dimensions of the client's life were used to improve care receiver behaviors, enhance caregiver well-being, and strengthen family relationships.

SUMMARY

Imagine your brain as a house filled with lights. Now imagine someone turning off the lights one by one. That's what Alzheimer's disease does. It turns off the lights so that the flow of ideas, emotions, and memories from one room to the next slows and eventually ceases. . . . there is no way to stop the lights from turning off, no way to switch them back once they've grown dim. At least, not yet. (Nash, 2000, p. 51)

As the population ages, social workers will increasingly be asked to assist clients and their families in dealing with dementia. There has been enormous progress in this area over the past 35 years. Today we certainly know much more about this disease. Unanswered questions remain about what makes the disease process begin in the first place and what factors contribute to its development. Why are some neurons more vulnerable and likely to die than others? Why does the prevalence of Alzheimer's disease increase with age? What is Alzheimer's disease? Who gets it? How does it develop? What course does it follow? What are critical areas for early diagnosis? What are the genetic factors in Alzheimer's disease development? What do we know about diagnosing Alzheimer's disease? What is the best treatment? What are the next steps needed toward advancing and creating promising leads on possible treatments?

In the absence of definitive treatments for Alzheimer's disease and related dementias, researchers in a variety of disciplines are utilizing psychosocial and behavioral intervention strategies designed to help individuals and their caregivers cope with and manage some of the difficult symptoms that commonly occur (Beck, 1998). Competency-based treatment and its attendant focus on strengths provides a perspective for the practitioner to explore the ways that clients and their families are successful in coping with the stresses associated with the cognitive disorders rather than dwelling on how they fail. The practitioner is mindful of the risks as well as the protective factors for the older adult with significant cognitive and/or physical impairments.

Practitioner Reflections

1. The purpose of this activity is to foster self-awareness. Reflect for a moment on your own expectations of your family taking care of you when you are older. Also consider:
   - What challenges have you faced as a family?
   - How have you dealt with those challenges?

2. Imagine you are the social worker in a nursing home and you have identified the need to start a lecture series for the families of patients. How would you approach the facility's administration about starting this lecture series? Design a promotional brochure that you would use to advertise the series. In addition, describe what topics you would plan to cover, and why.
   - Will topics differ for the families of newly admitted patients as compared to patients who have lived in the facility for at least six months?
   - How will you encourage families to attend a lecture series, and what obstacles might prevent their attendance?
   - As an alternative activity, imagine you are working with the families of patients admitted to the nursing home with Alzheimer's disease, as in the case of Jean Pfohl. What topics would you cover in a lecture series for these families?

3. Put yourself in the place of the social worker assigned to the case of Jean Pfohl. Her daughter, Nancy Conig, comes to you and explains that her father, Harry, has been hospitalized. Apparently he got up in the middle of the night for a glass of water, tripped over a chair in his apartment, and broke his hip. Nancy is asking for your help in telling her mother the "bad news." What would you advise Nancy to do?

4. Growing old in our society places individuals at greater risk for health problems and other difficulties. Many persons have recovered from negative life events and/or circumstances and adjusted successfully. Think of an older client you have known (or are currently working with) who has successfully overcome adversity. Identify the event or life circumstance that the person has overcome. Looking at the individual's social context, what effects did the client's difficulty have on his or her family, friends, or society? List the factors that led to that person's capacity to be resilient. How did these factors influence your interventions?

5. The case of Zelda "Jean" Pfohl underscores the importance of providing caregiver support. Her family struggled to understand and come to terms with Alzheimer's disease and the related changes in Jean's behavior. Caregiver support groups can provide helpful information, increase support networks, enhance feelings of competence in the caregiver role, and improve psychological functioning. Contact the Alzheimer's Disease and Related Disorders Association (ADRDA) for information about services in your area and identify what would be helpful if you were working with a client with Alzheimer's disease (and his or her family). The national ADRDA

headquarters can be reached at the following 24-hour contact center number: 1-800-292-3900.

6. The purpose of this activity is to increase your sensitivity about how one remembers. This exercise is to be completed with a colleague. Ask your partner to fill a bag with at least 15 small items one generally uses every day, such as a pen, pencil, paper clip, rubber band, and so forth. Your colleague will show you the items for one minute and then replace them in the bag. After a five-minute delay, you will attempt to list at least ten items. Discuss how you remembered the objects. What facilitated your memory, and what got in the way of remembering? Were you surprised (or disappointed) by how much you remembered?

SCHIZOPHRENIA AND OTHER PSYCHOTIC DISORDERS

The lifetime prevalence of schizophrenia in the United States has been reported as ranging from less than 1 percent to 1.5 percent. Worldwide prevalence ranges from 0.010 percent to 3 percent of the population. It is further estimated that approximately 2.8 to 3.0 million people have been diagnosed with schizophrenia and that the disorder affects men and women in equal numbers. Age at onset differs for men and women, however. Onset for the initial schizophrenic episode generally occurs between the ages of 15 and 25 for men and between 25 and 35 years for women. Although schizophrenia is rarely seen before or after these age ranges, this disorder has been reported to occur in children as young as 8 years old (Dulmus & Smyth, 2000), and onset in adults has been observed as late as age 50. Men tend to have a worse prognosis, but the reasons are not clear. Perhaps the differences are related to the earlier onset in men. Also, it has been suggested that women may be seen in a more favorable light by practitioners, who view their higher levels of verbal, social, and communicative functioning as evidence of an increased willingness to adhere to psychopharmacology or treatment modalities.

UNDERSTANDING SCHIZOPHRENIA AND OTHER PSYCHOTIC DISORDERS

Psychosis traditionally has been defined as the loss of reality testing and the impairment of mental functioning manifested by delusions, hallucinations, confusion, impaired memory, and the inability to function both personally and socially. Schizophrenia is a disorder of unknown origins, although there is growing evidence that genetic and biological factors are associated with its etiology. A number of causative factors have been implicated in schizophrenia, including genetic influences, neurotransmitter imbalances, brain configuration, and psychological stressors (Bray & Owen, 2001). Schizophrenia is characterized by loss of a sense of self, significant impairment in reality testing, and disturbances in feeling, thinking, and behavior. When this condition exists, the individual is unable to evaluate correctly the accuracy of his or her perceptions and thoughts.

"The first task in diagnosing any psychosis is to determine the extent of the psychotic symptoms" (Morrison, 1995, p. 139). Generally, the symptoms of schizophrenia include delusions, hallucinations, disorganized speech, disorganized behavior, and negative symptoms (American Psychiatric Association, 2000; Zide & Gray, 2001; Zimmerman, 1994), as described below.

- *Delusions*—Delusions are false and fixed beliefs based on incorrect reasoning or misrepresentation of the individual's reality. These beliefs are firmly maintained despite incontrovertible and obvious proof or evidence to the contrary. There are several types of delusions. The two most common are "delusions of grandeur" (a belief that one is special, famous, or important) and "delusions of persecution" (a belief that others are intent on harming the individual). Delusions may serve an important purpose for some individuals with a psychotic disorder by helping to reduce depression and to give added meaning to their lives.
- *Hallucinations*—Hallucinations exist in relatively few other psychiatric disorders and are experiences of sensory events without environmental stimulation. Auditory hallucinations or "hearing voices," a frequent psychotic symptom, are the most common type of hallucination in persons with schizophrenia. These "voices" usually are described as abusive and critical in nature and/or as commanding the individual to perform certain tasks (usually harmful). Tactile hallucinations are the second most common type. Individuals with tactile hallucinations often describe symptom sensations similar to electrical tingling, a burning sensation, or feeling "as if snakes and spiders are slithering inside my body around my chest, and up and down my legs."
- *Disorganized Speech*—Persons diagnosed with schizophrenia may display illogical, concrete thinking characterized by a marked inability to think in abstract or general terms, which includes incoherent speech, also known as loose association. These mental associations are not governed by logic and often include rhymes or puns. Some individuals mimic the speech patterns of those around them by articulating the specific tone or repeating overheard words or fragments of conversations. This is known as *echolalia*. The use of rhymes and puns rather than making a logical comment is called *clanging*. For example, the individual might comment, "Where should I lie? If I do lie, will I die? If I die, will I go way up in the sky?" Another example of disturbance in speech includes condensing or inventing new words, referred to as *neologism*. Some individuals incessantly repeat the same words or sentences over and over, which is called *perseveration*. Other manifestations of disorganized speech include failure to answer specific questions, known as *tangentiality* (going off on a tangent), or haphazard, arbitrary leaping from topic to topic, known as *derailment*. The speech patterns of these persons are so severely impaired that they are unable to communicate with others. Attempts at conversation are often characterized as vague, stereotyped, or very abstract.

- *Disorganized behavior*—Disorganized behavior involves physical actions that do not appear to be goal-directed, such as removing one's clothes in public, assuming (or maintaining) unusual postures, pacing excitedly or moving fingers and extremities in idiosyncratic, repetitive ways. Individuals with schizophrenia often have inappropriate affect—that is, laughing or crying at inappropriate times. The term *bizarre* refers to a pattern of conduct or demeanor that is so far removed from normative and expected experiences that most people would not understand it. Practitioners are often asked to determine whether a client's given behavior is bizarre. It is important to note that cultural factors play an important role in distinguishing between bizarre and culturally normative behaviors.
- *Negative symptoms*—The symptoms of schizophrenia are further divided into "positive" and "negative" categories. Most practitioners find these categorizations confusing. Zide and Gray (2001) offer a simple way to think about these terms: remember that "positive symptoms," or outward signs of the disorder, are present in the individual when they should be absent. For example, positive symptoms may include delusions, hallucinations, and severe disruptions in thinking, hostility, suspiciousness, or fear of being persecuted. Positive symptoms can vary widely from one person to another, and no symptom is common to everyone. Individuals who are diagnosed with a psychotic disorder must have at least one of these positive symptoms present. Symptoms classified as "negative" are those characteristics that are absent in the person when they should be present. For example, the person may show the relative absence of affect, motivation, social interaction, and/or spontaneity, as well as deficiencies in self-care (Danion, Werner, & Fleurot, 1999).

Schizophrenia is classified into five subtypes determined by the predominant symptoms:

- *Paranoid type*—These persons experience persecutory delusions, delusions of grandeur, auditory hallucinations, or fear they will be harmed or mistreated by others. However, they do not display negative symptoms, disorganized speech, or catatonic behavior.
- *Catatonic type*—Persons diagnosed with this subtype alternate between "retarded-like" immobility, stupor, and excited agitation.
- *Disorganized type*—People with this subtype experience delusions and hallucinations, but these are less noticeable than negative symptoms and disorganized speech and behavior.
- *Undifferentiated type*—The individual experiences a combination of some or all of the five basic types of psychotic symptoms but does not meet specific criteria for paranoid, catatonic, or disorganized subtypes.
- *Residual type*—The active phase of disturbance has not markedly improved and does not meet the criteria for inclusion of other schizophrenia subtypes. However, there are enough fragmentary symptoms in attenuated forms so that the individual can be described as "somewhat unusual, odd, or peculiar." A variety of different lifetime sequences exist; recovery of an individual's social function is seen more commonly than is complete recovery from residual symptoms.

It is worth noting that it is often difficult to fit all clients into specific sub-categories because they generally do not remain true to just one subtype classification. Other psychotic disorders listed in the DSM include the following:

- *Schizophreniform disorder*—These persons may experience manifestations of a schizophrenia-like picture, but on assessment the course of these symptoms is not characterized by the level of deterioration, chronicity, or duration of symptoms (less than six months) found in schizophrenia. To complicate the picture even further, these symptoms can disappear just as quickly as they emerge, perhaps because of a successful treatment regimen or for reasons that cannot be explained. To make a diagnosis of schizophreniform, the psychotic symptoms must last less than six months and include a prodromal, active, and residual phase. The individual appears to have full-blown schizophrenia but often subsequently recovers completely, with no residual after-effects.
- *Schizoaffective disorder*—Historically, those who demonstrated symptoms of schizophrenia and also presented with a mood disorder, such as depression, have been lumped together under the umbrella of schizophrenia. Some practitioners suggest that schizoaffective disorder is either a mixture of a mood disorder and schizophrenia, or a form of bipolar disorder (because individuals often respond well to medication, specifically lithium treatment). Others hold that this is an entirely separate type of psychosis. Still others believe this is simply a collection of confusing and contradictory symptoms. Depression frequently accompanies schizophrenia, and because of this, it becomes more difficult to distinguish schizophrenia from psychotic forms of mood disorders and schizoaffective disorder. The schizoaffective disorder presents with symptoms of psychosis and mood disturbances. If the periods of depression or mania are brief in relation to schizophrenia, the diagnosis of schizophrenia is used. However, if they are lengthy, a mood disorder or schizoaffective disorder should be considered. This diagnosis requires that both a mood episode and the psychotic features of schizophrenia, such as social impairment or poor self-hygiene, be present concurrently during a substantial and uninterrupted period of the overall course of the illness. During the same uninterrupted period of illness, there must be at least two weeks of delusions or hallucinations in the absence of a mood episode. It is important to rule out symptoms that are not better accounted for by other psychotic disorders or attributable to a general medical condition such as AIDS or dementia.
- *Brief psychotic disorder*—Brief psychotic disorder is infrequently diagnosed in clinical practice and unfortunately has received minimal professional attention. Symptoms always include one or more major symptoms of psychosis that usually have an abrupt onset but do not always encompass the complete characteristic patterns seen in schizophrenia. Symptoms include erratic emotions, screaming or muteness, impaired memory of recent events, and eccentric or "odd" behavior. This disorder is usually precipitated by some extreme or overwhelming stressful situation(s). These precipitating

stressors may include major life events that would cause any person significant emotional upheaval, such as the loss of a parent, a severe life-threatening accident, or the birth of a child. Practitioners should consider "the event" in relation to the individual's life, or stresses caused by event(s). In some instances the person may actually benefit from the symptoms as a result of being in the sick role; this is referred to as secondary gain. Typically, brief psychotic disorder lasts more than one day but less than one month, with an eventual return to the person's premorbid level of functioning. If symptoms persist beyond one month, the diagnosis would then be changed to one of the other psychotic categories, such as schizophreniform disorder. If symptoms occur within four weeks of childbirth—for example, if the mother threatens to harm or kill her infant, "with postpartum onset" should be specified. The practitioner should not consider this diagnosis when symptoms are culturally sanctioned or perceived as a normative coping response.

- *Delusional disorder*—As the name suggests, the central characteristics of a delusional disorder are a persistent belief that is contrary to reality and the absence of other schizophrenia-like symptoms. Individuals with delusional disorder imagine events that could be happening but are not. At face value these thoughts seem completely plausible in that they are non-bizarre. Individuals with this disorder tend not to have some of the other problems associated with schizophrenia, such as flat affect or other negative symptoms.

  The onset of delusional disorder is relatively late compared to some of the other disorders, occurring when a person is between 40 and 50 years old. It is not known why this disorder has such a late onset, although some suggest that perhaps these persons have led relatively normal lives and have felt no need for clinical support prior to the precipitating event (Rudnick & Kravetz, 2001). The later onset may not represent the beginning of the delusional disorder but rather the time when symptoms became more problematic and ego-dystonic. To meet the criteria for this diagnosis, the person must exhibit one or more positive symptoms of schizophrenia lasting less than one month (often precipitated by stressful situations) but lasting at least for one day. Unfortunately, we know relatively little about the biopsychosocial influences such as prevalence or the course of this illness. However, what we do know is that the disorder appears to be rare, is seen more often in women than men, and has a genetic component.

- *Shared psychotic disorder*—This is a very exotic and uncommon disorder. Relatively little is known about shared psychotic disorder (previously known as *Folie à Deux*), except that these individuals slowly develop delusions resulting from being in a symbiotic-like relationship with someone who does have delusions. Individuals who are more likely to receive this diagnosis are under the powerful influence of, or have a long-standing submissive relationship with (the relationship of a parent/child, husband/wife, or member of a cult group) someone who suffers from delusions. These individuals usually live together in social isolation and move frequently to escape their delusional difficulties. There are usually no associated features other than these shared delusions. The age of onset is variable, and the condition is seen more often in women than men. The development of these delusions is gradual, and the disorder usually remits spontaneously when the individual diagnosed with the primary disorder either resolves his or her delusions or is separated from the person not experiencing these delusions.

- *Psychotic disorder due to a general medical condition*—Many diseases produce psychotic-like symptoms, and a number of these diseases are relatively common; for example, AIDS, meningitis, hyper- or hypothyroidism. Sometimes when these individuals appear for treatment they are misdiagnosed as having schizophrenia or some other type of psychosis. The first step toward making a differential diagnosis is ruling out general medical conditions and/or substance use.
- *Substance-induced psychotic disorder*—This diagnostic category includes all psychoses caused by the direct effects of using one or more substances. The predominant symptoms are typically hallucinations or delusions. Depending on the category of substance used, symptoms can occur during acute intoxication or withdrawal. If it is determined that a person's hallucinations or delusions (or both) originate with the use of a substance, then the appropriate diagnosis is noted as substance withdrawal, substance intoxication, or a substance-induced psychotic disorder.

Competency-based treatment begins with an examination of the client's strengths and selection of counseling strategies emphasizing education, rehabilitation, family involvement, and consumer advocacy (Merinder, 2000). Exciting advances in pharmacology offer additional treatment opportunities and hope for persons struggling with psychotic disorders. The following discussion provides an overview of two key interventions commonly used when working with persons with schizophrenia or other psychotic disorders: hospitalization and biological therapy.

OVERVIEW OF MAJOR INTERVENTIONS

Competency-based treatment individualizes specific treatment modalities across the intrapersonal, interpersonal, and community domains of a client's life, while at the same time remaining attentive to the person's unique life experience. The competency-based treatment model centers on the strengths and the subjective well-being of individuals living with schizophrenia or other psychotic disorders. Biological advances have slowly evolved over the past 40 to 50 years in the area of neurosciences and serve to emphasize the medical aspects of mental illness. The use of antipsychotic medications has had a dramatic effect on reducing positive symptoms, especially delusions, hallucinations, and thought disorders. Although antipsychotic medications have become the major treatment focus, psychosocial interventions targeting the intrapersonal, interpersonal, and/or social domains augment these chemical approaches (Razali, Hasanah, & Khan, 2000). Most individuals benefit from receiving a combination of pharmaceutical treatment and counseling, and the competency-based model provides a framework for the practitioner to integrate interventions that promote client participation and involvement. In this way, the practitioner ensures that clients receive proper and effective treatment, including psychotropic medications when necessary to promote competent functioning.

Treatment can be organized around three phases: acute; transient or episodic; and the ongoing or maintenance phase. These phases are not clearly or easily delineated, and overlap occurs in the process of working with clients. The acute phase occurs during the individual's full exacerbation of symptoms. The transient or episodic phase follows the initial control of active symptoms. At this point, medication may be gradually reduced when maximal improvement is reached (Azorin, 2000). The focus of the ongoing or maintenance phase is to help keep the individual relatively symptom-free.

Hospitalization

During the acute phase, one of the first decisions confronting the practitioner is whether a person who displays schizophrenic-like symptoms requires inpatient treatment or can receive assistance on an outpatient basis. Usually it is the first episode with psychotic onset, including unusual manifestations of the schizophrenic disorder, that warrants hospitalization (Schuepbach, Keshavan, Kmiec, & Sweeney, 2002). Other considerations necessitating hospitalization include diagnostic reevaluation; medication stabilization; providing a safe environment (suicidal or homicidal ideation); and inappropriate or disorganized behavior affecting the person's ability to care for his or her basic needs.

Current trends in service provision and the reality of soaring medical expenses are minimizing the length and frequency of hospitalization in favor of treatment within one's own community. With this in mind, hospital discharge plans should include referrals to aftercare resources such as foster families, group living homes, adult congregate living facilities (ALF), halfway houses, and day-care programs. These resources can help provide therapeutic support in addition to offering social activities geared toward self-care, quality of life issues, social and/or family relationships, and work-related issues. Hospitalization discharge planning can be helpful in establishing linkages between the individual and their collaborative community support systems (Stuart & Arboleda-Florez, 2001). This linkage provides for continuity of care aimed at reducing excessive rehospitalizations, eliminating duplication of services, and promoting appropriate use of community supports.

Biological Therapies

The role of pharmacology in treating schizophrenia and other psychotic disorders is to help manage and/or bring under control ongoing psychotic manifestations, rather than to prevent a new episode. One of the first drugs on the market to treat schizophrenia was chlorpromazine, better known by its trade name Thorazine. This drug and its successors completely revolutionized the treatment of persons living with schizophrenia. The first of its type, Thorazine soon became the gold standard in the management of refractory schizophrenia. It enabled people to live outside a hospital setting, function within the community, and limit revolving cycles of hospitalizations. Prior to the advent of Thorazine, many individuals spent a majority of their lives locked up in institutions or hidden by family members in attics or basements (often under extremely primitive conditions). The author remembers working with a family who lived in a rural community. They allowed their 16-year-old son (later diagnosed with schizophrenia, paranoid type) to roam the yard tethered to a long rope. When they could no longer manage his paranoid outbursts, the family brought him in for treatment. I recall how surprised I was when I first saw the youngster in the waiting room tied to a chair. As if it had happened just yesterday, I can still remember looking at his parents and seeing the fear and defeat in their eyes.

While there are many drugs available for treating psychotic disorders, people respond to them differently because of variations in body chemistry, metabolism, age, or other non-specific factors. Various terms are used to describe the general category of antipsychotic drugs (e.g., neuroleptics and psychotropics) that are designed to induce what is known as a neuroleptic state. That is, psychomotor agitation, aggression, and impulsiveness are slowed down or decreased, and hallucinations, delusions, affective indifference, and indifference with one's external environment are diminished (Cohen, 2002; Salzman & Tune, 2001).

Antipsychotic medications can reduce and/or improve behaviors such as combativeness, tension, hyperactivity, hostility, and delusions. These medications also help alleviate feelings of disintegration or being overwhelmed, and they normalize psychotic symptoms (including hearing "voices") that would otherwise interfere with the quality of sleep. It is important to note, however, that some symptoms do not improve with the use of medication, such as problems with insight, judgment, and memory (Sajatovic, Madhusoodanan, & Buckley, 2000).

Dopamine receptor antagonists are viewed as the classic antipsychotic drug and appear to be effective in the treatment of approximately 25 percent of persons with schizophrenia. Unfortunately, some of these antipsychotic medications are highly associated with increased unpleasant side effects that include akathisia, tardive dyskinesia, and neuroleptic malignant syndrome (NMS).

Akathisia is a condition known to cause motor restlessness that may involve the entire body. It is most obvious in the person's inability to remain motionless, especially in the restless agitation of legs and feet. It is not considered a rare condition, but it is often mistaken for anxiety, or increased psychotic symptomatology (Tarsy, Baldessarini, & Tarasi, 2002). Akathisia often occurs within a few weeks to months after beginning antipsychotic therapy and is difficult to manage. Symptoms may be mitigated by decreasing the dosage, switching to another neuroleptic, or using a beta-blocker (propranolol/Inderol), benzodiazepine (diazepam/Valium), or vitamin E (Scully, 1996).

Tardive dyskinesia is a late-onset movement disorder that causes involuntary movements of the face, mouth, tongue, or jaw. Thrusting or protrusions of the tongue are usually the earliest symptom. Other indicators include lingual-facial hyperkinesia exhibited by puffing up of cheeks, puckering or pursing of the mouth, and jaw movements similar to chewing food. The predominant clinical explanation suggests that tardive dyskinesia results from long-term, high dosages of certain neuroleptic medications (Alptekin & Klvirlk, 2002; Caroff, Mann, Campbell, & Sullivan, 2002; Chari, Jainer, Ashley-Smith, & Cleaver, 2002; Chen, Bai, Pyng, & Lin, 2001; Gupta, Frank, & Madhusoodanan, 2002; Kane, 2001; Kumet & Freeman, 2002; Llorca, Chereau, Bayle, & Lancon, 2002; Lykouras, Agelopoulos, & Tzavellas, 2002; Rodnitzky, 2002; Rosenquist, Walker, & Ghaemi, 2002; Sherr, Thanker, & Tamminga, 2002). Clients should be screened every six months for early signs of this complication and maintained on the lowest effective dosages in order to minimize this serious complication. Tardive dyskinesia is irreversible, and current statistics suggest it occurs in as many of 20 percent of those who remain on neuroleptic medication for extended periods of time. Currently pharmacological efforts have focused on designing drugs that curb hallucinations without triggering the disabling Parkinsonian-like symptoms of tardive dyskinesia (Lauriello, 2001; Lerner, Miodownik, & Cohen, 2001; Sirota, Mosheva, Shabtai, & Korczyn, 2001).

Tardive dyskinesia usually appears later on in treatment, and it remains unclear why it tends to strike older men (Harvey, 2001; Sable & Jeste, 2002). Anticholinergics are most often the drug of choice for treating this undesirable side effect and ameliorating its symptoms. Some of the more commonly prescribed anticholinergic drugs include benztropine mesylate (Cogentin); trihexyphenidyl (Artane); procyclidine (Kemadrin); and amantadine (Symmetrel). Regrettably, these medications also produce their own side effects that include dry mouth, blurred vision, constipation, and urinary retention. Most people eventually adjust to these additional negative side effects, often finding them slightly more tolerable than those produced by the more powerful antipsychotic medications. Anti-anxiety medications, antihistamines, and beta-blockers are occasionally used to reduce some of these side effects, but unfortunately they often have their own set of side effects. It is important to note that all of the aforementioned medications have side effects.

Neuroleptic malignant syndrome (NMS) is the most severe and potentially life-threatening complication resulting from the use of antipsychotic medications. While this syndrome is considered rare, it is regularly reported in the professional literature and seen at least a few times by the most experienced practitioners working with clients medicated with neuroleptics. It affects all age groups, and depending on early recognition and treatment has a mortality of up to 20 percent (Reid, Balis, & Sutton, 1997). Although it can be mistaken for a worsening of psychotic symptoms, it is a serious complication resulting from neuroleptic treatment. This syndrome is characterized by an altered level of consciousness, severe muscular rigidity, sweating, hypertension, and fever. Laboratory findings include elevated white blood count (WBC), blood creatinine phosphokinase, liver enzymes, and myoglobin in plasma and myoglobinuria occasionally associated with renal failure; autonomic instability regulating the cardiovascular system (including the heart), endocrine system (including pituitary glands, adrenal glands, and the thyroid), and other bodily functions (including digestion and regulation of body temperature). Onset usually occurs usually over a one- to two-day period of time appearing after a period of gradual, progressive muscular rigidity. The treatment is fairly straightforward and involves immediate discontinuation of the neuroleptic medication and immediate treatment with dantrolene (Dantrium) (because of side effects that include fatigue, dizziness, and diarrhea, dantrolene is not indicated for long-term use), bromocriptine (Parlodel), or amantadine (Symmetrel), all of which are direct-acting skeletal muscle relaxants. Relief takes place within several hours, and the medication must be taken for seven days to minimize a reoccurrence. Intensive medical, cardiac, and renal support must also be established. Those with liver, kidney, and/or chronic lung diseases have specific contraindications assigned for the use of these muscle relaxants. Fortunately, 80 percent benefit from this combined regimen. Consideration concerning future antipsychotic treatment must include a careful and monitored regimen using a dopamine-blocking neuroleptic (after at least a two-week delay). Atypical neuroleptics such as clozapine (Clozaril) or risperidone (Risperdal) are considered safer and more effective than other neuroleptic medications. Table 4.1 outlines the recommended treatments for akathisia, tardive dyskinesia, and neuroleptic malignant syndrome.

TABLE 4.1   **SELECTED SIDE EFFECTS FROM MEDICATIONS COMMONLY PRESCRIBED FOR SCHIZOPHRENIA AND OTHER PSYCHOTIC DISORDERS**

Side Effect	Comments	Treatment
Akathisia	Causes motor restlessness often involving the person's entire body.	Treated by lowering dose, switching to another medication, or adding a beta-blocker (i.e., propranolol/Inderol), a benzodiazepine (i.e., diazepam/Valium), or vitamin E.
Tardive dyskinesia	Involves the involuntary movements of the person's face, mouth, tongue or jaw, and often includes physical fasciculations of the tongue (seen as thrusting or protrusions of the tongue).	Anticholinergics to ameliorate symptoms, such as benztropine mesylate/Cogentin, trihexyphenidyl/Artane, procyclidine/Kemadrin, amantadine/Symmetrel.
Neuroleptic malignant syndrome (NMS)	Considered to be a rare and potentially fatal toxic complication of antipsychotic drug treatment; symptoms can include an altered level of consciousness, severe muscular rigidity, sweating, hypertension, high fever, autonomic instability regulating the cardiovascular system (for example, rapid heartbeat).	Discontinue neuroleptic medication and treat with dantrolene/Dantrium, bromocriptine/Parlodell or amantadine/Symmetrel.

In 1989 the Food and Drug Administration (FDA) approved clozapine, and a new generation of medications became available to treat schizophrenia. Clozapine was referred to as the first major psychopharmacologic advancement in more than 30 years (Markowitz, Brown, & Moore, 1999), and it has served as a template and prototype for the development of other atypical agents that bind both serotonin and dopamine (Kapur et al., 1998).

Clozapine was available in the late 1960s but was subsequently withdrawn from the drug market because of its association with several life-threatening side effects. Clozapine was later reintroduced when it became apparent that it had some unique attributes differentiating it from the then-standard neuroleptics; that is, it was found effective for about one third of persons not responding to standard drugs, was found to improve an individual's overall functioning, and reduced the incidence of suicide.

While clozapine was considered more efficacious than the typical antipsychotics previously used, its use was not without risks. Clozapine was associated with a rare side effect known as *agranulocytosis*, a blood disorder involving significant reduction of white blood counts to the point where it could be fatal if not monitored appropriately (Alphs & Anand, 1999; Pies, 1998a, 1998b). Agranulocytosis occurs in 1 to 2 percent of those treated with clozapine and if undetected can result in death. The condition can develop precipitously or gradually, and although it can appear at any time it most often occurs within the first six months of treatment (Mark, Dirani, Slade, & Russo, 2002).

A recently completed meta-analysis of 30 clinical trials with a total of 2,530 participants confirmed that clozapine was more effective than conventional antipsychotic medications in reducing symptoms and postponing relapse for all participants, including those designated as treatment-resistant (Conley & Kelly, 2001; Wahlbeck, Cheine, Essali, & Adams, 1999). Several other studies found improvement in cognitive organization and functions, increased treatment compliance, improved quality of life, reduced risk for suicide attempts and aggression, and persistent efficacy in long-term treatment (Brieden, Ujeyl, & Naber, 2002; Glazer & Dickson, 1998; Glick, Murray, Vasudevan, & Marder, 2001; Hipplus, 1999; Malla, Norman, McLean, & Cheng, 1998; McGurk, 1999; Opler, 1999; Perris & McGorry, 1998; Rudnick, 2001). Clozapine is sometimes prescribed with some hesitancy because of its cost (Fichtner, Hanrahan, & Luchins, 1998; Glazer & Johnstone, 1997). A study conducted by Sasich, Torrey, and Wolfe in 1997 for the Health Research Group found the average 30-day supply of clozapine costs approximately $317. When added to the cost of other medications and related health care, the overall cost becomes even greater (Martina, Thakore, & Thakore, 2002).

Between 1994 and 1996 three additional atypical antipsychotic medications were approved by the FDA for first-line treatment of schizophrenia: risperidone (Risperdal), olanzapine (Zyprexa), and quetiapine (Seroquel) (Csernansky, Mahmoud, & Brenner, 2002; Lieberman, 1996a, 1996b; Miller et al., 2001; Narendran et al., 2001; Sacristan et al., 2000; Schulz, 2000; Small, Hirsch, & Arvanitis, 1997; Tollefson, Beasley, Tran, Street, & Krueger, 1997; Valenti & Pristach, 2001). These drugs do not produce many of clozapine's more troubling side effects, such as sedation, dizziness, dry mouth, and weight gain. Recent clinical studies suggest these newer drugs are at least as effective as standard antipsychotic medications for positive symptoms and more effective for the negative symptoms, such as apathy, social withdrawal, and/or inability to feel pleasure.

There is some historical evidence suggesting that risperidone's parent compound, the herb Rauwolfia serpentina (commonly referred to as Rauwolfia or Indian Snakeroot), was used many centuries ago for treatment of psychotic-like behavior. Written accounts found in a 3,000-year-old ancient Hindu medical text suggest the use of Rauwolfia for a condition of an "insanity-like behavior" that sounds very similar to a description of psychosis: "an abnormal condition of the mind, wisdom, perception, memory, character, creativity, conduct, and behavior" (Bhatara, Sharma, Gupta, & Gupta, 1997, p. 894). A principal component present in the root, stem, and leaves of the plant is Reserpine. It was later isolated from Rauwolfia by scientists and later still synthesized for use as an antipsychotic and also an antihypertensive agent. Ultimately risperidone's use for symptoms of hypertension was eventually discontinued because of its serious and undesirable side effects (Rivas-Vazquez, Blais, Rey, & Rivas-Vazquez, 2000).

Two drugs released in 1997 for clinical use in treating schizophrenia were quetiapine and ziprasidone. Quetiapine (Seroquel) blocks a variety of receptors but was found to be more receptive for serotonin type 2 than for dopamine type 2 receptors. Quetiapine has shown effectiveness against both positive and negative symptoms. Reported side effects include drowsiness and low blood pressure (Borison, Arvanitis, & Miller, 1996). Ziprasidone (Zeldox) originally encountered difficulty during the Food and Drug Administration's approval process because of concern for its cardiac safety. However, these issues were eventually resolved and the Food and Drug Administration (FDA) approved its use in early 2001 (Jibson & Tandon, 1998). Ziprasidone was found to be a strong blocker of serotonin type 2a receptors and a moderate blocker of dopamine type 2 receptors. Ziprasidone is associated with a reduced incidence of low blood pressure, weight gain, and sedation in comparison with other traditional anti-psychotics (Hirsch, Kissling, Baumi, & Power, 2002; Mark et al., 2002). Sertindole and zotepine are two new atypical agents that are not yet available on the U.S. market. Because of sertindole's potential for cardiovascular problems, it was pulled from the Food and Drug Administration approval process; however, it is currently available in Europe. Early reports suggested sertindole (Serlect) demonstrated some advantages over the standard drugs in reducing negative symptoms while producing fewer neurological side effects. Clinical studies are currently underway to examine the safety of sertindole for distribution in U.S. markets.

A novel neuroleptic agent considered to have a strong role in treating schizophrenia is pimozide. Current data suggests pimozide (Orap) is helpful in treating negative symptoms associated with psychotic disorders (Takhar, 1999). Unfortunately, its use in the United States has been limited to treatment of Gilles de la Tourette's syndrome (commonly referred to as Tourette's syndrome). Several promising experimental drugs may soon be released, including rimcazole, remoxipride, and tiospirone. Early data suggest that they may help treatment-resistant symptoms or be useful for people who have experienced severe toxic side effects from other medications.

Currently at least two dozen antipsychotic medications are available to the prescribing physician. These medications, considered the more conventional antipsychotic drugs, are often referred to as high-potency, mid-potency and low-potency. Those classified as high-potency are administered in relatively small doses for a therapeutic effect. Conversely, low-potency drugs require larger doses. However, the "potency" categorization does not influence the effectiveness of the drug since all of the antipsychotic medications demonstrate similar activity.

A number of antipsychotic drugs worth mentioning here include several in the low-potency category. Benzisoxazole (Risperidone), a serotonin-dopamine antagonist (SDA), has been proven effective for treating positive and negative symptoms of schizophrenia, with some improvement noted in cognitive functioning. It is also effective for persons who are treatment-resistant, although not to the extent that clozapine is effective (Bondolfi, Dufour, & Patris, 1998; Green, Marshall, Wirshing, & Ames, 1997; Lindenmayer, Iskander, Park, Apergi, & Czobor, 1998). Some of the more objectionable side effects, especially in the higher doses, include hypertension, irregular heartbeat, insomnia, weight gain, headache, and agitation (Mavangell, Yudofsky, & Silver, 1999). Another low-potency medication worth mentioning is mesoridazine (Serentil). Its effects are seen as more sedating but with fewer neurological reactions. The anticholinergic side effects include dry mouth, constipation, and dizziness.

Medications in the mid-potency category include perphenazine (Trilafon), trifluoperazine (Stelazine), thiothixene (Navane), chlorprothixene (Taractan), molindone (Moban), and trifluopromazine (Vesprin). High-potency drugs include loxapine (Loxitane), fluphenazine (Prolixin), and haloperidol (Haldol). These drugs are useful for treating schizophrenia, especially for its debilitating delusions and hallucinations. In time, it is hoped that neurological side effects will be of less concern and the ability to treat the negative symptoms will improve. While these "cutting-edge" drugs appear to hold much promise, questions about effectiveness will remain until they are available and in use for an extended period of time (Bentley, 1998). A key question still unanswered is whether these newer drugs can reduce cognitive deficits and thereby improve social and occupational functioning. Given what we know about clozapine and its successors, it appears that important changes in pharmacological treatment are imminent (Mark et al., 2002). Table 4.2 summarizes the medications commonly prescribed for schizophrenia and other psychotic disorders.

In sum, the use of psychotropic medications is integral to treating schizophrenia and has greatly increased over the past 30 years. Many mental illnesses were once traced to psychological factors but are now attributed to specific genetic components and/or chemical imbalances. Schizophrenia is a complex mental disorder, and each person's experience is unique. Understanding the risk factors is central to competency-based treatment, as it serves to help the practitioner better understand how people experience the stresses associated with mental illness. This understanding of how people cope with the diagnosis of schizophrenia reminds the practitioner to consider the client's strengths rather than focus exclusively on the negative aspects of mental illness.

TABLE 4.2	MEDICATIONS COMMONLY PRESCRIBED FOR SCHIZOPHRENIA AND OTHER PSYCHOTIC DISORDERS

Generic Name	Trade Name	Comments
chlorpromazine	Thorazine	Revolutionized treatment of refractory schizophrenia.
clozapine	Clozaril	Considered a safer and a more effective atypical neuroleptic.
risperidone olanzapine quetiapine	Risperdal Zyprexa Seroquel	Atypical antipsychotic medications that are considered more effective for "negative symptoms."
ziprasidone	Zeldox	Originally encountered problems with FDA approval; has fewer side effects than those found in other antipsychotic medications (i.e., less low blood pressure, weight gain, sedation).
pimozide	Orap	Used in the U.S. only for Tourette's syndrome.
benzisoxazole mesoridazine	Risperidone Serentil	Medications commonly referred to as "low-potency."
perphenazine trifluoperazine thiothixene chlorprothixene molindone trifluopromazine	Trilafon Stelazine Navane Taractan Moban Vesprin	Medications commonly referred to as "mid-potency."
loxapine fluphenazine haloperidol	Loxitane Prolixin Haldol	Medications commonly referred to as "high-potency."

RISKS ASSOCIATED WITH SCHIZOPHRENIA AND OTHER PSYCHOTIC DISORDERS

Intrapersonal Risks

People who are diagnosed with a psychotic disorder are often described as lonely, isolated, suspicious, irritable, ambivalent toward others, and/or having little insight into their problems. Their behavior appears erratic and inconsistent, and they have problems forming relationships and holding on to a job (Bricout & Bentley, 2000).

Some may show a strong dependency on people they are familiar with, such as family members, while others may be considered bothersome, annoying, or disturbing. Social networks and real friendships rarely exist, perhaps because people's delusions and hallucinations may frighten, estrange, and alienate others (Meeks & Hammond, 2001). Admittedly, this is a terribly bleak picture.

A number of risks are associated with a diagnosis of schizophrenia, which is considered the most severe of all psychiatric disorders. "Schizophrenia is a complex syndrome that inevitably has a devastating effect on the lives of the person affected and on family members" (Barlow & Durand, 2002, p. 421). While a great deal of research has been done to unearth the causes of this disorder, much remains unknown (Holzman, 2003). Schizophrenia has been described as a widespectrum disorder, with variations in the prognosis, onset, and etiology. Although at least 50 percent of people with schizophrenia improve significantly, many others experience schizophrenia as a chronic, lifelong illness fraught with taking medications and frequent psychiatric hospitalizations. It should be noted that people's experiences with schizophrenia depend on psychosocial factors, treatment remedies, and accurate diagnostic criteria. Positive symptoms are often prominently seen during exacerbations of the active phase of this mental disorder. Negative symptoms often persist during remissions, and future prognosis tends to be guarded.

Living with a diagnosis of schizophrenia can be quite devastating for some individuals and their families (Bennett, Bellack, & Gearon, 2001; Marder, 2001; Mueser et al., 2001). Factors associated with a better prognosis include acute onset, later life onset, previous good functioning at work or with personal relationships, and the ability to comply with the course of treatment (Hafner, 2000). Factors associated with a poorer prognosis include an early and insidious onset, family history of schizophrenia, evidence of social withdrawal, inappropriate or shallow affect, a prior diagnosis of schizoid personality disorder, schizoaffective disorder (Robinson, Woerner, Alvir, Bilder, & Goldman, 1999), schizophreniform or schizotypal personality disorders, and difficulties conforming to treatment regimens.

Other risk factors associated with the psychotic disorders include the misuse of alcohol and drugs, which is likely to worsen symptoms (especially when the person attempts to self-medicate) (Drake & Mueser, 2000). Living in poverty is another concern. Recent studies suggest people who rank in the lowest socioeconomic quartile appear to have an eightfold increase in their risk of schizophrenia over those ranked in the highest quartile. Homelessness is another risk factor that also poses challenges for treatment follow-up, maintenance, and relapse prevention. It is estimated that 11 percent of homeless persons meet the diagnostic criteria for schizophrenia (Jeste, 2002), and they tend to have a limited social network in which real friendships rarely exist (Dickey, 2000; Odell & Commander, 2000; Sullivan, Burnam, & Koegel, 2000). The incidence of marriage among people with schizophrenia is consistently reported to be lower than that of the general population. Medical problems and the related need for care represent another risk factor associated with psychotic disorders (Schwartz, Petersen, & Skaggs, 2001). Relapse appears to be somewhat influenced by two major factors: unsympathetic and non-supportive family environments, and medication non-compliance (Gray, Wykes, & Gournay, 2002; Pinikahana, Happell, Taylor, & Keks, 2002).

Treatment typically involves the use of neuroleptic drugs. These medications are usually administered in combination with a variety of psychosocial interventions aimed at reducing relapse, improving skill deficits, and promoting compliance in taking medications. For some persons, treatment is limited to symptom reduction, appropriate life management, and education (Cohen, 2002).

Interpersonal Risks

Current research has begun to pay more attention to the ways in which family interactions influence relapse prevention (Robinson, Woerner, & Schooler, 2000). Even though schizophrenia is better understood today than it was in the past, the diagnosis remains devastating and catastrophic, taking an enormous emotional, psychological, and social toll from everyone involved (Procyshyn, Thompson, & Tse, 2000). Schizophrenia interferes with almost every aspect of a person's psychosocial functioning, as it is manifested by disruptions in how one sees his or her social world and the manner in which one thinks, speaks, or even moves.

Attitudes toward those living with psychotic disorders have varied throughout history, but no matter what the era, those with mental illness have tended to be consistently ridiculed or scorned. In reality, schizophrenia is often a stealth disease with the potential to transform an ordinarily bright and friendly person into someone who is afraid to tell family members or friends about the voices no one else can hear or the things no one else can see. The practitioner must be careful to ensure that each person receives an accurate diagnosis, as other factors may explain puzzling behaviors (Farmer & Pandurangi, 1997).

Another risk factor to consider is suicide, a common cause of premature death among persons with schizophrenia (Siris, 2001). Estimates suggest that 50 percent of persons with a psychotic disorder attempt suicide at least once during their lifetime (Fenton, 2000; Nugent & Williams, 2001). Approximately 2 percent will commit suicide during the onset of their first psychotic episode or during resolution of the active phase (Miller & Mason, 1999). Gender does not appear to contribute or play a role in suicidal ideation, which has been linked instead to depression, hopelessness, prior suicide attempts, exacerbations of illness, and young age at onset (Rossau & Mortensen, 1997). The fact that many suicides occur shortly after discharge from the hospital suggests that providing more comprehensive aftercare and community support, particularly during the first three months post-discharge, would reduce suicide mortality during this high-risk time period (Fenton, McGlashan, Victor, & Blyler, 1997; Fenton, Mosher, Herrell, & Blyler, 1998; Husted & Ender, 2001; Lehman & Steinwachs, 1998). Often these persons look at suicide as the only reasonable alternative to living with the devastating and chronic symptoms of schizophrenia, and they are unlikely to communicate suicidal intent to their treating practitioner (Heila, Isometsa, Henriksson, & Marttunen, 1997).

Community and Environmental Risks

Although serious mental disorders are found in people of all races, ethnicities, and socioeconomic classes, minorities tend to be overrepresented among those most vulnerable and in need of mental health treatment. Unfortunately, members of minority groups tend to suffer a disproportionate burden from mental illness because of reduced access to services and lower quality of available care. In addition, they are less likely to seek help because of the stigma attached to mental health problems (Goode, 2001; Shaner, 1997). Stress also plays a role in the psychotic disorders, and evidence suggests a lack of support increases this risk (Link & Phelan, 1995). Looking beyond the tremendous emotional and physical burdens of living with a psychotic disorder, other concerns include its considerable financial expense (Johannessen, 2001; Knapp, 2000; Lindström & Bingefors, 2000; Martin, Miller, & Kotzan, 2001).

Cultural beliefs about mental illness represent another risk factor. In fact, because schizophrenia is a complex disorder, some theorists contend schizophrenia per se does not really exist but rather is a culturally created label for people who behave in ways that are outside accepted cultural norms (Barlow & Durand, 2002; Sarbin & Mancuso, 1980). Others assert that some cultures may be more or less "schizogenic," an archaic term describing a parent (usually the mother) who was described as cold, distant, rejecting, and who gave conflictual or double-bind messages. What should be seen as important is how mental illness is recognized or perceived within a person's culture. Kia Bentley (2002) aptly captures an important challenge facing the social work practitioner. "How do we know what to call psychopathology? What behaviors do we refer to as a mental illness?" (p. 50). Kaplan and Sadock (1998) posit,

> Overall, cultural differences appear more in the expression of signs and symptoms than in syndromes. Signs are what we, as clinicians, objectively observe in our clients; symptoms are those subjective experiences our clients describe to us when telling us what is bothering them; and syndromes are known conditions, made up of a number of configurations and signs and symptoms (as cited in Bentley, 2002, p. 52).

A negative stigma is attached to persons diagnosed with mental illnesses in our society (Kirk & Einbinder, 1994). Emphasizing disease and illness obscures the person's strengths, adaptability, and coping skills (Zide & Gray, 2001).

CASE ILLUSTRATION: RUDY ROSEN

To better illustrate the competency-based treatment model and differentiate among the various counseling theories and approaches, the following case illustrates the personal (or intrapersonal) experiences associated with schizophrenia by describing the impact of this disorder on a client, his family, and life span development, including the effects of frequent hospitalizations, medication, and chronic relapse. The case of

Rudy Rosen, first discussed in Zide and Gray's Psychopathology: A Competency-Based Assessment Model for Social Workers (2001), *is included here to serve as an exemplar of competency-based treatment for persons struggling with schizophrenia and to illustrate the practitioner's role in helping clients and their families tap into strengths in order to find ways to resolve the real-life problems associated with this diagnosis. The author acknowledges that many clients encountered in practice do not have family members who are actively involved in their lives, and for such people the social agency becomes a substitute family. Although this case illustration centers around family issues and concerns, many parallels can be drawn to those case situations in which the client does not have a family. For example, the Rosen family is exceptionally tolerant and accepting of Rudy's behavior. Many times an agency is called upon to provide services to clients whose behavior is much like Rudy's. In those instances the practitioner "accepts" the client's behavior unconditionally (much as a family member might do). Note that Mrs. Rosen refers to herself as Rudy's "jailer," but in reality she performs many case management functions.*

Rudy is a 76-year-old white male who was brought to the hospital because of a suicide attempt earlier this afternoon. I am the social worker on record and will recount my conversation with this couple. At this time, Mr. Rosen is non-responsive. I will speak with Mrs. Rosen regarding whatever history she can provide about today's suicide attempt.

According to Mr. Rosen's wife, Ruth, "Rudy tried to jump off the top floor of our apartment building, but a workman saw him and called the police. Thank heaven! I just don't know what got into Rudy. Why would he try to kill himself?" This worker asked if this had ever happened before. She replied, "Not like this." She continued, "When we were put in the ambulance (on our way to the hospital) I asked Rudy, 'What happened?' He didn't answer me right away and then whispered in my ear, 'I didn't try to kill myself. I wanted to fly down to the parking lot instead of taking the stairs.'" Mrs. Rosen mentioned that she had pressed Rudy to explain why he had been up on the roof. She recalled that he had whispered, "Three very mean-looking men have been following me." Mrs. Rosen went on to ask, "What do they have to do with you being on the roof?" He said, "They are very bad men who want to hurt me. They wait for me at the elevator or stairs. I'm afraid because they follow me everywhere." Mrs. Rosen went on, "I asked Rudy, 'Do you see these three men in the ambulance with us?'" She recalled that he had looked around and then slowly nodded his head "Yes." She added, "Then he turned his head away from me and tightly scrunched his eyes closed. He looked like he was shivering, and I think he wanted to pull the blanket covering him up over his eyes, but his arms were restrained. I wanted nothing more than to comfort him. The only thing I could do was put my hands over his eyes. I leaned down and whispered a made-up lullaby singsong, and crooned over and over and over, 'Everything's going to be all right; we're going to get through this together just like always. I'll take care of you, don't worry. I'm here for you.'" She went on, "His eyes stayed closed, and I'm not really sure if he heard me, but at least I said it." This worker commented,

"Mrs. Rosen, you have been his greatest source of protection. Perhaps once he's admitted we will be able to suggest other ways to help you deal with this."

Mrs. Rosen briefly supplied the following information: "Rudy was taken by Mobile Crisis Unit (MCU) to here (Regional Memorial, a large, metropolitan psychiatric hospital). He didn't want to stay, but he was admitted for 72 hours involuntarily for observation after a competency hearing."

At the time of admission, Rudy exhibited precursory hallucinations and delusions. He told this worker, "Three bad men are coming here because they want to hurt me. (Screaming) *Don't you see them? They're right there!*" (pointing to a corner in his room) It appeared to this worker Mr. Rosen was trying to protect his eyes as he attempted to tuck his face downward into the neck portion of his hospital gown. He was breathing rapidly and appeared agitated by the aforementioned event, but he remained quiet for a few minutes. He then said, "No one believes me. My wife and those rotten doctors poison my food and medicine." He leaned toward this worker, whispering, "Don't trust her, because she'll poison your food, too. I'm on to her." This worker responded, "Mr. Rosen, we will try our very best to help you get through this difficult time. I have a lot to offer in the way of support, education, and ways to prevent another relapse. We have family groups, rehabilitation programs—well, actually, all sorts of things that can be of help. Once you become stabilized maybe we can talk about learning new coping skills or ways to take your medicines correctly. I know I'm telling you lots of things all at once. I just wanted you to know I care about what's going on for you, and we will work on getting you better. I'll be back to check on you in a little while. Right now I need to meet with your wife."

As I walked away, I reflected (to myself) how glad I was to have had a lot of experience working with people who are living with schizophrenia. It could be scary talking to someone like Mr. Rosen who isn't making too much sense right now. Instead, I know it's his paranoid ideation. He must be a really special person behind all those symptoms for his wife to be so devoted to him. Mr. Rosen certainly doesn't trust me right now, but he doesn't trust anyone else either. Gaining his trust may be one of the most difficult things to achieve; however, I'm optimistic that with patience, education, and support he has a good chance for going back into remission.

During the intake process, Rudy's wife, Ruth, revealed to this social worker a litany of symptoms beginning when Rudy was initially diagnosed with paranoid-type schizophrenia approximately 25 years ago. At that time, Rudy had been employed as an automobile mechanic. According to his wife, "It seemed like one day Rudy began to really show bizarre behavior." She continued, "I vividly remember the first time Rudy came home from work and told me, 'Shhh, our telephone is bugged. Don't say anything inside the house; let's go outside where they can't hear us talking.'" I walked outside with him and asked, "What the devil do you mean, our phone is bugged?" He said, "The people at my work rigged the house phone because they want to hear everything I say."

Ruth recollected, "Rudy accused several fellow mechanics of stealing his tools and fooling around with his car battery. One day he came home all bent out of shape and yelling up a storm. He told me his car wouldn't start after work and he was convinced 'They did something.' I tried to reason with him by saying car batteries die all the time, and it isn't anyone's fault. When Rudy is in this frame of mind, he never listens to me. You know, he told me people follow him home all the time because they have 'something against me,' but I've never seen 'these people.' Even the smallest, most innocent thing can set him off. Like the time he told me 'someone screwed around with my watch.' I asked how he knew this. He told me, 'The windup stem fell out.'" Looking over to this social worker, Mrs. Rosen smiled, saying, "You might not remember windup watches, but in the olden days every watch had a stem you had to rotate to make the mechanism move inside and keep the watch running. I never could convince Rudy his watch stem just fell out because the watch was old. I guess that's the real heartbreak of living with some-one who has schizophrenia. Rudy never believes, trusts, or has faith in me. Most of the time our relationship is solely based on *my* commitment, devotion, and con-cern for him, but what about my needs?" (Mrs. Rosen closed her eyes and placed trembling hands over her mouth. She was quiet as she rocked back and forth in her chair. I respected her need for silence.) A short time later, she added, "I feel so guilty even saying those things out loud. I may think it, but putting it into words sounds as if I'm a heartless witch. I really didn't mean to imply that I resented Rudy or anything. It's just after so many years of his being in and out of the hospi-tal, the high cost of his antipsychotic and cardiac medications, my children not hav-ing a 'real dad,' and my own loneliness it got too much to hold inside." This worker responded, "That's an awful lot for anyone to deal with."

Ruth nodded her head and continued, "Soon after he was first diagnosed, Rudy began accusing me and our children of scheming against him. I tried to talk rationally with him about his unreasonable blaming attitude, but he wouldn't talk to me or the kids." This worker could sense how difficult it must be for Mrs. Rosen to recount these past events. Mrs. Rosen conveyed her willingness by continuing to recount Rudy's psychiatric history. "I remember Rudy used to run around the house screaming, 'You're *all* against me. You think I don't know, but I do.' I didn't know what to say to him. Sometimes he accused me of working with the police and his employer so we could put him in the 'crazy' hospital. Other times he'd rant and rave, saying I had poisoned his food. Or else, for no reason at all, he'd accuse our best friends of over 40 years of trying to get a free car from the car dealership where he worked as a mechanic. None of this was true. As if that wasn't enough, Rudy would just make up things out of thin air to blame on me. I felt so hurt. How could he think I'd want to hurt him? But, one of the social workers at that last hos-pital was real nice. She told me Rudy's mental disorder caused him to say these unkind things and once he got on the right medications he'd start feeling better."

During Rudy's initial hospitalization 25 years ago, he had a difficult time understanding his illness or why he had been put in the "hospital for crazy people." Rudy did not believe the opinions of his psychiatrist, social worker, or family doc-tor. Instead, he remained convinced that people were plotting against him, his home telephone was bugged, and his medicine would not help "because it's poi-soned." At that time, Rudy began a six-week trial course of Thorazine. His symp-toms subsequently abated, and he was later discharged. Rudy did relatively well over a long period of time, although he did have several episodes of first-rank symptoms whenever he refused to take his medications.

Mrs. Rosen said, "I tried really hard to manage Rudy at home, but whenever his symptoms became worse, I'd have to readmit him back into a psych hospital."

She added with a deep sigh, "I'm getting really good at getting Rudy into the hospital. Unfortunately, I've had way too much practice." She continued, "I was especially worried whenever Rudy became actively suicidal. It's really hard to keep watch on someone 24 hours a day. I really don't mean to complain, but I didn't get much rest." This social worker supported Mrs. Rosen's struggles by saying, "That must have been really difficult for you. Were you able to get help?" Mrs. Rosen shook her head from side to side, responding, "No, not really. It was just me. I can't tell you how overwhelmed and alone I felt with all of Rudy's craziness. Wait a minute, I almost forgot. I did get help during one of Rudy's hospitalizations when a social worker told me about the National Alliance of Mentally Ill folks. She was so helpful. I still remember her name; it's Mary Bischoff. That group was so helpful! It was such a miracle. For the first time I could talk with other people who had to deal with the same kind of stuff I did. It was such a relief, you know?"

She sighed and went on, "I know this might sound odd, but when I was able to share how I felt with those folks I also learned other ways to deal with Rudy's craziness. They told me his mental illness wasn't my fault. That was something I needed to hear. I just wish my children would have come to these groups. They could have learned so much about what's going with their father. They used to roll their eyes at me whenever I wanted to talk to them about why their father behaved the way he did. I guess they could have learned a bunch of things. They were teenagers back then, and I guess they couldn't deal with their 'crazy dad.' Maybe they wouldn't have taken it so hard when their father went in and out of the hospital. Me? I learned to appreciate the good days Rudy and I had together."

This social worker inquired, "Now that your children are adults, do you think they might be interested in coming to a family support group we have here at the hospital?" Mrs. Rosen responded, "I don't really know, but I'd sure like to see that happen. This might be a good time for our family to really talk to each other about all the problems we've had to deal with." I offered, "Is this something we could talk to them about?" She replied (with a smile), "Absolutely!"

A review of Rudy's family history revealed he was the youngest of five children. He has three siblings still living: a brother aged 90 and two sisters who are 87 and 85. A certain amount of vague history surrounds the oldest sibling, a sister named Kate, who died at age 38 while hospitalized in a mental institution more than 60 years ago. According to Mrs. Rosen, Rudy's sister had been hospitalized for what was then called "depression" shortly following the birth of her only child, Lila. After the mother's death, baby Lila was placed in an orphanage because the biological father and the maternal grandfather clashed over custody issues. According to Mrs. Rosen, "some money changed hands" and the child eventually began living in her maternal grandfather's home. Lila continued to have a close relationship with her biological father although she was raised in another home. No additional information was available regarding the cause of death or how long this sister was hospitalized.

Further exploration of family history reveals Rudy's mother was described as "being very strange" (by everyone in the family). She would accuse people of "being against her," out to hurt her, and (reported by others) "heard voices that were not heard by anyone else." Rudy's mother was considered to be "unfit and crazy" by all family members, and she played no role in his upbringing. An interesting aside: Rudy's parents had married each other twice and divorced twice. The history becomes somewhat more convoluted as to the reasons behind both the divorces and remarriages. According to Mrs. Rosen, "The family thought Rudy's father Sam loved his wife 'too much.' Pop put up with all her 'craziness' and 'eccentric behavior.' It seemed every time his wife returned home he gave her money and turned over valuable building properties. Then she'd leave again."

Mrs. Rosen described Rudy's mother as a "stunning beauty in her time, who was never without crowds of people around her." According to the family's folklore, Rudy's mother had to flee Russia when she caught the eye of a young Czarist prince. Apparently this prince wanted to kidnap her, and instead Rudy's mother managed to escape during the night (along with her mother and a younger brother). The family had to abandon everything they owned, including the family-run tavern and stagecoach stop. No other information was revealed.

Rudy's father, a "self-taught lawyer," was busy managing his lucrative law practice and the many tenement properties he owned in Brooklyn. Rudy's siblings at the time of his birth were 8, 11, 15, and 18 years old. Rudy's father was described as "loving and caring," and he and his older children helped raise Rudy. Rudy did not grow up with a lot of discipline and got into more than his fair share of trouble. No one in the family knew Rudy didn't attend school for six months during fifth grade (they later found out Rudy stayed in the basement and smoked cigarettes all day) until a truant officer showed up at their brownstone reporting, "Rudy's missed a lot of school." Another time Rudy stole his father's prized automobile and took it for a joy ride around Manhattan (when he was 11) until it ran out of gas.

As Rudy grew older his brother and sisters became busier with their own lives; and he was left in the primary care of the family's Polish housekeeper, Minnie. She cooked his meals, kept him company, got him ready for school (where he was often truant), and provided a bed for him in her own room. There is no explanation why this wealthy family did not provide Rudy with a room of his own.

Of noteworthy physical importance, both of Rudy's eardrums were punctured due to a serious infection when he was 5 years old. The etiology remains unknown; however, his father took him to the finest specialists of the time, and Rudy was treated for many years, including several surgeries for chronic ear infections. This condition left Rudy with a significant hearing deficit and necessitated wearing dual hearing aids for most of his life. Rudy also had a history of suffering from rheumatoid heart disease as a youngster; this caused him no further medical complications.

Mrs. Rosen reported, "One of Rudy's sisters, the one who is now 87, always exhibited 'bizarre-like' behavior. She would talk to people when no one else was in the room, and spit chewed food onto the floor, table, or on others saying, 'Somebody is trying to kill me and fooled with my food.'" No diagnosis has ever been determined. Ever since this sister became a widow 10 years ago, she has been under the care of a full-time companion.

Rudy and Ruth met when he was 5 and she was 3. Rudy's wealthy family owned a summer home in upstate New York where Ruth lived with her family year-round. Through the summer months spent together their relationship blossomed and they became childhood sweethearts. Ruth recalls working in her family's ice cream and candy shop and "counting the days until summer arrived." After Ruth graduated from high school in 1941, she and Rudy became engaged. Rudy did not graduate from high school and dropped out of school in the eleventh grade. Instead, he enrolled in an auto mechanic trade school. During this same time, World War II was in full force. Rudy had wanted to enlist in military service but had been rejected because of his chronic ear infections and loss of hearing. He got a job working for the war effort at a New Jersey shipyard.

Rudy and Ruth have been married more than 55 years and have two children, one daughter, 54, and a son, 50. Both children are professionals and live in nearby communities. Rudy is the grandfather of 6, with one great-grandson. He is retired and currently has no outside hobbies, interests, or friends. He is in poor cardiac health, having had quadruple heart bypass surgery five years ago. In addition, he has a pacemaker, suffers from congestive heart disease (CHD), has cataracts in both eyes, and continues to experience chronic ear infections. Rudy experiences severe tardive dyskinesia (TD) from his many years of taking high doses of antipsychotic drugs. His symptoms include hand tremors, tongue thrusting, and an unsteady gait. To maintain his physical health Rudy requires a cocktail of daily medications including Coumadin (a blood thinner to prevent stroke); Resperdil and Dyserel (for psychotic symptoms); Valium (for sleep); Cogentin (to reduce symptoms of TD); Wellbutrin, Paxil, Buspar (for his positive symptoms), and Synthroid (to slow his metabolism).

Mrs. Rosen retired as an executive office manager five years earlier. She said that since she retired she's become "Rudy's full-time nurse, appointment keeper, pharmacist, and jailer." Although she describes having had a "very good marriage" despite his illness, she had hoped their "golden years" would be filled with quality time spent going on vacations, participating in family activities, and having fun. Instead, "My days are spent driving Rudy from doctor to doctor, from dentist to hearing aid technicians to just about everywhere." She said, "Rudy has a difficult time keeping doctors because he eventually accuses them of cheating him, unethical behavior (they report directly to his ex-boss and the police), giving him the wrong medicine, and trying to kill him." She smiled sadly and added, "I guess you kinda figured out that Rudy needs to change doctors and dentists very often. I really can't blame them. If I were Rudy's doctor I wouldn't want to take care of someone who accused me of cheating and lying."

When this worker asked Mrs. Rosen how she had coped with Rudy's mental illness, she stated, "I don't have any time for myself. If I want to get my hair done I have to ask one of my kids to come over and keep an eye on their father. We don't have any social life to speak of anymore. Most of our friends, even those we've known for more than 40 years, don't ask us to join them for dinner or a movie. They feel too uncomfortable with Rudy's behavior, and never know when he's going to 'go off.' I can't really blame them, but I'm still lonely and feel isolated. Not many people really understand how hard it is to live with someone who is mentally ill. I think our friends view Rudy and me as being one person. Don't they know I'm not mentally ill?" This social worker offered support, reassurance, and validated Mrs. Rosen's feelings. Though Mrs. Rosen was familiar with the "routine" of hospitalizing her husband, I reaffirmed how a hospital stay can provide her husband with a safe and structured environment where he can receive 24-hour observation and evaluation. I further explained, "The hospital is a really good place for identifying Mr. Rosen's strengths and monitoring his responses to treatment regimens, including those for his tardive dyskinesia. Once he's discharged I will stay connected to you and your family and provide all kinds of referrals for support in the community or other networking supports. Maybe we can find a nearby day treatment program where Rudy won't feel so isolated, so you can finally have some free time for yourself." (This worker began to think of a few day care programs that could offer Rudy a structured therapeutic focus and social activities especially helpful in maintaining his progress once discharged.) "Is that something you would like?" Mrs. Rosen wiped away a few tears welling up in her eyes and then said, "I can't thank you enough for understanding what I've been going through and looking for Rudy's good side. I thought I was the only one in this world who could see his strengths. He's such a dear man when he isn't crazy."

She continued, "I have problems leaving Rudy alone, you know, like if I need to run an errand or be away from the apartment for any length of time." The social worker commented how difficult this must be for her and asked, "Have you been able to find anything to alleviate your loneliness?" Mrs. Rosen commented, "Those groups I used to go to were helpful. That's why I came up with this great idea, or so I thought. In order for me to get away even for a little while, I'd leave Rudy his medications in a small paper cup on the kitchen sink. Before I left, I'd *always* make sure to remind him about what time he had to take his medications." She added, "But now I sure can't allow him to take his medications unsupervised anymore. A couple of days ago I came home from the grocery store, and after putting the food away I went in the bathroom to put some hand soap in the closet. Well, you can imagine how shocked I was when I found several of Rudy's pills just laying on the bathroom floor next to the toilet. I cannot tell you how upset I was. Even now, I'm still steaming! I asked Rudy, 'Why didn't you take your medicine?' He said, 'I won't take that poison you and those damn crooked doctors gave me. I know you're all in cahoots. You want to kill me and get my retirement money.' He went on, 'I flushed all that stuff down the toilet.'" Mrs. Rosen was not sure how long this had been going on, but suspects this may have led to his current hospitalization when he once again began having active signs and symptoms of delusions and hallucinations.

This worker again reassured Mrs. Rosen, "Your husband is in good hands here. The next 72 hours will be the perfect time to re-evaluate Rudy's psychiatric situation." I explained, "I will request a psychiatric evaluation concerning his medication compliance and medication stabilization. It's been awhile since Mr. Rosen's medications have been reevaluated, and there are newer antipsychotic agents available without the more noted unpleasant side effects." While this worker understands prescribing medication is beyond the purview of social work practice, it can be helpful to know about medication use, including contraindications. As such, the practitioner remains current with the professional literature and remains knowledgeable as to the cutting edge of client care.

This worker asked Mrs. Rosen, "Do you have any questions about what we've just talked about?" She responded slowly, "No. I just want my Rudy to get better so he can come back home. I can't believe this is the very first time after all these years that I feel some hope about Rudy staying better." She reached for this worker's hands and holding tight said, "You probably hear this all the time but I have to say it anyway. Thank you, Mary, for really understanding what our life has been like, and thanks for all the choices you've offered us." I responded, "Thank you for the thank yous. I appreciate your faith in us and promise to do everything possible to return Rudy home." Mrs. Rosen then asked, "When can I see Rudy?" I looked at her and said, "How about right now?"

OPERATIONALIZING COMPETENCY-BASED TREATMENT

According to Sheafor and Horejsi (2003),

> Schizophrenia is a baffling and debilitating illness. About 1 percent of the population is afflicted with this disturbance of the thinking processes. . . . Many experts believe that a stressful environment, viral infections, and other physiological conditions may trigger the onset of this illness in those predisposed by heredity. . . . About one-fourth of those who have a schizophrenic episode get well and never have another episode. Some have occasional relapses. Between 20 and 30 percent develop symptoms that are persistent throughout life (p. 558).

Rudy Rosen was initially hospitalized almost 25 years ago, and Table 4.3 itemizes the risks, protective factors, and buffers in his life. Although Rudy's initial onset of schizophrenia, paranoid type, occurred later in life, the course was considered quite chronic. Rudy has had many exacerbations of positive and negative symptoms over his lifetime, especially when he did not take his medications. It is important to note the impact schizophrenia has had on this family and the associated struggles to cope with Rudy's symptomatic behavior. Rudy's wife, Ruth, has borne the emotional and financial brunt of his mental illness for the past 25 years. On the other hand, Rudy's children had to constantly cope with the loss of a meaningful parental relationship, and deal with their father's bizarre behavior and frequent hospitalizations. As adults, Rudy's children continue to struggle with their father's repeated hospitalizations, violent outbursts, paranoid ideation, and relapses. They are also a great source of support for their mother.

Working with Rudy Individually

Twenty-five years ago when Rudy was first diagnosed with schizophrenia his prognosis was considered bleak and hopeless. Thanks to the tenacious efforts of a loving and dedicated wife, however, he was able to live at home, raise two children, and hold a job. Although the Rosen family did not have the ideal Norman-Rockwell-like, picture-perfect lifestyle they were able to afford a home, purchase a car, educate two children, and establish some form of normalcy in between the times Rudy needed to be hospitalized. For too many others, unfortunately, living with schizophrenia means institutionalization, restraints, unwanted tranquilizers, and lost time. At first, Thorazine was the only drug available to treat schizophrenia and was used for years despite its life-threatening side effects.

TABLE 4.3	**RISKS, PROTECTIVE FACTORS, AND BUFFERS IN RUDY ROSEN'S LIFE**	

	Risk Factors	Protective Factors and Buffers
Intrapersonal	Schizophrenia, paranoid type Diagnosed 5 years ago Periodically suicidal Health concerns • Heart disease • Cataracts • Tardive dyskinesia	Taking psychotropic medications fairly regularly Periods of stable functioning
Interpersonal	Suspicious of others Bizarre behaviors; delusions; hallucinations Family history of mental disorders • Sister was "depressed" • Mother heard voices Wife "overwhelmed"	Married 55 years Supportive wife Family recognizes when Rudy needs to be hospitalized Children involved Family knows how to access resources
Social and Environmental	No hobbies or outside interests Isolated from long-time friends	Services available and accessible Retired auto mechanic Pension Family involvement in support groups Has adequate health insurance (Medicare) Financially stable

Today life is very different for those who are newly diagnosed, because schizophrenia has a wide range of courses and outcomes (Bustillo, Lauriello, & Keith, 1999; Cortese, 2002). The overall outlook for these persons continues to improve despite the presence of life events that often complicate treatment (Bachrach, 2000). Interestingly, 60 percent of those diagnosed with schizophrenia are able to achieve a full recovery or at least realize significant improvement. These persons may continue to have some hurdles to overcome but their prognosis remains quite good.

In this vignette the practitioner attempted to develop a supportive therapeutic alliance that focused on Rudy's medication compliance, recognized Rudy's inner chaos, and provided a measure of safety and trust in relationships outside of his family. It is important to view treatment as a long-term initiative rather than a short-term project to be completed in a matter of weeks or months. The therapeutic conversation began with a focus on educating Rudy and his family about the long-term consequences of schizophrenia and inviting them to talk about the struggles of living with someone with this disorder. By sharing problems, thoughts, and feelings, it is hoped Rudy may begin to understand more about himself and take a more active role in his treatment (Ribner & Knei-Paz, 2002; Young & Ensing, 1999). By talking with an objective, empathic practitioner, perhaps Rudy might begin to learn to differentiate reality from the distorted thoughts or cognitive disturbances characteristic of schizophrenia (Brenner & Pfammatter, 2000; Lecomte, Cyr, Lesage, & Wilde, 1999).

The "here and now" approach to the family's current hospitalization crisis addresses a number of their concerns, such as what will happen to Rudy during this hospital stay, what is his medical status, medication compliance, and other problems in daily living (Linhorst, Hamilton, Young, & Eckert, 2002; Young, Forquer, Tran, Starzynski, & Shatkin, 2000). Dilemmas associated with coping with the stresses associated with a diagnosis of schizophrenia, symptoms, taking medications, and forestalling relapse seem to be a reasonable focus of treatment (Marsh, 2002; Rudnick, 2001). The practitioner provides support, feedback, and reassurance to help Rudy concentrate on his day-to-day challenges. Once he has become stabilized, cognitive and behavioral approaches will be especially useful in reducing his positive and negative symptoms, emphasizing solving problems in living, and learning practical interpersonal skills (Dickerson, 2000; Garety, Fowler, & Kulpers, 2000; Gumley & Power, 2000; McQuaid, Granholm, McClure, & Pedrelli, 2000; Rector & Beck, 2001).

The therapeutic relationship is often influenced by the skills and expertise of the practitioner, especially the attributes of warmth, concern, and genuineness. Practitioners who are uncomfortable or unfamiliar with active symptomatology may rush to inaccurate conclusions or premature interpretations. It takes time to develop a sense of competence when working with clients who are actively psychotic, unwilling to take medication, and resist sustaining ongoing treatment (Sensky, Turkington, Kingdon, Scott, & Scott, 2000). In a perfect world the therapeutic alliance is characterized by a trusting relationship; however, this proves to be more difficult considering Rudy's paranoid ideation along with his strong defenses against becoming close or trusting anyone. Instead, Rudy becomes suspicious, aggressive, and hostile (Goff, Heckers, & Freudenreich, 2001). The practitioner remains patient, sincere, and at the same time honors Rudy's need for maintaining distance. Longer-term therapeutic goals will include providing Rudy with more information about his mental illness, ways to begin solving problems in living, setting reasonable expectations, learning to express his emotions appropriately, setting limits, managing stress, increasing self-esteem, enhancing his sense of empowerment, and learning when it is time to seek help (Boehm & Staples, 2002; Kopelowicz, Wallace, & Zarate, 1998; Lecomte et al., 1999).

On the other hand, the practitioner should also be comfortable working with someone like Rudy who has a complex diagnosis and a variety of complicated situations. In this case, the practitioner attempts to accurately assess Rudy's current situation including the influence of interpersonal and social or community concerns. Connecting clients with needed resources and community services is an essential worker activity. This family has coped with Rudy's diagnosis for almost a quarter of a century, and whether they wanted to or not they have had to deal with the consequences of schizophrenia. The practitioner complements their expertise with her knowledge of resources and programs, fostering a collaborative relationship with the Rosens.

Family Intervention

More than one-third of all persons with schizophrenia live with at least one family member. Some of the collateral work planned for the Rosens includes finding ways to support Rudy's medication adherence and identify signs suggesting deterioration or relapse. By involving Mrs. Rosen and extending an invitation to include her children, the practitioner has an opportunity to engage key members who play a vital role in helping to maintain Rudy's successful recovery (Leff, 2000; Segal, Akutsu, & Watson, 1998; Wykes, Tarrier, & Lewis, 1998; Zygmunt et al., 2002). By considering the family context, the practitioner has expanded opportunities to tap into the protective factors and buffers associated with Rudy's mental health struggles. Several studies suggest looking at strengths can be very effective at decreasing relapse while promoting improvements in client and family functioning (Herz, 1996; Pittenger, 1998). The burden experienced by family members who provide care following hospitalization has generated interest in including the family as active participants on the treatment team. This dynamic role serves to reduce the stress felt by family members and thereby reduce the risk of chronic client relapse. There is a growing body of professional literature regarding the relevance of constructing interventions aimed at therapeutic compliance and long-term outcomes (Atkinson, Coia, Gilmour, & Harper, 1996; Lieberman, Wallace, Blackwell, & Kopelwicz, 1998; Mueser et al., 2001; Oehl, Hummer, & Fleischhacker, 2000; Rivas-Vazquez et al., 2000; Wyatt, Damiani, & Henter-Ioline, 1998).

Mrs. Rosen has played a central supportive role in Rudy's care. The practitioner supports her realistic expectations of Rudy's behavior and also acknowledges the disappointment related to their retired life together. Over the years, Mrs. Rosen managed to maintain a loving relationship with her husband and provide a stable home environment for their children. The practitioner listened as Mrs. Rosen vented her frustration about the times when Rudy refused to take his medication. The process of reporting Rudy's disturbing behaviors to the practitioner serves two purposes. First, it affords Mrs. Rosen the opportunity to learn that her feelings are normal reactions. Second, she begins to explore strategies to minimize future relapses. This "conversation" with the practitioner models the elements important to relapse prevention; that is, increased communication, setting realistic goals, and exploring ways of coping with a family member's mental illness (Firth & Bridges, 1996; Pfammatter, Garst, & Teschner, 2000).

The combination of family-centered treatment together with adjunct psychopharmacological support appears to be effective at this time. Ideally, this treatment combination should offer stability for Rudy during this acute crisis; at a later time the worker can introduce individual and/or group therapy moving the Rosen family beyond considering relapse prevention strategies (Andres, Pfammatter, Garst, Teschner, & Brenner, 2000; Jackson & Birchwood, 1996; Miller & Mason, 2001). Although it was not stated directly, one gets the sense that Mrs. Rosen is concerned about who will care for Rudy when she is no longer able to do so.

Fortunately, Rudy has worked much of his adult life and has accrued adequate retirement benefits and medical insurance coverage. The increased financial responsibilities associated with his mental illness (such as expensive antipsychotic medications and multiple hospitalizations) have not become an issue for the Rosens.

Rehabilitation

Within the framework of rehabilitation it is essential to involve the person treated with antipsychotic drugs in programs aimed at making substantial functional gains and improving symptoms (Carpenter, Conley, Buchanan, & Breier, 1995). Considering Rudy's suspiciousness, emotional withdrawal from his family, and isolation, the practitioner reviews the potential benefits of rehabilitation programs for him. Normally, these programs emphasize social and vocational strategies to help individuals overcome difficulties associated with the diagnosis of schizophrenia and typically focus on vocational counseling, job training, problem-solving and money management skills, how to use public transportation, and social skills training. Rudy may benefit from the opportunity to learn more about his medication, such as how to watch for side effects and actively monitor himself. With a focus on social skills, Rudy may discover a hobby, thereby linking him with the community and reducing his isolation. Since rehabilitation programs are designed to aid individuals in bridging the gap between 24-hour supervised hospitalization and independent living in the community, it would be timely to refer Rudy to this type of community-centered support program when he is discharged from the hospital. There are a number of programs designed to bridge the gap between hospitalization and the community, including supervised housing, partial hospitalization providing day or night care, and living in a halfway house. Although Rudy's children are very involved and supportive of their mother in times of crisis, knowing that short-term residential care is available through rehabilitation programs may allay Mrs. Rosen's fears about the future. It can also help supply needed immediate relief from stressful situations by providing a protective atmosphere.

Group Work Interventions

Self-Help Groups   Self-help groups focus on the needs of the chronically mentally ill and have become a prominent alternative approach. Mrs. Rosen is already involved with perhaps the best-known self-help group, the National Alliance for the Mentally Ill (NAMI), which was developed by and composed of family members. Mrs. Rosen found a great deal of support and reassurance from others whose struggles were much like her own. NAMI is the oldest and largest organization of its kind in the United States, and its focus includes all aspects of mental illness and mental health issues. Based on the case discussion, it is difficult to gauge the empowering effects of a self-help group such as NAMI for the Rosen family. Through their participation over the years, they have come to realize that their experiences with Rudy are not unique. They and others have been able to find meaning in their lives through the struggles associated with chronic mental illness. The group is similar in format to other successful types of self-help initiatives providing group support for friends and family members. NAMI distinguishes itself through its advocacy on behalf of the needs and rights of persons with mental illness and their families. Advocating on behalf of others fosters resilience. The National Mental Health Consumers' Association is another resource. This association unites self-help organizations across the country and operates a Clearinghouse. (For additional information, please refer to the resources listed at the end of this chapter.)

Group Therapy Group programs have been used successfully in both inpatient and outpatient settings and are considered most useful after the acute symptoms of schizophrenia have subsided (Hepworth, Rooney, & Larsen, 2002; Miller & Mason, 1998). Although her children are a source of support to Mrs. Rosen, the entire family has struggled for more than 25 years with Rudy's psychotic symptoms. A support group focusing on building better communication, understanding Rudy's symptoms, and experiencing a sense of cohesiveness among members built on shared experiences may serve to extend the family's support system.

Rudy might also take advantage of group services. Once he is stabilized and his paranoid suspicions subside, Rudy may benefit from learning from the experiences of others, testing out his perceptions with other members of the group, and correcting distortions and maladaptive interpersonal behaviors by receiving feedback. A support group organized around mutual aid would also reduce Rudy's social isolation and perhaps improve his reality testing. According to Walsh (2002), those participating in group therapy have fewer hospital re-admissions than those who receive only social skills training. When people move past the acute phase of schizophrenia to continuation or maintenance, group therapy is most helpful in developing and maintaining relationships, tackling real-life problems, and rehabilitation (Toseland & Rivas, 1998).

Case Management

As the needs of the person with schizophrenia change and community responses become more fragmented, a variety of other providers and agencies may become involved in the person's care. The case manager is replacing the role of the single practitioner who coordinates services. Although she describes herself as Rudy's "jailer," Mrs. Rosen actually functions as a case manager for the family. She coordinates medical, psychiatric, social, and financial plans; for example, she makes all of Rudy's appointments and then transports him to those services. Analogous to the case manager's role, she focuses on solving problems, being an advocate for her husband, and providing support to maintain Rudy within the community. In this regard she may work toward gaining needed services, such as case-specific advocacy. During Rudy's current hospitalization she describes the range of supportive community-based services used by the family and remains open to the social worker's input and suggestions.

Conclusion

The competency-based treatment model provides a framework for the practitioner to consider the complexity, chronicity, and the many personal, social, and environmental problems the Rosen family has encountered. Although Rudy Rosen benefits from family and social supports that are not available to many persons struggling with schizophrenia, the impact of a diagnosis of schizophrenia remains the same. This case vignette illustrates the many domains in Rudy's life targeted by the practitioner: working with Rudy individually, involving his family, and considering community groups and rehabilitation programs helpful for persons with chronic mental illness. The counseling theories of crisis intervention and cognitive behavioral therapy, and the services provided through hospitalization and rehabilitation are highlighted. Although Rudy's diagnosis is made from a common set of symptoms, competency-based treatment provides the practitioner with a framework to make every attempt to individualize his experiences, provide needed support, promote coping and adaptation, and consider his symptoms within a social context. This orientation to practice helps the practitioner to move seamlessly among efforts aimed at helping Mrs. Rosen with her personal struggles living with a husband with schizophrenia while fostering the Rosens' connections to the community (Gehart & Tuttle, 2003).

SUMMARY

Schizophrenia has a chronic course that includes a prodromal phase, an active phase (characterized by delusions, hallucinations, or both), and a residual phase in which the disorder may either be spiraling down into remission or spiraling up into a relapse. To make the diagnosis of schizophrenia, the specific psychotic symptoms and behaviors must be present for at least one month during the active phase of the illness and this disturbance must persist for at least six months. The following is a diagnostic summary of schizophrenia:

- Schizophrenia is characterized by a multi-spectrum of cognitive and emotional dysfunctions, including symptoms of delusions, hallucinations, disorganized speech and behavior, and inappropriate emotions.
- Symptoms of schizophrenia are divided into positive and negative symptoms. Positive symptoms refer to the more outward signs and symptoms, or those that are present but should be absent. These include abnormal behavior or an excess or distortion of normal behavior, including delusions, hallucinations, and disorganized speech. Negative symptoms refer to the more inward

signs and symptoms, or those symptoms that are absent but should be present. They involve scarcity in normative behavior such as affect, speech, and motivation.

- Schizophrenia is subdivided into five categories. Persons with the paranoid type have prominent delusions or hallucinations, but their cognitive skills and affect remain relatively intact. Those with the disorganized type tend to exhibit marked disruption in speech and behavior; they also display flat or inappropriate affect. Persons with catatonic type have unusual and striking motor responses such as remaining in a "fixed position" (waxy flexibility), excessive activity, or being oppositional in remaining rigid. They show signs of odd mannerisms with their bodies and faces, such as grimacing. People who do not fit neatly into these subtypes would be categorized as undifferentiated type. Those who have had at least one episode of schizophrenia, but who no longer manifest major signs and symptoms of active phase, are diagnosed as the residual type.

Several other disorders are characterized by "a psychotic-like picture" and include symptoms such as hallucinations and delusions:

- *Schizophreniform disorder* (symptoms of schizophrenia experienced for less than 6 months)
- *Schizoaffective disorder* (symptoms of schizophrenia as well as symptoms of a mood disorder such as major depressive disorder or bipolar disorder)
- *Delusional disorder* (persistent delusions or beliefs that are contrary to reality, in the absence of the other characteristics of schizophrenia)
- *Brief psychotic disorder* (includes one or more "positive" symptoms such as delusions, hallucinations, disorganized speech or disorganized behavior occurring over the course of less than 30 days)
- *Shared psychotic disorder* (delusions are present as a result of an intensely close relationship with a person who has a delusional disorder)

As highlighted in the case of Rudy Rosen, schizophrenia is a severe, debilitating, and costly mental illness. Although first-generation antipsychotic agents were able to provide reasonable relief from some of his more undesirable symptoms, they failed to offer permanent relief. The second generation of antipsychotic drugs treated more of the symptoms associated with schizophrenia than the typical agents. While some second-generation agents can cause adverse side effects such as weight gain or sexual dysfunction, their use is considered in a more favorable light than first-generation agents. Despite these advances, Rudy and his family continued to struggle (Mathiesen, 2001; Rudnick, 2001; Thaker & Carpenter, 2001; Zide & Gray, 2001).

Schizophrenia is a complicated disorder, and its course and prognosis are unique for each person. Competency-based treatment organized the practitioner's interventions around Rudy's competence and strengths, coping capacities, familial or social relationships, cultural background, and environmental resources (Provencher et al., 2003; Robinson et al., 2000). Applying selected skills from multiple counseling theories and methods helped the practitioner participate collaboratively with Rudy and his wife and individualize their experiences with mental illness. The social worker's relationship was seen as one of warmth, support, and caring.

More information related to the topics discussed in this chapter can be found on the following websites:

- Association for the Advancement of Social Work with Groups (http://www.aaswg.org)
- The National Alliance for the Mentally Ill at 1 (800) 950-6264 or (http://www.nami.org)
- The National Alliance for Research on Schizophrenia and Depression (http://www.mhsource.com/narsad.html)
- The National Institute of Mental Health (http://www.nimh.nih.gov/)
- Online Dictionary of Mental Health (http://www.human-nature.com/odmh/)
- World Wide Web Resources for Social Workers (http://wwwnyu.edu/socialwork/wwwrsw/)

The author recognizes that websites can become outdated rather quickly or disappear altogether; therefore, this listing of suggested resources is provided as a starting point for the reader's own investigations.

PRACTITIONER REFLECTIONS

1. Persons with schizophrenia (and other psychotic disorders) are often oppressed and highly vulnerable to stress. In some instances, services are unavailable. They may find themselves discounted, treated like children, or ignored.
   - Thinking about your own community and the services available for persons with schizophrenia or other psychotic disorders, can you identify what may be needed but lacking?
   - What programs are in place? Identify how they are helpful.
   - List the qualities important for developing a relationship with persons with schizophrenia (or any of the psychotic disorders).
   - Looking inward, reflect on which of the listed qualities come easily to you and which ones you may need to develop. Also consider ways you can work on improving your relationship skills.
   - Interview a colleague and ask for his or her opinion about the essential qualities for developing (and maintaining) a relationship with someone who has schizophrenia (or one of the other psychotic disorders). Compare this list with the one you developed. Reflect on any differences you discover. (You may also want to ask this colleague what he or she does to improve relationship qualities and skills.)
2. Persons with schizophrenia may behave in bizarre and unpredictable ways. Self-awareness is an important aspect of competency-based treatment. Examine some of the feelings and emotions you experience when working with a person diagnosed with a psychotic disorder. How do these feelings manifest themselves in your thinking and behavior?

3. Clients bring their own self-concept to the therapeutic relationship, and often this self-concept is influenced by prior experiences with other professional helpers.

   - Reflecting on the case of Rudy Rosen, identify prior experiences he (and his family) had with previous practitioners. How do they influence the relationship with the social worker in this case illustration?
   - Think about one of your current clients and identify what factors in his or her experiences with prior helpers influence your relationship today.

4. The chapter reviews many of the adverse side effects associated with the use of pharmacologic agents. Research one of the antipsychotic medications used in treating schizrenia and make a list of side effects indicated.

   - Identify reasons why clients might not want to comply with taking the medication.
   - How would you intervene?
   - What are the advantages and disadvantages of taking medication for schizophrenia?

5. Rehabilitation programs are effective in helping persons with major mental illness after discharge from the hospital and focus on helping people live independently within the community. Plan a field trip to one such program in your community. Survey the services offered, such as vocational counseling, job training, problem-solving, money management skills, and how to use public transportation.

   - Does the program offer ancillary partial hospitalization such as day (or night) care, supported-living housing, or halfway housing?
   - In your opinion, what programs are most effective; and what services need to be added?

6. Imagine for a moment that you are the social worker assigned to the case of Rudy Rosen. You and Mrs. Rosen have been working together for some time and have developed a positive working relationship. During one of your conversations with her, Mrs. Rosen confides a "secret": she applied for and received welfare assistance some time ago when finances were tight. When the situation improved, financial benefits stopped but she continued using food stamps. "Everybody does it," she says, adding, "We've been through so much and every little bit helps." What would you do? (*Hint:* You might want to review the discussion in Chapter 1 addressing ethical factors in practice.)

7. The case of Rudy Rosen illustrates the times when clients may refuse to take their prescribed medications. If you were the social worker in this case, identify your obligations to Rudy. Consider the Code of Ethics and the client's right to self-determination.

MOOD DISORDERS

Mario, age 49, had recently retired from his job with the phone company. Now that he was at home all the time, his wife Nancy noticed how negative and pessimistic he seemed. She thought her husband, who had done well on the job, seemed unmotivated and detached from the rest of the family. Not sure if his attitude was related to his retirement, she encouraged him to go to the doctor for a checkup. Mario admitted that he always felt lousy and sort of empty, but "that's normal for me," he explained. He was surprised when his doctor diagnosed him as depressed.

Unfortunately, Mario is typical of many people who do not seek help because they believe it's "normal" for them to feel depressed. In addition, it is not uncommon for those who struggle with depression to attribute their symptoms to having the flu, feeling stressed, needing more sleep, or just not eating right.

An estimated 10 to 14 million Americans will have some form of a mood disorder in any given year (Clement & Greene, 2002; Kluger, 2003). More than 35 million adults have experienced one depressive episode at some point in their lives (Kluger, 2003). The mood disorders not only account for considerable pain and suffering but also cause significant disability and consequent loss of productivity. Depression has been ranked as the second leading cause of disability, surpassed only by heart disease (Nemeroff & Owens, 2002). Fortunately, most of the mood disorders are eminently treatable. According to Reid, Balis, and Sutton (1997), when the appropriate treatment is used, 70 to 90 percent of patients respond well. The three major treatments that have been effective in treating depression are antidepressant medications, psychotherapy, and electroconvulsive therapy (ECT) (Nemeroff & Owens, 2002).

Depression can affect one's outlook on life. Remember the old adage of seeing the world through rose-colored glasses? Unfortunately, depression clouds one's ability to view his or her world realistically. People who are depressed see their world with a sense of pessimism, sadness, or hopelessness. In other words, they see through dark-colored glasses.

A clinical depression is different from the experiences of sadness and disappointment experienced by everyone from time to time. Have you ever lost a bid for that coveted job, election, or promotion? Almost everyone has had a major loss or disappointment in his or her life. Feelings of sadness and discouragement are normal emotional reactions to difficult situations. A depressed mood can last for several days or weeks without causing concern. Although these feelings can be characterized as depression, they typically do not constitute the symptoms found in a mood disorder because they are relatively mild and of short duration. They don't keep you from going to work or spending time with friends and family. When they last more than a few weeks or get so bad that they interfere with a person's life, they could be symptoms of a mood disorder. People with a mood disorder may feel tired, worthless, helpless, and hopeless, but these feelings do not accurately reflect their true situation.

The mood disorders are separated into two major categories: unipolar and bipolar disorder. Unipolar disorder, known as depression, can range from mild to life-threatening. This category includes the major depressive disorders (single episode, recurrent) and dysthymia, a long-term, low-grade depression. Major depression is marked by more severe or exaggerated symptoms. Bipolar disorder, also referred to as manic depression, is the more distinct and dramatic of the mood disorders. The person suddenly shifts from one emotional extreme, or pole, to the other, usually with periods of normal behavior between the extremes. The manic phase is marked by feelings of happiness and high energy. The depressive phase is characterized by feelings of despair and hopelessness. Cyclothymia is composed of chronic, fluctuating mood disturbances with numerous periods of hypomanic symptoms and numerous periods of depressive symptoms for at least two years. Cyclothymia is considered a milder form of bipolar disorder (APA, 2000; Zide & Gray, 2001).

UNDERSTANDING MOOD DISORDERS

The mood disorders are one of the most researched sections in the *Diagnostic and Statistical Manual* (DSM), and the DSM provides a considerable amount of information regarding safe and effective treatments (APA, 2000; Barlow & Durand, 2005; Gabbard, 1995). Note Zide and Gray (2001), the mood disorders refer to a group of emotional disturbances that cause people to experience serious and persistent difficulty maintaining an even, productive emotional state. The term *affective disorder* is often used interchangeably with *mood disorder,* but the DSM attempts to define and differentiate between affect and mood. The DSM–IV–TR (APA, 2000) glossary defines *affect* as "a pattern of observable behaviors that is the expression of a subjectively experienced feeling state (emotion). Common examples of affect are sadness, elation, and anger" (p. 819). The term *mood* refers to "a pervasive and sustained emotion that colors the perception of the world" (APA, 2000, p. 825). Persons with a mood disorder generally show depression, elation, anger, and anxiety.

The Major Depressive Disorders

Depression is a chronic disorder that is recurrent in nature, causing significant impairment for the individual, his or her family, and employer (Simon, 2003). Major depressive disorder affects approximately 9.9 million American adults or about 5 percent of the United States population aged 18 and older in a given year (National Institute of Mental Health, 2001). Major depressive disorder, most often called major depression, is characterized by one (single episode) or more (recurrent) depressive episodes without a history of manic (abnormally exaggerated elation, joy, or euphoria), mixed (a combination of manic symptoms with feelings of depression or anxiety at the same time), or hypomanic (a less severe version of a manic episode that does not cause marked impairment in social or occupational functioning) episodes. A *single episode* in a person's lifetime is rare (Judd, 1997, 2000; Mueller et al., 1999; Solomon et al., 2000). As many as 75 percent of persons who have experienced a major depressive disorder will go through it again (Nietzel, Speltz, McCauley, & Bernstein, 1998). For all intents and purposes, unipolar depression is a chronic condition that waxes and wanes over time but seldom disappears. If two or more major depressive episodes occurred and were separated by periods of at least two months during which the person was not depressed, "major depressive disorder, *recurrent*" is diagnosed (APA, 2000; Barlow & Durand, 2005; Zide & Gray, 2001).

The possibility of major depression is considered when the following features have been present over a two-week period of time and represent a change from the person's earlier ways of coping (Zide & Gray, 2001):

- Despondent mood most of the day, nearly every day;
- Markedly diminished interest or pleasure in most activities;
- Vegetative features such as insomnia (cannot sleep) or hypersomnia (sleeping too much);
- Psychomotor agitation (hand wringing or restless pacing), or retardation (a slowing down in activities such as walking or talking);
- Fatigue and/or loss of energy;
- Feelings of worthlessness or excessive guilt;
- Inability to concentrate or think clearly;
- Recurring thoughts of death, or suicidal ideation;
- Significant distress or impairment in social, occupational, or other important areas of interpersonal functioning.

Individuals may describe feeling worthless, lacking energy, and being unable to experience pleasure (anhedonia). Bodily symptoms (vegetative features) are critical to the assessment of mood disorders and appear in the form of changes in sleep patterns, energy levels, or appetite fluctuations (Rubin, 1997). An external event often seems to precipitate an episode of depression, such as serious loss, a difficult relationship, or financial problems. More common, a combination of genetic, psychological, and environmental factors is involved in the onset of a depressive disorder.

Remick (2002) suggests the mnemonic "SIGECAPS" adapted from the DSM (2000) criteria for major depressive disorder to help the practitioner recognize the extent of a person's depression. The practitioner considers the presence of major depression if the person has a depressed mood (for example, sad or empty feeling) or loss of interest or pleasure most of the time for two or more weeks *plus* four or more of the following symptoms:

S = Sleep	Is the person experiencing insomnia or hypersomnia nearly every day?
I = Interest	Does the person experience a markedly diminished interest or pleasure in nearly all activities most of the time?
G = Guilt	Does the person experience excessive (or inappropriate) feelings of guilt or worthlessness most of the time?
E = Energy	Does the person have a loss of energy or seem fatigued most of the time?
C = Concentration	Does the person have a hard time thinking or concentrating?
A = Appetite	Has the person experienced an increase or decrease in appetite?
P = Psychomotor	Can psychomotor agitation (or retardation) be observed?
S = Suicide	Does the person have recurrent thoughts of death (or suicidal intention)?

If the person meets two or three of the "SIGECAPS" criteria, the possibility of dysthymia is considered.

Bipolar Disorder

Bipolar disorder, also known as manic depression, is marked by extreme changes in mood, thought, energy, and behavior. A person's mood can alternate between the "poles" of mania (highs) and depression (lows). This change in mood or mood swing can last for hours, days, weeks, or months. Typically, an episode evolves over a period of a few days. Bipolar disorder differs significantly from clinical depression, although the symptoms for the depressive phase of this diagnosis are similar. This similarity in symptoms complicates diagnosis (Dunner, 2003). The severity of the mood swings and the way they disrupt normal life activities distinguish bipolar mood episodes from ordinary mood changes. The practitioner may observe psychotic symptoms (such as delusions) or perceptual disturbances (such as hallucinations).

There are two types of bipolar disorder. The patterns and severity of symptoms (or episodes) of highs and lows determine the classification.

Bipolar I Disorder   One or more manic episodes or mixed episodes (symptoms of both a mania and a depression) occurring nearly every day for at least one week, as well as one or more major depressive episodes characterize bipolar I disorder. This is the most severe form of the depressive illnesses and is marked by extreme manic episodes. The literature indicates bipolar I disorder has a poorer prognosis than major depressive disorder (Zide & Gray, 2001). Symptoms of mania (the highs) of bipolar disorder include

- Increased physical and mental activity
- Heightened mood, exaggerated optimism and self-confidence
- Excessive irritability, aggressive behavior
- Decreased need for sleep without experiencing fatigue
- Grandiose delusions, inflated sense of self-importance
- Poor judgment (including inappropriate social behavior)
- Racing speech, racing thoughts, flight of ideas
- Impulsiveness, poor judgment, distractibility
- Increased sexual desire
- Reckless behavior, and in the most severe situations delusions and hallucinations.

    Symptoms of the lows of bipolar disorder include

- Prolonged sadness (or unexplained crying spells) or "empty mood"
- Significant changes in appetite and sleep patterns
- Irritability, anger, worry, agitation, anxiety
- Feelings of hopelessness, pessimism, indifference
- Loss of energy, persistent lethargy, or being "slowed down"
- Feelings of guilt, worthlessness, helplessness
- Inability to concentrate, indecisiveness
- Inability to take pleasure in former interests (including sex), social withdrawal
- Unexplained aches and pains that do not respond to treatment
- Recurring thoughts of death or suicide, suicide attempts.

Bipolar II Disorder   Bipolar II disorder is characterized by one or more depressive episodes accompanied by at least one hypomanic episode. Hypomanic episodes have symptoms similar to manic episodes but are less severe, and they must be clearly different from the person's non-depressed mood. For some people the hypomanic episodes can cause interpersonal difficulties (like trouble on the job), and for others these episodes are not severe enough to cause notable problems.

To identify other key variations in the bipolar disorders, two additional aspects are considered: rapid cycling and a seasonal pattern. *Rapid cycling* occurs when four or more separate bipolar episodes (in any combination) are experienced in a one-year period. Those with a *seasonal affective pattern* tend to experience episodes during a particular time of the year, such as late fall or early winter (Zide & Gray, 2001).

The Minor Mood Disorders

Dysthymia   Dysthymia is a chronic, less severe type of depression. The practitioner may encounter a person who has a poor appetite (or overeats), suffers from insomnia (or oversleeps), and experiences low energy or fatigue. Because functioning is not greatly impaired, individuals are often unaware that they have an illness. This disorder has been referred to as a long-term, low-grade depression because the individual must have a chronically depressed mood for most of the day for most days for at least two years. To be diagnosed with dysthymia, the person must exhibit two or more of the following symptoms (APA, 2000; Zide & Gray, 2001):

- Increased or decreased sleep
- Increased or decreased appetite
- Low energy
- Low self-esteem
- Poor concentration or decision-making ability
- Hopelessness.

Persons with diagnoses of both dysthymia and major depression are said to experience "double depression." An example might be a person who shows a chronic state of mild depression with periodic major depressive episodes.

Cyclothymia   Cyclothymia is characterized by chronic fluctuating moods involving episodes of hypomania and depression over a period of at least two years. People with cyclothymia may exhibit symptoms of low mood, lethargy, feelings of despair, problems eating and sleeping, and difficulty concentrating. It is not unusual for people to regard their chronic low mood as normal or the way they have always been (Zide & Gray, 2001). The episodes of both depressive and hypomanic symptoms are shorter, less severe, and do not occur with regularity as found in the bipolar II or I disorders. However, these mood swings impair interpersonal functioning, causing problems at home or on the job.

Suicide and the Mood Disorders

Unfortunately, the mood disorders are associated with a significant risk for suicide, one of the top ten causes of death in the United States (Bronisch, 2003; Nemeroff & Owens, 2002). In 2000, 29,350 people died by suicide in the United States (Minino, Arias, Kochanek, Murphy, & Smith, 2002). Depression and the depressive phase of bipolar disorder are associated with symptoms such as intense sadness, hopelessness, lethargy, loss of appetite, sleep disturbance, decreased ability to perform usual tasks, or a loss of interest in once-pleasurable activities. Taken together, they may lead a person to consider suicide (Farmer et al., 2001). More than 90 percent of people who kill themselves have a diagnosable mental illness, and the most common underlying condition is a depressive disorder (Minino et al., 2002). The pervasive perception of hopelessness associated with depression makes it important for the practitioner to evaluate a person's risk of suicide. The risk factors for suicide frequently occur in combination and include the following (Brown, Beck, & Steer, 2000; Zide & Gray, 2001): family history of suicide, exposure to the suicidal behavior of others (including peers or even in the media), family violence (including physical or sexual abuse), previous attempts, depression, anxiety and exhaustion, verbalization of suicidal ideation, concern for family being left behind, making plans for death, having specific access to means, firearms in the home, incarceration, substance abuse, and adverse life events. Suicidal ideation has also been linked to an unstable sense of self-esteem (De Man & Gutierrez, 2002). On one day the person may feel relatively good and on another day they may suffer from a negative self-image. As a consequence, they have no stable base from which to deal with the demands of life, making them more vulnerable to the risk of suicidal ideation. The practitioner also considers the person's age, gender, health, marital status, and employment status. While it is important to consider the risk factors that correlate with suicide, they do not necessarily predict suicide (Joiner & Rudd, 2000; Mann, Waternaux, Hass, & Malone, 1999; Orbach, 1997). One of the most potentially lethal antecedents of suicide is a state of mind known as "tunnel vision" in which the person views death as the only viable alternative (Aguilera, 1994; James & Gilliand, 2005). In this instance, the person has the feeling that life is so excruciating that death is the only way to ease the pain. This sense of emotional torment coupled with a detailed plan for suicide that includes a specific time, place, and method increases the likelihood of suicide (Barlow & Durand, 2005).

Suicidal ideation varies in severity from transient thoughts that life is not worth living through making plans and finally attempting to kill oneself (Beck, 1986; Dyer & Kreitman, 1984). Eight out of ten persons give some sign of their intentions. Those who do talk about suicide, threaten to commit suicide, or call suicide crisis centers are 30 times more likely than average to kill themselves. A suicide attempt is a clear indication that something is gravely wrong in the person's life. Clearly, precipitants should be addressed as well as the lack of coping mechanisms suicidal persons have at their disposal. It is not uncommon for suicidal people to believe they have no coping mechanisms left, as the ones they have used did not work for them. How the individual approaches the event (or stressor) is more significant than the actual stressfulness of the event. A careful assessment of suicide danger (or extent of lethality) is important and provides the opportunity for the practitioner to offer reassurance that once the depressive symptoms are alleviated, the self-destructive impulses are also very likely to dissipate as well.

Suicidal behavior is complex and there is no single therapeutic approach that works for all suicidal persons or people with suicidal tendencies. However, when the practitioner suspects a significant risk of suicide, a number of steps should be taken to prevent the person from acting on unrealistic self-destructive impulses. The specific steps will vary with each situation. The practitioner should gather information about any plans that have been formulated as well as the availability of means. The most commonly used method of suicide for both men and women is firearms. The second most common method for men is hanging, and for women it is self-poisoning including drug overdose. The practitioner's first priority is to prevent suicide. If the threat is very real, the practitioner considers restricting the person's freedom and detaining him or her involuntarily for a period of time. Alternatively, the practitioner may make arrangements with a relative or loved one for careful monitoring. A written agreement, usually referred to as a contract, may be developed with the person to ensure safety and provide alternatives to self-injury. If hospitalization is warranted, it is important for the practitioner to know specific state statutes and regulations regarding an involuntary and emergency admission. In all instances, the practitioner communicates his or her concern to the person (and family) and gathers as much information as possible in order to understand the specific circumstances surrounding suicidal ideation.

OVERVIEW OF MAJOR INTERVENTIONS

The mood disorders present a substantial therapeutic challenge, and the last dozen years have seen a dramatic increase in the number of treatment options available. Treatment includes both attention to acute mood episodes and management of a chronic, waxing and waning illness. Some persons may experience a single and nonrecurring depressive mood event while others may experience chronic neurochemical imbalances that challenge treatment efforts. Age, the type and severity of depression, responses to past treatment, a person's general medical status, and/or stressful life circumstances influence the type of treatment intervention used. Up until the mid-twentieth century, the available treatments for the mood disorders were largely supportive and palliative. Today, these disorders are seen as serious and potentially life-threatening conditions that have clearly defined mood, cognitive, motor, somatic, and neurobiological concomitants.

Biological Therapies

Recognizing the biochemical components of the mood disorders, treatment has increasingly included pharmacotherapy. Certain medications alter levels of norepinephrine or serotonin to alleviate the symptoms of depression (Blier, 2001). Twenty years ago there were few treatment options available for persons with unipolar illness beyond the original tricyclic antidepressants and the difficult to use first generation monoamine oxidase inhibitors (Joffe, 2002). Currently, the use of antidepressant medication is considered to be effective (ranging from 60 to 70 percent) in the treatment of depression (Austrian, 2000; Bentley & Walsh, 2001; Dziegielewski, 2001).

The "classes" of medications most often prescribed for depression are the heterocyclics (HCAs), selective serotonin reuptake inhibitors (SSRIs), serotonin/norepinephrine reuptake inhibitors (SNRIs), and monoamine oxidase inhibitors (MAOIs). Generally, the medications need to be taken by a person for two to six weeks to become effective. Mood-stabilizing medications such as lithium, or anticonvulsants such as carbamazepine or valproate, are commonly used for bipolar disorder.

Heterocyclics   The HCAs include tetra-, tri-, bi-, and unicyclic antidepressants distinguished by the number of rings in their chemical structures. They are believed to be effective by increasing the level of norepinephrine in the brain synapses (the place where brain cells or neurons are connected to each other), although they may also affect serotonin levels. Persons are usually started at low dosage levels and then the dosages are increased over a period of one or two weeks until the therapeutic benefits are achieved. The HCAs are listed below:

- *Secondary tricyclics*—This category includes desipramine (Norpramin), nortriptyline (Pamelor, Aventyl), and protriptyline (Vivactyl).
- *Tertiary tricyclics*—Commonly prescribed medications in this class are amitriptyline (Elavil), clomipramine (Anafranil), doxepin (Adapin, Sinequan), imipramine (Tofranil, SK-Pramine, Janimine, others), and trimipramine (Surmontil).
- *Tetracyclics*—Examples of tetracyclic antidepressants include maprotiline (Ludiomil) and mirtazapine (Remeron). This medication works at somewhat different biochemical sites. It affects serotonin but at a post-synaptic site (after the connection between nerve cells). It also increases histamine levels, causing the person to feel drowsy. For this reason, the medication is usually taken at bedtime. It can also be prescribed for people who have trouble falling asleep.
- *Other*—Examples of other classes of heterocyclic medications include
    Dibenzoxazepine—amoxapine (Asendin);
    Triazolopyridine—trazodone (Desyrel).

While the side effects vary for each person, the most common are dry mouth (or xerostomia), constipation, bladder problems such as urinary retention and hesitancy, impaired sexual functioning, blurred vision, dizziness, drowsiness, and increased heart rate.

Selective Serotonin Reuptake Inhibitors   The next category of medications is the selective serotonin reuptake inhibitors (SSRIs) and the serotonin/norepinephrine reuptake inhibitors (SNRIs). These medications increase the amount of the neurochemical serotonin in the brain. The brains of people who are depressed have low levels of serotonin. The SSRIs work by selectively inhibiting or blocking serotonin reuptake in the brain. This block occurs at the synapse. Serotonin is one of the chemicals in the brain that carries messages across these connections or synapses from one neuron to another. SNRIs reduce uptake of both serotonin and norepinephrine. SSRIs and SNRIs represent a relatively new class of medications that seems to be growing in use, primarily because they produce fewer side effects than HCAs. As such, they are often seen as "first-line" treatment for depression.

- *Selective serotonin reuptake inhibitors (SSRIs)*—These medications are considered "atypical" because they differ chemically from the cyclic antidepressants and the monoamine oxidase inhibitors (MAOIs). Some of the commonly prescribed medications in this category include bupropion (Wellbutrin), citalopram (Celexa), fluoxetine (Prozac), fluvoxamine (Luvox), paroxetine (Paxil), and sertraline (Zoloft). The common side effects of the SSRIs are anxiety and restlessness, constipation, dry mouth, headache, nausea and vomiting, and sedation. Bupropion, because of its atypical chemical structure, does not fit neatly into the SSRI class; in other words, it could be considered to be in a class by itself. The most common side effects of bupropion are headaches, restlessness, and nausea. Interestingly, bupropion is approved by the Food and Drug Administration (FDA) for use in weaning people from addiction to cigarettes.

- *Serotonin/norepinephrine reuptake inhibitors (SNRIs)*—This class of medications appear to have particularly robust effects on both the norepinephrine and serotonin systems. The dual serotonin and norepinephrine reuptake inhibitors do not affect other chemicals that are impacted by the cyclic antidepressants, thereby reducing the incidence of adverse effects. This class of medication includes venlafaxine (Effexor), which shares many of the side effects of the SSRIs.

Monoamine Oxidase Inhibitors   The monoamine oxidase inhibitors (MAOIs) are effective for some people with major depression who do not respond to other antidepressants. This class of medications includes the earliest developed antidepressants. The MAOIs elevate the levels of neurochemicals in the brain synapses by inhibiting monoamine oxidase (the main enzyme that breaks down neurochemicals such as norepinephrine). When monoamine oxidase is inhibited, the norepinephrine is not broken down and thus the amount of norepinephrine in the brain is increased. MAOIs also impair the ability to break down tyramine, and therefore it is important for those taking MAOIs to carefully monitor their diet and avoid high-tyramine foods (for example, aged cheese such as Camembert or Edam, sauerkraut, aged meat, sausages, cold cuts, alcohol (notably, beer and red wine, especially Chianti), caffeinated beverages, chocolate, yeast extracts, yogurt and sour cream, pickled herring or smoked fish, sardines, and anchovies). Examples of MAOIs are deprenyl (Eldepryl), phenylzine (Nardil), and tranylcypromine (Parnate). The most common side effects are constipation, dizziness, dry mouth, hypotension, insomnia, nausea, sexual difficulties, skin reaction, weakness, and weight gain. In addition, the MAOIs can interact with over-the-counter cold and cough medications to cause dangerously high blood pressures.

Mood Stabilizers and Other Medications   Lithium (Lithium carbonate, Lithonate, Eskalith, Lithobid, Lithane, Lithium citrate, Cibalith-S) is a mood stabilizer that is effective in reducing symptoms of mania, depression, and mood instability. Lithium is also considered the "gold standard" for treating persons with bipolar disorder (Frank, Swartz, & Kupfer, 2000; McIntyre, 2001; Walsh, 1998). Lithium treatment is often compromised by poor adherence; that is, when people begin to feel better they stop taking the medication (Dharmendra & Eagles, 2003). Because the difference between toxic and therapeutic levels is not extreme, individuals who take this drug must have their blood levels carefully monitored. Common side effects may include weight gain, nausea, diarrhea, hand tremor, muscle weakness, dulling and memory difficulties, drowsiness, increased thirst, or increased urination. If a person does not respond to lithium, anticonvulsants have proven to be effective, particularly carbamazepine (Tegretol) or valproate (Depakote). The most frequent side effects are gastrointestinal difficulties. Oxcarbazepine, a derivative of carbamazepine, has been used in Europe and may show promise for use in the United States (Reinstein, Sonnenberg, Hedberg, Jones, & Reyngold, 2003).

Stimulants such as methylphenidate (Ritalin) or dextroamphetamine (Dexedrine) are used for treating depression when the person seems unresponsive to other medications. The stimulants are most commonly used along with other antidepressants or other medications (for example, the mood stabilizers). On rare occasions stimulants are used alone.

Table 5.1 summarizes the medications commonly prescribed for mood disorders, together with their side effects.

The most effective medications have complex pharmacologies, and efforts to develop more effective biological treatments are ongoing (Roth, Sheffler, & Kroeze, 2004). A number of aspects of the current biological therapies could be improved upon. The first is efficacy. After six to eight weeks, only 35 to 40 percent of persons treated with standard doses of the most commonly prescribed antidepressants return to levels of premorbid functioning without any significant depressive

TABLE 5.1   **CLASSES OF MEDICATIONS COMMONLY PRESCRIBED FOR THE MOOD DISORDERS**

Class	Generic Name	Trade Name	Common Side Effects
HCAs—Tertiary tricyclics	amitriptyline clomipramine doxepin imipramine trimipramine	Elavil Anafranil Adapin, Sinequan Tofranil, SK-Pramine, Janimine, others Surmontil	• Dry mouth (or xerostomia) • Constipation • Bladder problems such as urinary retention and hesitancy
Secondary tricyclics	desipramine nortriptyline protriptyline	Norpramin Pamelor, Aventyl Vivactyl	• Impaired sexual functioning • Blurred vision
Tetracyclic	maprotiline mirtazapine	Ludiomil Remeron	• Dizziness • Drowsiness
Dibenzoxazepine	amoxapine	Asendin	• Increased heart rate
Triazolopyridine	trazodone	Desyrel	
Selective Serotonin Reuptake Inhibitors (SSRIs)	bupropion citalopram fluoxetine fluvoxamine paroxetine sertraline	Wellbutrin Celexa Prozac Luvox Paxil Zoloft	• Anxiety and restlessness • Constipation • Dry mouth • Headache • Nausea and vomiting • Sedation
Serotonin/ Norepinephrine Reuptake Inhibitors (SNRIs)	venlafaxine	Effexor	• Shares many of the side effects of the SSRIs.

(*continued*)

| TABLE 5.1 | CONTINUED | | |

Class	Generic Name	Trade Name	Common Side Effects
Monoamine oxidase inhibitors (MAOIs)	deprenyl phenylzine tranylcypromine	Eldepryl Nardil Parnate	• Constipation • Dizziness • Dry mouth • Hypotension • Insomnia • Nausea • Sexual difficulties • Skin reaction • Weakness • Weight gain
Others—Mood stabilizers	lithium	Lithium carbonate Lithonate Eskalith Lithobid Lithane Lithium citrate Cibalith-S	• Weight gain • Nausea • Diarrhea • Hand tremor • Muscle weakness • Dulling and memory difficulties • Drowsiness • Increased thirst or increased urination
Anticonvulsants	carbamazepine valproate	Tegretol Depakote	• For those not responding to lithium—gastrointestinal symptoms
Stimulants	methylphenidate dextroamphetamine	Ritalin Dexedrine	• Most commonly used along with other antidepressants

symptoms, and we do not know why this happens (Nemeroff & Owens, 2002). The second problem area revolves around tolerability. Each medication has side effects. The third area for improvement is the slow response to treatment. Often a person needs to take a medication for several weeks before knowing if it will work for them. Also, once an effective dose has been determined, the length of time required for a person to take medication varies; some people may need to take medication all of their lives, while others may need to take medication for several months. Unfortunately, some people stop taking medication as soon as they feel better, causing symptoms to return. Others stop because they do not like the side effects.

It is important for the practitioner to educate individuals about the known risks of medication and the consequences of discontinuing treatment prematurely. Decisions about who is a good candidate for pharmacotherapy should be made on a case-by-case basis (Hadjipavlou, Hiram, & Yatham, 2004). Unfortunately some individuals perceive biological therapy as a sign that they are not working hard enough to get better or have some kind of character defect. It is helpful for the practitioner to explore these assumptions and the related stigma associated with the mood disorders.

Natural or Herbal Treatments

Complementary or alternative treatments have become increasingly popular in recent years. There is growing interest in the antidepressant properties of Omega-3, SAM-e, the natural herb St. John's wort (hypericum), and others. Available primarily in health food stores, these preparations have few side effects. Some herbal treatments like St. John's wort are equivalent to low doses of other antidepressants (APA, 2000). However, this herb may interfere with the beneficial effects of some medications. Different brands may have different concentrations of the active substance, so there is no guarantee that they may contain the appropriate ingredients. European studies have demonstrated the efficacy of St. John's wort (Linde et al., 1996), but North American studies showed the compound to be no more effective than a placebo in major depressive disorder (Shelton et al., 2001).

Electroconvulsive Therapy (ECT)

When medication and psychotherapy have not been helpful, electroconvulsive therapy (also known as shock therapy) or electroshock therapy (EST) may be considered. ECT generally works more rapidly than the currently available antidepressant medications. Unfortunately, this therapy has often been negatively portrayed in the media, making it seem painful or frightening. The popular movie "One Flew Over the Cuckoo's Nest" shows the protagonist, Jack Nicholson, being forced into a room, strapped to a table, and subjected to "shock therapy." In reality, ECT is a safe and effective treatment administered by a physician, most often a neurologist and psychiatrist. By inducing a controlled seizure, ECT creates a generalized brain activity that seems to produce a massive neurochemical release in the brain. The process consists of applying small amounts of electrical current to the brain and inducing convulsions that usually last for 20 to 90 seconds. Before beginning ECT, the individual is anesthetized and given muscle-relaxing medications to prevent bone breakage from the convulsions. Once treatment is completed, the person is awake within 5 to 10 minutes. The average length of treatment is 6 to 10 sessions every other day (or less if the person improves). ECT seems to relieve symptoms of depression within one to two weeks after beginning treatments. It is effective for the major depressive disorders and especially for persons who have medical complications, extreme exhaustion, or lethal catatonia, or who are unresponsive to antidepressant medications (Barker, 1996; De Murtas, Tatarelli, Girardi, & Vicini, 2004). Side effects are generally limited to short-term memory loss and confusion that disappears after a week or two. In some instances, a person may experience long-term memory problems.

Other Treatments

For seasonal affective disorder (SAD) and depressions associated with seasonal exacerbations and remissions, such as some forms of dysthymia, light therapy has been used to correct abnormal circadian stimuli (sleep-awake cycle) and associated neurotransmitter imbalance. Individuals using this treatment spend regular therapeutic sessions bathed in light from a full-spectrum light source. Some studies suggest that good results can be obtained regardless of the time of light exposure (Wirz-Justice et al., 1993), making light therapy flexible and practical for affected individuals. A light visor is another recent innovation increasing the convenience of this treatment, but its efficacy is unknown.

RISKS ASSOCIATED WITH THE MOOD DISORDERS

Delineating the risk factors associated with the mood disorders is a complex task. Along with genetic and biochemical vulnerability, research has shown that stressful life events and circumstances are also contributors (Dunner, 2003; Remick, 2002; Simon, 2003). However, the buffers and protective factors in a person's life can mediate reactions. In stressful situations, people use different coping strategies, some of which may reduce the risk of major depression. The following discussion should not be considered "the final word" on the risks associated with the mood disorders; instead, its purpose is to help the practitioner begin to appreciate the complex vulnerabilities associated with this diagnostic category. While each risk factor is discussed separately, in reality the mood disorders are associated with a combination of factors. Overall, the extent and severity of risk factors combined tend to increase a person's probability of having a mood disorder.

Intrapersonal Risks

Age is a risk factor associated with the mood disorders, as the incidence of these disorders is especially high among older people (Barnow & Linden, 2000; Blazer, 2003). Masand and Gupta (2003) note that age-related deterioration of cortical areas and neurochemical changes, social isolation, and sensory deficits place older people at increased risk for developing depression. In addition, the mood disorders are likely to be underdiagnosed in this population; for example, elderly suicide attempters with depression are often diagnosed only after the attempt (Suominen, Isometsa, & Lonnqvist, 2004). Older persons commonly seek help from the family physician for symptoms of depression such as unexplained fatigue or weight loss. Further contributing to problems with adequate diagnosis, physicians fail to diagnose depression in about half of all depressed elderly individuals. The risk for depression should be considered for older people who have vague somatic symptoms or overlapping symptoms of medical illness, frequently use health care services, and have persistent but unexplained pain, headache, fatigue, insomnia, loss of appetite, or gastrointestinal symptoms (Charney, Reynolds, Lewis, et al., 2003).

The risk for depression increases for hospitalized elderly persons with myocardial infarction, congestive heart failure, stroke, hip fracture, cancer, or alcohol abuse who have a delayed recovery, do not comply with rehabilitation programs or refuse treatment entirely (Bush et al., 2001; Musselman, Evans, & Nemeroff, 1998). In long-term care settings, risk for depression may be found in persons who are apathetic, withdrawn, or agitated or who show increased dependency, functional decline, or delayed rehabilitation.

Gender also plays a role. Women are at least twice as likely to experience a depressive episode within a lifetime as men (Blazer, Kessler, McGonagle, & Swartz, 1994; Remick, 2002). Childbirth, menopause, and hormonal factors seem to be the major precipitants. Archie Bunker, the main character known for his sarcastic wit in the television sitcom "All in the Family," once referred to menopause as "mental pause." At this stage of life a woman's body begins to change, and some women do not like what they see; for example, they may have a bigger belly, wrinkles, or gray hair (Brink, 2002). Aside from falling short of our cultural standards for youth and beauty there is nothing inherently wrong with these changes; however, the associated hormonal factors can play a significant role in triggering depression.

The children of women who are depressed also seem to be affected. There is increasing evidence that these youngsters have increased problems in school and with behavior, and have lower levels of social competence and self-esteem than their classmates whose mothers do not have depression (Goodman & Gotlib, 1999).

Depression tends to co-occur for those with limited functional status and with chronic general medical conditions such as cancer, heart disease, or HIV/AIDS. Depression is thought to result from disruption of a person's normal brain chemistry, and the current thinking on the development of depressive disorders suggests that stress-induced vulnerability in genetically susceptible people may induce a cascade of responses in the brain (Remick, 2002). Abnormalities in the functioning of the brain's central serotonergic system are found to be involved in the pathogenesis of depressive illness and suicidal behavior (Du, Faludi, Palkovits, Bakish, & Hrdina, 2001).

The personal quality of perfectionism may also be a risk factor for depression (Blatt, 1995; Ferguson & Rodway, 1994; Hewitt & Flett, 1993). People who value achievement and strive to meet perfectionistic standards may perceive the experience of failure as being more devastating than it is for those with less exacting personal standards. This keen sense of defeat increases a person's stress and vulnerability. Perfectionism has also been linked to suicide (Blatt, 1995). Another personality quality associated with depression is cognitive style. Beevers et al. (2003) studied the extent of cognitive changes during depression and found that those individuals with dysfunctional attitudes or thought content and extreme thinking experienced a recurrence of depressive symptoms, even after treatment.

Interpersonal Risks

Mood disorders seem to have a strong genetic component (Todd, 2003; Todd & Botteron, 2001, 2002). In particular, children of depressed parents are at an increased risk (Nunes et al., 1998; Weissman, Warner, Wickramaratne, Moreau,

& Olfson, 1997). Close relatives of individuals with mood disorders are also at a higher risk of developing either depression or manic depression than the general population (Malhi, Moore, & McGuffin, 2000; Potash & De Paulo, 2000). The risk of a major depression increases 1.5 to 3.0 times if the diagnosis is present in a first-degree relative as compared with no such diagnosis in a first-degree relative (Bland, 1997).

The mood disorders also carry significant risk of death and disability. About 15 percent of persons with a mood disorder die by their own hand (Bostwick & Pankratz, 2000). Suicidal behavior seems to cluster in families, and studies show that half of those committing suicide have a diagnosis of depression (McGuffin, Marusic, & Farmer, 2001). The presence of depression is considered to be a long-term risk; that is, 70 percent of persons with depression can experience a recurrence during their lifetime (Murphy et al., 2000; Remick, 2002). The correlates of depression, such as social isolation, may be seen as risk factors as well as consequences of depression (Charney et al., 2003).

Stress plays an important role in depression (Remick, 2002) and stressful influences such as negative family relationships, serious illness, death of a loved one or some other major loss or change, and substance abuse can increase a person's risk (Charney, 2003). As well, those who have poor social support, have experienced a hospitalization over the past year, and have diminished visual acuity are at a higher risk for depressive symptoms (Miller et al., 2004). Marital status is another risk factor linked to depression. Individuals who are divorced, separated, or widowed are at a higher risk for depression than their married counterparts (Badger & Rand, 1998; Blazer et al., 1994). However, Callahan and Turnbull (2001) observe that depression is also correlated with unhappy marriages and marital distress, especially among women.

Stressful events in childhood are also seen as predisposing factors for major depression in adulthood (Callahan & Turnbull, 2001). Read et al. (2001) found that a history of childhood trauma, particularly sexual and physical abuse, was a risk factor for depression and suicide in adults. However, the vulnerability to adult onset of depression is seen more as a downward spiral of negative circumstances beginning in childhood. Callahan and Turnbull (2001) offer the example of a child who loses his or her mother. This loss may place the youngster at increased risk for neglect or impaired personality development that may potentially result in inadequate coping mechanisms and difficulty forming relationships. These factors combine to challenge the person's ability to respond to the losses and stresses found in adult life.

Community and Environmental Risks

Cultural beliefs can contribute to the risks associated with the mood disorders. We live in a culture that prizes strength in men, and they are socialized early on to believe there is little to be gained in exhibiting feelings. Our society perceives the mood disorders as a sign of psychic weakness, and this increases the difficulty of detecting (and treating) depression in men (Kluger, 2003).

For the population at large, environmental factors such as discrimination, lower levels of education, or poverty can also trigger depression (Callahan & Turnbull, 2001; Scarinci, Beech, Naumann et al., 2002; West, Reed, & Gildengorin, 1998). Unfortunately, there are striking differences in the quality of mental health care available to various groups of people in the United States. Ethnic minority groups tend to bear a heavier burden from unmet mental health needs and thus suffer a greater loss to their overall health and productivity. While racial and cultural minority groups tend to have lower rates of depression than the dominant American majority, members of some ethnic groups are more likely to experience certain stressful life events that correlate with a higher risk for depression, such as the ecological conditions of poverty and discrimination confronting many African Americans (Stevenson, Reed, Bodison, & Bishop, 1997). Kaslow et al. (2002) studied suicide in low-income African American women and identified high levels of emotional distress and depression, a sense of hopelessness about the future, and alcohol and drug problems as risk factors associated with suicide attempts.

Case Illustration: Anita Richards

People who struggle with major depression have a constant risk of recurrence over their life spans up to the age of 70 or more (Angst, Gamma, Sellaro, Lavori, & Heping, 2003). Ramana et al. (1995) conducted a two-year follow-up study on the course of depression and found that up to 40 percent of persons relapsed within the first 10 months after recovery from a depressive episode. Dysfunctional attitudes and social and interpersonal difficulties seem to challenge a person's recovery (Rafanelli, Park, & Fava, 1999). The case of Anita Richards, first described in Psychopathology: A Competency-Based Assessment Model for Social Workers *by Zide and Gray (2001), illustrates these challenges. Anita was admitted to the hospital psychiatric unit after being brought in by the Mobile Crisis Unit who responded to her suicide threat made over the telephone. She had attempted to slash her wrists with a razor blade.*

The psychosocial history reveals that Anita is a 38-year-old Hispanic divorced mother with four children aged 15, 12, 11, and 9. According to her medical records she was treated for "major depressive disorder, recurrent." She had been fired about six months previously for showing up late for work and had been unable to find work since that time. Because of her financial difficulties, Anita's children were in the custody of relatives. The oldest two lived with their father in another state, and her younger two lived with Anita's mother. Ms. Richards expressed a desire "to get them back as soon as I can." Her relationship with her mother was seen as hostile and unsupportive. Little was known about her husband. She had recently broken up with her boyfriend, apparently due to sexual difficulties. In addition to diminished libido, Ms. Richards reported difficulties eating and sleeping. She summed up her life by

> *saying, "It's all hopeless. I have nothing going for me. I'm a real loser."*
> *She also reported difficulty concentrating and no interest in formerly*
> *pleasurable activities like watching television. Her medical history was*
> *unremarkable, and she denied experiencing manic or psychotic behavior.*
>
> *Anita attributed her prior hospitalization to "crying jags" that she*
> *could not seem to stop. She had been prescribed antidepressant medication*
> *but had stopped taking it because of the side effects of weight gain and*
> *constipation. She had a history of incarceration for selling drugs (cocaine)*
> *but denied drug and alcohol use. The prior social worker noted the need to*
> *further explore the potential for substance abuse.*

This is Anita's fifth admission over a three-year span for major depressive episode. Once at the hospital, Anita was given a physical exam, her vital signs were recorded and the required admissions forms were completed. The intake worker, noting her severely depressed state, commented, "Of course you're depressed, honey. Who wouldn't be what with all those things going on in your life right now?" Once in her room, Anita tried to sleep. She wondered what her hospitalization would be like this time.

The practitioner had just graduated with her master's degree and this was her first job. She was feeling a little nervous but confident that she was well trained and up to the professional challenges ahead. After a week of orientation learning about policies, hospital forms, and fire drill procedures, she was really looking forward to seeing her own clients. She was finally on the hospital's psychiatric unit and on her way down the hall to see her client, Anita Richards. A tech in the nurses' station called her over and said, "Oh, you must be the new one around here. I see you're assigned to the Richards case. Well, everybody has to get initiated some time or another, but that one's a doozey! She's a 'repeater.' You know, in and out of the hospital. Folks like that give us the reputation of being a revolving door. Ha! We'll always have a job. Good luck with that case, sweetheart, and don't worry if you make a mistake. She'll be back again soon and you'll have another chance to get it right." The practitioner tells herself that she really ought to say something to the tech about that "attitude," but being new and so nervous she just takes a deep breath and continues walking toward Anita Richards's room. She wonders if all the staff members in the psychiatric unit are so pessimistic.

Entering Anita Richards's room, the practitioner finds her lying in bed facing the wall. The room is dark and Anita is so still it seems that she might be sleeping. She looks so small and somehow desolate. The practitioner finds it hard to believe that this rumpled lump of clothes and blankets is someone with a jail record for selling crack cocaine. She gently calls Anita's name. Anita rolls over and stares straight ahead, avoiding eye contact. She looks tired, and there is an unmistakable sadness in her eyes. The practitioner introduces herself. Anita's gaze shifts to the practitioner, who sits down in a chair next to the bed. Anita begins the conversation by acknowledging how desperate she is to snap out of her "crying jags."

> ANITA: *I'm really tired of feeling like this. I just don't get it. I know I should*
> *have kept taking those damn pills, but I started gaining weight again. So I*
> *stopped . . . but just for a little while, and started them again, but I hated it so*

I quit again. I know when I was here last time they tried to adjust my meds, but no luck. It was just the same all over again. These new and improved pills just made me feel dizzy, and I can hardly sleep through the night. Oh God! Will it ever stop?

WORKER: *You sound really discouraged. Have you ever felt like this before?*

ANITA: *Well, I felt bad the last time I was here, but I can't remember feeling this bad. You know, the last time I was tired of fighting life. This time I just feel numb. I feel like I'm already dead and somebody should just put me out of my misery. Guess I really freaked out the Mobile Crisis folks this time. Next thing you know, the police were at my door and I was on my way back in here.*

WORKER: *What is it like to have this dead feeling?*

ANITA: *Well, it's hard to put into words. I just feel like I'm on empty all the time. I have no drive, no energy, no nothing. Just to get up is a struggle. I can't focus on anything. I feel so tired but I can't sleep. Believe it or not, I was really pretty good on the job. Waitressing is not rocket science, you know? But I was really good with the customers. If I served somebody the wrong drink I'd feel so guilty that I had to make it up to them and right away. My customers just loved the attention. Then I started to show up late a coupla times and, well, the rest is history. Next thing you know I'm fired. I used to love work, but right now even that seems like too much. I guess I'm just damaged goods. Who would want to hire a 'sicko' anyway?*

WORKER: *Your cynicism makes me wonder if you aren't covering up a lot of pain.*

ANITA: *So how would you feel?*

WORKER: *I'd certainly feel empty and scared, too.*

ANITA: *Well, that's how I've been feeling for a long time, but now it's even worse. Just put me out of my misery and leave me alone with my antidepressants.*

WORKER: *You want to kill yourself?*

ANITA: *Can you think of why I might want to live?*

WORKER: *How about your kids?*

ANITA: *They don't know me like this. They think I'm just down on my luck a little and they'll be coming back as soon as I get back on my feet in the money department. They know me as somebody who's pretty together.*

WORKER: *You think that's all they care about, the money? You don't sound like you're thinking much of yourself right now.*

ANITA: *Who would love me this way? Even my jerk of a boyfriend had the good sense to leave me. All I do is sit around and cry. I really feel rotten. I hate myself. Hell! I don't deserve to live.*

WORKER: *I know we just met, but it seems to me there's a lot more to you. We've only been talking about the part of you that brought you in here, but you have a whole character. There are other parts of you . . . your mind, your spirit, your personality.*

ANITA: *(Silence)*

WORKER: *(After respecting her need to be quiet.) What's going on inside you right now?*

ANITA: *(Her eyes begin to fill up with tears.) I'm just letting what you just said sink in. Nobody ever talked to me like that before. I feel so down right now, but I need to know that this is not what I'm all about. What you just said, I never thought about my life like that before. I really want to find me again.*

WORKER: *I know this is hard. I just want you to tell me that you won't give up on yourself without a fight.*

ANITA: *Well, people always did say I was persistent, and I'm not afraid of hard work. I figure I'll have to take responsibility for me. I guess I'll need to stay here a while to try out this new attitude.*

During the course of Anita's hospitalization, her medication was readjusted and she participated fully in the inpatient therapy programs. She continued to see the practitioner individually, and their work emphasized coping strategies such as learning more about her depression and medication with its attendant side effects. The practitioner encouraged Anita to take an assertive role in her treatment. They talked about the meaning of her medication, and the practitioner worked with Anita's physician around adjustment. She also taught Anita how to approach the physician about her medication. Together they brainstormed ways Anita could maintain a healthy lifestyle. This included avoiding alcohol and drugs, engaging in satisfying activities, taking medication, and participating in follow-up counseling. Specific suggestions for preventing relapse were explored, such as how Anita could monitor her symptoms, identify personal warning signs of decompensation (for example, sleep difficulties), and cope with stress. While she was in the hospital, Anita began charting her moods and made a list of lifestyle changes (for example, improving her diet, getting more exercise, and engaging in pleasurable activities). Armed with this knowledge Anita recognized that her recovery process would be fraught with challenges. The practitioner explored community resources designed to buffer these challenges and offered suggestions such as the telephone hotline called Hopeline or 1-800-SUICIDE (1-800-784-2433). Once home, Anita wrote a letter to the practitioner. An excerpt follows:

Working with you helped me to make sense of my terrifying fear and hopeless despair. I want to thank you for your professionalism, availability, and your patience with me. You were the first one who affirmed my strengths and challenged me to give up that side of myself that was so depressed. For the first time I believe, or better yet I have learned to believe, that I might someday be able to contend with all of this. Some days are really hard and others not so bad. On the bad days I remember what you said. I'll go for a walk or when it's really tough I'll call one of the kids. With each passing day I get a little stronger and that gives me more hope.

OPERATIONALIZING COMPETENCY-BASED TREATMENT

The challenge of working with someone who has as many problems as Anita Richards is not a new one for social workers. The practitioner in this vignette was new to the job, a little nervous about being assigned to Anita, and really did not

TABLE 5.2	THE RISKS, PROTECTIVE FACTORS, AND BUFFERS IN ANITA RICHARDS'S LIFE	
	Risk Factors	**Protective Factors and Buffers**
Intrapersonal	• Sees herself as a failure • Several hospitalizations for major depression • Side effects from antidepressants • Noncompliant with her medication • Suicidal	• Called Mobile Crisis Unit • Persistent • Works hard • Creative (sells drugs "to make a living") • Willing to learn about her depression and medication • Believes she can get better • Willing to take responsibility for her treatment
Interpersonal	• Recently lost her job (6 months ago) • Sells drugs to make a living • Divorced • Boyfriend recently broke up with her • Relatives have custody of her children	• Loves her children • Worked for five years • Good relationship with her customers (waitressing) • Develops a relationship with the social worker • Copes with stress by reaching out for help • Plans to change her lifestyle
Social and Environmental	• Single parent • Financial problems • Prior hospitalizations for depression • Incarcerated • Previously stopped treatment	• Emergency services (Mobile Crisis Unit) accessible & available • Psychiatric hospital services available

know what exactly had happened to contribute to the client's relapse and return to the hospital. All too often, clients have no choice in the selection of the nature and quality of the professional services they receive. "Although this may appear to be stating the obvious, the lack of such positive contacts in their histories as clients underscores the gap between social work theory and actual practice" (Ribner & Knei-Paz, 2002, p. 386). Table 5.2 summarizes the risks, protective factors, and buffers in Anita Richards's life.

Working with Anita Richards Individually

The therapeutic alliance seems more important than any specific intervention strategy in determining outcomes of treatment for depression (Krupnick, 1996). The nature of the relationship with the practitioner seemed to make a critical difference in the work with Anita Richards. Gagne (1999) conducted extensive interviews with persons diagnosed with mental illness and asked them about their struggles. They identified a loss of self and hope; loss of connection; loss of roles and opportunities; multiple and recurring traumas; devaluing and disempowering programs, practices, and environments; and stigma and discrimination from others. Their barriers to recovery were identified as persistent symptoms, lack of access to helpful treatment, devaluing experiences, feelings of hopelessness and powerlessness, low expectations of others, lack of opportunity for valued roles, lack of connection to others, stigma and shame, and financial insecurity. These variables aptly apply to Anita Richards. Important aspects of her recovery included a sense of hope and connections with others. The practitioner approached Anita's discussion of suicide with a sense of hopefulness when she reached into Anita's profound feelings of loss and helped her to explore reasons for living. Careful not to talk her out of her feelings or to rationalize them, the practitioner simply asked, "How about your kids?" A sense of hope may be the most vital factor in recovery, but unfortunately many people encounter a mental health system that instead instills a sense of hopelessness (Marsh, 2000). The staff member's unsolicited comments to the practitioner about Anita being "another one of those repeaters" certainly conveyed a sense of pessimism about Anita's potential for recovery.

The personal accounts of those who have been diagnosed with mental illness offer unique insights for practitioners and suggest implications for effective treatment. The social stigma associated with having a mental illness exerts a powerful influence on one's sense of self and identity. Anita's depression created profound changes in her thinking, feelings, and behavior. The chronic course of her depression was only emphasized, and the responses of others in her life reinforced her sense of being a failure: her boyfriend left, she was fired from her job, and relatives took over the care of her children. Her feelings of hopelessness seemed compounded by her recognition that she once again felt suicidal and had to be readmitted to the hospital. Further, the social consequences of her re-hospitalization had an impact. Bassman (2000), who was once diagnosed with a mental illness, describes a similar ordeal: "Once hospitalized you are marked with a diagnosis and that label becomes an indelible tattoo burned into your sense of self. You may successfully hide your experiences from others, but you will always have to deal with that shadow" (p. 1402). Observe Young and Ensing (1999), "One's sense of self becomes altered, damaged, or even destroyed as a result of mental illness" (p. 220). While Anita's diagnosis of major depression seemed to have taken over all aspects of her life, however, she continued to be a unique person who was not fully defined by her diagnosis. Unfortunately Anita felt like a failure—in her words, "damaged goods" and a "sicko"—when she came to the practitioner's attention on her hospital re-admission. The practitioner did not react to her cynicism but remained objective and invited a conversation about Anita's underlying pain. The transcript illustrates the practitioner's focus on the uniqueness of Anita's character beyond her depression by asking about her "spirit" and personality. Lynch (2000) notes, "In my journey toward health, the most helpful experiences were with professionals who saw me as a person first, who adapted their treatment according to my need" (p. 1431). Lynch goes on to define the qualities of a helpful practitioner. They include flexibility, patience, and availability; being someone who affirms strengths and conveys acceptance, dignity, respect, and hope. Similarly, Ribner and Knei-Paz (2002) asked clients from multiproblem families to describe a successful helping relationship. They identified factors that provided a sense of equality such as love, friendship, and a non-judgmental stance. Helpful practitioners were described as flexible and willing to go the extra distance. Bassman eloquently summarizes these professional attributes as human contact that "can penetrate the despair and hopelessness" (p. 1404). The practitioner reflected the core conditions required for an effective relationship with Anita: genuineness, caring, acceptance, and empathy (Hepworth, Roney, & Larsen, 2002).

Working with the Family

Anita seems to be one of those clients who can easily fall through the cracks of the service delivery system. Remick (2002) observes that it is not unusual for clients to minimize or exaggerate their symptoms of depression, making it hard for the practitioner to obtain a clear picture of the extent of their condition. Many times a client is seen by those who do not know them well, and this points to the importance of consulting with family members. Anita seemed to have a strained relationship with her mother despite the fact that she was caring for Anita's two younger children. Unfortunately, Anita had recently broken up with her boyfriend, and there seemed to be no one close to her who could help the practitioner to make an accurate assessment.

Another problem was the attitudes of hospital staff. When Anita was readmitted, the intake worker seemed rather quick to minimize and explain away Anita's symptoms by saying, "Of course you're depressed, honey. Who wouldn't be what with all that's going on in your life right now?" These challenges, coupled with the stigma associated with depression (Sirey et al., 2001), seemed to make it all the more difficult for Anita to get the help she needed. Fortunately, as shown in this vignette, the practitioner took Anita's thoughts of suicide seriously and broached the topic with compassion and a nonjudgmental attitude.

Working with the Community

According to the United States Department of Health and Human Services (2003), about 30,000 people kill themselves per year. In addition, between 300,000 and 600,000 people annually survive a suicide attempt and about 19,000 of those survivors are permanently disabled because of the effects of the attempted suicide (Stone, 1999; United States Department of Health and Human Services, 2003). Recurrent depression and severity of depression are associated with serious suicidality (Goldney, 2003; Joiner, Pettit, & Rudd, 2004) and persons like Anita with major depressive disorder, recurrent episodes, are at a significant risk for suicide. Looking at Anita's psychiatric history, she showed many of the significant predictors of suicide such as previous psychiatric hospitalization, previous suicide attempts, and previous pharmacotherapy, in addition to being unemployed (Brown et al., 2000). Research has shown that persons whose feelings of hopelessness do not significantly change with treatment are more likely to commit suicide (Ivanoff & Fisher, 2001). In this vignette, Anita planned to use her hospitalization to "stay here a while to try out this new attitude."

Notwithstanding the high prevalence of depression, only one-third of persons struggling with depression receive adequate help (Judd et al., 1996; Manji, Moore, Rajkowska, & Chen, 2000). Despite our understanding of the specific psychological variables that could be modified by clinical intervention, the most frequent error seems to be not asking enough questions about a person's symptoms (Remick, 2002). What can be done? Joiner, Pettit, and Rudd (2004) recommend ongoing and objective assessment of symptoms and regular monitoring of suicide risk level. Remission with symptom resolution should be the therapeutic goal, along with a more holistic approach to treat the full range of clinical symptoms that contribute to the burden of those struggling with major depression (Joffe, 2003). Competency-based treatment provides a multi-dimensional framework to operationalize this holistic approach by systematically looking at the entire person and his or her multiple connections to others in addition to the diagnosis of depression.

SUMMARY

The mood disorders fall into two categories: unipolar and bipolar disorders. The unipolar disorder, depression, ranges from mild (diagnosed as *dysthymia*) to severe (diagnosed as *major depression*). Unlike the normal shifts in mood that most people experience, the symptoms of depression are more extreme and frequently incapacitating. Bipolar disorder is characterized by dramatic shifts between mania and depression. *Bipolar I* disorder refers to severe manic symptoms accompanied by one or more periods of major depression. *Bipolar II* has the same pattern, but the symptoms are less severe. *Cyclothymic* disorder refers to a chronic or cyclic mood disturbance. The symptoms of each disorder were outlined along with the risks associated with the mood disorders.

In sum, individuals who suffer from the mood disorders will more than likely display one or more of the following symptoms:

- Feelings of worthlessness, hopelessness, helplessness, total indifference, and/or extreme (or inappropriate) guilt;
- Prolonged sadness;
- Unexplained crying spells;
- Jumpiness, irritability, or agitation;
- Loss of interest or pleasure in activities formerly enjoyed (or relationships);
- Difficulty concentrating or remembering details;
- Significant change in appetite or body weight;
- Difficulty in falling asleep, or oversleeping;
- Physical ailments that cannot be explained;
- Recurrent thoughts of death (or suicide attempts).

Individuals who suffer from manic-depressive disorder will show one or more of the following symptoms during the manic phase:

- Excessively euphoric or expansive mood;
- Irritability and anger that is inconsistent with the situation;

- Hyperactivity;
- Grandiose ideas or delusions;
- Extreme optimism;
- Lack of good judgment;
- Flight of ideas (or racing thoughts);
- Increased talkativeness;
- Disorganized, racing thoughts;
- Decreased need for sleep;
- Physical agitation, sudden rage, irritability, or paranoia;
- Excessive involvement in activities that have a high potential for risky consequences.

Treatments including the major biological therapies, electroconvulsive treatment, herbal remedies, and light therapy were described. Suicide is often associated with the mood disorders, and the case of Anita Richards emphasizes this risk. The complications she experienced centered on employment problems and stressful relationships with her family. Despite these adverse life events, the case illustrates competency-based practice by highlighting the importance of the relationship between the practitioner and Anita.

Practitioner Reflections

1. Imagine for a moment that you met a colleague who had graduated from your social work program. You decided to have lunch together and catch up on old times. Your colleague is working in a community mental health center. You notice that this colleague refers to the persons he or she works with as "sickos," "those hopeless depressives," "nut cases," and other derogatory terms. What would you do? Identify some of the possible reasons someone might behave this way.
2. Further imagine that this colleague has what would normally be considered too much to drink over lunch. What would you do? Is there a provision in the National Association of Social Work Code of Ethics to guide your response?
3. Marilyn Monroe, a popular movie star, struggled with depression and committed suicide at the age of 36. Read her biography and identify the risks, protective factors, and buffers in Marilyn's life. Imagine that you are her social worker and have been asked to intervene shortly before her death. What would you do? Be sure to reflect on the strengths and buffers in her life as you develop your "competency-based treatment plan." Following are some suggested biographies:
   - Hyatt, K. (1996). *Marilyn: Story of a woman.* New York: Seven Stories Press.
   - Guiles, F. L. (1992). *Legend: The life and death of Marilyn Monroe.* Lanham, MD: Scarborough House.

4. Most people, at some time in their lives, will experience the grief that accompanies a tragedy and bereavement. How would your interventions differ if you were helping someone with a major depression versus a "normal" reaction?

5. Imagine that a current client on your caseload has committed suicide. What would you do?
   - Does your agency have any policies and procedures in place for clients who may be actively suicidal?
   - As an alternative, imagine that your colleague in the office next to you had a client who committed suicide. You've been working together for about three years and know each other pretty well professionally. Since the incident, your colleague does not seem the same; that is, she (or he) is increasingly withdrawn, sometimes comes in late for work (or leaves early), does not participate actively in staff meetings anymore, does not seem to care about the clients, and so on. What would you do?

6. Anita Richards, illustrated in this chapter, has many of the risk factors associated with suicide. On an intrapersonal or personal level she has a sense of hopelessness and defeat, has previously attempted suicide, and abuses substances. Interpersonally her boyfriend just left, relatives have custody of her children, the relationship with her mother seems strained, and she seems isolated, alone, and lacking in social support. From the environmental perspective, she was jailed overnight for selling cocaine and recently fired from her job.
   - What programs are available in your practice community that could help someone like Anita Richards?
   - Identify potential barriers or obstacles a client like Anita Richards would encounter in seeking help.
   - Are additional services needed?
   - Since most clients do not seek help for suicidal ideation, what outreach services are in place (or what might be needed) in your community?

ANXIETY DISORDERS

Although almost ten years have passed, I still remember those butterflies in the pit of my stomach as if it were just yesterday. My heart was pounding, and I swear I could actually hear it thumping in my chest. My hands were sweating and I just couldn't seem to sit still. My head was spinning and I had to struggle just to concentrate. Strangely, no one around me seemed to notice. I tried really hard to stay calm and breathe evenly so I wouldn't faint dead away. At the same time I tried to mentally re-create the peace and serenity I felt while sitting on the beach and looking at the ocean. My breakfast of toast and eggs felt like a lump in my stomach, and I was starting to feel nauseated. I wondered if this was what it felt like to go crazy. Gosh! I was so threatened by that licensure exam! I had to pass or else! It would have been so embarrassing to tell everybody that I had failed and would have to retake the test. I kept telling myself that I was prepared for the exam and had studied hard. I had always been a good student and had taken a lot of exams during my school years. I had faced challenges before in my life and successfully mastered them. Why was I so anxious about taking this test?

Everyone has experienced anxiety at one time or another. It is as much a part of life as eating and sleeping. In fact, some anxiety is considered normal and even adaptive. Under the right circumstances, anxiety can even be useful as it heightens alertness and readies the body for action. When we are faced with an unfamiliar challenge, anxiety often spurs us to prepare for the upcoming event. In the above vignette, the anxiety associated with taking the exam became an early warning system that served as an alert to take anticipatory action by studying hard. Beyond a certain point, however, anxiety can cause problems. For example, anxiety about taking an exam may become so intense that a person cannot concentrate on the questions and ends up failing the test.

As noted by Zide and Gray (2001), anxiety is a normal reaction to anything that is perceived as a threat to a person's lifestyle, values, self, or loved ones. Anxiety can appear when things go wrong and also when good things happen or there are changes in one's life. Waiting for important news or living in a situation that is unpredictable and uncontrollable generates a feeling of anxiety, which can also be described as a general state of apprehension and psychological tension.

The term *anxiety* is often used casually in conversation; for example, you may be waiting for a bus and tell someone that you feel "anxious" about the possibility of being late for an important meeting. The concept of fear might be used to describe the same thing; that is, you may say you are "afraid" that you will be late for that important meeting.

Fear is an immediate alarm reaction to danger in which a person feels mental tension because of a specific, external reason. Anyone in a dangerous and unfamiliar situation feels fear. In the short run, this emotion is adaptive because it energizes one to cope with danger. Fears are abnormal when they become overwhelming and interfere with a person's daily life.

Anxiety disorders differ from normal states of anxiety in that the apprehension is out of proportion to the situation and unduly prolonged. In relation to the anxiety disorders, the word *anxiety* refers to an unpleasant and overriding mental tension that has no apparent or identifiable cause. It is a mood state in which the person anticipates future danger or misfortune with apprehension. In this context, anxiety is characterized by marked negative affect, apprehension about the future, and bodily symptoms of tension.

As a group, the anxiety disorders affect almost 9 percent of Americans during any six-month period and are considered to be the most common and most successfully treated types of mental illness (APA, 2000). However, symptoms associated with anxiety disorders can become so severe that some people are almost totally disabled; for example, they may be too terrified to leave their home.

Anxiety disorders include panic attack, agoraphobia, panic disorder without agoraphobia, panic disorder with agoraphobia, agoraphobia without history of panic disorder, specific phobia, social phobia (or social anxiety disorder), obsessive-compulsive disorder, post-traumatic stress disorder, acute stress disorder, generalized anxiety disorder, anxiety disorder due to a general medical condition, substance-induced anxiety disorder, and anxiety disorder not otherwise specified (APA, 2000). Note that panic attack (PA) and agoraphobia are not codable or diagnosable disorders in the DSM (APA, 2000). The conditions reviewed in this chapter are characterized by anxiety and behavior calculated to ward it off. Attention will be focused primarily on those anxiety disorders social workers are most likely to encounter in practice: agoraphobia, panic disorder with and without agoraphobia, specific and social phobias, obsessive-compulsive disorder, post-traumatic stress disorder (PTSD), and generalized anxiety disorder (GAD).

UNDERSTANDING ANXIETY DISORDERS

Agoraphobia

The most disabling fear disorder is agoraphobia. Zide and Gray (2001) explain that the term *agoraphobia* is taken from the Greek language and literally means "fear of the marketplace." In ancient Greece, the *agora* was the public meeting place in the center of town where people conducted their social, political, business, and religious activities. Interestingly, one of the most stressful places for persons struggling with agoraphobia in today's world is the shopping mall, the contemporary version of the *agora*. Although agoraphobic behavior is initially linked to occasions of panic, it can become relatively independent of panic attacks. Anxiety seems to diminish for persons who think they are in a "safe" place. People often restrict themselves to a safety zone that may include their home or immediate neighborhood, and any movement beyond this zone creates mounting anxiety. The agoraphobic avoidance is determined by the extent to which people expect they might have another panic attack rather than by how many attacks they have actually had. However, most people with agoraphobia continue to have panic attacks at least a few times a month.

Agoraphobia usually begins with a panic attack that seems to occur for no apparent reason (McNally, 2003). People who are having a panic attack may think they are dying or otherwise losing control. The attack is so frightening that they begin to avoid situations that they think may provoke another one. Since the panic attacks occur without warning, the person takes elaborate precautions to be in a safe place and agoraphobia develops. Because the person exerts so much effort to avoid a panic attack, agoraphobia can be considered a "fear of fear" rather than a fear of places. The fundamental fears of agoraphobia typically involve characteristic clusters of situations that include being outside the home alone; in a crowd or standing in a line; on a bridge; or traveling in a bus, train, plane, or car where escaping might be difficult or help might be unavailable if the person has a panic attack. Individuals may report a specific fear, such as being in a crowded movie theater, driving in tunnels, or going to parties, but the underlying fear is being away from a safe place, usually home (or a familiar person). In severe cases, the person is totally unable to leave the house. The prospect of simply walking outside may fill them with debilitating fear, and this condition may last for years. Some individuals may rely heavily on other family members to do the shopping or run errands as well as accompany them outside the safety zone.

Some people experience anxiety and panic without developing agoraphobia. Although they may experience a significant change in behavior related to their panic attacks, they do not develop anxiety about being in places or situations where escape might be difficult or embarrassing. Similarly, some people develop agoraphobia without a history of panic disorder.

The criteria for panic disorder with agoraphobia are listed below (APA, 2000; Zide & Gray, 2001):

- The person experiences recurrent and unexpected panic attacks;
- At least one of the attacks has been followed by one month (or more) of the following:
   (a) Persistent concern about having additional panic attacks;
   (b) Worry about the consequences of the attack (for example, feeling that they are having a heart attack or "going crazy");
   (c) A significant change in behavior related to the panic attacks.

Craske (1999), Dattilio and Salas-Auvert (2000), and Zuercher-White (1999) caution that while the anxiety disorders are a leading mental health problem, the prognosis for persons struggling with panic disorder with agoraphobia is guarded. Fewer than half of these individuals become symptom-free. They caution the practitioner to set treatment goals aimed at helping the person to achieve a "relative" improvement in anxiety levels rather than striving for a "cure."

Agoraphobia without a history of panic disorder, by far the least common type of agoraphobia (APA, 2000), is present when

- There is an absence of a history of recurrent unexpected panic attacks;
- The avoidance behavior results from fear of incapacitation or humiliation due to sudden panic-like symptoms rather than from fear of a full panic attack. Other reasons for avoidance must also be distinguished from other physiological factors (for example, drug abuse or a medication or a general medical condition); and
- The anxiety (or phobic avoidance) is not explained by another mental disorder (such as social phobia, specific phobia, obsessive-compulsive disorder, posttraumatic stress disorder or separation anxiety).

Agoraphobia without a history of panic disorder is considered when:

- The presence of agoraphobia is related to fear of developing panic-like symptoms (such as dizziness);
- Criteria have not been met for panic disorder;
- The disturbance is not due to the direct effects of a substance or a general medical condition;
- If a medical condition is present, the fear is clearly in excess of that usually associated with the condition.

Specific Phobia

The specific phobias, formerly known as simple phobias, involve excessive or unreasonable fear of objects (or situations) that are unrelated to fear of unexpected panic attacks or fear of embarrassment. Most of us are afraid of the usual kinds of events such as going to the doctor or dentist for a checkup. However, once we have kept the dreaded appointment the fear usually dissipates and does not rule our life to the point where we completely avoid such activities in the future. Phobias are extreme and irrational fears. Note Zide and Gray (2001), when people are engulfed in a phobic episode, they usually feel inundated by an overwhelming terror that literally obscures almost all other experiences. In the most severe form, a phobia becomes extremely incapacitating. The person may experience profuse sweating, a racing heartbeat, a feeling of choking or smothering, dizziness (or light-headedness), and trembling, to list a few typical sensations.

Four common phobias are listed below:

- *Animal type*—Animal phobia is defined by an excessive or unreasonable fear of animals and insects.

- *Natural environment type*—Children may, at a very early age, develop fears of situations or events that occur in nature, such as fear of the water, thunderstorms, heights, hurricanes, floods, and tornadoes.
- *Blood-injection/injury type*—This subtype tends to run in families, and the individual almost always differs in his or her physiological reaction from persons with other types of phobias (Ost, 1992). It is more prevalent in females and persons with less education (Bienvenu & Eaton, 1998).
- *Situational type*—Individuals with this type of phobia have difficulty using public transportation or being in enclosed places. This condition differs from panic disorder with agoraphobia because individuals never experience a panic attack outside the context of their phobic object or situation.

Social Phobia

Social phobia (or social anxiety disorder) is distinguished by significant and persistent fear and avoidance of social situations in which embarrassment or humiliation may occur (Munson, 2001). Exposure to the feared situation produces an immediate anxiety response. The holiday season, for example, can bring about such intense feelings of anxiety and dread that some individuals completely avoid all social gatherings. Social phobia can be limited to one type of situation or, in its most severe form, may be so broad that the individual experiences symptoms almost anytime he or she is around others. It has an estimated incidence in the United States of 4 to 5 per 1,000 persons per year (Neufeld, Swartz, Bienvenu, Eaton, & Cai, 1999). Social phobia occurs in women twice as often as in men. This disorder can severely hamper one's social life and lead to considerable impairments in interpersonal functioning and difficulties with work, school, or family relationships. Social phobia is commonly referred to as performance anxiety; that is, the person fears performing in a public forum because of the risk of being seen as inept, foolish, or inadequate and thereby suffering disgrace, humiliation, or embarrassment (Zide & Gray, 2001).

The fear of situations in which a person can be watched by others, such as public speaking, is considered the most common type of social phobia, followed by fear of trembling when writing in public. These phobias are more severe forms of the occasional shyness and social anxiety that everyone experiences at some time or another. Other forms of social phobia involve physiological functions, such as worrying about choking on food when eating in a public place or psychogenic urinary retention (being unable to urinate when others are present, also referred to as "having a bashful bladder"). The various types of social phobia can be diverse, and it is important for the practitioner to ascertain the parameters of the person's anxiety-evoking stimuli; for example, test anxiety; severe fears of blushing, trembling, or sweating; dysmorphophobia (or the unrealistic belief that aspects of one's physical appearance will evoke ridicule from others); dating anxiety; or sports performance anxiety, to list a few. In some instances the social performance situation is avoided or is endured, but it remains significantly dreaded.

Physical symptoms often accompany the anxiety of social phobia and may include blushing, profuse sweating, trembling, and other symptoms of anxiety such as difficulty talking and nausea or other stomach discomfort. These physical symptoms can then become an additional focus of the person's fear. As the person with social phobia worries about experiencing these physical symptoms, the chances of developing them increase, thus creating a vicious cycle.

Social phobia is defined by the following diagnostic criteria (APA, 2000; Zide & Gray, 2001):

- A marked and persistent fear of one or more social or performance situations in which the person is exposed to unfamiliar people or to possible scrutiny by others. The individual fears that he or she will act in a way (or show anxiety symptoms) that will be humiliating or embarrassing;
- Exposure to the feared social situation almost invariably provokes anxiety;
- The person recognizes that the fear is excessive or unreasonable;
- The feared social or performance situations are avoided or else endured with intense anxiety or distress;
- The avoidance, anxious anticipation, or distress in the feared social or performance situation(s) interferes significantly with the person's normal routine, occupational or academic functioning, or social activities or relationships; or there is marked distress about having the phobia.

Here, too, problems cannot be attributed to substance abuse, a general medical condition, or another mental disorder. For young adults under age 18, symptoms must have lasted at least for six months. The one specifier for social phobia, "generalized," applies to fears that include most social situations rather than being more definitive (or specific), such as a fear of speaking in public.

Obsessive-Compulsive Disorder

Many of us can recall reciting the childhood rhyme, "Step on a crack, break your mother's back," as we walked down sidewalks avoiding those "cracks" in our old, familiar neighborhood. In retrospect, we are not sure why we avoided those cracks, but we were convinced that in some way we could protect our mother against harm by performing the ritual. While this is a somewhat simplistic example, most of us can identify with it (Zide & Gray, 2001). Now imagine a person who has spent his or her entire life trying to avoid stepping on cracks and is afraid that a mis-step will bring disaster. Persons with obsessive-compulsive disorder are plagued with recurrent (and unwanted) obsessions or compulsions or both.

While the symptoms of obsessive-compulsive disorder can be bizarre, it is a surprisingly common disorder. It is about twice as prevalent as Alzheimer's disease (Chapter 3), affecting 1 to 2 percent of the population. It occurs equally often in men and women and can strike at any age. Approximately 5 million persons will develop obsessive-compulsive disorder (OCD) during their lifetime (Cooper, 1999). Obsessions are terrifying, repeated, unwanted and intrusive thoughts, and compulsions are ritual acts. Counting is a common compulsion.

Remember hearing a catchy jingle on TV and being unable to get it out of your mind? You just kept hearing it over and over in your head. Most of us have experienced this kind of temporary obsession. Consider the experience of the person with OCD who struggles with this every single minute of every hour of every day, day after day. Persons with obsessions are plagued with involuntary, persistent thoughts or impulses that are distasteful. These thoughts can be fleeting and momentary or they can be lasting ruminations. The most common obsessions focus on a fear of hurting others or violating socially acceptable behavior standards by swearing or making inappropriate sexual advances. They can also involve religious or philosophical issues that the person seems unable to resolve. People with compulsions go through senseless and repeated and involuntary ritualistic behaviors designed to prevent or produce a future event. People with OCD generally recognize the irrational aspect of the obsession or compulsion and attempt to subdue the thoughts or behaviors. Sometimes they manage to resist, and they experience a great deal of anxiety that is relieved by giving in to the obsession or compulsion. People with OCD encounter extreme distress, especially when their thoughts or behaviors interfere with daily routines, work, or other interpersonal activities (Black, Gaffney, Schlosser, & Gabel, 1998).

Compulsions are repetitive behaviors such as hand washing or checking. They may include mental or physical acts such as silently repeating words or counting objects over and over. The rituals are unrelated to a specific event. For instance, the person may constantly touch a particular object in a certain way and repeat the behavior numerous times in order to do it right! Some compulsions are relatively simple and others are exceedingly elaborate. Howard Hughes was known to have suffered from obsessions and compulsions (Dolnick, 1994). Hughes, who was a wealthy businessman in the aviation industry, was able to hire aides to help him cope with his disorder. For example, before using a spoon, Hughes was reported to have instructed his attendants to wrap it in tissue paper, seal it with cellophane tape, and then to place a second piece of tissue around the protective wrappings. When he finished using the spoon, Hughes discarded the tissue into a specially provided container.

Obsessive-compulsive disorder has two components: obsessions and compulsions. *Obsessions* are defined as recurrent and persistent thoughts, impulses, or images that at some point are experienced as intrusive and inappropriate, causing anxiety or stress (APA, 2000). Some people fear that they will commit violent or aggressive actions against themselves or others; for example, a mother who loves her child may struggle with the thought of hurling the youngster into oncoming traffic. People with obsessions may battle against intrusive sexual, offensive, or blasphemous thoughts; for example, they may be tormented by intolerable impulses to shout obscenities in public places (and find they just cannot get them out of their head) or be afraid to ride a bus for fear that if someone sat down beside them they would reach over and touch the stranger's breast or crotch inappropriately. Furthermore, these thoughts, impulses, or images are not simply excessive worries about real-life problems, and the person tries to ignore, suppress, or neutralize them with another thought or action. Finally, a person with obsessions recognizes that these thoughts, impulses, or images are a product of his or her own mind.

Compulsions are defined as repetitive behaviors such as constantly checking and rechecking doors to make sure they are locked. Checking seems to affect men more than women. Compulsions may also be mental acts (such as praying, counting or repeating words, numbers, tunes, or sounds silently) that the person feels driven to perform in response to an obsession or according to a rigid set of "rules." Washing and cleaning rituals are another form of compulsions. The person may have a fear of contagion that is averted through excessive hand washing. Women seem to be affected more often by this compulsion than men are. People may spend hours washing and cleaning to the point where their hands are raw and bleeding. Some people experience an overwhelming concern for order and tidiness and hoarding; for example, they may pick up small pieces of garbage on the street and then store them until their home becomes crowded with bags full of trash. Hoarders cannot throw anything away because if they do, they believe something terrible will happen to them or to those they care about. Checking and cleaning comprise the overwhelming majority of compulsive rituals. Compulsions are behaviors (or mental acts) aimed at preventing or reducing stress or avoiding some dreaded event or situation, but they are not connected with what they are designed to neutralize or prevent or are clearly obsessive.

The diagnosis of obsessive-compulsive disorder is made when symptoms become severe enough to cause excessive anxiety, are time-consuming (take up more than one hour a day) and significantly interfere with the person's normal routine, work or school functioning, or usual social activities or relationships. At some point during the course of the disorder, the person has recognized that the obsessions or compulsions are excessive and unreasonable. OCD places formidable burdens on the individual, his or her family, and on other interpersonal relationships. There is one specifier, "with poor insight"; this refers to the person who generally does not recognize that the obsessions and compulsions are excessive or unreasonable.

Post-Traumatic Stress Disorder

Shay (1995) chronicles the experiences of a Vietnam veteran who had been having problems sleeping for the past 20 years. The veteran would get up at least five times during the night to circle his room, and he described himself as feeling watchful or vigilant. On some occasions he would repeat this behavior 10 or 15 times. The veteran always kept a weapon nearby to protect himself, such as a baseball bat or a knife. In post-Vietnam America, practitioners have encountered many military veterans suffering from post-traumatic stress disorder (PTSD). Notes Waters (2003), some 3 million men and women returned home after serving in Vietnam and it is estimated that about one-third, nearly one million veterans, developed post-traumatic stress disorder. Nearly 500,000 continue to struggle with the disorder. However, PTSD is not a new phenomenon and Vietnam was not the first war to traumatize its soldiers. During World War I, 80,000 British soldiers were discharged for a condition described at that time as "shell shock." During World War II, nearly 400,000 American soldiers were sent home with psychiatric problems. Those who served in World War II, the Korean conflict, the Persian

Gulf War, and now the most recent wars in Afghanistan and Iraq can potentially become victims of the disorder. Estimates of PTSD among veterans of the Persian Gulf War are running as high as 8 percent (Wolfe, Erikson, & Sharkansky, 1999). Additionally, PTSD occurs in those who have experienced or witnessed life-altering events such as the natural disasters of hurricanes Hugo in 1989 and Andrew in 1992; the unprecedented four hurricanes Charley, Frances, Ivan, and Jeanne occurring over a two-month period in the southern United States during the late summer of 2004; the 1997 North and South Dakota floods; or the aftermath of terrorist attacks in New York City and Washington, DC, on the now-infamous date of September 11, 2001.

Most individuals experience symptoms in the initial days or weeks after a traumatic event, and women are more than twice as likely as men to develop the disorder. The risk of developing PTSD varies. Factors include prior trauma, the ability to cope with stress, the intensity of the stressful event, feelings of betrayal or victimization, and access to support groups.

For PTSD to be diagnosed, six criteria must be met (APA, 2000; Zide & Gray, 2001). The individual must:

- Have experienced, witnessed, or been confronted with a traumatic event (or events) involving the threat of death, serious injury, of loss of physical integrity to which the person responds with fear, helplessness, or horror;
- Have re-experienced the event in one (or more) of the following ways: recurrent and intrusive distressing recollections of the event including images or thoughts; dreams about the event; a sense that the event is recurring (includes illusions, hallucinations, and dissociative flashback episodes); intense distress when reminded of the event; or physiological reactivity to event-related cues;
- A minimum of three symptoms of avoidance and numbing, including avoidance of thoughts, feelings, or conversations about the event; avoidance of activities, places, or people that are reminders of the event; inability to remember important parts of the experience; decreased participation in significant activities; sense of detachment or estrangement from others; inability to experience a full range of emotions (for example, being unable to have loving feelings) or a restricted sense of the future (for example, not expecting to marry, have children, or live a normal life span);
- A minimum of two symptoms of increased arousal, including difficulties falling or staying asleep, irritability (or outbursts of anger), trouble concentrating, heightened startle response, or hypervigilance;
- Symptoms lasting for more than one month; and
- Impaired functioning at school or work, in relationships, or other important areas of functioning.

In addition, there are three specifiers for PTSD:

- *Acute*—symptoms have been present for less than three months;
- *Chronic*—symptoms have lasted three months or more;
- *Delayed onset*—symptoms begin at least six months after the stressor.

Recent research is adding to our understanding of the risk factors associated with PTSD. Individuals who have been abused as children or have had other previous traumatic experiences are more likely to develop the disorder (Widom, 1999). The emotional numbing response that occurs after a trauma has also received attention, as there is evidence that this distancing from feelings may make some people more prone to develop PTSD (Feeny et al., 2000). When people are in danger, they produce high levels of natural opiates that can temporarily mask pain. Individuals with PTSD continue to produce those higher levels after the danger has passed, which may lead to the inability to experience the full range of emotions, or blunted affect, associated with the diagnosis (Yehuda, 1998).

Generalized Anxiety Disorder

In any given year, 4 million Americans struggle with generalized anxiety disorder (GAD). Generalized anxiety disorder represents a "residual" entity consisting of persistent anxiety without the panic attacks, phobias, obsessions, and compulsions that define the other anxiety disorders. For generalized anxiety to be diagnosed, it must be experienced independently of symptoms that define the other anxiety disorders. The main features of GAD are unrealistic or excessive anxiety and worry that bothers the person most of the time for at least six months, and somatic symptoms such as increased muscular tension, autonomic hyperactivity, and hyperarousal. The chief characteristic of generalized anxiety disorder is a continuous, uncontrollable feeling of anxiety or worry, often described as a feeling of foreboding and dread, that occurs on a majority of days during a six-month period and is not brought on by physical causes such as disease, drugs, or drinking something with too much caffeine, such as coffee (APA, 2000; Barlow & Durand, 2005; Zide & Gray, 2001). Symptoms include feelings of restlessness or being "keyed up," difficulty in concentrating, irritability, muscle tension and jitteriness, sleep disturbance, and unwanted, intrusive worries. It is not uncommon for people struggling with GAD to visit their doctor several times before getting help for the diagnosis.

OVERVIEW OF MAJOR INTERVENTIONS

Competency-based treatment provides a framework for the practitioner to integrate the use of multiple strategies that address the physiological, affective, cognitive, and behavioral symptoms found in the anxiety disorders. The practitioner focuses on understanding the person's symptoms of anxiety within the total context of his or her life. The client's family, cultural values, and community environment may provide valuable insights to help the practitioner understand how the person's symptoms have developed over time. The helping relationship is characterized by mutual negotiation of objectives and priorities between practitioner and client. The strategies highlighted in the following section are targeted to relieve specific symptoms prevalent among the anxiety disorders, in a sequential fashion, based on severity (Sanderson, 1997). They exemplify the key counseling theories supporting competency-based practice; for example, the practitioner provides assurance that is anchored in psychosocial treatment, psychoeducation to explain somatic symptoms, and cognitive-behavioral interventions to organize the process of managing or resolving conflicts. In other instances, the practitioner may use more complex interventions aimed at helping the individual acquire coping mechanisms by revising maladaptive attitudes, acquiring new skills, and making changes in life style; for example, relaxation techniques may be combined with pharmacotherapy. The combination of psychological and biological interventions aimed at soothing a neurobiology disregulated by trauma seems to enhance the outcome of therapy (Lydiard, 2000; Walker & Kjernisted, 2000; Zarate & Agras, 1994).

Assessment Considerations

The anxiety disorders may co-occur with mood disorders such as major depression; medication side effects; substance-related dependence or withdrawal; or disorders of the endocrine, neurologic, cardiorespiratory, and immune systems (Moreno & Delgado, 2000). It is important for the practitioner to discern the influence of these other factors; for example, someone struggling with alcohol dependence in addition to an anxiety disorder is unlikely to respond to the practitioner's interventions until abstinence is achieved. There may be overlap between the anxiety disorders, making the boundaries between them poorly defined (Lydiard, 2000). The complexity of assessment highlights the importance of obtaining a thorough psychosocial history, beginning with the first session and continuing throughout treatment. This inquiry should be structured and emphasize functioning in the six Ps, as described below (Sperry et al., 1992).

- *Presentation*—The practitioner explores the intensity, duration, and severity of the person's symptoms.
- *Predisposing factors*—The factors in the client's life that predispose him or her to anxiety are explored; for example, the practitioner may inquire, "If you were not struggling with your anxiety (or phobia, or compulsion), what would you be doing instead?"
- *Precipitant*—The practitioner inquires about the onset of the symptoms of anxiety: are there any specific stressors, or do they come "out of the blue"?
- *Pattern*—Detailed information about the client's behavior patterns is obtained; for example, since avoidance is most likely a major behavior pattern, ascertaining the full range of avoidance behaviors is helpful in treatment planning. Other patterns common to the anxiety disorders, especially panic and/or agoraphobia, include dependency, low self-esteem, and interpersonal sensitivity.
- *Perpetuants*—Perpetuants are the factors that maintain anxiety and interfere with the client's progress; for example, a spouse who feels needed or important to the client can receive secondary gain from the person's condition.
- *Prognosis*—The client's doubts about the efficacy and/or outcome of treatment (or their ability to be involved actively in treatment) is explored.

Of these six factors, the three most important ones are presentation, pattern, and prognosis.

The anxiety disorders commonly include motor tension, autonomic hyperactivity (characterized by shortness of breath, palpitations, sweating, dizziness), vigilance, and scanning. Each of the specific disorders includes further characteristic features. Many persons with the anxiety disorders try to control their anxiety by avoiding certain situations. This avoidance may lead to further interpersonal and social or environmental problems; for example, social phobia may limit a person's chances for promotion by preventing him or her from making speeches or giving presentations at work.

Biological Interventions

There may be instances when biological therapy is helpful in treating persons struggling with the anxiety disorders. However, medical intervention is not considered a "magic bullet" but an adjunct to help an individual cope with the difficulties associated with the most severe physical symptoms of panic and anxiety. Psychotropic medications may influence the course of treatment beyond physiological reactions, and there are some cautions to keep in mind. For example, clients may become dependent on the sedative-hypnotic effects of drugs and believe that taking medication is more crucial to their well-being than learning to manage anxiety through behavioral approaches (Buelow & Herbert, 1995). Another problem is that some individuals become accustomed to the anxiety-reducing effects of medications and become less tolerant of the discomforts caused by the kind of anxiety that is a natural part of life. Conversely, the effects of medication may fail to match the individual's expectations for improvement, particularly if he or she believes the illness is a deserved punishment (Kaplan & Sadock, 1996). Culture and personal beliefs can also exert an influence. It is important for the practitioner to understand how a person explains his or her illness and to explore cultural ideas about taking medication (Sperry, 1995). It is also helpful to know about the person's specific fantasies about taking medication and its effects.

The anxiety-reducing effects of biological therapy may decrease the client's motivation for self-improvement; for example, if no anxiety exists for the client who is taking medication, then no series of cognitive-behavioral exercises aimed at diminishing stress can effectively take place. As a parallel, medication may be seen as a magical cure that can eliminate symptoms. Finally, some individuals may perceive the need to take medication as a suggestion that they are weak or incapable of taking care of their own problems. The need for medication might also imply that the disorder is more serious than it actually is (Sansone & Shaffer, 1997).

Social, financial, and psychological costs can also influence a person's attitudes about medication. The family system may be a source of support (or distress), and the practitioner may want to ask the client if he or she would like other family members' help in following through with the treatment regimen. The family may be able to provide valuable insights and information about medication side effects during the course of biological treatment.

First introduced in the 1950s, the benzodiazepines (BZDs) are the largest class of anti-anxiety medications that can relieve symptoms within a short time. They have relatively few side effects; drowsiness and loss of coordination are the most common. Fatigue and mental slowing (or confusion) can also occur. The most common adverse effect of the BZDs is drowsiness, and the individual should be advised not to drive or operate dangerous machinery while taking the drug. Some persons may also experience dizziness. The most adverse effects occur when other sedative drugs are taken concurrently. Before beginning treatment it is also important to reduce or stop ingesting stimulants such as nicotine or caffeine.

Therapeutic effect is attained by increasing the efficiency with which the GABA neurotransmitter binds with its receptors (Bentley & Walsh, 2001; Kaplan & Sadock, 1996; Walsh & Bentley, 2002). (Chapter 2 reviews the biological therapies.) The BZDs are absorbed into the gastrointestinal tract and have a rapid effect. The benefits of the drugs are that they can be taken orally and do not present a high potential for overdose; as a cautionary note, they can be physically addictive with continuous use at some dose levels. Most persons with generalized anxiety disorder are treated for about two to three months for acute symptoms, at which point the drug is gradually withdrawn.

Medications known as the beta-blockers, which are often used to treat heart conditions and high blood pressure, are also used to control anxiety. Propranolol (Inderal, Inderide) is a commonly used beta-blocker. Buspirone (Buspar) is an antianxiety medication that is chemically unrelated to the BZDs and has also become widely used for anxiety disorders. Because it is not potentially addictive and produces fewer negative side effects, clients who have taken the BZDs for an extended period of time are often changed over to buspirone.

Remarkable progress has been made in the approaches to treating anxiety disorders in the last decade. Biological interventions are quite varied. Table 6.1

TABLE 6.1   **ANTI-ANXIETY MEDICATIONS—THE BENZODIAZEPINES LISTED BY GENERIC AND TRADE NAMES**

Generic Name	Trade Name
Alprazolam	Xanax
Chlordiazepoxide	Librax, Libritabs, Librium
Clonazepam	Klonopin
Clorazepate	Azene, Tranxene
Diazepam	Valium
Flurazepam	Dalmane
Halazepam	Paxipam
Lorazepam	Ativan
Oxazepam	Serax
Prazepam	Centrax
Temazepam	Restoril
Triazolam	Halcion

summarizes the benzodiazepines commonly used for the anxiety disorders highlighted in this chapter. Longer-term use is indicated for panic disorder, social phobia, and generalized anxiety disorder. Short-term use is indicated for persons with posttraumatic stress disorder (Bentley & Walsh, 2001). Therapeutic benefit varies in duration of action in different people, depending on symptoms and body chemistry. This summary is intended to acquaint the practitioner with the biological therapies commonly prescribed for specific anxiety disorders in order to better assist clients, their families, and other members of the mental health care community involved in the client's treatment.

Panic and Agoraphobia

Persons with panic typically seek help from their physician because they believe that their symptoms reflect a catastrophic medical event such as a heart attack or stroke (Mahoney, 2000). Concentrating primarily on the physical aspects of the problem, these physicians generally prescribe medications such as anxiolytics or antidepressants (Mavissakalian & Ryan, 1997) while the person's life context may go unexplored (Randall, 2001). People with panic disorder often suffer from two kinds of anxiety: the panic attack itself and the anticipation of the panic. The second type of anxiety is frequently associated with agoraphobia. Most heterocyclics (HCAs), monoamine oxidase inhibitors (MAOIs), and several atypical BZDs are of benefit in treating the panic component. The MAOIs are infrequently used as a first-line drug because there are other equally effective alternatives that do not require adherence to a special diet (or avoiding high-tyramine foods). The HCA anti-depressant imipramine (Tofranil) is most commonly prescribed. Those who fail to respond to imipramine may be switched to phenelzine (Nardil). The BZDs alprazolam (Xanax) or clonazepam (Klonopin) are also prescribed. The BZDs have the advantage of reducing the anticipatory component of anxiety.

Persons struggling with panic disorder are generally aware of their bodies and related physical reactions, and look for an explanation for their dysphoric somatic sensations. Behavior therapy appears most effective for panic disorder, even when no phobic avoidance is present. Persons can be taught to reproduce somatic sensations of "panic" (for example, to exercise or hyperventilate) in order to desensitize themselves to triggers of panic. Relaxation, aimed at modifying catastrophic thinking, and learning to breathe in a measured fashion is also helpful. Also referred to as "natural breath," the person focuses on deep, relaxed breathing or abdominal breathing. These techniques address connections between the mind and the body or the interplay of the emotions and the brain; for example, how the body remembers trauma. Those who struggle with panic disorder with agoraphobia may benefit from exposure in vivo. Instead of recreating the situation in the practitioner's office, the person is taken to the actual feared situation. The practitioner instructs the person to voluntarily enter phobic situations until it is possible to experience these situations without discomfort. The practitioner may supervise a practice session or alternatively, a spouse or friend may accompany the person to provide support. According to Brook (1993), some individuals can benefit from group in vivo exposure and relearning. Perhaps the most popular example of this type of group are those programs conducted on planes in airports designed specifically to help participants tackle their fear of flying.

Specific Phobia

Of all the phobias, specific phobias are the most responsive to exposure therapy. Despite struggling with a specific phobia, some persons are able to function fairly well and may not even seek professional help. For instance, if someone struggles with a natural environment type of phobia such as a fear of drowning in the ocean and lives in a location with limited or no ocean access, he or she may be able to cope with this kind of fear without professional intervention. Because of the situation-specific nature of the symptom, such as fear of spiders or the sight of blood, medication is usually not indicated. In some cases, a limited course of BZD might be prescribed to enable the person to engage in an unavoidable situation.

Some persons benefit from exposure in vivo to more easily confront feared situations. Exposure works well when paired with some form of new learning. The practitioner may model how to enter the specific phobic situation and then encourage the client to repeat the same behaviors.

Social Phobia

The choice of treatment depends on the subtype of the disorder. The MAOI phenelzine (Nardil) is highly responsive to the more generalized form of social phobia involving most social gatherings or social encounters. The SSRI paroxetine (Paxil) has also been approved for social phobia. For those whose difficulties are limited to a single situation, such as speaking in public, the beta-adrenergic blocking drug atenolol (Tenormin) may be helpful. The beta-blockers are not addicting but are prescribed less often than the BZDs because they have a brief effect, lasting only a few hours. The antianxiety medications (or BZDs) may reduce the person's subjective distress and perhaps even improve performance. Alprazolam (Xanax) and clonazepam (Klonopin) have also been found useful in reducing the symptoms of social phobia. However, because of the tendency to use the drug before confronting phobic situations thus potentially increasing a person's dependence, these medications should be used sparingly.

Two behavioral strategies are often employed with social phobia: anxiety management training and cognitive restructuring. Anxiety management training is aimed at reducing the anxiety believed to be the basis of the distress in social settings. This training involves exposure to the phobic situation. However, opportunities for real-life (or in vivo) exposure may prove difficult, and in these cases the practitioner may use a substitute situation. For example, someone struggling with a fear of speaking in public may "practice" by participating in a Toastmasters Club. Cognitive restructuring may be used to reduce the perceived consequences of physiological symptoms (for example, blushing or sweating palms) or other dysfunctions and replace negative expectations in the situation with positive ones.

Additional strategies such as relaxation training, exposure to internal cues, and distraction may also be used. When people begin to feel the symptoms of anxiety, they may distract themselves by visualizing a more relaxing situation. Social skills training may be of benefit for those who feel awkward or inept in interpersonal social situations. This training may also include assertiveness and communication skills.

Despite the availability of effective treatment interventions for social phobia, most adults do not receive mental health care for their symptoms (Olfson & Guardino, 2000). Several barriers inhibit individuals from seeking treatment and the most common seems to be not knowing where to go for help. Many individuals believe they should be able to handle their symptoms by themselves. Another barrier is lack of insurance coverage or inability to afford treatment. Socially anxious people are often ashamed of their symptoms and embarrassed to discuss them with friends or appropriate health care professionals. Problems with clinical detection of the disorder can also play a role in preventing a person struggling with social phobia from seeking help. Many health care professionals are unfamiliar with social anxiety, unaware of the availability of effective treatments for social phobia, or fail to appreciate the relationship between social anxiety and social phobia.

Obsessive-Compulsive Disorder

The first medication specifically used in the treatment of obsessive-compulsive disorder was the tricyclic antidepressant clomipramine (Anafranil). Combined treatment consisting of behavior therapy and clomipramine (Anafranil) is the treatment of choice for most persons with obsessive-compulsive disorder. The dose is usually kept as low as possible because of an increased risk of seizures in higher doses. Some side effects are poorly tolerated by some people, such as lethargy, weight gain, and sexual dysfunction. The SSRIs fluoxetine (Prozac), fluvoxamine (Luvox), paroxetine (Paxil), and sertraline (Zoloft) may be useful in obsessive-compulsive disorder and also tolerated better than clomipramine. MAOIs such as phenelzine (Nardil) may also be effective. Trazodone (Desyrel) is another psychotropic medication that may sometimes be beneficial.

With the onset of obsessive-compulsive disorder, people with ordinary lives can suddenly find themselves tormented by unwanted and unwelcome thoughts and compelled to carry out meaningless rituals. On the one hand they recognize these rituals as "crazy" and yet on the other hand they feel powerless to resist. Behavior therapy consists of exposure plus response prevention, a process whereby rituals are actively prevented and the person is systematically and gradually exposed to the feared thoughts or situations. The practitioner assists the person to design and implement a homework-based exposure and response prevention program. Generally, three hours a day of graduated exposure and response prevention tasks is recommended at the outset and gradually decreased as symptoms remit (Barlow, 2002). This may be combined with modeling techniques. It is important for the practitioner to evaluate the person's perception of their obsessional concerns. For instance, if the person views his or her behavior as realistic and "normal" given their circumstances, they will do less well with exposure-oriented interventions. However, the technique of "thought stopping" may be of benefit, especially if the person improves with medication.

Symptoms may subside or even disappear and then reappear in a new and different form. These reappearances can certainly upset one's sense of security, and relapse prevention is an integral part of treatment. Relapse prevention plans target high-risk circumstances and triggers to obsessions or compulsions and provide a strategy for anticipating and dealing with them. Adverse life events and depression are often associated with the reemergence of OCD symptoms.

OCD has been described as the most pervasive and potentially disabling anxiety disorder (Hollander & Stein, 1997; Hyman & Pedrick, 1999; Steketee, 1999). More often than the other anxiety disorders it is associated with serious comorbid disorders such as depression or schizotypal disorder, thus increasing the treatment challenges. For those persons whose symptoms do not respond to therapy, additional consultation may be indicated. In some cases, obsessive-compulsive disorder may involve a brain abnormality (Schwartz et al., 1996) and neurosurgery occasionally may be indicated. Despite the challenges, almost 70 percent of cases respond to treatment. In most instances, after the danger has passed and the person is able to recognize that there is no cause for fear, the alarm signal in the brain turns off. For some, false alarms keep sending out mistaken fear signals in the brain. As a result, the individual continues to perceive a constant state of danger and tries repeatedly to reduce the resulting anxiety through obsessions or compulsions.

Post-Traumatic Stress Disorder

PTSD treatment combines medication with therapy, but because the disorder is caused by emotionally traumatic events or circumstances, the treatment of choice is support combined with cognitive interventions. The medication most frequently prescribed is imipramine (Tofranil). It seems to be effective in dampening the hyperarousal associated with PTSD and in reducing intrusive recollections. Sedating tricyclics such as amitriptyline (Elavil) may be useful in promoting sleep as well as in reducing daytime anxiety. MAOIs, such as phenelzine (Nardil), are also helpful in some cases. In addition to the antianxiety and antidepressant effects, these drugs inhibit rapid eye movement sleep. Their stimulating effects may help interrupt the inertia and social withdrawal experienced by some persons. However, the MAOIs carry the risk of hypertensive crises and require strict adherence to a tyramine-free diet. Tyramine-rich foods to be avoided while taking MAOIs include aged cheese (for example, Camembert or Edam), alcohol (particularly beer and wines, especially Chianti), sausages, cold cuts, or pickled or smoked fish. (Refer to Chapter 5 for a more complete listing.) Some of the SSRIs that are effective with other anxiety disorders, such as fluoxetine (Prozac) and paroxetine (Paxil), might be helpful in relieving the severe anxiety and panic attacks prominent in this disorder.

Most psychotherapy interventions focus on helping the person to re-experience the traumatic event (or events) and to restore a sense of mastery and meaning in life. Exposure therapy is a well-established treatment that requires the person to focus on and describe the details of a traumatic experience (Rothbaum, 2002). This may include confrontation with a frightening yet safe stimulus that continues until the person's anxiety is reduced. Exposure therapy is also referred to as flooding, imaginal, in vivo, prolonged, or directed exposure. The practitioner must be careful to ensure that the re-exposure experience will be therapeutic rather than traumatic. In some events or situations, it is difficult to recreate a trauma, and therefore imagined exposure (where the trauma and related emotions are systematically recreated through a conversation with the practitioner) is more frequently used. Another complication to the re-exposure technique is that persons who experience a trauma often automatically (and unconsciously) repress memories of the troubling event. In this case, when the memories flood back through "re-exposure," the person can dramatically re-live the event. This can be a frightening experience for both the client and the practitioner, and generally re-exposure is best carried out gradually (Foa & Meadows, 1997). Walsh (1998) suggests another technique called "making meaning of adversity" (p. 51) or helping the person to put his or her experience into a personal narrative. For example, the soldier who has seen the remains of a close friend killed in action on the battlefield may "make meaning" of this episode and the pain associated with losing a loved one by reflecting on how deeply they cared for each other. This meaning attributed to loss may carry over to other friendships, and the person may deepen his or her appreciation for these relationships (Walsh, 1999).

People with PTSD may persistently re-experience the traumatic event through memories, dreams, or intense psychological distress. They subsequently tend to avoid any stimuli associated with the trauma. To reduce the anxiety associated with situations or objects that are not dangerous, the practitioner may use systematic desensitization combined with cognitive restructuring and instruction in appropriate coping skills. Therapy is often combined with relaxation, meditation, or other techniques that have a soothing or calming effect on the person. Groups can also offer support and provide opportunities to learn coping strategies.

Generalized Anxiety Disorder

Interventions for generalized anxiety disorder need to take into account the person's age, severity and chronicity of symptoms, specific details (or content of the anxiety) of the person's life, and the presence of co-existing personality disorders. Many persons first turn to their family doctor, who offers reassurance about physical health. When the anxiety is mild, providing information about the disorder is helpful. Several self-help books and audiotapes on this topic are available; see, for example the popular book entitled *Peace from Nervous Suffering* by Claire Weekes or her audiocassette entitled *Pass Through Panic*. People who are suffering from severe anxiety may benefit from medication combined with cognitive and behavioral strategies that include relaxation training, breathing exercises, exposure to internal cues, distraction, and correction of cognitive distortions. Meditation may be a useful adjunct. Support may be helpful for persons struggling with stressful life circumstances.

If medication has been prescribed, it is usually discontinued after a period of time. To avoid client dependence on medication, the practitioner can work with the client to develop an individualized relapse prevention plan that addresses how to prevent or deal with high-risk circumstances. The person's future worries about anxiety episodes are discussed and role-playing may be used to rehearse responses to potentially problematic situations.

Diazepam (Valium) is a widely prescribed anti-anxiety drug against which the BZDs are measured. It not only reduces anxiety but also promotes sleep and muscle relaxation. More potent medications, such as alprazolam (Xanax), may be more effective but also create more dependence. Rebound anxiety is known to occur in a substantial minority of persons when the BZDs are discontinued. Buspirone (Buspar) is a new BZD alternative. It apparently has no addictive potential and is not sedating. Tricyclic antidepressants, such as impramine (Tofranil), also appear to be effective. The antidepressants venlafaxine (Effexor) and paroxetine (Paxil) have also been used for generalized anxiety disorder.

Summary

Generalized anxiety may be secondary to another disorder such as depression, post-traumatic stress disorder, or hypomania. A careful assessment is the first step in planning treatment in order to distinguish between a primary anxiety disorder and anxiety that is a manifestation of another disorder. However, when a person does not respond to treatment interventions as expected, the practitioner may need to consider the following questions (Davies, Dubovsky, Gabbert, & Chapman, 2000):

- Is anxiety secondary to a medical disorder? The practitioner begins intervention planning with a referral for a medical exam even when the person's anxiety seems clearly related to psychosocial stresses.
- Does the person have delirium or dementia? A person with early cognitive dysfunction can be anxious as a reaction to the diminishing ability to keep track of his or her environment.
- Is anxiety caused by a medication? It is helpful for the practitioner to learn about all the medications that a person may be taking and to work with the appropriate health care professional, for example the person's physician, to discontinue any other medications that are not absolutely necessary.
- Is anxiety substance-induced? Many individuals drink large quantities of caffeinated beverages such as coffee or soda without considering their impact. Some popular herbal preparations, such as kava, that are intended to relieve anxiety can actually cause anxiety in susceptible persons.
- Is anxiety secondary to another psychiatric disorder? Some disorders, such as depression, have prominent symptoms of anxiety. Antidepressants may initially improve symptoms but over time their effectiveness diminishes resulting in a return of symptoms often accompanied by increased mood instability.

- Is the person adhering to treatment interventions? Some individuals may be concerned about the costs of medication or the frequency of taking their medication. Medication side effects may be another cause for non-compliance.
- Is the family exacerbating the person's anxiety? Some family members may be covertly threatened by the person's recovery; for example, a husband who feels needed by his chronically anxious wife's dependency may unintentionally feel threatened by her recovery.
- Is the person's medication effective? Certain medications may be effective early in the course of uncomplicated anxiety disorders, but complex and chronic symptoms may require combinations of biological treatments.
- Does the treatment plan focus excessively on biological treatment? Interventions that emphasize medication may reinforce passivity and thus increase a person's anxiety. As discussed earlier, a number of the anxiety disorders are responsive to cognitive-behavioral techniques that encourage the person's active involvement in the mastery of symptoms.
- Are there any barriers to treatment? When a person's adaptive skills are organized around anxiety, improvement may mean giving up the "sick role" and the secondary gains associated with the illness.
- Is the practitioner's countertransference interfering with treatment? Individuals struggling with anxiety may provoke a reaction in the practitioner; for example, unrealistic optimism about a client's recovery may contribute to overlooking the presence of substance use or other variables that can negatively affect treatment interventions.

In sum, when anxiety is a central part of psychological, social, or other problems in living that the person seems unable to resolve in any other way, competency-based treatment provides a framework to address the multiple dimensions in the person's life. The practitioner formulates a systematic and integrated approach to treatment that sets the stage for a collaborative relationship characterized by support and identification of strengths.

RISKS ASSOCIATED WITH ANXIETY DISORDERS

There is no one simple risk associated with the complex symptoms characterizing the anxiety disorders. Looking at the intrapersonal domain, there is increasing evidence that a person may inherit a tendency to be tense or uptight (Barlow & Durand, 2005; Gray & McNaughton, 1996). Research into areas of the brain associated with anxiety and panic continues to inform our understanding of the disorder. Intrapersonal risks consider perceptions about how much control one may have over his or her life, ranging from confidence in ourselves to deep uncertainties. Interpersonal risks may be associated with stressful relationships or a difficult job. A child's worries and feelings of anxiety or panic may be reinforced by interactions with a parent who is fearful and anxious. Social and environmental risks are increased by a life style characterized by stress and anxiety.

Intrapersonal Risks

Research into the neurobiology of anxiety and panic is in an early stage, and the role of the brain in the development of anxiety disorders is being investigated. Anxiety has been found to be linked with specific brain circuits, especially the GABA-benzodiazepine system. Depleted levels of this neurotransmitter are associated with increased anxiety, but the relationship is complicated. The noradrenergic system has also been implicated in anxiety, and studies of normal anxiety suggest that the serotonergic neurotransmitter system is involved (Lesch et al., 1996).

Looking at inherited vulnerabilities, a child whose parent has an anxiety disorder is seven times more likely to have an anxiety disorder than other children (Woodruff-Borden, 2002). Personality dynamics are also offered to explain the panic associated with anxiety disorders. Persons with intense angry feelings of which they may be totally or partly unaware are at higher risk of panic and anxiety disorders than the general population (Busch, Milrod, and Singer, 1999). Typically, persons struggling with panic tend to minimize these feelings. As the practitioner attempts to explore these feelings, unacknowledged rage is found to be an increasingly important part of a client's mental life at the time of panic onset. Symptoms "come out of the blue" (APA, 2000, p. 397) and are related to the person's lack of conscious awareness of the relevant stressors or life events and ensuing intrapsychic reactions. Although panic attacks often occur in the backdrop of conflicted hostility, for some persons the attacks take on a significance of their own (Compton, 1998; Kessler, 1996). Freud considered anxiety to be a reaction to danger surrounding the reactivation of an infantile fearful situation (Breuer & Freud, 1959). Behaviorists view anxiety as the product of early classical conditioning (Bandura, 1986). The particular way we react to stress seems to run in families. These psychological explanations offer insight into the person's vulnerability to anxiety in later life.

Obsessive-compulsive disorder may be associated with Group A beta-hemolytic streptococcal infection (such as scarlet fever or strep throat) for a small subset of children (APA, 2000). The symptoms may appear abruptly or take an episodic course in which exacerbations are temporary related to the streptococcal infections. A case known to the author involved a 13-year-old boy (whom we will call Paul) who came to the attention of a social worker in the school setting. The youngster had just finished seventh grade and had recently moved from a rural part of Florida to urban Miami. The transition was not easy for Paul as he struggled to adjust to coming from a small school where everyone knew everyone else to a big, crowded one where he felt anonymous. Paul began to devote more time to sports after school, and his family initially viewed it as their son's attempt to adjust to his new surroundings. Soon Paul began to carry out a self-imposed fitness training routine at home. He became fanatical about exercise and would work out for hours at a time. Sometimes his parents would find him out in the backyard doing push-ups long after dark. Coaxing Paul to come inside for dinner or to watch some TV to relax before going to bed became a source of conflict, and his parents tried to get him to stop exercising altogether. He was losing a great deal of weight and looked gaunt and tired. His behavior spiraled out of control; symptoms included checking doors, compulsive showering, and repeating sentences or words. In school Paul's behavior became increasingly disruptive; for example, he had to tap his pencil on his desk a specified number of times while holding it in a certain position before using it. Despite the distraction to the other students, he would repeat this behavior over and over until the pencil was finally in the "right" place. Taking exams became another struggle. Before he could write something on a test paper, Paul had to count up to 25 between every word he wrote. In gym class, Paul had to make sure his sneakers were tied "just so." If not, he would take them off and retie them. Paul would repeat this behavior so often that sometimes he would miss the entire gym class just putting on his sneakers. A medical evaluation revealed the presence of a strep infection that had not produced the usual sore throat symptoms. There was no way to tell how long the infection had been present, but it seems to have triggered the youngster's obsessive-compulsive symptoms.

With certain anxiety disorders, such as post-traumatic stress disorder, there is growing evidence of predisposing genetic and biochemical factors. A person's exposure to trauma may trigger biological vulnerabilities to anxiety. Anyone who has encountered a dangerous situation can remember feeling that their senses were more acute than usual, a condition that is commonly referred to as an adrenaline rush. Increased levels of epinephrine (or adrenaline) and norepinephrine (or noradrenaline), the two primary fight-or-flight hormones, increase the brain's alertness, enhance memory, and quicken the heartbeat. When the stress becomes overwhelming, too much of these hormones can induce confusion and impair learning and memory. Floods of epinephrine and norepinephrine not only increase and accompany emotional and neurobiological arousal; they can also trigger flashbacks in previously traumatized people. Although the underlying brain chemistry is not well understood, repeated adrenaline rushes seem to progressively sensitize brain chemistry to produce even greater floods of adrenaline at lower thresholds. There is recent evidence to suggest that trauma may effect long-lasting damage to the hippocampus, a structure located deep in the brain (Butler, 1998). Regardless of the protective factors and buffers in the person's environment, these biological influences may cause ongoing symptoms that disrupt his or her life.

Interpersonal Risks

Stress is also implicated in the anxiety disorders, and women seem more vulnerable than men to day-to-day stress (Domar & Dreher, 2001). A woman's multiple roles (such as spouse, mother, housekeeper, employee, caretaker, or friend) and the constant need to balance conflicting demands can increase the stress and pressure she feels. The burdens of caring for an ailing relative tend to fall on the woman in the family and also increase her stress (as illustrated in the case vignette found in Chapter 3). As noted by Domar and Dreher (2001), one woman in four becomes a caretaker between ages 35 and 44, and more than one in three between ages 55 and 64.

Stressful life events can increase one's vulnerability to anxiety, and many of these events are interpersonal in nature. Examples include marriage, divorce, difficulties at work, or the death of a loved one. Social pressures, such as attempting to get promoted, might also be a source of stress that is great enough to trigger anxiety.

Community and Environmental Risks

As mentioned previously, many women struggle to balance work and family. Some experience feelings of guilt because they think they are not doing a good enough job in either arena. Despite advances, our culture is still not designed to accommodate working women. Domar and Dreher (2001) point out that the level of stress some women experience is similar to that of soldiers in combat.

While it could be argued that stress and anxiety are a natural part of life, some life style conditions can increase one's vulnerability. In our chaotic twenty-first century society, many persons live and work under high levels of stress. Many of us know persons with hectic lifestyles characterized by overworking, overeating, or talking on the phone while simultaneously doing something else like cooking or watching television (euphemistically referred to as multi-tasking). A friend of the author would skip breakfast and grab a donut on the way to work, routinely eat lunch at her desk, snack on candy bars, and generally arrive home late and exhausted. Today it's easy to find a store open 24 hours, a fast-food chain providing instant meals for the person on the run, and cell phones offering instant access no matter where you are. Life can be fast-paced and many individuals struggle with role overload as they try to balance the multiple and often conflicting demands of work, family, and other interests.

Instant gratification is expected, and our society has grown to accept the benefits of medication at the risk of the "medicalization" of anxiety (Buelow & Herbert, 1995). Over ten years ago, Garvey (1990) observed that about 65 million prescriptions for benzodiazepine medications were written each year. This is an enormous number given that some degree of anxiety is normal and even necessary to protect us from harm.

Social workers must be attentive to the ecological considerations of poverty and powerlessness. Poverty seems to be associated with poor health care and higher mortality rates. The continuous environmental stressors related to poverty include crime, discrimination, inaccessibility of services, and inadequate housing.

Summary

There are differences of opinion about the main causes of the anxiety disorders (Austrian, 2000; Barber & Crits-Christoph, 1995; Johnson, 1999; Kutchins & Kirk, 1997; Miller, 2002). The extent to which psychological factors are involved in increasing a person's vulnerability is unclear, but certain variables seem to play a role, including the suppression of negative thoughts and feelings, pessimism, feelings of powerlessness, and lack of social support. The current research calls for attention to the connections between the mind and the body, including individual variations in the person's biological vulnerabilities; psychological factors like personality traits, emotional inhibition, explanatory styles, perceptions, and emotions; how people behave under stress and how they manage it; and social networks.

CASE ILLUSTRATION: JADA WU

The most common phobia for which people seek treatment is agoraphobia, characterized as a fear of being away from a safe person or place. For people who experience panic attacks, concerns about having additional panic attacks may develop into agoraphobia. In either case, agoraphobia limits the client's interaction with the outside world. The case of Jada Wu illustrates this diagnosis and the related pressures of meeting the demands of her job as a flight attendant and its interplay with her Asian American culture. [Ms. Wu's diagnosis is described in detail in Zide and Gray's Psychopathology: A Competency-Based Assessment Model for Social Workers *(2001).] In this case vignette, the practitioner looks for potential strengths and resources and builds them into the treatment plan. The practitioner recognizes Ms. Wu's resilience by reminding her that she has had many successes prior to her diagnosis, affirms her coping skills, and determines what competencies can be applied to the current situation. Building on Ms. Wu's strengths captures a natural nexus that enhances the likelihood of her ability to address the fears of when her panic attacks are going to occur again and successfully helps her to modify her behavior.*

Agoraphobia is a set of phobias often set off by a panic attack involving the basic fear of being away from a safe place or person. Jada is scared that she is "going to die" because of her loss of control. Her physical symptoms included shaking, breathing hard, and sweating. Jada Wu is a 27-year-old airline flight attendant who was referred for counseling by her company's Employee Assistance Program (EAP). The social worker at the local counseling center, Mary Wear, observed that Ms. Wu was a very attractive woman of Chinese descent. She was well groomed, of medium height, and wore her long hair in a fashionable braid hanging down the center of her back. She described a lifestyle that included a well-balanced vegetarian diet. Relevant psychosocial history noted that Jada's parents were originally from Beijing and had immigrated to Florida about 25 years previously, when Jada was 2 years old. Jada recalls a "traditional" Chinese American upbringing in which festivals and holidays were celebrated. While she was growing up, Jada participated actively in the family's restaurant business. She loved waiting on tables and making sure her customers were satisfied. Many of the "regulars" specifically asked for Jada and she would share special dishes that were not on the menu but could be easily prepared in the kitchen just for them. After high school she went on to attend (and eventually graduate from) college. This created some degree of tension at family gatherings, reported Jada. She further distanced herself from the family business when she took the job at the airline.

The practitioner explored Jada's common responses to her anxiety and whether Jada experienced agoraphobia. This assessment included what she had tried as interventions to panic and anxiety and to what extent these had helped. Jada acknowledged problems leaving her home, and relying on her sister to take her grocery shopping. She also described feeling uncomfortable at the local shopping mall. When asked about her current level of functioning, Jada replied that she was always worried about when one of her panic attacks was going to occur again. She felt that passengers expected their flight attendants to always be perky and cheerful—to act as if they had no problems of their own. Sometimes her mother would drive her to her job at the airport.

The social worker's assessment identified a number of strengths in this client's situation. The airline company supported her by providing employee assistance services. Jada was successful at her job, had a good support system in her friends and family, maintained a healthy lifestyle, was intelligent, related easily to others, and was motivated to seek counseling. Jada had insight into her problems, and she followed through on the counseling referral. However, she also appeared to have an underlying sense of tension and worry. After introductions, Jada Wu began the session by describing her symptoms and recounting her decision to seek treatment.

> MS. WU: *You know, when I went to the doctor for my physical (exam) he said that everything checked out but gave me a prescription for Xanax anyway. At first I was excited thinking that I had conquered this thing. Boy, was I wrong! Now I'm afraid to go without the pills, but I don't know if I want to be dependent on them for the rest of my life. They make me feel so tired; even when I first wake up I just feel so groggy. I'm embarrassed about these attacks. I feel so ashamed and I really don't want anybody to know. My parents would be so disgraced if they knew that I had to get help outside of the family. I just know that they would be stigmatized if anybody found out in our community. Mind you, I'm not looking for a cure here; I just don't want to depend so much on medication.*

Jada goes on to say that her panic episodes start suddenly, develop rapidly, and are over in about 30 or 40 minutes. Sometimes they happen every day. They are not always the same but frightening nonetheless. One time she remembers feeling cold. Her heart was beating rapidly and she felt like she couldn't breathe. Jada was afraid she was going to die right then and there. Jada said she worried about having more attacks and was most fearful of something happening when she was at work. To make sure she would be safe when she was at work, Jada had been taking the Xanax before leaving the house. Jada concluded by asking the social worker if she thought she was crazy.

> MS. WEAR: *You've come to the right place. It has taken a lot of courage, and that's certainly a sign that you are not crazy. I believe that if we put our heads together we can figure out how to manage these episodes and even find*

ways to help you to be more relaxed. With some hard work, I think we can make some great progress in about 10 sessions. How does that sound to you?

MS. WU: *You know, Mary, I really wanted to solve this on my own but I can see that my efforts really didn't work out so well. I pride myself on thinking just like an American, but all this emotional distress feels like a sign of weakness to me. I used to think that the only thing I needed was more discipline in my life, but now I think it's something else. I'm not sure what to do . . . maybe I need more willpower.*

MS. WEAR: *I'd like to explain what we'll be doing over the next couple of weeks. You've been struggling with this for some time now and are the expert on the problem. I know some strategies that have been helpful for panic episodes like this, but we need to work together to figure out what will be the best plan for you. We're going to do something called cognitive-behavioral therapy to understand the connections between thoughts and behaviors. Once we identify the thoughts and feelings that accompany your panic attacks, we're going to work on modifying your responses to them. There's a lot that can be done. I would like to show you some systematic relaxation techniques. By learning how to relax, you can reduce the anxiety and stress that sets the stage for panic attacks. We'll also focus on some breathing exercises. By learning to control your breathing, you'll avoid the hyperventilation or pattern of rapid, shallow breathing that exacerbates those panic attacks.*

MS. WU: *Working hard with you for 10 sessions sounds pretty good right now. I'm not looking for a cure, you know, but just to get back on track with my life a little more!*

MS. WEAR: *Let's begin by taking a close look at the internal sensations associated with panic. Remember, we will go slowly and you can stop at any time. Ready? (Jada nods affirmatively.) I'm going to ask you to bring on some of the sensation of a panic attack by spinning around to trigger dizziness. (The client stands up, takes off her shoes, moves to the center of the room, and begins to spin. She becomes short of breath, slightly disoriented, and stops suddenly.)*

MS. WU: *I'm going to have a heart attack . . . I just know it!*

MS. WEAR: *Jada, replace those thoughts with "It's only dizziness, and I can handle it!" Okay now, repeat after me . . .*

MS. WU: *It's only dizziness . . . I can handle it!*

(At this point Jada seemed a bit surprised by her ability to actually change her thoughts.)

MS. WEAR: *Be proud of yourself for the great progress you've made so far! Focus on thinking about how good you will feel when you succeed again. Let's turn our attention now to some breathing techniques that I think might be another way to control your anxiety. You be the judge. (Jada nodded affirmatively and looked eager to learn another anxiety management technique.) I like to call it natural breath, but it's really a deep, relaxed way of breathing or abdominal breathing. Okay, let's get started. First, I would like you to relax and quietly breathe. Now, become aware of your breathing and nothing else. (Jada takes a few deep breaths.) Focus on sinking down into your body and breathing. As you are breathing, visualize a bright ball of energy in the middle of your body just behind your navel. Gently and slowly inhale and visualize the air going all the way down to that ball of energy. Then exhale slowly and visualize all the air leaving the ball of energy.*

MS. WU: *Wow! This is great! I'm really beginning to feel relaxed!*

MS. WEAR: *Outstanding! And you can practice this at home, too. Don't fight your feelings or try to wish them away. Okay, on a scale of 1 to 10, where the number 10 is when the fear is barely noticeable and 1 is when the fear is the worst, give your feeling a number.*

MS. WU: *Well, when I first stopped spinning I would say that I was really up there…like maybe 2 or 3. But now, I would say that maybe I'm an 8. This is really amazing, Mary.*

MS. WEAR: *Notice that it does not stay at that low level for more than just a few minutes! Remember that facing the fear will make it less intense. I would like you to combine this breathing technique with visualization. The trick is to hold positive thoughts rather than to allow your mind to be overrun by negative ones. When you find yourself thinking about the fear, focus on and carry out this breathing-visualization combination.*

The practitioner and Jada began to brainstorm visual images, and Jada described the serenity she felt walking along the beach on a hot summer day. The social worker instructed Jada to incorporate this visualization along with the deep, relaxed breathing.

The work over the next few sessions centered on helping Jada to identify the triggers of her panic attacks and to practice the anxiety management and relaxation techniques she had learned. Jada seemed to especially like the mind-body connection evoked by the breathing-visualization techniques, saying it helped her to feel "at one" with herself. By the sixth session, Jada reported that she had had a better week than she remembered for a very long time and attributed this to being able to identify the early warning signs of her panic attacks. Managing her panic attacks proved to be more challenging, and sometimes Jada was unable to fully stop them. However, she was making progress and was pleased with her efforts. Two additional strategies to help "distract" from the thoughts and feelings associated with Jada's panic attacks were introduced. The first one was to count backward from 100 by 3s. The other was to wear a rubber band on her wrist. Instead of focusing on the fear, Jada was to distract herself by snapping the rubber band. She began to notice that when she stopped adding to those frightening thoughts, they began to fade. Jada was instructed to stay in the present and notice what is really happening instead of what she thought might happen.

The combination of Jada's improved ability to identify triggers of her panic attacks, her ability to talk herself through these situations, and the success of taking concrete steps helped her to gain confidence and trust in her ability to face future episodes. At the end of their sessions, Jada planned to practice her new behaviors. The social worker asked if Jada would be interested in joining a support group for persons with similar struggles, but she declined, indicating that she would like to try things on her own for now.

OPERATIONALIZING COMPETENCY-BASED TREATMENT

The competency-based framework for treatment considers the dynamic interplay of biology and psychology, social and cultural factors, and the individual's resilience and perceived coping abilities. There are ethnic differences in perceptions of mental health, and people differ in their experience of pain, what they label as a symptom, how they communicate about their pain or symptoms, their beliefs about its cause, their attitudes toward helpers, and the treatment they desire or expect (McGoldrick, Giordano, & Pearce, 1996). In this case vignette, the practitioner regards the total context of the client's life and attempts to cope with stressors given the existing risks and vulnerabilities (Slattery, 2004). As illustrated in Jada Wu's experiences, this social context includes cultural expectations as well as beliefs about the diagnosis and related problems. Jada's symptoms caused intrapersonal, interpersonal, occupational, and social difficulties.

The vignette highlights competency-based treatment interventions that are tailored to the client's unique needs and expectations rather than organized around a single method or modality. This does not mean that the approaches were "watered down" but that they were adapted to fit the client's cultural context and world view (Wachtel, 2002). Jada Wu was involved actively in the treatment process as a collaborator in solving her problems. Goals were set that were feasible for the client to accomplish while at the same time challenging and realistic (Hubble, Duncan, & Miller, 1999; Walter & Peller, 1992). Table 6.1 highlights the risks, protective factors, and buffers in Jada Wu's life.

Working with Jada Individually

In addition to limiting her social interactions, Jada felt guilty over the shame she believed she had brought to her family by seeking outside help for her problems. She also blamed herself, thinking that she needed more discipline or will power or to control her panic attacks. While Jada claimed that she thought "just like an American," she did have some internalized stigma from her cultural heritage. Acculturation can create serious emotional strain for ethnic clients (Diller, 2004), and conflict between her upbringing and her chosen career had created additional stress on Jada. The practitioner listened to what Jada communicated and respected her shifting cultural context (Atkinson, Morten, & Sue, 1998). Although Jada was able to acknowledge that her fears were unreasonable, she was still unable to change her behavior. Jada's agoraphobia affected her job as a flight attendant, and the need to hide her symptoms from co-workers (and her family) increased her difficulties around getting help when the feelings became too acute. Even though she had collapsed on the job, Jada did not seek treatment on her own. She endured significant distress and required support with activities like grocery shopping or riding to work. The potential stigma her panic attacks would bring to her family seemed to play a significant role in Jada's delay in seeking help. In addition, there were periods when Jada was able to obtain some degree of relief through avoidance strategies.

TABLE 6.2	**THE RISKS, PROTECTIVE FACTORS, AND BUFFERS IN JADA WU'S LIFE**	
	Risk Factors	**Protective Factors and Buffers**
Intrapersonal	Agoraphobia with panic disorder	Intelligent, attractive, and well groomed
	• Scared she's going to die (heart attack)	Maintains healthy lifestyle— well-balanced vegetarian diet
	• Feels loss of control	Insight into problems
	• Shaking, breathing hard, sweating	Motivated
	Ashamed of symptoms	Followed through with counseling referral
	Fears disgracing her family	Concerned about reliance on medication (Xanax)
	Unsuccessful prior attempts to cope with symptoms	
	Becoming anxious about work	
Interpersonal	Demanding job as flight attendant	Successfully worked in family business growing up
	Restricting social activities	Currently working (for airlines)
	Family observes "traditional" customs, creating acculturation tensions	Family is close-knit and helpful
Social and Environmental	Family immigrated from China	Asian culture
		College graduate
	Job expectations for performance (to be cheerful all the time)	Employer supportive
		Has insurance coverage
	Single	Appropriate counseling services readily available

However, when she became concerned about an increasing dependence on taking medication for her panic attacks, Jada followed through with her employer's referral for counseling through the Employee Assistance Program. The social worker set the stage for a collaborative relationship by pointing out that Jada was the "expert" about her problems (de Jong & Berg, 2002) and the practitioner knew strategies that had proven effective for persons struggling with panic attacks with agoraphobia. Working together with Jada, the practitioner adapted cognitive-behavioral strategies to help Jada cope effectively with the sensations of panic and replace her alarmist thoughts with more appropriate ones. The combination of visualization and natural breathing was normative to the value placed on harmony by Jada's Chinese American cultural heritage (Kitano & Nakaoka, 2001; Lee, 1997; Lum, 1999, 2000, 2003).

The social worker listened carefully to what Jada communicated about her panic attacks and stayed focused on the issues for which Jada was seeking help; for example, Jada did experience some degree of tension about being the first woman in her family to complete college and move out and live on her own. Taking a job with the airline had meant that Jada was the first family member to work outside of the family business. The collectivist orientation of her culture conflicted with Jada's individualistic desire for autonomy and independence from her family, creating tension for her. The family's world view valued living with parents and submerging one's individual self for the collective good (Sue, Sue, & Sue, 2000; Sue & Sue, 1999; Sue, 1999). These "tensions" were not the concerns that Jada had brought to the practitioner and thus were not addressed.

The practitioner was explicit in explaining cognitive-behavioral therapy to Jada, who was uncomfortable at the start of the counseling relationship. Practicing cognitive-behavioral techniques provided structure for their work together. The practitioner acknowledged what Jada was experiencing during the first appointment and pointed out that she was not weak or crazy. To avoid those interventions that are disempowering, the practitioner worked with Jada's motivation for change and focused on her strengths. The practitioner declared her counseling expertise and then relied on basic listening skills to check out Jada's response by asking, for example, "How does that sound to you?" (Greenberg, 1997; Ivey & Ivey, 2003; Ivey, Ivey, & Simek-Morgan, 1997). In this way the practitioner focused on verifying whether her understanding was accurate by communicating that understanding to Jada. Next, the practitioner began to help Jada identify other ways of looking at her problem. The scaling question ("on a scale of 1 to 10, where the number 10 is when the fear is barely noticeable and 1 is when the fear is the worst, give your feeling a number") encouraged Jada's critical reflection on the presenting problem. It was important for the practitioner to understand what was normative and culturally valued by Jada (Cox & Ephross, 1998) and she followed the client's lead in identifying the problem rather than attempting to impose her own ideas (de Jong & Berg, 2002; Prochaska, 1999; Walter & Peller, 1992). A collaborative relationship was fostered, with Jada's perspectives and experiences as a focal point.

Family Intervention

Although Jada's family members were not directly involved with the practitioner, they were very much a part of the intervention picture. As Jada had "Americanized" by going to college and working outside the home, she had seemed less bound by her family's traditional ways. Culture undoubtedly influenced the family's reaction to Jada's symptoms. Jada knew that her inability to control her "fears" and the need to take medication would be a source of shame to her family. Instead of openly sharing her panic episodes she disguised her symptoms as physical ailments; for example, rather than describing what was really wrong with her, she told her family she was getting a fever.

Jada's family was very supportive and brought on some symptom relief by their presence. The social isolation that usually accompanies agoraphobia affected family members as well. In this case vignette, Jada's mother was available to drive her to the airport, and her sister had started to take her grocery shopping. In these instances, there is some danger that such dependency could disrupt relationships within the family. For Jada, however, their efforts were a source of support.

Environmental Intervention

Working within the airline industry was a source of stress for Jada. She felt that she always had to put on a bright face, even when she was feeling the disabling symptoms of her panic attacks. There seemed to be the societal expectation that flight attendants are consistently cheerful and problem-free. Jada's airline did provide counseling services through its employee assistance program, and her insurance coverage supplemented the costs of additional counseling. Fortunately, Jada was able to locate a social work practitioner with expertise in the kind of help she needed: cognitive-behavioral therapy.

Conclusion

Competency-based treatment provided the framework to adapt skills and information to the client's cultural context. The practitioner was not wedded to any particular theoretical orientation or practice model. To exclusively rely on a single treatment approach would have been too restrictive for addressing Jada's complex problems and life circumstances associated with her diagnosis. Instead, the work was based on the belief that there are options in the ways people perceive and interact in society, and the social worker explored the full range of the client's life and experiences. Jada was not looking for a "cure," and so the practitioner focused on supporting her increased self-mastery and achievements.

The case of Jada Wu illustrates how a client's shifting cultural beliefs can be integrated into cognitive-behavioral techniques aimed at anxiety management. Jada's cultural heritage and background were additional resources for the practitioner to tap into to foster resilience. At the heart of the competency-based perspective is the recognition that all clients have the innate ability to change. Working from a strengths perspective, the social worker collaborated with Jada with respect to problem definition, planning, and action steps. This approach recognizes that individuals are resilient and have the capacity to rebound from problems (Saleebey, 1997). The core practice skills and techniques highlighted were (a) engaging the client; (b) contracting between the client and social worker; (c) enhancing the client's self-esteem and competence; (d) paying attention to culture; and (e) respecting the client's focus for treatment.

SUMMARY

The anxiety disorders can fill a person's life with overwhelming anxiety and fear. The case illustration of Jada Wu highlights the diagnosis of panic disorder with agoraphobia and discusses the social worker's competency-based interventions.

The major types of anxiety disorders described in this chapter are agoraphobia, panic disorder with and without agoraphobia, specific phobias, social phobia, obsessive-compulsive disorder, post-traumatic stress disorder, and generalized anxiety disorder. Figure 6.1 summarizes these disorders.

Each of the anxiety disorders has distinct features, but they all share the common theme of excessive and irrational fear and dread. The specific characteristics of the anxiety disorders are described below:

- *Panic disorder*—Episodes of intense fear strike often and without warning. They can occur at any time. An attack generally peaks within 10 minutes, but some symptoms may last longer. Accompanying physical symptoms can include chest pain, heart palpitations, shortness of breath, dizziness, abdominal stress, feelings of unreality, and a fear of dying.
- *Agoraphobia*—Panic disorder may progress to the more advanced stage where the individual becomes afraid of being in any place (or situation) where escape might be difficult or help is unavailable in the event of a panic attack.
- *Specific phobia*—Intense fear of something that poses little or no actual danger. These fears are not extreme; they are irrational fears of a particular thing such as being in escalators, tunnels, water, dogs, or injuries involving blood.
- *Social phobia (or social anxiety disorder)*—Persistent dread of situations in which the person is exposed to possible scrutiny by others and is afraid of doing something that will lead to embarrassment or humiliation. Social phobia can be limited to only one type of situation or, in its most severe form, may be so broad that the individual experiences symptoms almost anytime he or she is around other people.
- *Obsessive-compulsive disorder*—Symptoms consist of repeated, unwanted thoughts or compulsive behaviors that seem impossible for the person to stop or to control. The disturbing thoughts or images are called obsessions and the rituals that are performed to try to prevent or get rid of them are called compulsions. Rituals such as counting, prolonged hand washing, and repeatedly checking for danger take up much of the person's time and interfere with other activities. Individuals recognize that what they are doing is senseless but they are unable to stop.
- *Post-traumatic stress disorder*—Persistent symptoms occur after a person experiences a traumatic event or ordeal in which grave physical harm occurred or was threatened. Precipitating events can include violent personal assaults, natural or human-caused disasters, accidents, or military combat. Anniversaries of the traumatic event can be very difficult. Common symptoms include nightmares, flashbacks, dulled emotions, depression, anger, irritability, and being easily distracted or startled. PTSD is diagnosed only if the symptoms last more than a month; symptoms usually begin within months of the trauma and the course of the illness can vary. Occasionally, the illness does not appear until years after the traumatic event.

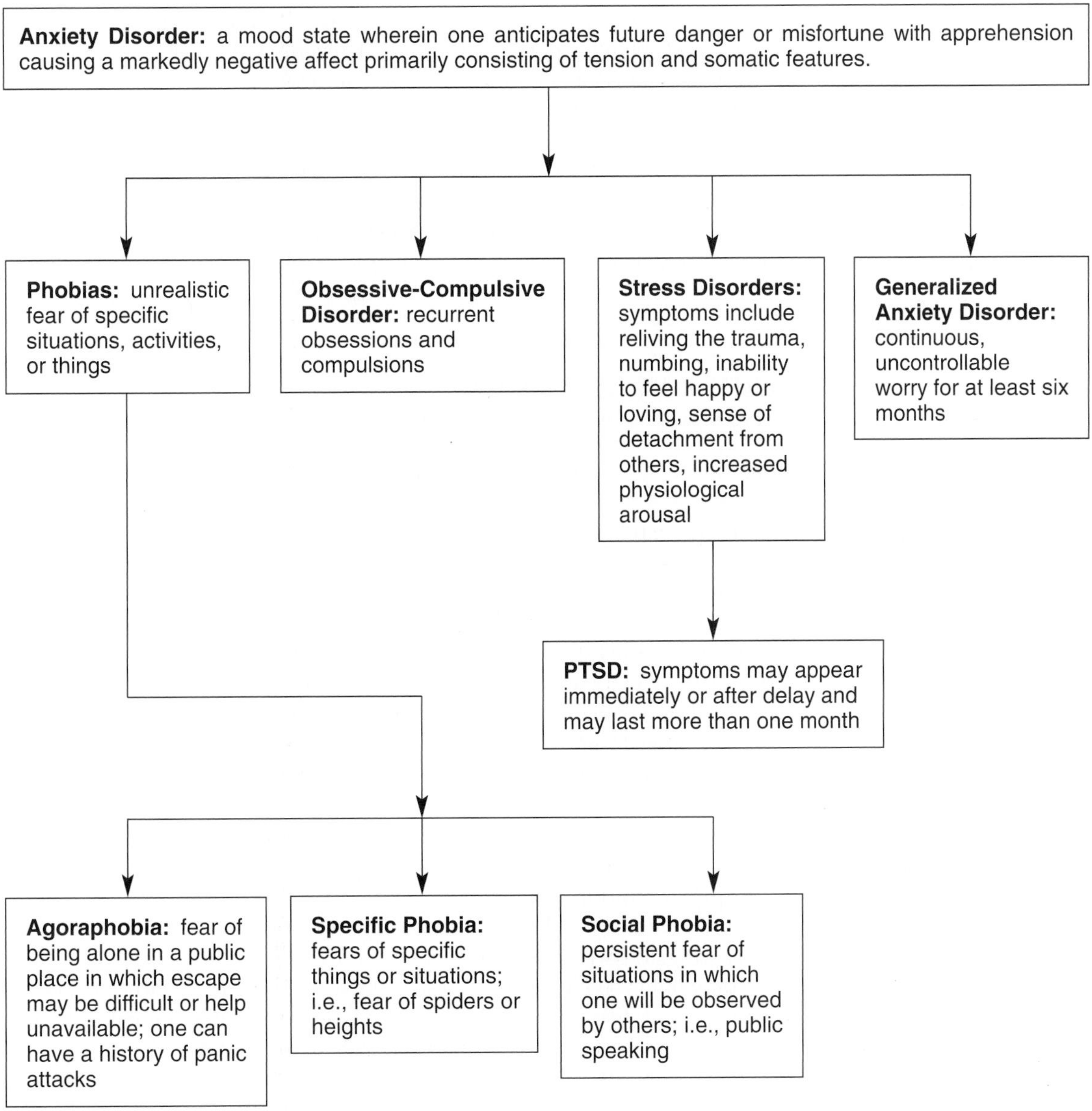

Anxiety Disorder: a mood state wherein one anticipates future danger or misfortune with apprehension causing a markedly negative affect primarily consisting of tension and somatic features.

Phobias: unrealistic fear of specific situations, activities, or things

Obsessive-Compulsive Disorder: recurrent obsessions and compulsions

Stress Disorders: symptoms include reliving the trauma, numbing, inability to feel happy or loving, sense of detachment from others, increased physiological arousal

Generalized Anxiety Disorder: continuous, uncontrollable worry for at least six months

PTSD: symptoms may appear immediately or after delay and may last more than one month

Agoraphobia: fear of being alone in a public place in which escape may be difficult or help unavailable; one can have a history of panic attacks

Specific Phobia: fears of specific things or situations; i.e., fear of spiders or heights

Social Phobia: persistent fear of situations in which one will be observed by others; i.e., public speaking

FIGURE **6.1**

OVERVIEW OF ANXIETY DISORDERS

- *Generalized anxiety disorder*—Constant, exaggerated worrisome thoughts and tension about everyday routine and life events and activities (lasting at least six months) characterize generalized anxiety disorder (GAD). Persons struggling with GAD always anticipate the worst, even when there is little supporting evidence. GAD is often accompanied by physical symptoms such as fatigue, trembling, twitching, muscle tension, headache, difficulty swallowing or nausea, irritability, sweating, and hot flashes. People may also feel light-headed or short of breath. Some may have to go to the bathroom frequently. Persons with GAD seem unable to relax, although they usually realize that their anxiety is more intense than the situation warrants.

PRACTITIONER REFLECTIONS

1. Websites tend to come and go rather quickly. The following websites were operational at the time this book was written. Visit one of the following and evaluate how the information provided could be useful for a client such as Jada Wu highlighted in this chapter. Be attentive to the fact that some clients may not have access to a computer or the Internet and may be unfamiliar with this kind of technology. Consider the impact of cultural considerations such as using English as a second language. Conversely, describe the advantages of this source of information for working with clients. Suggested sites are listed below:
   - The National Center for PTSD at **http://www.ncptsd.org.**
   - The National Institutes of Mental Health website provides an array of information on the anxiety disorders (and specific disorders such as obsessive-compulsive disorder, panic disorder, post-traumatic stress disorder, social phobia and generalized anxiety disorder) at **http://www.nimh.nih.gov.**
   - Can you identify additional websites that may be helpful to clients who are struggling with anxiety disorders?
   - How would you incorporate these sources of information into your work?
2. Everyone feels fear at times, but a phobia is an exaggerated, unrealistic fear of a specific situation, activity, or object. Reflect on what you fear the most or interview someone who you know has a specific fear. Ask yourself (or the person interviewed):
   (a) How would I respond if I could not avoid encountering the object of my fear?
   (b) How much am I willing to rearrange my life to avoid this feared thing or situation?
   (c) Reflecting on my answers to these questions, is my fear a "phobia" or a normal source of apprehension?
3. For generalized anxiety disorder, interventions should be tailored for the individual based on age, severity and chronicity of symptoms, social context, and

any potential co-existing disorders. For mild anxiety, providing information about the disorder to clients is useful and self-help materials are a great resource. Visit your local bookstore and browse through the section of self-help books. Select a book that targets the topic of anxiety, and preview the publication with an eye toward how you might use this with a client who has generalized anxiety disorder. As an alternative, preview the book by Claire Weekes entitled *Peace from Nervous Suffering* mentioned in this chapter. This author also has a videocassette by the same title. Would the audiotape format have any advantages or disadvantages over a book?

- Self-help books and manuals are available for other anxiety disorders. Review the following materials and evaluate how you might use them with a client with obsessive-compulsive disorder:

   Hyman, B., & Pedrick, C. (1999). *The OCD workbook.* Oakland, CA: New Harbinger.

   Van Noppen, B., Pato, M., & Rasmussen, S. (1997). *Learning to live with OCD.* New Haven, CT: Obsessive-Compulsive Foundation.

- Identify additional self-help information you might use with a client and review the materials with a colleague who is also familiar with the anxiety disorders.

- What are the advantages and potential disadvantages of providing self-help books or tapes for your clients?

4. Culturally competent practitioners seek out education, consultation, and training opportunities to improve their understanding and effectiveness in working with culturally diverse populations. Recall the case of Jada Wu discussed in this chapter and identify the steps you would take to learn more about her culture. Generalize this learning to your work with clients who may be from other cultural backgrounds.

5. The following activities are adapted from Barlow and Craske (1994) and are designed to help you to become more aware of the sensation of panic. It is recommended that you complete these exercises with a trusted colleague and then talk about your sensations associated with "panic" with each other. Be careful to interrupt or stop the activity if you are feeling uncomfortable. If this happens, discuss with your partner your thoughts about what this sensation might be like for the person who is experiencing a panic attack and who feels no sense of control over these unexpected or unanticipated sensations.

- To produce the sensation of dizziness or disorientation, rapidly shake your head from side to side for about 30 seconds. As an alternative activity, find a chair that spins. Have your partner spin you around for about one minute. If you are unable to find this kind of chair, you can also stand and spin around for about one minute. Be sure to be near a comfortable chair or couch so that you can immediately sit down when done. You might also invoke the feeling of nausea by this spinning activity.

- To evoke the sensation of chest tightness and smothering feelings, hold your breath for as long as you can. Have your partner time you for at least 30 to 45 seconds, but try to go for a longer period of time.

- Hyperventilate (breathe deeply and quickly, using a lot of force) for about one minute. Be sure to sit down while doing this. This activity may produce feelings of unreality, shortness of breath, tingling, cold or hot sensations, dizziness, or even a headache.
- To bring about the sensation of lightheadedness, place your head between your legs for about 30 seconds and then lift it quickly.
- To experience muscle tension, weakness, and trembling, tense every part of your body for about one minute without causing pain. Be sure to tense the muscles in your arms, legs, stomach, back, shoulders, and face—everything! You may also try holding a push-up position for as long as you can.

SOMATOFORM, FACTITIOUS, AND MALINGERING DISORDERS

My Aunt Carol always loved company, but after a while I used to dread going to see her. She was my father's middle sister. That side of the family was really pretty healthy . . . but not Aunt Carol! It seemed that all she talked about was her latest ailment. At first it was kind of interesting, especially when I was in high school and thinking about a career as a nurse. She had this uncanny ability to exaggerate even the slightest headache into some kind of rare brain tumor. At first we used to joke about Aunt Carol's "disease of the month" but after a while her preoccupations got to be really boring. It seemed she had little else to talk about! We used to wonder how Uncle Jerry could stand it! Apparently Aunt Carol had a better relationship with her doctors than her own husband! Guess that's why Uncle Jerry was always down in the basement working on some project. What's going on with Aunt Carol?

In the United States, hundreds of thousands of individuals visit their physician with complaints that cannot be explained by physical disease (Phillips, 2001). For some people, much like the author's Aunt Carol, the preoccupation about health or appearance can become so intense that it dominates their life. These problems can be classified as somatoform disorders (APA, 2000). The key feature of this class of disorders is the presence of physical complaints that cannot be explained completely by a medical condition, substance use, or another mental disorder.

In 1859, a French physician named Pierre Briquet provided the first formal description of the somatoform disorders. Known for his willingness to listen to his patients at great length, he described individuals who had seemingly endless lists of ailments but no supporting medical basis for their symptoms (Stone, 1997). Briquet's observations advanced the idea that people were usually afflicted early in life, and their symptoms were manifested by recurrent, unexplained, somatic complaints noted in many organ sites (Zide & Gray, 2001). The disorder, included in the *Diagnostic and Statistical Manual* (DSM) as somatization disorder in 1980 (APA, 1980), was originally referred to as hysteria or Briquet's syndrome. Hysteria was primarily seen as a physical disorder.

During the Middle Ages, the concept of hysteria shifted from a medical condition to a spiritual disorder emerging from demonic possession. North and Guze (1997) observe that a seventeenth-century English physician by the name of Thomas Sydenham noticed that hysteria could disguise almost any medical disease. The term *neurosis* was adopted a century later to describe a type of nervous energy or nervous force thought to play an important part in the etiology of certain illnesses having medical, neurological, or emotional underpinnings (Fabrega, 1991; North, 2002).

During the latter part of the nineteenth century, understanding of the psychological and organic disorders became more differentiated, and so did our understanding of hypochondriasis, hysteria, and neurasthenia (or unexplained fatigue and lassitude). "The term *hypochondriasis* has carried multiple meanings in modern as well as historical cultures, and therefore it is an imprecise term that may encompass a wide variety of contexts" (North & Guze, 1997, p. 277). Hypochondriasis has ancient roots. The Greeks referred to "hypochondria" as the region of the body below the ribs. The organs in this area were believed to affect the person's mental state. As the etiology of the disorder was refined, physical complaints without a clear cause continued to be labeled as "hypochondriasis" (Barsky, 1992). In hypochondriasis, the individual has an overwhelming and unrelenting preoccupation with physical symptoms and the threat seems so real that no amount of reassurance, even from a physician, is helpful.

Another term was introduced during the late nineteenth century, dysmorphophobia, to describe people having a disproportionately negative attitude toward parts of their bodies (Berrios & Kan, 1996). Coined by Enrico Morselli, dysmorphophobia was characterized as an "imagined ugliness" (Phillips, 1991). It was referenced in European literature during the 1960s and 1970s and formally introduced in the United States when it was included in the DSM-III–R (APA, 1987).

UNDERSTANDING SOMATOFORM, FACTITIOUS, AND MALINGERING DISORDERS

Somatization can be defined as a process where the individual, such as Aunt Carol mentioned above, consciously or unconsciously uses bodily symptoms (or the body) for psychological gain or personal gain. When considering the various factors relevant to the somatization process, it is helpful to distinguish between "illness" and "disease." Disease is defined as "a pathological condition of the body that presents a group of clinical signs, symptoms, and laboratory findings peculiar to it and setting the condition apart as an abnormal entity differing from other normal or pathological conditions" (Thomas, 1997, p. 552). Illness refers to those experiences associated with disease that ultimately affect the individual's state of being and social functioning (Zide & Gray, 2001). Somatoform disorders, factitious disorders, and malingering represent degrees of illness behavior distinguished by somatization. With factitious disorders and malingering, unlike somatoform disorders, the physical symptoms are intentional. Diagnostic categories are often thought of as a continuum of abnormal illness behavior. How do the person's symptoms serve to resolve life circumstances or express psychological conflicts? Despite the individual's motivation, competency-based treatment provides a blueprint for the practitioner to intervene in ways that are attentive to the personal, interpersonal, and social context of the person's illness behavior while being mindful of the degree to which he or she is suffering or unable to engage in usual activities.

The DSM lists five basic somatoform disorders: somatization disorder, conversion disorder, pain disorder, hypochondriasis, and body dysmorphic disorder. Related disorders are factitious disorders and malingering. The factitious disorders are characterized by physical and psychological symptoms that are intentionally produced or feigned so the person may assume the sick role. Malingering also involves feigning symptoms, but the person is motivated by some kind of an incentive such as avoiding work or achieving financial gain through insurance benefits. Unlike the malingering and factitious disorders, the physical symptoms characterizing the somatoform disorders are not intentionally manufactured. The combination of imagined and intentional physical symptoms, and the individual's emotional response to them, make it difficult for the practitioner to correctly diagnose these syndromes. Therefore, it is important to recommend a thorough medical screening before any intervention is attempted. The first disorder to be discussed is somatization disorder.

Somatization Disorder

Somatization disorder is considered to be very rare. It begins early in life, affects mostly women, and is characterized by recurring, multiple, clinically significant complaints. The person with somatization disorder will seek medical attention for almost every ache or pain. People with this disorder may begin to reinvent or create changes in their condition regarding the intensity, duration, severity, or level of impairment in their health and medical problems. The person's symptoms become a part of life. If the individual gains some relief, new complaints emerge. Hardly a year passes without the experience of some intense physical discomfort. Caution Zide and Gray (2001), it is important for the practitioner to listen carefully when people talk about their medical history. When an individual who has somatization disorder is asked to describe when symptoms first started, the information given may be somewhat inaccurate, vague, and uncertain. Additionally, the person may exaggerate about when the symptoms first began and dramatize the description. A red flag in a client's medical background is a complicated medical history fraught with multiple diagnoses, failed treatments, and voluminous medical records. Some persons may show indifference while describing a seemingly tragic medical event (known as *la belle indifference*). It may be helpful for the practitioner to explore the extent to which a person suffering from a somatoform disorder wants to get better, versus what it would entail for them to give up physical symptoms that are sometimes used to control or manipulate others, hold on to a relationship, or divert attention from other problems. Of note, *alexithymia* is the term used to describe an inability to identify and articulate one's feelings and needs, or a tendency to experience and express emotions through physical symptoms.

Somatization criteria require the presence of at least eight symptoms (APA, 2000; Barlow & Durand, 2005; Munson, 2001; Zide & Gray, 2001). For those reporting fewer than eight symptoms, the diagnosis of undifferentiated somatization disorder may be applied. Somatization disorder should be considered if the following conditions are met:

- Onset starts before the age of 30 and the individual has a history of many physical complaints over the past several years;
- Treatment is sought for these physical symptoms, or the individual has experienced significant impairment in social, occupational, or other important areas of interpersonal functioning;
- Individual symptoms occur at any time during the course of the disturbance (these symptoms do not have to be concurrent):
  - Pain symptoms (four or more) related to different sites or functions, such as the head, abdomen, back/spine, joints, extremities, chest, rectum; or related to bodily functions (such as during sexual intercourse, menstruation, or urination);
  - Gastrointestinal symptoms (two or more, excluding pain), such as nausea, bloating, vomiting (other than during pregnancy), diarrhea, intolerance of certain foods;
  - Sexual symptoms (at least one, excluding pain), such as indifference to sex, difficulties with erection or ejaculation, irregular menses, excessive menstrual bleeding, or vomiting throughout an entire pregnancy.
  - Pseudoneurological symptoms (at least one), such as poor balance or poor coordination, paralysis or localized weakness, difficulty in swallowing or feeling a lump in the throat, loss of voice, urinary retention, hallucinations, loss of touch or pain sensation, double vision, blindness, deafness, or seizures or other dissociative symptoms such as amnesia or loss of consciousness (other than fainting). None of these are limited to pain; that is, pain in itself is not enough to assess the presence of a pseudoneurological symptom.
- For each of the symptoms noted above, one of the following additional conditions must also be met:
  - Symptoms cannot be fully explained by a general medical condition (upon appropriate physical or laboratory exam) or by the use of substances; or
  - When there is a related general medical condition, the reported impairment or physical complaints exceed what would generally be expected (based on history, physical exam, or laboratory findings).
- The person does not consciously feign or intentionally produce his or her symptoms (as found in factitious disorder, which involves maintaining the sick role for secondary gain) or in malingering (such as to achieve some material gain) (APA, 2000; Zide & Gray, 2001).

In sum, a person must suffer from a particular number of physical complaints from four categories: four pain symptoms; two gastrointestinal symptoms; one sexual symptom; and one pseudoneurological symptom. This history of many physical complaints begins before 30 years of age and lasts for several years, resulting in treatment or impaired functioning. The person's symptoms cannot be explained by a general medical condition and if one is present, complaints are beyond what could be expected for the disorder. Finally, symptoms are not intentional or feigned.

Conversion Disorder

The essential feature of conversion disorder is the presence of symptoms affecting voluntary motor or sensory function that suggest a neurological or other general medical condition. Individuals with conversion symptoms frequently come to the practitioner's attention via emergency services, such as a hospital emergency room. With some exceptions, this disorder has a somewhat better outcome than somatization disorder. Individuals are less likely to have chronic or disabling illnesses (Kent, Tomasson, & Coryell, 1995). Most conversion reactions often disappear spontaneously over hours or days, either gradually or (less commonly) all at once. This loss of symptoms may be due to the lessening of some underlying anxiety-provoking trigger, or to the adoption of more efficient ways to deal with problems or to the loss of secondary (unconscious) gain. For example, others may ignore the person's "sick role." In some cultures, conversion symptoms can appear suddenly in groups of people as part of a phenomenon that is sometimes referred to as mass hysteria (Ford, 1995).

The criteria for conversion disorder are listed below (APA, 2000; Zide & Gray, 2001):

- One or more symptoms affecting voluntary motor or sensory function, suggesting a neurological or other medical condition;
- Psychological factors associated with interpersonal conflicts or other social stressors;
- Symptoms are not intentionally produced or feigned as in factitious or malingering disorder;
- Symptoms are not fully explained by a general medical condition, medication, effects of a substance, or culturally sanctioned behaviors;
- Symptoms are not limited to pain or sexual dysfunction;
- Symptoms do not occur solely during somatization disorder, and no other medical disorder better explains them;
- Symptoms cause clinically significant impairment.

It is important to distinguish among the subtypes of this disorder:

- Motor symptom deficit (including difficulties such as swallowing, poor balance or gait, paralysis or weakness in arms or legs, loss of voice, and urinary retention)
- Sensory deficit (such as losing the sensation of touch or pain, blindness or deafness)
- Seizures or convulsions
- Mixed presentation.

There is no generally accepted explanation for how a psychological stress can convert into symptoms, and the Freudian interpretation of defense mechanisms remains the prevalent explanation (Crimlisk, Bhatia, Cope, Marsden, & Ron, 1998). To bridge the gap left by the traditional overreliance on psychodynamic theory, neuropsychology has emerged to offer alternative explanations for the cognitive processes that may cause clinical symptoms (Spence, 1999). Neuropsychologists study the brain and the rest of the nervous system in order to gain a better understanding of aspects of human behavior such as volition, memory, and motor and sensory control.

Pain Disorder

An important feature of pain disorder is that the client feels actual discomfort, regardless of its cause (Aigner & Bach, 1999). Criteria for this diagnosis include a preoccupation with pain for at least 6 months and pain that is either grossly in excess of what would be expected from physical findings or for which no underlying organic pathology can be detected. The pain causes significant distress for the person, and dysfunction is not intentional. Psychological factors are considered to play a role in the onset of pain, and the pain is not better explained by another mental disorder. Pain disorder, like conversion disorder, requires the practitioner to consider intrapersonal factors that play a role in the development or maintenance of symptoms (Zide & Gray, 2001).

The assessment for pain disorder is based on the following criteria (APA, 2000; Zide & Gray, 2001):

- Pain that occurs in more than one anatomical site is the presenting problem and the predominant focus for seeking clinical attention (the pain is severe enough to warrant clinical attention);
- The pain causes distress that impairs social or occupational functioning;
- Intrapersonal factors are considered important in the onset, severity, and exacerbation of pain (or these factors support maintenance of the pain);
- The person does not consciously feign the pain symptoms (as seen in malingering or factitious disorder);
- The pain is not explained by a mood, anxiety, or psychotic disorder, and it does not meet the criteria for dyspareunia (that is, pain that occurs during or after sexual intercourse).

Pain that lasts for less than six months is considered acute. If pain lasts longer, it is labeled as chronic.

Hypochondriasis

Some 20 billion dollars per year in wasted medical resources are expended on persons with hypochondriasis in the United States (Lemonick, 2003). With the recent proliferation of medical information that is available through the Internet, it seems likely that the problem has been getting worse. Today, people can go on the Web and learn about new diseases and new presentations of old diseases that they have never heard about before. Physicians refer to this phenomenon as "cyberchondria"

(Lemonick, 2003). For those struggling with hypochondriasis, severe anxiety is focused on the possibility of having a serious disease. No amount of reassurance seems helpful for very long, and people live in constant terror that they are dying of some awful disease or even several awful diseases at once. While anxiety is a central feature of the diagnosis, it is expressed by the individual's preoccupation with bodily symptoms, which are misinterpreted as indicative of illness or serious disease. The individual's concerns persist after medical evaluation does not substantiate the presence of "illness" and are not of delusional intensity. The person can acknowledge the lack of a medical cause of the concern but physical signs and symptoms are *interpreted* as evidence of having an actual physical illness. Significant distress or dysfunction is present and lasts for more than six months. Because of this focus on illness, the person usually turns first to the family physician for help and comes to the social worker's attention after a realistic medical condition has been ruled out.

Assessing somatic symptoms is challenging for the practitioner. When working with clients from different cultural backgrounds who may have differing perceptions of physical signs, it is important to be attentive to the client's construction of the illness experience. This is particularly meaningful when the practitioner has a different cultural background. For example, *"dhat"* (a culture-specific disorder prevalent in India) is an anxious concern about losing semen, a process that occurs naturally during sexual intercourse (Barlow & Durand, 2005; Castillo, 1997). *Dhat* is associated with a vague mix of physical symptoms including dizziness, weakness, and fatigue, all of which are attributed to semen loss. Attempting to tell a client from India that *dhat* syndrome is something imagined would obviously discount the client's cultural schemas and explanations. Ideally, the source of the client's distress should be addressed through a process more culturally familiar to the client, such as symbolic healing, in addition to the more prevalent explanatory models. With its attention to the full range of the client's experiences, competency-based treatment enables the practitioner to construct culturally relevant interventions— for example, including folk healers (refer to Chapter 8 for a more detailed case illustration), in conjunction with other treatment models. Counseling is not a culturally universal concept, and therefore it is important to identify and learn from culturally indigenous practices of health and healing.

Body Dysmorphic Disorder

A central feature of dysmorphic disorder (historically called dysmorphophobia) is the individual's persistent belief that his or her appearance is somehow defective. Virtually any part of the body may be the focus of some imagined defect. The preoccupation causes distress and functional impairment. The individual's concerns persist despite medical evaluation and reassurance and are not of delusional intensity. The individual can acknowledge the lack of a medical cause of the concern. The duration of the disturbance is more than six months.

The more common symptoms that the social worker will encounter in practice involve facial flaws such as wrinkles, spots and/or texture of the skin, excessive facial hair, and the shape of the nose, jaw, mouth, eyes, or eyebrows (Zide & Gray, 2001).

If there happens to be some very slight physical defect present, the concern is grossly exaggerated and in excess of what would be considered "normal." While the person's appearance causes a great deal of distress, he or she appears normal to others. The preoccupation with physical appearance includes extreme self-consciousness and embarrassment, excessive importance given to appearance in self-evaluation, avoidance of activities, body camouflaging, and a pattern of constant body checking (Rosen & Reiter, 1996). To illustrate, imagine that you have a mole on the side of your nose about the size of the period at the end of this sentence. Take your hand and make it into a fist. Place your fist on the side of your nose where this "mole" is located. For the person struggling with body dysmorphic disorder, this tiny mole seems to be as big as your fist!

The social and cultural environment can play a role in diagnosis, and it is important for the practitioner to be aware of this influence. Some racial and ethnic minority persons may have been the target of discrimination or harassment based solely on their appearance. If this has happened on a consistent basis, the individual may be preoccupied with how they look, particularly those "defects" defined by the dominant group. The practitioner should be mindful that persons who have encountered discrimination based on their appearance might want to alter how they look based on these very real experiences. As Castillo (1997) observes, many Jewish American women are born with a "Jewish nose" and undergo cosmetic surgery to fix their "defect." He goes on to note that the "defect" is not imaginary but has been constructed by prevailing cultural schemas.

Re-Thinking Cultural Influences

Undifferentiated somatoform disorder and somatoform disorder not otherwise specified are included in this chapter to help the practitioner carry out interventions attentive to those behaviors that do not quite meet the categories discussed earlier and to avoid stigmatizing or stereotyping clients. Here, too, culture may play a role in understanding a person's manifestation of physical illness, a central feature of the somatoform disorders. Additionally, culture can influence the type and frequency of symptoms. What may be considered "pathology" by people outside the group may actually represent culturally acceptable and adaptive behaviors (Gilgun, 1996); for example *neurasthenia* is one of the most commonly diagnosed disorders in China. The symptoms of headaches, insomnia, and related vague somatic complaints are considered to be related to stress rather than to pathology. Somatic symptoms have far more importance in the Chinese culture and physical complaints are used as cultural idioms expressing emotional distress. Therefore, the person primarily notices and reports somatic symptoms and is less attentive to expressing emotional distress. However, the practitioner, trained in the DSM classification system in which *neurasthenia* is not listed, may pay more attention to the symptoms they consider significant and "see" the symptom picture differently; for example, as the person complains about not sleeping well the practitioner may be thinking about the symptoms supporting a diagnosis of depression rather than hearing the story of someone who is "stressed."

Because competency-based practice is attentive to the full range of the client's life including social and environmental influences, culturally relevant interventions are a fundamental aspect of this model. Specific interventions, adapted from Van Voorhis (1998) can be summarized as follows:

- *Listen carefully to the client's "story."* This involves listening to what clients have to say instead of interpreting the client's experiences from the dominant cultural view of mental illness.
- *Assess the intrapersonal, interpersonal, and community/environmental effects of a diagnosis on clients (and families).* As the client tells his or her "story," the practitioner listens for:
  - Effects of the diagnosis of mental illness on the client's life span, time, energy, mobility, or identity;
  - The extent to which the client feels alienated from self or others because of the diagnosis;
  - Strengths, resources, and sources of personal power utilized in response to the diagnosis, particularly the protective factors and/or resilience and buffers that help clients respond to adversity;
  - The primary pattern of coping and ways clients experience problems related to having a diagnosis.
- *Be self-aware.* The practitioner should critically assess his or her own ideas about a particular disorder and explore how these assumptions could be projected onto the work with clients.
- *Intervene to enhance the person's identity before (or without) the diagnosis.*

By carefully listening to the client's "story" and considering the client's social context, the practitioner connects with each person's unique perceptions of mental illness. This process fosters an understanding of the client's unique experiences with the diagnosis. The client and his or her uniqueness as a human being struggling with mental illness moves into the foreground of competency-based treatment, and the diagnosis of illness recedes into the background. Understandably, this involves a mutually empathic, collaborative relationship that is at the heart of competency-based practice. By validating the client's experiences regarding the diagnosis, the practitioner acknowledges not having all the answers. Mutual collaboration affirms the client's capacity to resolve problems. In sum, competency-based treatment synthesizes concepts from a range of practice theories into a meaningful whole and avoids objectifying clients by their diagnosis. Among the other somatoform categories, the following section addresses undifferentiated somatoform disorder followed by somatoform disorder not otherwise specified.

Undifferentiated Somatoform Disorder

This disorder was almost eliminated from the DSM-IV because of its lack of specificity but ultimately kept because of its relevance to primary health care settings (Frances, First, & Pincus, 1995). Although it has its own diagnostic category, undifferentiated somatoform disorder is really just somatization disorder with fewer than eight symptoms. This diagnosis is considered when one or more physical complaints lasting for more than six months cannot be explained by a general medical condition. The remaining criteria are the same as those for somatization disorder.

Somatoform Disorder Not Otherwise Specified

This category is reserved for disorders that do not meet the full criteria of the other disorders described in this chapter. An example would be a woman's false belief that she is pregnant, associated with the objective signs of a pregnancy (pseudocyesis) such as an enlarged abdomen, nausea, amenorrhea, breast engorgement, perception of fetal movements, and labor pains at the "due date." Another symptom cluster includes non-psychotic hypochondriacal symptoms that would meet the criteria for hypochondriasis except that they do not last for the required six months. Unexplained symptoms that last for less than six months and are not caused by another psychological disorder may fall into this category. A relatively new phenomenon is environmental illness, a polysymptomatic disorder associated with immune system dysfunction and allergy-like sensitivity to many compounds found in chemicals, food, clothing, perfumes, and airborne substances (Neligh, 1996). Two conditions that are related to the somatoform disorders are factitious disorder and malingering disorder.

Related Disorders: Factitious and Malingering

The factitious disorders are defined by physical and psychological symptoms intentionally produced so that a person may assume the sick role, whereas malingering involves feigning symptoms.

Factitious Disorder   This category includes people who display physical and psychological symptoms that have been intentionally produced, under voluntary control, and deliberately used to pursue a desired goal. The diagnosis is based on a careful examination of behavior, motivation, and medical history. Medical records are particularly helpful in identifying suspicious circumstances and inconsistencies in the person's description of symptoms (Krahn, Li, & O'Connor, 2003). Factitious disorder has the following criteria (APA, 2000):

- Intentional production or feigning of physical (or psychological) signs/symptoms;
- Motivation to assume the "sick role";
- Absence of external incentives such as the prospect of economic gain.

Subtypes of this disorder include factitious disorder with predominantly psychological signs and symptoms, factitious disorder with predominantly physical signs and symptoms; and factitious disorder with combined psychological signs and physical symptoms. Munchausen by proxy, a variant of factitious disorder, occurs within the context of a relationship between parent and child. It is recorded under the subtype of "with predominantly physical signs/symptoms." This disorder occurs when the caregiver, usually the parent, deliberately falsifies the child's medical history and subjects the child to unnecessary medical procedures and unneeded hospitalizations. A false medical description may be provided, laboratory samples may be contaminated, and injuries may be inflicted on the child.

Malingering Disorder   Malingering disorder differs from factitious disorder in that the motivation for symptom production in malingering disorder involves an external incentive (for example, avoidance of criminal prosecution or military duty) whereas in factitious disorder external incentives are absent. The "illness" provides opportunities for a temporary escape from harsh situations. The person deliberately and consciously feigns illness or grossly exaggerates physical (or psychological) symptoms), pretending to be suffering from an illness that is nonexistent.

OVERVIEW OF MAJOR INTERVENTIONS

Somatization Disorder and Undifferentiated Somatoform Disorder

Although somatization disorder and undifferentiated somatoform disorder differ in severity, treatment approaches are similar. People with either one of these disorders rarely seek counseling on their own; instead, they may engage in "doctor shopping" that leads to costly, inappropriate, and potentially dangerous overutilization of health care services (Campo & Garber, 1998; Cloninger, 1987, 1996). Typically, these individuals are seen and treated over and over without success by their physician who finally, in frustration, refers them for counseling. However, for the person struggling with somatization disorder, the effects of psychosomatic symptoms are very real. The symptoms may be physically, emotionally, and behaviorally genuine but without the physiologic signs; for example, a person may believe that he or she is actually having a heart attack, but testing reveals that the heart is functioning normally. Some psychosomatic symptoms may create actual physical damage, such as hemorrhaging from involuntary vomiting. Since somatization disorders are chronic, practitioners need to be aware of their own feelings toward clients who just do not seem to get any better.

It is helpful to listen carefully to the language people use to describe how somatization disorder affects their lives (and the lives of their family members), and negotiate a mutually agreeable understanding of "the problem" (McDaniel, Hepworth, & Doherty, 1995). McCahill (1995) adds that it is important for the practitioner to candidly discuss the diagnosis with the client. This disorder must be separated from factitious disorder (in which the person knowingly feigns illness) and from malingering (in which the person feigns illness for conscious and secondary gain). The primary goal of intervention is *not* to eliminate the person's physical complaints. Maxmen and Ward (1995) suggest that instead of raising false hopes the practitioner should accept clients "as they are." Non-complaining behaviors are reinforced and complaining behaviors are ignored (and if at all possible, the family is taught to do likewise).

Another intervention strategy is to develop a close collaboration with other professionals (Bentley & Walsh, 2001; McDaniel, Hepworth, & Doherty, 1995), particularly the client's physician, since the individual with somatization disorder may have a real physical illness that may be concurrent or hidden (or later develop). General principles to guide the practitioner's work include coordination of efforts among multiple health and mental health care professionals; attention to life stresses; observation for co-morbid disorders (for example, major depression); and maintenance of ongoing, supportive contacts with the client.

Cognitive-behavioral group interventions that are beneficial include development of coping strategies, assertiveness training, taking control of one's own life, problem solving, risk taking, and recognizing and continuing positive changes (Kashner et al., 1995; Kroenke & Swindle, 2000; White & Freeman, 2000). An additional source of support can be found in mutual aid groups centering on sharing methods of coping with physical problems and increasing one's ability to perceive and express emotion (Schopler & Galinsky, 1996; Walsh & Hewitt, 1996). Another helpful intervention consists of participation in psychoeducational groups organized around a didactic presentation followed by small-group discussion to facilitate peer communication (Gabbard, 1995). Suggested topics could include learning how to be more assertive with health care professionals; developing strategies for taking more control and increasing the positive aspects of one's life; problem solving; and personal risk taking. Lock and Giammona (1999) suggest using multiple strategies aimed at rehabilitation, including behavioral shaping, supportive and family therapies, and a milieu approach on an inpatient psychiatry unit for those with severe somatoform disorders.

Fritzsche and Larisch (2003) describe a psychosocial treatment model consisting of the following steps: (a) taking a thorough symptom history and exploring the person's own perception of his or her illness; (b) developing alternative perceptions of the illness by understanding the relationship between physical and psychological factors; and (c) reducing the impact of stress in the person's life. The authors underscore the importance of eliciting the client's trust and cooperating with other involved health care professionals.

Conversion Disorder

Effective treatment of conversion disorder requires utilizing a range of skills, which Ford (1995) has organized around the "three Ps" of predisposition, precipitating stressors, and perpetuating factors. Similar to the competency-based model, each "P" considers the various dimensions of the client's life and serves as a shorthand way to conceptualize and formulate treatment interventions. Briefly:

- *Predisposition*—This aspect includes a consideration of (a) personality factors and past experiences; (b) impaired ability to communicate, and (c) underlying neurological (or co-morbid) disorders.
- *Precipitating stressors*—These stresses are often related to interpersonal difficulties (such as an impending divorce) or traumatic events (such as sexual abuse).
- *Perpetuating factors*—These features are found in secondary gain or the degree to which the conversion solves the person's problems. Ford (1995) cautions that social expectations within some cultures may lessen the individual's outward expression of certain feelings.

Treatment goals are aimed at relieving symptoms and addressing the various interpersonal or social factors that produced them. The treatment process includes a careful assessment of symptoms, candid discussion of the diagnosis with the person and his or her family, psychoeducation, and a "rehabilitative mindset" (Campo & Negrini, 2000). Reid, Balis, and Sutton (1997) describe an intervention called "pseudotreatment." In this approach, a person's conversion symptoms receive a specific (and face-saving) treatment targeting the apparent physiologic condition. Zide and Gray (2001) describe case experiences with a young woman who developed blindness (without supportive medical or neurological data) after witnessing a robbery. After being given a "special shot" in the hospital emergency room, this client experienced a spontaneous recovery. This face-saving measure did not confront the client's reasons for her blindness, and it is recommended that the practitioner follow up on this intervention with honesty about the "treatment" to avoid legitimating symptoms. Intervention in the person's social environment is also known to be helpful (Kukleta, Dufek, & Rektor, 1997) but not always possible; for example, who could have foreseen that this young woman would be a witness to a robbery? Many conversion symptoms spontaneously disappear within a few weeks to months of onset, and it may be helpful to reassure people that they will soon recover (Maxmen & Ward, 1995). There is emerging evidence that those individuals who experience a change in their life circumstances after the onset of symptoms will have a better prognosis (Binzer & Kullgren, 1996).

A number of short-term interventions can reduce or eliminate symptoms. Hypnosis is one treatment for conversion symptoms. Hypnotic phenomena and conversion symptoms share many features; for example, areas of the brain activated by paralysis induced by hypnosis are similar to those activated in hysterical paralysis (Halligan, Athwal, Oakley, & Frackowiak, 2000). Through hypnotic suggestion, the function of the affected organ may be restored and will be remembered when the person awakes. The amobarbital-assisted interview, in which an altered state of consciousness is achieved by the use of intravenous medication, is another approach. Amobarbital has been the traditional medication of choice, but lorazepam is also recommended as a substitute. Methylphenidate may be used to maintain wakefulness and facilitate the person's verbal production. In the altered state of consciousness, the person may relax and new information may be provided to effect a return of function (or partial function) to the affected body part.

Behavioral therapy is also frequently used for treating persons with conversion disorder; specific techniques include relaxation and biofeedback. Through biofeedback, intact sensory organs and innervation can be demonstrated, and muscle activity can be shown. This self-directed process provides the affected person with concrete evidence of the intact physiological functioning of the disabled body part. Donohue, Thevenin, and Runyon (1997) report success with the cognitive-behavioral technique of contingency management targeting specific symptoms. Contingency management procedures involve working with the client to specify desired behaviors, the tasks to be performed to achieve these desired behaviors, and the tasks that will be done by the client and those that will be carried out by the practitioner. A deadline is usually established for completing these tasks. The advantage of contingency management is that it serves to guide clients as to the specific actions they need to take in order to improve their problematic situations.

Pain Disorder

Interventions for pain disorder are intended to relieve pain (acute or chronic), decrease the person's disability and reliance on medications, and increase quality of life. Treatment approaches for acute and chronic pain are often similar, but there are some significant differences between acute and chronic pain. The primary goal for acute pain is relief. In contrast, chronic pain is more complex involving not only the pain but also underlying emotional and psychological antecedents, pain-related dysfunction or disability, comorbid disorders (for example, depressed mood, including major depression and dysthymic disorder), and factors sustaining the pain. A person's emotional reaction and capacity to cope with the fluctuating course of pain disorder can influence treatment. It is helpful for the practitioner to intervene early to prevent complications (Magni et al., 1994; Verma & Gallagher, 2000).

For those with chronic pain, a pain clinic may be the person's last hope. Because of the complexity of pain and the variety of medications prescribed, these clinics are usually found in larger medical institutions such as hospitals. Pain clinics primarily are multidisciplinary and use multiple modalities aimed at reinforcement for decreasing pain behavior as well as decreased use of medication and a lessened perception of pain (Barlow & Durand, 2005). The therapies most often used are biofeedback, nerve blocks, trigger point injections, acupuncture, physical therapy, and transcutaneous electrical nerve stimulation (TENS). The effectiveness of TENS has been inconsistently supported by research (Reid, Balis, & Sutton, 1997). Various types of relaxation and meditation procedures are also used (either alone or in combination with other approaches), but the reported results are fairly modest (Taylor, 1999). It seems the physical interventions for pain control have more of a placebo value; nonetheless, they are effective. Pain clinics offer individual and group therapy programs with particular attention to the personality and family dynamics operative in the individual's pain syndrome. The family may also be involved through educational programs and learning how to plan for activities of daily living. Insight-oriented psychodynamic psychotherapy is sometimes used but cognitive-behavioral techniques aimed at identifying and correcting distorted attitudes, beliefs, and expectations are generally recommended (Gabbard, 1995; Reid, Balis, & Sutton, 1997). Those who have a reduced activity level because of their pain may benefit from physical therapy.

Chronic pain is frequently associated with depression, and several antidepressant medications have also been shown to have analgesic effects (Stoudemire, 1994). The tricyclic antidepressants, including amitriptyline (Elavil) (which may be too sedating for some individuals), nortriptyline (Pamelor), imipramine (Tofranil), desipramine (Norpramine), clomipramine (Anafranil), and doxepin (Sinequan), have been found to be effective. Nontricyclic antidepressants such as maprotiline (Ludiomil) or trazodone (Desyrel) and the monoamine oxidase inhibitors (MAOIs) may also be useful, but the evidence of their effectiveness is not as strong as it is for the use of tricyclic antidepressants (Max et al., 1992).

Many additional medications have also been used. Low doses of neuroleptics, such as haloperidol (Haldol) and chlorpromazine (Thorazine), have been prescribed as adjuncts to analgesics (separate from their antipsychotic properties). Anticonvulsants such as phenytoin (Dilantin), carbamazepine (Tegretol), and sodium valproate (Depakene) have also been found to be effective. The benzodiazepines, too, are used as adjuncts in managing chronic pain but because of the side effects associated with chronic use, they may make it more difficult for the person to function. The benzodiazepines are prescribed more frequently for the sleep problems that accompany the pain (King & Strain, 1996).

One variable affecting treatment interventions for pain revolves around legal considerations. As discussed earlier, the subjective experience of pain may not always be clearly related to the degree of physical pathology. When someone may be financially compensated for their pain because of a lawsuit or a worker's compensation claim, it can be difficult to determine whether the person is distorting his or her pain experience for personal financial gain (Weintraub, 1995). This is not to say that most individuals who seek help are malingering. They may be receiving conflicting advice from physicians, lawyers, family members, and/or friends regarding the actual requirements for receiving compensation for an injury; for example, a certain level of physical inactivity may be necessary for compensation. People may also be afraid that if they can function sufficiently despite the pain, their financial compensation may be taken away. It may be prudent for the practitioner to discuss these issues and assist people to determine what is in their best interests.

Hypochondriasis

Until recently, hypochondriasis was seen as a disorder with no effective treatments, but there is increasing evidence that both psychotherapy and medication can be effective (Magarinos, Zafar, Nissenson, & Blanco, 2002). Pharmacological treatment of comorbid conditions (for example, depression, panic disorder, or obsessive-compulsive disorder) seems to be helpful. It appears that antidepressants, especially the selective serotonin reuptake inhibitors (SSRIs) hold promise (Magarinos et al., 2002). Those with hypochondriasis may actually represent three different groups with similar problems (Fallon, Klein, & Liebowitz, 1993; Fallon, Liebowitz, Salman, et al., 1994; Fallon, Qureshi, Laje, et al., 2000). The first group is considered to have a variant of obsessive-compulsive disorder. People in the second group have a problem that looks more like depression, often triggered by something that makes the person feel guilty, such as an extramarital affair. The third group consists of people who somatize; that is, they focus an inordinate amount of attention on their bodies. For them, a slight muscle spasm that most people would not even notice feels like someone has kicked them in the stomach.

Reassurance seems to be beneficial for some people. This is surprising since, by definition of having the diagnosis, reassurance about symptoms of illness is not effective for very long. Kellner (1992) summarizes a series of interventions that have proven to be helpful: consistently providing clients with the facts about their difficulties; clarifying the difference between pain and the experience of pain; explaining how emotions can affect the perception of physical sensation; demonstrating how selective attention and suggestion contribute to overestimating a symptom's seriousness; emphasizing that life goes on despite physical symptoms; and being empathic and accepting of the person's overwhelming, persistent preoccupation with physical symptoms.

Barsky (1996) and Warwick and Salkovskis (1990) report success with cognitive-behavioral therapy. In this approach, individuals are trained to take their attention away from symptoms and counter panicky thoughts with self-reassurance; for example, they are taught to remind themselves that a headache almost never means a brain tumor. Clark and colleagues (1998) provide evidence to support the efficacy of cognitive-behavioral therapy. In a study conducted by Avia et al. (1996), group therapy seemed helpful in producing significant reductions in illness-related fears and attitudes, somatic symptoms, and dysfunctional beliefs. Because individuals with hypochondriasis have a high rate of other disorders, it is also important to screen for comorbid conditions. The most consistent intervention associated with improvement is collaborative efforts between health care providers and practitioners (Magarinos et al., 2002).

Body Dysmorphic Disorder

Persons with body dysmorphic disorder are generally resistant to treatment (Rosen, 1995) and the most effective intervention appears to be an accurate diagnosis that ultimately prevents unnecessary and sometimes harmful treatments or surgeries. Despite the fact that this disorder is relatively common (Albertini & Phillips, 1999; Perugi, Akiskal, & Lattanzi, 1998; Phillips et al., 2000) and causes severe distress and functional impairment (Cotterill, 1996; De Marco et al., 1998; Phillips, 2002), research on the treatment of body dysmorphic disorder has been limited (Phillips, 2000; Phillips et al., 2001).

Cognitive-behavioral techniques reported to be helpful include cognitive restructuring of private body talk to reduce the undue importance given to physical appearance, exposure to avoided body image situations, and response prevention of body checking and grooming behaviors (Rosen, 1995; Wilhelm, Otto, Lohr, & Deckersbach 1999). Maintenance or booster sessions are recommended to prevent relapse in people with severe symptoms of BDD.

Medication has been used with mixed results, and more studies are needed (Grant, 2001; Phillips, 2000; Phillips et al., 2000; Phillips, Albertini, Siniscalchi, Khan, & Robinson, 2001). Because of the comorbidity of BDD with major depression and obsessive-compulsive disorder, the use of selective serotonin reuptake inhibitors (SSRIs) is considered a first-line approach (Anderson, 2003). Antipsychotic medications should be limited to augmentation treatment with other agents, such as the SSRIs, even for those experiencing delusions (Phillips, 2002). Atypical antipsychotic medications, such as olanzapine (Zyprexa), quetiapene (Seroquel), ziprasidone (Geodon), and risperidone (Risperdal) may be more effective and better tolerated than the typical antipsychotic medications such as haloperidol (Haldol) and chlorpromazine (Thorazine). Medication alone does not address all symptoms of BDD and is generally combined with therapy, particularly cognitive-behavioral interventions.

Many persons with BDD turn to surgery to treat their symptoms, but this approach is controversial. BDD appears to be comorbid with obsessive/compulsive disorder, major depression, or other psychiatric conditions, and these conditions may be missed or underdiagnosed. An accurate diagnosis is important when surgery is considered because the person with co-existing disorders is generally dissatisfied with the outcome of surgery. In fact, surgical interventions rarely improve the person's situation and may even make matters worse (Cunningham & Feinmann, 1998). Because of the poor response, surgery is generally not recommended (Phillips et al., 2001).

Factitious Disorder

Most individuals with factitious disorder will not admit the "factitious" nature of their symptoms (even when confronted with incontrovertible evidence), thus complicating treatment. Even with the gentlest confrontation, individuals usually react with hostility and reject any offers of help. It is important to evaluate for any genuine medical disease. Several non-confrontational counseling approaches can be helpful. One is to allow the individual to relinquish the factitious symptom in a face-saving way (Klonoff & Moore, 1986). For instance, an individual may be taught biofeedback techniques as a strategy to gain control over the factitious symptoms. A related intervention is aversive conditioning. Solyom and Solyom (1990) describe a case in which uncomfortable electrical stimulation was applied to the leg muscles of an individual with paraplegia. The person was informed that the length of treatments would increase if they were not effective, and he quickly regained the ability to walk. Instead of confrontation, the individual was able to "save face" by claiming that the electrical stimulation treatments were effective and had healed him. Face-saving measures help the practitioner to avoid getting into a power struggle and embarrassing the client.

A second technique called inexact interpretations has been described. The practitioner provides an interpretation about the person's condition that is partially correct but incomplete (Eisendrath, 1989; Eisendrath, Rand, & Feldman, 1996). For example, the practitioner "interprets" the person's underlying psychodynamics but does not identify the factitious nature of the disorder. Eisendrath (1989) reports the case of a young woman who was guilt-ridden as a consequence of childhood abuse. After her boyfriend proposed marriage, she developed unexplained septicemia. The practitioner suggested (or interpreted) to the young woman that she might feel a need to punish herself when good things happen such as the marriage proposal, but the practitioner did not connect the guilt feelings with the client's physical symptoms. Several days later the young woman admitted to faking her symptoms and entered into counseling.

A third technique is the use of a therapeutic double bind. The individual is informed that a differential diagnosis for the presenting symptoms includes a factitious etiology. In other words, if the medical treatment is ineffective it will confirm the presence of factitious disorder.

Overall, little is known about the successful treatment of factitious disorders. Part of the difficulty is that many of these individuals abruptly leave counseling or prematurely terminate treatment and it is hard to follow up with them. Co-occurring disorders that are frequently reported include substance abuse and suicide (Popli, Masand, & Dewan, 1992).

Malingering Disorder

The practitioner usually encounters individuals with malingering disorder in outpatient settings where they are less likely to subject themselves to invasive medical procedures (Overholser, 1990). They are often facing litigation or some type of criminal prosecution. It is difficult to detect malingering. Once a diagnosis is made, it is natural for the practitioner and other health care providers to react with negative feelings of anger or frustration in response to the individual's deception even when they understand the situation intellectually. The first step is for the practitioner to acknowledge that these feelings exist, and then it is equally important to seek the help of a supervisor to process these reactions instead of projecting them onto the client. A nonjudgmental attitude is fundamental to social work practice, and treatment is more effective if the practitioner is able to relate to people with malingering disorder "as they are."

RISKS ASSOCIATED WITH SOMATOFORM, FACTITIOUS, AND MALINGERING DISORDERS

Intrapersonal Risks

Stress is a risk factor for persons with somatization disorder. Periods of distress seem to coincide with the onset of new symptoms and increased health care-seeking behavior; for example, Swartz et al. (1998) found 95 percent of those with somatization disorder had visited a health care provider in the previous 6 months compared with only 56 percent of other community residents. According to Katon (1993), individuals who felt emotionally distressed were more likely to seek medical services than to go in for mental health counseling.

Clients with a positive self-image and a confident sense of self are rarely seen by social workers. A poor self-image increases one's risks, and people with somatization disorder tend to regard themselves as being in poor health. Smith, Monson, and Ray (1986) compared the perceptions of persons with chronic medical conditions (for example, hypertension, rheumatoid arthritis, chronic obstructive pulmonary disease, or insulin-dependent diabetes mellitus) with those of people with somatization disorder. Individuals with somatization disorder perceived their overall health status as "sicker than the sick."

Brodsky (1984) observes that persons with somatization disorder have learned to develop a repertoire of maladaptive coping strategies that are used to withdraw from usual life activities (or to engage, manipulate, or punish others). They are unmotivated to seek help, and the very problems that should lead them to seek counseling services may impair their judgment (Zapka, McCusker, Stoddard, & Morrison, 1990).

There is emerging evidence of a biological predisposition increasing the risk for somatization disorder. It does seem to run in families and has a component of inheritance (Andreasen & Black, 1995; Katon, 1993). Neurophysiological studies are in the preliminary stages and require more investigation. One model with some support suggests a dysfunction in the brain circuit mediating the behavior inhibition system (running from the septal area through the hippocampus to the orbital frontal cortex). This dysfunction has been implicated in somatization disorder as well as in substance abuse, antisocial personality disorder, and possibly attention deficit hyperactivity disorder (Cloninger, 1987, 1996; Lilienfeld, 1992).

Interpersonal Risks

The diagnosis of somatization disorder is often associated with childhood experiences that include pain (or serious illness) in a family member (Hartvig & Sterner, 1985). Brodsky (1984) identified several family factors that can increase the risk of a diagnosis of somatization disorder: the individual is raised in a family with a history of multiple physical complaints; parent(s) were seen as demanding and unrewarding when the child was healthy but caring and loving when the child was sick; a home environment in which one (or both) parents suffered from multiple illnesses; and an environment where other coping mechanisms for handling psychosocial crises were unavailable. Persons with somatization disorder are noted for their chaotic lives reflected in interpersonal relationship difficulties such as multiple marriages or problems at work.

Gender is another risk factor. Women, in particular, with a reported history of childhood sexual and/or physical abuse are more likely to experience somatic complaints later in life (Pribor, Yutzy, Dean, & Wetzel, 1993; Slavney, 1994).

Community and Environmental Risks

Socioeconomic status, culture, and ethnicity create risks. One barrier to receiving services is inadequate health insurance coverage (Crow, Smith, McNamee, & Piland, 1994) and a related issue is the person's "out-of-pocket" expenses such as copayments. Looking at those assessed with somatization disorder, Ford (1995) notes that in the United States, unmarried, poorly educated women of color are most at risk to be assessed as having the disorder. Pomeroy and Wambach (2003) observe that persons with somatoform disorders tend to be somewhat "unsophisticated"; that is, they live in rural communities, belong to a lower socioeconomic class, and are relatively uneducated about medical and/or psychological problems.

Piccinelli and Simon (1997) addressed the influence of ethnicity on symptoms reported and help-seeking behaviors. Somatization disorder is found to be more common among African Americans (Adebimpe, 1994) than among members of other groups, and they are likely to turn to natural helping networks such as friends, relatives (Sussman, Robbins, & Earls, 1987), or clergy (Brown, Ahmed, Gary, & Milburn, 1995) before seeking professional counseling.

CASE ILLUSTRATION: BRAD JONES

Malingering involves a pattern of behavior similar to that of someone with a genuine medical disorder (Zide & Gray, 2001). The following case discussion provides a transcript of the "conversation" between a client diagnosed with malingering disorder and the social worker, Nancy Ellen Walker. The practitioner struggled with the client's abrupt termination of the session. Thinking that she might have missed something important, Ms. Walker brought the case to her clinical supervisor. To prepare for the supervisory conference, the supervisor asked Ms. Walker to provide a process recording (a verbatim account of what transpired) of the perplexing interaction that had occurred. The supervisor also asked her to identify her feelings and reactions to the client's behavior. These reactions are noted in parentheses in the interview transcript. The supervisor reminded Ms. Walker that regardless of whether the client's physical problems are real or imagined, they are real to him. The supervisor went on to agree that the client's reaction seemed out of proportion to what the problem might actually be and asked Ms. Walker to think about why the client might have become so defensive during the interview. The supervisor commented, "You know, Nancy Ellen, this guy is really different from you. He works as a short-order cook, and I'm wondering if he even graduated from high school. Do you think any of this might have influenced your judgment about him?" This comment set the stage for a discussion of the areas of diversity that may have potentially influenced Ms. Walker's responses to her client. [This case was first introduced in Zide and Gray's Psychopathology: A Competency-Based Assessment Model for Social Workers *(2001).]*

Brad Jones entered the social worker's office in obvious distress. "Ow, ow, that hurts, oh my gosh, ow, my neck hurts something terrible," said Mr. Jones as he was attempting to sit down. The social worker, Ms. Nancy Ellen Walker, noticed that the late afternoon sun streamed into her office and seemed to shine directly into Mr. Jones's eyes. Thinking that it might be uncomfortable for him, she asked if he would like to move to another chair. Rather quickly and with surprising agility Mr. Jones got up and moved. For an instant, Nancy Ellen remembered the casual comment she had heard from a co-worker when this case had been assigned to her. The co-worker was familiar with the referral source, Mr. James Martino, a well-known personal injury attorney, and said to Nancy Ellen, "Be careful, honey, this guy takes on a lot of fakers! He makes his living by getting some really fab insurance settlements!" Nancy Ellen reflected on her case assignment, thinking, "Oh, great! Here's another one to manipulate the system!"

Nancy Ellen was a graduate social work student newly assigned to this agency, and she really wanted to do well. Social work was a new career for her and she was anxious about her work, particularly the prospect of having to diagnose someone. She was relieved that she had decided to take her classes concurrently with her internship; that way she could learn about psychopathology and counseling skills while she was actually seeing clients. Returning her focus to Mr. Jones, Nancy Ellen found herself wondering just how "real" his discomfort was.

Mr. Jones began the interview by stating he had been involved in a rear-end collision and subsequently missed a great deal of work. He described enduring "a tremendous amount of pain . . . constant neck pain and terrible headaches." He went on, "I feel dizzy most all the time, and I don't sleep a wink most nights. As if that isn't bad enough, my chest hurts when I try and take a deep breath, and I really feel lousy."

Nancy Ellen asked how she might be of help, and Mr. Jones replied, "You know, I'm not asking for anything special. I just want to reclaim damages I got from the woman who rear-ended me, destroyed my car, ruined my health, and cost me my job." Glancing down at the intake sheet, Nancy Ellen noticed that Mr. Jones had been employed sporadically as a short-order cook. Curiously, his car was listed as a rather late model Ford. "It couldn't be worth much," she thought. She also noted that his fee for the session was only a few dollars based on the agency's sliding scale for low-income clients. She wondered how much he had actually lost financially and began to have some suspicions about the extent of Mr. Jones's truthfulness. Is he malingering? she wondered.

The transcript of the interview follows, with Ms. Walker's reactions noted in parentheses.

> MS. WALKER: *Mr. Jones, can you tell me about what is currently going on for you?* (I figure that if I shift the conversation to this guy's current concerns, then it will be easier to find out what he really needs and establish a working contract between us for what the agency can do. Somehow this guy makes me uncomfortable. I don't like it when I think somebody is trying to pull a fast one on me. In my social work practice class last week we talked about how important is to be nonjudgmental with people, but I'm wondering what you're supposed to do when you don't even like the client.)
>
> MR. JONES: *I can't begin to tell you how much pain this accident has caused me. I mean, I can't do anything for myself anymore. I had to move into a limited nursing care facility. Do you know anything about what they are like?*
>
> MS. WALKER: *Could you tell me?* (Boy! This guy is good! By focusing on what I know or rather, don't know about nursing care facilities, he can shift the focus away from his physical ailments. This way, he put me on the spot.)
>
> MR. JONES: *Well, it's a place you live where they cook your meals, do your laundry, and clean your room. I didn't want to move into a place like that, but Mr. Martino—that's my lawyer—told me that I wouldn't have to strain myself having to do all this stuff for myself. He thought it would be best, especially since I'm in so much pain.*
>
> MS. WALKER: *Where did you live before the accident?* (Mr. Jones seems to be easily influenced by his lawyer. Maybe I'm just being overly cautious about the possibility he might be faking his symptoms. It takes a lot to get admitted into a nursing facility, and he really does look uncomfortable.)
>
> MR. JONES: *I lived here and there. You know, sometimes with friends, and sometimes with family members. Hey, aren't we here to talk about how much pain I'm having?*

MS. WALKER: *Yes, could you tell me more about that?* (Wow! This is fascinating. It makes me remember a lecture we had in our practice class just last week. The professor said that when clients change the subject it usually means something. I'll bet this guy is really homeless, but he doesn't want to admit it!)

MR. JONES: *Well, yeah, I ran up a lot of financial costs as a result of that nitwit smashing into my car. Now I'm taking lots of medicine, but none of it seems to help. I was wondering if maybe one of the docs here could give me something to help relax, you know, for my muscle spasms and all?*

MS. WALKER: *Mr. Jones, have you ever been involved in any kind of lawsuit before this one?* (This is getting overwhelming. First he mentions transient living arrangements, then he's taking a lot of medication, and now he asks for more medication! Maybe he's a drug abuser. Changing the subject and shifting the focus back to his pain certainly means he really doesn't want to explore any of these areas further!)

MR. JONES: *What do you mean, like a slip and fall accident or something like that?*

MS. WALKER: *Well, yes, something like that.* (I wonder. His answer sounds like he's had some past experience with accidents.)

MR. JONES: *You probably won't believe this, but I did fall down once when I was walking out of a department store. It was really storming something fierce, and the exit ramp was very slippery. I broke my glasses, hurt my back, and wore a neck brace, and I had to walk with a cane for six months. Oh, wait a minute. I just remembered there was one other time. I worked at some diner, as a short-order cook, you know? My arm got burned when I was cooking some eggs in hot grease. But it was really nothing like this.*

MS. WALKER: *What do you make of what has happened?* (Well, he's right, I don't believe him!)

MR. J: *Hey, are you gonna be like all the rest of them social workers?*

WORKER: *What do you mean?* (Now he attacks me! Great! What do I do next?)

MR. JONES: *You know, suggesting that I just want to make some money out of this accident.*

MS. WALKER: *Has someone accused you of that?* (Hmmmmmmm. I wonder where he got that idea?)

MR. JONES: *Yeah. It's not like I'm trying to get away with something. Why does everybody think I'd try to do a thing like that? Listen, I'm outta here. Send the bill to my lawyer.*

Mr. Jones abruptly stood up and walked out. Interestingly, he showed no indication of having the debilitating physical pain so much in evidence earlier. The social worker was startled by his abrupt departure.

OPERATIONALIZING COMPETENCY-BASED TREATMENT

The case of Brad Jones highlights the importance of establishing a collaborative relationship with the client. An important first step is to achieve a working alliance in which clients perceive the practitioner as a capable and trustworthy ally in their

TABLE 7.1	THE RISKS, PROTECTIVE FACTORS, AND BUFFERS IN BRAD JONES'S LIFE	
	Risk Factors	**Protective Factors and Buffers**
Intrapersonal	Questionable physical symptoms: • neck pain • "terrible" headaches • dizziness most of the time • sleeping problems • chest pains Suspicious of the social worker's intentions History of prior "accidents": • slipped and fell in a department store • burned his arm at work Challenging and manipulative coping style	Resourceful Able to survive by his sheer wit Able to cope despite "illnesses," accident, job loss, housing loss, and transportation loss
Interpersonal	No secure employment Prior negative experiences with social workers Potential for exploitation from his attorney	Able to work sporadically as a short-order cook Receives support from friends and family Willing to see the social worker at the clinic
Social and Environmental	Lost his car Lost his job Transient living arrangements Uncertainties about meeting basic needs	Able to access services (i.e., from the limited nursing care facility) Hired an attorney to obtain benefits Surviving in his environment despite obstacles

personal struggles (Safran & Muran, 1998). In this vignette, the practitioner struggled with Brad's symptoms of malingering, a difficult disorder to accurately diagnose. The social worker, Nancy Ellen Walker, is new to the profession, uncertain about making a diagnosis, and anxious about her performance. As a result, she has a hard time conveying to Brad that she recognizes his distress. Nancy Ellen misses the opportunity to make a "connection" with the client because her focus is on gathering data. Table 7.1 summarizes the risks, protective factors, and buffers in Brad Jones's life.

Working with Brad Individually

Transference is a near-universal phenomenon that is found in almost every relationship (Krause & Merten, 1999). The concept of transference is another way to think about the session with Brad. As a part of psychodynamic theory, Freud (1924) considered transference (which occurs when the client responds to the practitioner as a significant authority figure) as an obstacle to treatment. Psychodynamic theory carries a negative connotation for some practitioners who believe it is irrelevant to contemporary practice. However, these ideas call attention to the subtleties of the worker-client relationship (Walsh, 2002a). Developing a positive relationship characterized by understanding the client's strengths and limitations *and* being aware of one's feelings about the client is a prerequisite to striving for change (Floersch, 2002; Hepworth, Rooney, & Larsen, 2002; Walsh, 2000). By acknowledging and processing his or her feelings, the practitioner keeps the focus on the client and selects appropriate interventions.

Traditionally, psychoanalytic explanations of transference referred to the client's projection of thoughts, feelings, and perceptions toward the practitioner, who comes to represent a person from the client's past, such as a parent, sibling, other relative, or teacher (Jacobs, 1999; Parrott, 2003; Teyber, 2000). Both positive and negative feelings can be transferred (Binder & Strupp, 1997). Clients are unaware of the functional importance of these feelings in the counseling relationship. The emotional reactions that the client has toward the practitioner are distortions that have been unrealistically transferred from past relationships, especially during vulnerable or affect-laden moments. When these types of traditional transference reactions happen, they distort the client's perceptions of and emotional responses to the practitioner. The contemporary definition of transference more broadly refers to all of the feelings, perceptions, and reactions that the client has toward the practitioner, whether realistic or distorted. Culture can also be a likely source of influences on client behavior within the therapeutic situation (Mallinckrodt, 1996). Teyber (2000) suggests these reactions do not necessarily represent pathology and almost always hold at least a kernel of truth. For example, when Brad reacted defensively to Nancy Ellen by asking her if she understood what it was like to live in a limited nursing care facility, his question may have been based on the reality that she was challenging his story and unable to grasp what was most important to him. It is helpful for the practitioner to be aware of the transference and not take it personally; when the latter situation occurs it is called countertransference. In this regard, a certain client may inadvertently evoke issues in the practitioner's life that have not been resolved. The practitioner may thus unconsciously displace onto the client feelings, attitudes, and behaviors that belong to the practitioner's past (Jacobs, 1999; Szybek, Gard, & Linden, 2000).

Contemporary definitions of countertransference assume that some of the practitioner's reactions (both conscious and unconscious) exist independently of the client's feelings (Jacobs, 1999). Clients struggling with a mental illness face multiple life circumstances, events, and interpersonal difficulties that can provoke a range of both conscious and unconscious reactions from the practitioner (Brody & Farber, 1996). The difficulties associated with accurately diagnosing malingering disorder and the tentative, skeptical manner in which Brad Jones related to the social worker set the stage for a number of reactions on her part. Common and potentially problematic countertransference reactions practitioners experience include the following (Gelso, Hill, Mohr, Rochlen, & Zack, 1999; Hepworth, Rooney, & Larsen, 2002; Schoenwolf, 1993; Walsh, 2002a):

- Needing clients to be dependent;
- Needing to be liked by clients;
- Needing to control the relationship;
- Demonstrating too much curiosity about the details of a client's life;
- Becoming aggressive and confrontational with clients or reacting negatively to clients who are assertive;
- Feeling uncomfortable with certain types of emotional expression, such as anger;
- Over-identifying with clients whose problems are similar to one's own;
- Encouraging clients to denounce authority figures; and
- Idealizing clients.

In this vignette, Nancy Ellen was curious about the details of Brad's symptoms and asked a lot of questions. She was also quite uncomfortable with his challenging manner. In most instances, the client's reactions can accurately capture aspects of the interaction with the practitioner. Therefore, it is helpful for the social worker to acknowledge the potential validity of the client's reactions and to explore what he or she may have done to activate the client's responses. Brad challenged Nancy Ellen's understanding of what it is like to live in a limited nursing care facility, and in retrospect she might have responded, "When you ask me if I know anything about what nursing care facilities are like, I'm wondering if I'm making you uncomfortable by asking too many questions. Could we talk about that?" If the client responds affirmatively, both can explore what needs to happen for the client to feel more comfortable in the interview. If Brad were to deny any negative response to Nancy Ellen's questioning behavior, then at least she would have conveyed her concern about the quality of their interaction. She might follow up with, "Great! But if I do something that makes you uncomfortable, will you let me know?" It is difficult to explore non-defensively how one might have upset a client, particularly for a beginning practitioner like Nancy Ellen who is anxious about her performance. However, this approach affirms the validity of the client's reactions and provides the opportunity for the client to see that the practitioner doesn't always have to be "the expert." Another strategy to invite collaboration and to make the practitioner's work more accountable to the client is to ask situating questions (Madsen, 1999). This refers to the practice of clearly identifying the intentions that guide our work. As she began to explore Brad's physical status Nancy Ellen might have said to Brad, "I'm thinking about asking a number of questions about how you are currently feeling; how would that work for you?" In this way, Nancy Ellen could have shared her thoughts and assumptions with Brad and invited his feedback. Brad would have had the opportunity to better understand (if he had chosen to do so) the rationale behind her questions or comments. The willingness to risk exposing one's vulnerabilities is easier said than done, but it can set the stage for establishing an equal and collaborative practitioner-client relationship that is a fundamental aspect of competency-based practice.

Teyber (2000) suggests strategies aimed at using transference reactions to conceptualize clients. These strategies can be applied to Nancy Ellen's work with Brad Jones. One approach is to inquire about the client's feelings and reactions toward the practitioner. A well-timed question can yield a wealth of information. The practitioner may consider asking any of the following questions:

- "Brad, when you find yourself thinking about getting help from our clinic, what kinds of thoughts do you have about me and our work together?"
- "As you were driving to our session today, how did you feel about coming in?"
- "Brad, I've been asking you a lot of questions about your illnesses. What are you feeling toward me right now as we talk about this sensitive issue?"

As the client's reactions are made more overt, the practitioner can attempt to respond with a level of immediacy and authenticity not often found in other relationships. Teyber (2000) observes that it is difficult for beginning practitioners to recognize clients' distortions, and this difficulty can cause practitioners to respond to clients defensively. Encouraging a discussion of the clients' subjective reactions toward the practitioner may bring to light new issues or information that would not have been accessible otherwise. In this vignette, Brad alludes to problems with housing, work, and transportation. Exploring the transference may reveal aspects of the same problems that the client is having with others; for instance, Brad shares with Nancy Ellen that he has had unproductive conversations with other social workers who suggested that he might "just want to make some money out of this accident." The emotional reactions of some clients may not fit the present circumstances but will make better sense when placed within their original context. Real-life issues may have caused clients to feel the way they do. In this vignette, the practitioner has very little information about Brad's life history and prior experiences, but by attempting to clarify the transference distortion in their current interaction she may find that his feelings begin to make better sense.

Supervision of Practice

Troubled by the client's abrupt termination, Nancy Ellen reviews this case with her clinical supervisor. Typically, practice struggles revolve around a lack of knowledge, skill, self-confidence, or objectivity on the part of the practitioner (Dougherty, 2000). While there is no simple formula for deciding which intervention strategy will be effective, supervision helps the practitioner manage the tensions embodied in the helping relationship with the client where the dynamics of power and vulnerability can undermine even the best of intentions. The supervisor takes on several roles, including listener, expert, teacher, facilitator, mentor, coach, advisor, and evaluator (Dougherty, 2000; Falvey, 2002). Supervision is a core aspect of clinical training, and the primary goal is improvement of the supervisee's ability to work effectively with a particular client as well as generalize learning to other similar situations (Sumerall et al., 1998). Instead of telling the supervisee what to do next, the supervisor models a reflective stance and encourages openness, active inquiry, and vulnerability (Coburn, 1997). One's practice and related decisions influence the lives of others. As illustrated in this vignette, the practitioner brings her own sense of reality and personal needs to bear on her clinical decisions. The supervisor gently challenges the social worker by telling her that whether Brad's physical problems are real or not, they are real to him. Together, Nancy Ellen and her supervisor begin to reflect on the reasons why Brad might have become so defensive during the interview. This shifts the focus of the conversation toward the client's concerns and provides a backdrop to explore the practitioner's unease about the session. Helping Nancy Ellen to process her feelings about Brad's defensive behavior enables her to better understand her own feelings about the client.

The case also illustrates a conflict of values between the social worker and the client. Throughout the session Nancy Ellen remained skeptical about Brad's account of his pain and discomfort. She wondered if he was lying. With a client who is acting out values that contradict the personally held values of the practitioner—in this case, honesty—how can the social worker remain honest, congruent, and respectful? Welch (1998) underscores the importance of being nonjudgmental, a core social work principle, and suspending one's own personal values for a professional value that has demonstrated itself to be helpful: the creation of a climate of understanding, respect, and genuineness. How can Nancy Ellen be genuine when she has values that seem so different from Brad's? Genuineness requires the practitioner to convey respect and focus on an empathic understanding of the client's situation.

The supervisor attempts to help Nancy Ellen to explore how her personal values may affect the values she holds about counseling. The aim of supervision is to promote the development of Nancy Ellen's skills and to foster her self-awareness. Integral to this heightened self-awareness is understanding the impact of bias on the kinds of issues one attends to, the potential interventions one selects, and how responsive one is to the client. According to Cooper and Lesser (2002), "The supervisor is selective and goal oriented, focusing on those aspects of a personal theme which can be directly related to actual problems in the supervisee's work with clients" (p. 35). In this vignette, a number of factors affected the social worker. First, she was a student and new to the profession as well as to the agency. Knowing that she would receive a grade at the end of the term for her performance, Nancy Ellen was highly motivated to succeed; her personal values were to work hard, please her superiors, and do well. For Nancy Ellen, this meant that she would carefully uphold agency policies and follow procedures "to the letter." When a co-worker commented about the client's potential for abuse of agency services, this remark set the stage for Nancy Ellen's responses to the client. As a consequence, she lost sight of the full meaning of the client's behavior and unwittingly concluded, "Here's another one to manipulate the system."

Streeck (1999) notes that practitioners may interact with clients in ways that unintentionally reveal how they regard the behavior of the client. Through speech and behavior, the practitioner demonstrates his or her assessment about what the client has expressed. Without conscious thought, the practitioner responds to the client's subtle behaviors, including the affective coloring of remarks, choice of words, voice, and intonation. Nancy indicated in her process recording notes that this client overwhelmed her and she struggled with her negative reactions to him. Could this struggle somehow have been conveyed to Brad? Self-awareness is fundamental to competency-based treatment, and supervision can help the practitioner understand what is played out during sessions (Fryo, Hardell, & Cederroth, 1999). Together, the supervisor and Nancy Ellen attempted to sort out the central problem that was reflected in the client's attitude toward her and to the session. Armed with this level of understanding, they could begin to explore alternative responses. Brad had come to the practitioner's attention because of suspected "malingering," a diagnosis based on a claim of symptoms or diseases that either are exaggerated or do not exist. Several adaptational models have been advanced to explain malingering (LoPiccolo, Goodkin, & Baldewicz, 1999). In retrospect, Nancy Ellen might have considered how Brad was trying to adapt to the numerous adverse circumstances in his life; for example, he had lost his job and car, and he was limited to transient living arrangements. Seeing his "deception" as adaptive may have shifted the conversation to a focus on Brad's strengths.

Nancy Ellen has a good relationship with her supervisor and actively sought guidance. Sumerel and Borders (1996) note, "A good alliance with the supervisor is important if the supervisee is to feel comfortable revealing significant information, particularly negative reactions" (p. 21). It is difficult for supervisees to talk with their supervisors about experiences that may evoke strong feelings (Walsh, Gillespie, Greer, & Eanes, 2002). However, the more open and honest the practitioner can be, the more the supervisor can understand the dynamics of the session with the client and facilitate the learning process. According to Pearson (2000), it is important for the supervisor to approach the supervisee in a warm, supportive, and instructional manner when critiquing the supervisee's practice. Gorman (1999) adds that treating supervisees as competent professionals who can expect to benefit from appropriate examination of their work is a mark of collegial respect. Note Miller and Stiver (1997), it is easier for practitioners to talk about difficult experiences when they feel their supervisor is engaged with them in their work, an approach based on mutual empathy. Hess (1999) observes that a positive supervision experience is exemplified by a practitioner who feels "safe" and knows that the supervisor wants him or her to do well. Recognizing possible sources of practitioner anxiety in supervision is paramount. Liddle (1986) identifies four areas:

- Given that supervisors assign grades and provide recommendations, performance and evaluation are inextricably linked, which motivates practitioners to strive for perfection rather than competence and allows little room to discuss errors and uncertainties in supervision;
- Performance anxiety reflects a struggle to live up to a set of standards in order to feel competent;
- The practitioner's personal problems (or unresolved issues) may be another source of anxiety, especially when supervision touches on these sensitive areas;
- The practitioner may be afraid of negative consequences for trying new behaviors such as responding with empathy to a client like Brad Jones who is lying or manipulative.

Looking for symptoms and formulating a diagnosis was new to Nancy Ellen, which caused her to feel some uncertainty about how to approach Brad. Not wanting to label or stigmatize someone with a mental illness, Nancy Ellen was anxious about assigning a diagnosis. As a result, she asked a lot of questions in the session with Brad to satisfy her doubts about his behavior and the related suspicions that he might be trying to abuse the agency's services. With this focus on her own performance, she failed to notice the impact of her questions on the client. Clearly, Nancy Ellen's biases influenced the issues she attended to and the interventions she selected—that is, her singular reliance on questioning Brad about his presenting symptoms. The supervisor encouraged Nancy Ellen to begin to think about the areas of diversity that may potentially influence her judgment; for example, Brad's socioeconomic status, educational level, and background. Self-awareness is integral to competency-based practice and requires an understanding of the impact of one's values as well as the ability to separate personal values from professional values during the counseling process. The clinical supervisor helps the practitioner to minimize judgment errors that can lead to mistakes and ultimately professional liability. Formal training, supervision, and the wisdom that comes with experience contribute to one's competence. Becoming a competent practitioner requires thoughtful reflection of one's practice, a conscientious effort to be attentive to the multiple perspectives in the client's life, and the ability to acknowledge the uncertain consequences of one's work (Pope & Vasquez, 1998).

SUMMARY

This chapter reviewed the various somatoform disorders: somatization disorder; conversion disorder; pain disorder; hypochondriasis; body dysmorphic disorder; undifferentiated somatoform disorder; and somatoform disorder not otherwise specified. The key feature is the presence of physical complaints that suggest a general medical condition, but the physical complaints cannot be completely explained. These disorders are difficult to assess and even though the person may be faking, they are still "ill." The related disorders of factitious and malingering were also included in the discussion. In factitious disorders, a person's physical and psychological symptoms are intentionally produced or feigned to assume the sick role. Malingering also involves feigning symptoms, but the person is usually motivated by some type of incentive such as economic gain, avoiding criminal prosecution, or obtaining drugs. The case of Brad Jones, suspected of "malingering," was included to highlight the challenges involved in developing a competency-based relationship that exemplifies self-awareness, collaboration, and taps into client strengths.

PRACTITIONER REFLECTIONS

1. Social workers practice in an environment where managed care programs and behavioral health services are very much a part of a client's care. There can be instances when these organizations and their values can conflict with core values of the profession and the social worker's ethical behaviors.

Imagine for a moment that you have been working with someone you suspect is struggling with one of the somatoform disorders. How would you respond to a case coordinator from a managed care company who asks you to share detailed information about this client? Give a specific example of the information you would provide about this hypothetical client.

2. Persons struggling with somatoform disorders have been known to go "doctor shopping" to find relief from their symptoms. Keeping the NASW Code of Ethics in mind, discuss how managed care requirements can be seen as consistent with the code. As an alternative, identify where you think managed care requirements could be seen as inconsistent with the social work profession's Code of Ethics.

3. Standards of what is considered "normal" appearance and beauty differ by culture. In the United States, having an appearance consistent with the dominant culture brings acceptance. Persons who differ from this standard may want to alter their appearance. The pop singer and media figure, Michael Jackson, has had multiple surgeries and procedures to alter his ethnic appearance. Should he be considered as an example of body dysmorphic disorder? If no, explain why not. If yes, explain. If Michael Jackson was your client, how would you treat him?

4. Imagine that you are the social worker in an acute care medical hospital. You are doing routine case finding and stop by to assess a woman admitted with aplastic anemia. Reviewing the chart, you note that the patient's white blood cell and platelet counts are at life-threateningly low levels. While you are chatting with the patient, her friend stops in to visit and asks for a moment of your time. You agree and see the friend alone in the hallway outside of the patient's room. This friend reveals information indicating that the patient has been self-administering chemotherapy drugs. Would it be appropriate for you to convey your "suspicions" of a factitious disorder diagnosis to the physician caring for this patient?

5. In the case of Brad Jones, the client abruptly ends the session with the practitioner. If you were seeing someone closely resembling this gentleman and this type of incident occurred in your practice, what would you do? Be as specific as you can.

6. Imagine you are the social worker assigned to Brad Jones. After he has abruptly ended the session, you walk over to your office window to collect your thoughts before seeing your next client. As you glance out, you notice Brad walking over to a bicycle in the parking lot. No mistaking that this is Mr. Jones! With surprising agility and no evidence of pain or discomfort, he bends over and unlocks his bike. Brad turns toward the building, raises his right fist, and gives an obscene gesture ("the finger") in your direction. He then hops onto his bike and quickly pedals off down the highway. Identify the ethical dilemma in this incident and describe what you would do.

DISSOCIATIVE DISORDERS

Have you ever driven to work and, as you pulled into the parking lot, realized that you had lost track of time and distance? If so, you've experienced *dissociation,* or split awareness. One side of you was driving and paying attention to the other drivers and the condition of the road, and at the same time another part of you was daydreaming. Dissociation also occurs when a person must deal with an extremely stressful event and feels dazed, strange, or unreal. For people who suffer from dissociative disorders, however, their consciousness, behavior, and identity are more severely split or altered and they cannot just snap out of it. The dissociative disorders are characterized by altered perceptions and a sense of detachment from one's own self, from the world, or from memories. The disturbance can be sudden, gradual, transient, or chronic.

The categories of dissociative disorders have been expanded and refined over time. Given the personal struggles associated with the diagnosis and the high costs of misdiagnosis to insurers, accurate identification of the disorders is essential. Progress toward recovery varies. For example, individuals who experience dissociative amnesia will usually get better on their own and be able to "remember" what they had forgotten (Barlow & Durand, 2005). At the other extreme, treatment for persons with dissociative identity disorder is typically a long, slow, and challenging process, although there have been many documented successes (Ellason & Ross, 1997; Ross, 1997). Once the condition has been diagnosed, the practitioner may begin the work by conveying the "good news" that many who struggle with a dissociative disorder can be successfully treated. This does not diminish the challenges associated with coming to terms with traumatic experiences and their consequences but can help to set the stage for hope and optimism, an important feature of competency-based treatment.

In 1952, with the publication of the first edition of the DSM, only one dissociative disorder was noted: dissociative psychoneurotic reaction. The second edition included two diagnostic categories: depersonalization neurosis and dissociative type of hysterical neurosis. Four categories were introduced in the DSM–III, and in the current edition (DSM IV-TR) they underwent a name change in which the role of dissociation in each disorder was highlighted. Existing categories include dissociative identity disorder (formerly multiple personality disorder); dissociative amnesia (formerly psychogenic amnesia); dissociative fugue (formerly psychogenic fugue); and depersonalization disorder. As will be seen in this chapter, the roles played by social and cultural factors are more evident in the dissociative disorders than in some of the other diagnostic categories.

The nature of dissociative disorders is controversial, and the DSM–IV Task Force Chair raised questions about whether these disorders exist (Frances, 1995). Many wonder if the person is faking symptoms or could be more troubled than they really are. Take the case of Kenneth Bianchi, known as the "Hillside Strangler." In the late 1970s he raped and murdered 10 young women in the Los Angeles area and left their bodies naked and in full view on the sides of various hills. Despite overwhelming evidence against him, he continued to claim his innocence. His attorney brought in a clinical psychologist who hypnotized Mr. Bianchi. When the psychologist asked whether there was another part of him with whom he could speak, Bianchi answered, "Steve." Another expert clinical psychologist and psychiatrist, Martin Orne, was called in to testify and refuted the diagnosis of dissociative identity disorder. His refutation was based on the lack of evidence of different "personalities" before Bianchi's arrest and the failure of psychological tests to show differences among the personalities. Interestingly, several psychopathology textbooks were found in Bianchi's room.

Critics wonder if dissociative identity disorder may be created through suggestive and occasionally unreliable techniques, such as hypnosis or the power of suggestion (Acocella, 1999; Merskey, 1992, 1995; Spanos, 1996). Richard Kluft, a psychiatrist who is an expert in dissociative identity disorders, claims that it may require between 2-1/2 and 4 hours of continuous and uninterrupted interviewing for the person to reveal a dissociated personality. Some have suggested that in the course of such a lengthy interview these clinicians may have actively created personalities through suggestion or intimidation (Loftus, 1996).

Understanding Dissociative Disorders

Dissociative Identity Disorder

Dissociative identity disorder or DID (formerly referred to as multiple personality disorder) is a more covert than overt condition. Making the diagnosis is challenging, and people suffering from DID may be misdiagnosed initially. It is not unusual for the practitioner to encounter people with DID in gynecological outpatient programs, neurology wards, pain clinics, drug and alcohol units, and prisons (Middleton & Butler, 1998). They are also represented among those with a history of suicide, may present themselves for treatment in multiple ways, have had many diagnoses and yet respond poorly to treatments directed at such assumed conditions, and frequently have had long careers as clients. This controversial diagnosis involves the presence of two or more distinct identities or personality states that frequently take control of the person's behavior.

In general, we are associative thinkers; that is, our experiences are recorded with an association consisting of four components: *behavior*, or what was done; *affect*, or the emotions experienced; *sensation*, or what the body felt in all of the senses; and *knowledge*, or the story line and explanations. This characterization of association was first proposed by Bennett Braun and has become known as the BASK model of cognition (Braun, 1988). Dissociation occurs when these components are broken off from each other and stored separately. A barrier of amnesia separates them. For the individual with DID, each personality state, or *alter* (the abbreviated term for the different identities or personalities who perceive, relate to, and think about the environment and self), can be experienced as if it has a distinct history and identity.

People with DID can have as many as 100 different identities all simultaneously coexisting within them. However, the median number of an individual's personalities ranges from 5 to 10 (Ellason & Ross, 1997; Kluft, 1996, 1999b; Ross, 1997). Each can have a separate name. Some of the identities may have their own behavior, tone of voice, and physical gestures. In other instances, only a few characteristics are distinct. The transition from one personality to another is referred to as a switch. This switch is instantaneous, and the person may physically change; for example, posture, patterns of facial expression and/or language, and even physical disabilities may emerge. For example, Chris Sizemore, the real-life subject of the book and movie *The Three Faces of Eve*, showed a transient microstrabismus (divergence in conjugate lateral eye movements) in one of her "personalities" (Eva Black) that was not observed in the other personalities. The frequency of switching seems to decrease with age, and there is some evidence to suggest that one of the personalities usually becomes dominant (Zide & Gray, 2001).

The defining feature of DID is the person's failure to integrate various aspects of identity, memory, and consciousness. The inability to recall personal information is beyond what could be characterized as ordinary forgetfulness. The person experiences memory gaps for recent and past personal history. There is a growing body of literature suggesting that DID is an extreme subtype of post-traumatic stress disorder (Butler, Duran, Jasiukaitis, Koopman, & Spiegel, 1996). DID places greater emphasis on the process of dissociation than on the symptoms of anxiety. The practitioner usually encounters the "host" identity, which is the personality that seeks out treatment and carries the individual's legal name. The host personality attempts to hold various fragments of identity together, but when the process does not work well, the person ends up being overwhelmed. The person may not be aware of the presence of these alters and confused about what is going on. By the time persons with DID enter therapy, the assemblage of personalities and their intricate system of functioning have often sabotaged the person's coping abilities (Fine, 1999).

The client's life history contains long-standing and frequent instances of physical and/or sexual abuse, most often incest (Zide & Gray, 2001). The individual, as a young child, learned to survive by means of a psychobiological mechanism that allowed the mind to escape what the body was experiencing. The child then existed in a world of fantasy where these abusive experiences were blunted (Solomon, 1997). Although the use of dissociation begins in childhood, the presence of a dissociative identity is often not accurately diagnosed until adulthood. By this time, the dissociation is well entrenched as a way to cope. Without treatment, the disorder can last a lifetime.

In contrast to people who develop DID, persons with dissociative amnesia and dissociative fugue seem to lead generally normal daily lives with no apparent impairment until their daily lives are suddenly disrupted by a life event and they develop symptoms that are difficult to understand. These individuals have had no prior neurological or organic disorders.

There are a number of culturally accepted dissociative experiences. For example, *ataque de nervios* refers to a Latin American trance syndrome (Oquendo, 1995). Trembling, heart palpitations, heat in the chest rising to the head, faintness and seizure-like episodes characterize it. Sometimes the person experiences hallucinations. It is attributed to acute anxiety-provoking experiences, particularly related to family conflict, fear, and grief (Lewis-Fernandez, 1994; Oquendo, 1995; Zide & Gray, 2001). Another example is *falling out,* a trance syndrome found among Southern Black persons in the United States and the Bahamas. The individual falls down in a trance and is unable to move, yet he or she can hear and understand surrounding events. Similarly, *indisposition* occurs in Haitian persons. The person falls to the ground and is not able to understand anything that is said or heard (Castillo, 1997).

Dissociative Amnesia Disorder

Dissociative amnesia is an inability to recall important personal information that is usually of a traumatic or stressful nature. This lapse of memory cannot be attributed to normal forgetfulness or explained by absentmindedness. The memory loss is usually reversible. There are five patterns of memory disturbance:

- *Localized amnesia* or circumscribed amnesia is the inability to recall traumatic events within hours or days of the event, which usually was profoundly disturbing;
- *Selective amnesia* is the recollection of some aspects of traumatic events within hours or days of the event;
- *Generalized amnesia* is the failure to recall all of the experiences during a person's lifetime;
- *Continuous amnesia* is an inability to remember all events from a specific time to the present;
- *Systematized amnesia* is a loss of memory involving specific categories of information.

Localized and selective amnesia are encountered more often than the other three patterns.

Dissociative Fugue Disorder

Fugue states are unusual and yet dramatic expressions of dissociation. Dissociative fugue (formerly known as psychogenic fugue) is characterized by sudden, unexpected travel from one's home or place of work associated with the inability to recall one's past, confusion about personal identity, or assumption of a new identity. Often the person leaves behind a difficult and troubling situation that on some level is believed to be intolerable (Zide & Gray, 2001). Fugue states, when durable and prolonged, create distress and anxiety for the person's family when the individual travels away from home or work. In some instances major management difficulties are created for those in the community involved in locating the missing person, such as the police, rescue workers, and the practitioner. Despite the disturbance caused by their sudden disappearance, it is unlikely that persons with dissociative fugue will cause harm to themselves either deliberately or by neglect (Macleod, 1999).

Cross culturally, *pibloktoq* (sometimes called *arctic hysteria*) can be found among native Arctic peoples. It is characterized by short-lived episodes (from 5 to 60 minutes) of extreme anxiety responses in which the individual tears off his or her clothes and runs into the snow or across the ice, screaming incoherently. *Pibloktoq* is attributed to intense fear and imagined (or actual) personal abuse. *Grisi siknis* (spirit attack) is found among the Miskito Indians of Central America. Among the North American Navajo tribe it is called *frenzy witchcraft*. These disorders are characterized by trance, amnesia, and leaving home. These experiences differ from dissociative fugue disorder in that the person acts wildly, runs aimlessly, and sometimes assaults others or harms him- or herself. *Amok* is a Southeast Asian trance syndrome characterized by a sudden and short-lived (ranging from a few minutes to one hour) outburst of unrestrained violence, usually of a homicidal nature. It is preceded by a period of anxious brooding, and the person ends up feeling exhausted. It appears to be attributed to interpersonal conflict, intolerably embarrassing or shameful situations, loss of honor, and personal abuse (Barlow & Durand, 2005; Castillo, 1997).

Depersonalization Disorder

Depersonalization disorder is a fascinating yet poorly studied condition (Zide & Gray, 2001). Depersonalization is the subjective experience of unreality in one's sense of self and the outside world. The experience can occur on a continuum from a transient episode to chronic course. Depersonalization disorder is distinguished by persistent or recurrent episodes in which the person experiences feelings of detachment or estrangement from the self, resulting in considerable distress or impairment. It is important to rule out the presence of other mental disorders as well as substance use or a general medical condition. Persons with depersonalization disorder may describe the experience as feeling like living in a dream, feeling "foggy," or not being able to feel their own body. The depersonalization experience is highly subjective, and reality testing remains intact. Once thought to be a relatively rare disorder, depersonalization may be more widespread than expected, with onset typically beginning in mid-adolescence (Simeon et al., 1998).

OVERVIEW OF MAJOR INTERVENTIONS

The dissociative process is responsible for much avoidance and amnesia. Some symptoms, such as amnesia and depersonalization, appear in more than one disorder. Ironically, the anxiety and discomfort associated with dissociative responses in the person play a central role in the treatment process. Further dissociation may be triggered as the practitioner strives to identify cues or triggers that provoke memories of trauma (and or dissociation) and to neutralize them by enabling re-association and re-integration. Since there is considerable overlap in the presentation of the dissociative disorders, they are frequently discussed together.

Trauma is closely connected with amnesia (Brown, van der Hart, & Graafland, 1999; Kluft, 2000; Lowenstein, 1996, 1997; Vermetten & Bremner, 2000; Wiztum, Maragalit, & van der Hart, 2002), and many of the same treatment concepts apply to amnesia and post-traumatic stress disorder: creating a safe and stable environment, establishing a strong therapeutic alliance and reassuring the person about safety, working through traumatic issues, and stabilizing gains so the person can reintegrate his or her life (Reid, Balis, & Sutton, 1997).

Dissociative Identity Disorder

Cases of dissociative identity disorder are rare, and the intervention process is more complicated and lengthy than it is for amnesia. The author is familiar with a case in which the client has been in treatment for almost 20 years. Most of the treatment information described in the literature reflects the experience and case reports of practitioners and treatment centers. No single modality seems to have been systematically studied (Maldonado, Butler, & Spiegel, 2002; Searles, 2001). Given the complexity of the disorder, many individuals have been misdiagnosed (International Society for the Study of Dissociation, 1997). The average person with DID spends about 6.8 years in the mental health care system prior to the establishment of a correct diagnosis and receives an average of 2.3 incorrect diagnoses. These averages may be even higher in rural or economically depressed areas. Obtaining an accurate early assessment is the most important single factor in effective treatment (Steinberg & Hall, 1997). However, given the increased recognition of the dissociative disorders and the development of specialized diagnostic instruments such as the SCID-D-R or Structured Clinical Interview for DSM-IV Dissociative Disorders-Revised (Steinberg, 2000; Steinberg & Hall, 1997) considerable progress has been made.

Before 1980, few cases of DID had been diagnosed anywhere in the world. Since that time tens of thousands of cases have been reported (Acoella, 1999; Kenny, 1986; Loftus, 1996; Nathan, 1994; Pendergrast, 1995). By 1985 psychiatrist Richard Kluft claimed to have treated 250 persons with "multiple personality disorder" (Kluft, 1987). Earlier interventions had focused on attempts to reintegrate identities through long-term psychotherapy. Kluft (1993, 1996, 1999b) ascribes high, medium, or low treatment trajectories according to prognosis, ranging from good to poor. Those with a poor prognosis have experienced a number of adverse life conditions and events, such as significant self-harm through suicidality or self-mutilation and the presence of comorbid disorders such as depression, eating disorders, substance use, or borderline personality disorder. The prognosis is considered guarded for persons who have highly differentiated and specialized alters or who are invested in maintaining the differentiation (Ellason & Ross, 1997; Ross, 1997). Many are frightened, angered, or ashamed by having a diagnosis of DID (Kluft, 1996, 1999a, 1999b). With the growing recognition of the connection between the diagnosis of DID and child abuse, feeling "defective" in some way adds to the treatment challenges. Kluft's (1993) work with persons struggling with DID convinced him that "the reality of the abuse may be denied with more vigor and endurance than the diagnosis itself" (p. 153). Many individuals fear exposure and may try to minimize or hide their symptoms. Kluft (1993) further observed that denial, suppression, or derealization of the diagnosis may reoccur throughout the course of treatment.

The International Society for the Study of Dissociation (ISSD) developed a set of treatment guidelines (ISSD, 1997). They are not intended to replace the practitioner's clinical judgment but to summarize what has been found to be of benefit for persons with DID. These guidelines underscore the importance of an accurate and early diagnosis as a first step in treatment. The person should be asked about episodes of amnesia, fugue, depersonalization, derealization, identity confusion, and identity alteration as well as age regressions, autohypnotic experiences (spontaneous or purposeful hypnotic trance states produced by the person), and hearing voices, usually internal (Fine, 1999; Kihlstrom, 2001; Putnam & Lowenstein, 1993; Steinberg & Hall, 1997). Screening tools such as the Dissociation Questionnaire (Vanderlin, Van Dyck, Vandereycken, Vertommen, & Verkes, 1993) and structured interview tools such as the SCID-D-R (Steinberg, 1994, 2000; Steinberg & Hall, 1997) are recommended to detect the disorder and/or to confirm the diagnosis.

The treatment goals identified by ISSD are symptom stabilization, control of dysfunctional behavior, restoration of functioning, and improvement of relationships. When indicated, close coordination with other professionals is recommended. Treatment interventions may include education, bibliotherapy, and nonverbal techniques such as art therapy, movement therapy, sand tray therapy, and recreational therapy. The sand tray is a technique adapted from play therapy in which the person works in a tray of sand to create an expression of thoughts and feelings. In this way, the person has the opportunity to share their trauma experiences with the practitioner in a safe way. The individual may also be encouraged to keep a journal as a part of ongoing treatment. Cognitive behavioral techniques can be employed to help explore and alter dysfunctional trauma-based belief systems. Antidepressant drugs are also used as therapeutic adjuncts.

In some instances, hypnosis can be incorporated as an adjutant. It is commonly used for calming, soothing, containment, ego strengthening, and memory retrieval as well as increasing communication between alternate personalities or bringing alternate personalities into communication with the therapist. However, it is not recommended in the treatment of elderly individuals due to the older person's greater vulnerability to the physical stress of abreactions (the emotional release or discharge after recalling a painful experience that has become repressed because it was consciously intolerable) and the possibility of organic compromise of cognitive functions (Kluft, 1993). Positive experiences with hypnosis, such as the induction of trance for relaxation or similar induction imagery, may be more useful for the older client. The ISSD (1997) guidelines caution that memory processing through hypnosis can potentially increase the likelihood that some retrieved images may be fantasized.

Current treatment approaches emphasize working with the client to identify cues or triggers that provoke memories of trauma and/or dissociation and to develop strategies to neutralize them (Rosik, 2003). Accordingly, treatment interventions have moved from processing memories to behavior management and cognitive restructuring. Less emphasis is placed on examining the past and more on establishing a personally rewarding present-day life for the person with DID. Psychodynamic issues are addressed as they manifest in the person's present psychosocial functioning (Kluft, 1999b). Abreactive models of treatment or the planned processing of traumatic material have given way to the pacing of treatment to avoid crises, ego strengthening, and the maintenance of adequate functioning in the present. Confronting the abuser is no longer encouraged as a part of treatment initiatives since it has led to lawsuits filed by accused abusers (Kihlstrom, 2001). Practitioners are more careful to monitor suggestiveness and to avoid uncritical endorsement of the veracity of recovered memories. Novel techniques, such as Eye Movement Desensitization and Reprocessing (EMDR) aimed at speeding the processing of trauma, are gaining acceptance (Rosik, 2003).

The support offered through more traditional "talking therapies" may not adequately meet the concrete and environmental needs of those who have been severely traumatized and are struggling with dissociative identity disorder. According to Wakeman (2002), the process of dredging up traumatic memories may stalemate the therapeutic relationship. By helping the person identify resources and strengths to build on, the practitioner can shift the focus to psychiatric rehabilitation. Interventions are aimed at "doing with" as opposed to "doing for" or "doing to." This shift in focus can be empowering. Psychiatric rehabilitation emphasizes the here-and-now wherein the practitioner looks for opportunities to reframe problems into more solvable descriptions. The work is characterized by a sense of hope. No matter how severe the illness, the practitioner strives to identify possibilities and to encourage the person to take small steps toward recovery.

Dissociative Amnesia and Dissociative Fugue

Persons with dissociative amnesia or dissociative fugue disorder usually get better on their own and are able to remember what they have "forgotten." There may be instances when the practitioner helps the person to recall what occurred during the amnesic or fugue states, and usually the help of family or friends is enlisted. In more difficult situations, hypnosis or benzodiazepines may be used (Maldonado, Butler, & Spiegel, 2002; Van der Hart, van der Kolk, & Boon, 1998).

Degun-Mather (2001) summarizes the benefits of hypnosis for persons with dissociative fugue:

- Offers a supportive technique to reduce anxiety and promote stabilization and grounding; for example, the person is introduced to a "special place" or an "anchor" and taught self-hypnosis to produce feelings of calm by a post-hypnotic suggestion;
- Serves as an uncovering technique whereby the person can talk through traumatic events and transform the fragmented memories into a narrative;
- Re-creates state-dependent memory for easier recall and narration in therapy sessions; for example, the same mood in which the events were first experienced can be created;
- Helps the person to re-associate with dissociated feelings;
- Facilitates re-association and integration; and
- Allows the cognitive re-evaluation of traumatic events to be mainly client-led.

The first task of treatment for persons with dissociative fugue is the restoration of safety and well-being. Since the disorder is characterized by travel away from home, Macleod (1999) describes the novel technique of using a locator or tracking device to find the individual.

Depersonalization Disorder

Depersonalization disorder is poorly understood, and little systematic research has been conducted into the treatment of this syndrome (Baker et al., 2003; Sachdev, 2002; Simeon, Guralnik, & Schmeidler, 2001; Simeon et al., 1998). Unfortunately, the symptoms are sometimes misinterpreted as indicative of a more severe mental illness or brain dysfunction (Hunter, Phillips, Chalder, Sierra, & David, 2003). It is helpful for the practitioner to understand both the symbolic and physical trauma associated with the depersonalization experience. A careful medical evaluation is recommended to rule out other conditions (Gabbard, 1995). The most common immediate precipitants of the disorder are reported to be severe stress, depression, panic, marijuana ingestion, and hallucinogen ingestion (Simeon, Knutelska, Nelson, & Guralnik, 2003). Hypnosis directed at creating a safe environment and/or group therapy aimed at normalizing the person's view of him- or herself may be of benefit (Reid, Balis, & Sutton, 1997).

RISKS ASSOCIATED WITH DISSOCIATIVE DISORDERS

Intrapersonal Risks

Individual biological or psychological differences may contribute to increasing the risks of having a dissociative disorder. Although difficult to pinpoint, there is some evidence of a biological vulnerability to DID (Waller & Ross, 1997). Persons who are suggestible or easily hypnotized are also considered to be at a higher risk

(Butler, Duran, Jasiukanitis, Kooperman, & Spiegel, 1996). Kluft (1996, 1999a, 1999b) highlights four factors that may place someone at higher risk of having a dissociative disorder: an inherited predisposition to dissociation; chronic trauma usually beginning in early childhood; severe trauma; and a lack of positive nurturing and support.

Interpersonal Risks

Childhood abuse, usually sexual or physical, is associated with the development of DID (Lewis, Yeager, Swica, Pincus, & Lewis, 1997; Ross, 1997). Abusive experiences are described as bizarre and sadistic; for example, being tortured with matches, steam irons, razor blades or glass, forced to have sex with animals, insertion of objects, exposure to pedophile rings and child prostitution arranged by parents, involvement in pornographic photography, and sexual relationships with a sibling. The author can recall one client's experiences as a young child with sexual humiliation and degradation at the hands of her stepfather, who subjected her to abuse that is too horrible to describe. He would meticulously record these events by taking photographs. After the pictures were developed she would be forced to kneel (usually undressed) with her hands tied behind her, sometimes for hours at a time, and instructed to look at the photos to contemplate her "lessons" in obedience. Middleton and Butler (1998) report that physical abuse, neglect, abandonment, and a range of emotional traumas including death threats by the primary abuser(s) generally accompany sexual abuse. Other forms of trauma have been reported, such as being abandoned, placed in foster care or institutions, or locked in rooms or cupboards. It goes without saying that the lack of a stable and supportive family environment increases risk. In many cases, clients describe abuse from close family members, including one or both parents. A lack of social support during or after the abuse is another risk factor associated with the development of dissociative identity disorder.

Many dissociating people lead chaotic lives and re-enact the trauma, chaos, and neglect they may have experienced while growing up. For those with total amnesia, loss of a place where the individual can feel secure and comfortable and weak family relationships place one at higher risk for dissociative symptoms (Ishikura & Tashiro, 2002). In addition, these individuals are at increased risk for other disorders such as major depression, addictions, eating disorders, somatization, borderline personality disorder, and/or anxiety disorders (Garnefski & Diekstra, 1997; Hall, 2003; Rodriguez, Ryan, Van de Kemp, & Foy, 1997). Stressful or traumatic situations, such as war, disasters, spouse abuse and childhood abuse, place one at risk for dissociative amnesia. Individual crises accompanied by the mental strain associated with these life events, and also extramarital relations by the client or his/her spouse correlate with the development of dissociative fugue (Ishikura & Tashiro, 2002).

The diagnostic validity of dissociative identity disorder continues to be controversial, with some professionals regarding the diagnosis as a modern variant of "hysteria" or attention-seeking behavior (Foote, 1999). This debate may invalidate the abuse experiences for the person, and others may need to advocate for him or her. Extreme invalidation, both from the person's family of origin and/or from health care systems, can also increase risks for those with dissociative styles (Wakeman, 2002).

Community and Environmental Risks

Contemporary trends in society play a role in influencing perspectives on the dissociative disorders. One of the most controversial issues associated with the dissociative disorders is the accuracy of memories of early trauma, particularly sexual abuse. In some cases a careless practitioner has evoked false or inaccurate memories and caused harm to innocent people. Victims who have been wrongly accused have formed the False Memory Syndrome Foundation. The foundation underscores the importance of educating society (and especially the legal profession) about the damage caused by convicting innocent people based on "false memories." Judicial decisions, or even the threat of litigation, can potentially affect the practitioner's assessment and treatment efforts. It is human nature to be intimidated by reports of a colleague who is being sued.

The growth of managed care and the attendant treatment requirements and limitations provide another example of how societal trends can influence perspectives about the dissociative disorders. Faced with the prospect of a client who may need intensive long-term intervention, the practitioner is required to carefully document goals and necessary procedures to keep therapeutic costs within pre-set limits. The prevailing attitudes of the general public can also influence illness perceptions. As a society we tend to avoid pain, and the presence of those who have suffered severe abuse (as is commonly found among individuals with DID) may make others around them feel uncomfortable. Who wants to listen to the disquieting accounts of severe ongoing developmental trauma and abuse dating from early childhood at the hands of a relative or close friend?

CASE ILLUSTRATION: JEAN REDHORSE OSCEOLA

The experience of depersonalization and related symptoms does not automatically imply the presence of psychopathology. In premodern societies, depersonalization is typically experienced and diagnosed as a set of various culture-bound symptoms related to a spirit attack or spirit possession. Depersonalization is somewhat different from the other dissociative disorders in that the key symptom of this disorder is depersonalization rather than dissociation. The person experiences persistent or recurrent feelings of being detached from his or her mental processes or body, accompanied by significant emotional distress or impairment. As will be seen in the following case of Jean Redhorse Osceola, first described in Psychopathology: A Competency-Based Assessment Model for Social Workers *by Zide and Gray (2001), the client describes feeling as if part of her body is detached from the rest of her. Although Jean Redhorse initially perceived her symptoms as "weird," she began to feel frightened when she could not control her "spells." With the exception of these episodes, she appears to be a typical teenager. To fit the criteria for depersonalization, the person's reality testing must remain intact. Jean Redhorse denies hearing voices or having hallucinations. The person may feel a lack of control of his or her actions, speech, or thoughts. Jean Redhorse describes feeling as if her experiences "just sorta happen" and this scares her, causing considerable distress. Jean Redhorse is a member of the Seminole tribe and lives on the Hollywood reservation, one of six reservations in Florida. The practitioner is not a native person, and the following case accents the major features of a competency-based relationship in which the practitioner considers the social realities of First Nations people to foster the client's resilience and buffer the stresses in her life.*

The school social worker, Barbara Mazzuchi, greeted Jean Redhorse Osceola in the waiting room outside the guidance counselor's office. Since the last time they had talked, Barbara noticed that Jean Redhorse had grown taller and matured into a graceful young adult. The person who now sat before her exuded a quiet dignity. Barbara immediately thought of the indomitable spirit and proud heritage of the Seminole tribe. She was surprised at how much she remembered about the tribal history Jean Redhorse had taught her when they first worked together. Despite three Seminole wars, they were the only Indian tribe never to surrender to the United States. Jean Redhorse had stressed to Barbara that the Seminoles of Florida refer to themselves as the "unconquered people." They are the direct descendants of just 300 Indians who managed to elude capture by the United States army in the nineteenth century. Ironically, on this day Jean Redhorse looked defeated.

Barbara thought back on her first meeting with Jean Redhorse. The youngster had been about 12 years old at the time. She had recently transferred into a new school and had experienced a number of problems adjusting. Many of the other children had made fun of Jean Redhorse, calling her derogatory names related to her cultural status as a Native Seminole. The youngster's mother maintained a strong respect for "the old ways." Jean Redhorse and her mother lived in an open, palm-thatched dwelling called a "chickee." Both wore the brightly colored clothing that reflected an evolution of traditional styles. Jean Redhorse was raised in the rich Seminole heritage and traditions, but she stood out in the new school where there were few Native Americans. Barbara had never worked with this population before. She recalled that even though her favorite television channel was "Home and Garden Television" (HGTV), she found it hard to imagine what it would be like to live in an open, thatched-roof structure. Barbara knew it would be important to understand the traditional Seminole ways as part of her work with Jean Redhorse and to be nonjudgmental about a life style so different from her own. "That's Social Work 101," she thought. However, Barbara knew that it was important to recognize that she brought her own background of privilege and lack of personal experience with oppression and disenfranchisement to their relationship. Barbara's curiosity about First Nations cultures, her interest in the history of the Seminole tribe, and a willingness to learn from her client had seemed to characterize their earlier relationship. Barbara found herself to be an eager student, and Jean Redhorse was a willing teacher. Eventually Jean Redhorse had transitioned into her new school and their work together had ended.

Jean Redhorse brightened when she saw the social worker again. "Oh! Ms. Mazzuchi, I'm so glad it's you! You're the only one who pronounces my name, Osceola, (pronounced as Asi-Yaholo) correctly!" Barbara was genuinely glad to see Jean Redhorse but noticed the tears in the young woman's eyes and observed that she looked very tired. They went to the social worker's office. Barbara commented, "I'm really impressed, Jean Redhorse. You have been doing so well in school. I understand that you are on the honor roll just about every semester!" After a long silence, Jean Redhorse replied with a sad voice and tears welling up in her eyes, "I guess so, but my mother and the rest of the clan are worried about me. It's my 'crazy talk,' they say." There was another silence while Barbara patiently waited for Jean Redhorse to go on. "It's just that I've had a hard time concentrating in school, and it's getting worse. If this keeps up, I'm afraid I'm going to be in trouble with all my teachers. There's the one teacher, Ms. Wojcik, who was surprised I did so well in her chemistry class, you know? I heard it from the other kids that she doesn't expect much from people like us. She thinks all 'Injun kids' . . . that's what she calls us . . . are either dropouts or drunks. I guess I don't care what she thinks, but the others really seemed concerned about me. I don't want to let them down," said Jean Redhorse.

Barbara gently pointed out that Jean Redhorse had mentioned to one of her teachers that she "felt like a robot" and "I can see myself standing outside of my body." Jean Redhorse replied, "Listen. I don't want to be here. I want to go home. I don't want somebody to lock me up and tell me that I'm crazy or something." Jean Redhorse then began to cry. The social worker gently asked, "When did you start having these feelings?" Jean Redhorse responded, "Well, it really started the last time I saw you. I didn't tell you because I thought I could handle it. Since then, I've had these feelings now and again. They seem to come over me when I get stressed out about something. It feels so weird. I used to just go and be by myself for a while and that would help. Sometimes I'm fine, but even then it's like I'm not myself."

Barbara asked, "Has there been anything that's happened that you think might be related to these feelings?" Jean Redhorse looked thoughtful and after some time responded. "I remember that my father left my mother around the time I first started seeing you. He was arrested, I think, but he never came back. Oh, how my Mom loved my Dad! I remember the stories of how they met at the American Indian Exposition of '84 in Anadarko, Oklahoma. Did you know it's the oldest Indian-owned and operated fair in the world? He was a proud Navajo, and it was love at first sight! Mom loved to dance, and in those days they would go every year to the Wichita Annual Dance in the Wichita Tribal Park. Mom was so sad after he was gone and cried a lot. It was hard for us. She was homesick, and so we moved back home to the Seminole reservation in Hollywood, Florida. And then I had all those problems getting used to the new school. That's where you came in. Remember? You know, I almost forgot the time when those welfare workers came to our chickee and almost took me away from her. They said something about the house being dirty, and there was not enough food. They asked Mom a lot of questions about her drinking, too. She never drank, but that didn't seem to make a difference to those people. They asked their questions anyway. That was a scary time! If it weren't for my uncle, Bobby Jumper, they probably would have taken me away. Well, he's not really my 'uncle' but part of my clan. Our ancestors traded in Fort Lauderdale in the early 1900s. Did you know that about me?"

Barbara observed, "Okay, let me understand. You've had these feelings happen several times since then." Jean Redhorse responded, "Yeah. Maybe once or twice a year but then they would seem to go away . . . at least for a while. Now that I'm close to graduation, they seem to come on more often. It's getting really hard. I'm stressed out so much. Mom is happy with the idea that I'll be graduating. She never made it past the tenth grade. I'll be the first, you know? Sometimes I think it would be easier to drop out of school, but I know my family would disapprove. They are all so proud of me." She looked down. Barbara inquired if being one of the few members of the Seminole tribe in her school also added to her stress, and Jean Redhorse nodded affirmatively. Barbara then asked Jean Redhorse if she'd been feeling sad or down in the dumps lately. Jean Redhorse denied feeling depressed or suicidal. She also denied having experienced blackout spells, convulsions, headaches, dizziness, or trauma to her head. She denied hearing voices, having hallucinations, or feeling that other people were plotting against her. She claimed she was alcohol- and drug-free. While some of her friends had tried pot once or twice, she never had. Barbara Mazzuchi commented to Jean Redhorse that her mother had been called at work and asked to come to the school immediately. When Ms. Osceola arrived, Ms. Mazzuchi asked Jean Redhorse if it would be okay to have her join them.

Ms. Osceola began, "My daughter had this 'thing' several times before, but it doesn't amount to much of anything. It's just her 'crazy talk.' Listen, I have way too much to do to waste my time coming down to school when she gets into one of her 'spells.' I just wish she would eat a good breakfast, ya know?" Barbara replied, "Can either you or Jean Redhorse tell me anything more about this?" Jean Redhorse was the first to respond. "Well, sometimes it looks like my arms and legs get really big, or really small. Sometimes I even feel like I'm floating up in the air. You know, like floating outside my body and above my head. You know, it's not like I'm crazy or anything because I know it's happening, but the first time it was so weird. Now it's getting a little scary. I feel like I have no control over it. It just sorta happens." The social worker noticed that Ms. Osceola sat quietly, listening to her daughter. She remembered Ms. Osceola's prior negative experiences with social workers when she had first moved to the reservation and wondered if this might have something to do with her annoyance about being called into the school today. In addition, it seemed that her daughter's symptoms were hard for her to understand.

Barbara began by thanking Ms. Osceola for coming to see her on such short notice and despite a busy schedule at her job. She went on to acknowledge that

Jean Redhorse's "crazy talk" seemed puzzling for everyone, including the school, Jean Redhorse herself, Ms. Osceola, their family, and even tribal community members. Ms. Osceola sat silently, neither agreeing nor disagreeing, but Barbara had a feeling that she seemed to be listening more intently. Barbara believed that her next comment would be important. She thought that Jean Redhorse appeared to be a typical teenager in every way with the exception of the "spells" she experienced. Considering her client's culture and its interplay with coping behaviors, Barbara asked, "Ms. Osceola, is there someone that you know who could be helpful with Jean Redhorse's 'spells,' or is this something that you would like me to look into?" After what felt like a very long silence to Barbara, Ms. Osceola responded. Her words seemed deliberate and selected with great care. She said, "Well, as a matter of fact, I do. Everyone says that Ronnie Brave Heart Gray has the wisdom to help. The elders tell me that she has had much training in matters like this." Ms. Osceola went on, "Her special skills were identified when she was very young, and she apprenticed for a long time with the medicine man Billy Miller who was willing to take her on. Thirty years, I think. It was very intensive training, and Billy always decided what tasks Ronnie Brave Heart was ready to perform and what she needed to learn. She has much knowledge about our healing ways." Ms. Osceola went on to share with Barbara her concerns about involving the medicine woman in her daughter's care. Apparently Ms. Osceola was troubled about how the school personnel might react and apprehensive that the state would be contacted again to investigate her and her home. Barbara pointed out to Ms. Osceola that as the school social worker, she would work with the school staff to help them understand what would be helpful for Jean Redhorse. She asked how Ronnie Brave Heart would be contacted and what could be expected. Once again, she felt like the student as she learned about tribal healing customs from Ms. Osceola. Jean Redhorse listened to their conversation with interest and seemed excited to discover she did not have some kind of serious mental illness. Something could be done to help. Barbara remarked, "I will be glad to be available to Ronnie Brave Heart Gray, if she would like to talk with me. If that's the case, I'll just need your written consent to release information."

The interview concluded with plans to involve the medicine woman and a discussion about when Barbara would see Jean Redhorse and Ms. Osceola again. Since it was difficult for Ms. Osceola to take time off from work to come to the school, Barbara offered to see her at the reservation. The social worker found herself thinking, "I wonder how many youngsters are out there just like Jean Redhorse who seem to get 'lost' in the system. I'm going to talk with the principal first thing tomorrow morning about developing an informational workshop series for the teachers. After all, they are the first to come into contact with these kids." Since it had been awhile since Barbara had been out to the reservation, she looked forward to the prospect of a home visit.

Barbara went to see Jean Redhorse and her mother about one month later. Jean Redhorse was excited once again about school, and her depersonalization symptoms had abated. Ms. Osceola was greatly relieved and looking forward to her daughter's graduation.

OPERATIONALIZING COMPETENCY-BASED TREATMENT

A community context replete with ethnic and cultural diversity characterizes social work practice in the twenty-first century. The United States 2000 Census reflects a marked increase in minority populations. Between 1980 and 2000, the minority population increased by 41.3 million while the white, non-Hispanic population increased by only 13.7 million ("A rapid move to diversity," 2001). During a period of 20 years the minority population has more than doubled, and this growth is expected to continue. The case vignette illustrates the importance of moving away from stereotypical treatment approaches that may have marginalized Jean Redhorses's experiences and instead moving toward effectively integrating culturally relevant social work practice skills into the field of mental health. Jean Redhorse Osceola challenged the practitioner not only to recognize the symptomatic behavior of depersonalization but also to develop a greater understanding of herself, her own culture, her experiences as a privileged member of society, and the places where her own beliefs intersected with the client's world. As Guadalupe and Lum (2005) point out, the concept of intersectionality helps the practitioner to recognize "the multidimensional nature of people and contextual aspects to highlight the importance of persons, events, and experiences in the environmental situation" (p. xxi). For example, Jean Redhorse was proud of her Seminole heritage, but she also experienced oppression and discrimination due to her status as a First Nations person in her high school. This was further complicated by her struggles with a diagnosis of depersonalization. Additionally it was important for the practitioner, Barbara Mazzuchi, to be nonjudgmental, self-reflective, and willing to learn from her client and from the tribal community. Competency-based treatment provided a framework for blending the practitioner's knowledge about the multiple dimensions of Jean Redhorse's life, her Seminole tribal culture and history, and the realities of her environment (see Table 8.1). This understanding helped the practitioner to select culturally relevant interventions.

Working with Jean Redhorse Individually

Atkinson, Morten, and Sue (1998) observe that American Indians have been characterized as "aliens in their own land" for the past century. Stress increases as Indians adapt to the dominant culture, and certainly being one of the few Native Americans in her school heightened Jean Redhorse's stress. She describes numerous pressures, beginning with the difficult adjustment to her school when she was 12 years old, the disappearance of her father, and the family's subsequent relocation to the Seminole reservation. Current stresses include negative perceptions of her as a Seminole Indian from one of her teachers and pressure from family and others for her to graduate from high school. Despite these life events and circumstances, Jean Redhorse showed much strength; for example, she adjusted to her new school and eventually became an honor roll student. The practitioner assessed the culture-based sources of Jean Redhorse's social and environmental stress as well as the factors that supported her functioning. As seen in this case vignette, Jean

TABLE 8.1	THE RISKS, PROTECTIVE FACTORS, AND BUFFERS IN JEAN REDHORSE OSCEOLA'S LIFE	
	Risk Factors	**Protective Factors and Buffers**
Intrapersonal	Feels detached from her body	Denies drug/alcohol abuse
	Scared by detachment experiences, which are happening with increasing frequency	Denies • Blackouts • Convulsions • Dizziness • Head trauma • Hallucinations • Paranoid thoughts
	Stressed about school and impending graduation	Bright, personable student
Interpersonal	Chemistry teacher's negative attitude toward First Nations Peoples	Successful transition to new community/school
	Mother's past negative experiences with social workers	Good student
		Prior positive relationship with social worker
	Mother puzzled by daughter's symptoms	Other teachers concerned about Jean's symptoms and progress
	Father "disappeared"	Mother involved in daughter's life
		Family and clan proud of Jean Redhorse
Social and Environmental	Cultural barriers (few members of the Seminole tribe in the school)	Strong sense of community
	Negative stereotypes of First Nations People held by some	Value placed on family (including clan), traditions, and cultural continuity
		Access to a competent, well-trained medicine woman
		Strong respect for all people

Redhorse's culture was a source of strength for her, and her past heritage as a member of an "unconquered people" became a part of how she coped (Lum, 2004).

At one point in the interview Barbara interjects, "Okay, let me understand . . ." and attempts to comprehend the full range of Jean Redhorse's symptoms of dissociation. The practitioner did not assume the presence of psychopathology and carefully ruled out the presence of other syndromes such as depression or substance use.

Working with the Family

First Nations peoples tend to underutilize services based on perceptions that service providers are unresponsive to their needs (Lum, 2004). Ms. Osceola had a negative experience with the previous social worker who had investigated her home. Her fear, mistrust, and the insensitivity of the prior experience reduced her willingness to seek help. Ms. Osceola saw coming to the school about her daughter's behavior as a "waste of time." It was important for the practitioner to not be afraid of the client's anger as Ms. Osceola directed her negative feelings toward Barbara. Instead of taking the anger personally, the practitioner listened patiently and began her response by thanking Ms. Osceola for coming in. This shifted the focus to this mother's very real concerns about her daughter's puzzling behavior. There is the added possibility that Ms. Osceola may have initially seen the practitioner as a member of the White establishment who had come into her home and conducted what was described as a humiliating and insensitive experience. Ms. Mazzuchi resisted the temptation to "interpret" the significance of the home visit and was attentive to the client's account of what had happened. This served to respect her client's feelings rather than discount, patronize, or demean them through well-intended "explanations."

Ms. Osceola's hostile attitude changed when the current social worker, Barbara Mazzuchi, attempted to connect dominant mental health counseling approaches with traditional healing practices by involving a medicine woman in her daughter's care. Sue and Sue (1990, 1999) underscore the value of harmony with nature that is so much a part of Native American cultures. This concept underlies Native beliefs about mental health and illness. For Jean Redhorse, having symptoms of depersonalization reflected the existence of disharmony between herself and the natural world. Her healing was facilitated by interventions aimed at restoring harmony.

To find an intervention that was a good match, Barbara assessed the importance of culture in this family and their adherence to "traditional ways." For symbolic healing to be effective, it is important for the practitioner and the client to agree on the appropriate treatment (Castillo, 1997). While the use of traditional healers to help and heal should be a priority over all other forms of intervention (Atkinson, Morten, & Sue, 1998), the challenge for non-Native practitioners is to know the difference between when clients use culture as a defense against meaningful change and when Native cultural beliefs are genuine (Diller, 2004). The best source of information on whether an intervention is a good cultural fit will come from the client, and it is important to acknowledge the client as the expert (Lum, 2003). This stance is compatible with the helping relationship characterized by competency-based treatment. More than 20 years ago Morgan (1981) compared the Native American healer to the prototypic family physician. In Native American societies:

- Well-being is based on a harmony or equilibrium of forces including the social and psychological;
- Both the healer and the ill person share a system of beliefs about the nature of the world and the nature of the "disease";
- The person's sickness is a shared responsibility with family members, and all participate in healing rites;
- The healer involves the person, his or her family, and others;
- Rather than focusing on disease (seen as a pathological condition of the body that presents a group of clinical signs, symptoms, and laboratory findings peculiar to it), the healer focuses on illness (or those experiences associated

with disease that ultimately affect the person's state of being and social functioning), directing attention to the person's reactions to the disease, rather than just the disease itself;

- The healer enlists the participation of others through ceremonial rituals, songs, and/or dances;
- The healer gives more than a pill; instead, both a remedy and a ritual ceremony are given;
- The healer is surrounded with helpers who support the ceremony and the person;
- The helpers assess the person's belief in the healer; and
- The helpers welcome the person, give the person time, listen, answer questions, and explain before the ceremony and afterward.

Ms. Osceola already knew of a medicine woman who had been identified at a young age as having special gifts. This healer had apprenticed with a medicine man for almost 30 years and would bring the wisdom of spiritual legends and healing for insight into Jean Redhorse's emotional and behavioral problems. When Ms. Osceola voiced her concerns about how using a medicine woman would be perceived by the school, Barbara supported her client by offering to educate the school personnel about this treatment approach. Empowerment was fostered when the practitioner acknowledged, validated, and respected indigenous healing practices. Walters (1999) observes that First Nations peoples "have survived by taking the best of both worlds" (p. 163). It becomes important for the practitioner to carefully distinguish between the level of a client's assimilation and traditionally held beliefs and develop treatment interventions accordingly (Diller, 2004). Another strength of First Nations cultures is their respect for all people and parts of creation. These strengths were integrated into the practitioner's efforts.

In this case vignette, the practitioner recognizes that she comes from a cultural background that is different from that of Jean Redhorse, and she demonstrates the essential qualities of self-reflection, open-mindedness, a nonjudgmental attitude, humility, and a willingness to learn from her client (Lum, 2003, 2005; Weaver, 1999, 2000, 2005). The foundation of the helping relationship was based on a core social work value of treating the client and her family with respect and dignity. Self-awareness is also important when working with First Nations people. When Barbara learned that Jean Redhorse and her mother lived in a chickee, the practitioner recognized the difference in her own cultural values and biases from those of her client. She reflected on her own preferences such as enjoying a home-oriented television station and began to appreciate how she may have been influenced by her own culture. If one is going to work with a client whose world view is fundamentally different from one's own, it is important to understand the many places where one's own culture intersects with that of the client (Guadalupe & Lum, 2005; Lum, 2005). This paradigm shift is helpful to avoid labeling culturally relevant behavior as deviant or abnormal (Diller, 2004) and to see "differences" as strengths. The practitioner values the client's beliefs and knowledge and focuses on how people create meaning in their lives (Walsh, 1998). From this perspective, the practitioner becomes a partner or facilitator in the helping process instead of the "expert" who can solve the client's problems.

When working with First Nations peoples in particular, it is also important to be patient and allow for silence (Sutton & Broken Nose, 1996; Weaver, 1999). This silence may connote respect, that the client is forming his or her thoughts, or that the client is waiting for a sign from the practitioner that it is the right time to speak. Rather than interpret silence from Jean Redhorse or her mother as resistance, Barbara Mazzuchi saw this as another form of communication between them. On many occasions, the social worker waited for responses from Jean Redhorse or her mother and was careful to pace the interview so as to allow the Osceola family additional time to respond to her questions or statements.

Working with the Community

Competency-based treatment considers community influences, and the social worker's interventions were grounded in an understanding of Jean Redhorse's cultural resources; for example, spirituality, her support systems found in the clan, historic patterns of assimilation and adaptation, as well as formal and informal services. By including a medicine woman, Ronnie Brave Heart Gray, as well as being mindful of the influence of the clan, the practitioner respected the Osceola family's need to maintain linkages with their cultural and spiritual resources to bring about healing and social support. This inclusion of indigenous community helpers buffered Jean Redhorse's stresses and helped her to recover her sense of wholeness and meaning. These meanings were especially important to Jean Redhorse, a Native American.

Competency-based treatment also involves activism and advocacy (Lum, 2003, 2005; Weaver, 2005). Oppression has had a significant effect on Native peoples. Concerned about Jean Redhorse's perceptions of negativity toward Native Americans from her chemistry teacher, Barbara Mazzuchi decided that it would be helpful if the school faculty could learn more about the Seminole culture. The social worker hoped that by increasing the teachers' competence (including the chemistry teacher) then their responses to students would be more appropriate. She planned to develop a workshop series to accomplish this goal. The practitioner enjoyed a good relationship with the school principal and had offered many similar programs in the past with success. She realized this would not resolve all of the problems associated with the negative stereotyping of minorities by some faculty members but could be a first step in a positive direction. Competency-based treatment includes striving for social justice by working to overcome oppression and discrimination. In this case illustration, the practitioner began with her own agency and practices.

As illustrated in this vignette, competency-based treatment is uniquely suited for practice with vulnerable individuals and families. Moreover, this approach is attentive to the reciprocal interactions that occur between individuals and their environment, while at the same time considering the influence of culture and ethnicity across the intrapersonal, interpersonal, and community/environmental domains in the client's life. More simply, the client is not seen as separate from the context in which he or she lives (Guadalupe & Lum, 2005). Jean Redhorse's experiences with a mental disorder disrupted the usual "goodness of fit" important to adaptation. When the practitioner drew upon Native healing approaches, the focus shifted to the client's adaptive interaction with all elements of her environment.

In summary, competency-based treatment enabled the practitioner to consider the interconnectedness and interrelatedness of the Osceola family to the dominant American society from a strengths-based perspective. Integral to the practitioner's understanding of Jean Redhorse's symptoms of depersonalization disorder was the consideration of First Nations peoples' values, adaptive responses, and coping skills. By introducing indigenous strategies to help and heal, the practitioner took into account the uniqueness of the individual as well as group meanings associated with the social realities of First Nations people. In particular, the cultural emphasis on restoring harmony drew upon Jean Redhorse Osceola's strengths and resilience from her identity as a Seminole.

SUMMARY

In summary, the dissociative disorders often seem related to the tendency for the person to escape psychologically from memories of traumatic events. The disorders are characterized by disruptions in the usually integrated functions of consciousness, memory, identity, or perception of one's environment. The disorders discussed in this chapter included dissociative identity disorder, in which new identities, or alters, may be formed; dissociative amnesia, where the person may be unable to remember important social information; dissociative fugue, or a memory loss combined with an unexpected trip (or trips); and depersonalization disorder, in which the person temporarily loses a sense of reality regarding the self and the external world.

The case vignette provided the opportunity to examine the symptoms of depersonalization disorder as a combination of both clinical and cultural issues. When the practitioner perceived the client's behavior within the larger context of her culture, the range of treatment interventions expanded. The practitioner recognized the influence of culture on help-seeking behaviors, problem-solving strategies, concepts of health and healing, and the role of spirituality. By involving the tribal medicine woman, healing was understood within the context of spiritual beliefs. Competency-based treatment was operationalized around tapping into Jean Redhorse Osceola's culture as a resource and source of strength. The practitioner followed her client's lead in identifying problems and their solutions rather than attempting to impose her own ideas (Prochaska, 1999; Walter & Peller, 1992). The therapeutic relationship was characterized by trust and collaboration.

PRACTITIONER REFLECTIONS

1. Imagine that you are on a jury. The case involves a defendant who was charged with kidnapping and brutally raping and killing eight young women who were known to the police as prostitutes. The bodies were left in places

where they could be easily found. The defendant claims that he suffers from dissociative identity disorder and has no memory of committing the murders. His defense attorney brings in a well-known psychiatrist with expertise in the dissociative disorders who testifies that the man has a true case of dissociative identity disorder. What questions would you want to ask about this case?

2. Dissociative identity disorder, or DID, poses many challenges for the practitioner. For example, persons with the diagnosis lack a coherent sense of identity and often have deficits in forming relationships and caring for themselves. Another challenge consists of the difficulties of validating the diagnosis. Additionally, clients may have "false memories" of their abuse. Imagine you are working with someone who has been diagnosed with DID. Describe how you would develop a therapeutic relationship with your client. Be attentive to what factors would facilitate the therapeutic alliance and what could potentially get in the way.

3. The following book has been written for persons suffering symptoms of dissociation as well as for their family members and friends: Steinberg, M., & Schnall, M. (2000). *Stranger in the Mirror.* New York: Cliff Street Books. The book includes a questionnaire designed to help the reader to self-assess the presence and severity of symptom-related behaviors for the core symptoms of dissociation, which are amnesia, depersonalization, derealization, identity confusion, and identity alteration. The book is intended to provide insight into what dissociation looks like, feels like, and what to do about it.

    • Review the book and decide whether you would loan it to a client and his or her family.

    • In general, do you think self-help books are helpful? Describe the advantages and disadvantages of reading self-help books.

    • Can you identify any other self-help resources useful for the dissociative disorders?

4. The case of Jean Redhorse Osceola illustrates the social worker's ability to interact with her client in a way that was knowledgeable and respectful of the client's social context. While it is not possible to know everything about every diverse group one encounters in practice, practitioners using the competency-based model of practice will attempt to be knowledgeable about the culture, history, and contemporary realities of the people they encounter in practice. Discuss with your supervisor or a colleague how you would learn about other groups of persons different from yourself (for example, people of another culture, race, ethnicity, age, gender, social class, spirituality, or gender identification). Also consider the following questions:

    • How would you go about engaging persons from this group?

    • Are there any particular skills that would be helpful in this work?

    • Do current laws or social policies have adverse consequences for this group?

    • What has fostered this group's resilience and survival within the dominant culture?

EATING DISORDERS

- *Nancy is 23 years old, just under 5 feet 6 inches tall, wears a size 2, and weighs only 90 pounds. Even though she looks thin, she always seems to be on a diet. She is obsessive about what she eats, constantly reads food labels, and carefully avoids consuming any kind of fat.*
- *Carol lives in a beautiful house that looks as if it belongs in the pages of an interior design magazine. Carol is a wonderful hostess, but she has a peculiar habit of eating quickly and then excusing herself to use the bathroom. Interestingly, food disappears rapidly from her kitchen cabinets.*
- *Susan's weight is about average for her height and size. Like her sister Carol, she has some eating habits that could be considered odd. She can eat a lot during one meal and will tell you in a most convincing manner that she can control her weight by dieting.*

What do all of these women have in common? Each shows symptoms of eating disorders.

Many of us remember being told as children that we could not have dessert until we had eaten everything on our plate. Most of us take food for granted. We eat two or three meals a day and may have a few between-meal snacks. We know we should eat more fruit and vegetables but figure a sweet treat now and then won't hurt. For most of us, food is not only a necessity but also a source of pleasure. Our eating habits are controlled by factors such as appetite, the availability of food, family and peer influences, or cultural practices. Some people can be described as skinny, while others are characterized as plump. Some can eat anything they want without gaining weight, while others struggle constantly to shed a few pounds. Almost everyone worries every now and then about their weight, but people with eating disorders take concerns to extremes, developing abnormal eating habits that ultimately threaten their well-being. Adolescent and young adult women account for about 90 percent of people with disordered eating patterns, but older women and men can also develop eating disorders. An increasing number of people from ethnic minority groups are falling prey to these illnesses.

Obesity is a significant health problem in the United States. As noted by Taubes (1998), half of all American adults are overweight and at least 25 percent under age 19 can be considered overweight or obese. Why are people in our society getting fatter? This weight-gain epidemic has been attributed to several causes (Robinson, 1999):

- Low-cost, high-fat foods are easily available;
- We have developed a habit of eating high-calorie food on the run rather than sitting down to enjoy a leisurely meal;
- We have become dependent on an increasing number of devices that reduce physical exertion, such as the television remote control; and
- We have developed a preference for watching television and engaging in other sedentary activities rather than exercising.

Many people subsist on foods that are convenient, high in fat, and cheap, such as quarter-pound hamburgers, fries, chips, tacos, sweets, and pizzas (Pinel, Assanand, & Lehman, 2000). Snack machines are loaded with food and beverages that are high in calories, fat, and sugar and low in nutritional value. Moreover, food portions have become gargantuan (Critser, 2003). We take the well-being of our bodies for granted and don't pay attention to our health unless our lives are disrupted by illness or disease.

Most people overeat from time to time, and many of us can recall the feeling of having eaten more than we should have. Eating disorders such as anorexia nervosa, bulimia nervosa, and binge eating are among the hardest of all mental illnesses to comprehend and among the most difficult to diagnose and treat. Persons with disordered eating tend to deny that they are sick and resist treatment, making this syndrome the deadliest of all psychiatric disorders. The eating disorders involve serious disturbances in one's eating behaviors ranging from an extreme and unhealthy reduction of food intake to severe overeating. An estimated 50,000 people who are currently struggling with an eating disorder will eventually die as a result of it (Sohn, 2002). Persons with anorexia relentlessly pursue becoming so "thin" through diet and exercise that they are below 85 percent of their ideal body weight and at a high risk of heart attacks, arthritis, osteoporosis, and other serious health problems. Persons with bulimia eat uncontrollably and then compensate by throwing up, taking laxatives, or exercising obsessively to the point that the body's chemical balance is not working properly.

The eating disorders affect a relatively small segment of the population. For example, in 2000 an estimated 1 percent of American women suffered from anorexia (Schindehette, Sandler, Nelson, & Seaman, 2003). More than 90 percent of people struggling with eating disorders are females from families of upper socioeconomic status who live in a socially competitive environment (Barlow & Durand, 2005; Zide & Gray, 2001). The late Princess of Wales, Diana, is perhaps the most visible example of someone who suffered from an eating disorder. She battled bulimia for 7 years and recalled bingeing and vomiting four or more times a day during her honeymoon (Morton, 1992).

UNDERSTANDING EATING DISORDERS

Anorexia Nervosa

An English physician, Sir William Gull, first introduced the term anorexia nervosa in 1868 to describe a "want of appetite" attributed to the individual's mental state (Gull, 1874/1964). Persons with anorexia tend to be ritualistic about the food they eat, cutting it into tiny pieces or eating only one specific food at a specific time of day. Those with anorexia nervosa usually do not lose their appetite but focus their energy on curbing food intake. A client known to the author restricted herself to one lettuce leaf each day. On alternate days she added two almonds to her diet, and each almond had to be broken into pieces. When the nut segments were ingested, they were not to be chewed but swallowed whole. After each morsel she would drink a glass of water.

Anorexia nervosa involves a person's refusal to maintain a minimally normal body weight, which is defined as at least 85 percent of the body weight that is considered appropriate based on age and height (as measured by standardized height and weight charts, body mass index calculations, or pediatric growth charts). The amount of weight loss is an important factor in determining whether one is struggling with anorexia. The person fears gaining weight, and this fear is not abated by significant weight loss. The assessment criteria for anorexia nervosa are listed below (APA, 2000; Zide & Gray, 2001):

- Refusal to maintain weight at or above a minimally normal weight for age and height (for example, a woman who should weigh 100 pounds weighs less than 85 pounds);
- Despite being considerably underweight, continuing to be fearful of gaining weight or becoming "fat";
- Distorted perception of body weight or body shape, or denial of the serious health consequences of their present low weight;
- In women who are of post-menarche status, an absence of at least three consecutive menstrual cycles (amenorrhea).

Fairburn and Cooper (1998) define an eating binge as ingesting a much larger amount of food than individuals would normally eat under similar circumstances. Purging is defined as any activity aimed at ameliorating the perceived negative effects of a binge on the body shape and weight (Agras, 1994; Kinder, 1997; Zide & Gray, 2001). Purging may include vomiting or ingesting large quantities of diuretics (or water pills) or laxatives to keep from gaining weight. Anorexia nervosa is divided into two subtypes based on the method the person uses to limit calorie intake. In the *restricting type* of anorexia, the individual severely limits caloric intake during the current episode and does not regularly engage in binge eating or purging behavior. In the *binge eating/purging type* of anorexia, the individual regularly engages in binge eating or purging behavior such as self-induced vomiting or misuse of laxatives, enemas, or diuretics.

Bulimia Nervosa

Bulimia nervosa, which is a more common condition than anorexia, was first introduced almost 25 years ago in the *Diagnostic and Statistical Manual—III* (DSM) (APA, 1980). The symptoms are less obvious than the starving symptoms of anorexia nervosa. In fact, some individuals with this disorder may even be slightly overweight. Persons with bulimia nervosa, like those with anorexia nervosa, are concerned with body weight and have a morbid fear of becoming fat, but most tend to keep nearly normal weight. The onset of symptoms may take place when an attempt to diet is closely followed by purging behaviors (Zide & Gray, 2001). While purging may seem to be a convenient method to overeat without gaining weight, it often quickly becomes a destructive process that cannot be easily controlled. Yager (1994) observes that stressful life circumstances often trigger a binge, and food becomes a temporary "fix" to soothe and reduce emotional tension.

People with bulimia nervosa differ from those with anorexia nervosa primarily in the fact that the individual with bulimia is usually of normal weight or overweight. In practice, it can be difficult to distinguish between the two disorders, since eating patterns for both can include binge eating and purging. While the distinguishing factors for anorexia nervosa are the failure to maintain 85 percent of normal body weight (and the presence of amenorrhea), bulimia nervosa is characterized by a person's repeated episodes of uncontrollable binge eating alternating with repeated and desperate measures to prevent weight gain (APA, 2000; Zide & Gray, 2001). Binges usually occur in secret, last as long as eight hours, and may result in an intake of up to 20,000 calories. The preferred foods are usually high in calories and easily ingested, such as junk food high in sugar or fat rather than fruits and vegetables (Cooke, Guss, Kissileff, & Devlin, 1997).

The assessment criteria for bulimia nervosa are listed below (APA, 2000; Zide & Gray, 2001):

- Recurrent episodes of binge eating are characterized by both of the following:
  1. Eating occurs during a discrete period of time; and
  2. The individual experiences a lack of control over eating during the episode.
- Recurrent and inappropriate compensatory methods are used to prevent weight gain (such as self-induced vomiting, fasting, excessive exercise, and misuse of laxatives, enemas, diuretics, or other medications);
- Binge eating and inappropriate compensatory methods occur at least twice a week for three months;
- Self-image is unduly influenced by body shape and weight;
- The disturbance does not occur exclusively during an episode of anorexia nervosa. (Of note, a majority of those with bulimia have never had anorexia but it is not uncommon to find a past history of many anorexic features.)

Those with *purging type* counteract the effects of eating either by vomiting or using compensatory methods such as ingesting large amounts of laxatives or diuretics, or (less frequently) administering enemas to purge their bowels. Excessive exercise and fasting measures are considered *nonpurging type*. Exercise, in this case, means exercising for more than an hour just to keep from gaining weight after binge eating. Fasting is defined as not eating for at least 24 hours. Unfortunately, fasting usually backfires, causing increased hunger and leading to greater overeating. Approximately two thirds of persons with bulimia nervosa are "purgers" (Barlow & Durand, 2005).

Binge Eating Disorder

Eating disorder not otherwise specified (NOS) is used when the individual does not meet full criteria for an eating disorder. Binge eating disorder, or recurring episodes of binge eating without regular compensatory behaviors associated with bulimia nervosa, falls into this category. Binge eating disorder is probably the most common eating disorder. This syndrome is similar to bulimia except that individuals are not fixated on body shape and weight. Binge eating disorder (BED) has been called by several names, including bulimia, nonpurging bulimia nervosa, and compulsive overeating (APA, 2000; Zide & Gray, 2001). Interestingly, individuals who meet the preliminary criteria for BED are often found in weight-control programs (Barlow & Durand, 2005).

The criteria for binge eating disorder include the following (APA, 2000; Zide & Gray, 2001):

- Recurrent episodes of binge eating must occur, and in these episodes:
  1. Eating occurs during a discrete period of time, and
  2. The individual lacks control over what or how much food is eaten.
- The binge eating episode usually has three or more of the following characteristics:
  1. Consuming food more rapidly than would be considered "normal";
  2. Eating food until one feels uncomfortably full or overstuffed;
  3. Eating large quantities of food even when not physically hungry;
  4. Eating alone because of embarrassment about the quantity of food eaten;
  5. Feeling disgusted or guilty after overeating.
- Marked distress regarding binge eating is present;
- The binge eating occurs, on average, at least twice a week over a period of at least six months;
- Binge eating is not combined with the regular use of inappropriate alleviative behaviors (such as fasting) and does not occur solely during the course of either anorexia or bulimia.

Most individuals with binge eating disorder have tried to control it on their own but have not been successful for very long. They may try to hide their problematic eating and feel ashamed about what they are doing. Often the person becomes so successful at concealment that even family members and close friends do not know about the binges. Similar to bulimia nervosa, persons struggling with binge eating disorder eat large amounts of fats and sugars. They can get sick because they may not be getting the right amount of nutrients. Investigative clinical trials are being conducted to determine whether binge eating disorder should be classified as a separate DSM category, but the proposal is controversial.

The Role of Obesity

Obesity is not considered a psychiatric disorder and does not appear in the DSM (APA, 2000). It is medically defined as having an excess of fat tissue and a weight of at least 20 percent over what is considered normal for a person's age and build (Stunkard, 1980). Notes Austrian (2000), obesity can be characterized as mild, moderate, or severe. Persons who are 5 to 39 percent over their ideal weight are considered mildly obese. Those who are 40 to 99 percent over their ideal weight are moderately obese, and those who are 100 percent or more over ideal weight are considered severely obese. Obese persons may develop eating disorders, and a small percentage of persons with bulimia nervosa are obese (Zide & Gray, 2001). Greater numbers of obese persons engage in binge eating behaviors. The social environment has important implications for the development and maintenance of obesity. Although obesity can occur across the social spectrum, it is predominantly found in people from the lower socioeconomic groups (von Bulow & Braiman, 2001). It is also more prevalent among downwardly mobile people.

OVERVIEW OF MAJOR INTERVENTIONS

Strategies for treating the eating disorders range from prevention to treatment. The trend has been toward multidisciplinary management with the involvement of physicians, nutritionists, and other professionals such as social workers (APA, 2001; NCCMH, 2004; Richards et al., 2000; Wolfe, 2003). Successful programs combine multiple methods such as individual, family, and group treatment. Persons with eating disorders and, where appropriate, family and significant others should be provided with education and information about the nature, course, and treatment of eating disorders including information about self-help groups and support groups.

Treatment for anorexia involves restoring the weight a person has lost as a result of severe dieting and purging; addressing the person's psychological disturbances such as distortion of body image, low self-esteem, and interpersonal conflicts; promoting healthy eating; and achieving long-term remission and recovery. Whenever possible, the person should be seen as soon as possible and treated before reaching a stage of severe emaciation. Careful monitoring for those at severely low weight or falling weight should be a priority. Early diagnosis and intervention increases the rate of success. Earlier thinking about family interventions for the eating disorders was rooted in the notion that families played a causal role in the development of anorexia nervosa through patterns of interaction characterizing the "anorexogenic family." It is now widely agreed that family interventions that mobilize family resources rather than treating dysfunction tend to be more effective (Eisler et al., 2000).

The primary goal in treating people with bulimia is to reduce or eliminate binge eating and purging behavior. This goal may be achieved through nutritional rehabilitation, psychosocial intervention, and medication management strategies.

The intent is to establish a pattern of regular, non-binge meals, improve attitudes related to the eating disorder, encourage healthy but not excessive exercise, and resolve the co-occurring conditions such as mood or anxiety disorders, if present. Treatment strategies for binge eating disorder are similar to those for bulimia.

Persons with disordered eating come to the attention of the practitioner in a number of ways. Some complain of eating problems on their own, while others seek treatment under duress from parents or loved ones. The practitioner in a medical setting may see someone who has developed physical problems as a result of the bodily abuse of massive food intake and/or restriction. These individuals may have gastrointestinal problems, esophageal tears, dermatological problems, or cardiac problems. Practitioners in counseling settings or in private practice may also encounter a client with anorexia nervosa or bulimia nervosa. Feelings of guilt, anxiety, self-loathing, and shame are often associated with disordered eating.

Assessment

Assessment of individuals with eating disorders should be comprehensive and address physical, psychological, and social aspects of each person's situation, including an assessment of risk to self. Persons with eating disorders frequently will not recognize or admit that they are ill. Many are ambivalent about treatment, and the practitioner should recognize the challenges of working with a reluctant client. There is a secretive nature to the eating disorders and it is important for the practitioner to look carefully for clues to disturbances in eating patterns (Zide & Gray, 2001). A person who is struggling with anorexia nervosa may exhibit dry or scaly-textured skin that is yellowish in color; lanugo (baby fine hair or peach fuzz found on the trunk, face, and extremities); and intolerance of cold temperatures. On a hot summer day the person may wear a heavy sweater. Because of the extreme loss of body fat and muscle mass, the person is often described as stooped or hunched-over with dull, lifeless hair, a pale or sallow complexion, and poor posture. To conceal an extremely thin frame, the person may wear loose, baggy clothing.

The telltale signs that a person is struggling with bulimia nervosa are skin lesions, abrasions, small lacerations, or raised calluses found on the dorsal (top) surface of the fingers and knuckles resulting from frequent attempts to vomit. The dorsal lesions are known as Russell's signs and are the result of repeated and constant friction of fingers being scraped back and forth across the person's teeth during attempts to induce vomiting (Daluiski, Rahbar, & Means, 1997). Other purging complications may include infection of the parotid or salivary glands, giving the person a puffy or "chipmunk" facial appearance. The front teeth are vulnerable to stomach acids brought up by frequent vomiting, and the tooth enamel may be eroded and look "moth eaten." The person may feel tired, weak, and experience a mild cognitive disorder or seizures (Zide & Gray, 2001).

The National Institute for Clinical Excellence (NICE) advocates guidelines for treating eating disorders (Baggott & Bartlett, 2004). (A copy of the treatment guidelines may be obtained from www.nice.org.uk.) NICE recommends asking individuals with a suspected eating disorder a few simple questions—for example, inquiring whether they think they have an eating problem or are worried about weight (Gough, 2003). Zide and Gray (2001) caution the practitioner to be attentive to nonverbal communication when asking about eating habits, since people may withhold information or minimize the extent of their eating behaviors. Additional questions to consider asking are the following (Anstine & Grinenko, 2000):

- Do you feel you should be dieting?
- How many diets have you been on in the past year?
- Do you feel dissatisfied with your body size?
- Does your weight affect the way you feel about yourself?

Other signs to look for include menstrual disturbances or menstrual cessation (amenorrhea) and gastrointestinal symptoms. The sooner one receives help for an eating disorder, the more favorable the prognosis will be. The Eating Disorder Examination (EDE) is considered to be the "gold standard" assessment tool of anorexia nervosa and bulimia nervosa and, when used in conjunction with other behavioral measures, is helpful in planning interventions (Guest, 2000).

Ethnocultural identity can be a factor when treating the eating disorders. Harris and Kuba (1997) suggest the practitioner incorporate knowledge of the meaning of food and cultural eating patterns into therapeutic and relapse prevention interventions. It is helpful to establish treatment goals that are consistent with cultural eating patterns, such as periods of religious fasting. The authors also suggest the person will benefit from a strong support system but it must be defined broadly; for example, the practitioner may develop a supportive peer group, community, and family, and identify healthy role models. To provide a sense of self and culture as well as buffer negative messages from the dominant culture, it is useful to foster a sense of cultural belonging while helping the person to maintain a positive self-identity. For some, developing a spiritual base may help them feel grounded enough to explore the issues that underlie their eating disorder.

A culturally aware assessment of eating disorders includes inquiry into the following areas:

- Are the person's eating patterns typical of her (or his) culture?
- Is the person's sense of beauty typical of her (or his) culture?
- How does the person's cultural/racial identity interact with and change her (or his) body satisfaction, concept of beauty, and eating patterns?
- Might cultural self-hatred be reflected in the use of food? For example, does she (or he) restrict food intake as a reflection of self-loathing?
- Does the person engage in self-destructive eating patterns other than those outlined in the DSM? (For example, the person may engage in compulsive eating and ritual dieting after binge-eating episodes.)

Treating a person with an eating disorder is challenging, and it may take many cycles of care before recovery occurs. Notes Wolfe (2003), between 20 and 30 percent of those struggling with eating disorders drop out of treatment. Denial about the severity of illness and cognitive impairment associated with malnourishment pose significant obstacles (Kahn & Pike, 2001); for example, the central characteristics of the illness can be perceived as functional and valuable by people who have anorexia nervosa. They may be ambivalent about recovery and resistant to intervention. The symptoms of anorexia nervosa are largely ego syntonic and the person often attempts to conceal purging behaviors. It is not uncommon for the individual with an eating disorder to minimize symptoms or fail to talk about essential issues. A person's struggle with an eating disorder can go undetected for many years, and society may reinforce the hidden disorder by being complimentary about the person's thinness (Bagley, Character, & Shelton, 2003). Self-starvation has much to say about social and cultural contexts that value a person's slenderness (Krusky, 2002).

The most effective approach for treating people with eating disorders will include an early assessment coupled with a comprehensive plan of treatment involving medical care and monitoring, counseling, nutritional counseling, and when appropriate, medication management. A comprehensive initial evaluation should consider the presence of secondary psychopathology associated with disordered eating, such as family and interpersonal problems, co-existing personality disorders, depression and/or substance abuse. The first task confronting the practitioner is to determine whether the person is in any immediate danger and requires hospitalization or may be treated on an outpatient basis. The eating disorders can be life-threatening, and the practitioner also needs to know when to make a referral to a medical doctor. Hospitalization is recommended when the person's physical condition has become medically precarious. Inpatient care should continue until the person's normal weight has been attained and is stable. For those individuals who have more severe illness or who have been inpatients for a longer period of time, transitional care or a "step-down" program may be helpful. A gradual termination of treatment enables the person to practice new skills and gain the confidence needed to face the typical stresses of daily life.

Prevention

A person's early concerns about being overweight are a predictive factor of later symptoms. The eating disorders cannot be attributed to a failure of will power but are a real medical illness in which maladaptive patterns of eating take on a life of their own. Achieving complete recovery from an eating disorder is a challenge. Only about half of those with anorexia and bulimia recover enough to maintain a healthy weight and positive self-image. Ten percent of cases remain chronic and unremitting. Without intervention up to 20 percent of persons with an eating disorder die prematurely. Disordered eating behaviors are often associated with secrecy and shame. The defense mechanisms of denial and resistance are the two major psychological obstacles to be confronted in treatment.

Perhaps the best treatment intervention is prevention (Merriam & Murray, 1997; Wright, 2000; Mizes & Palermo, 1997). Social workers are employed in a variety of settings and can be found in non-clinical locations such as schools or colleges. In these "neutral" settings, psychoeducational interventions can be developed to target those at risk for eating disorders (Schweitzer, Bergholz, Dore, & Salimi, 1998). Educational programs aimed at reducing the risk factors associated with the drive for thinness and increasing protective factors have been found to be successful (Abood & Black, 2000; Buddeberg-Fischer & Reed, 2001; Sapia, 2001). Practitioners can also provide consultation and training for peer counselors, coaches, or teachers to help them identify risk factors (Heller, 2002). Competency-based treatment considers the community and environmental domains of a client's life. Within this framework, practitioners can expand their range of intervention to develop prevention programs in diverse arenas such as dance schools or companies, community recreation centers, and exercise clubs.

Self-Help Programs

Self-help programs such as Weight Watchers, Take Off Pounds Sensibly (TOPS), or Overeaters Anonymous (OA) can be helpful, particularly for those with milder forms of disordered eating (McAleavey, Fiumara, & Zelvin, 2001; Ronel & Libman, 2003). Many individuals are more likely to participate in self-help groups than to seek the assistance of a mental health professional. Weight Watchers is a successful organization that combines dietary recommendations with group support in an environment analogous to a pep rally. The format for OA is similar to Alcoholics Anonymous, with a "12-step" program in which the major goal is abstinence. For OA members, abstinence is defined as freedom from compulsive overeating and eating only three meals a day with no snacks (Malenbaum, Herzog, & Wysbak, 1988). Some meetings specifically focus on women struggling with anorexia nervosa or bulimia nervosa.

Biological Therapy

The eating disorders have a high co-morbidity with the depressive spectrum disorders. Medications used for treating people with anorexia nervosa include major tranquilizers, minor tranquilizers, antidepressants, lithium, anticonvulsants, insulin, and appetite stimulants, but there has been no consensus about their efficacy (von Bulow & Braiman, 2001). The side effects of drug treatment, particularly involving the heart, should be carefully considered because of the compromised cardiovascular function of many individuals with anorexia nervosa. Some co-morbid conditions, such as depression or obsessive-compulsive features, may spontaneously resolve themselves when the person gains weight.

In contrast, women with bulimia nervosa have been responsive to antidepressant medications, particularly tricyclic antidepressants (Kaye, Strober, Stein, & Gendall, 1999; Wilson et al., 1999) such as desipramine (Norpramin) or imipramine (Tofranil), and monoamine oxidase inhibitors (MAOIs) such as phenelzine (Nardil) (Walsh et al., 1982; Walsh, Stewart, Roose, Gladis, & Glassman, 1984; Walsh & Kahn, 1997). Caution is suggested when prescribing MAOIs because of the difficulty of maintaining a low-tyramine diet. Certain SSRIs have independent actions on psychiatric symptoms other than depression; for example, fluoxetine (Prozac), sertraline (Zoloft), and paroxetine (Paxil) have been used successfully for treating people with bulimia (Mayer & Walsh, 1998; von Bulow & Braiman, 2001). The antidepressant drugs alone do not have long-lasting effects on bulimia nervosa, although they may enhance the effects of psychosocial treatment. Another biological treatment that holds promise is light therapy, similar to that used for people with seasonal affective disorder. In an earlier study conducted by Lam, Goldner, Solyom, and Remick (1994), individuals with seasonal bulimic symptoms showed positive short-term improvement.

RISKS ASSOCIATED WITH EATING DISORDERS

Intrapersonal Risks

Gender seems to place one at risk of developing an eating disorder, as 90 percent of eating disorders occur in girls and women. Most often these conditions begin to develop during adolescence. Eating disorders run in families, suggesting that genes may also play a role in the risk of developing an eating disorder (Sohn, 2002). However, genetic predisposition seems to interact with cultural pressures and psychological conflicts. For example, ballerinas, models, actresses, and jockeys who want to excel in their career are under considerable professional pressure to be thin (Brumberg, 2000).

Body image dissatisfaction is the strongest predictor of disordered eating, and shame also plays an important role (Greenberg, 2002). Those with eating disorders are intensely preoccupied with how they appear to others. They may suffer from low self-esteem, feelings of helplessness, and intense dissatisfaction with the way they look. These individuals also tend to see themselves as frauds and may feel like an impostor with their family and friends (Smolak & Levine, 1996). In addition, women who tend to have very rigid, fixed thought patterns, be depressed, perfectionistic, and more self-critical about themselves and what they eat than those with healthy eating patterns are also more likely to be at risk for developing an eating disorder (Pomeroy & Wambach, 2003; Walsh & Devlin, 1998). Other risk behaviors are cigarette smoking, anxiety-depression, and/or substance abuse (alcohol use) (Croll, Neumark-Sztainer, Story, & Ireland, 2002; Granner, Abood, & Black, 2001; Moorehead, 2001; Sinha & O'Malley, 2000).

Interpersonal Risks

Dysfunctional family relationships continue to be a target of blame for the development of eating disorders. Family members who are struggling with their own psychiatric difficulties and eating problems may increase a person's risk for eating disorders (Moorehead, 2001). There is also a relationship between general parental "controlling-ness" and eating disorder symptomatology (Pizer, 2002). Family factors linked to anorexia nervosa include enmeshed family systems, blurred boundaries between parents and children, and a lack of separation and individuation. In addition, family issues surrounding achievement, food, weight, and exercise create an atmosphere supportive of anorexia nervosa (Bachner-Melman, 2003). Family factors increasing the risk for developing bulimia nervosa include chaotic family dynamics, power imbalances, lack of flexibility, and the lack of clear family structure (Moreno, Selby, Aved, & Besse, 2000; Pomeroy & Wambach, 2003). However, genetics and biology may be equally important contributors. Although certain family dynamics and cultural influences seem to place a person at higher risk for an eating disorder, it seems increasingly likely that hormones and brain chemicals in particular individuals push them to the brink of starvation (Sohn, 2002).

An early study by Polivy and Herman (1993) linked dieting to bingeing. In addition, if the individual has friends who tend to use extreme dieting measures or other drastic weight loss techniques, there is an increased risk for developing an eating disorder. As a parallel, being overweight can be considered a risk factor for disordered eating. Research has found that a person's weight can increase vulnerabilities for teasing from others, body dissatisfaction, and/or dieting (Stice, 1999).

Community and Environmental Risks

In our culture, there is ample reinforcement for developing eating disorders. Both anorexia and bulimia occur more often in modern, industrialized societies where food is abundant and beauty is associated with thinness (Castillo, 1997). Over the past 100 years, standards of beauty, particularly for females, have changed several times and the cultural ideal for women has been getting thinner in recent decades. During the latter part of the nineteenth century, the ideal was a full-figured woman with large hips and breasts. The 1920s era popularized the flat-chested "flapper" style. The Depression era of the mid-1930s, when food was scarce for many, returned the more rounded figure as the fashion ideal. The popular actresses Diana Dors, Marilyn Monroe, and Jayne Mansfield exemplified female beauty during the 1950s. This post-war ideal was curvy, buxom, and "womanly." Throughout the 1960s big breasts and hips remained stylish. Today, by contrast, many women struggle to look like the skinny, angular, and boyish television character Ally McBeal, portrayed by actress Calista Flockhart. The contemporary perfect image is a combination of big breasts and no hips, perhaps reflecting our culture's ambivalence about female beauty.

The fact remains that American women are under increasing pressure to lose weight to be considered attractive. Research has shown that exposure to the ideal thin standard of female beauty presented in the media contributes to body image disturbance in women (Posavac, Posavac, & Weigel, 2001). Reinforcement of thinness by family members, peers, and the mass media contributes to the development of eating disorders, since such pressure promotes internalization of unrealistic ideals of thinness that lead to body dissatisfaction and dieting (Stice, 1999). Cultural standards regarding an appropriate body shape seem to be a major determinant of how women perceive and evaluate their bodies. Those who routinely compare their bodies with images of beauty contained in advertising and the broader media are at greater risk for eating disorders. Our society sends conflicting and ambiguous messages, and being fit and slim is depicted as a positive personality attribute. For many women, looking good is more important than being healthy. This creates intense pressure to be thin, and the media reinforce these images. For example, one finds constant reminders about food in television commercials and in magazine advertisements. Open almost any magazine and it will more than likely contain articles about the most recent diet, advertisements for health spas and clubs, or clothes for almost every sport. Levine and Smolak (1996) refer to this as "the glorification of slenderness," and these messages are primarily aimed at women. Although most people know what they need to do in order to be physically fit, it is difficult to achieve the levels of fitness and physical shape idealized today. With improved nutrition, the size and weight of the average woman has increased over the years, compounding the difficulty of achieving the exaggerated contemporary standard of thinness.

The cultural ideal for men has also undergone change. Until relatively recently, heavily muscled men were laborers, and this was considered a sign of being a member of the working class. Within the past 15 years, middle-class men have been under pressure to be muscular, macho, and strong (Bordo, 2000). Having a well-toned body implies that a man has the money to join a gym and work out. This exercise regimen helps men to lose weight while simultaneously "buffing up" or gaining muscle tone (or weight) in selected parts of their body. In a culture of growing equality between the sexes and challenges to masculinity, men want to look strong and "manly" (Pope, Phillips, & Olivardia, 2000; Tanofsky, Wilfley, Spurrell, Welch, & Brownell, 1997).

There is growing evidence to support prejudice against obese persons in the United States (Brownell & O'Neil, 1993). Those who consider themselves to be overweight often feel inferior and unacceptable, and their self-esteem is diminished. This pervasive "fear of fatness" seems to be integral to Western cultural norms (Weiss, 1995).

CASE ILLUSTRATION: MARY MCDANIEL

The following vignette illustrates one client's experience with an outreach initiative targeting prevention of health problems in an employee assistance program. In response to rising health insurance costs, the company initiated a comprehensive wellness campaign. As part of these endeavors, the practitioner developed an educational flyer on good health habits and nutrition that was included in employee paychecks. After reading the flyer, Mary McDaniel, a company employee who struggles with bulimia nervosa, referred herself for counseling. The case illustrates a combination of individual, family, and group counseling organized around cognitive-behavioral strategies; for example, asking the client to maintain a food log aimed at helping to clarify the relationship between binge/purge behaviors and specific feelings, thoughts, and external events. Adjunctive meetings included participation in a time-limited support group and a referral to Overeaters Anonymous. This added assistance created an environment in which to explore some of the underlying issues associated with Mary's disordered eating patterns while working to reduce symptomatic eating behaviors. A series of small successes restored her sense of self-esteem, thus shifting the focus of treatment to the positive aspects of Mary's struggles with bulimia. Mary McDaniel's symptoms of bulimia nervosa were first introduced in Psychopathology: A Competency-Based Assessment Model for Social Workers *by Zide and Gray (2001).*

Mary McDaniel explained to the practitioner, "I eat a tremendous amount of food, and I don't care what the food is." She added, "You know how milk and orange juice usually sour the stomach? I don't care when it comes to anything like that. I eat whatever is in the pantry. The best way I can explain it is that it's sort of like a 'feeding frenzy.' I gulp food down, and most of the time I don't even taste it."

Mary continues, "A typical day for me starts after my kids go off to school and my husband leaves for work. I usually have an extra hour before I have to leave the house. During this time I usually eat anything I can stuff in my mouth. I start with some ice cream and when I'm done with that I munch on bags of cookies. They are much easier to put in my mouth and eat when I'm getting dressed. I always try and eat soft things, because they're easier to vomit up. I don't like to eat stuff like pretzels or hard candies. I also don't like to eat spicy stuff, like hot peppers, garlic, and onions. They are terrible to bring up!"

"Before I leave for work, I have just enough time to vomit up everything I already ate. I'm pretty good at that, and I don't usually need to stick my fingers down my throat anymore." Mary continues, "When I'm driving to work, I always have a bag of M&Ms or cookies in the car; or else I stop and buy a dozen Dunkin Donuts. You know, it's stuff I can eat without having to take my eyes off the road. Usually I throw up before I get to work, and I always keep a couple of mason jars under the front seat of my car for that purpose."

Mary's thoughts about herself and her disordered eating can be seen in the following statement. She remarked, "I used to pride myself on what a nice person I was, but now I'm nothing but a horrible pig. I feel terrible, but I don't know how to stop. I've tried stopping so many times. I just can't give up the food, but if I don't vomit, use laxatives or enemas, I start putting on the pounds. This is no way to live." Mary believed that somehow her eating had become a "bad habit," and she decided that she needed to tell her husband about it. After much inner turmoil, she told him and was initially relieved at his accepting response. He told her that he had been puzzled by the way food would sometimes disappear, "but now everything makes sense." Mary recalled that she had felt encouraged when her husband said he would do whatever she needed and support her in any way he could to help her to stop this habit. "I thought that if he knew, then it would help me to stop bingeing and purging. Boy! Was I wrong! It only made things worse for me. I learned my crazy eating is not a 'habit.' I just couldn't stop. It's almost like a compulsion for me. My husband, Ken, was so accepting when I first told him, and now I feel guilty that I let him down. I can't stop, and now I don't want to disappoint him. He's so proud of me. It's almost like food has become a wedge between us."

Mary's psychosocial history revealed that when she was about 15 her parents had seemed to drift apart and go their own separate ways without ever divorcing. Her father ran his own construction business and was quite successful. She recalled that while she was growing up he was always buying gifts for her and her two younger sisters, but after Mary started high school his business began to decline. She described her father as an alcoholic who also used marijuana occasionally, usually on weekends. After she married, her father started attending Alcoholics Anonymous. "He had a few relapses but has been sober for the last 10 years," she added.

Her mother was always overweight and had a "tremendous appetite." When pressed for details, Mary explained, "She simply ate everything is sight. We used to laugh it off but I really couldn't stand it. When we would finish eating, she would literally stuff everything remaining on the table in her mouth. If you had something left over on your plate she would reach over and ask, 'Are you going to finish that?' It didn't matter what was there. She would eat it. It could be cold mashed potatoes, cake, whatever!" Her mother reportedly had been attractive when she first married Mary's father but gradually seemed to let herself go. "She seemed depressed, and not interested in much except for her soap operas. I think she sometimes took antidepressants, and I'm sure that didn't help with her weight problems," stated Mary.

Mary remembered that when she was about 8 years old her mother had suddenly been hospitalized. Not much was said at the time, but afterwards Mary was able to piece things together from what she overheard from relatives. Apparently her mother had attempted suicide. Her father was out drinking at the time, but when he came home he rushed over to the hospital, leaving Mary with his brother. To cheer her up, this uncle took her out for ice cream. On the way into town he pulled over to the side of the road, pulled up her skirt, put his hand down her pants and fondled her. He threatened that if she ever said anything to anyone about it, her mother would never come home. Mary remembered feeling confused and scared, so she kept their "little secret" to herself. Shortly afterward her uncle joined the Marines and never returned to her home town so she did not have to face him. Mary adds, "I heard he married a couple of times." She continued, "I felt so ashamed. It was hard, but I shared this with my husband early on in our marriage. I thought that I had come to terms with what my uncle had done to me. Now, I'm not so sure. Ever since my husband told me that he wants to have another child the memories of this event have come flooding back. If I just close my eyes I can remember everything, even the shabby upholstery in my uncle's pickup. Needless to say, it kind of ruins sex with my husband. You might say I'm just damaged goods," she adds.

When Mary noticed the flyer in her paycheck describing good health and nutrition habits she decided to see the employee assistance social worker, Paul Niglio. She stated, "I'm just sick and tired of being sick and tired. I feel bloated all the time, and my throat hurts so much. I just hate that feeling. I figured what the hell! So I came over to see what you could do. I don't know anybody else with a problem like this, and I figured if you know someone I can talk to it might improve things." Paul acknowledged her concerns and supported Mary's initiative in taking the first step by reaching out for help. He also provided information about Overeaters Anonymous and offered details on how to connect with a particular group of women who had problems much like hers. Paul then checked her

company insurance coverage, and together they went about setting up an appointment with Rain View Center, a local agency with a treatment program for people
with eating disorders.

Before going to Rain View, Mary completed a thorough medical exam with her
family doctor and released her records to the agency. She was in good overall
health, but her doctor recommended monitoring her electrolyte levels. Treatment
aimed at changing a person's eating habits may temporarily effect a chemical
imbalance. Mary was introduced to her practitioner, Diane Leo, and immediately
took a liking to her. Diane explained the program and Mary learned that in
addition to individual sessions she would also be attending a 12-session group
consisting of other women with eating problems like hers. The group was
described as a place where Mary would not have to feel so alone and isolated with
her symptoms. Her practitioner explained, "I hope that everybody in the group will
support each other in their recovery here at Rain View." The practitioner described the group format. The group would meet weekly for 90 minutes.
Preliminary sessions would provide members with information and dispel any misconceptions about bulimia. The group would also learn about the pressures that
the media convey to create insecurities in women about their bodies. At this point
Mary blurted out, "Gosh! You mean that I'm not entirely responsible for my preoccupation with food and weight?" Diane thought Mary seemed to be really hard
on herself. The practitioner continued to describe the group, adding that there
would be some guest speakers from the staff. She explained, "We'll have our nurse,
the nutritionist, and the doctor attending various sessions to talk about the medical
consequences of bulimia nervosa." Finally, the group sessions would focus on nutrition and nourishing one's body. "We like to think that nourishing the body does
not equal weight gain and body dissatisfaction," said Diane. Mary indicated that
she liked this sense of collaboration in her recovery. "For the first time in a long
time I'm starting to feel some sense of relief," she said.

At the midpoint of the session, the practitioner commented, "Small incremen-
tal changes seem to be the most effective way to reach recovery. I want to challenge that 'all or none' thinking of yours, Mary. To get started, I would like to ask
you to self-monitor your food intake. This food record will provide the foundation
for our work together. I would like you to write down the details of your eating,
such as the circumstances and moods surrounding your behavior. I'll give you a list
of what to look for, like the time and place where you eat, if you ate with anybody,
your mood, hunger level, purging activities, type, frequency, and duration of activities, consumption of basic food groups, and your observations and reactions. I
know it sounds pretty extensive, but by helping to identify what you eat and how
bingeing is triggered, we can get on the way toward looking at your eating behavior
a little differently. I know this sounds like a lot of work, so let's start by taking some
really small steps. How does that sound to you?" Mary nodded affirmatively, and
Diane continued, "Look at each eating episode as a meal, snack, or binge. Then together we can explore whether the eating episode led to a binge. It's sort of like
putting the pieces of a puzzle together. Are you up for the challenge?" Mary
responded, "You know, I think of food so much anyway, this food log thing would
fit right in. What's different is that now I'm self-monitoring all those purging

episodes as well as the thoughts and feelings associated with each one. By sharing it with you I don't have to feel so alone in this. I think we're on to something. I never looked at it in quite this way before."

After working with Mary for three sessions, Diane asked Mary if her family would be willing to come to an appointment with her. Mary agreed, and the session with her family lasted for approximately one hour. It quickly became apparent to Diane that certain dynamics prevailed in this family. Mary's sons, Jerry (8) and Ricky (10), were drinking soda in the waiting room while waiting for the family's appointment. Once they were in session and the topic of Mary's disordered eating came up, both boys suddenly decided they had to go to the bathroom. Her husband, Ken, followed them, indicating he wanted to make sure the boys were all right. Once again, Mary was left feeling alone and isolated. In individual sessions Mary was usually very articulate and insightful, but with her family she was quiet and seemed emotionally distant. The practitioner inquired if this distant behavior was usual for Mary, and her husband responded, "I don't know what happened. For a while there we were so happy, and with Mary's job the money situation has been good, so I thought this would be the perfect time for us to have another child. We always wanted a little girl so the boys could have a baby sister. Well, ever since we started talking about another baby things have turned upside down. Like you pointed out, Mary is just like that at home, too. It's like she's someplace else. The boys are involved in Little League and we're busy most nights so we always try to get together for dinner at least once on the weekend, but that's when things seem to be the worst. I almost feel like food has come between us. I'm walking on eggshells around her, and I'm afraid to say anything because I don't want to upset Mary or the boys. I just don't know what to do anymore."

Diane acknowledged his concerns and provided information about eating disorders. This gave the family ideas about alternative ways to respond to the illness. Together they explored how to improve their communication. The family decided at their next "family meal" they would establish rules of conduct and each family member had a task. As the family's understanding of what was going on increased, they were able to be more supportive of each other and have their emotional needs addressed. In turn, Mary felt encouraged, and this helped to decrease her sense of isolation. In separate sessions the practitioner also worked with the couple around their sexual relationship.

Mary worked very hard throughout treatment and at termination was no longer bingeing and purging. By self-monitoring her food intake, she was able to recognize how her bingeing was triggered and to develop a series of strategies for self-control. For instance, Mary planned her eating for specific places and specific times. That strategy helped her to avoid eating while driving to work. She learned what foods "triggered" a binge and structured her activities to avoid potential binge situations. For example, she would go for a walk or meet with a friend. By establishing regular eating patterns Mary was able to distinguish between feeling "fat" and feeling "full." She had expanded the type of food that she ate to include more fruit and vegetables instead of high-calorie sweets. She had also developed healthy exercise patterns. Mary understood that setbacks could occur and planned to use OA meetings as her relapse prevention plan.

OPERATIONALIZING COMPETENCY-BASED TREATMENT

Mary's symptoms are typical of bulimia nervosa. She had binge/purge cycles; used laxatives, diuretics, enemas; and felt unable to restrain how much she ate. Despite feeling unhappy about herself, Mary was unable to stop her eating pattern and perceived her behavior as out of control. Mary had a positive family history for substance use, and there were questions about her mother's eating patterns and possible depression. The case also illustrates many supportive factors and buffers in Mary's life. Unlike the experience of many with eating disorders, she initiated counseling, lacked associated medical problems, and was motivated to process feelings associated with her symptoms of bingeing and purging.

Working with Mary Individually

Knowledge of the risks and protective factors in a client's life (Table 9.1) can guide intervention and prevention efforts (Croll, Neumark-Sztainer, Story, & Ireland, 2002). The protective factors in Mary McDaniel's life were her motivation to seek help and her determination to understand the interplay of her bulimic behavior with her self-esteem. She seemed connected to her family and saw them as a source of support to her. This support became readily apparent when she started to keep a journal of her eating patterns. Mary's resilience was also quite evident throughout her struggles with bulimia. There had been a time in Mary's life when she had felt good about herself. Despite her current struggle, she did well on the job. The McDaniel case vignette illustrates a key concept of competency-based treatment. Someone with an eating disorder can identify and build on strengths, resilience, and protective factors as long as the practitioner looks for them in the treatment process. Conversely, a mindset that looks only for pathology can undermine the individual's capacity for change. Competency-based treatment provides a specific path for the practitioner's expectations for success that ultimately influences perceptions of the client's struggle.

Cognitive-behavioral therapy seems to be effective in treating bulimia nervosa (Agras, Walsh, Fairburn, Wilson, & Kraemer, 2000; Bulik, 1998; Cooper, Coker, & Fleming, 1996; De Angelis, 2002; Spangler, 1999; Thiels, Schmidt, Treasure, & Garthe, 1998; Wilson et al., 1999). For Mary, it helped her to learn how to keep track of her eating and change unhealthy eating habits. In this case illustration, the practitioner encouraged Mary to keep a food log that helped clarify the relationships among her feelings, thoughts and external events, and her bingeing and purging. The food diary served as a way for Mary to become more aware of the types of situations that triggered her bingeing, and she was able to replace destructive thoughts and behaviors with more positive ones. When Mary was able to begin to perceive herself as efficacious in this task, she began to regain a sense of competence and thus experienced a more positive level of self-esteem.

The practitioner and Mary worked together to focus on health rather than weight. Mary began to understand that her eating disorder was only part of the problem. Triggered by her husband's desire to have another child, memories of the

TABLE 9.1	THE RISKS, PROTECTIVE FACTORS, AND BUFFERS IN MARY McDANIEL'S LIFE	
	Risk Factors	**Protective Factors and Buffers**
Intrapersonal	Struggles with bulimia nervosa	Self-referred for counseling
	Self-esteem concerns	Intelligent, motivated, and articulate
	Has feelings of shame	Shows qualities of courage and tenacity
	Feels responsible for the eating disorder	Uncomplicated bulimia nervosa
	Feels isolated in her struggle	Lacks associated medical problems
	History of sexual abuse	
Interpersonal	Father has history of alcoholism	Mary is connected to her family
	Mother has history of suicidal behavior and suspected eating disorder/depression	Husband supportive
		Successful at work
	Food has become a "wedge" in the marital relationship	Family participates actively in treatment
	Family communication problems	Good relationship with the social worker
	Family tendency to avoid conflict	
Social and Environmental	Vulnerable to societal expectations of "thinness"	Attends Overeaters Anonymous
		Company provides coverage for counseling
		Has access to available resource specializing in eating disorders

earlier episode of sexual abuse came flooding back, leaving Mary feeling upset, isolated, and confused. Mary also felt a sense of shame that was not just around her body and eating but about her personal experience of sexual abuse. Shame is a common experience for women with eating disorders and involves feelings of inferiority and powerlessness (Swan & Andrews, 2003). As Mary began to better understand some of these underlying issues, cognitive-behavioral skills aimed at reducing her disordered eating behaviors were introduced. Mary showed a great deal of courage and tenacity in her struggle to recover from disordered eating. Her challenges were many and entailed facing herself, the world, and her future without the use of bulimia as a coping mechanism. The practitioner believed that Mary was doing the very best that she could. Diane and Mary established a therapeutic relationship characterized by a mutually influencing partnership as Mary slowly began to trust herself to create or re-create a more healthy self.

It is important for the practitioner who works with persons struggling with eating disorders to be aware of his or her personal feelings and attitudes (Vandereycken & Beumont, 1998). Although the practitioner's personal history is not central to this case vignette, the author would like to note that the practitioner in this case had recovered from her own eating disorder at an earlier point in time. Although this experience created a greater opportunity for countertransference issues that can arise in the therapy process, this particular practitioner worked hard to maintain her objectivity and used supervision to address the potential for these problems. Eating, weight management, and body image concerns are prevalent issues in our culture, and the practitioner is not immune to eating disorders. The practitioner's self-awareness is an important aspect of competency-based practice.

Unlike the majority of individuals with eating disorders, Mary was highly motivated to seek help. Typically, most are resistant to taking on the work of change and their resistance plays itself out in interpersonal relationships. The practitioner must be comfortable with these predictable behaviors in order to be able to challenge them as they occur throughout the recovery process.

Working with the Family

Mary's family seemed to have developed a pattern of communication that avoided conflict. In this way, the family was able to deny Mary's eating disorder, thus adding to the difficulties of treatment. Rather than confront Mary about her strange eating behaviors or the mysterious disappearance of food, the family remained silent. When her sons felt a degree of tension around the dinner table they would usually make up some kind of excuse to leave the table. It was difficult for Mary's husband to discuss his feelings about what was going on between them. Somehow food had triangulated their relationship.

The practitioner worked with family members to help them understand Mary's eating disorder and learn new techniques for coping with their problems. Involving the family afforded a context to discuss Mary's disordered eating. This discussion opened therapeutic possibilities by providing a format for Mary to talk about her "secret" without judgment from her husband and children (Carr, 2000; Dallos, 2001; Levitt, 2001; Nylund, 2002). In this way, Mary was able to externalize her eating problems and remember who she was outside the realm of bulimia. Family members were able to gain insight and learn from each other, improve communication, provide support and encouragement, and alleviate Mary's sense of isolation.

The practitioner also provided education and support to Mary's husband throughout the treatment process so that he could remain supportive to Mary and assist her recovery. If family members are not part of the treatment process and solution, they may become part of the problem. Mary felt that food had become a wedge between herself and her husband. Her eating disorder "triangulated" their relationship and became an integral component of the marital system for this couple. By educating Mary's husband about how the system might be perpetrating and prolonging the disease syndrome, the practitioner could recruit his assistance in alleviating it.

Working with the Group

As shown in this case vignette, group therapy was an effective method of intervention, especially when combined with other treatment methods such as individual and family work (McKisack & Waller, 1997; Peterson & Mitchell, 1999; Riess, 2002; Riess & Dockray-Miller, 2001; Tantillo, 1998). The support provided to Mary through group membership decreased her sense of isolation so that she no longer had to feel alone in her struggle. Additionally, the group dynamics sustained her behavioral and attitudinal changes. The major benefit of group intervention is that it provides a curative culture for persons who struggle with disordered eating (Black, 2003).

Mary showed many behaviors characteristic of an addict. She would take in greater amounts of food than she had intended, would experience withdrawal symptoms, and then take in more food to alleviate her withdrawal. The employee assistance social worker's referral to Overeaters Anonymous provided Mary with a 12-step program that focused on this addictive behavior. While there is some debate about the effectiveness of OA (McAleavey, Fiumara, & Zelvin, 2001), the mutual aid provided by other group members offered Mary support with her struggles. Knowing that others were also battling with disordered eating bolstered Mary's efforts to look at the deeper issues related to her eating disorder.

Group work has increasingly been seen as the modality of choice for those struggling with bulimia nervosa (von Bulow & Braiman, 2001). Our culture promotes an unrealistic image of a beautiful body, and acceptance by a group of peers about how one looks rather than how one "should" look can be reassuring. Gitterman and Shulman (1994) underscore the value of mutual aid provided by groups. Bringing together individuals who are working together on a common problem or "all in the same boat" can be very successful for those who have an eating disorder. The group Mary McDaniel attended at the Rain View Center used a combination of cognitive-behavioral techniques, psychoeducation, mutual aid, and psychosocial therapy (Reiss & Dockray-Miller, 2001). The cognitive-behavioral techniques were designed to eliminate extreme dietary restrictions, increase the consumption of a wider variety of foods, and decrease cognitive distortions that maintained disordered eating. The psychoeducational phase provided information and dispelled common misconceptions about the factors that cause and maintain symptoms of bulimia nervosa. Mutual aid was evident through the validation of members' experiences that served to foster trust and a sense of universality within the group. Membership provided an opportunity to form empathic relationships with others struggling with bulimia, to gain mutual understanding, and to receive emotional support. The interpersonal interactions within the group supported change, growth, and symptom improvement.

In sum, eating disorders affect every aspect of the person's lifestyle, personality, attitudes, values, quality of relationships, and overall functioning. The disorders may evoke depression and fear, thereby limiting the person's quality of life. What sets an eating disorder apart from other diseases is its integrative nature; that is, it affects the person's mind, body, emotions, and personal relationships. Each person's experience with disordered eating is different. Because of their complexity, the eating disorders require a comprehensive, multicomponent intervention program involving medical care, nutritional counseling, and when appropriate, medication management (Foreyt, Poston, Winebarger, & McGavin, 1998; Kalodner, 1998). Coordinating this program may involve establishing a team of professionals such as physicians, nurses, nutritionists, and social workers. Competency-based treatment sets the stage for tapping into a client's strengths and provides a framework for the practitioner to select the skills and techniques needed to effectively prevent, diagnose, and treat individuals struggling with disordered eating and to assist their families. This framework provides the practitioner with the grounding needed to begin working collaboratively with the individual. With eating disorders even more than with any of the psychiatric disorders, it is important to involve the client and understand his or her worldview since beliefs about one's appearance are strongly linked to cultural and societal beliefs.

SUMMARY

Eating disorders have grown to epidemic proportions (Murray, 2003). Our society is preoccupied with weight and dieting. According to the American Psychiatric Association's guidelines for the treatment of persons with eating disorders (2001), 50 percent of fourth-grade girls have dieted, and the figure rises to 90 percent by age 17. Eating disorders occur in men but are up to ten times more common in women. Obsessive-compulsive or addictive-type behavior involving food characterizes the eating disorders. It is difficult to determine the predisposing cause of an eating disorder. Vulnerable individuals may begin with a simple diet that often results in malnutrition and produces changes in brain chemistry. The person becomes obsessed with consuming or not consuming food.

Severe restriction of food intake leads to anorexia nervosa, causing a range of serious medical problems associated with starvation, such as amenorrhea in females, hypothermia, low blood pressure, low mineral levels, and electrolyte imbalances. Anorexia nervosa has the highest mortality rate of any of the psychiatric illnesses (Baggott & Bartlett, 2004). An estimated one thousand women die each year of anorexia nervosa in the United States. Many of the deaths are related to heart attacks and suicide (APA, 2001). Bingeing-purging-starving behavior is associated with bulimia nervosa. Medical problems associated with bulimia nervosa can include fluid and electrolyte abnormalities, loss of stomach acid (due to vomiting), and a significant loss of dental enamel (APA, 2000).

The roles of environmental and cultural factors in the development of eating disorders are well accepted. The American ideal for white women has been getting thinner and thinner. Relatively recently, pressures have increased for men to become muscular and strong. Paradoxically, men are expected to lose weight while simultaneously buffing up or gaining weight in selected parts of the body. Eating disorders exist primarily in young, white American women, but people from other cultures are not invulnerable to pursuing the dominant image of beauty. Acculturation, immigration, and ethnic identity exert an influence on the presenting symptoms of disordered eating (Kempa & Thomas, 2000).

The major features of anorexia nervosa, bulimia nervosa, and binge eating disorder were reviewed in this chapter:

- *Anorexia nervosa* refers to those with have a distorted body image causing them to see themselves as overweight even when they are dangerously thin. Often these individuals refuse to eat, exercise compulsively, and develop unusual habits such as not eating in front of others. They tend to lose excessively large amounts of weight and be in danger of actual starvation amidst plenty. Anorexia nervosa is characterized by extreme weight loss, body image disturbance, and an intense fear of becoming fat. Anorexia is generally accompanied by the absence of at least three consecutive menstrual cycles in young women.

- *Bulimia nervosa* refers to persons who eat excessive quantities of food and then purge their bodies of the food and much-feared calories by using laxatives, diuretics, enemas (less common), vomiting and/or exercising. These behaviors often occur in secrecy and the person feels disgusted and ashamed of bingeing while at the same time feeling relieved of tension and negative emotions once the stomach is empty again. It is highly unusual for a person with bulimia to vomit in public. Bulimia nervosa is characterized by secretive binge eating episodes followed by self-induced vomiting, fasting, excessive exercise or the use of laxatives, diuretics, or the manipulation of other medications.

- Frequent episodes of out-of-control eating characterize *binge eating disorder,* which is similar to bulimia nervosa except that persons with binge eating disorder do not purge themselves of excess calories. According to DSM diagnostic categories, binge eating disorder is an example of an eating disorder not otherwise specified (EDNOS), and involves similar criteria to bulimia nervosa but does not include the use of compensatory behaviors.

All persons with disordered eating share a disturbance in perception of body shape and weight. Persons with anorexia nervosa differ in one very important way from those with bulimia: they are extremely successful in their efforts to lose weight. The person struggling with bulimia is not trying to lose weight. The chief motivation seems to be the avoidance of becoming fat, and binges are followed by induction of vomiting or other compensatory methods such as using large amounts of laxatives to purge one's bowels. Individuals with binge eating disorder experience marked distress related to binge eating but do not engage in extreme compensatory behaviors.

Cognitive-behavioral therapy is the mainstay for treating clients with anorexia and bulimia nervosa. Cognitive-behavioral therapy, on an individual basis and in the group format, is designed to help the person gain control of unhealthy eating behaviors and alter distorted and rigid thinking associated with the syndrome. The family is also involved in treatment, and the focus is on the person's current circumstances and relationships. Antidepressant medications, such as selective serotonin reuptake inhibitors (SSRIs), are helpful for those struggling with co-morbid symptoms of depression, anxiety, or obsessions. Because of the complexity of eating disorders, treatment interventions are comprehensive and other professionals, such as physicians, nurses, and/or nutritionists may be involved in the person's care. Short-term interventions focus on nutritional rehabilitation and the restoration of normal eating, while longer-term treatment goals are established to address associated psychological family, social, and behavioral problems.

PRACTITIONER REFLECTIONS

1. Imagine that you have been invited to speak to a local high school class about eating and nutrition. Outline the key points of your presentation, focusing on information about anorexia nervosa, bulimia nervosa, binge eating, cultural influences on perceptions of "thinness," and the presence of other intrapersonal factors such as low self-esteem, depression, and/or substance use. Knowing that a "lecture" would be boring to the students, consider what interactive activities you would like to include in your presentation. Are there any self-help books, videos, or websites you would recommend to these students?

2. Many practitioners find it challenging to work with persons with anorexia nervosa since attempts to offer support and treatment are often met with resistance or are undermined. A central tenet of the social work profession is the client's self-determination and the right to make his or her own decisions. An ethical practice dilemma for the practitioner is whether persons with anorexia nervosa should have their treatment choices respected or overridden. Imagine for a moment that you are working with someone who is struggling with anorexia nervosa and who makes harmful decisions about treatment, especially if death or serious harm could result. Are there instances in which a client with anorexia nervosa can or should be treated without his or her consent? What is the legislation in your state regarding the compulsory treatment of anorexia nervosa, such as force-feeding?

3. Prejudice against people who are obese is pervasive in the United States. Write down as many possible examples you can think of about how persons who are obese may experience oppression on an organizational (or macro) level, on a local community and small-group (meso) level, and on an individual, family (micro) level. Select two or three examples for each practice level and describe how you would attempt to address this prejudice.

4. Self-awareness is an important part of competency-based practice. Our society places an emphasis on physical appearance as a measure of attractiveness, particularly for females. Critically assess your own ideas of physical attractiveness and eating behavior and determine how these concepts might possibly be projected onto your client.

5. Individuals from non-Western cultural groups are at less risk for developing eating disorders than are Westerners. Problems arise when persons from another culture internalize the dominant Western cultural values regarding thinness as a requirement for female beauty. Imagine you are working with an immigrant family and the mother confides her "worries" that the youngest child in the family, a girl, is developing what sounds very much like disordered eating patterns. What would you do?

6. The acute management of severe weight loss is usually provided in a hospital setting where intravenous feeding can address the person's medical and nutritional needs. Nasogastric feeding is reserved for the rare patient who is extremely unable to recognize her (or his) illness, to accept the need for treatment, or to tolerate the guilt accompanying active eating even when performed to sustain life. Imagine that you are the social worker in a large acute care medical hospital. You have just read the chart on a young woman who was recently admitted for complications related to anorexia nervosa. You are seeing her as a part of routine case finding. As you enter the room, she furtively moves her hand away from the tube inserted into her nose feeding nutrients into her body. You are not sure about exactly what you saw since it happened so quickly, but you think she may have been pinching the tube to prevent nutrients from entering her body. What would you do?

THE PERSONALITY DISORDERS

Personality disorders affect between 5 and 10 percent of the adult population in the United States (Ellison & Shader, 2003; MacFarlane, 2004). Significantly, about half of those who seek counseling are diagnosed with a personality disorder. This means practitioners can expect that approximately half of their clients will be struggling with a personality disorder. Up to 30 percent of people who require mental health services have at least one personality disorder, which tends to complicate treatment of the primary presenting problem found on Axis I (Dingfelder, 2004). Most such persons experience a chronic impairment of social and occupational functioning, an increased propensity for disordered eating and/or substance abuse, and frequent involvement with the legal system.

Personality disorders encompass a range of diverse conditions that have originated from very different clinical, theoretical, and research findings. Some reflect psychodynamic thinking, while others have a genetic basis. Despite this diversity, most would agree that the personality disorders describe inflexible and maladaptive patterns of behavior that cause distress to the person or impairment of the ability to function (Rey, 1996). People with personality disorders have an enduring pattern of inner experience and behavior that deviates markedly from the expectations of their culture. Because of the long-term and enduring nature of the associated behaviors, personality disorders are rarely diagnosed in children. A personality disorder is considered a variant of character traits that goes far beyond the normative range found in most people (Zide & Gray, 2001). The person usually responds poorly to change, has trouble forming relationships, and has interpersonal problems in a variety of arenas such as work or school.

Every person has personality traits that are considered normative in his or her culture of origin. When diagnosing a personality disorder, the practitioner evaluates the person's behavior within a cultural context and avoids pathologizing when personality traits of a particular group may vary from Western cultural expectations. Competency-based practice provides a framework for understanding people in their social contexts by exploring the biological, psychological, sociological, sociocultural, and environmental factors in each person's life. By looking at the full range of life experiences and events, the practitioner differentiates the symptoms of a personality disorder from problems generally associated with the expression of habits, customs, religious or political values, or acculturation following immigration. Merging the DSM format with the competency-based model provides a balanced approach for understanding personality and helps the practitioner to consider alternate perspectives, explanations, and treatments.

In 1952, the *Diagnostic and Statistical Manual* (DSM) described 27 personality disorders and organized them into five specific headings: personality pattern disturbance, personality trait disturbance, sociopathic personality disturbance, special symptom reactions, and transient situational personality disorders (APA, 1952). The subsequent edition of the DSM reduced the number of personality disorders from 27 to 12 categories (APA, 1968). Additionally, the concept of Axis II was introduced, separating the personality and developmental disorders from the clinical syndromes noted on Axis I. The DSM-III-R then described 11 personality disorders and divided them into three clusters (APA, 1987). The DSM IV-TR (2000) notes ten distinct personality disorders and groups them into three clusters as described below.

- Cluster A—Individuals are seen as odd and eccentric. The personality disorder types are paranoid, schizoid, and schizotypal.
- Cluster B—Individuals appear highly emotional, dramatic, or erratic. The personality disorder types are antisocial, borderline, histrionic, and narcissistic.
- Cluster C—These individuals are seen as anxious and fearful. The personality disorder types are avoidant, obsessive-compulsive, and dependent.

A person must meet the general criteria for personality disorders before being diagnosed with a specific type. The criteria are defined as follows (APA, 2000):

- An enduring pattern of inner experience and behavior that deviates markedly from the expectations generally found in one's culture. The person's personality dysfunction is pervasive and inflexible. The onset is in adolescence or young adulthood. (*Note:* If a child is given a diagnosis of personality disorder, the symptoms and behaviors must be present for at least one year. The one exception is antisocial personality disorder, which cannot be diagnosed in individuals under 18 years of age.) The disorder is stable over time, leading to distress and impairment. The pattern is evident in two (or more) of the following:
  1. Cognition is impaired; this can include distorted ways of perceiving oneself, others, and events.
  2. Affectivity can be dysfunctional and abnormal in range, intensity, lability, and appropriateness of emotional responses.
  3. Interpersonal functioning is impaired and distressed.
  4. Impulse control is poor.
- The enduring pattern of dysfunction is inflexible and pervasive in a large number of personal and social situations.
- The enduring pattern leads to clinically significant distress or impairment in social, occupational, or other areas of functioning.
- The enduring pattern is stable over a long period of time, and the onset can be established to have occurred in adolescence or early adulthood.

- The enduring pattern of dysfunction is not better accounted for by another mental disorder.
- The enduring dysfunctional pattern is not due to the direct physiological effects of substance use or a general medical condition.

UNDERSTANDING PERSONALITY DISORDERS

Personality comprises a number of factors generally described as traits, states, dimensions, domains, and types. *Traits* are described as long-standing characteristics that endure over time and in various situations (Millon & Davis, 2000). *States* are typically time-limited conditions such as anxiety or depression that can be associated with a specific personality type. *Dimensions* comprise clusters of traits. *Domains* are clusters of dimensions: for example, being conscientious, good-natured, or agreeable. The ten specific *types* of personality disorders described in the following section arise from the historical traditions found in the DSM of dividing the domains of personality disorders. The following discussion provides an overview of the basic features of each personality disorder noted in the DSM-IV-TR. Table 10.1 summarizes the major characteristics of each personality disorder, organized by cluster.

The personality disorders are syndromes that are not easy to separate from each other; for example, there are strong similarities between features of the avoidant and dependent personality or between histrionic and narcissistic personality disorder. The enduring nature of the behaviors, their impact on relationships and social functioning, and the person's perception of the symptoms as not being foreign (or ego syntonic) add to the diagnostic challenges. The lack of clear boundaries between normality and illness make this group of conditions more difficult to conceptualize than the other mental disorders. Some individuals may exhibit behaviors that would qualify them for several different disorders, while a wide range of people may fit different criteria for the same disorder although they may have very different "personalities." Each person is unique, and the personality disorders can be seen as extreme examples of behavioral tendencies that everyone has. However, the personality disorders tend to disrupt people's lives and, to different degrees, the lives of those around them. While people can possess very different personality disturbances, these disorders have something in common: they are considered problematic to treat and pose challenges for successful resolution or management. Notes Dingfelder (2004), people with borderline personality disorder, the most commonly treated personality disorder, quit treatment programs about 70 percent of the time.

Our discussion of the specific disorders begins with the personality disorders in cluster A.

Cluster A Personality Disorders

Cluster A comprises the "odd and eccentric" group consisting of the paranoid, schizoid, and schizotypal personality disorders.

Paranoid Personality Disorder   In paranoid personality disorder, the person's behavior is characterized by pervasive distrust and suspicion. The motives of others are interpreted as malevolent. These individuals rarely seek help on their own. Others close to them in their social environment such as a spouse or an employer usually refer them to treatment. The person is often characterized as hostile, irritable, or angry, and refusing to take responsibility for his or her own actions and feelings. These people are apt to see insult where none exists and are quick to take offense when none was intended. They are generally hard to get along with. To be diagnosed with this disorder, the person must have four or more of the following characteristics (APA, 2000):

- Feels exploited, harmed, or deceived by others without justification;
- Preoccupied with unjustified doubts about others' loyalty;
- Reluctant to confide in others for fear the information will be used to cause harm to him or her;
- Reads hidden meaning into harmless or innocent remarks;
- Persistently bears grudges;
- Perceives attacks on reputation or character that are not evident to others;
- Has recurring doubts, without justification, about fidelity of spouse or others.

Before considering pathology, the practitioner must first consider the person's social or cultural context (Castillo, 1997). Sometimes members of minority groups or immigrants are behaving according to the values or customs of their country of origin, even though their behavior may resemble the symptoms of paranoid personality disorder. In addition, people who have experienced severe child abuse, physical assault, war trauma, or sexual assault may also show symptoms that look very much like a paranoid personality disorder. It is helpful for the practitioner to remember that symptoms can develop in instances where there has been actual persecution, discrimination, abuse, or humiliation.

Schizoid Personality Disorder   Zide and Gray (2001) pose the following questions, "Do you know someone you consider a 'loner'? Someone who would rather stay home to watch television than accept an invitation to a party?" (p. 259) To begin to understand the impact of isolation on someone with a schizoid personality disorder, magnify this preference many times over. These individuals seem reserved, indifferent, or detached and frequently lead quiet, distant, reclusive, and unsociable lives. They seem to have little need or desire for emotional ties to others. Beneath this veneer of indifference, however, the person is often lonely and desires close relationships. The essential feature of schizoid personality disorder is a pervasive pattern of detachment from social relationships and a restricted range of emotional expression, along with one or more of the following symptoms (APA, 2000):

- Does not desire or enjoy close relationships with others, including family members;
- Almost always chooses solitary activities;
- Has little (or no) sexual interests or experiences with others;

TABLE 10.1 OVERVIEW OF PERSONALITY DISORDERS

Paranoid	Schizoid	Schizotypal	Cluster A
Suspicious and distrustful of others' motives as malevolent	Socially restricted	Perceptual disturbances; interpersonal deficits	**Odd and Eccentric**
1. Believes that others seek to harm him or her	1. No desire for close friendships	1. Ideas of reference	
2. Preoccupied with unjust doubts about others' loyalty	2. Chooses solitary activities	2. Odd beliefs	
3. Reluctant to confide in others	3. No interest in sex	3. Unusual perceptions	
4. Reads hidden meanings into communication	4. Takes little pleasure in activities	4. Odd thinking and speech	
5. Bears grudges	5. Lacks friends	5. Suspicious or paranoid ideation	
6. Counterattacks or reacts angrily	6. Indifferent to praise or criticism	6. Behavior appears odd, eccentric	
7. Has recurrent suspicion about fidelity of partner	7. Cold, detached, or flat affect	7. Inappropriate affect	

Antisocial	Borderline	Histrionic	Narcissistic	Cluster B
Violent; blatant disregard for others; behavior present before 15 years old; must be 18 before diagnosed	Unstable relationships; poor self-image; marked impulsivity	Excessive emotionality; attention seeking	Requires excessive admiration	**Emotional, Dramatic, or Erratic**
1. Failure to conform to social norms	1. Frantic efforts to avoid being abandoned	1. Uncomfortable when not center of attention	1. Grandiose	
2. Dishonest for own profit and purposes	2. Unstable, chaotic relationships	2. Provocative behavior	2. Fantasizes about unlimited success, power	
3. Irritability and/or aggressiveness	3. Impulsive spending, sex, substance abuse	3. Uses physical attraction to draw attention to self	3. Striking sense of entitlement	
4. Impulsivity	4. Suicidal	4. Self-dramatization	4. Lacks empathy	
5. Reckless disregard for self or others	5. Feeling "empty"	5. Rapidly changing, shifting emotions	5. Believes self "special" and others ordinary	
6. Irresponsible	6. Inappropriate, intense behavior, or difficulty controlling anger	6. Highly suggestible	6. Interpersonal relationships exploited; others manipulated	
7. Lack of remorse	7. History of mutilating		7. Envious of others and thinks others are jealous of him or her	
			8. Arrogant	

Avoidant	Obsessive-Compulsive	Dependent	Cluster C
Inhibited, feels inadequate	Orderly, perfectionistic, inflexible	Needs to be taken care of; clinging behavior with others	**Anxious, fearful**
1. Avoids meaningful relationships with others	1. Preoccupied with rules, regulations	1. Difficulty making everyday decisions	
2. Unwilling to get involved unless "guaranteed" they will be liked	2. Quest for perfection interferes with completion	2. Desires others to assume responsibility	
3. Shows restraint because they fear shame or ridicule	3. Overly conscientious	3. Lacks initiative	
4. Preoccupied with criticism or rejection	4. Hoards objects	4. Goes to excessive lengths to obtain support	
5. Feels inadequate	5. Rigid and stubborn	5. Feels uncomfortable or helpless	
6. Views self as inept, inferior	6. Reluctant to delegate tasks	6. Urgently seeks another relationship	
7. Reluctant to take risks, might be embarrassed		7. Preoccupied with fears of being left alone	

Reprinted with permission from *Psychopathology: A Competency-Based Assessment Model for Social Workers* by Zide/Gray (Belmont, CA: Wadsworth, 2001), p. 253.

- Takes little pleasure from activities;
- Lacks close friends except close relatives;
- Appears indifferent to the praise or criticism of others;
- Shows emotional coldness, detachment, and flat affect.

There are some instances where a person may show behaviors that look like schizoid personality disorder but instead are an adaptation to a painful social environment. In this instance, the person adapts to the "pain" by focusing his or her attention inwardly and essentially detaches from the environment. In some cultures, to be detached is thought to be a positive and valued behavior. For example, Hindu yogis are considered saintly for their ability to become detached and unmoved by events.

Schizotypal Personality Disorder   There is evidence that schizotypal personality disorder has a strong genetic component, and there seems to be a genetic link between this personality disorder and schizophrenia. It is estimated that 10 to 20 percent of people with this disorder eventually develop schizophrenia. The major features of schizotypal personality disorder are anxiety in social relationships, accompanied by eccentricities of behavior characterized by superstition, preoccupation with paranormal phenomena, magical thinking, or use of rituals in everyday situations (APA, 2000). These individuals show strikingly odd or strange mannerisms in addition to having an active fantasy life (Zide & Gray, 2001). Like persons with schizoid personality disorder, they can be described as loners, but their solitary pursuits and isolation may originate from strained social anxiety that does not diminish with familiarity.

In addition to social and interpersonal deficits marked by acute discomfort and diminished capacity for close relationships, the person shows five or more of the following symptoms (APA, 2000):

- Ideas of reference (excluding delusions of reference);
- Odd beliefs or magical thinking that influences behavior and is inconsistent with subcultural norms, such as superstition, belief in clairvoyance, telepathy, or a "sixth sense";
- Unusual perceptual experiences;
- Odd thinking and speech;
- Suspicion or paranoid ideation;
- Inappropriate or constricted affect;
- Peculiar behavior or appearance;
- No close friends other than close relatives;
- Excessive social anxiety that does not diminish with familiarity and tends to be associated with paranoid fears rather than negative self-judgments.

When considering the presence of a schizotypal personality disorder, it is helpful to evaluate a person's cognitive and perceptual distortions within a cultural context. For example, certain religious beliefs and rituals can appear to be schizotypal in nature, such as belief in a life beyond death, presence of the "evil eye," or the ability to speak in tongues. A belief in supernatural powers is commonplace and normative in some pre-modern societies (Castillo, 1997). However, the description of "normal behaviors" in the DSM presumes a person with a modern education and the social skills of working- or middle-class individuals. It is important to consider subcultural differences when diagnosing a schizotypal personality disorder, as feelings of not fitting in may be present among many diverse groups in the United States, such as poor people, ethnic minorities, or immigrants.

Cluster B Personality Disorders

Cluster B comprises the "dramatic, emotional, or erratic" group of disorders. This includes the antisocial, borderline, histrionic, and narcissistic personality disorders.

Antisocial Personality Disorder   The behavior of a person with antisocial personality disorder is characterized by "a pervasive pattern of disregard for and violation of the rights of others that begins in childhood or early adolescence and continues into adulthood" (APA, 2000, p. 701). This diagnosis is reserved for persons over age 18 who have had a history of symptoms of conduct disorder before the age of 15. The person must have three or more of the following symptoms (APA, 2000):

- Failure to conform to norms and laws, as evidenced by repeatedly performing acts that are grounds for arrest;
- Deceitfulness, as indicated by repeated lying, use of aliases, or conning others for profit or pleasure;
- Impulsivity or failure to plan ahead;
- Irritability and aggressiveness, as shown in repeated fights or assaults;
- Reckless disregard for the safety of self or others;
- Consistent irresponsibility, as shown by repeated failure to sustain consistent work or honor financial obligations;
- Lack of remorse, as indicated by being indifferent to or rationalizing having hurt, mistreated, or stolen from another.

The DSM notes that antisocial personality disorder is often associated with members of lower socioeconomic and urban groups (APA, 2000). In some settings, features of antisocial behavior may be protective and even preferred to less aggressive and less violent alternatives. As mentioned earlier, sociocultural factors should be considered when assessing personality development.

Borderline Personality Disorder   Persons with borderline personality disorder are characterized by a pattern of instability in interpersonal relationships, self-image, and affect, and a marked impulsivity that begins by early adulthood and is present in a variety of social contexts. The impulsivity is potentially self-damaging; for example, these individuals may gamble, spend money irresponsibly, go on eating binges, abuse substances, engage in unsafe sex, drive recklessly, show recurrent suicidal behavior or self-mutilating behavior (APA, 2000). The key feature of this instability is the fear of abandonment and rejection. These are persons who are extremely sensitive to their social environment and appear to have an intense, unmet need for affection and for personal closeness. The major characteristics of borderline personality disorder include the following (APA, 2000; Zide & Gray, 2001):

- Frantic efforts to avoid real or imagined abandonment (excluding suicidal or self-mutilating behavior);
- A pattern of unstable and intense relationships characterized by extremes of idealization and devaluation;
- Identity disturbance marked by unstable self-image or sense of self;
- Impulsivity in areas of functioning that can cause self-damage, such as spending, sex, drugs, reckless driving, eating (suicidal or self-mutilating behavior are excluded);
- Recurrent suicidal behavior, gestures, or threats, or self-mutilating behavior;
- Affective instability due to marked reactivity of mood (usually lasting a few hours and only rarely more than a few days);
- Chronic feelings of emptiness;
- Inappropriately intense anger or difficulty controlling anger; and
- Transient stress-related paranoid ideation or severe dissociative symptoms.

The behaviors that compose this disorder are fairly stable, and it is not uncommon for the practitioner to see a client with borderline personality disorder in the mental health care system (Zide & Gray, 2001). While this is considered a chronic disorder and individuals do not change very much, most will experience a lessening of symptoms as they reach their middle years.

Histrionic Personality Disorder   Some people show behaviors that could be described as "hysterical," but the person with a histrionic personality disorder has far greater problems relating to others. This disorder is characterized by a pattern of excessive emotionality and attention seeking that is present in a variety of contexts. Zide and Gray (2001) note that the following adjectives are often used to describe someone with histrionic personality disorder: colorful, dramatic, extroverted, excitable, and emotional. Beneath this presentation is a deep-seated inability to maintain strong, reciprocal, and long-lasting friendships. Onset occurs in early adulthood, and the person must show five or more of the following symptoms (APA, 2000):

- Discomfort when he or she is not the center of attention;
- Interaction with others involves sexually seductive or provocative behavior;
- Displays rapidly shifting and shallow emotions;
- Consistently uses physical appearance to draw attention to self;
- Has an impressionistic style of speaking that lacks detail;
- Prone to self-dramatization, theatrical, and exaggerated expression of emotion;
- Is suggestible and easily influenced by others or circumstances; and
- Sees relationships to be more intimate than they actually are.

Expressions of emotion can vary by culture, gender, and age. Interestingly, the DSM uses the example of a personality that may behave in a "macho" style (APA, 2000, p. 712). However, in many Hispanic subcultures the concept of a "macho" male is not considered inappropriate and would not be diagnosed as pathology.

Women are more frequently diagnosed with histrionic personality disorder than men are, and this may be a reflection of Western ideas and values about how women should behave. A woman who is flamboyant and sexually aggressive may not fit into the type of behavior our contemporary American society considers "normal" for females; that is, being quiet, demure, and passive in sexual and interpersonal relationships.

Narcissistic Personality Disorder A heightened sense of self-importance and unrealistic notions of inflated self-worth characterize the person with a narcissistic personality disorder. This self-aggrandizing behavior disguises an underlying fragile sense of self-worth. These individuals often see themselves as unique and special, deserving extraordinary treatment. As Zide and Gray (2001) observe, a narcissistic person's sense of entitlement is striking. The individual with narcissistic personality disorder shows a pervasive pattern of grandiosity (in fantasy or behavior), need for admiration, and lack of empathy beginning by early adulthood and present in a variety of contexts. The person shows five or more of the following symptoms (APA, 2000):

- Has a grandiose sense of self-importance, exaggerates achievements and talents, and expects to be recognized as superior without appropriate achievement;
- Is preoccupied with fantasies of unlimited success, power, brilliance, beauty, or ideal love;
- Believes he or she is special and unique and should only associate with high-status people or institutions;
- Requires excessive admiration;
- Has a sense of entitlement—for example, the unreasonable expectation of favorable treatment or others' automatic compliance with his or her expectations;
- Is interpersonally exploitive, taking advantage of others to get his or her needs met;
- Lacks empathy or is unwilling to recognize or identify with the feeling and needs of others;
- Often envious of others or believes others are envious of him or her; and
- Shows arrogant, haughty behaviors or attitudes.

Most individuals diagnosed with this disorder are men (APA, 2000). Taking into account the sociocultural context, this gender difference can be expected because male dominance is the norm in the United States (Castillo, 1997).

Cluster C Personality Disorders

Cluster C represents the "anxious and fearful" group of disorders. This cluster includes the avoidant, dependent, and obsessive-compulsive personality disorders.

Avoidant Personality Disorder The diagnostic category of avoidant personality disorder was introduced into the DSM–III in 1980 and has a shorter history in the psychiatric literature than most of the other personality disorders

(APA, 1980; Zide & Gray, 2001). Some clinicians argued there was too little distinction among the avoidant, schizoid, and dependent personality disorders to warrant a new diagnostic category. Further, persons who are "shy" can be misdiagnosed as having an avoidant personality. As the name suggests, this diagnostic category is reserved for those who are highly sensitive to the opinions of others and avoid most social relationships (Barlow & Durand, 2005). Persons with this disorder are characterized by a pervasive pattern of social inhibition, feelings of inadequacy, and hypersensitivity to negative evaluation beginning in early adulthood and occurring in a number of contexts. Individuals must show four or more of the following symptoms (APA, 2000):

- Avoids occupational activities that involve significant interpersonal activity because of fears of criticism, disapproval, or rejection;
- Is unwilling to get involved with others except when certain of being liked;
- Shows restraint in intimate relationships for fear of being shamed or ridiculed;
- Is preoccupied with being criticized or rejected in social situations;
- Is inhibited in new interpersonal situations because of feelings of inadequacy;
- Views self as socially inept, unappealing, or inferior to others; and
- Is unusually reluctant to take personal risks or to engage in new activities because they may prove embarrassing.

Some individuals with avoidant personality disorder are able to function when they are in a safe or protected social environment. They are able to marry and may have families but it is important for them to be surrounded by familiar relationships and life circumstances that do not demand spontaneity. It is helpful to consider a person's sociocultural context and to consider how a pattern of what looks like social avoidance fits in with the person's social expectations when making the diagnosis of avoidant personality disorder. For example, new immigrants may show avoidant behaviors that could be considered appropriate and adaptive as they struggle to cope with the stresses of new social circumstances and unfamiliar surroundings.

Dependent Personality Disorder   The key features of dependent personality disorder are an excessive need to be taken care of, associated with submissive, clinging behavior and a fear of independence (APA, 2000). These are individuals who show a pervasive pattern of extreme inability to act independently of others. They go to great lengths to avoid undertaking or assuming positions of responsibility or leadership. These are not simply people who are "unsure about whether to order a tuna salad or a sandwich for lunch" (Zide & Gray, 2001, p. 292). They want others to make decisions for them in all aspects of their lives. The disorder begins in early adulthood, occurs in a number of contexts, and the individual has four or more of the following symptoms (APA, 2000):

- Has difficulty making common, everyday decisions without excessive advice and reassurance from others;
- Needs others to assume responsibility for most major areas of his or her life;
- Has difficulty expressing disagreement with others because of fear of loss of support or approval (this does not include realistic fears of retribution);

- Has difficulty initiating projects or doing things on his or her own initiative because of a lack of self-confidence in judgment or abilities;
- Goes to excessive efforts to obtain nurturance and support from others to the point of volunteering to do things that are unpleasant;
- Feels uncomfortable or helpless when alone out of a fear of being unable to care for himself or herself;
- Urgently seeks another relationship as a source of care and support when one relationship ends; and
- Has unrealistic fears of and preoccupation with being left to take care of himself or herself.

Culture factors may play a role when making this diagnosis. Some cultures accentuate many of the "qualities" that could be attributed to a dependent personality such as an emphasis on passivity, politeness, and deferential treatment (APA, 2000). This may be in stark contrast to the majority behaviors in the United States where individualism and personal autonomy are highly valued personality attributes.

Obsessive-Compulsive Personality Disorder   The obsessive-compulsive personality disorder is often confused with obsessive-compulsive disorder (OCD). Persons with this latter disorder are distinguished by obsessive thinking and compulsive behavior. Persons with obsessive-compulsive personality disorder often have difficulties making decisions, may appear excessively moralistic and are often characterized as headstrong. They are inordinately careful and pay extraordinary attention to detail. The individual may become so involved in making every detail of a project perfect that the project ultimately is never finished. These individuals are oblivious to the fact that others may become very annoyed about the delays and inconvenience that can result from this behavior. The person is emotionally constricted and adheres to a high degree of orderliness, perfectionism, and mental and interpersonal control at the expense of flexibility, openness, and efficiency (APA, 2000; Zide & Gray, 2001). The person meets four or more of the following criteria (APA, 2000):

- Is preoccupied with details, rules, lists, orders, organization, or schedules to the extent that the major point of the activity is lost;
- Shows perfectionism that interferes with task completion;
- Is excessively devoted to work and productivity to the exclusion of leisure activity and friendships;
- Is overly conscientious, scrupulous, and inflexible about morals, ethics, or values;
- Is unable to discard old and worthless objects even when they have no sentimental value;
- Is reluctant to delegate tasks or to work with others unless they submit to exactly his or her way of doing things;
- Adopts a miserly spending style toward self and others; and
- Shows rigidity and stubbornness.

In sum, people with obsessive-compulsive personality disorder tend to take life very seriously. These are people who go by the book and pay careful attention to the letter of the law. This is the individual in the fast lane of the highway who drives at exactly 55 miles an hour because that's the speed limit, whereas others are traveling at an average speed of 75 miles per hour.

OVERVIEW OF MAJOR INTERVENTIONS

Until the mid-1970s, many practitioners felt the personality disorders were essentially untreatable conditions. The fact that the personality disorders develop in early adulthood and are a natural way for the person to behave and to define themselves complicates treatment. People can grow and change throughout life. While many persons with personality disorders are deeply troubled, there is an increasing consensus that they can be helped although the degree of improvement may vary. Treatment outcomes improve for the person who seeks out treatment on his or her own and takes responsibility for problems. These are the individuals who use treatment to learn ways to modify the expression of their problematic personality traits. Intervention is less effective for the person who denies responsibility, projects his or her difficulties onto the environment, or claims to be powerless to change.

Treatment interventions can be conceptualized in terms of levels (Sperry, 1995a, 1999):

- The first level involves symptoms;
- The second level addresses personality features that are related to the environment and can be modified;
- The third level involves personality features that are related to character; and
- The fourth level involves personality functions related to temperament.

Sperry (1995a, 1999) observes that the first two levels are considered relatively uncomplicated. Medication or behavioral treatments may quickly remit symptoms. Various methods such as group therapy and/or involving the family combined with psychotherapy are often helpful at level three. Level four characterizes a person's temperament and human nature and is considered difficult to change. Rather than focusing on a cure, treatment can be seen in terms of a continuum and the idea of success broadened to consider an optimal level of functioning for the individual (Blocher, 2002; Cortright, 1997; Sperry, 1995a, 1999).

Contemporary interventions integrate neurobiological and temperamental dimensions of a person's personality (Cloninger, 1987, 1999, 2000; Cloninger, Svrakic, & Przybeck, 1993; Millon & Davis, 2000). Individual, family, and group modalities may be combined with medication and various theoretical approaches such as cognitive-behavioral or interpersonal treatment. In the past, psychodynamic approaches, particularly psychoanalysis and long-term psychoanalytically oriented psychotherapy, were considered the treatment of choice (Stone, 1993). Interventions are currently more structured and focused on the here and now, and practitioners are taking a more active role. One recent advance is dialectical behavioral therapy.

Dialectical Behavior Therapy

Dialectical behavior therapy (DBT) was first developed as a treatment for parasuicidal women with borderline personality and has successfully been adapted to other populations (Robbins, 2002, 2004). DBT assumes that the person's core difficulty is one of emotional dysregulation and that this dysregulation is exacerbated and maintained, in part, by being invalidated by others. Therapy is organized along a fourfold hierarchy. The first set of priorities attends to the person's suicidal or parasuicidal behaviors and ideation. The second set of priorities addresses the behaviors that interfere with therapy. The third involves behavior that interferes with the person's quality of life. The fourth set of DBT priorities addresses skills deficits commonly associated with individuals with borderline personality disorder. The practitioner may also focus on decreasing behaviors related to post-traumatic stress, improving self-esteem, and negotiating individual priorities with the client. Interventions are behavioral and focus on skills training, collaborative problem solving, contingency clarification and management, and on the observable present. DBT is an integration of cognitive-behavioral intervention strategies and Zen practices (Heard & Linehan, 1994). Borrowing from the eastern religion of Zen, DBT begins with a concept called radical acceptance; that is, the practitioner assumes a stance of total acceptance. Dialectical refers to the philosophy supporting this approach or the tension between opposites. This tension is manifest in the expectation that clients are required to accept themselves as they are while at the same time they are actively trying to change. The practitioner balances supportive acceptance and change strategies. For example, the practitioner may point out to the client that he or she has two options. One is to accept things as they are and stay miserable, and the other option is to try to change.

Marsha Linehan, a psychology professor at the University of Washington, was instrumental in the development of DBT, which includes weekly one-on-one practitioner and group training sessions focusing on skill development in the areas of mindfulness, interpersonal effectiveness, emotion modulation, and distress tolerance (Linehan, 2000). Mindfulness is a form of awareness that can diffuse negativity, aggression, and compulsivity without suppressing emotions or indulging them (Marlatt & Kristeller, 1999). Mindfulness skills are techniques that enable one to become more clearly aware of the content of experience and to develop the ability to stay with that experience in the present moment. Interpersonal effectiveness skills focus on effective ways of achieving one's objectives with other people; for example, learning to ask for what one wants in an effective way, to say no and have it taken seriously, to build relationships, and to maintain self-esteem in interactions with others. Emotion modulation skills are ways of changing distressing emotional states (and improving distress tolerance) and include techniques for putting up with these emotional states if they cannot be changed for the time being. For a detailed explanation of the DBT skills, the reader is directed to a skills training manual written by Marsha Linehan (1993), *Skills Training Manual for Treating Borderline Personality Disorder*. Linehan recommends skills training to be carried out in a group context, ideally by someone other than the individual practitioner. Phone contact with the therapist between sessions should be offered to clients as an added measure of support in applying the skills the client is learning. Since persons with borderline pathology are challenging to the practitioner, another recommended mode is therapist consultation consisting of groups of practitioners who come together to provide professional support and ongoing training in DBT methods.

Similar to competency-based treatment, the DBT treatment process emphasizes a collaborative relationship in which the practitioner and client work together. A working assumption of DBT is that clients cannot fail. If things are not improving, it is the treatment that is failing (Linehan, 1991; Shearin & Linehan, 1994). In particular, the practitioner avoids viewing the client's efforts with pessimism. Empirical evidence seems to back DBT's efficacy in reducing self-destructive behaviors, reducing hospital admissions, and improving social adjustment (Koerner & Linehan, 2000; Linehan, Armstrong, Suarez, Allmon, & Heard, 1991; Scheel, 2000; Verheul et al., 2003).

Residential Treatment

In some instances, particularly during times of crisis such as a suicide gesture, an individual with a personality disorder may need to be hospitalized for a short period of time. When the home environment does not provide needed structure, the person may benefit from a specialized therapeutic community offering supervision, confrontation around the consequences of unhelpful or destructive behavior, group meetings with peers, and/or a structured work program.

Biological Therapy

There are no specific drug treatments for personality disorders, but medication can be effective if it focuses on Axis I disorders and/or specific symptoms characteristic of persons with personality disorders. The one possible exception is avoidant personality disorder. The newer antidepressant venlafaxine (Effexor), a serotonin/norepinephrine reuptake inhibitor, appears to be effective at reducing avoidant personality traits. Medications effective for treating social phobia have also been found to be effective with avoidant personality disorder (Altamura, Piolo, Vitto, & Mannu, 1999; Reich, 2000, 2002). Selective serotonin reuptake inhibitors (SSRIs) may divert impulsiveness, the tendency to worry, and depressed mood; medications in this category include paroxetine (Paxil), fluoxetine (Prozac), sertraline (Zoloft), and fluvoxamine (Luvox).

Reich (2002) summarizes the efficacy of various classes of psychotropic medications directed to the basic dimensions that underlie the personality. For cluster A disorders characterized by a paranoid, mild thought disorder, an atypical antipsychotic such as risperdone (Risperdal) may be effective. Low-dose neuroleptics may be useful for schizotypal and passive disorders.

Looking at the cluster B disorders, serotonin blockers can be useful for the impulsivity and aggression found in the borderline and antisocial personality disorders. Cyclic antidepressants or serotonin blockers may be useful for the affective instability characterizing borderline and histrionic personalities. Persons with bipolar characteristics may benefit from mood-regulating medications such as lithium and anticonvulsants such as carbamazepine (Tegretol) and valproate (Depakene) (Akiskal, 1996; Stein, Frenkel, Islam, & Hollander, 1995). For individuals in whom rejection sensitivity is prominent, a MAOI may be effective. Naltrexone (Re Via), a synthetic opioid antagonist with no opioid agonist properties, may be a useful adjunctive for persons with self-harming behavior.

Serotonin blockers and MAOI agents may be useful for avoidant personality disorder, a cluster C disorder. For those individuals with prominent anxiety but without impulsivity, an SSRI may be considered. If the individual responds, long-acting benzodiazepine or clonazepam (Klonopin) can be added or even used as the sole medication. If these fail, beta-blockers or atypical antipsychotics may be tried (Reich, 2002).

RISKS ASSOCIATED WITH PERSONALITY DISORDERS

We are only beginning to understand the personality disorders. As in most mental disorders, multiple factors play a role and it is difficult to isolate one major risk contributing to the development of personality disorders. The personality "system" needs to be considered in its totality, emphasizing the interrelationships among the intrapersonal, interpersonal, community, and environmental domains of a person's life.

Intrapersonal Risks

Individuals are born with genetically determined temperaments or dispositions to respond to the environment in certain ways (McCrae et al., 2000; Rothbart, Ahadi, & Evans, 2000). These temperaments remain stable over time and may later form specific personality traits. Personality traits are heritable, but Kagan (1998) cautions that a given temperament depends, in part, on how extreme the person's trait is in infancy. While most traits are highly influenced by genes (Plomin, DeFries, McClearn, & McGuffin, 2001), one's genetic predisposition does not imply genetic inevitability. According to Paris (1997), the risks of developing a personality disorder can best be understood in the context of gene-environment interactions.

Attachment research contends that early-life relational deficits lead to both neurophysiological brain deficits and psychological deficits (Siegel, 1999). In particular, a sensitive and responsive parent helps the infant grow the connections in the orbitofrontal cortex of the brain by communicating with the baby (or providing reciprocal attention) through eye contact, facial expressions, tone of voice, touch, and so forth. Securely attached children show neural pathways for resilience and are better able to handle emotional assaults (Ainsworth, Behar, Waters, & Wall, 1978). Distinct patterns or styles of attachment in early life can be detected, and infants with what is called a secure style show more emotional resilience than those with insecure styles of attachment (Ainsworth, Behar, Waters, & Wall, 1978; Erdman & Caffery, 2003). Vulnerability is greatest for infants who are insecurely attached to their parents, and insecure attachment is associated with inconsistent parenting styles or emotional unavailability (Ainsworth et al., 1978). Insecure attachment influences the development of personality disorders (Brennan & Shaver, 1998).

Interpersonal Risks

According to Harris (1999), traditional thinking has assumed that parents exert a crucial influence on the development of one's personality. Parents with impulsive or depressive personality traits may increase a person's risk for developing borderline personality disorder. Neglectful parenting has also been implicated as a significant predictor for a borderline personality diagnosis; in particular, neglect by both caretakers represents a significant risk (Zanarini & Frankenburg, 1997). A childhood history of verbal, emotional, physical, and/or sexual abuse or neglect can significantly impair functioning in adulthood, and research has confirmed that these factors are associated with the development of personality disorders (Herman, Perry, & van der Kolk, 1989; Zanarini, 1997; Zanarini et al., 2000).

Although genetic predispositions and parenting styles can modify and shape a child's temperament, they are not the sole contributors to personality (Kagan, 1998). Peers, like parents, can cause a person to emphasize some aspects of personality and downplay others. This is not a linear, cause-and-effect relationship since one's temperament and disposition may influence how one behaves within the group. However, most people go along with the group and mold their personalities according to the pressures of the group (Arroyo & Zigler, 1995). One's temperaments, learned habits, and beliefs about abilities influence responses to others, the persons with whom one chooses to associate, and the situations sought out (Bandura, 1986, 2001; Cervone, 1997). Other environmental influences including chance events that cannot be predicted can also contribute to one's "personality" (Rutter, Pickles, Murray, & Eaves, 2001). In sum, even traits that are highly heritable are not fixed, and one's experiences can strengthen or diminish them (Caspi, 2000).

Community and Environmental Risks

Culture also affects one's behavior and personality traits. Culture may exert just as powerful an influence on one's personality as any biological determinants (Cvetkovich & Earle, 1994). Cultural norms define which personality traits are valued, how one expresses emotions, and the value placed on relationships. Key aspects of personality begin with the culture in which one is raised (Cohen, 2001).

In the case vignette that follows, the client's childhood history includes many of the risk factors for developing a personality disorder.

CASE ILLUSTRATION: SUZIE HUTCHFIELD

There are two general approaches to treating persons with personality disorders. One is embedded in psychoanalysis and the other in cognitive-behavioral approaches. Earlier explanations of the personality disorders were rooted in psychoanalytic thinking. Historically, the personality disorders were considered to exist within the individual and the treatment of choice was to restructure the personality. Psychoanalysis and related supportive psychotherapies attempted to uncover the unconscious elements involved in the person's patterns of thinking. This approach required a long-term, analytically oriented process of psychotherapy that would delve deeply into the person's psyche in order to effect a profound change in personality.

Prompted by changes in the service delivery system and the growing influence of managed care, a number of innovations were developed to provide quicker methods of characterological transformation (Barlow & Durand, 2005; Berkow, 1992; Eisendrath, 1998). These developments led to the second treatment approach, which is to treat the symptoms (usually those that have brought the client to the practitioner's attention) and bolster the positive aspects of the client's personality. This treatment category focuses on modifying behavior rather than finding the underlying reasons for the individual's psychological structure. This field includes dialectical behavior therapy. Of all the approaches that are available, the cognitive-behavioral orientations have the strongest scientific basis to support efficacy (Gunderson & Gabbard, 2000; Linehan, 2000; Livesley, 2004; Robbins, 2002, 2004; Ryle, 2004).

The case of Suzie Hutchfield was first presented in Zide and Gray's (2001) Psychopathology: A Competency-Based Assessment Model for Social Workers *to describe someone struggling with borderline personality disorder. This vignette illustrates the practitioner's attempts to develop an accepting relationship with the client while balancing confrontation of her destructive behaviors. The specific skills highlighted in this case were drawn from a combination of the therapy approaches of crisis intervention, solution-focused therapy, cognitive-behavioral techniques, and psychoeducation.*

The session takes place in a community mental health center. The agency provides time limited crisis-oriented emergency services and short-term treatment. Those requiring longer-term help are linked with other practitioners in the community. When Suzie Hutchfield called to confirm her appointment she indicated that she wanted "someone to help me." Her appointment was scheduled for later that week. On the intake form Suzie noted that she felt depressed and empty. She didn't think she could stand to feel that way any longer. She remembered the phone number of the community mental health center from the resources given to her as a part of her discharge plan from the hospital.

You go out to the reception area to greet Suzie and find her restlessly flipping through a magazine and nervously pulling at a fingernail. She is slightly overweight but well-groomed, wearing a pair of navy slacks and a tropical shirt—the "uniform" of waitresses at a local delicatessen. Her curly hair is over-bleached to a light blonde color and somewhat tousled, giving her a slightly untamed look. She is wearing a considerable amount of makeup, and her mascara seems to accentuate her eyes. For an instant you think Suzie appears quite healthy and does not look like the person who sounded so desperate when she called about her appointment.

You introduce yourself as the social worker assigned to her case and invite Suzie to come with you to your office. Suzie eagerly agrees and begins talking as she walks down the hall with you toward your office. "The shrink at the hospital told me that this was a good place to come to talk to someone," Suzie remarks. Somewhat warily she enters your office, and her eyes are drawn to your professional license and social work diploma hanging on the wall. "Well, I can see you've been around the block once or twice. The last social worker I saw at the hospital was one of those graduate students. I think she was afraid of me! Do you think you can handle me?" asks Suzie.

You respond by telling Suzie what she can expect of counseling. She interrupts, "Yeah, yeah! I know the routine and all that sh_t about confidentiality. I know that if I come in here and tell you that I'm thinking about suicide and crap like that you'll call in the Gestapo and 'presto' I'm back in the crazy house! Besides, I haven't thought much about suicide this week!" You note Suzie's inference about suicide and decide to wait before fully exploring the issue since it might be too soon in the interview. You are hoping to build more of a relationship with Suzie before delving into the topic.

Behind her air of aggressiveness and bravado you get the sense that Suzie is quite fragile and scared to engage with you in a meaningful way. You respond, "You know, I'm sure you already know how much work counseling is, so I don't want to 'candy coat' things for you. I think I may be able to help you and I'll sure do my best, but you have to make a commitment to our work together. There might be times it may feel uncomfortable. Will you give me a chance?" You later learn that one of the things that Suzie liked about you right away was your honest and forthright manner. She felt that you were somehow able to look beyond her anger and "see" that she was a pretty decent person behind the borderline symptomatology. You continue, "Maybe we could begin by you telling me why you made the appointment for today." The following is an excerpt of the session.

Suzie describes a childhood history with an abusive, alcoholic father. "He was no Prince Charming. He used to beat me and my younger brother up real good, and then he'd go drink his booze in front of the television set." She currently works as a waitress in a local delicatessen. Despite a college education, she admits to having a series of jobs that "don't last too long." She goes on to add, "I've been married three times, and once I married the same man twice. Did I confuse you?" She continues, "Anyway, I can't seem to get it right even though I'm 42 years old. You know, I'm a single mom of two girls, and even at home I can't get things right. My oldest daughter, Candy, is 16 and a real piece of work. She should be making A's but skips school a lot. One of these days some goody-two-shoe social worker is gonna haul me to jail because that kid's always truant. Now my little girl, Heather, she's the best. She's 11 years old and a better kid you never saw. Don't that beat all. I got one good kid and one bad one."

"What did you ask? Oh yeah, I remember now. My boyfriend, Bob, just moved in, but I'm not so happy about this arrangement. I think he's been cheating on me, but he tells me he's not. Twice last week I followed him after he left for his motorcycle repair shop. Anyway, he drove right over to his ex-girlfriend's house and stayed there for two hours! When he came home, I confronted him, and he told me some cock-and-bull story that she needed some 'house maintenance' done. Some maintenance! I've been through this with him before, many, many times. I throw him out, and then he swears this is the last time, but it never is, and I still take him back."

Suzie continued, "You know, there's nothing I hate more than being alone, and if it means taking that bum back, well at least I know what I have, ya know? It's not that I need him. I've had lots of men in my life. I always have a man waiting in the wings. You never know what can happen. I really just don't want to ever be alone."

Suzie goes on to describe her earlier hospitalization for "the cuts and the cocaine." During that time she met an orderly and they "found a broom closet and made out a coupla times." Suzie has been hospitalized several times after attempting suicide by cutting her wrists. "You know, sometimes I feel so empty I'll do something really exciting for fun. My old social worker tried to tell me that I do these crazy things for attention. She's so stupid! Now, on the other hand, you seem to be real smart and like you can help me. What do you think?"

I reflected, "It sounds like you sometimes feel really empty when you're not in a relationship with someone."

Suzie looked thoughtful for a moment and replied, "Some days when I wake up I feel like I'm already tired. It's like being in this big black hole, and no matter what I do or how hard I try it just surrounds me. It's awful! But when I'm in a relationship it sorta lifts me a little but that's really not enough. I get scared and do anything just to avoid being alone. Even putting up with that jerk of a boyfriend, you know? At first I get angry with him and I usually feel justified. Then the anger causes me to feel shattered into tiny pieces. Then I can't seem to think straight and I start to question everything. You know, like 'Should I be angry? Maybe he really is a good guy.' Then I start to feel guilty, afraid, and crazy. Then I hate myself for being so stupid."

Gently, you ask, "And when all this happens, how does that make you feel?"

Suzie replies, "Oh, that's an easy one cause it happens so often. I feel down in the dumps and worthless. Like I said when I called this place, I feel so depressed and empty. I don't think I can stand to feel this way any longer."

You ask, "Have you ever tried to hurt yourself?"

"Well, when it first started, I didn't try to hide it. I cut my wrists a coupla times but no one seemed to notice, if you can believe that! So I felt I needed it to be seen so that someone would help me. The more I felt that I needed help, the less it seemed to be available. So I started with the drugs—cocaine, ya know? Well that made the cuts a lot easier. That's what put me in the hospital last week. Since I got out I've had pretty good days. I've been productive and not depressed. I haven't done anything serious lately."

You then proceed to contract with Suzie that when she starts to feel suicidal "you will not do anything before talking to me." She nods affirmatively and states, "No one ever went the 'extra mile' for me. All those other therapists didn't seem to hold out much hope for somebody like me."

For the remainder of the interview you explain the expectation that Suzie will attend Alcoholics Anonymous, Narcotics Anonymous, participate in weekly individual counseling sessions, and participate in a group program provided by the staff team. The interview concludes with plans to set treatment goals in the next session. You ask, "When we meet next time, I would like you to imagine that we are having our last session. I would further like you to imagine that as we look back on our work together that we have been successful. What would have to change in order for you to know that we have been successful?"

The next session begins with Suzie's comment that all she thought about over the week was "that crazy question." Suzie states, "The answer is easy. All I have to do is make the commitment to change. It's up to me. I can decide to do something or I can get dramatic and fall to pieces. That's it in a very large nutshell! I mean I can change my life. I know it will be hard work, but I believe it can be done. I'm not going to buy into the pessimism that I can't change. Now we're not talking about coping either, we're talking about change! You know, all this time I've been trying to manage my emotional static but now I just want to turn it off completely!"

You inquire, "What's the first small thing you will notice that's different when that happens?"

Suzie responds, "I guess it's what you might call basic therapeutic communication 101. I figure this won't work overnight and I imagine talking has got to be the best way. I know this sounds corny but when I am very angry and not in danger of losing control, it's best if you could just listen to me and help me to explore my anger without judging. I don't want you to think I'm a bad person or anything like that. Help me to understand what's going on . . . really understand. That kind of thing will be really different for me. You could say something like, 'It sounds like when this or that happens it really unhinges you.' Sorta like echoing my feelings. Hearing you say it will help me to look at my anger."

You indicate to Suzie, "I'm impressed at how at how quickly you came up with this, and I wonder how you did that."

She replies, "I've had this on my mind for a really long time. I figure until someone can formulate what's going on inside me this therapy thing won't go anywhere." Suzie adds, "I guess this isn't going to be easy, but I know I need some help to stay on track right now. Do you really think you can help me sort through all this crap?"

Suzie's individual sessions at the center were coupled with a group work program provided by the staff team aimed at reducing problematic interpersonal dynamics. The group provided education and opportunities for socialization. For example, during one session the symptoms of borderline pathology were explained and members encouraged to discuss the implications for them. The group was co-facilitated by various staff members and one community practitioner. About two years ago, the social worker currently assigned to work with Suzie had been concerned when she saw several clients relapse after being discharged from the mental health center. She researched the problem and learned that the clients had a hard time connecting with community-based therapy services for longer-term counseling. Apparently the clients felt deserted and abandoned by the center, and these feelings made it harder to develop yet another relationship with a new therapist. As a result, the practitioner advocated for the mental health center to include practitioners from the community as group co-facilitators. In this way, clients could meet the practitioner while they were still participating in the mental health center's programs. The counseling referral at discharge would then be perceived as an extension of agency services. This program seemed to be working well, and the practitioner was planning to follow up with another research project to evaluate the apparent success of this group work program.

Suzie's relationship with the practitioner had its ups and downs. She was often angry, volatile, and challenged the social worker. Despite several relapses, the practitioner remained optimistic and confident that Suzie's efforts would pay off in the long run. According to Suzie, "No matter how hopeless I felt, my social worker always believed I could do better. She was so respectful. I know I gave her a hard time, but she just kept coming back. Somehow I didn't feel like a 'mental case' with her. She was the first professional who really listened to me." Treatment goals included developing increased self-awareness with greater impulse control and increased stability of relationships. With this increased awareness and capacity for self-observation and introspection, Suzie was able to confront and better understand the self-destructive path of her anger. At termination, she was no longer feeling suicidal, she was less angry, and she was better adjusted socially. Suzie observed, "For the first time I'm sort of feeling that things could be better." She was referred to one of the group community-based co-facilitators for longer-term therapy and seemed to be looking forward to the opportunity to reinforce the gains she had made at the mental health center.

OPERATIONALIZING COMPETENCY-BASED TREATMENT

The competency-based treatment model provides the practitioner with a framework for attending to the relational and systemic influences that often reinforce and complement personality styles and the personality disorders. This multidimensional perspective helps the practitioner to carefully select skills from various therapeutic approaches that apply to the individual's unique interpersonal matrix and take into consideration the multiple influences in the person's life (see Table 10.2). It should be noted that the practitioner would have liked to have included Suzie's family in her care, but their inaccessibility during the times when services were provided at the mental health center prohibited their involvement.

TABLE 10.2	THE RISKS, PROTECTIVE FACTORS, AND BUFFERS IN SUZIE HUTCHFIELD'S LIFE	
	Risk Factors	**Protective Factors and Buffers**
Intrapersonal	Struggles with borderline personality disorder	Intelligent, insightful, motivated, and articulate
	Low self-esteem	Shows qualities of tenacity
	Anger (toward men)	
	Poor impulse control	
	History of suicide, drug and alcohol abuse, physical and emotional abuse	
	Splitting in how she sees her daughters (i.e., one is "good" and the other is "bad")	
Interpersonal	Hostile relationship with father	Concerned about her two daughters
	Married 3 times	Participates actively in treatment (i.e., able to discuss her behaviors; participates in groups)
	Single parent	
	One daughter truant	
	Current boyfriend just moved in; tenuous relationship	Good relationship with the social worker
Social and Environmental	A diagnosis commonly seen as "difficult," "challenging," and stigmatizing	Attends Alcoholics Anonymous and Narcotics Anonymous
		Available continuum of care from hospitalization to outpatient to community-based longer term counseling resources
		Practitioner knowledgeable of borderline pathology
		Mental health center services are client-centered (i.e., linking clients to community practitioners)

Working with Suzie Individually

The relationship between practitioner and client is generally considered the cornerstone of treatment for someone struggling with a personality disorder (Gunderson & Gabbard, 2000). This work is complicated by the fact that these individuals rarely seek help until they are in serious trouble or in a crisis

(Bender, Dolan, & Skodol, 2001; Bender et al., 2003), because the problematic personality traits are so deeply entrenched that they seem ego-syntonic (or normal) to the client. Suzie came to the mental health center at a time in her life when she couldn't stand to feel depressed and empty any longer.

Suzie Hutchfield's presenting problems were fundamentally social in nature and challenged her ability to perceive the practitioner as helpful. It was not unusual for Suzie to make desperate attempts to maintain flawed relationships. For example, although her current boyfriend was cheating on her she maintained that she still loved him. However, she also met someone else when she was hospitalized for another suicide attempt. Suzie's relationship style underscores the importance of understanding the internal dynamics of the client's thoughts and their relationship to the practitioner. The practitioner has a good understanding of psychopathology, and she knows that persons with borderline personality disorder often struggle with severe internal turmoil associated with extraordinary social dysfunction, certain kinds of vulnerability, and emotional instability. With this understanding, the practitioner was able to relate to Suzie as a person with unique qualities who also happened to be struggling with internal turmoil. In turn, Suzie perceived the practitioner as someone who went the "extra mile" for her.

In this case illustration, the practitioner intervened during a time of crisis in Suzie's life. According to Heller and Johnson (2001), research suggests that intervention that prevents a client's suicide in the crisis phases of the disorder suggests individuals have a good chance of having a satisfying life at a later point in time. The psychosocial assessment data notes that Suzie was able to stay in the protected hospital environment until the immediate threat of suicide had passed. Suzie subsequently followed up with her discharge plan for outpatient counseling and came in to the appointment at the mental health center asking for "someone to help me." The practitioner focused on helping Suzie cope with the stressors that seemed to trigger her self-destructive behaviors. The practitioner also provided support and worked with Suzie to help her to better understand her anger. This concrete focus coupled with Suzie's practical suggestion (to talk about feelings) ultimately helped to solidify the therapeutic relationship.

As discussed earlier, there are a variety of treatments for the personality disorders but their success depends on both the practitioner and the client. The practitioner must have the technical skills and emotional capacity to accept the client without judgment, and the client needs to be motivated to change. Ideally, the relationship with the practitioner will provide the client with a model that can be used outside of the counseling realm.

In this illustration, the practitioner recalled her training in psychopathology, particularly what she had learned about persons with personality disorders. She was able to recognize that people like Suzie are generally in a great deal of psychic pain because of their behavior. They can also cause profound pain in the people with whom they are in contact.

The practitioner extended her understanding of Suzie's struggles by trying to understand how the world looked from the client's perspective. To facilitate this process, the practitioner asked herself the following questions [adapted from

Madsen's work (1999) with multi-stressed families]:

- *In what context might Suzie's behavior make sense?* The practitioner realized it might be difficult for Suzie to trust professionals after multiple hospitalizations and failed prior treatment attempts.
- *What might be the positive intent behind the behavior I find frustrating?* Suzie grew up with her father's abuse and prediction that she was never going to make much of herself, so her hostile, angry approach to relationships could be seen as a struggle to survive.
- *How can I come to respect and appreciate that positive intent even if I don't condone the behavior?* The positive effects of Suzie's feisty and argumentative relational style represented her efforts to seek help despite a continuing pattern of rejection (beginning with her father) and failed relationships.
- *What can I learn from this client?* As Suzie felt understood and validated by the practitioner, despite a fiery temper, she was able to develop a relationship characterized by mutual appreciation. In turn, the practitioner's belief in the client's resiliency was reaffirmed.

Working with the Group

Persons with borderline personality disorders are at high risk for developing substance abuse disorders, and about 80 percent attempt suicide at some point during treatment (Barlow & Durand, 2005; Zide & Gray, 2001). These problems seemed to complicate Suzie's treatment. Suzie minimized her pattern of drinking by commenting, "I'm not a drug addict or nothing like that. I just wanna smoke a little weed, drink a little wine, have a good time, and I don't hurt anybody," but she was referred to Alcoholics Anonymous (AA) and Narcotics Anonymous (NA) meetings in addition to participating in a group program at the mental health center. Using groups that emphasize improving interpersonal dynamics and integrating education and socialization fits well with a managed care environment (Hurdle, 2001). Group work is a cost-effective way to augment services.

Suzie had difficulty with authority but she was able to benefit from the self-help groups and the center's group program. It seemed that group members were able to challenge Suzie's maladaptive and impulsive patterns without being perceived as trying to manipulate and control her. By making use of peer relationships and the repetition offered in AA and NA, Suzie was able to utilize peer pressure to impose restraint and to modify her self-destructive behavior. At the same time, the 12-step format provided concrete tools for coping. As members shared their own experiences, it was easy for Suzie to identify destructive patterns of coping in others before looking at herself. The groups also provided a supportive forum in which Suzie could develop new and better relationships outside of therapy. The benefits of group work enhanced the gains made in Suzie's individual work with the practitioner.

Working with the Community

Suzie made dramatic improvements. At termination of services she was no longer suicidal, was beginning to feel less angry, and was better adjusted socially. Typically, however, progress for persons struggling with personality disorders is often slow and gradual, and relapses can be expected. During the course of their work together, Suzie was able to understand the characteristics of borderline disorders and began to explore what this meant to her in individual and group sessions. The community mental health center primarily provided time-limited, crisis-oriented services. Considering the gains Suzie had made, the practitioner referred Suzie to a community-based practitioner for longer-term counseling. The mental health center social worker noticed that many clients like Suzie struggled with these follow-up referrals and initiated a research project to further explore the problem. As a result, community-based practitioners were invited to co-facilitate the center's groups. This practice provided clients with a stronger link to the community, and the social worker planned to use her research skills for another study to verify the effectiveness of the agency's change in services.

In sum, the case of Suzie Hutchfield illustrates the competency-based approach to treatment that provides the practitioner with flexibility in sequencing, combining, and shifting various approaches and modalities. The practitioner was able to select specific intervention skills and methods that emphasized a systemically based, relational oriented approach to counseling Suzie. Together, client and practitioner co-collaborated treatment efforts as much as possible. Crisis intervention services provided Suzie with an appointment when she felt desperate for "someone to help me" after discharge from the hospital for a recent suicide attempt. By exploring Suzie's vision of a successful last session, the miracle question from solution-focused therapy was modified and served to help set treatment goals and identify the first small steps toward progress. When Suzie was quickly able to come up with specific and concrete steps to use therapy, the practitioner provided a therapeutic compliment. By turning the compliment into a question, the practitioner gained insight into Suzie's commitment to the counseling process. Psychoeducation helped to foster an understanding of the features of borderline personality disorder and its implications for Suzie.

SUMMARY

The personality disorders can be thought of as a dysfunction in the personality system of an individual, his or her relationships, and the total ecosystem. They are deeply ingrained, inflexible, maladaptive patterns of relating, perceiving, and thinking that are severe enough to cause impairment in the person's functioning or considerable distress. Problems can manifest themselves in a variety of ways but are most clearly evident in patterns of relationships and behavior that tend to be maladaptive to the person's sociocultural setting.

There are many different personality disorders, and symptoms vary depending on the specific subtype. Those addressed in this chapter are summarized as follows:

- *Paranoid personality disorder*—Persons with this disorder are highly suspicious of other people and are usually unable to acknowledge their own negative feelings toward others. They are often hypersensitive to their social environment, looking for clues that selectively validate prejudices or biases.
- *Schizoid personality disorder*—Persons with this disorder show a lifelong pattern of social isolation and indifference to others. They do not desire or enjoy close relationships (even with family members), and they avoid social activities that involve significant interpersonal contact. Persons with this disorder appear aloof and detached, and their behavior could be characterized as eccentric. They often react to disturbing experiences with apparent detachment and are unable to show hostile or aggressive feelings. Symptoms of schizoid personality disorder include shyness, oversensitivity, social withdrawal, frequent daydreaming, and avoidance of close or competitive relationships.
- *Schizotypal personality disorder*—The features of this disorder are various oddities of thinking, perception, communication, and behavior that are not severe enough to meet the criteria for schizophrenia. People with this disorder manifest a disturbance in thinking expressed as magical thinking, ideas of reference, or paranoid ideation. They often show marked peculiarities in communication. They may use words deviantly but never to the point of the loosening of associations or incoherence found in those struggling with schizophrenia. Frequently, persons with schizotypal disorder are socially isolated and show constricted or inappropriate affect that interferes with establishing rapport in face-to-face interactions with others.
- *Narcissistic personality disorder*—Persons with narcissistic personality disorder have a grandiose sense of self-importance and consider themselves to be unique. These individuals have an obsessive self-interest. They are preoccupied with fantasies of limitless success and need constant attention and admiration from others. Interpersonal relationships lack empathy and appear to be exploitative. They seem to vacillate between the extremes of over idealization and devaluation of others.
- *Histrionic personality disorder*—People with histrionic personality disorder are usually able to function at a high level and can be successful at work and in social relationships. Problems seem to arise in more intimate relationships where deeper involvement is required. However, these individuals often do not see their own situation realistically and tend to overdramatize and exaggerate. Someone with a histrionic personality can be described as having a pervasive pattern of excessive emotionality and attempting to gain attention from others in strange and unusual ways. They may go through frequent job changes as they become easily bored and have trouble dealing with frustration. Because they tend to crave novelty and excitement, they may place themselves in risky situations. Failure or disappointment is usually blamed on others.

- *Antisocial personality disorder*—Antisocial personality disorder is characterized by chronic behavior that manipulates, exploits, or violates the rights of others. The behavior of these individuals is often seen as criminal, and they are described as callous, irresponsible, impulsive, and unable to feel guilt or to learn from experience or punishment. They tend to have a low frustration tolerance and to blame others when things go wrong. To be diagnosed, the person must have first shown behavior that qualifies for a diagnosis of conduct disorder during childhood. Those with this disorder are often angry and arrogant but can be superficially witty and charming. They may be adept at flattery and manipulating the emotions of others. Substance abuse and legal problems often accompany an antisocial personality diagnosis.

- *Borderline personality disorder*—Persons with this disorder are characterized by a pervasive pattern of instability in interpersonal relationships, self-image and feelings, along with marked impulsivity. Frequently, their behavior is potentially physically self-damaging. Persons with borderline personality disorder tend to be impulsive in areas that may create self-harm, such as drug use, drinking, or other high-risk behaviors. They may display an unstable mood with marked shifts. There may be chronic feelings of emptiness, boredom, or brief episodes of psychosis.

- *Avoidant personality disorder*—Avoidant personality disorder is characterized by a long-standing and complex pattern of feelings of shyness, inadequacy, social inhibition, and extreme sensitivity to rejection and what others think about them. Feelings of loss and rejection are so painful to the individual that they will choose loneliness rather than risk rejection by trying to connect with others.

- *Dependent personality disorder*—Individuals struggling with this disorder do not trust their ability to make decisions. They may be devastated by separation and loss and may go to great lengths to stay in a relationship even if their partner is abusive.

- *Obsessive-compulsive personality disorder*—This disorder should not be confused with obsessive-compulsive disorder, or OCD, a psychotic condition that shares some of the same symptoms with obsessive-compulsive personality disorder. Persons with obsessive-compulsive personality disorder believe that their preoccupations are appropriate. These are people who tend to be high achievers and become upset if others disturb their rigid rules and routines.

The exact cause of personality disorders is unknown, but prevailing thinking considers the role of genetic and environmental factors. People with personality disorders usually do not seek out treatment on their own. There is no single medication that has been shown to be consistently effective. The case of Suzie Hutchfield underscores the importance of a helping relationship in which the practitioner balances support while confronting Suzie's self-destructive behaviors. Skills from crisis intervention and solution-focused approaches illustrate the practitioner's attempts to co-collaborate with the client, tap into strengths, and set the tone for a hopeful future. Competency-based treatment provides a framework to consider the whole person, emphasizing interrelationships among the intrapersonal, interpersonal, community, and environmental domains in a person's life.

PRACTITIONER REFLECTIONS

1. The personality disorders are highly culture-bound. Behavior that is considered deviant in one culture might be expected or normal in another. Your cultural background will influence your response to the following question, particularly whether your culture emphasizes individualism or community. Individualist cultures accentuate the independence of the individual over the needs of the group. Collectivist cultures accentuate group harmony over the wishes of the individual, and the self is defined in the context of relationships and the community.

   Take as much time as you like to answer the question: "Who are you? I am _____."

   The ways you define yourself influence many aspects of your life, including the personality traits you value, how you express emotions, and how much value you place on relationships.

2. Persons with a personality disorder rarely seek help on their own but wait until they are in serious trouble or their families pressure them into treatment. The reason for this "reluctance" is that the problematic traits are so deeply entrenched that they seem ego-syntonic to the person. A strong therapeutic alliance between practitioner and client contributes to success. Select one of the personality disorders described in this chapter and discuss how you would go about engaging the client and developing a relationship in which the client perceives you as being trustworthy and effective.

3. Self-awareness is important to competency-based practice. This activity is designed to encourage you to assess your own conceptions of normal personality development and determine how these conceptions may be projected onto the client. Reflect on a client you are currently seeing (or may have seen in the recent past), and consider how your family background, gender, age, race, religious beliefs, culture, or ethnicity may influence your understanding of the client's emotions and/or behavior. Can you identify behaviors of this client that would be seen as socially or occupationally impairing in the dominant American society but may be normative in social interactions for other groups?

CHAPTER

11

SUBSTANCE-RELATED DISORDERS

- *Lois Slinger is a highly successful stockbroker with a cocaine habit that costs her at least $2,000 a week.*
- *Eddie Rodriguez is a 20-year-old ranch hand working in Ocala, Florida. He says he doesn't have a drinking problem, but he is appearing in court for 3 DUIs and two counts of "disturbing the peace."*
- *Jerry Bischoff, a 17-year-old teen, was brought to the local emergency room. According to his friends, "JB" was coming down from a "meth" high after attending his high school senior prom.*
- *Katie Rose, a 42-year-old mother of two, has difficulty sleeping at night; she frequently buys "Seconal" from a neighbor for whom it is prescribed by a doctor.*
- *Jan Sella, 63 years of age, "sips" on a bit of sherry every day. She says, "It's good for my health, and the doctors say a little 'sip' of alcohol gets the blood running." Her children feel differently. They grumble, "Mother has a drinking problem. We know this because we buy her at least three new bottles of sherry every week."*

What do all of these people have in common?

Although no one knows exactly when early humans discovered the intoxicating effects of alcohol, there is evidence that it was used 10,000 years ago (Potter, 1997). Interestingly, several Sumerian excavation sites revealed remnants of a form of beer dating back to 8,000 BC. It was thicker than today's brews and contained vitamins and amino acids. Five thousand years later, burial tombs in Egypt revealed written accounts of a type of "wine" made around 3,000 BC. Until the late nineteenth century, most adults drank primarily wine or various forms of beer because available drinking water was considered too dangerous to ingest.

Throughout history, human beings have known about and experimented with using naturally occurring stimulants, including coca leaves, betel nut, coffee beans, tobacco, and khat leaves. When used in their natural form these stimulants heightened physical sensations and accelerated mental processes in the central nervous system. It has been well documented that for many centuries the Chinese used medicinal teas that included ephedrine (a stimulant) as one of the major active ingredients. Physiological effects include increased blood pressure, rapid heart rate, higher body temperature, and/or constriction of peripheral blood vessels (vasodilatation). When using or ingesting stimulants, the person generally experiences an increased level of energy and alertness, feelings of pleasure (or euphoria), a heightened sense of well-being, self-confidence, and decreased fatigue and appetite (Benshoff & Janikowski, 2000).

In 1992 the National Longitudinal Alcohol Epidemiologic Survey, a national household survey, found that approximately 7.5 percent of the U.S. population (14 million Americans) abuse and/or are dependent on alcohol. According to the National Drug and Alcoholism Treatment Unit Survey, more than 700,000 people receive treatment for alcohol abuse on any given day (National Institute on Alcohol Abuse and Alcoholism, 1997). Of those receiving treatment, almost 14 percent receive either residential or inpatient hospital treatment and 86 percent are treated as outpatients.

More recently, the 2000 National Household Survey on Drug Abuse estimated that 6.5 percent of the total U.S. population (14.5 million Americans) abused or were dependent on either alcohol or illicit drugs (Epstein, 2002). Further, an estimated 1.7 percent of Americans (3.9 million out of the total U.S. population) did not receive any form of specialized treatment and thus fell into the drug abuse "treatment gap" (Epstein, 2002, p. 3). During the 12 months prior to the 2000 survey, approximately 1.3 percent of the population (or 2.8 million people) reported having received some form of treatment for problems related to substance abuse or dependence. Treatment continues to be provided at specialized settings such as inpatient or outpatient rehabilitation facilities and outpatient mental health centers.

The 1999 National Household Survey on Drug Abuse estimated that 1.6 million Americans had used prescription pain relievers non-medically for the first time during the previous year (Office of Applied Studies, 2000). This represents a significant increase since the 1980s, when generally fewer than 500,000 first-time users per year were reported. From 1990 to 1998, the number of non-medical new users of pain relievers increased by 181 percent; tranquilizer use increased by 132 percent; sedative use increased by 90 percent; and stimulant use increased by 165 percent. Prescription drug abuse affects many Americans, and there is growing alarm over increased abuse among older adults (Emlet, Hawks, & Callahan, 2001; Gurnack & Johnson, 2002; Marks, 2002).

The prevalence of heavy drinking or alcohol abuse among the elderly ranges from 2 percent to 20 percent (Menninger, 2002; Pennington, Butler, & Eagger, 2000; Rigler, 2000). Older adults, their relatives, and caregivers tend to downplay the existence of substance abuse problems, and the symptoms of alcohol and drug abuse are often misinterpreted as signs of dementia or depression. Moreover, older people have the highest rate of non-compliance regarding directions for taking medication; are at increased risk for injuries related to falling, such as hip and thigh fractures; and are vulnerable to drug-related cognitive impairment and physical dependence (Adams & Jones, 1998; Azmitia, 2001; Brennan & Moos,

1996; Rigler, 2000). Levin and Kruger (2000) call substance abuse among our elders an "invisible epidemic" (p. 1). Once substance abuse has become a problem, older people are often isolated from the traditional avenues to treatment. For instance, they may no longer drive and are thus unlikely to be arrested for driving under the influence. Further, the elderly are usually retired and consequently do not experience alcohol-related problems on the job. This is an age cohort that is likely to view alcohol abuse as a moral failure and therefore may be reluctant to ask for help with alcohol problems. Lastly, the social isolation associated with failing health may reduce social activities but may not preclude drinking at home. For older people who are hospitalized, 11 percent to 20 percent of acute care hospital admissions are related to alcoholism (Adams, Zhong, Barboriak, & Rimm, 1993). Life events such as the loss of loved ones, the onset of health problems related to the aging process, and the failure of caregivers to recognize and confront drug and alcohol use may contribute to the development and continuation of substance abuse among older people (Bleechem, 2002; Benshoff & Harrawood, 2003; Benshoff & Janikowski, 2000).

UNDERSTANDING SUBSTANCE-RELATED DISORDERS

Addressing the effects of substance abuse on the individual, the family, and the community poses significant challenges for the social work profession (Gruber, Fleetwood, & Herring, 2001). This chapter is organized around substance-related disorders found in the *Diagnostic and Statistical Manual* (DSM). Several terms commonly used in conjunction with alcohol, drugs, and related substances are intoxication, abuse, dependence, and withdrawal. *Intoxication* is the development of a series of symptoms, often involving psychological or behavioral changes, directly related to consumption of a substance and its influence on the central nervous system (CNS). *Abuse* represents maladaptive patterns of substance use leading to clinically significant impairment or distress (American Psychiatric Association, 2000; Crump & Milling, 1996; Farr, Bordieri, Benshoff, & Taricone, 1996). *Dependence* occurs when an individual requires increasing quantities of the substance to reach the same level of mood alteration because the substance's effects diminish significantly with continued use. *Withdrawal* develops when a person stops using a substance but continues to crave it. Withdrawal symptoms can include convulsions, depression, tremors, and/or severe abdominal pain.

Substance-related terminology has become more complicated in recent years. Morse and Flavin (1992) describe alcohol addiction as a

primary, chronic disease with genetic, psychosocial and environmental factors influencing its development and manifestations. The disease is often progressive and fatal. It is characterized by impaired control over drinking, preoccupation with the drug alcohol, use of alcohol despite adverse consequences, and distortions in thinking (p. 1013).

People who experience both a mental disorder and substance-related disorder concurrently are described as having a *dual diagnosis* (Doweiko, 2002). Although specific treatment for mental illness and substance-related problems developed separately, both conditions need to be treated simultaneously. Historically, many treatment programs insisted that client mental health issues be addressed only after a period of sobriety. Treatment generally focused on psychiatric issues and fell short of recognizing the role of substances in the symptoms being observed. Today there is broader recognition that the most viable way to meet the needs of clients with co-occurring substance-related and mental health concerns is through interdisciplinary teamwork and integrated treatment plans (Hendrickson, Schmal, & Ekleberry, 2004; Lewis, Dana, & Blevins, 2002).

The social use of a substance is defined by traditional social standards and subdivided into *occasional* and *regular* patterns of use. Substance abuse occurs when an individual uses a substance with no legitimate medical need to do so (Minkoff, 2001). Although most persons take medications as directed by their physician, abuse of and addiction to prescription drugs is a worldwide public health problem.

Asking clients about their drug of choice was once considered an important indicator that supposedly helped define the addictive process. It was previously assumed that the specific types of drugs people used (especially when they had a choice) provided important clues about the nature of their addiction. Current thinking no longer puts much emphasis on a person's choice of drug, especially because it is rare for a person to use just one substance (Walters, 1994).

Some people experiment with psychoactive substances for a brief period of time, and no further serious psychosocial or medical sequelae occur. For others, substance use may lead to more destructive drug-taking patterns of abuse or dependence. This chapter begins with a brief overview of some of the more commonly misused substances. However, due to the scope of this book the discussion should not be considered inclusive of all drugs used and substances of abuse.

Substances that are abused because of their psychoactive properties include central nervous system depressants, central nervous system stimulants, opioids or narcotics, hallucinogens, cannabis, anabolic steroids, and over-the-counter drugs.

Central Nervous System (CNS) Depressants

Central nervous system depressants include chloral hydrate (Noctec); barbiturates (Phenobarbital, Seconal, Tuinal); benzodiazepines (Ativan, Xanax, Versed, Tranxene); and others (Equanil, Miltown, Noludar, Placidyl). Central nervous system (CNS) depressants are substances that slow normal brain function. Because of this property, some CNS depressants are used in the treatment of sleep and anxiety disorders, panic attacks, and acute stress reactions. The more commonly used medications for these purposes include barbiturates such as mephobarbital (Mebaral) and pentobarbital sodium (Nembutal), and benzodiazepines such as alprazolam (Xanax) or diazepam (Valium). Shorter-acting and more sedating benzodiazepines include triazolam (Halcion) and estazolam (ProSom) (Longo & Johnson, 2000).

CNS depressants act on the human brain by affecting the neurotransmitter gamma-aminobutyric acid (GABA). As discussed in Chapter 2, neurotransmitters are chemicals in the brain that facilitate communication between brain cells. Ultimately, CNS depressants work by decreasing brain activity and producing a drowsy or calming effect considered beneficial to those suffering from sleep or anxiety disorders. While many benefits are associated with treatment using barbiturates and benzodiazepines, they do have serious potential for abuse when not used as prescribed. Over a period of time the body develops a tolerance for the drug and larger doses are needed to achieve the same initial effects. Withdrawal from benzodiazepines can be problematic but rarely life threatening. On the other hand, withdrawal from prolonged use of other CNS depressants can cause life-threatening conditions.

Central Nervous System (CNS) Stimulants

As the name suggests, stimulants are a class of drugs that boost brain activity and cause increased attention, alertness, and energy; elevated blood pressure; and an accelerated heartbeat and respiration. Stimulants are prescribed for health conditions such as narcolepsy, attention-deficit hyperactivity disorder, and cases of depression that do not respond to other forms of treatment. Historically, stimulants were very popular for the treatment of obesity (appetite suppressants) and for persons suffering with asthma. Stimulants have chemical structures similar to the family of brain neurotransmitters known as monoamines (which include dopamine and norephinephrine). Some of the more commonly prescribed stimulants include dextroamphetamine (Dexedrine), methylphenidate (Ritalin), and sibutramine hydrochloride monohydrate (Meridia). Stimulants increase the amounts of these neurotransmitters in the brain and subsequently raise the blood pressure and heart rate, constrict blood vessels, elevate levels of blood glucose, and open up pathways in the respiratory system. Serious consequences of stimulant overuse may include dangerously high body temperatures; arrhythmias (disruption of the normal rhythm of the heart); and in some cases, cardiovascular failure or fatal seizures.

Opioids or Narcotics

Opioids are most often prescribed for their effective analgesic and pain-relieving properties; for example, they can relieve coughing and diarrhea (Belgrade, 1999). Medications that fall within this class of drugs are referred to as narcotics and include morphine (used before or after surgery to alleviate severe pain) and codeine (used for its milder pain efficacy). Other related pain-relieving drugs include oxycodone (OxyCotin), propoxyphene (Darvon), hydrocodone (Vicodin), meperidine (Demerol), and hydromorphone (Dilaudid).

The most commonly prescribed narcotic and opioid medications include morphine (street names include "Miss Emma," "monkey," and "white stuff"); codeine (street names include "Captain Cody," and "schoolboy"); hydrocodone (Vicodin);

oxycodone (OxyCotin, Percodan); methadone (Dolophine); propoxyphene (Darvon, Demerol, and Talwin); and LAAM (L-alpha-acetyl-methadol) or Levomethadyl acetate. Opioids include heroin (street names include "brown sugar," "H," "horse," "skunk," and "junk"); and opium.

Opioids act on the body by attaching themselves to specific proteins called opioid receptors found in the brain, spinal cord, and gastrointestinal tract. When these drugs attach themselves to certain opioid receptors, they obstruct or block the transmission of pain messages to the brain. Depending on the amount taken, they can produce drowsiness, cause constipation, depress respiration, and also produce euphoric states. When taken as prescribed, opioids can be used to manage pain effectively. However, chronic use of opioids can quickly bring about a tolerance for these drugs, and the user must then consume higher doses to achieve the same initial effects (Joransson, Ryan, & Dahl, 2000). Long-term use can lead to physical dependence as the body adapts to the drug's presence. If use is reduced or stopped, symptoms of withdrawal will occur, including restlessness, muscle and bone pain, insomnia, vomiting, diarrhea, and involuntary leg movements.

Cocaine

Cocaine is one of the world's oldest known drugs, and the coca leaves from which it is extracted have been ingested by human beings for thousands of years. Pure cocaine was first extracted from the leaf of the Erythroxylon coca bush, which predominantly grows in the higher elevations of Peru and Bolivia. By the late 1800s and early 1900s cocaine was used worldwide when it was mixed into tonics and elixirs to treat a wide variety of illnesses. In its pure chemical form, cocaine hydrochloride has been an abused substance for more than 100 years. Cocaine, a narcotic, was regarded as the illicit drug of choice during the 1980s and 1990s because of its extensive popularity and seemingly endless supply during this period. Cocaine is available in two forms. Cocaine hydrochloride is a water-soluble pure salt derivative that may be taken orally once it is dissolved into a liquid form or used intranasally. Street names for this kind of cocaine include, "blow," "toot," "nose candy," "girl," and "coke." Cocaine that is separated from the HCl base (fat soluble) then becomes smokable. Street names for this kind of cocaine include "crack" cocaine, "freebase," or "rock" (National Institute on Drug Abuse, 1999). Cocaine can also be administered or dispersed through rectal exposure (referred to as "booty bumping") or intravenous use (referred to as "shooting," "slamming," or "mainlining").

The initial use of a small amount of cocaine often produces tachycardia (rapid heartbeat), irregular respiration, elevated blood pressure and body temperature, dilated pupils, and hallucinations. These symptoms are often followed by bizarre, erratic, or violent behavior, blurred vision, chest pain, muscle spasms, convulsions (sometimes leading to death), coma, heart failure, or brain failure that causes respiratory arrest (Stevens, 2002). Long-term psychological effects of cocaine use include emotional problems (difficulties at school and work, isolation from family and friends). The cocaine "high" may be replaced with feelings of restlessness, anxiety, irritability, mood swings, paranoia, and weight loss. Long-term physical effects associated with ingesting cocaine through the nose include damage to the sinus cavity (nasal membrane erosion causing holes inside the nose or inflamed nasal passages) and increased risk of respiratory infections. Injecting the drug creates a heightened risk of contracting hepatitis C and/or HIV. Those who habitually inject cocaine or other drugs eventually end up with unusable, deteriorated, and collapsed veins. As a result, other avenues are found to administer these drugs; for example, they are introduced intramuscularly (referred to as "muscling"), injected subcutaneously (just underneath the skin, referred to as "skin popping") or injected between the toes (Inaba & Cohen, 1997).

Hallucinogens

Hallucinogens, also referred to as psychotomimetics or psychedelics, alter perception. There are two basic groups of hallucinogens: natural and manufactured forms. Natural forms include mescaline (street names include "mescal," "buttons," "peyote," and "cactus") and psilocybin (street names include "magic mushroom," "purple passion," "shrooms"). In its synthetic and chemical form it is most notably recognized by its synthesized alphabet symbols; e.g., LSD, PCP, TCP, and Angel Dust. First developed by German chemist Albert Hoffman in 1938, LSD or lysergic acid diethylamide is perhaps the most well-known hallucinogen and remains one of the most potent psychotropic and mind-altering drugs ever developed. LSD (street names include "Acid," "Blotter," "Cubes," "yellow sunshines," and "Microdot") is usually sold in three forms: a liquid form suspended in small glass vials; thin squares of gelatin-like substance (often referred to as "hits"); or drops administered to small pieces of perforated paper (commonly referred to as "blotter acid"). This last form of LSD is often printed with a small cartoon-like design—for example, Bart Simpson, Popeye, or Donald Duck. Because of its form and similarity to a candy treat known as "Dots" it is particularly dangerous to small children who may ingest this drug by mistake.

Ecstasy is the newest addition to the hallucinogens. Scientifically known as MDMA (3-4-methylenedioxymethamphetamine), ecstasy is a semi-synthetic drug that acts simultaneously as a stimulant and a hallucinogen. It was patented by Merck Pharmaceutical Company in 1914 and abandoned for 60 years (Greer & Tolbert, 1998) until it was reintroduced during the late 1970s and early 1980s when psychiatrists and psychotherapists began using it to facilitate psychotherapy. It stimulates the central nervous system and produces hallucinogenic effects. The effects of the drug last 3 to 6 hours and include feelings of empathy, openness, and well-being. Other effects include increases in body temperature, blood pressure, and heart rate. Users may also experience persistent jaw clenching and teeth gnashing and will put a pacifier or lollipop in their mouth for protection. Ecstasy usually comes in the form of different colored tablets or capsules, which are swallowed, but it can also be crushed, snorted, or smoked. Street names are "XTC," "E," "ECCY," "X," "M&M," "beans," "adam," "rave," "disco biscuits," "burgers," "hug drug," "love drug," "lover's speed," "fantasy," "clarity," "mitsubishes," or "Rolexes" (Beebe & Walley, 1991; Henry, Jeffreys, & Dawling, 1992). The different names often come from the small image stamped on the top of each tablet or from the shape of the tablet itself. Considered a designer drug, ecstasy is often associated with "raves" or all-night underground parties with techno music and extensive drug use (SAMHSA, 2000). People who take ecstasy at rave dances report they enjoy dancing and feeling close to others (Beck & Rosenbaum, 1994). Ecstasy is now being used in a number of other social settings (SAMHSA, 2000).

With the possible exception of PCP, these hallucinogens alter how the brain experiences time, reality, and the environment (Doweiko, 2002). For example, users of hallucinogens often experience synesthesia, or "seeing" of sounds and "hearing" of colors. Signs of hallucinogen abuse include mood and behavior changes; distorted sense of sight, hearing, and touch; distorted image of self and time perception; warm skin temperature (excessive perspiration and noticeable body odor); unusually dilated pupils; acute anxiety, depression, and increased suicide risk; and unpredictable flashback episodes that may occur weeks or months (or more rarely, years) after use (Batzer, Ditzler, & Brown, 1999).

Cannabis

Cannabis is a green or gray mixture of dried, shredded flowers, stems, and leaves of the hemp plant (Cannabis sativa/indica). The main active chemical in cannabis is THC (delta-9-tetrahydrocannabinol) which kicks off a series of cellular reactions users experience when smoking (less often eating, as in pot brownies) the drug. THC travels throughout the body, including the brain, to produce its many effects. THC attaches to sites called cannabinoid receptors on nerve cells in the brain, affecting the way those cells work. Cannabinoid receptors are abundant in parts of the brain that regulate movement, coordination, learning and memory, higher cognitive functions such as judgment, and pleasure. Short-term consequences of cannabis use include difficulty learning and maintaining memory; distorted perception; difficulty thinking and problem-solving; loss of coordination; and increased heart rate, anxiety, and panic attacks. Health problems from long-term use include respiratory problems (regardless of the THC content) caused by the amount of tar inhaled and levels of carbon monoxide absorbed that are three to five times greater than those associated with tobacco smoking. Street names for cannabis include "marijuana," "dope," "herb," "weed," "gangster," "chronic," "joints," "skunk," "reefer," "pot," "Acapulco gold," "hemp," and "boom." Although cannabis remains a Schedule 1 drug (forbidden class) in the United States, it has been used in medical practices to relieve glaucoma or reduce the nausea associated with chemotherapy in cancer patients (Kandel & Chen, 2000; Mathre, 2001).

Anabolic Steroids

Anabolic steroids include testosterone (Delatestryl, Depo-Testosterone), nandrolone (Durabolin), and Androl-50 (Oxymetholone). Street names include "roids" or "juice." Anabolic steroids are the more familiar name for synthetic substances related to the male sex hormones known as androgens (Bagatell & Bremner, 1996; Blue & Lombardo, 1999). Anabolic steroids promote the growth of skeletal muscle (anabolic effects) and the development of male sexual characteristics (androgenic effects). Anabolic steroids were developed in the late 1930s mainly to treat hypogonadism, a condition in which the male testes are defective and do not produce sufficient amounts of the male hormone testosterone to support normal physical development and sexual functioning. The primary medical use was to treat delayed puberty and some types of impotence (National Institute on Drug Abuse, 2000). Shortly after the development of these drugs, it was found that using anabolic steroids helped facilitate the growth of skeletal muscles in laboratory animals. When this unanticipated feature became public knowledge, body builders and weightlifters began using anabolic steroids to create larger and stronger muscles. Steroid abuse has become widespread within the athletic world, and random drug testing to ensure the integrity of competitive sports has been instituted by the International Olympic Committee, the U.S. Olympic Committee, and other organizations that supervise athletic events.

Consequences of anabolic steroid abuse include increased energy, sexual arousal, mood swings, distractibility, forgetfulness, and confusion (Porcerelli & Sandler, 1998). Those who frequently misuse anabolic steroids often become dependent on these drugs, as evidenced by continuation of use in spite of physical problems (insomnia, fatigue, and loss of appetite) and diminished social relationships (fighting, aggression, and at-risk behaviors) (Dobs, 1999; National Institute on Drug Abuse, 2000). Anabolic use in men is associated with a wide range of adverse side effects ranging from deep-pitting facial acne, enlarged breasts, and increased aggression to more severe life-threatening effects such as heart attacks and liver cancer (Pope, Phillips, & Olivardia, 2000). Adverse side effects in women may include hirsutism (excessive facial or body hair growth in unusual places, and loss of scalp hair), masculinization (deeper voice), and clitoral hypertrophy (increased size). Most of these side effects are reversible after anabolic steroid use is discontinued, but unfortunately some persist.

Anabolic steroids can be used in a variety of ways. They can be administered orally, injected intramuscularly, or rubbed on the skin in the form of a gel or cream. For optimum advantage the anabolic user might alternate methods of drug use, such as by combining two or more different anabolic steroids (oral and/or injectable types together). This multiple steroid use supposedly produces an effect on muscle size that is greater than the effect of using these drugs separately. Pyramiding is another method used to achieve heightened anabolic steroid efficacy. The principle behind pyramiding is manipulating the dosing cycle, which generally takes place over a period of 6 or 12 weeks. At the beginning of the cycle, the individual will use a lower dose of anabolic steroid, also known as stacking, and then slowly begin increasing his or her dose. During the second half of this cycle the drug is gradually decreased to zero. Sometimes this regimen is followed by a second cycle in which the person continues to work out but does not use anabolic agents, also known as cycling. Some abusers believe pyramiding allows their body time to adjust to the high doses, and during the drug-free cycle the body's hormonal system is allowed to recuperate. As with stacking, the perceived benefits of pyramiding and cycling have not been empirically substantiated (National Institute on Drug Abuse, 2000).

Over-the-Counter Substances

Caffeine   Coffee was first discovered in the Middle East and had spread to Europe by the thirteenth century. Caffeine belongs to the drug class known as xanthenes and is considered the most widely used stimulant in the world. It has been estimated that up to 92 percent of the United States population consumes some form of caffeine on a regular basis (Winger, Hofmann, & Woods, 1992). When ingested in small amounts, the caffeine found in coffee decreases fatigue and increases alertness, heart rate, and blood pressure. The body's absorption of caffeine peaks about 30 minutes after oral ingestion, with the maximum central nervous system (CNS) impact taking place within two hours. The effects of caffeine last approximately 3 hours, with 90 percent of the drug metabolized or absorbed by the body and the other 10 percent excreted through the urinary tract. Caffeine works by blocking the brain's receptors for a neurotransmitter/neuromodulator known as adenosine. Adenosine acts as an inhibitor, producing sedation; caffeine blocks the receptors for adenosine and results in a mild stimulating effect on the central nervous system (Ray & Ksir, 1993). Excessive use of caffeine can cause irritation of the stomach lining, psychomotor agitation (nervousness, restlessness, or jitteriness), muscle twitching, diuresis (increased urinary output), tachycardia (rapid heart rate), arrhythmia (abnormal heart rhythm), irritability, and difficulties sleeping. Physical factors such as body weight, metabolism, and physical tolerance influence the effects of caffeine. On the average, caffeine dependence occurs when 500 mg of caffeine, or approximately 5 cups of coffee (110–150 mg per 6-oz serving) are consumed per day. Withdrawal from the caffeine found in coffee has been well documented, with symptoms that include headaches and feelings of lethargy. Interestingly, abrupt cessation after long-term caffeine use may result in anxiety, depression, marked fatigue, nausea, or vomiting.

Caffeine is found not only in coffee but in lesser amounts in teas, soft drinks, cocoa/chocolate, headache remedies, and certain over-the-counter stimulants. The amount of caffeine is about 2 to 5 mg in a 6-oz serving of decaffeinated coffee, 30 to 60 mg in a 12-oz serving of cola, or 20 to 50 mg in a 6-oz serving of tea.

Alcohol   The term *alcohol* refers to any type of fermented or distilled liquor that contains ethyl alcohol (or ethanol), such as beer, wine, or whisky. The term *drugs* refers to a wide range of materials such as cocaine, cannabis, and amphetamines that alter mood or consciousness and are ingested through smoking or other means of consumption (Copeland, Swift, Roffman, & Stephens, 2001; Hughes, 1993; Hughes, Gust, Skoog, Keenan, & Fenwick, 1991; Hughes, Goldstein, Hurt, & Shiffman, 1999; Solowij et al., 2002). The term *substance* refers to both drugs and alcohol, hence the term *alcohol and other substance-related abuse* (Kirst-Ashman & Hull, 1999).

Early and subtle indications of problematic alcohol use may include drinking to reduce feelings of anxiety or depression, covert drinking, anticipatory or defensive drinking, and/or gulping drinks. Early signs of problematic use may include accidental overdoses, behavior changes, blackouts, and dangerous or aggressive activities while intoxicated. Later indications of greater problem severity include rationalizing drinking behavior, hiding alcohol, and drinking regularly during morning hours. Later sequelae include the loss of non-using friends, impaired relationships with family and/or co-workers, problems in occupational or social functioning, and prevalence of medical or legal problems.

Listening to how clients describe their alcohol use helps define changes in patterns of using alcohol (or other substances) and dependence. Common client responses regarding their struggles with alcohol include the following remarks:

- "I can stop drinking anytime I want to. I just don't want to quit right now."
- "I never drink before I get home from work, so that proves I don't have a drinking problem."
- "I'm not like those other guys. I can control my drinking. No problem."
- "What's the big deal? I don't drink booze. I only drink beer, and everyone knows beer doesn't count for anything."

Although the terms "problem drinking" and "alcoholism" sometimes are used interchangeably, researchers in the substance-related field have distinguished between the two concepts. The current professional literature suggests that relative to persons described as alcoholics, those characterized as "problem drinkers" have a shorter problem drinking history, greater social and economic stability, and greater personal resources. Typically, they have not experienced major losses due to their drinking nor have they exhibited severe withdrawal symptoms such as delirium tremens or seizure upon cessation of past drinking. While they may occasionally experience problems from drinking they do not have a history of severe physical dependence on alcohol. The definition of a standard drink may vary; however, it is commonly defined as 12 oz of beer, 5 oz of wine, or 1.5 oz of distilled spirits (Lauer & Lauer, 2002).

Nicotine   Nicotine is the psychoactive ingredient found in Nicotiana tabacum (tobacco plant). The Mayan culture planted and cultivated tobacco more than 2000 years ago, and First Nations people have known about (and used) tobacco for many centuries. Methods of tobacco use include cigarettes, cigars, smokeless tobacco (chewing), and pipe smoking. Patterns of use vary from the individual who may smoke one cigarette per day to those who smoke non-stop (sometimes referred to as chain-smoking) throughout the day. No matter how often it is ingested, nicotine acts the same way once it enters the bloodstream. Tobacco smoke is immediately absorbed by the lungs and within seven seconds reaches the smoker's brain. When taken in small dosages, nicotine mimics the effect of acetylcholine, causing the release of acetylcholine and norepinephrine. When nicotine reaches the brain, the user experiences a sense of release from stress or even feelings of euphoria. Additional physical effects may include an accelerated heart rate, elevated blood pressure, and an increase in the strength of heart contractions.

Nicotine and caffeine are documented as the most widely used stimulants worldwide, and almost as well documented are the attempts made to discontinue nicotine use. Available over-the-counter nicotine gum and patches have been reported successful in helping people stop smoking. Along with these self-help measures, support groups and/or group therapy have been used (Abrams et al., 2003; Hall, Muñoz, & Reus, 1996; Plasse, 2000). Unfortunately, approximately 20 percent of those who successfully quit smoking become dependent on the gum itself

(Hughes, 1993; Hughes, Goldstein, Hurt, & Shiffman, 1999; Hughes, Gust, Skoog, Keenan, & Fenwick, 1991). Additionally, a substantial number of smokers relapse once they stop using the gum or patch (Cepeda-Benito, 1993). Several new treatments have shown encouraging results, including nicotine nasal spray, a nicotine inhaler, and bupropion hydrochloride (Zyban) (Hughes, 1993; Hughes et al., 1991, 1999). Research studies suggest nicotine is the most addictive drug in existence and results in cravings that last a lifetime, persisting even after withdrawal (Hurt & Robertson, 1998; Inaba & Cohen, 1997).

Inhalants   Inhalants are breathable chemical vapors that produce psychoactive (mind-altering) effects. Although many people are exposed daily to volatile solvents and other inhalants in their homes and workplace environments, we tend not to think of inhalable substances as drugs because most of them were not intended to be used in that way. Their popularity is largely a matter of availability, as they can be cheaply obtained at any grocery or home improvement store. Although it is illegal to breathe inhalants, it is not illegal to possess or purchase them (Espeland, 1997). Inhalants fall into the following categories:

- Industrial or household solvents, such as gasoline, certain glues, and model cement.
- Art or office supply solvents, such as felt-tip marker and/or correction fluids.
- Gases used in household or commercial products, such as propane tanks, butane lighter material, whipping cream aerosols, and refrigerant gases.
- Household aerosol propellants, such as hair or deodorant sprays, nail polish, air freshener, fabric protector sprays, and spray paints.
- Medical anesthetic gases, such as nitrous oxide (laughing gas), ether, or chloroform.
- Nitrites including cyclohexyl that are currently available to the general public. (Amyl nitrite, a volatile and highly flammable clear liquid used as a vasodilator, especially for anginal pain, is available by prescription only; and butyl nitrite, which is used in disinfectants, emulsifying agents, and some pharmaceuticals, is illegal for anything other than its intended use.)

Although most inhalants differ in their makeup, nearly all abused inhalants produce effects similar to anesthetics that slow down the body's functions. To produce the full range of desired inhalant effects, the person breathes in through the nose or mouth sufficient concentrations to cause intoxicating effects. The process known as sniffing refers to spraying or pouring an inhalant onto a rag and placing it into a bag. The user then places the bag over their face and breaths in deeply the highly concentrated amounts of chemicals. This process induces a short-lived, lightheaded, euphoric state. Unfortunately, the devastating downside of inhalant use can include short-term memory loss, heart failure, hearing loss, peripheral neuropathies (numbness), limb spasms, damage to the central nervous system, brain, bone marrow, liver, and kidneys, blood oxygen depletion, and death. The signs of inhalant abuse includes problems in school or work, chemical breath odor, red or runny nose or eyes, dazed or drunken appearance, irritability, and disappearance of household chemical items.

OVERVIEW OF MAJOR INTERVENTIONS

Substance-related disorders can be treated in a variety of settings. Each setting influences the services a person may receive and also the venue in which services are delivered. The following is a brief overview of the settings of service:

- *Community settings* focus on appropriate identification of clients with substance-related issues; provide brief intervention; and refer to specialized treatment programs.
- *Detoxification centers* are the first step in treatment and offer several choices: remaining at home; attending a non-medical detoxification center (if medically stable); or seeking an inpatient medical setting. The focus is short-term and designed to oversee the client's safe withdrawal from substances; to monitor the client's progress and if necessary refer for medical assistance; to provide personal and emotional support; to assess potential for further intervention; to work with the client (and family) to develop an appropriate intervention plan; and to link the client with appropriate community and agency resources (Prater, Miller, & Zylstra, 1999).
- *Residential rehabilitation programs* tend to have a great deal in common with each other whether the facility is run by a general hospital, a free-standing medical treatment unit, or a social agency. These programs focus on the psychological aspects of substance-related disorders rather than the physiological factors, and on education rather than medicine. Ideally, the time the client spends in the rehabilitation setting should provide an opportunity to develop personal recovery goals, learn skills needed to prevent relapse, prepare for re-entry into the community, and plan on living an abstinent life style (Rabinowitz & Marjefsky, 1998).
- *Therapeutic communities* were historically staffed by persons involved in their own recovery process; however, through the years social workers have increasingly become involved. Cohen (1985) identifies 12 characteristics that therapeutic communities have in common: an arduous admission policy; charismatic leadership; emphasis on personal responsibility; mutual assistance (considered a core value); self-examination and confession; structure and discipline; a system of rewards and punishments; status as an extended family; sustained separation from society; staff members not identified as authority figures; valuing of honesty; and an emphasis on working toward abstinence.
- *Methadone-maintenance programs* were pioneered by Dole and Nyswander (1965) in New York during the 1960s. It was posited that methadone use would be a viable treatment substitute for heroin and would free the client from the pressures and significant dangers of illegally obtaining heroin. Methadone was seen as a positive alternative to heroin because it was legal, administered orally (versus injection of heroin), did not produce the level of euphoria of heroin, and blocked both the effects and withdrawal symptoms of the abused opiates. For many years, it was assumed that no other

treatment but methadone was necessary. Today we know that methadone maintenance cannot occur in a vacuum but needs to take place within the context of a treatment plan that includes counseling and other efforts at rehabilitation.

- *Outpatient counseling agencies* run a gamut of settings ranging from comprehensive community mental health agencies to the offices of private practitioners. Outpatient counseling offers a high degree of individualization, treatment plans including both short- and long-term goals, and an opportunity for the client to try out new behaviors.
- *Employee assistance programs (EAP)* are not a treatment modality but were designed to help employees in the work setting and as an avenue to help companies resolve (in a fair manner) problems related to worker productivity. The EAP worker acts as both a human resource consultant to the organization and a service provider to the employee.

To address the unique needs of each client, treatment is provided in a wide variety of settings. Within these settings, clients benefit from interventions along a continuum of care.

Motivational Enhancement

Motivation is a key element in treatment and recovery, influencing a client's progress through the stages of change from considering change to following the planned action into sustained recovery (Smith & Meyers, 2004). Motivational enhancement therapy (MET) is an approach to treating alcoholism that has been receiving increased clinical attention in recent years. This approach recognizes that motivation is an important first step toward any action or change of behavior (Connors, Donovan, & DiClemente, 2001; DiClemente, 2003; DiClemente, Bellino, & Neavins, 1999; Miller & Rollnick, 2002; Sanchez-Craig, 1995; Sanchez-Craig, Davila, & Cooper, 1996; Straussner, 2004; Wild, Cunningham, & Hobdon, 1998).

MET is based on a client-centered model that creates a supportive and non-threatening environment in which clients are encouraged to explore the consequences of their drinking. This approach does not guide the individual through a step-by-step recovery but strives to motivate clients to use their own resources to change their behavior. The focus is toward raising a person's awareness of the impact of alcohol on his or life and encouraging a commitment to behavioral change.

One MET technique is called "motivational interviewing." It takes what clinicians traditionally conceptualize as denial and "normalizes" it so it is viewed as one stage in a person's ability to change—namely, ambivalence. The practitioner asks the individual about difficulties caused by drinking or drug use, enabling the client to examine his or her habits objectively. The worker provides structured feedback, encouraging the client to make future plans while at the same time attempting to maintain (or increase) the client's motivation to continue to change (Fisher & Harrison, 2000).

The evidence suggests that a motivational approach holds considerable promise for facilitating positive outcomes in drinking-reduction interventions (Walitzer & Connors, 1999). The next few years should yield interesting and important information about the feasibility and effectiveness of methods used to help motivate and move clients through the stages of change in resolving substance abuse problems.

Biological Therapies

The biopsychosocial framework supporting competency-based treatment underscores the importance of considering the neurobiological aspects of the client's substance abuse (Erikson & Wilcox, 2001). Recent knowledge about how psychoactive drugs work on the brain led researchers to explore altering the ways drugs are experienced by people (who are) dependent and/or addicted to them (O'Brien, 1996). Neuroscience research in the past ten years suggests the possibility of developing medications to improve the efficacy of concurrent psychological or behavioral therapies (Litten & Allen, 1998; Litten, Allen, & Fertig, 1996). These investigations implicate specific neurotransmitter systems in the development of addiction, suggesting that medications aimed at modifying the activity of these systems may interfere with the development of alcoholism. In addition, some individuals may be biologically predisposed to alcohol dependence. Studies suggest persons may benefit from medication designed to ameliorate the biochemical abnormalities that presumably underlie their susceptibility (Johnson & Ait-Daoud, 1999). Pharmacotherapy treatment of alcoholism often includes the use of two different types of medications: aversive medications (which deter the person from drinking) and anti-craving medications (which reduce the person's desire to drink alcohol).

A commonly recognized biological therapy involves the use of substitutes, or more specifically, agonist substitutes. An *agonist* is "a substance that binds to a receptor and stimulates the same type of cellular activity as a neurotransmitter, thereby increasing its effect" (Bentley & Walsh, 2001, p. 52). Agonist substitution involves providing the individual with a safer drug: for example, prescribing methadone, which has a chemical make-up similar to the addictive drug, heroin (Strain, Bigelow, Liebson, & Stitzer, 1999; Strain, Stitzer, & Liebson, 1993). Agonist substitutes for nicotine are used in treating people who are addicted to cigarette smoking, for example. The other treatment consideration involves the use of antagonists to modify the natural events in the synapse along pathways in certain areas of the brain so that using the drug of choice no longer produces the euphoric desired effect. An *antagonist* "binds to a receptor but fails to stimulate its activity, thereby decreasing the effect of the neurotransmitter" (Bentley & Walsh, 2001, p. 52).

In addition to looking for ways to block the euphoric or elevated effects of using psychoactive drugs, other methods focus on making the ingestion of the abused substance exceedingly unpleasant. One such aversive pharmacological treatment is disulfiram (Antabuse), which is used with people who are alcohol dependent. Antabuse was the first drug of its type to be released and has been available nationwide since the late 1940s. This drug helps prevent the breakdown of acetaldehyde, a by-product of alcohol. The resulting buildup of acetaldehyde causes those who begin to drink alcohol after taking Antabuse to experience severe reactions, including nausea, vomiting, difficulty breathing, elevated heart rate and respiration. These reactions may endanger the life of the person (Thomas, 1997). Unfortunately, non-compliance is a major concern, and if people skip their daily dose of Antabuse for a few days they are able to resume their drinking without aversive side effects.

Opioid Antagonists

Opioid peptides are a class of neurotransmitters that produce physiological effects similar to those of morphine and heroin. In humans, these opioid peptides modulate the effects of other neurotransmitters, thereby influencing a broad range of physiological functions (Froehlich, 1997; Herz, 1997; O'Connor, 2000). In 1994 the U.S. Food and Drug Administration (FDA) approved the medication naltrexone (ReVia) for alcoholism treatment based on results of two randomized, double-blind placebo-controlled clinical trials (O'Malley, Jaffee, Rode, & Rounsaville, 1996; Volpicelli, Alterman, Hayasgida, & O'Brien, 1992; Volpicelli, Watson, King, Sherman, & O'Brien, 1995; Volpicelli et al., 1997). Naltrexone reduces the craving for alcohol. In addition, naltrexone makes the use of alcohol less rewarding for persons who have relapsed, so that the individual is less likely to continue to drink. Apparently two major reasons prevent the wide clinical acceptance of naltrexone (Center for Substance Abuse Treatment, 1998; Garbutt, West, Carey, & Lohr, 1999; O'Malley, Jaffee, Rode, & Rounsaville, 1996). In a three-month follow-up study, O'Malley and colleagues (1996) found the effectiveness of naltrexone appeared to dissipate over time. Medication noncompliance was another significant problem. Many addicts just discontinue taking the drug on their own. Further large-scale clinical trials are needed to establish naltrexone's clinical effectiveness (Jaffee et al., 1996; Volpicelli et al., 1997).

Specific Glutamate Antagonists

Acamprosate (calcium acetylhomotaurinate), an amino acid derivative that affects both gamma–aminobutyric acid and excitatory amino acid (e.g., glutamate) neurotransmission, has been studied throughout Europe and has been in regular use for the past 14 years under the brand name Campral. Although its action is not wholly understood, it is believed the drug normalizes abnormalities in two neurotransmitter systems in the brain called glutamate and GABA systems (Sass, Soyka, Mann, & Zieglgänsberger, 1996). The drug appears to interact with a certain type of receptor (e.g., the N-methyl-D-aspartate or NMDA receptor) that is located on the surface on some brain cells and helps to mediate the effects of another important brain chemical, glutamate. Acamprosate appears to ease the discomfort of long-term abstinence from alcohol, thus reducing the risk of relapse (Carpenter, 2001; Irvin, Bowers, Dunn, & Wang, 1999; Sherman, 2000; Spanagel & Zieglgänsberger, 1997).

Acamprosate is receiving increased attention in Europe through controlled clinical trials, and results suggest significant abstinence rates among persons recovering from alcohol use (Sass et al., 1996). Acamprosate has also been used in the treatment of chronic alcohol abuse in Canada and is being studied for use with persons recently detoxified in the U.S. (Kranzler, 2000; Mason, Salvato, Williams, Ritvo, & Cutler, 1999). Large-scale clinical studies support the effectiveness of Acamprosate indicating twice as many patients remained abstinent from alcohol for up to one year after treatment with Acamprosate compared with those who received only a placebo (Geerlings, Ansoms, & Van Den Brink, 1997; Sass et al., 1996; Swift, 1999). The drug has prompted a great deal of clinical interest in finding ways to reduce alcohol cravings.

Serotonergic Medications

Serotonin plays an important role in regulating diverse physiological functions, including sleeping patterns, sensory perception, mood states, temperature regulation, pain suppression, and body rhythms such as appetite (Lovinger, 1997). The class of medications known as SSRIs have primarily been used in the treatment of mood disorders, particularly major depression (refer to Chapter 5). Over the past two decades the effects of serotonergic agents in the treatment of alcoholism has been well studied. Fluoxetine (Prozac) has been used in those situations where the person has alcohol abuse/addiction and a concurrent depressive disorder (Doweiko, 2002). However, the findings of clinical trials using SSRIs for the treatment of persons struggling with alcoholic use without co-occurring psychiatric disorders have been equivocal, and further research is indicated (Cornelius, Salloum, Ehler, Jarrett, & Perel, 1997; Fils-Aime et al., 1996; Johnson, 2001; Kranzler, 2000).

Buspirone Buspirone (Buspar) is commonly used to treat anxiety disorders (refer to Chapter 6). Research has suggested that buspirone may be useful in diminishing the anxiety and worry associated with abstinence (Meza & Kranzler, 1996; Schuckit, 1996) rather than in reducing the rewarding effects of alcohol-related behaviors per se. Any potential benefit from this medication is probably limited to those with alcohol dependency and co-occurring anxiety disorders, but further research is needed (Malec, Malec, & Dongier, 1996).

Ondansetron The most promising serotonergic medication for treating alcoholism appears to be the $5HT_3$ antagonist ondansetron, which has been shown to reduce alcohol intake (Johnson et al., 2000). Drawing on the knowledge that early-onset alcoholism might reflect a serotonergic system dysfunction, Johnson and Ait-Daoud (1999) conducted research that used a serotonin-blocking agent that focused its effects on the $5HT_3$ receptor subtype. Findings showed the use of ondansetron reduced the person's desire to drink and the subjective experience of pleasure if the individual did drink. These findings are consistent with literature positing serotonin dysfunction among early-onset alcoholism (Swann, Johnson, Cloninger, & Chen, 1999).

Dopamine Antagonists   Although medications that directly affect dopamine functioning would appear to be promising candidates for alcoholism treatment, experimental results have not been encouraging (DiChiara, 1997). A variety of dopamine antagonists, such as the antipsychotic medications haloperidol (Haldol) and tiapride have been shown to decrease alcohol use. However, an important side-effect quandary associated with using these medications is their potential to produce neurological side effects such as movement disorders and seizures.

Exploring the New Vistas of Pharmacotherapy   Expanded large-scale clinical trials exploring effective pharmacotherapy that include an examination of the mu receptor antagonist nalmefene and antagonists of the delta opioid receptor (e.g., naltriben and naltrindole) in alcoholic populations are needed. Zofran, a medication typically used to prevent the side effects of nausea during chemotherapy, has been reported as beneficial in the treatment of early-onset alcoholism (those who started drinking heavily before the age of 25). Sertaline (Zoloft), an antidepressant, was found in several studies to be helpful in reducing drinking in those with late-onset alcoholism.

Calcium Channel Antagonists   Calcium has many physiological functions throughout the body and is required for nerve cell activity. Medications that interfere with the passage of calcium into cells (for example, calcium channel blockers) are prescribed to treat hypertension and other cardiovascular conditions; examples include nifedipine (Adalat) and verapamil (Calan). There are some clinical suggestions that these medications may decrease alcohol consumption (Rush & Pazzaglia, 1998). However, further studies are needed.

The specialized role of self-help groups, particularly Alcoholics Anonymous, in treating substance abuse is addressed next.

Twelve-Step and Self-Help Groups

Looking at the risks and vulnerabilities for those who are struggling with substance abuse, self-help groups are beneficial in diminishing isolation and denial on a personal level and providing opportunities for mutual aid and fellowship (Felix-Ortiz, Salazar, Gonzalez, Sorenson, & Plock, 2000). Of all the treatments for alcohol misuse, Alcoholics Anonymous is, without question, the most popular self-help model (Rotgers, Morgenstern, & Walters, 2003). This "12-step" program was developed by Alcoholics Anonymous (AA) founders William "Bill W" Wilson and Robert "Dr. Bob" Holbrook Smith in 1935. Central to its design, Alcoholics Anonymous works independently from the established medical community. It is predicated on two assumptions: alcoholism is a disease, and persons struggling with alcohol use must acknowledge their addiction to alcohol and its destructive power over them. Within this approach, addiction to alcohol is seen as more powerful than any single individual, and therefore the individual must look to others to help overcome his or her addiction. AA aims at helping people by providing a new social network (through group meetings and/or daily telephone contact) that replaces the alcohol abuser's usual circle of friends who drink with them. AA's social network provides its members with fellowship, inspiration, and support toward the goal of reaching and maintaining abstinence.

Since its inception in 1935, Alcoholics Anonymous has progressively expanded to include over 25,000 groups holding more than 30,000 meetings all over the world (Nathan, 1993; Saporito, 2001). Alcoholics Anonymous inspired the development of numerous other self-help groups, including Narcotics Anonymous, Al-Anon, Adult Children of Alcoholics, Nar-Anon Family Group, Overeaters Anonymous, Emotions Anonymous, and Co-dependents Anonymous. Other 12-step type programs include Women for Sobriety (WFS), Secular Organizations for Sobriety, SMART Recovery, and Rational Recovery Systems (RR) (Miller, 1999).

From the 1940s through the early 1980s a few studies were conducted regarding AA, but they did not directly evaluate the AA's effectiveness. Rather, the researchers examined AA's organizational structure, functioning, and history. Given the limited empirical base at that time, many clinicians and researchers doubted whether AA truly helped its members recover from alcohol dependence (Humphries, 1999). In the 1990s the National Institute on Alcohol Abuse and Alcoholism (NIAAA) sponsored several collaborative studies to look at the AA program. The benefits were supported through the use of reliable measures. The improved methodological quality of research reduced the skepticism in the treatment community about AA's effectiveness and increased practitioner interest in facilitating connections between substance-related treatment and 12-step self-help groups. In a survey by Room (1993), over 3 percent of the adult population in the United States reported having attended an AA meeting. In AA, participants take part in a series of mental, written, and verbal activities that can lead to recovery and abstinence. Several clinical trials found those who regularly participated in AA meetings and followed its guidelines were more likely to have a positive outcome (Emrick, Tonigan, & Montgomery, 1993; Fiorentine & Anglin, 1996; Fiorentine & Anglin, 1997; Fiorentine, 1999).

Detoxification

For many, drinking alcohol is just a pleasant way to kick off one's shoes and relax; for example, a person might drink a few beers while watching Monday night football. However, people with alcohol use disorders drink to excess, endangering both themselves and others. For most adults, moderate alcohol use is ingesting no more than two drinks a day for men and one drink for women and older persons. Moderate use that is considered relatively harmless lies at one end of the continuum that moves through alcohol abuse to alcohol dependence. People with alcoholism (technically referred to as alcohol dependence) have lost reliable control of their alcohol use. It really doesn't matter what kind of alcohol someone drinks or even the amount ingested, as the alcohol-dependent person is unable to stop drinking once he or she starts. The use of alcohol is characterized by tolerance; that is, the need to drink more to achieve the same "high" and the presence of withdrawal symptoms if drinking is suddenly stopped. Some people with drinking problems work very hard to resolve them. Often with the support of family and friends, individuals are able to achieve sobriety on their own and without outside intervention. There are others with drinking problems who cannot stop drinking through willpower alone and require outside help (Franken & Hendriks, 1999).

The abrupt termination of alcohol consumption in one who has consumed alcohol regularly often leads to a variety of clinical symptoms that are collectively called alcohol withdrawal syndrome (Giannini, 2000; Saitz, 1998). Symptoms range from mild irritability, insomnia, and tremors to potentially life-threatening medical complications such as hallucinations, delirium tremens, or seizures (American Psychiatric Association, 2000). Consequently, before an individual begins long-term alcoholism treatment, he or she often requires a detoxification period. Under strict medical supervision the person becomes alcohol-free. There are several advantages of outpatient detoxification; specifically, the individual may be able to use the same facility for both detoxification and subsequent long-term outpatient treatment, and may be more easily able to maintain family and social supports (Hayashida, 1998; Sayre, Schmitz, Stotts, & Averill, 2002). However, outpatient detoxification is not appropriate for everyone. Individuals who are at risk for life-threatening symptoms, have serious medical conditions, are suicidal or homicidal, live in disruptive family settings, or cannot travel daily to the treatment facility are not candidates. Finally, individuals undergoing outpatient treatment are at an increased risk of relapse, especially during or shortly after detoxification, because they have easier access to alcohol than they would have in an inpatient setting (Hayashida, 1998; Mattick & Hall, 1996).

Detoxification is the process of removing drugs or other harmful substances from an individual for a sufficient length of time to allow for the restoration of adequate physiological and psychological functioning. The first goal is to help the client achieve detoxification in a safe and comfortable way and then foster motivation to enter rehabilitation treatment. Detoxification is generally offered either in residential or hospital inpatient programs. In both cases, the individual is provided with highly structured services that include rest, proper diet, health care, medication, emotional support, and social services (Fuller & Hiller-Sturmhöfel, 1999) including group therapy, individual therapy, and education about alcoholism. Additionally, professional staff members are available around-the-clock to help manage the individual's acute medical and psychological problems, especially during the initial treatment period of detoxification. Effective detoxification programs include careful physical and psychiatric examinations, provide appropriate treatment of withdrawal symptoms, and make an effort to prevent future medical difficulties and relapse. Examinations conducted by a physician provide critical information regarding the client's diagnosis, management, and assessment of potentially life-threatening complications such as sepsis (severe blood infection) or severe malnutrition (Zide, 2002). Further, people who are going through detoxification may need to be treated for delirium or for mood and affective disturbances exhibited by symptoms of panic, anxiety, depression, and transient or persistent hallucinatory phenomena.

Because of escalating health care costs, the focus in recent years has shifted away from inpatient treatment for all stages of alcohol recovery (Adrian, 2001; Hudson, 2001). Outpatient detoxification programs that are less expensive than inpatient treatment are currently emphasized (Finney, Hahn, & Moos, 1996). The vast majority of individuals with alcohol dependency problems are treated in outpatient facilities where the services offered include day hospital programs (the individual goes to the hospital for several hours a day, several days a week). This type of program was developed as an alternative to inpatient programs and allows the person to maintain his or her family roles while at the same time receiving treatment. Less intensive outpatient treatment generally involves group sessions, individual, family, or couple sessions, and aftercare, all of which provide maintenance support after the client has received the initial inpatient or intensive outpatient treatment.

RISKS ASSOCIATED WITH SUBSTANCE-RELATED DISORDERS

Intrapersonal Risks

Begleiter and Kissin (1995) observe that some people seem to have a biological vulnerability for substance abuse, particularly alcohol dependence. Heavy drinking may result in difficulty walking, blurred vision, slurred speech, slowed reaction times, or impaired memory (National Institute on Alcohol Abuse and Alcoholism, 2004). Some impairments are apparent after only one or two drinks and others may result in persistent and longer-term brain defects. Prolonged heavy drinking increases the risk of damage to the liver that can lead to a serious and potentially fatal brain disorder known as hepatic encephalopathy (Butterworth, 2003). Hepatic encephalopathy can cause changes in mood and personality, anxiety and depression, and severe cognitive effects such as shortened attention span along with problems with coordination such as shaking or flapping of the hands (referred to as asterixis).

In addition, those with a family history of alcoholism and/or drug addiction are at a higher risk for developing substance abuse problems. Researchers have also identified intrapersonal (or personal) factors contributing to an increased risk, including low self-esteem, low self-confidence, greater rebelliousness, impulsivity, and co-occurring mental disorders (Chilcoat & Johanson, 1998; Goldman, 1998; Hanson, 2001; Hilarski & Wodarski, 2001). Further, individuals who are alienated from conventional norms and institutions, such as school or family, and who lack respect for authority or are vulnerable to peer pressure are at an increased risk for drug abuse (Jessor & Jessor, 1977). Age is another factor. Those between the ages of 21 and 24 are at the greatest risk for drug use (Kandel & Chen, 2000).

Sexual orientation and gender identity can also pose risk factors for the substance-related disorders (Cruz & Peralta, 2001). Emerging research suggests that alcohol, tobacco, and drug related problems may be higher among gay, lesbian, and bisexual people due to marketing strategies of pharmaceutical, alcohol, and tobacco conglomerates that specifically target these communities (Cabaj, 1997; Drabble, 2000; Pecoraro, 2000; Ungvarski & Grossman, 1999; Warn, 1997).

Gender is another risk factor (Comfort, Loverro, & Kaltenbach, 2002; Karroll & Memmott, 2001; Zelvin, 1997). Women tend to experience more adverse consequences associated with alcoholism. For example, women are more likely than men to develop cirrhosis (Loft, Olesen, & Dossing, 1987), damage of the heart muscle such as cardiomyopathy (Fernandez-Sola et al., 1997), or nerve damage such as peripheral neuropathy (Ammendola et al., 2000). Among women, there is also a high correlation between substance-related disorders, the stigma associated with drug use, and past or current sexual victimization (Blume, 1998; El-Bassel, Ivanoff, Schilling, & Gilbert, 1995; El-Bassel, Schilling, Irwin, Faruque, & Gilbert, 1997; Liebschutz, Mulvey, & Samet, 1997; Marcenko, Kemp, & Larson, 2000; Simpson, 2002); use of family protective services (Littell & Tajima, 2000; Rittner & Dozier, 2000; Smith, 2002); recovery issues (O'Dell, Turner, & Weaver, 1998). Women who are alcohol dependent during pregnancy are at risk of delivering babies with fetal alcohol syndrome and related conditions (Albert, Klein, Noble, & Zahand, 2000; Chasnoff, Anson, & Laukea, 1998; Coles, Kable, Drews-Boysch, & Falek, 2000; Hayes, 1997; Ramlow, White, Watson, & Leukefied, 1997). Hanson (2001) observes that in all ethnic and cultural groups, young men tend to be at greater risk for illegal drug use.

Parental addiction places children at risk for physical, social, and psychological problems (Freeman, Parillo, Collier, & Rusek, 2001; Hurcom, Copello, & Oxford, 2000; Messman-Moore & Long, 2002; Sher, 1991, 1997). Parental alcoholism has also been directly linked to conduct disorders, poor academic performance, inattentiveness (Owings-West & Prinz, 1987), antisocial personality disorder (Silverman, 1989), and suicide (Cornelius, Kirisci, & Tarter, 2001; Hurcom, Copello, & Oxford, 2000; Nugent & Williams, 2001). Lastly, children of an alcoholic parent (or parents) are at a greater risk of using alcohol or other drugs of abuse (Sher, Walitzer, Wood, & Brent, 1991).

Conversely, the elderly population is also at risk (Marks, 2002; Rigler, 2000; Schilling & El-Bassel, 1998). In our culture, it is easy to ignore or overlook the fact that older people may struggle with alcoholism. Often medication taken for other medical conditions interacts adversely with alcohol use. The author recalls overhearing a conversation among a group of elders seated at the next table in a local restaurant. After the group had ordered a round of alcoholic drinks, the conversation drifted to how each had altered their medication earlier in the day to plan for the drink. Some commented on how expensive it is to drink outside of the home.

Does culture play a role in substance-related disorders (Jones-Webb, 1998; Markward, Dozier, Hooks, & Markward, 2000)? Native Americans between the ages of 25 and 44 years drink more than members of other ethnic groups and suffer the highest rates of drinking-related accidents (Nixon, Phillips, & Tivis, 2000; Taylor, 2000). African-Americans and people in other non-dominant cultures tend to see problems with addiction as secondary to other critical issues including racism, poverty, and oppression (Jones-Webb, 1998; Markarian & Franklin, 1998; Randolph, Stroup-Benham, Black, & Markides, 1998; Stewart, 2002). Treatment approaches are not always attentive to cultural differences. As Inclan and Hernandez (1992) so aptly state:

> The clinical approach to codependence, when examined cross-culturally, emerges as a value laden Anglo cultural narrative whose applicability to poor Hispanic patients need review. The changes the client and family are

implicitly expected to accomplish for recovery from this disease are in conflict with an important Hispanic family value: familism. Therefore, the question arises: are the client and family expected to change their cultural family values and beliefs for the sake of recovery? (p. 246).

Interpersonal Risks

From a systems perspective, a substance disorder can promote a dysfunctional family system when the unit adapts to the addiction of one of its members. Alcoholism, for example, becomes the "family secret" and the family's rules and rituals are organized around the person's addiction. Heath and Stanton (1998) observe that the alcohol use of one parent may even help the family to cope with other problems. Family life revolves around the pathology of a single member and dysfunctional family systems are maintained as the member's substance abuse becomes a stabilizing force within the family (Hurcom, Copello, & Oxford, 2000). This process of adaptation leads to unhealthy family themes where individuals are left on their own to struggle with the dysfunction within the family (Bradshaw, 1988). For example, a mother's drug addiction might leave an older sibling to assume responsibility for preparing meals for the rest of the family. For some families, "chaos (covert or overt), inconsistency, unpredictability, blurring of boundaries, unclear roles, arbitrariness, changing logic, and perhaps violence and incest" (Brown & Lewis, 1995, p. 285) become the norm (Dube, Anda, Felitti, Croft, & Edwards, 2001; Lauer & Lauer, 2002; Medrano, Hatch, Zule, & Desmond, 2002).

Community and Environmental Risks

Almost 20 years ago, Akers (1985) observed that the United States is a "drug-saturated society." Over-the-counter and prescription drugs are increasingly promoted in television advertisements and exert a powerful influence on societal attitudes. The societal context influences a person's decision to use mood-altering substances, and the cumulative effects of substance abuse correlate with other community and environmental risk factors such as poverty, unemployment, discrimination, and poor health care. People living in communities characterized by poverty are at greater risk to use drugs (Chilcoat & Johanson, 1998; Myers, 2002). Neighborhoods where services are inadequate and residents feel alienated have also been linked with addictive behaviors (Hawkins et al., 1992; Turner, 1997; van Dalen, 2001). Persons who are homeless are at increased risk for substance-related disorders (Carroll & Trull, 2002; Cohen, 2001; Rodell, Benda, & Rodell, 2001; Sosin & Bruni, 2000).

Culture also influences the risk for substance use. The protective factors that exist in more traditional ethnic cultures, such as an emphasis on cooperation, sharing, communality, group support, interdependence, and social responsibility, are believed to mitigate against the social alienation associated with substance abuse (Diller, 2004). Unfortunately, as ethnic group members acculturate, their substance use patterns begin to approximate those of the dominant group. However, Castillo (1997) notes,

> because the symptoms of substance dependence usually involve physiological changes such as substance tolerance and withdrawal that are relatively invariant regardless of cultural influences, the concept of substance dependence remains relatively constant across cultural boundaries for many substances (p. 165).

In the United States, the predominant definition of alcoholism defines the condition as a progressive physical disease for which there is no cure (Castillo, 1997; Doweiko, 2002). According to the philosophy of Alcoholics Anonymous, the only successful treatment strategy is complete abstinence. The approach to treatment is detoxification followed by an in-patient stay in a treatment facility where the person is introduced to the AA model of being powerless over the "disease." This cultural construction can affect a person's subjective experience of illness, how they describe their struggle with substance use, and interactions with others. Ultimately, effective and successful treatment depends on an appreciation of both the uniqueness of each client and the social milieu in which they are being served (Friedman, 2000; Lewis, Dana, & Blevins, 2002).

CASE ILLUSTRATION: LUKE ROSSEY

The following case vignette highlights various aspects of working with a client who is well known to the mental health community. Mr. Rossey was previously diagnosed with antisocial personality disorder (refer to Zide & Gray, 2001) and currently presents with a substance-related disorder.

Following his most recent court appearance for driving under the influence (DUI), driving without a valid driver's license, resisting arrest including battery on the arresting officer, and three outstanding warrants for prior arrests, Mr. Rossey was remanded to Kenninger's Drug Rehabilitation Program, an inpatient drug and alcohol treatment center. Mr. Rossey's sister, Sara, accompanied him to the intake interview.

I escorted Sara and Mr. Rossey into my office, and once they were settled I began some preliminary introductions. I briefly made a cursory assessment of Mr. Rossey and his sister. He was dressed in threadbare and somewhat dirty clothing and appeared disheveled. It looked as if he was in immediate need of a hot shower, clean clothes, and a cooked meal. Sara Rossey was on the verge of tears and held tightly onto her brother's hand. I made a mental note to remind myself to introduce Mr. Rossey to Ricky Coniglio, BSW, one of our top-notch case managers who has a reputation for cutting through "the red tape" and who could enable Mr. Rossey to have his needs cared for immediately. But that's later. This is now.

I introduced myself and explained my job as a social worker at Kenninger's. I described my role of helping Luke through the intake process, detoxification, and later participation in our program. I asked Mr. Rossey and his sister why they felt they were here at Kenninger's. Mr. Rossey said, "I don't like to be called Mr., so you can just call me Luke." He then said softly to his sister, "You tell the shrink the whole damn pitiful story. I'm too tired." And so Sara supplied the following intake information.

"My brother Luke is 23 years old and he works as a cable installer, at least this week, that is. My brother has had at least 20 different jobs, and he just can't seem to keep any of them." She added that her brother was really a smart person. When he was in high school, Luke's IQ "scored somewhere up in the 160s." She continued, "Luke was small for his age and lots of times some of the bigger kids in the neighborhood would pick on him and tease him. While nobody could ever prove it, I always suspected that Luke drowned two dogs and a kitten, because they were the pets of the two boys who used to make the most fun of him."

Luke perked up at this remark and added, "I never did anything like that. Those boys were always lying and trying to get me into trouble."

Sara went on, "Anyway, after that, Luke sorta got a reputation as 'the bad boy.' Our dad died from a drug overdose when Luke was only six years old. As we grew up, our mother filled in the blanks about our father. Dad had lots of problems not only with drugs, but alcohol too. Mom told us he would go to the bar with his friends on Friday night and not come home until Sunday night. Mom said Dad used to waste his whole paycheck on alcohol. She told us that just after Luke was born our dad went to prison for two years. We never really knew the reason, but we figured out it was for some kind of domestic altercation with our grandmother . . . the one on my mother's side of the family."

Sara took a sip of water, paused, and then continued, "Mom raised the two of us all by herself, but she just couldn't seem to control Luke. When he was about 13 or so he got involved with a bunch of gang-banger punks. Then Luke started to fail in school, had lots of suspensions, and stole anything he could from his classmates. A couple of times he threatened to 'kill' one of his teachers. Said he was going to 'burn the school down.' Even in those days threats like that were pretty big deals."

Sara continued, "Luke was sent to juvie hall for assaulting a police officer while the poor ol' cop was just trying to break up a street fight. Some kind of court-appointed shrink told the judge that Luke had a poor childhood and was the victim of something called 'conduct disorder.' The court just slapped Luke's wrist and sent him to some country club youth ranch for nine months. When he got out he went right back to his old ways. He boozed it up all the time and took any kind of drug he could get his hands on. He was busted for selling drugs to an undercover narc and eventually court ordered into a drug treatment program. Some program! He'd go in for a week and later check out, and go right back to the streets and trouble. He had some DUIs and a few warrants out for his arrest, but I don't know all the details."

Sara began to cry quietly into an obviously shredded and worn tissue. With tears once again threatening to brim over her eyes, Sara continued, "I'm sorry. I just can't seem to keep all of Luke's stuff straight. I hope I'm not jumping around too much."

This worker reassured her that everything she said was understood. I glanced over to Luke but could not tell if he was dozing or listening. I decided not to rouse him. Sara continued, "Everything came to a head after Luke stole an antique heirloom wedding ring from our mom. She finally threw him out of the house and told him to 'never come back.' Luke joined the Army, but soon after he got into some trouble there too. I found out he got court-martialed for beating up his commanding officer. I'm not really sure of what happened, but the Army tossed Luke out."

"When Luke returned home, his girlfriend Alyssa told him she was 5 months pregnant. Luke called her a liar, and she began to raise the baby all by herself. I don't know exactly what happened, but when he heard the baby was born, Luke went over to see him. The story I got was that Alyssa let Luke name the baby. He must have had a change of heart, because he named the baby Lucas Webster Rossey. That little guy looks just like Luke, too. And that's the name that went on the baby's birth certificate. Luke really took an interest in the baby. When the baby came home from the hospital Luke started bringing over bags of diapers and cans of formula. He went over Alyssa's parents' house to help bathe and feed Lucas. All Luke could talk about was that baby and how smart he was. I guess I got my hopes up thinking how things might be turning around for Luke. I was so hopeful. I don't know what happened to cause his drinking and drugging again. I just want him to get help and stay away from alcohol and drugs. Now that Luke has a son he has to realize that he has more to live for than ever before."

Luke was subsequently admitted to the detoxification phase of Kenninger's program. He was immediately given time to care for his personal needs, and this was followed with a hot meal and clean clothes. Afterward, he underwent a medical and psychiatric evaluation as the first step toward recovery. His course of treatment was unremarkable. He began to sleep and eat better and interacted with staff members and other residents. He even gained a little weight, making him look much better.

Two weeks later Luke was seen by this social worker and introduced to the next phase of treatment. The following is a brief synopsis of our first conversation.

After introductions were remade I asked Luke why he thought he had been court-ordered to the Kenninger program. He did not acknowledge any problems, but rather stated, "I was in the wrong place at the wrong time. If it weren't for that damn cop I wouldn't be here. The cops have it in for me." I then began to ask him a series of questions to gather further information.

"Luke, what kinds of things happened during your life that would cause you to be court ordered for treatment of your alcohol and drug usage?"

He replied, "I don't see what everybody's problem is. I drink and smoke. Hell, everybody does!"

"I understand from what Sara told me your first day here that your father had a history of alcohol problems. Has this been a problem for anyone else in your family?"

He replied, "No. Just my old man died a drunk. So what?"

"Luke, when was the last time you used alcohol or drugs?"

He replied, "Now, now, now" (wagging his index finger at me), "don't you go trying to trip me up. If I tell you anything, I sure could get into a heap of trouble with my parole officer. I figure the less I say in here the less you can tell on me."

This seemed like the perfect segue to re-introduce confidentiality issues with Luke. We spoke about what kinds of things would remain between us and what types of things would be reported to his probation officer. He seemed doubtful but said he'd "give it a shot."

"Luke, can you tell me the names of the different drugs you've tried?"

He replied, "Well, I could tell you that, but I don't know if I remember them all. Let's see . . . hmm . . . I used to use 'boom' (hashish), reefer (marijuana), red birds 'n' yellow jackets (barbiturates), hog (PCP), pancakes and syrup (codeine), smack or is it horse (heroin), Miss Emma (morphine), and shrooms (psilocybin) when I can find em. Hey, Mrs. Social Worker, how'd I do?"

Before I could reply, he continued (shaking his index finger at me once again), "You forgot to ask me about alcohol. That's a drug, too, isn't it?"

I replied, "Yes, it is."

Luke stated, "I'm just like my ol' man, because I like the juice. I guess I was about 8 or 10 years old when I had my first drink of beer. Right away, I liked the way it made me feel. Soon after that I started drinking the stuff regularly. Then I took it from the liquor cabinet in the living room. Mom never drank, so she never knew I was drinking. To keep her from finding out I made a bunch of tea and poured it into the bottles to make them look like they were the real thing. Ha."

"Luke, what is your drug of choice?"

He replied, "Well, I have two favorites and both for different reasons. I love smoking crack, but it's not cheap; and I like alcohol because it is cheap." I made a note of how Luke used drugs.

"Could you describe your pattern of use?"

He shrugged his shoulders and replied, "When I can get crack I use it. When I can get liquor I drink it. What else is there left to say?" (He smiled at this, and my first thought was that he was smiling like a Cheshire Cat.)

"When you were in 'detox' before, what helped you stay sober?" He replied, "These places are all the same to me. Once you're there they fill your head with stuff like 'just say no,' or 'trust in a higher power.' And then there's the HALT stuff. You know, 'hungry, angry, lonely, and tired.' If they're not mouthing fancy sayings to you then they're trying giving you a bunch of psycho tests. I am not into that!"

He spoke passionately for a few minutes about his previous treatment experiences. I then reminded him of the parts to the question he had not responded to. He continued, "I've been in all those places you mentioned, and detox is the worst. I have been able to stay away from drugs and booze for a few weeks, but I always go back to what makes me feel good. I mean, why live life if you can't enjoy it. Right?" It was this worker's impression that Luke has not achieved success for any length of time previously until now.

"When you were in treatment, what did you find was most helpful?"

He replied, "I remember this one social worker who was cool. She didn't harp or nag at me if I did something wrong. We used to talk about the things I did right and how I could keep on the right track." I explored where his previous treatment had occurred and the name of this social worker. He replied, "I think her name was Terry Blake or something like that, and she was working someplace downtown." This worker did not inform Luke (at that time) that Theresa Blake was currently employed at this clinic. I needed to make sure she was available, as it had crossed my mind that perhaps Luke could be transferred to her caseload.

Later that same afternoon, I walked over to Terry's office and luckily found her at her desk catching up on some paperwork. I told her about Luke, and she said she remembered him. She told me, "I'll be happy to transfer him to my caseload." I was pleased to hear that Terry would work with Luke. She is a very capable practitioner who has a great deal of experience working in the addiction field. In addition to being a licensed clinical social worker and having her certified addiction professional (CAP) credentials, she works with clients using a cognitive-behavioral approach. She runs several treatment groups and alcohol education groups for families, partners, and significant others. Terry is also responsible for coordinating the various aftercare and 12-step programs offered at Kenninger. She is also extremely patient and giving. It seemed to me that Luke was really challenging when we talked about his substance use, and Terry's qualities would be a real asset to the work ahead.

I asked Terry how she might approach working with Luke again. She replied, "First step, right off the bat, is he must want to be drug-free. If he doesn't, then anything I try to do or say will just go in one ear and out the other. So what I might start out with is asking Luke, 'What do you really want?' I know that sounds like basic social work, but it's where you have to begin. From there we might talk about what he wants to see happen from our work together. For me, I like to formally write out a contract between myself and my client as a way to delineate and clarify exactly what we are going to do, how we're going to do it, and what we are working toward."

Terry continued, "I remember Luke as being a very bright young man. I think he might respond well to a cognitive-behavioral approach. You know, I really like this approach because together we work as a team. Generally, my focus is to help Luke recognize what triggers his drinking and drug-using behaviors and how he copes with cravings. I like to use role-playing and homework assignments and then talk about them in the next session. I also focus on ways to manage negative moods, and looking for other reasons for living than a focus on drinking. As a social worker, I'm troubled so many people believe once they stop drinking or using drugs their problems are automatically cured. It's like when someone who drank or used drugs out of control and hasn't for 30 days, well, things must be OK now. That way of thinking is really a misconception. Rather than thinking 'cure'" (Terry used her fingers to motion the application of quotation marks), "we have to start educating folks that successful treatment must be seen as a process and continuum. I'll tell you what, the 12-step program has the right idea. Members are encouraged to work on their sobriety 'one day at a time.' Oh, goodness me! I do go on and on. I've probably talked your ear off. Sorry."

This worker asked Terry specifically what cognitive-behavioral techniques she generally uses. "Well, there are a lot of really neat ways to work within this approach, and I especially like using 'self-monitoring,' 'goal setting', 'self-talk', and 'modifying drug-using behavior.' You know as well as I do that all sorts of therapy techniques or medication support aren't going to be enough. Luke's going to need to stay connected to the aftercare program after the formal treatment is completed. Actually, the term 'aftercare' is misleading because its services should not be viewed as short-term but as a continuum of care to prevent relapse. Also, Luke must take part in the center's alcohol and drug education program and regularly attend a 12-step program if he wants to remain successful. From experience we know that Luke is not going to recover alone, because it's a process. We'll make a concerted effort to involve his family and friends. (Tapping her finger to her cheek) I remember he had a sister who was very supportive of him. Is she still in the picture?"

This worker replied, "Yes, in fact, Sara provided most of the intake information you'll read. I don't know whether or not you remember, but Luke's mother also lives nearby. Sara said the relationship between Luke and his mom is strained, but perhaps repairing their relationship might be one goal to work on. Also, I know you aren't aware of this, but Luke has an infant son named Lucas. I wish I had enough time to tell you the whole story, but the short version is before Luke went into the service his girlfriend Alyssa became pregnant. After he was dishonorably discharged a few months later he came back home. According to Sara, Luke wanted nothing to do with Alyssa at first, said she was lying, and denied being the baby's father. I'm really not sure what happened, and this is something you'll probably want to talk with him about, but Luke started going over to Alyssa's parents' house and visiting the baby. He proudly described giving Lucas his evening bath. He also brings over diapers and baby food. Actually, it was the only time I saw Luke smile during our two sessions together."

Terry went on, "I'm always glad when we come across client support and strengths. Certainly we want Luke not only to become successful, but live chemical-free and be able to handle the impending threat of relapse. Part of our work will include examining specific situations that might lead to a 'slip.' Together we'll certainly discuss Luke's negative emotions, interpersonal conflicts, social pressures, and life style issues associated with past relapses. Also, part of our work will be to try and figure out what sort of sequence of warning signs he must learn in order to recognize and prevent a relapse. This time around we can focus on exploring positive things in Luke's life—for example, his relationships with Sara, Lucas, Alyssa, and his mother.

"First off, though, Luke and I'll try and formulate a treatment plan." She readily clicked off the following elements, and I remembered thinking that she was really good at working in the substance abuse field. Terry noted, "We'll need a problem statement that includes describing Luke's life history and drug use; long-term goals—for example, how he plans to remain abstinent from using all chemicals. We'll also need short-term objectives, such as how Luke plans to remain abstinent from all chemicals for 30 days; attending one AA or NA meeting every day for 90 days . . . No excuses! Going to all Kenninger's program and educational lectures; three individual counseling sessions every week; becoming a member in a support group four times per week; and taking part in one family counseling session each week." She added, "I guess you could say Luke and I have our work cut out for us."

We said our goodbyes, and I must admit I had a good feeling about Luke's chances to get through our program and get his life on track.

OPERATIONALIZING COMPETENCY-BASED TREATMENT

The issues surrounding substance abuse and how they affect the individual, his or her family, and the community remain a major challenge to the social work profession (Gruber, Fleetwood, & Herring, 2001). The competency-based model of treatment provides a framework in which to examine health-promoting behaviors across the life course and focus on those environments in the client's life that promote health, family, and community well-being. Looking at Luke Rossey's history of substance use beginning at about 8 years of age, it becomes important for the social worker to begin identifying those protective factors and buffers that could potentially help sustain him throughout treatment; particularly since Luke has had several prior attempts to treat his substance abuse (refer to Table 11.1). Some of these factors include strong and positive bonds with his son Lucas, a connection (though strained) with family members in his life; a brief period of success in the military, and conventional patterns of behavior related to his substance use (Friedman, 2000; Johnson, 2000; Okundaye, Smith, & Lawrence-Webb, 2001).

TABLE 11.1 THE RISKS, PROTECTIVE FACTORS, AND BUFFERS IN LUKE ROSSEY'S LIFE

	Risk Factors	Protective Factors and Buffers
Intrapersonal	Polysubstance abuse • Drugs • Alcohol	Intelligent
		Brief periods of abstinence from drugs/alcohol
	Denial of substance abuse	Good overall health
	History of substance abuse beginning at age 8	Cooperative with social worker (in past treatment experience)
	Prior attempts at treatment	
	Prior diagnosis of antisocial personality disorder	Periods of relatively stable functioning
Interpersonal	Unable to hold a job	Sister (Sara) involved during the intake interview
	Father died of drug overdose	
	Family history of alcohol abuse (father)	Positive (prior) relationship with the social worker
	Dishonorable discharge from military services (U.S. Army)	Cooperative with rehabilitation programs for periods of time
	Strained relationship with mother	Brief periods of success in military service, school, work
		Involved with substance abuse programs (past and current)
Social and Environmental	Court charges pending • DUI • Resisting arrest • Battery • Prior arrest warrants	Range of services available and accessible
	Prior legal involvement while an adolescent	Continuum of services provided by the agency and monitored by a case manager

Although Luke's sister had participated in the intake interview, she was hesitant to become involved further. Treatment began with Luke's admission into detoxification.

Working with Luke Individually

In this case vignette, the social worker, Terry Blake, plans on having a conversation with Luke about whether he will consider a treatment plan that includes total abstinence (Walitzer & Connors, 1999). Luke was mandated into treatment as a consequence of legal charges associated with his drug use: DUI, resisting arrest, and battery on the arresting officer. After the preliminary intake interview, he was subsequently admitted into detoxification. During this phase of treatment, medications will certainly help decrease the intensity of substance-related cravings. However, when partnered with the competency-based model, focusing on the strengths in Luke's life taps into his ability to persist in the face of obstacles and to move forward with the challenges associated with his substance abuse treatment regimen. Saleebey (1996) refers to this as "a practice based on the ideas of resilience, rebound, possibility, and transformation" (p. 297).

Treatment for Luke's substance disorder centers on several areas, and the first step is to help him through the withdrawal process. While the ultimate goal of all substance-related treatment is to enable the client to achieve lasting abstinence, the immediate goals for Luke are to reduce substance use, improve his ability to function, and minimize the medical, social, and personal complications of abuse. Treating people with substance-related issues is not a simple matter of finding just the right drug or the best way to change thoughts or behaviors (Barlow & Durand, 2005; Haack, 1998; Moore, 2002). Luke's case vignette is exemplary of the many clients who come into treatment programs juggling several other life events and circumstances in addition to substance-related problems, such as unemployment, domestic violence, other forms of drug abuse, and involvement with the legal system (Alexander, 1996; Alterman et al., 1998; Beeder & Millman, 1995; Bellack & DiClemente, 1999; Daly & Pelowski, 2000; Gomez, Primm, Tzolva-Iontchev, & Perry, 2000; Gortner, Gollan, & Jacobson, 1997; Howard & McCaughrin, 1996; Lehman & Dixon, 1995; Lown & Vega, 2001; Modesto-Lowe & Kranzler, 1999; RachBeisel, Scott, & Dixon, 1999; Ryan, Delva, & Gruber, 2001).

Dual Diagnosis Considerations

Clients who enter treatment for substance abuse should be continually evaluated for concurrent emotional problems (Ziedonis & Brady, 1997). Although this aspect of Luke's history was not explored in the case vignette, Luke Rossey had been previously diagnosed with an antisocial personality disorder (Zide & Gray, 2001). Personality disorders, characterized by persistent and pervasive ways of behaving, can make substance abuse treatment particularly challenging (Ball & Cecero, 2001; Sacks, 2000). Although Luke was readily accepted into the detoxification program and favorably remembered by his former social worker, Terry Blake, most clients unfortunately are rejected because of a dual diagnosis (Polcin, 1992). In these instances, clients can "fall through the cracks" of service delivery systems and not receive the kind of help they really need.

Many of the diagnostic criteria for antisocial personality disorder are common to drug dependent individuals. The case vignette underscores the importance of the practitioner's careful (and ongoing) assessment in order to try to discern when Luke's personality characteristics emerged: were these behaviors in place before his drug use or after Luke began abusing drugs? As the case vignette notes, he had been reported to have started abusing drugs at an early stage of development, approximately age 8. Buelow and Buelow (1998) list the following features of antisocial personality disorder typically found in many clients who are drug dependent: "(1) failure to conform to social norms or laws; (2) conning; (3) impulsivity or failure to plan ahead; (4) irritability and aggressiveness; (5) reckless disregard for self or others; (6) consistent irresponsibility; (7) lack of remorse as indicated by rationalizing" (p. 155). The case vignette raises the question of whether Luke's antisocial traits are really secondary to his drug abuse.

Case Management

Upon admission into detoxification Luke was assigned to a case manager in order to assure the coordination of treatment, current and longer-term, and the resources of all who would be involved in his care. Case management in the field of substance abuse raises a number of concerns (Najavits, Crits-Christoph, & Dierberger, 2000; Sullivan, 2002). Many clients like Luke Rossey come into treatment programs with a history of legal charges (often related to substance abuse) and prior unsuccessful recovery attempts. The case manager's role is to advocate for his or her client. For those involved with the judicial system, this places the practitioner in a potentially awkward position to challenge the appropriateness of the legal charges against the client. Still others perceive the case manager's role as professional "enabling" (Sullivan, Hartmann, Dillon, & Wolk, 1994).

Sullivan (1996, 2002) further observes that those struggling with addiction often interact with others by "denial" and "deceit." These interpersonal ways of relating threaten the case manager-client relationship, in which the qualities of collaboration and cooperation are important. In addition, the competency-based model is built on a relationship of mutuality and genuineness. Rapp (2002) suggests the case manager should confront and reexamine assumptions about clients while at the same time emphasizing strengths.

Cognitive-Behavioral Therapy

One of the greatest challenges for social workers involved in the treatment of clients with substance-related disorders is the prevention of relapse. Many factors are involved in triggering a relapse. Some are internal to the individual, such as a craving for alcohol (Anton, 1999), and others are external, including social pressure to drink, problems in relationships with others, death or serious illness of a family member, or the loss of a job. Environmental cues can also be associated with drinking, such as the smell of alcohol when visiting a tavern, pub, or bar. In Luke's case, his social worker plans to begin their work together by uncovering relapse areas specifically risky for him (Miller, 1999).

Cognitive-behavioral interventions were among the first alcoholism treatment approaches to demonstrate efficacy in reducing drinking in randomized clinical trials (Chaney, O'Leary, & Marlatt, 1978; Oei & Jackson, 1980). Studies support the effectiveness of cognitive-behavioral treatment especially for alcohol problems or poly-substance use when combined with the adjunctive use of medication (Hwang, 1999; Irvin et al., 1999; Ouimette, Finney, & Moos, 1997; Walitzer & Connors, 1999). Over the past 30 years, numerous cognitive-behavioral approaches have been developed to treat substance-related disorders, and the case vignette highlights the practitioner's intentions to use self-monitoring, goal setting, and self-talk with Luke (Miller, Westerberg, & Waldron, 1995; Najavits, 2001).

Cognitive-behavioral treatment provides clients with the skills to recognize and cope with urges to drink by helping them to recognize what triggers drinking, manage negative moods, and orient their social life to focus on something other than drinking. Individuals are presented with techniques and strategies to heighten their awareness of drinking and to reduce drinking and associated risks. To help Luke identify high-risk situations for relapse, particularly ways to deal with his negative moods, the social worker proposes to use role play and homework assignments to help him learn and rehearse different strategies for coping with those situations.

Conclusion

There are many ways to effectively treat persons who struggle with substance-related disorders. The case of Luke Rossey involves the practice methods of individual counseling, involving the family whenever possible, and group work (i.e., self-help groups such as Alcoholics Anonymous). As well, the counseling theories of crisis intervention and cognitive-behavioral therapy, and the services of detoxification including pharmacotherapy, case management, and aftercare are illustrated. At first glance, appropriate treatment goals for substance-related disorders appear quite evident and yet, as the case shows, each person's experiences with substance abuse are different. An individual's decision to use mind-altering substances is made within a sociocultural context, and it is important to recognize there are also cultural differences in substance dependence (Castillo, 1997). As social workers we strive to help all our clients achieve their optimal levels of functioning for as long as possible, and Luke's case vignette illustrates the many resources needed to reach out to clients with substance disorders. The competency-based treatment model guides the practitioner's selection and integration of the many approaches and techniques helpful for the effective treatment of substance disorders. This framework organizes the choices about what will be effective for each individual.

SUMMARY

Substance-related issues remain a serious medical, economic, and societal problem (Galanter, 1998). Clinical literature suggests the potential development of pharmacogenetic strategies to help treat alcohol dependence (Gordis, 2001). One focus is on identification of genetic variations that mediate the differential medication effects in subgroups of clients with alcohol dependence; for example, research in genes coding for the serotonin transporter (or the 5-HT_3 receptor proteins) may someday provide efficacious medications to customize pharmacological treatment (Johnson & Ait-Daoud, 1999; Litten & Allen, 1998; Litten, Allen, & Fertig, 1996).

The continually evolving strengths perspective within social work has provided practitioners with an alternative to practice models that stress pathology and sickness. The underpinnings of competency-based treatment for alcohol and substance-related disorders incorporate resiliency, healing, and wellness (Amodeo & Fassler, 2001; Benard, 1997a; Berg, 1994; Brun & Rapp, 2001; Cade & O'Hanlon, 1993; Cowager, 1994; DeJong & Miller, 1995; Fraser, Richman, & Galinsky, 1999; Homrich & Horne, 2000; Quick, 1996; Saleebey, 1996) while developing a plan of intervention that considers the client's interpersonal and environmental systems (Bentley, 2002). A strengths-based approach is especially important for people struggling with substance disorders who may, because they have so frequently been viewed in terms of what they have failed to do, have learned to define themselves in terms of their limitations and inabilities.

The competency-based treatment model provides a tool for the practitioner to integrate the fundamental principles that characterize treatment of substance abuse clients:

- No single treatment is appropriate for all clients, and the treatment modality should match the type of setting, intervention, and services to a client's specific needs (McNair & Roberts, 1997).
- Motivation and reinforcing factors should be addressed, especially as they pertain to intrapersonal (or personal), interpersonal, and the environmental aspects of a person's life (Read, Kahler, & Stevenson, 2001).
- Effective interventions focus on empathic and non-confrontational styles.
- Education about substance disorders promotes teaching skills that help keep people from using alcohol or drugs (Lochman, 2000).
- Optimal success occurs when programs and services are readily available; clients may not follow through with treatment interventions if services are not immediately available or accessible.
- Effective practice concentrates on responding to multiple client needs and should include addressing substance use as well as associated difficulties such as medical, psychological, social, occupational, and legal issues.
- Treatment needs to be flexible and adaptable while providing continual assessment of the client's current needs (as the client's course of treatment may change).

- For ultimate effectiveness the client should remain in treatment for an "adequate period" of time, and the term "adequate" depends on individual need. However, three months in treatment appears the most optimal. In addition, programs and services should include strategies that help prevent clients from leaving treatment prematurely.
- The practice methods of individual counseling, family and/or group work are important. Treatment should address client motivation, skills employed to resist drug use, replacement of substance-using activities with constructive and rewarding non-drug-using activities, and improvement of problem-solving abilities.
- Effective intervention approaches are built on strengths and call on the client's active efforts to achieve recovery and to help set goals to do so. The promotion of active coping and goal setting is considered essential.
- Medications are an important element of treatment for many clients. Clients who are addicted and/or abusing drugs and also have coexisting mental disorders (dual diagnosis) should have both disorders treated in an integrated way (Kelley & Benshoff, 1997; Skodol, Oldham, & Gallaher, 1999).
- Medical detoxification is only the first stage of addiction treatment.
- Treatment does not need to be voluntary in order to be effective. The endorsement and/or support of the client's family, criminal justice system (Wilson, Rojas, Haapanen, & Duxbury, 2000), or employment setting significantly increases the chances of treatment entry, retention, and successful completion.
- Potential drug use throughout the treatment process must be monitored. Such monitoring can provide early evidence of drug use so that treatment can be adjusted.
- Intervention programs should provide assessment for HIV/AIDS, hepatitis B and C, tuberculosis, and other infectious diseases (Harsch, Pankiewicz, Bloom, Rainey, & Cho, 2000; Lewis, Boyle, Lewis, & Evans, 2000; Rotheram-Borus, Murphy, Kennedy, & Kulinski, 2001; Wilson et al., 2000). This information can help clients avoid high-risk behavior and learn better ways to manage their lives (Broadbent, 1998; Coyle, Needle, & Normand, 1998; DiBisceglie & Bacon, 1999; Dieperink, Willenbring, & Ho, 2000; Latkin, 1998; Needle, 1998).
- Recovery from substance use should be considered a long-term process (National Institute on Drug Abuse, 1999).
- Prevention programs should be long-term, developmentally specific, age-specific, and culturally sensitive (Lee, 1997).
- Family prevention programs can teach skills for better family communication, discipline, rule making, and talking about drugs.
- Community prevention programs need to help strengthen norms against drug use in all drug abuse prevention settings, including the family, the school, the workplace, and the community.

A number of websites sponsored by national organizations may be helpful to the practitioner working with persons who have substance abuse problems:

www.nida.nih.gov   National Institute on Drug Abuse (NIDA)

www.samhsa.gov/centers/csat/csat.html   Center for Substance Abuse Treatment (CSAT)

www.health.org   National Clearinghouse for Alcohol and Drug Information

www.cdc.gov/ncidod/diseases/hepatitis/c/edu/Info/default.htm   Centers for Disease Control and Prevention

www.niaaa.nih.gov   The National Institute on Alcohol Abuse and Alcoholism (NIAAA)

www.samhsa.gov   Substance Abuse and Mental Health Services Administration (SAMHSA)

PRACTITIONER REFLECTIONS

1. Substance-related disorders should be viewed as occurring along a continuum instead of thinking of addiction or alcoholism as an "either/or" dichotomy. This chapter presents the idea that the treatment setting is selected for each client to meet his or her own needs and goals. What implications might these ideas have for working with Luke Rossey?

2. Plan to attend a meeting of a self-help recovery group in your local community, such as Alcoholics Anonymous. Observe member participation, note what seems to be helpful, and reflect on your own personal reaction. Can you think of any barriers to participating in such a group and if so, how might they be addressed? Do you think the program is responsive to persons of various cultural groups (for example, First Nations people)?

3. Imagine that Luke Rossey had been assigned to your caseload.
   • What additional information would you want to know about him? Why? How might this information affect your work with him?
   • Reflect on what you would do if Luke had been in recovery for some time and then started making subtle changes in his life; for example, he stopped attending his 12-step meetings, stopped visiting his young son Lucas, and began to associate with alcohol-using friends. What would you do? Be as specific as you can.

4. Interview a friend or colleague who has given up an "addiction"; for example, cigarettes or coffee. Find out what was the person's greatest struggle and how this was addressed. Did this person give up the addiction several times? If so, what had happened and why did they continue to struggle to give up the addiction?

5. Beginning with the case vignette of Luke Rossey, identify the risks and vulnerabilities associated with *all* clients who struggle with substance-related disorders. Be as comprehensive as you can. Thinking about your own experiences working with clients, identify protective factors and buffers that

might be helpful for working with clients who have substance-related disorders. You might want to complete this "practice reflection" with a colleague or with your supervisor and compare your listing.

6. The purpose of this activity is to foster an understanding of the ways in which your own cultural background and social context influence your thinking about substance-related disorders.

   - Begin by reflecting on your basic assumptions about substance use, and think about how your assumptions are likely to affect your work with clients who struggle with a substance disorder. Be particularly attentive to your beliefs about culture, ethnicity, race, gender, social class, religion, and life style.

   - Identify other cultural beliefs about substance-related disorders. How might cultural differences in substance dependence affect treatment?

References

Aambo, A. (1997). Tasteful solutions: Solution-focused work with groups of immigrants. *Contemporary Family Therapy, 19*(1), 63–79.

Abarbanel, G., & Richman, G. (1990). The rape victim. In H. J. Parad & L. G. Parad (Eds.), *Crisis intervention book 2: The practitioner's sourcebook for brief therapy* (pp. 93–118). Milwaukee, WI: Family Service America.

Ablon, S. J. (2002). Validity of controlled clinical trials of psychotherapy: Findings from the NIMH treatment of depression collaborative research program. *American Journal of Psychiatry, 159*(5), 775–783.

Abood, D., & Black, D. R. (2000). Health education prevention for eating disorders among college female athletes. *American Journal of Health Behavior, 24*(3), 209–219.

Abrams, D. B., Niaura, R., Brown, R. A., Emmons, K. M., Goldstein, M. G., & Monti, P. M. (2003). *The tobacco dependence treatment handbook: A guide to best practices.* New York: Guilford.

Ackerman, N. W. (1958). *The psychodynamics of family life.* New York: Basic Books.

Ackerson, B. J., & Harrison, W. D. (2000). Practitioners' perceptions of empowerment. *Families in Society, 81*(3), 238–244.

Acocella, J. (1999). *Creating hysteria: Women and multiple personality disorder.* San Francisco: Jossey-Bass.

Adams, J. F., Piercy, F. P., & Jurich, J. A. (1991). Effects of solution-focused therapy's "formula first session task" on compliance and outcome in family therapy. *Journal of Marital and Family Therapy, 17*(3), 277–290.

Adams, W. L., & Jones, T. V. (1998). Alcohol and injuries in elderly people. *Addiction Biology, 3,* 237–238.

Adams, W. L., Zhong, Y., Barboriak, J. J., & Rimm, A. A. (1993). Alcohol-related hospitalizations of elderly people: Prevalence and geographic variation in the United States. *Journal of the American Medical Association, 270,* 1222–1225.

Adebimpe, V. R. (1994). Race, racism, and epidemiological surveys. *Hospital and Community Psychiatry, 45,* 27–31.

Adler, A. (1936). The neurotic's picture of the world. *International Journal of Individual Psychology, 2,* 3–10.

Adrian, M. (2001). Do treatments and other interventions work? Some critical issues. *Substance Use and Misuse, 36*(13), 1759–1780.

Agras, W. S. (1994). Disorders of eating: Anorexia nervosa, bulimia nervosa, and binge eating disorder. In R. I. Shader (Ed.), *Manual of psychiatric therapies* (2nd ed., pp. 59–67). Boston: Little, Brown.

Agras, W. S., Walsh, T., Fairburn, C. G., Wilson, G. T., & Kraemer, H. C. (2000). A multi center comparison of cognitive-behavioral therapy and interpersonal psychotherapy for bulimia nervosa. *Archives of General Psychiatry, 57,* 459–466.

Aguilera, D. (1994). *Crisis intervention: Theory and methodology* (7th ed.). St. Louis: Mosby.

Aguilera, D. C. (1998). *Crisis intervention: Theory and methodology* (8th ed.). St. Louis, MO: C. V. Mosby.

Aigner, M., & Bach, M. (1999). Clinical utility of DSM-IV pain disorder. *Comprehensive Psychiatry, 40*(5), 353–357.

Ainsworth, M. (1973). The development of mother-infant attachment. In B. Caldwell & H. Ricciuti (Eds.), *Review of Child Development Research* (pp. 1–94). Chicago: University of Chicago Press.

Ainsworth, M., Behar, M., Waters, E., & Wall, S. (1978). *Patterns of attachment: A psychological study of the strange situation.* Hillsdale, NJ: Erlbaum.

Akers, R. L. (1985). *Deviant behavior: A social learning approach* (3rd ed.). Belmont, CA: Wadsworth.

Akiskal, H. S. (1996). The prevalent clinical spectrum of bipolar disorders: Beyond DSM-IV. *Journal of Clinical Psychopharmacology, 16*(2), (Suppl. 1), 4S–14S.

Albert, V., Klein, D., Noble, A., & Zahand, E. (2000). Identifying substance abusing delivering women: Consequences for child maltreatment reports. *Child Abuse and Neglect, 24*(2), 173–183.

Albertini, R. S., & Phillips, K. A. (1999). 33 cases of body dysmorphic disorder in children and adolescents. *Journal of the American Academy of Child and Adolescent Psychiatry, 38,* 453–459.

Alexander, M. J. (1996). Women with co-occurring addictive and mental disorders. *American Journal of Orthopsychiatry, 66,* 61–70.

Alphs, L. D., & Anand, R. (1999). Clozapine: The commitment to patient safety. *Journal of Clinical Psychiatry, 60*(Suppl. 12), 39–41.

Alptekin, K., & Klvirlk, B. B. (2002). Quetiapine-induced improvement of tardive dyskinesia in three patients with schizophrenia. *International Clinical Psychopharmacology, 17*(5), 263–266.

Altamura, A., Piolo, R., Vitto, M., & Mannu, P. (1999). Venlafaxine in social phobia: A study in selective serotonin reuptake inhibitor non-responders. *International Clinical Psychopharmacology, 14,* 239–245.

Alterman, A. I., McDermott, P. A., Cacciola, J. S., Rutherford, M. I., Boardman, C. R., McKay, J. R., & Cook, T. G. (1998). A typology of antisociality in methadone patients. *Journal of Abnormal Psychology, 107,* 412–422.

American Psychiatric Association (APA). (1952). *Diagnostic and statistical manual of mental disorders* (1st ed.). Washington, DC: APA.

American Psychiatric Association (APA). (1968). *Diagnostic and statistical manual of mental disorders* (2nd ed.). Washington, DC: APA.

American Psychiatric Association (APA). (1980). *Diagnostic and statistical manual of mental disorders* (3rd ed.). Washington, DC: APA.

American Psychiatric Association (APA). (1987). *Diagnostic and statistical manual of mental disorders* (3rd ed., revised). Washington, DC: American Psychiatric Association.

American Psychiatric Association (APA). (2000). *Diagnostic and statistical manual of mental disorders* (4th ed., text revision). Washington, DC: American Psychiatric Association.

American Psychiatric Association. (2001). Practice guidelines for the treatment of patients with eating disorders (revision). *American Journal of Psychiatry* (Suppl.), *157,* 1–39.

Ammendola, A., Gemini, D., Innacone, S., Argenzio, F., Ciccone, G., Ammendola, E., Serio, L., Ugolini, G., & Bravaccio, F. (2000). Gender and peripheral neuropathy in chronic alcoholism: A clinical-electroneurographic study. *Alcohol and Alcoholism, 35,* 368–371.

Amodeo, M., & Fassler, I. (2001). Agency practices affecting social workers who treat substance-abusing clients. *Journal of Social Work Practice in the Addictions, 1*(2), 3–19.

Anderson, R. C. (2003). Body dysmorphic disorder: Recognition and treatment. *Plastic Surgical Nursing, 23*(3), 125–128.

Andreasen, N. C., & Black, D. W. (1995). *Introductory textbook of psychiatry* (2nd ed.). Washington, DC: American Psychiatric Press.

Andreasen, N. C., & Black, D. W. (2001). *Introductory textbook of psychiatry* (3rd ed.). Washington, DC: American Psychiatric Publishing.

Andres, K., Pfammatter, M., Garst, F., Teschner, C., & Brenner, H. D. (2000, April). Effects of a coping-oriented group therapy for schizophrenia and schizoaffective patients: A pilot study. *Acta Psychiatrica Scandinavica, 101*(4), 318–322.

Angell, M. (2000). Is academic medicine for sale? (Editorial) *New England Journal of Medicine, 342,* 1516–1518.

Angst, J., Gamma, A., Sellaro, R., Lavori, P., & Heping, A. (2003). Recurrence of bipolar disorders and major depression: A life-long perspective. *European Archives of Psychiatry and Clinical Neuroscience, 253*(5), 236–241.

Anstine, D., & Grinenko, D. (2000). Rapid screening for disordered eating in college-aged females in the primary care setting. *Journal of Adolescent Health, 26*(5), 338–342.

Anton, R. F. (1999). What is craving? Models and implications for treatment. *Alcohol Research and Health, 23,* 165–173.

Aponte, H. J. (1992). Training the person of the therapist in structural family therapy. *Journal of Marital and Family Therapy, 18*(3), 269–281.

Aponte, H. J. (1994). *Bread and spirit: Therapy with the new poor.* New York: W. W. Norton.

Aponte, H. J. (2002). Structural family therapy. In A. R. Roberts & G. J. Greene (Eds.) *Social workers' desk reference* (pp. 263–272). Oxford: Oxford University Press.

Aponte, H. J., & DiCesare, E. J. (2000). Structural theory. In F. M. Dattilio & L. Bevilacqua (Eds.), *Comparative treatment of couples' problems* (pp. 45–57). New York: Springer.

Aponte, H. J., & DiCesare, E. J. (2002). Structural family therapy. In J. Carlson & D. Kjos (Eds.), *Theories and strategies of family therapy* (pp. 1–18). Boston: Allyn & Bacon.

Aponte, H. J., & VanDeusen, J. M. (1981). Structural family therapy. In A. S. Gurman & D. P. Kniskern (Eds.), *Handbook of family therapy* (pp. 310–360). New York: Brunner/Mazel.

Araoz, D. L., & Carrese, M. A. (1996). *Solution-oriented brief therapy for adjustment disorders.* New York: Brunner/Mazel.

Arnold, M. (1960). *Emotion and personality* (Vol. 1). New York: Columbia University Press.

Aro, H. (1994). Risk and protective factors in depression: A developmental perspective. *Acta Psychiatrica Scandinavia, 377*(Suppl.), 59–64.

Aronson, J. A. (1996). *Inside managed care: Family therapy in a changing environment.* New York: Brunner/Mazel.

Arroyo, C., & Zigler, E. (1995). Racial identity, academic achievement, and the psychological well being of economically disadvantaged adolescents. *Journal of Personality and Social Psychology, 69,* 903–914.

Association for the Advancement of Social Work with Groups. (1999). *Standards for social work practice with groups.* Akron, OH: Author.

Atchley, R. C. (1994). *Social forces and aging: An introduction to social gerontology* (7th ed.). Belmont, CA: Wadsworth.

Atkinson, D. A., Morten, G., & Sue, D. W. (1998). *Counseling American minorities* (5th ed.). Boston: McGraw-Hill.

Atkinson, J. M., Coia, D. A., Gilmour, W. H., & Harper, J. P. (1996). The impact of education groups for people with schizophrenia on social functioning and quality of life. *British Journal of Psychiatry, 168,* 199–204.

Austrian, S. G. (2000). *Mental disorder, medications, and clinical social work* (2nd ed.). New York: Columbia University Press.

Avia, M. D., Ruiz, M. A., Olivares, M. E., Crespo, M., Guisado, A. B., Sanchez, A., & Varela, A. (1996). The meaning of psychological symptoms: Effectiveness of a group intervention with hypochondriacal patients. *Behavior Research and Therapy, 34*(1), 23–31.

Azmitia, E. C. (2001). Impact of drugs and alcohol on the brain through the life cycle: Knowledge for social workers. *Journal of Social Worker Practice in the Addictions, 1*(3), 41–63.

Azorin, J. M. (2000). Acute phase of schizophrenia: Impact of atypical antipsychotics. *International Clinical Psychopharmacology, 15*(4), S5–S9.

Bachner-Melman, R. (2003). Anorexia nervosa from a family perspective—Why did nobody notice? *American Journal of Family Therapy, 30*(1), 39–50.

Bachrach, L. L. (2000). Psychosocial rehabilitation and psychiatry in the treatment of schizophrenia: What are the boundaries? *Acta Psychiatrica Scandinavica, 102*(407), 6–10.

Badger, L. W., & Rand, E. H. (1998). Mood disorders. In J. B. W. Williams & K. Ell (Eds.), *Advances in mental health research: Implications for practice* (pp. 49–117). Washington, DC: National Association of Social Workers Press.

Bagatell, C. J., & Bremner, W. J. (1996). Androgens in men—uses and abuses. *New England Journal of Medicine, 334*(1), 707–714.

Baggott, J., & Bartlett, J. (2004, January 12). How should we treat eating disorders? *Clinical Pulse,* 36–41. Retrieved May 16, 2005 from the World Wide Web: http://www.pulse-i.co.uk.html.

Bagley, C. A., Character, C., & Shelton, L. (2003). Eating disorders among urban and rural African American and European American Women. *Women and Therapy, 26*(1–2), 57–59.

Baker, D., Hunter, E., Lawrence, E., Medfrod, N., Patel, M., Senior, C., Sierra, M., Lambert, M. V., Phillips, M. L., & David, A. S. (2003). Depersonalization disorder: Clinical features of 204 cases. *British Journal of Psychiatry, 182*(5), 428–433.

Ball, S. A., & Cecero, J. J. (2001). Addicted patients with personality disorders: Traits, schemas, and presenting problems. *Journal of Personality Disorders, 15*(1), 2–83.

Ballard, E. L., Nash, F., Raiford, K., & Harrell, L. E. (1993). Recruitment of Black elderly for clinical research studies of dementia: The CERAD experience. *Gerontologist, 33*(4), 561–565.

Bandura, A. (1969). *Principles of behavior modification.* New York: Holt, Rinehart & Winston.

Bandura, A. (1977). *Social learning theory.* Englewood Cliffs, NJ: Prentice-Hall.

Bandura, A. (1986). *Social foundation of thought and action: A social cognitive theory.* Englewood Cliffs, NJ: Prentice-Hall.

Bandura, A. (2001). Social cognitive theory: An agentic perspective. *Annual Review of Psychology, 52,* 1–26. Palo Alto, CA: Annual Reviews.

Barber, J. P., & Crits-Christoph, P. (Eds.). (1995). *Dynamic therapies for psychiatric disorders (Axis I).* New York: Basic Books.

Barker, R. L. (1996). *The social work dictionary.* Washington, DC: NASW Press.

Barlow, D. H. (2002). *Anxiety and its disorders: The nature and treatment of anxiety and panic* (2nd ed.). New York: Guilford Press.

Barlow, D. H., & Craske, M. G. (1994). *Mastery of your anxiety and panic, II.* Albany, NY: Graywind Publications Inc.

Barlow, D. H., & Durand, V. M. (2002). *Abnormal psychology* (3rd ed.). Pacific Grove, CA: Brooks/Cole.

Barlow, D. H., & Durand, V. M. (2005). *Abnormal psychology: An integrative approach* (4th ed.). Belmont, CA: Wadsworth/Thomson Learning.

Barnard, C. P. (1994). Resiliency: A shift in our perception? *The Journal of Family Therapy, 22*(2), 135–144.

Barnard, C. P., & Corrales, R. B. (1979). *The theory and technique of family therapy.* Springfield, IL: Charles C. Thomas.

Barnow, S., & Linden, M. (2000). Epidemiology and psychiatric morbidity of suicidal ideation among the elderly. *Crisis: The Journal of Crisis Intervention and Suicide Prevention, 21*(4), 171–180.

Barsky, A. J. (1992). Amplification, somatization, and the somatoform disorders. *Psychosomatics, 33,* 28–34.

Barsky, A. J. (1995, April). Essential aspects of mediation in child protection cases. University of Toronto, unpublished dissertation.

Barsky, A. J. (1996). Hypochondriasis. *Psychosomatics, 37*(1), 48–56.

Bartle, E. E., Couchonnal, G., Canada, E. R., & Staker, M. D. (2002). Empowerment as a dynamically developing concept for practice: Lessons learned from organizational ethnography. *Social Work, 27*(1), 32–44.

Bassman, R. (2000). Agents, not objects: Our fights to be. *Journal of Clinical Psychology: In Session, 56*(11), 1395–1411.

Bateson, G. (1991). *A sacred unity: Further steps to an ecology of mind.* New York: Harper/Collins.

Bateson, G., Jackson, D., Haley, J., & Weakland, J. (1963). Toward a theory of schizophrenia. *Behavioral Science, 1*(4), 251–264.

Batzer, W., Ditzler, T., & Brown, C. (1999). LSD use and flashbacks in alcoholic patients. *Journal of Addictive Diseases, 18*(2), 57–63.

Beck, A. T. (1963). Thinking and depression. 1. Theory and therapy. *Archives of General Psychiatry, 9,* 324–333.

Beck, A. T. (1964). Thinking and depression. 2. Theory and therapy. *Archives of General Psychiatry, 10,* 561–571.

Beck, A. T. (1967). *Depression: Clinical experimental and theoretical aspects.* New York: Hoeber.

Beck, A. T. (1986). Hopelessness as a predictor of eventual suicide. *Annals of the New York Academy of Sciences, 487,* 90–96.

Beck, A. T., & Weishaar, M. E. (1995). Cognitive therapy. In R. J. Corsini & D. Wedding (Eds.), *Current psychotherapies* (5th ed., pp. 229–261). Itasca, IL: F. E. Peacock.

Beck, C. K. (1998). Psychosocial and behavioral interventions for Alzheimer's disease patients and their families. *The American Journal of Geriatric Psychiatry, 6*(2), Suppl. 1, S41–S48.

Beck, J., & Rosenbaum, M. (1994). *Pursuit of ecstasy: The MDMA experience.* Albany: State University of New York Press.

Becvar, D. S., & Becvar, R. J. (1996). *Family therapy: A systemic integration* (3rd ed.). Boston, MA: Allyn & Bacon.

Beebe, D. K., & Walley, E. (1991). Substance abuse: the designer drugs. *American Family Physician, 43,* 1689–1698.

Beeder, A. B., & Millman, R. B. (1995). Treatment of psychopathology and substance abusers. In A. Washton (Ed.), *Psychotherapy and substance abuse* (pp. 76–102). New York: Guilford.

Beers, C. (1980). *A mind that found itself: An autobiography.* Pittsburgh: University of Pittsburgh Press.

Beevers, C. G., Keitner, G. I., Ryan, C. E., & Miller, I. W. (2003). Cognitive predictors of symptom return following depression treatment. *Journal of Abnormal Psychology, 112*(3), 488–496.

Begleiter, H., & Kissin, B. (Eds.). (1995). *The genetics of alcoholism.* New York: Oxford University Press.

Belcher, J. R., & Ephross, P. H. (1989). Toward an effective practice model for the homeless mentally ill. *Social Casework, 70,* 421–427.

Belgrade, M. J. (1999). Opioids for chronic nonmalignant pain. *Postgraduate Medicine, 106*(6), 115–124.

Bellack, A. S., & DiClemente, C. C. (1999). Treating substance abuse among patients with schizophrenia. *Psychiatric Services, 50,* 75–80.

Benard, B. (1997). Fostering resiliency in children and youth: Promoting protective factors in the school. In D. Saleebey (Ed.). *The strengths perspective in social work practice* (2nd ed., pp. 167–182). White Plains, NY: Longman Press.

Benard, B. (1997a). *Turning it around for all youth: From risk to resilience* (ERIC Clearinghouse on Urban Education, Institute for Urban and Minority Education (No. 126). Available: http://eric-web.tc.columbia.edu/digests/dig/126.

Bender, D. S., Dolan, R. T., & Skodol, A. E. (2001). Treatment utilization by patients with personality disorders. *American Journal of Psychiatry, 158,* 295–302.

Bender, D. S., Farber, B. A., Sanislow, C. A., Dyck, I. R., Geller, J. D., & Skodol, A. E. (2003). Representations of therapists by patients with personality disorders. *American Journal of Psychotherapy, 57*(2), 209–236.

Bennett, M. E., Bellack, A. S., & Gearon, J. S. (2001). Treating substance abuse in schizophrenia: An initial report. *Journal of Substance Abuse Treatment, 20*(2), 163–175.

Benshoff, J. J., & Harrawood, L. K. (2003). Substance abuse and the elderly: Unique issues and concerns. *Journal of Rehabilitation, 69*(2), 43–48.

Benshoff, J. J., & Janikowski, T. P. (2000). *The rehabilitation model of substance abuse counseling.* Pacific Grove, CA: Brooks/Cole.

Bentley, K. J. (1998). Psychopharmacological treatment of schizophrenia: What social workers need to know. *Research on Social Work Practice, 8*(4), 384–405.

Bentley, K. J. (Ed.). (2002). *Social work practice in mental health: Contemporary roles, tasks, and techniques.* Pacific Grove, CA: Brooks/Cole.

Bentley, K. J. (2003). *Psychiatric medication issues for social workers, counselors, and psychologists.* New York: Haworth Press.

Bentley, K. J., & Taylor, M. F. (2002). A context and vision for excellence in social work practice in contemporary mental health settings. In K. J. Bentley (Ed.), *Social work practice in mental health: Contemporary roles, tasks, and techniques* (pp. 1–17). Pacific Grove, CA: Brooks/Cole.

Bentley, K.J., & Walsh, J. (1996). *The social worker and psychotropic medication.* Pacific Grove: Brooks/Cole.

Bentley, K. J., & Walsh, J. (1998). Advances in psychopharmacology and psychosocial aspects of medication management: A review for social workers. In J. B. W. Willliams & K. Ell (Eds.), *Advances in mental health research: Implications for practice* (pp. 309–342). Washington, DC: NASW Press.

Bentley, K. J., & Walsh, J. (2001). *The social worker and psychotropic medication: Toward effective collaboration with mental health clients, families, and providers* (2nd ed.). Belmont, CA: Wadsworth/Thomson Learning.

Berg, I. K. (1994). *Family based services: A solution-focused approach.* New York: Norton.

Berg, I. K., & de Jong, P. (1996). Solution-building conversations: Co-constructing a sense of competence with clients. *Families in Society, 77*(6), 376–390.

Berg, I. K., & Hopwood, L. (1991). Doing with very little: Treatment of homeless substance abusers. *Journal of Independent Social Work, 5,* 109–199.

Berg, I. K., & Kelly, S. (2000). *Building solutions in child protective services.* New York: Norton.

Berg, I. K., & Miller, S. D. (1992). *Working with the problem drinker: A solution-focused approach.* New York: Norton.

Berg, I. K., & Reuss, N. H. (1997). *Solutions step by step.* New York: Norton.

Berkman, B. (1996). The emerging health care world: Implications for social work practice and education. *Social Work, 41*(5), 541–551.

Berkow, R. (Ed.). (1992). *The Merck manual of diagnosis and therapy* (16th ed.). Rahway, NJ: Merck Research Laboratories.

Berman-Rossi, T. (2001). Older persons in need of long-term care. In A. Gitterman (Ed.), *Handbook of social work practice with vulnerable and resilient populations* (2nd ed., pp. 715–768). New York: Columbia University Press.

Berrios, G. E., & Kan, C. S. (1996). A conceptual and quantitative analysis of 178 historical cases of dysmorphophobia. *Acta Psychiatrica Scandinavia, 94*(1), 1–7.

Bertolino, B., & O'Hanlon, B. (2001). *Collaborative, competency-based counseling and psychotherapy: A basic manual for interviewing, intervention, and change.* Boston: Allyn & Bacon.

Beyebach, M., Morejon, A. R., Palenzuela, D. L., & Rodriguez-Arias, J. L. (1996). Research on the process of solution-focused therapy. In S. D. Miller, M. A. Hubble, & B. L. Duncan (Eds.), *Handbook of solution-focused brief therapy* (pp. 299–334). San Francisco, CA: Jossey-Bass.

Bhatara, V. S., Sharma, J. N., Gupta, S., & Gupta, Y. K. (1997). Rauwolfia serpentina: The first herbal antipsychotic. *American Journal of Psychiatry, 154,* 894–899.

Biegel, D. E. (1995). Caregiver burden. In G. L. Maddox (Ed.). *The encyclopedia of aging: A comprehensive resource in gerontology and geriatrics* (pp. 138–141). New York: Springer.

Biegel, D.E., Song, L., & Milligan, S. E. (1995). A comparative analysis of family caregivers' perceived relationship with mental health professionals. *Psychiatric Services, 46,* 477–482.

Bienvenu, O. J., & Eaton, W. W. (1998). The epidemiology of blood-injection-injury phobia. *Psychological Medicine, 28*(5), 1129–1136.

Binder, J., & Strupp, H. (1997). "Negative process": A recurrently discovered and underestimated facet of therapeutic process and outcome in the individual psychotherapy of adults. *Clinical Psychology: Science and Practice, 4,* 121–139.

Binzer, M., & Kullgren, G. (1996). Conversion symptoms: What can we learn from previous studies? *Nordic Journal of Psychiatry, 50,* 143–152.

Black, C. (2003). Creating curative communities: Feminist group work with women with eating issues. *Australian Social Work, 56*(2), 127–140.

Black, D. W., Gaffney, G., Schlosser, S., & Gabel, J. (1998). The impact of obsessive-compulsive disorder on the family: Preliminary findings. *Journal of Nervous and Mental Disease, 186*(7), 440–442.

Blagys, M. D. (2002). Distinctive activities of cognitive-behavioral therapy: A review of the comparative psychotherapy process literature. *Clinical Psychology Review, 22*(5), 671–706.

Bland, R. C. (1997). Epidemiology of affective disorders: A review. *Canadian Journal of Psychiatry, 42*(4), 367–377.

Blatt, S. J. (1995). The destructiveness of perfectionism: Implications for the treatment of depression. *American Psychologist, 50,* 1003–1020.

Blazer, D. G. (2003). Depression in late life: Review and commentary. *Journal of Gerontological and Biological Sciences, Medical Science, 58 A,* 249–265.

Blazer, D. G., Kessler, R. C., McGonagle, K. A., & Swartz, M. S. (1994). The prevalence and distribution of major depression in a national community sample: The national co-morbidity study. *American Journal of Psychiatry, 15*(7), 979–986.

Bleechem, M. (2002). *Elderly alcoholism: Intervention strategies.* Springfield, IL: Charles C. Thomas.

Blier, P. (2001). Norepinephrine and selective norepinephrine reuptake inhibitors in depression and mood disorders: Their pivotal roles. *Journal of Psychiatry and Neuroscience Supplement, 26*(4), s 1–3.

Blocher, D. (2002). *Counseling: A developmental approach* (4th ed.). New York: Wiley.

Blue, J. G., & Lombardo, J. A. (1999). Steroids and steroid-like compounds. *Clinics in Sports Medicine, 18,* 667–687.

Blume, S. B. (1998). Addictive disorders in women. In R. J. Frances & S. I. Miller (Eds.), *Clinical textbook of addictive disorders* (2nd ed.). New York: Guilford.

Bockoven, J. S. (1963). *Moral treatment in American psychiatry.* New York: Springer.

Bodenheimer, T. (2000). Uneasy alliance—Clinical investigators and the pharmaceutical industry (Health policy report). *New England Journal of Medicine, 342,* 1539–1544.

Boehm, A., & Staples, L. H. (2002). The functions of the social worker in empowering: The voices of consumers and professionals. *Social Work, 47*(4), 449–460.

Bogart, T., & Solomon, P. (2000). Procedures to share treatment information among mental health providers, consumers, and families. *Psychiatric Services, 50,* 1321–1325.

Bondolfi, G., Dufour, H., & Patris, S. (1998). Risperidone versus clozapine in treatment-resistant chronic schizophrenia: A randomized double-blind study. *American Journal of Psychiatry, 155,* 499–504.

Booker, J., & Blymer, D. (1994). Solution-focused brief residential treatment with "chronic mental patients." *Journal of Systemic Therapies, 13*(4), 53–69.

Borden, W. (2000). The relational paradigm in contemporary psychoanalysis: Toward a psycho-dynamically-informed social work perspective. *Social Service Review, 74*(3), 352–379.

Bordo, S. (2000). *The male body.* New York: Farrar, Straus and Giroux.

Borison, R. L., Arvanitis, L. A., & Miller, B. G. (1996). A comparison of five fixed doses of Seroquel (ICI-204, 636) with haloperidol and placebo in patients with schizophrenia. *Schizophrenia Research, 18,* 132.

Boscolo, L., Cecchin, G., Hoffman, L., & Penn, P. (1987). *Milan systemic family therapy: Conversations in theory and practice.* New York: Basic Books.

Bostwick, J. M., & Pankratz, V. S. (2000). Affective disorders and suicide risk: A re-examination. *American Journal of Psychiatry, 157,* 1925–1932.

Boszormenyi-Nagy, I. (1987). *Foundations of contextual therapy: Collected papers of Ivan Boszormenyi-Nagy.* New York: Brunner/Mazel.

Boszormenyi-Nagy, I., & Framo, J. L. (Eds.). (1965). *Intensive family therapy.* New York: Harper and Row.

Bourgeois, M., Schulz, R., & Burgio, L. (1996). Interventions for caregivers of patients with Alzheimer's disease: A review and analysis of content, process, and outcomes. *International Journal of Aging Human Behavior, 43*(1), 35–92.

Bowen, M. (1960). A family concept of schizophrenia. In D. D. Jackson (Ed.), *The etiology of schizophrenia.* New York: Basic Books.

Bowen, M. (1978). *Family therapy in clinical practice.* New York: Jason Aronson.

Bowlby, J. (1969). Attachment and loss (Vol. 1). *Attachment.* New York: Basic Books.

Bowlby, J. (1973). Attachment and loss (Vol. II). *Separation anxiety and anger.* New York: Basic Books.

Bradley, S. S. (2003). The psychology of the psychopharmacology triangle: The client, the clinicians, and the medication. *Social Work in Mental Health, 1*(4), 29–50.

Bradshaw, J. (1988). *Bradshaw on the family.* Deerfield Beach, FL: Health Communications, Inc.

Braun, B. G. (1988). The BASK model of dissociation. *Dissociation, 1*(1), 4–23.

Braun, K. L., Takamura, J. C., Forman, S. M., Sasaki, P. A., & Meininger, L. (1995). Developing and testing outreach materials on Alzheimer's disease for Asian and Pacific Islander Americans. *Gerontologist, 35*(1), 122–126.

Bray, N. J., & Owen, M. J. (2001). Searching for schizophrenia genes. *Trends of Molecular Medicine, 7*(4), 169–174.

Breggin, P. R. (1997). *Brain-disabling treatments in psychiatry: Drugs, electroshock, and the role of the FDA.* New York: Springer.

Breggin, P. R., & Cohen, D. (1999). *Your drug may be your problem: How and why to stop taking psychiatric medications.* Cambridge, MA: Perseus.

Brekke, J. (1990). Crisis intervention with victims and perpetrators of spouse abuse. In H. J. Parad & L. G. Parad (Eds.), *Crisis intervention (Book 2): The practitioner's sourcebook for brief therapy* (pp. 67–75). Milwaukee, WI: Family Service America.

Brems, C. (2000). *Dealing with challenges in psychotherapy and counseling.* Belmont, CA: Brooks/Cole.

Brennan, C. D. (1999). Delirium: Making the diagnosis, improving the prognosis. *Geriatrics, 54*(3), 28–30.

Brennan, F., Downes, D., & Nadler, S. (1996). A support group for spouses of nursing home residents. *Social Work with Groups, 19*(3/4), 71–81.

Brennan, K., & Shaver, P. (1998). Attachment styles and personality disorders: Their connection to each other and to parental divorce, parental death, and perceptions of parental caregiving. *Journal of Personality, 66,* 835–878.

Brennan, P. L., & Moos, R. H. (1996). Late-life drinking behavior. *Alcohol Health and Research World, 20*(3), 197–205.

Brenner, H. D., & Pfammatter, M. (2000). Psychological therapy in schizophrenia: What is the evidence? *Acta Psychiatrica Scandinavica, 102*(407), 74–77.

Breton, M. (1995). The potential for social action in groups. *Social Work with Groups, 18*(2/3), 5–13.

Breuer, J., & Freud, S. (1959). Studies on hysteria (1895). In Strachey J. London (Ed.), *The standard edition of the complete psychological works of Sigmund Freud* (Vol. 1, pp. 1–183). London: Hogarth Press.

Bricout, J. C., & Bentley, K. J. (2000). Disability status and perceptions of employability by employers. *Social Work Research, 24*(2), 87–95.

Brieden, T., Ujeyl, M., & Naber, D. (2002). Psychopharmacological treatment of aggression in schizophrenic patients. *Pharmacopsychiatry, 35*(3), 83–89.

Brill, H. (1980). State hospitals should be kept for how long? In J. A. Talbot (Ed.), *State mental hospitals: Problems and potentials* (pp. 147–160). New York: Human Sciences.

Brink, S. (2002). Emotions. *U.S. News and World Report, 133*(19), 68–70.

Broadbent, R. S. (1998). Harnessing peer networks as an instrument for AIDS prevention: Results from a peer-driven intervention. *Public Health Reports, 113*(Suppl. 1), 42–57.

Broden, S. (1994). The therapeutic use of humor in the treatment of eating disorders: Or, there is life even after fat thighs. In B. Kinoy (Ed.), *Eating disorders: New directions in treatment and recovery* (pp. 92–99). New York: Columbia University Press.

Brodsky, C. M. (1984). Sociocultural and interactional influences on somatization. *Psychosomatic, 25,* 673–680.

Brody, E. M., & Farber, B. A. (1996). The effects of the therapist experience and patient diagnosis on countertransference. *Psychotherapy, 33*(3), 372–380.

Bronfenbrenner, U. (1989). Ecological systems theory. *Annuals of Child Development, 6,* 187–249.

Bronisch, T. (2003). Depression and suicidal behavior. *Crisis: The Journal of Crisis Intervention and Suicide Prevention, 24*(4), 179–180.

Brook, D. (1993). Group psychotherapy with anxiety and mood disorders. In H. Kaplan & B. Sadock (Eds.), *Comprehensive group psychotherapy* (3rd ed., pp. 374–393). Baltimore: Williams & Wilkins.

Brookmeyer, R., Gray, S., & Kawas, C. (1998). Projections of Alzheimer's disease in the United States and the Public Health: Impact of delaying disease onset. *American Journal of Public Health, 88*(9): 1337–1342.

Brown, D. R., Ahmed, F., Gary, L. E., & Milburn, N. G. (1995). Major depression in a community sample of African Americans. *American Journal of Psychiatry, 152,* 373–378.

Brown, G. K., Beck, A. T., & Steer, R. A. (2000). Risk factors for suicide in psychiatric outpatients: A 20-year prospective study. *Journal of Consulting and Clinical Psychology, 68*(3), 371–377.

Brown, P., van der Hart, O., & Graafland, M. (1999). Trauma-induced dissociative amnesia in World War I combat soldiers. II. Treatment dimensions. *Australian and New Zealand Journal of Psychiatry, 33,* 392–398.

Brown, S., & Lewis, V. (1995). The alcoholic family: A developmental model of recovery. In S. Brown (Ed.), *Treating alcoholism.* New York: Jossey-Bass.

Brownell, K. D., & O'Neil, P. M. (1993). Obesity. In D. H. Barlow (Ed.), *Clinical handbook of psychological disorders: A step-by-step treatment manual* (2nd ed., pp. 318–361). New York: Guilford.

Brumberg, J. J. (2000). *Fasting girls: The history of anorexia nervosa.* New York: Vintage.

Brun, C., & Rapp, R. C. (2001). Strengths-based case management: Individuals' perspectives on strengths and the case manager relationship. *Social Work, 46*(3), 278–288.

Buckley, W. Q. (1967). *Sociology and modern systems theory.* Englewood, NJ: Prentice-Hall.

Buddeberg-Fischer, B., & Reed, V. (2001). Prevention of disturbed eating behavior: An intervention program in Swiss high school classes. *Eating Disorders, 9*(2), 109–124.

Budman, S. H., Cooley, S., Demby, A., Koppenaal, G., Koslof, J., & Powers, T. (1996). A model of time-effective group psychotherapy for patients with personality disorders: The clinical model. *International Journal of Group Psychotherapy, 46*(3), 329–355.

Buelow, G. D., & Buelow, S. A. (1998). *Psychotherapy in chemical dependence treatment: A practical and integrative approach.* Pacific Grove, CA: Brooks/Cole.

Buelow, G., & Herbert, S. (1995). *Counselor's resource on psychiatric medications: Issues of treatment and referral.* Pacific Grove, CA: Brooks/Cole.

Bulik, C. M. (1998). Women and disordered eating. In S. E. Romans (Ed.), *Folding back the shadows: A perspective on women's mental health* (pp. 177–191). Dunedin, New Zealand: University of Otago Press.

Busch, F. N., Milrod, B. L., & Singer, M. B. (1999). Theory and technique in psychodynamic treatment of panic disorder. *The Journal of Psychotherapy Practice and Research, 8,* 234–242.

Bush, D. E., Ziegelstein, R. C., Tayback, M., Richter, D., Stevens, S., & Zahalsky, E., et al. (2001). Even minimal symptoms of depression increase mortality risk after acute myocardial infarction. *American Journal of Cardiology, 88,* 337–341.

Bustillo, J. R., Lauriello, J., & Keith, S. J. (1999, January-February). Schizophrenia: Improving outcome. *Harvard Review of Psychiatry, 6*(5), 229–240.

Butler, K. (1998). The biology of fear. In S. O. Lilienfeld (Ed.), *Looking into abnormal psychology: Contemporary readings* (pp. 36–42). Pacific Grove, CA: Brooks/Cole.

Butler, L. D., Duran, R. E. R., Jasiukaitis, P., Koopman, C., & Spiegel, D. (1996). Hypnotizability and traumatic experience: A diathysis stress model of dissociative symptomatology. *American Journal of Psychiatry, 153,* 42–63.

Butterworth, R. F. (2003). Hepatic encephalopathy: A serious complication of alcoholic liver disease. *Alcohol Research and Health, 27*(2), 143–145.

Cabaj, R. P. (1997). Gays, lesbians and bisexuals. In J. H. Lowinson, P. Ruiz, R. B. Millman, & J. Langrod (Eds.), *Substance abuse: A comprehensive textbook* (3rd ed.). New York: Williams and Wilkins.

Cade, B., & O'Hanlon, W. H. (1993). *A brief guide to brief therapy.* New York: Norton.

Callahan, J., & Turnbull, J. E. (2001). Depression. In A. Gitterman (Ed.), *Handbook of social work practice with vulnerable and resilient populations* (2nd ed., pp. 163–204). New York: Columbia University Press.

Campo, J. V., & Garber, J. (1998). Psychological and psychiatric issues in the pediatric setting. In R. T. Ammerman & J. V. Campo (Eds.), *Handbook of pediatric psychology and psychiatry* (Vol. 1, pp. 137–161). Boston: Allyn & Bacon.

Campo, J. V., & Negrini, B. J. (2000). Case study: Negative reinforcement and behavioral management of conversion disorder. *Journal of the American Academy of Child and Adolescent Psychiatry, 39*(6), 787–790.

Caplan, G. (1964). *Principles of preventive psychiatry.* New York: Basic Books.

Caplan, R. B., in collaboration with Caplan, G. (1969). *Psychiatry and the community in nineteenth-century America.* New York: Basic Books.

Caplan, T., & Thomas, H. (2001). The forgotten moment: Therapeutic resiliency and its promotion in social work groups. *Social Work with Groups, 24*(2), 5–26.

Carlson, J. (2002). Strategic family therapy. In J. Carlson & D. Kjos (Eds.), *Theories and strategies of family therapy* (pp. 80–97). Boston, MA: Allyn & Bacon.

Carlson, J., & Kjos, D. (1998). *Family therapy with the experts: Strategic family therapy with James Coyne.* Boston, MA: Allyn & Bacon.

Caroff, S. N., Mann, S. C., Campbell, E., & Sullivan, K. A. (2002). Movement disorders with atypical antipsychotic drugs. *Journal of Clinical Psychiatry, 63*(Suppl 14), 12–19.

Carpenter, S. (2001). Mixing medication and psychosocial therapy for alcoholism. *Monitor on Psychology, 32*(5), 17–22.

Carpenter, W. T., Conley, R. R., Buchanan, R. W., & Breier, A. (1995). Patient response and resource management: Another view of clozapine treatment of schizophrenia. *American Journal of Psychiatry, 152,* 827–832.

Carr, A. (2000). Evidence-based practice in family therapy and systemic consultation: I: Child-focused problems. *Journal of Family Therapy, 22*(1), 29–60.

Carroll, J. J., & Trull, L. A. (2002). Drug-dependent homeless African-American women's perspectives of life on the streets. *Journal of Ethnicity in Substance Abuse, 1*(1), 27–45.

Carter, B., & McGoldrick, M. (1989). *The changing family life cycle: A framework for family therapy* (2nd ed.). Boston: Allyn & Bacon.

Carter, B., & McGoldrick, M. (2005). *The expanded family life cycle: Individual, family, and social perspectives* (3rd ed.). New York: Pearson.

Caspi, A. (2000). The child is father of the man: Personality continuities from childhood to adulthood. *Journal of Personality and Social Psychology, 78,* 158–172.

Castillo, R. J. (1997). *Culture and mental illness: A client-centered approach.* Pacific Grove, CA: Brooks/Cole.

Center for Substance Abuse Treatment (1998). *Naltrexone and alcoholism treatment.* (Treatment Improvement Protocol #28). Rockville, MD: Center for Substance Abuse Treatment.

Cepeda-Benito, A. (1993). Meta-analytical review of the efficacy of nicotine chewing gum in smoking treatment programs. *Journal of Consulting and Clinical Psychology, 61,* 822–830.

Cervone, D. (1997). Social-cognitive mechanisms and personality coherence. *Psychological Science, 8,* 43–50.

Chamberlin, J. (1997). A working definition of empowerment. *Journal of Progressive Human Services, 20*(4), 43–46.

Chaney, E. G., O'Leary, M. R., & Marlatt, G. A. (1978). Skill training with alcoholics. *Journal of Consulting and Clinical Psychology, 46,* 1092–1104.

Chari, S., Jainer, A. K., Ashley-Smith, A., & Cleaver, M. (2002). Quetiapine in tardive dyskinesia. *International Journal of Psychiatry in Clinical Practice, 6*(3), 175–177.

Charney, D. S., Reynolds, C. F., Lewis, L., Lebowitz, B. D., Sunderland, T., Alexopoulos, G. S., Blazer, D. G., Katz, I. R., Meyers, B. S., Arean, P. A., Borson, S., Brown, C., Bruce, M. L., Callahan, C. M., Charlson, M. E., Conwell, Y., Cuthbert, B. N., Devanand, D. P., Gibson, M. J., Gottlieb, G. L., Krishnan, K. R., Laden, S. K., Lyketsos, C. G., Mulsant, B. H., Niederehe, G., Olin, J. T., Oslin, D. W., Pearson, J., Persky, T., Pollock, B. G., Raetzman, S., Reynolds, M., Saltzman, C., Schulz, R., Schwenk, T. L., Scolnick, E., Unutzer, J., Weissman, M. M., & Young, R. C. (2003). Depression and bipolar support alliance consensus statement on the unmet needs in diagnosis and treatment of mood disorders in late life. *Archives of General Psychiatry, 60*(7), 664–672.

Charny, I. W. (1966). Integrated individual and family psychotherapy. *Family Process, 5,* 179–198.

Chasnoff, I. J., Anson, A. R., & Laukea, K. A. (1998). *Understanding the drug-exposed child: Approaches to behavior and learning.* Chicago: Imprint Publications.

Chen, J., Bai, Y., Pyng, L., & Lin, C. (2001). Risperidone for tardive dyskinesia. *American Journal of Psychiatry, 158*(11), 1931–1932.

Chilcoat, H. D., & Johanson, C. (1998). Vulnerability to cocaine abuse. In S. T. Higgins and J. L. Katz, (Eds.), *Cocaine abuse: Behavior, pharmacology and clinical applications* (pp. 313–341). San Diego: Academic Press.

Clark, D. M., Salkovski, P. M. N., Hackmann, A., Wells, A., Fennell, M., Ludgate, S., Ahmad, S., Richards, H. C., &

Gelder, M. (1998). Two psychological treatments for hypochondriasis: A randomized controlled trial. *British Journal of Psychiatry, 173,* 218–225.

Clement, J. A., & Greene, G. J. (2002). Assessment and treatment for persons with bipolar disorder. In A. R. Roberts & G. J. Greene (Eds.), *Social workers' desk reference* (pp. 575–581). New York: Oxford University Press.

Cloninger, C. (1987). A systematic method for clinical description and classification of personality variables: A proposal. *Archives of General Psychiatry, 44,* 573–588.

Cloninger, C. (1996). Somatization disorder. In T. A. Widiger, A. J. Frances, H. A. Pincus, M. R. Ross, & W. W. Davis (Eds.), *DSM-IV sourcebook* (Vol. 2, pp. 885–892). Washington, DC: American Psychiatric Press.

Cloninger, C. (Ed.). (1999). *Personality and psychopathology.* Washington, DC: American Psychiatric Press.

Cloninger, C. (2000). A practical way to diagnosis of personality disorders: A proposal. *Journal of Personality Disorders, 14,* 99–108.

Cloninger, C., Svrakic, D., & Przybeck, R. (1993). A psychobiological model of temperament and character. *Archives of General Psychiatry, 50,* 975–990.

Coburn, W. J. (1997). The vision in supervision: Transference-countertransference dynamics and disclosure in the supervision relationship. *Bulletin of the Menninger Clinic, 61*(4), 481–495.

Cohen, D. (2001). Cultural variations: Considerations and implications. *Psychological Bulletin, 127,* 451–471.

Cohen, D. (2002). Research on the drug treatment of schizophrenia: A critical appraisal and implications for social work education. *Journal of Social Work Education, 38,* 217–239.

Cohen, D. (2003). The psychiatric medication history: Context, purpose and method. *Social Work and Mental Health, (1)*4, 5–28.

Cohen, M. B. (1998). Perceptions of power in client/worker relationships. *Families in Society, 79,* 433–442.

Cohen, M. R. (2001). Homeless people. In A. Gitterman (Ed.), *Handbook of social work practice with vulnerable and resilient populations* (2nd ed., pp. 628–650). New York: Columbia University Press.

Cohen, S. (1985). *The substance abuse problems. Vol. 2: New issues for the 1980s.* New York: Haworth Press.

Coles, C. D., Kable, J. A., Drews-Boysch, C., & Falek, A. (2000). Early identification of risk for effects of prenatal alcohol exposure. *Journal of Studies on Alcohol, 61*(4), 607–616.

Comfort, M., Loverro, J., & Kaltenbach, K. (2002). A search for strategies to engage women in substance abuse treatment. *Social Work in Health Care, 31*(4), 59–70.

Compton, A. (1998). An investigation of anxious thought in patients with DSM–IV agoraphobic/panic disorder: Rationale and design. *Journal of the American Psychoanalytic Association, 46,* 691–721.

Compton, B. R., Galaway, B., & Cournoyer, B. R. (2005). *Social work processes* (7th ed.). Belmont, CA: Thomson Learning.

Congress, E. (1998). *Social work values and ethics.* Chicago: Nelson-Hall.

Congress, E. P., & Lynn, M. (1997). Group practice in the community: Navigating the slippery slope of ethical dilemmas. *Social Work with Groups, 20*(3), 61–74.

Conley, R. R., & Kelly, D. L. (2001). Management of treatment resistance in schizophrenia. *Biological Psychiatry, 50*(11), 898–911.

Connel, G., Bumberry, W., & Mitten, T. (1999). *Reshaping family relationships: The symbolic therapy of Carl Whitaker.* New York: Brunner-Routledge.

Connors, G. J., Donovan, D. M., & DiClemente. (2001). *Substance abuse treatment and the stages of change.* New York: Guilford.

Conrad, B. S. (1998). Maternal depressive symptoms and homeless children's mental health: Risk and resiliency. *Archives of Psychiatric Nursing, 12,* 50–58.

Cook, J. A., Pickett, S. A., Razzano, L., Fitzgivvon, G., Jonikas, J. A., & Cohler, J. J. (1996). Rehabilitation services for persons with schizophrenia. *Psychiatric Annals, 26,* 97–104.

Cooke, E. A., Guss, J. L., Kissileff, H. R., & Devlin, M. J. (1997). Patterns of food selection during binges in women with binge eating disorder. *International Journal of Eating Disorders, 22*(2), 187–193.

Cooper, D. (1967). *Psychiatry and antipsychiatry.* London: Tavistock.

Cooper, M. (1999). Treatment of persons and families with obsessive-compulsive disorder: A review article. *Crisis Intervention and Time-Limited Treatment, 5*(1–2), 25–36.

Cooper, M. G., & Lesser, J. G. (2002). *Clinical social work practice: An integrated approach.* Boston: Allyn & Bacon.

Cooper, M. G., & Lesser, J. G. (2005). *Clinical social work practice: An integrated approach* (2nd ed.). Boston: Allyn & Bacon.

Cooper, P. J., Coker, S., & Fleming, C. (1996). An evaluation of the efficacy of supervised cognitive behavioral self-help for bulimia nervosa. *Journal of Psychosomatic Research, 40,* 281–287.

Copeland, J., Swift, W., Roffman, R., & Stephens, R. (2001). A randomized controlled trial of brief cognitive-behavioral interventions for cannabis use disorders. *Journal of Substance Abuse Treatment, 21*(2), 55–64.

Corcoran, J., Stephenson, M., Perryman, D., & Allen, S. (2001). Perceptions and utilization of a police-social work crisis intervention approach to domestic violence. *Families in Society, 82*(4), 393–398.

Corcoran, K. (1997). Managed care: Implications for social work practice. In R. L. Edwards (Ed.), *Encyclopedia of social work* (19th ed., 1997 supplement, pp. 191–200). Washington, DC: NASW Press.

Corcoran, K., & Vandiver, V. (1996). *Maneuvering the maze of managed care.* New York: Free Press.

Corey, G. (2000). *The theory and practice of group counseling* (5th ed.). Pacific Grove, CA: Brooks/Cole.

Corey, G. (2001). *The theory and practice of group counseling* (6th ed.). Pacific Grove, CA: Brooks/Cole.

Corey, G., & Bitter, J. (2001). Family systems theory. In G. Corey (Ed.), *Theory and practice of psychotherapy* (6th ed., pp. 382–453). Pacific Grove, CA: Brooks/Cole.

Corey, G., Corey, M. S., & Callahan, P. (2003). *Issues and ethics in the helping professions* (6th ed.). Belmont CA: Brooks/Cole.

Cornelius, J. R., Salloum, I. M., Ehler, J. G., Jarrett, P. J., & Perel, J. M. (1997). Fluoxetine in depressed alcoholics: A double-bind, placebo-controlled trial. *Archives of General Psychiatry, 54*(8), 701–705.

Cornelius, J., Kirisci, L., & Tarter, R. E. (2001). Suicidality in offspring of men with substance use disorder: Is there a common liability? *Journal of Child and Adolescent Substance Abuse, 10*(4), 101–109.

Corsini, R. J. (Ed.) (1981). *Handbook of innovative psychotherapies.* New York: Wiley.

Corsini, R. J., & Wedding, D. (Eds.). (1995). *Current psychotherapies* (5th ed.). Itasca, IL: F. E. Peacock.

Corsini, R. J., & Wedding, D. (Eds.). (2000). *Current psychotherapies* (6th ed.). Itasca, IL: F. E. Peacock.

Cortese, L. (2002). New hope in pharmacotherapy for schizophrenia. *Hospital Physician, 50,* 21–28.

Cortright, B. (1997). *Psychotherapy and spirit.* Albany, NY: State University of New York Press.

Costin, L. (1986). Lathrop, Julia Clifford. In W. I. Trattner (Ed.), *Biographical dictionary of social welfare in America* (pp. 478–481). New York: Greenwood Press.

Cotterill, J. A. (1996). Body dysmorphic disorder. *Dermatology Clinic, 14,* 457–463.

Courtois, C. (1990). Adult survivors of incest and molestation. In H. J. Parad & L. G. Parad (Eds.), *Crisis intervention book 2: The practitioner's sourcebook for brief therapy* (pp. 139–160). Milwaukee, WI: Family Service America.

Cowager, C. D. (1994). Assessing client strengths: Clinical assessment for client empowerment. *Social Work, 39,* 262–268.

Cowager, C. D. (1997). Assessing client strengths: Assessment for client empowerment. In D. Saleebey (Ed.), *The strengths perspective in social work practice* (2nd ed., pp. 59–73). New York: Longman.

Cowan, P. A., Cowan, C. P., & Schulz, M. S. (1996). Thinking about risk and resilience in families. In M. Hetherington & E. A. Blechman (Eds.), *Stress, coping, and resilience in children and families* (pp. 1–38). Mahwah, NJ: Lawrence Erlbaum.

Cox, C. B. (1996). Discharge planning for dementia patients: Factors influencing caregiver decisions and satisfaction. *Health and Social Work, 21*(2), 97–104.

Cox, C. B., & Ephross, P. H. (1998). *Ethnicity and social work practice.* New York: Oxford University Press.

Coyle, G. L. (1962). Concepts relevant to helping the family as a group. *Social Casework, 43,* 347–354.

Coyle, S.L., Needle, R. H., & Normand, J. (1998). Outreach-based HIV prevention for injecting drug users: A review of published outcome data. *Public Health Reports, 113*(Suppl. 1), 19–31.

Craighead, W. E., Milkowitz, F. J., & Frank, E. (2002). Psychosocial treatments for bipolar disorder. In P. E. Nathan & N. M. Gorman (Eds.), *A guide to treatments that work* (2nd ed., pp. 263–275). London: Oxford University Press.

Craske, M. G. (1999). *Anxiety disorders: Psychological approaches to theory and treatment.* Boulder, CO: Westview.

Cress, C. (2001). *Handbook of geriatric care management.* Boston: Jones and Bartlett.

Crimlisk, H. L., Bhatia, K., Cope, H., Marsden, C. D., & Ron, M. A. (1998). Slater revisited: Six-year followup of patients with medically unexplained motor symptoms. *British Medical Journal, 316,* 582–586.

Critser, G. (2003). Fat land: How Americans became the fattest people in the world. Boston: Houghton Mifflin.

Croll, J., Neumark-Sztainer, D., Story, M., & Ireland, M. (2002). Prevalence and risk and protective factors related to disordered eating behaviors among adolescents: Relationship to gender and ethnicity. *Journal of Adolescent Health, 31*(2), 166–175.

Crow, M. R., Smith, H. L., McNamee, A. H., & Piland, N. F. (1994). Considerations in predicting mental health care use: Implications for managed care. *Journal of Mental Health Administration, 21*(1), 5–23.

Crump, M. T., & Milling, R. N. (1996). The efficacy of substance abuse education among dual diagnosis patients. *Journal of Substance Abuse Treatment, 13,* 141–144.

Cruz, J. M., & Peralta, R. L. (2001). Family violence and substance abuse: The perceived effects of substance use within gay male relationships. *Violence and Victims, 16*(2), 161–184.

Csernansky, J. M., Mahmoud, R., & Brenner, R. (2002). A comparison of risperidone and haloperidol for the prevention of relapse in patients with schizophrenia. *New England Journal of Medicine, 346*(1), 16–22.

Cummings, S. M. (1996). Spousal caregivers of early stage Alzheimer's patients: A psychoeducational support group model. *Journal of Gerontological Social Work, 26,* 83–98.

Cummings, S. M., Long, J. K., Peterson-Hazan, S., & Harrison, J. (1998). The efficacy of a group treatment model in helping spouses meet the emotional and practical challenges of early-stage care giving. *Clinical Gerontologist, 20*(1), 29–45.

Cunningham, S. J., & Feinmann, C. (1998). Psychological assessment of patients requesting orthognathic surgery and the relevance of body dysmorphic disorder. *British Journal of Orthodontics, 25,* 293–298.

Currie, S. R. (2002). Clinical significance and predictors of treatment response to cognitive-behavior therapy for insomnia secondary to chronic pain. *Journal of Behavioral Medicine, 25*(2), 135–153.

Custer, W. S., Kahn, C. N., & Wildsmith, T. F. (1999). Why we should keep the employment-based health insurance system. *Health Affairs, 18*(6), 47–53.

Cvetkovich, G. T., & Earle, T. C. (1994). Risk and culture. In W. J. Lonner & R. Malpass (Eds.), *Psychology and culture.* Boston: Allyn & Bacon.

Dallos, R. (2001). ANT-Attachment Narrative Therapy: Narrative and attachment theory approaches in systemic family therapy with eating disorders. *Journal of Family Psychotherapy, 12*(2), 43–72.

Daluiski, A., Rahbar, B., & Means, R. A. (1997, Oct.). Russell's sign. Subtle hand changes in patients with bulimia nervosa. *Clinical Orthopaedics and Related Research, 343,* 107–109.

Daly, J. E., & Pelowski, S. (2000). Predictors of dropout among men who batter: A review of studies with implications for research and practice. *Violence and Victims, 15*(2), 137–160.

Dancu, C. F., & Foa, E. G. (1992). Posttraumatic stress disorder. In A. Freeman & F. M. Dattilio (Eds.), *Comprehensive casebook of cognitive therapy* (pp. 79–88). New York: Plenum Press.

Dane, B. O., & Miller, S. O. (1992). *AIDS: Intervening with hidden grievers.* Westport, CT: Auburn House.

Danion, J. M., Werner, R., & Fleurot, O. (1999). Improvement of schizophrenic patients with primary negative symptoms treated with amisulpride. *The American Journal of Psychiatry, 156*(4), 610–616.

Dattilio, F. M., & Freeman, A. (1994). *Cognitive-behavioral strategies in crisis intervention.* New York: Guilford Press.

Dattilio, F. M., & Kendall, P. C. (1994). Panic disorder. In F. M. Dattilio & A. Freeman (Eds.), *Cognitive and behavioral treatment strategies in crisis intervention* (pp. 46–66). New York: Guilford Press.

Dattilio, F. M., & Salas-Auvert, J. A. (2000). *Panic disorder: Assessment and treatment through a wide-angle lens.* Phoenix: Zeig, Tucker, and Company.

Davies, R. D., Dubovsky, S. L., Gabbert, S., & Chapman, M. (2000). Treatment resistance in anxiety disorders. *Bulletin of the Menninger Clinic, 64*(3 Suppl. A), A22–A36.

Davis, L. (1986). Role theory. In F. J. Turner (Ed.), *Social work treatment: Interlocking theoretical approaches* (3rd ed., pp. 541–563). New York: Free Press.

Davis, S., & Meier, S. (2001). *The elements of managed care.* Pacific Grove, CA: Brooks/Cole.

De Angelis, T. (2002). Promising treatments for anorexia and bulimia: Research boosts support for tough-to-treat eating disorders. *Monitor on Psychology, 33*(3), 1–7.

de Jong, P. (2002). Solution-focused therapy. In A. R. Roberts & G. J. Greene (Eds.), *Social workers' desk reference* (pp. 112–116). New York: Oxford University Press.

de Jong, P., & Berg, I. K. (1997). *How to interview for client strengths and solutions.* Pacific Grove, CA: Brooks/Cole.

de Jong, P., & Berg, I. K. (1998). *Interviewing for solutions.* Pacific Grove, CA: Brooks/Cole.

de Jong, P., & Berg, I. K. (2002). *Interviewing for solutions* (2nd ed.). Pacific Grove, CA: Brooks/Cole.

de Jong, P., & Miller, S. D. (1995). How to interview for client strengths. *Social Work, 40*(6), 729–741.

De Man, A. F., & Gutierrez, B. I. B. (2002). The relationship between level of self-esteem and suicidal ideation with stability of self-esteem as moderator. *Canadian Journal of Behavioural Science, 34*(4), 235–238.

De Marco, L. M., Li, L. C., Phillips, K. A., & Mc Elroy, S. L. (1998). Perceived stress in body dysmorphic disorder. *Journal of Nervous and Mental Disease, 186*(11), 724–726.

De Murtas, M., Tatarelli, R., Girardi, P., & Vicini, S. (2004). Repeated electroconvulsive stimulation impairs long-term depression in the neostriatum. *Biological Psychiatry, 55*(5), 472–477.

de Shazer, S. (1982). *Patterns of brief family therapy.* New York: Norton.

de Shazer, S. (1985). *Keys to solution in brief therapy.* New York: Norton.

de Shazer, S. (1988). *Clues: Investigating solutions in brief therapy.* New York: Norton.

de Shazer, S. (1990). What is it about brief therapy that works? In J. K. Zeig & S. L. Gilligan (Eds.), *Brief therapy: Myths,* *methods, and metaphors* (pp. 90–99). New York: Brunner/Mazel.

de Shazer, S. (1991). *Putting difference to work.* New York: Norton.

de Shazer, S. (1994). *Words were originally magic.* New York: Norton.

Deblinger, E. (1992). Child sexual abuse. In A. Freeman & F. M. Dattilio (Eds.), *Comprehensive casebook of cognitive therapy* (pp. 159–167). New York: Plenum Press.

Deegan, P. E. (1992). The independent living movement and people with psychiatric disabilities: Taking back control over our own lives. *Psychosocial Rehabilitation Journal, 15*(3), 3–19.

Degun-Mather, M. (2001). The value of hypnosis in the treatment of chronic PTSD with dissociative fugues in a war veteran. *Contemporary Hypnosis, 18*(1), 4–13.

DeJong, P., & Miller, S. D. (1995). How to interview for client strengths. *Social Work, 40,* 729–736.

Dharmendra, M. S., & Eagles, J. M. (2003). Factors associated with patients' knowledge of and attitudes towards treatment with lithium. *Journal of Affective Disorders, 75*(1), 29–34.

DiBisceglie, A. M., & Bacon, B. R. (1999). The unmet challenge of hepatitis C. *Scientific American, 281*(4), 80–85.

DiChiara, G. (1997). Alcohol and dopamine. *Alcohol Health & Research World, 21*(2), 108–114.

Dickerson, F. B. (2000). Cognitive behavioral psychotherapy for schizophrenia: A review of recent empirical studies. *Schizophrenia Research, 43*(2–3), 71–90.

Dickey, B. (2000). Review of programs for persons who are homeless and mentally ill. *Harvard Review of Psychiatry, 8*(5), 242–250.

DiClemente, C. C. (2003). *Addiction and change: How addictions develop and addicted people recover.* New York: Guilford.

DiClemente, C. C., Bellino, L. E., & Neavins, T. M. (1999). Motivation for change and alcoholism treatment. *Alcohol Health & Research World, 23*(2), 86–92.

Dieperink, E., Willenbring, M., & Ho, S. B. (2000). Neuropsychiatric symptoms associated with hepatitis C and interferon alpha: A review. *American Journal of Psychiatry, 157,* 867–876.

Dietz, C. A. (2000). Reshaping clinical practice for the new millennium. *Journal of Social Work Education, 36*(3), 503–521.

Diller, J. V. (2004). *Cultural diversity: A primer for the human services* (2nd ed.). Pacific Grove, CA: Brooks/Cole.

Dingfelder, S. F. (2004). Treatment for the 'untreatable': Despite the difficult-to-treat reputation of personality disorders, clinical trials of treatments show promise. *Monitor on Psychology, 35*(3), 46–51.

DiNitto, D., with Cummins, L. K. (2005). *Social welfare: Politics and public policy* (6th ed.). Boston: Allyn & Bacon.

Dixon, L., Adams, C., & Lucksted, A. (2000). Update on family psychoeducation for schizophrenia. *Schizophrenia Bulletin, 26*(1), 5–20.

Dixon, L., McFarlane, W., Hornby, H., & Murray, R. (1999). Dissemination of family psychoeducation: The importance of consensus building. *Schizophrenia Research, 36,* 339.

Dobs, A. S. (1999). Is there a role for androgenic anabolic steroids in medical practice? *Journal of the American Medical Association, 281,* 1326–1327.

Dolan, Y. (1997). I'll start my diet tomorrow: A solution-focused approach to weight loss. *Contemporary Family Therapy, 19*(1), 41–48.

Dole, V. P., & Nyswander, M. E. (1965). A medical treatment for diacetyl morphine (heroin) addiction: A clinical trial with methadone hydrochloride. *Journal of the American Medical Association, 193,* 646ff.

Dolnick, E. (1994). Obsessed. *Health, 8,* 78–84.

Domar, A. D., & Dreher, H. (2001). *Self-nurture: Learning to care for yourself as effectively as you care for everyone else.* New York: Penguin Books / G. P. Putnam's Sons.

Donohue, B., Thevenin, D. M., & Runyon, M. K. (1997). Behavioral treatment of conversion disorder in adolescence: A case of globus hystericus. *Behavior Modification, 21*(2), 231–251.

Dougherty, A. M. (2000). *Psychological consultation and collaboration: A casebook* (3rd ed.). Pacific Grove, CA: Brooks/Cole.

Doweiko, H. E. (2002). *Concepts of chemical dependency* (5th ed.). Pacific Grove, CA: Brooks/Cole.

Drabble, L. (2000). Alcohol, tobacco, and pharmaceutical industry funding: Considerations for organizations serving lesbian, gay, bisexual, and transgender communities. *Journal of Gay and Lesbian Social Services, 11*(1), 1–26.

Drake, R. E., & Mueser, K. T. (2000). Psychosocial approaches to dual diagnosis. *Schizophrenia Bulletin, 26*(1), 105–116.

Du, L., Faludi, G., Palkovits, M., Bakish, D., & Hrdina, P. D. (2001). Serotonergic genes and suicidality. *Crisis: The Journal of Crisis Intervention and Suicide Prevention, 22*(2), 54–60.

Dube, S. R., Anda, R. F., Felitti, V. J., Croft, J. B., & Edwards, V. J. (2001). Growing up with parental alcohol abuse: Exposure to childhood abuse and neglect, and household dysfunction. *Child Abuse and Neglect, 25*(12), 1627–1640.

Duehn, W. D. (1994). Cognitive-behavioral approaches in the treatment of the child sex offender. In D. K. Granvold (Ed.), *Cognitive and behavioral treatment: Methods and applications* (pp. 125–134). Pacific Grove, CA: Brooks/Cole.

Duhl, B. S., & Duhl, F. J. (1981). Integrative family therapy. In A. S. Gurman & D. P. Kniskern (Eds.), *Handbook of family therapy* (pp. 483–513). New York: Brunner/Mazel.

Dulmus, C. N., & Smyth, N. J. (2000). Early-onset schizophrenia: A literature review of empirically-based interventions. *Child and Adolescent Social Work Journal, 17*(1), 55–69.

Dunkle, R. E., & Norgard, T. (1995). Aging: Overview. In R. L. Edwards (Ed.), *Encyclopedia of social work* (19th ed., pp. 142–153). Washington, DC: National Association of Social Workers Press.

Dunner, D. L. (2003). Clinical consequences of under-recognized bipolar spectrum disorder. *Bipolar Disorders, 5*(6), 456–463.

Durrant, M. (1995). *Creative strategies for school problems.* New York: Norton.

Dyer, J. A., & Kreitman, N. (1984). Hopelessness, depression and suicidal intent in parasuicide. *British Journal of Psychiatry, 144,* 127–133.

Dziegielewski, S. (2001). *Social work practice and psychopharmacology.* New York: Springer.

Dziegielewski, S. (2002). Social work and herbal medicine. In A. R. Roberts & G. J. Greene (Eds.), *Social workers' desk reference* (pp. 651–657). New York: Oxford Press.

Early, T. J., & GlenMaye, L. F. (2000). Valuing families: Social work practice with families from a strengths perspective. *Social Work, 45*(2), 118–129.

Eaton, Y. M., & Roberts, A. R. (2002). Frontline crisis intervention: Step-by-step practice guidelines with case applications. In A. R. Roberts & G. J. Greene (Eds.), *Social workers' desk reference* (pp. 89–96). New York: Oxford Press.

Ebenstein, H. (1998). Single-session groups: Issues for social workers. *Social Work with Groups, 21*(1/2), 49–60.

Edinburg, G. M., & Cottler, J. M. (1995). Managed care. In *Encyclopedia of social work,* (Vol. 2, pp. 1635–1642). Washington, DC: NASW Press.

Edlund, A., Lundstrom, M., Lundstrom, G., Hedqvist, B., & Gustafson, Y. (September–October, 1999). Clinical profile of delirium in patients treated for femoral neck fractures. *Dementia, Geriatrics, and Cognitive Disorders, 10*(5), 325–329.

Eisendrath, S. J. (1989). Factitious physical disorders: Treatment without confrontation. *Psychosomatics, 30,* 383–387.

Eisendrath, S. J. (1998). Psychiatric disorders. In L. M. Tierney, S. V. McPhee, & M. A. Papadakis, *Current medical diagnosis and treatment* (37th ed.). Stamford, CT: Appleton & Lange.

Eisendrath, S. J., & Lichtmacher, M. D. (2001). *Current medical diagnosis and treatment* (40th ed.). New York: McGraw-Hill.

Eisendrath, S. J., Rand, D. C., & Feldman, M. D. (1996). Factitious disorders and litigation. In M. D. Feldman & S. J. Eisendrath (Eds.), *The spectrum of factitious disorders* (pp. 65–81). Washington, DC: American Psychiatric Publishing.

Eisler, I., Dare, C., Hodes, M., Russell, G., Dodge, E., & Le Grange, D. (2000). Family therapy for adolescent anorexia nervosa: The results of a controlled comparison of two family interventions. *Journal of Child Psychology and Psychiatry and Allied Disciplines, 41,* 727–736.

El-Bassel, N., Ivanoff, A., Schilling, R., & Gilbert, L. (1995). Preventing AIDS/HIV in drug-abusing incarcerated women through skills building and social support enhancement: Preliminary outcomes. *Social Work Research, 19,* 131–141.

El-Bassel, N., Schilling, R., Irwin, K., Faruque, S., & Gilbert, L. (1997). Sex trading and psychological distress among women recruited from the streets of Harlem. *American Journal of Public Health, 87,* 66–70.

Elie, M., Cole, M. G., Primeau, F. J., & Bellavance, F. E. (1998). Delirium risk factors in elderly hospitalized patients. *Journal of General Internal Medicine, 13*(3), 204–213.

Ell, K. (1995). Crisis intervention: Research needs. In *Encyclopedia of social work* (19th ed.). Washington, DC: National Association of Social Workers.

Ellason, J. W., & Ross, C. A. (1997). Two-year follow up of inpatients with dissociative identity disorder. *American Journal of Psychiatry, 154,* 832–839.

Elliott, K. S., Di Minno, M., Lam, D., & Tu, A. M. (1996). Working with Chinese families in the context of dementia. In G. Yeo and D. Gallagher-Thompson (Eds.), *Ethnicity and the dementias* (pp. 89–108). Washington, DC: Taylor and Francis.

Ellis, A. (1962). *Reason and emotion in psychotherapy.* New York: Lyle Stuart.

Ellison, J. M., & Shader, R. I. (2003). Pharmacologic treatment of personality disorders: A dimensional approach. *Manual of psychiatric therapeutics* (3rd ed.). Philadelphia: Lippincott / Williams & Wilkins Publishers.

Emlet, C. A., Hawks, H., & Callahan, J. (2001). Alcohol use and abuse in a population of community dwelling, frail older adults. *Journal of Gerontological Social Work, 35*(4), 21–33.

Employee Benefit Research Institute. (1995). *Date book on employee benefits* (3rd ed.). Washington, DC: Author.

Emrick, C. D., Tonigan, J. S., & Montgomery, H. (1993). Alcoholics Anonymous: What is currently known? In B. S. McCrady & W. R. Miler (Eds.), *Research on Alcoholics Anonymous: Opportunities and alternatives* (pp. 41–76). New Brunswick, NJ: Rutgers Center of Alcohol Studies.

Engel, G. L. (1977). The need for a new medical model: A challenge for biomedicine. *Science, 196,* 120–136.

Engel, G. L. (1980). The clinical application of the biopsychosocial model. *American Journal of Psychiatry, 137,* 535.

Engel, G. L. (1997). From biomedical to biopsychosocial: Being scientific in the human domain. *Psychosomatics, 38*(6), 521–528.

Epple, D. M. (2002). Senile dementia of the Alzheimer type. *Clinical Social Work Journal, 30*(1), 95–110.

Epstein, J. F. (2002). *Substance dependence, abuse and treatment: Findings from the 2000 National Household Survey on drug abuse (NHSDA Series A-16).* Rockville, MD: Substance Abuse and Mental Health Administration, Office of Applied Studies.

Erdman, P., & Caffery, T. (Eds.). (2003). *Attachment and family systems: Conceptual, empirical and therapeutic relatedness.* New York: Brunner/Routledge.

Erikson, C. K., & Wilcox, R. E. (2001). Neurobiological causes of addiction. *Journal of Social Work Practice in the Addictions, 1*(3), 7–22.

Espeland, K. E. (1997). Inhalants: The instant, but deadly high. *Pediatric Nursing, 23*(1), 82–86.

Fabrega, H. (1991). Somatization in cultural and historical perspective. In L. J. Kirmayer and J. M. Robbins (Eds.), *Current concepts of somatization and clinical perspectives* (pp. 181–199). Washington, DC: American Psychiatric Press.

Fairburn, C. G., & Cooper, Z. (1998). The schedule of the eating disorder examination. In C. G. Fairburn & G. T. Wilson (Eds.), *Binge eating: Nature, assessment and treatment.* New York: Guilford.

Fallon, B. A., Klein, B. W., & Liebowitz, M. R. (1993). Hypochondriasis: Treatment strategies. *Psychiatric Annals, 23,* 1–8.

Fallon, B. A., Liebowitz, M. R., Salman, E., Schneier, F. R., Jusino, C., Hollander, E., & Klein, D. F. (1994). Fluoxetine for hypochondriacal patients without major depression. *Journal of Clinical Psychopharmacology, 1*(6), 438–441.

Fallon, B. A., Qureshi, A. I., Laje, G., & Klein, B. (2000). Hypochondriasis and its relationship with obsessive-compulsive disorder. *Psychiatric Clinics of North America, 23*(3), 605–616.

Falloon, I. R. H., & Liberman, R. P. (1983a). Interactions between drug and psychosocial therapy in schizophrenia. *Schizophrenia Bulletin, 3,* 544–554.

Falloon, I. R. H., & Liberman, R. P. (1983b). Behavioral family interventions in the management of chronic schizophrenia. In W. R. McFarlane (Ed.), *Family therapy in schizophrenia* (pp. 117–137). New York: Guilford.

Falvey, J. E. (2002). *Managing clinical supervision: Ethical practice and legal risk management.* Pacific Grove, CA: Brooks/Cole.

Fanger, M. T. (1995). Brief therapies. In R. L. Edwards (Editor-in-Chief), *Encyclopedia of social work* (19th ed., Vol. 1, pp. 323–334). Washington, DC: NASW Press.

Fanolis, V. (2001). The use of crisis teams in response to violent or critical incidents in schools. *Smith College Studies in Social Work, 71*(2), 271–278.

Farmer, A., Redman, K., Harris, T., Webb, R., Mahmood, A., Sadler, S., & McGuffin, P. (2001). The Cardiff sib-pair study: Suicidal ideation in depressed and healthy subjects and their siblings. *Crisis: The Journal of Crisis Intervention and Suicide Prevention, 22*(2), 71–73.

Farmer, R. L., & Pandurangi, A. K. (1997). Diversity in schizophrenia: Toward a richer biosocial understanding for social work practice. *Health and Social Work, 22*(2), 109–116.

Farr, C. L., Bordieri, J. E., Benshoff, J. J., & Taricone, P. F. (1996). Rehabilitation needs of individuals in treatment for alcohol dependency. *Journal of Applied Rehabilitation Counseling, 27*(1), 17–22.

Fava, G. (2003). Depressing antidepressant news. *Journal of Clinical Psychiatry, 64*(123), 123–133.

Feeny, N. C., Zoellner, L. A., Fitzgibbons, L. A., & Foa, E. B. (2000). Exploring the roles of emotional numbing, depression, and dissociation in PTSD. *Journal of Traumatic Stress, 13*(3), 489–498.

Feldman, L. B. (1985). Integrative multi-level therapy: A comprehensive interpersonal and intrapsychic approach. *Journal of Marital and Family Therapy, 11,* 357–372.

Feldman, L. B. (1992). *Integrating individual and family therapy.* New York: Brunner/Mazel.

Felix-Ortiz, M., Salazar, M. R., Gonzalez, J. R., Sorenson, J.L., & Plock, D. (2000). A qualitative evaluation of an assisted self-help group for drug-addicted clients in a structured outpatient treatment setting. *Community Mental Health Journal, 36*(4), 339–350.

Fellin, P. (1996). *Mental health and mental illness: Policies, programs, and services.* Itasca, IL: F. E. Peacock.

Fenton, W. S. (2000). Depression, suicide, and suicide prevention in schizophrenia. *Suicide and Life Threatening Behavior: The Official Journal of the American Association of Suicodology, 30,* 34–49.

Fenton, W. S., McGlashan, T. H., Victor, B. J., & Blyler, C. R. (1997). Symptoms, subtype and suicidality in patients with schizophrenia spectrum disorders. *American Journal of Psychiatry, 154,* 199–204.

Fenton, W. S., Mosher, L. R., Herrell, J. M., & Blyler, C. R. (1998). Randomized clinical trials of general hospital and residential alternative care for patients with severe and persistent mental illness. *American Journal of Psychiatry, 155,* 516–522.

Ferguson, K. L., & Rodway, M. R. (1994). Cognitive behavioral treatment of perfectionism: Initial evaluation studies. *Research on Social Work Practice, 4,* 283–308.

Fernandez-Sola, J., Estruch, R., Nicolas, J. M., Pare, J. C., Scanella, E., Antunez, E., & Urbano-Marquez, A. (1997). Comparison of alcoholic cardiomyopathy in women versus men. *American Journal of Cardiology, 80*(4), 481–485.

Fichtner, C. G., Hanrahan, P., & Luchins, D. J. (1998). Pharmacoeconomic studies of the atypical antipsychotic: Review and perspective. *Psychiatric Annals, 28,* 381–396.

Figley, C. R. (1995). *Compassion fatigue: Secondary traumatic stress disorders from treating the traumatized.* New York: Brunner/Mazel.

Figley, C. R. (2002). *Treating compassion fatigue.* New York: Routledge.

Fillenbaum, G. G., Heyman, A., Huber, M. S., & Woodbury, M. A. (1998). The prevalence and 3-year incidence of dementia in older black and white community residents. *Journal of Clinical Epidemiology, 51*(7): 587–595.

Fils-Aime, M. I., Eckardt, J. J., George, D. T., Brown, G. L., Mefford, I., & Linnoila, M. (1996). Early-onset alcoholics have lower cerebrospinal fluid 5-hydroxyindoleacetic acid levels than late-onset alcoholics. *Archives of General Psychiatry, 53*(5), 211–216.

Fine, C. G. (1999). The tactical-integration model for the treatment of dissociative identity disorder and allied dissociative disorders. *American Journal of Psychotherapy, 53*(3), 361–377.

Finklestein, L. (1987). Toward an object-relations approach in psychoanalytic marital therapy. *Journal of Marital and Family Therapy, 13*(3), 287–298.

Finney, J. W., Hahn, A. C., & Moos, R. H. (1996). The effectiveness of inpatient and outpatient treatment for alcohol abuse: The need to focus on mediators and moderators of setting effects. *Addiction, 91,* 1773–1796.

Fiorentine, R. (1999). After drug treatment: Are 12-step programs effective in maintaining abstinence? *American Journal of Drug and Alcohol Abuse, 25*(1), 93–116.

Fiorentine, R., & Anglin, M. D. (1996). More is better: Counseling participation and the effectiveness of outpatient drug treatment. *Journal of Substance Abuse Treatment, 13,* 341–348.

Fiorentine, R., & Anglin, M. D. (1997). Does increasing the opportunity for counseling increase the effectiveness of outpatient drug treatment? *American Journal of Drug and Alcohol Abuse, 25*(3), 369–382.

Firth, M., & Bridges, K. (1996). Brief social work intervention for people with severe and persistent disorders. *Journal of Mental Health, 5*(2), 135–143.

Fish, J. M. (1996). Prevention, solution-focused therapy, and the illusion of mental disorders. *Applied and Preventive Psychology, 5*(37), 37–40.

Fisher, G. L., & Harrison, T. C. (2000). *Substance abuse: Information for school counselors, social workers, therapists, and counselors* (2nd ed.). Boston: Allyn & Bacon.

Flacker, J. M., & Marcantonio, E. R. (1998). Delirium in the elderly: Optimal management. *Drugs and Aging, 13*(2), 119–130.

Fletcher, R. H. (1999). Who is responsible for the common good in a competitive market? *Journal of the American Medical Association, 281*(12), 1127(1).

Fletcher-Janzen, E., & Reynolds, C. R. (2003). *Childhood disorders: Diagnostic desk reference.* Indianapolis: Wiley/Jossey-Bass.

Floersch, J. (2002). *Meds, money, and manners.* New York: Columbia University Press.

Foa, E. B., & Meadows, E. A. (1997). Psychosocial treatments for posttraumatic stress disorder: A critical review. *Review of Psychology, 48,* 449–480.

Foa, E. B., Rothbaum, B. O., Riggs, D. S., & Murdock, T. (1991). Treatment of PTSD in rape victims: A comparison between cognitive-behavioral procedures and counseling. *Journal of Consulting and Clinical Psychology, 59,* 715–723.

Folsom, D., & Jeste, D. V. (2002). Schizophrenia in homeless persons: A systematic review of the literature. *Acta Psychiatrica Scandinavica, 105,* 404–413.

Foote, B. (1999). Dissociative identity disorder and pseudo-hysteria. *American Journal of Psychotherapy, 53,* 320–344.

Ford, C. V. (1995). Dimensions of somatization and hypochondriasis. *Neurologic Clinics, 12,* 241–253.

Foreyt, J. P., Poston, W. S. C., Winebarger, A. A., & McGavin, J. K. (1998). Anorexia nervosa and bulimia nervosa. In E. J. Mash & R. A. Barkley (Eds.), *Treatment of childhood disorders* (2nd ed., pp. 647–691). New York: Guilford Press.

Fortune. (2000). How the industries stack up. Retrieved October 17, 2000, from http://www.fortune.com/indexw.jhtml?channel=artcol.jhtml&doc_id=00001423

Fowler, D., Garety, P., & Kuipers, E. (1998). Cognitive therapy for psychosis: Formulation, treatment, effects and service implications. *Journal of Mental Health, 7*(2), 123–134.

Fox, K. J. (1999). Changing violent minds: Discursive correction and resistance in the cognitive treatment of violent offenders in prison. *Social Problems, 46*(1), 88–103.

Fox, P. (1984). Social work ethics and children: Protection vs. empowerment. *Children and Youth Services Review, 6,* 319–328.

Fox, P. (1992). Implications for expressed emotion within a family therapy context. *Health and Social Work, 17*(3), 207–213.

Framo, J. L. (1970). Symptoms from a family transactional viewpoint. In N. W. Ackerman (Ed.), *Family therapy in transition.* Boston: Little, Brown.

Framo, J. L. (1982). *Explorations in marital and family therapy: Selected papers of James L. Framo.* New York: Springer.

Frances, A. (1995). *DSM-IV audio review.* Washington, DC: American Psychiatric Press.

Frances, A., First, M. B., & Pincus, H. N. (1995). *DSM-IV guidebook: The essential companion to the diagnostic and statistical manual of mental disorders.* Washington, DC: American Psychiatric Association.

Francis, J. (1997). Outcomes of delirium: Can systems make a difference? *Journal of the American Geriatric Society, 45,* 247–248.

Frank, E., Swartz, H. A., & Kupfer, D. J. (2000). Interpersonal and social rhythm therapy: Managing the chaos of bipolar disorder. *Biological Psychiatry, 48,* 593–604.

Franken, I. H. A., & Hendriks, V. M. (1999). Predicting outcome of inpatient detoxification of substance abusers. *Psychiatric Services, 50,* 813–817.

Franklin, C., & Jordan, C. (1999). *Family practice: Brief systems methods for social work.* Pacific Grove, CA: Brooks/Cole.

Franklin, C., & Streeter, C. L. (1992). Social support and psychoeducation interventions with middle-class dropout youth. *Child and Adolescent Social Work, 9*(2), 131–153.

Fraser, J. S. (1995). Process, problems, and solutions in brief therapy. *Journal of Marital and Family Therapy, 21*(3), 265–279.

Fraser, M. W., Richman, J. M., & Galinski, M. J. (1999). Risk, protection, and resilience: Toward a conceptual framework for social work practice. *Social Work Research, 23*(3), 131–143.

Freeman, R. C., Parillo, K. M., Collier, K., & Rusek, R. W. (2001). Child and adolescent sexual abuse history in a sample of 1,490 women sexual partners of injection drug-using men. *Women and Health, 34*(4), 31–49.

Freud, S. (1924). *A general introduction to psychoanalysis.* New York: Boni and Liveright.

Friedman, B. D. (2000). Building a spiritual based model to address substance abuse. *Social Thought, 19*(3), 23–38.

Fristad, M. A., Gavazzi, S. M., & Soldano, K. (1999). Naming the enemy: Learning to differentiate mood disorder "symptoms" from the "self" that experiences them. *Journal of Family Psychotherapy, 10*(1), 81–88.

Fritzsche, K., & Larisch, A. (2003). Treating patients with functional somatic symptoms. *Scandinavian Journal of Primary Health Care, 21*(3), 132–136.

Froehlich, J. C. (1997). Opioid peptides. *Alcohol Health & Research World, 21*(2), 97–136.

Fryo, K., Hardell, C., & Cederroth, K. W. (1999). Problem-oriented sessions: Presentation of a method for therapeutic work within a narrow time frame. *Psychodynamic Counseling, 5*(4), 465–481.

Fuller, R. K., & Hiller-Sturmhöfel, S. (1999). Alcoholism treatment in the United States: An overview. *Alcohol Research & Health, 23*(2), 69–77.

Gabbard, G. O. (Ed.). (1995). *Treatment of psychiatric disorders* (2nd ed.). Washington, DC: American Psychiatric Press.

Gabbard, G. O., & Kay, J. (2001). The fate of integrated treatment: Whatever happened to the biopsychosocial psychiatrist? *American Journal of Psychiatry, 158*(12), 1956–1963.

Gagne, C. (1999, August). Recovery from mental illness: Results from the Recovery Research Project. Paper presented at the annual meeting of the American Psychological Association, Boston.

Galanter, R. (Ed.) (1998). *Recent developments in alcoholism, Vol. 14: The consequences of alcoholism: Medical, neuropsychiatric, economic, and cross-cultural.* New York: Plenum.

Gallagher-Thompson, D., Talamantes, M., Ramirez, R., & Valverde, I. (1996). Service delivery issues and recommendations for working with Mexican American family caregivers. In G. Yeo & D. Gallagher-Thompson (Eds.), *Ethnicity and the dementias* (pp. 137–152). Washington, DC: Taylor and Francis.

Gambrill, E. (1983). *Casework: A competency-based approach.* Englewood Cliffs, NJ: Prentice-Hall.

Gambrill, E. (1997). *Social work practice: A critical thinker's guide.* New York: Oxford University Press.

Garbutt, J. C., West, S. L., Carey, T. S., & Lohr, K. N. (1999). Pharmacological treatment of alcohol dependence: A review of the evidence. *JAMA, 281*(14), 1318–1325.

Garety, P. A., Fowler, D., & Kulpers, E. (2000). Cognitive-behavioral therapy for medication-resistant symptoms. *Schizophrenia Bulletin, 26*(1), 73–86.

Garland, J. A., Jones, H., & Kilodney, R. (1965). A model for stages of development on social work groups. In L. A. Frey & S. Bernstein (Eds.), *Explorations in group work* (pp. 12–53). Boston: Boston University School of Social Work.

Garmezy, N. (1993). Children in poverty: Resiliency despite risk. *Psychiatry, 56,* 127–136.

Garnefski, N., & Diekstra, R. F. W. (1997). Child sexual abuse and emotional and behavioral problems in adolescents: Gender differences. *Journal of American Academy of Child and Adolescent Psychiatry, 36,* 323–329.

Garner, D. M. (1994). Bulimia nervosa. In A. Freeman & F. M. Dattilio (Eds.), *Comprehensive casebook of cognitive therapy* (pp. 169–176). New York: Plenum Press.

Garner, D. M., & Friedman, L. J. (1994). Eating disorders. In F. M. Dattilio & A. Freeman (Eds.), *Cognitive-behavioral strategies in crisis intervention* (pp. 137–160). New York: Guilford.

Garrett, K., & Rice, S. (1998). Psychoeducational multiple-family groups. *The Journal of Baccalaureate Social Work, 3*(2), 89–99.

Garson, S. (1986). *Out of our minds.* Buffalo, NY: Prometheus.

Garvey, M. (1990). Benzodiazepines for panic disorder. *Postgraduate Medicine, 90*(5), 245–246, 249–252.

Gaugler, J. E., Leitsch, S. A., Zarit, S. H., & Pearlin, L. I. (2000). Caregiver involvement following institution-alization: Effects of preplacement stress. *Research on Aging, 22*(4): 337–359.

Geerlings, P. J., Ansoms, C., & Van Den Brink, W. (1997). Acamprosate and prevention of relapse in alcoholics. *European Addiction Research, 3*(3), 129–137.

Gehart, D. R., & Tuttle, A. R. (2003). *Theory-based treatment planning for marriage and family therapists* (pp. 172–191). Pacific Grove, CA: Brooks/Cole.

Geldmacher, D. S., & Whitehouse, P. J. (1996). Evaluation of dementia. *The New England Journal of Medicine, 335*(5): 330–336.

Gelfand, D. M., & Drew, C. J. (2003). *Understanding child behavior disorders* (4th ed.). Belmont, CA: Wadsworth/Thomson.

Gelman, S. (1999). *Medicating schizophrenia: A history.* New Brunswick, NJ: Rutgers University Press.

Gelso, C. J., Hill, C. E., Mohr, J. J., Rochlen, A. B., & Zack, J. (1999). Describing the face of transference: Psycho-dynamic therapists' recollect transference in cases of successful long-term therapy. *Journal of Counseling Psychology, 46*(2), 257–267.

Gendron, C., Poitras, L., Dastoor, D. P., & Perodeau, G. (1996). Cognitive-behavioral group intervention for spousal caregivers: Findings and clinical considerations. *Clinical Gerontologist, 17*(1), 3–19.

General Accounting Office. (2000, May 10). *Mental health parity.* Washington, DC: Author.

Gergen, K. J. (1985). The social construction movement in modern psychology. *American Psychologist, 40,* 266–275.

Germain, C. (1973). An ecological perspective in casework practice. *Social Casework, 54,* 323–330.

Germain, C. (1991). *Human behavior in the social environment: An ecological view.* New York: Columbia University Press.

Germain, C., & Gitterman, A. (1995). Ecological perspective. In J. G. Hopps and G. Lloyd (Eds.), *Encyclopedia of social work* (19th ed.), (pp. 816–824). Washington, DC: NASW Press.

Germain, C., & Gitterman, A. (1996). *The life model of social work practice.* New York: Columbia University Press.

Giannini, A. J. (2000). An approach to drug abuse, intoxication and withdrawal. *American Family Physician, 61,* 2763–2774.

Gibelman, M. (2002). Social work in an era of managed care. In A. R. Roberts & G. J. Greene (Eds.), *Social workers' desk reference* (pp. 16–22). New York: Oxford Press.

Gibelman, M., & Schervish, P. H. (1997). *Who we are: A second look.* Washington, DC: NASW Press.

Gilgun, J. F. (1996). Human development and adversity in ecological perspective. Part I: A conceptual framework. *Families in Society, 77,* 395–402.

Gingerich, W. J., de Shazer, S., & Weiner-Davis, M. (1988). Constructing change: A research view of interviewing. In E. Lipchik (Ed.), *Interviewing.* Rockville, MD: Aspen.

Gingerich, W. J., & Eisengart, S. (2000). Solution-focused brief therapy: A review of the outcome research. *Family Process, 39,* 477–498.

Gingerich, W. J., & Wabeke, T. (2001). A solution-focused approach to mental health intervention in school settings. *Children and Schools, 23*(1), 33–47.

Ginsberg, L. (1995). *Social work almanac* (2nd ed.). Washington, DC: NASW Press.

Gitterman, A. (Ed.). (2001). *Handbook of social work practice with vulnerable and resilient populations* (2nd ed.). New York: Columbia University Press.

Gitterman, A. (2001a). Vulnerability, resilience, and social work with groups. In T. Kelly, T. Berman-Rossi, & S. Palombo (Eds.), *Group work: Strategies for strengthening resiliency* (pp. 19–33). New York: Haworth.

Gitterman, A., & Shulman, L. (1994). *Mutual aid groups: Vulnerable populations and the life cycle.* New York: Columbia University Press.

Gladding, S. T. (1995). *Group work: A counseling specialty.* New York: Merrill.

Gladstone, J., & Reynolds, T. (1997). Single-session group work intervention in response to employee stress during workforce transformation. *Social Work with Groups, 20*(1), 33–50.

Glazer, S. (2002). Treating anxiety. *CQ Researcher, 12*(5), 99–110.

Glazer, W. M., & Dickson, R. A. (1998). Clozapine reduces violence and persistent aggression in schizophrenia. *Journal of Clinical Psychiatry, 59*(Suppl.), 8–14.

Glazer, W. M., & Johnstone, B. M. (1997). Pharmacoeconomic evaluation of antipsychotic therapy for schizophrenia. *Journal of Clinical Psychiatry, 57*(Suppl. 10), 50–54.

Glenmullen, J. (2000). *Prozac backlash: Overcoming the dangers of Prozac, Zoloft, Paxil and other antidepressants with safe, effective alternatives.* New York: Simon and Schuster.

Glick, I. D., Murray, S. R., Vasudevan, P., & Marder, S. R. (2001). Treatment with atypical antipsychotics: New indications and new populations. *Journal of Psychiatric Research, 35*(3), 187–191.

Goff, D. C., Heckers, S., & Freudenreich, O. (2001). Schizophrenia. *Medical Clinics of North America, 85*(3), 663–689.

Goldenberg, I., & Goldenberg, H. (1991). *Family therapy: An overview* (3rd ed.). Pacific Grove, CA: Brooks/Cole Publishing Company.

Goldenberg, I., & Goldenberg, H. (1996). Family therapy. In R. J. Corsini & D. Wedding (Eds.), *Current psychotherapies* (5th ed., pp. 356–385). Itasca, IL: F. E. Peacock.

Goldenberg, I., & Goldenberg, H. (1997). *Family therapy: An overview* (4th ed.). Pacific Grove, CA: Brooks/Cole.

Goldenberg, I., & Goldenberg, H. (2000). *Family therapy: An overview* (5th ed.). Pacific Grove, CA: Brooks/Cole.

Goldman, M. S. (1998). Alcohol abuse and dependence: The process of empirical validation. In K. S. Dobson & K. D. Craig (Eds.), *Empirically supported therapies: Best practices in professional psychology* (pp. 327–358). Thousand Oaks, CA: Sage.

Goldney, R. D. (2003). Depression and suicidal behavior: The real estate analogy. *Crisis: The Journal of Crisis Intervention and Suicide Prevention, 24*(2), 87–88.

Goldstein, E. (1995). *Ego psychology and social work practice.* (2nd ed.). New York: Free Press.

Goldstein, E. G., & Noonan, M. (1999). *Short-term treatment and social work practice: An integrative perspective.* New York: The Free Press.

Goldstein, M. (1996). Psychoeducational family interventions in psychotic disorders. *New Trends in Experimental and Clinical Psychiatry, 12*(2), 71–79.

Gomberg, R. M. (1958). Trends in theory and practice. *Social Casework, 39,* 73–83.

Gomez, M. B., Primm, A. B., Tzolva-Iontchev, I., & Perry, W. (2000). A description of precipitants of drug use among dually diagnosed patients with chronic mental illness. *Community Mental Health Journal, 36*(4), 351–362.

Goode, E. (2001). Disparities seen in mental health for minorities. *The New York Times,* (late edition), Section A, p. 1, col. 2.

Goodman, S. H., & Gotlib, I. H. (1999). Risk for psychopathology in the children of depressed mothers: A developmental model for understanding mechanisms of transmission. *Psychological Review, 106,* 458–490.

Gordis, E. (2001). Improving the old, embracing the new: Implications of alcohol research for future practice. *Social Work in Health Care, 33*(1), 17–41.

Gorman, H. E. (1999). Interpreting transference in supervision of psychoanalytic psychotherapy. *American Journal of Psychoanalytic Psychotherapy, 53*(4), 452–467.

Gortner, E. T., Gollan, J. K., & Jacobson, N. S. (1997). Psychological aspects of perpetrators of domestic violence and their relationships with the victims. *The Psychiatric Clinics of North America, 20,* 337–351.

Gosden, R., & Beder, S. (2001). Pharmaceutical agenda-setting in mental health policy. *Ethical Human Sciences and Services, 3,* 147–159.

Gough, R. (2003, September 22). GPs fail to pick up eating disorders, says NICE guidance. *Pulse* 20. Retrieved May 16, 2005 from http://www.pulse-i.co.uk.html

Granner, M. L., Abood, D. A., & Black, D. R. (2001). Racial differences in eating disorder attitudes, cigarette, and alcohol use. *American Journal of Health Behavior, 25*(2), 83–99.

Grant, J. E. (2001). Successful treatment of nondelusional body dysmorphic disorder with olanzapine: A case report. *Journal of Clinical Psychiatry, 62*(4), 297.

Grant, R. W., & Casey, D. A. (2000). Geriatric psychiatry: Evolution of an inpatient unit. *Administration and Policy in Mental Health, 27*(3), 153–156.

Granvold, D. K. (1994). Cognitive-behavioral divorce therapy. In D. K. Granvold (Ed.), *Cognitive and behavioral treatment: Methods and applications* (pp. 222–242). Pacific Grove, CA: Brooks/Cole.

Granvold, D. K., & Jordan, C. (1994). The cognitive-behavioral treatment of marital distress. In D. K. Granvold (Ed.), *Cognitive and behavioral treatment: Methods and applications* (pp. 174–197). Pacific Grove, CA: Brooks/Cole.

Gray, J. A., & McNaughton, N. (1996). The neuropsychology of anxiety: Reprise. In D. A. Hope (Ed.), *Perspectives on anxiety, panic and fear (The 43rd Annual Nebraska Symposium on Motivation)* (pp. 61–134). Lincoln: Nebraska University Press.

Gray, R., Wykes, T., & Gournay, K. (2002). From compliance to concordance: A review of the literature on interventions to enhance compliance with antipsychotic medication. *Journal of Psychiatric and Mental Health Nursing, 9*(3), 277–284.

Gray, S. W., & Zide, M. R. (1998, April). *Managing supervisory dilemmas through maximizing the strengths of supervisees.* Barry University, School of Social Work, Alumni Conference, Miami Shores, Florida.

Gray, S. W., Zide, M. R., & Wilker, H. (1998). *Using the solution-focused brief therapy model in bereavement groups in the rural community: Resiliency at its best.* Twentieth Annual Group Work Symposium, Miami, Florida.

Gray, S. W., Zide, M. R., & Wilker, H. (2000). Using the solution-focused brief therapy model with bereavement groups in rural communities: Resiliency at its best. *Hospice Journal, 15*(3), 13–30.

Green, M. F., Marshall, B. D., Wirshing, W. C., & Ames, D. (1997). Does Risperidone improve verbal working memory in treatment-resistant schizophrenia? *American Journal of Psychiatry, 154,* 321–330.

Greenberg, G. (1997). Right answers, wrong reason: Revisiting the deletion of homosexuality from the DSM. *Review of General Psychology, 1,* 256–270.

Greenberg, K. K. (2002). The relationship between shame, guilt, and body image dissatisfaction to disordered eating symptomatology in female undergraduates. *Dissertation Abstracts International, A: The Humanities and Social Sciences, 62*(12), 4332-A.

Greenberg, L. S., & Johnson, S. M. (1988). *Emotionally-focused therapy for couples.* New York: Guilford.

Greene, R. R. (2002). *Resiliency: An integrated approach to practice, policy, and research.* Washington, DC: NASW Press.

Greene, R. R., & Livingston, N. C. (2002). A social construct. In R. R. Greene (Ed.), *Resiliency: An integrated approach to practice, policy, and research* (pp. 63–93). Washington, DC: NASW Press.

Greenstone, J. L., & Leviton, S. C. (2002). *Elements of crisis intervention.* Belmont, CA: Wadsworth.

Greer, G., & Tolbert, R. A. (1998). A method of conducting therapeutic sessions with MDMA. *Journal of Psychoactive Drugs, 30*(4), 371–379.

Gruber, K. J., Fleetwood, T. W., & Herring, M. W. (2001). In-home continuing care services for substance-affected families: The bridges program. *Social Work, 46*(3), 267–277.

Gruetzner, H. (1997). *Alzheimer's: A complete guide for families and loved ones.* New York: Wiley.

Guadalupe, K. L., & Lum, D. (2005). *Multidimensional contextual practice: Diversity and transcendence.* Belmont, CA: Thomson Brooks/Cole.

Guest, T. (2000). Using the eating disorder examination in the assessment of bulimia and anorexia: Issues of reliability and validity. *Social Work in Health Care, 31*(2), 71–83.

Gull, W. W. (1874/1964). Anorexia nervosa. *Transaction of the Clinical Society of London, 7,* 22–28. Reprinted in R. M. Kaufman & M. Heiman (Eds.), *Evolution of psycho-somatic concepts, anorexia nervosa: a paradigm.* New York: International Universities Press.

Gumley, A. I., & Power, K. G. (2000). Is targeting cognitive therapy during relapse in psychosis feasible? *Behavioural and Cognitive Psychotherapy, 28,* 161–174.

Gunderson, J. G., & Gabbard, G. O. (Eds.). (2000). *Psychotherapy for personality disorders.* Washington, DC: American Psychiatric Press.

Gupta, S., Frank, B., & Madhusoodanan, S. (2002). Tardive dyskinesia: Legal issues and consent. *Psychiatric Annals, 32*(4), 245–248.

Gurnack, A. M., & Johnson, W. A. (2002). Elderly drug use and racial/ethnic populations. *Journal of Ethnicity in Substance Abuse, 1*(2), 55–71.

Gutheil, I. A., & Tepper, L. M. (1997). The aging family: Ethnic and cultural considerations. In E. P. Congress (Ed.), *Multicultural perspective in working with families* (pp. 89–105). New York: Springer Publishing Company, Inc.

Gutierrez, L. M. (1990). Working with women of color: An empowerment perspective. *Social Work, 35,* 149–154.

Gutierrez, L., DeLois, K., & GlenMaye, L. (1995a). Understanding empowerment practice: Building on practitioner-based knowledge. *Families in Society, 76,* 534–542.

Gutierrez, L., DeLois, K., & GlenMaye, L. (1995b). The organizational context of empowerment practice: Implications for social work administration. *Social Work, 40,* 249–258.

Gutierrez, L., Parsons, R., & Cox, E. O. (1998). *Empowerment in social work practice: A sourcebook.* Pacific Grove, CA: Brooks/Cole.

Haack, M. R. (1998). Treating acute withdrawal from alcohol and other drugs. *Nursing Clinics of North America, 33,* 75–92.

Haddock, G., Barrowclough, C., & Tarrier, N. (2002). Cognitive behaviour therapy for patients with co-existing psychosis and substance use problems. In A. Morrison (Ed.), *A casebook of cognitive therapy for psychosis.* (pp. 265–280). New York: Brunner-Routledge.

Haddock, G., Tarrier, N., Morrison, A. P., Hopkins, R., Drake, R., & Lewis, S. (1999). A pilot study evaluating the effectiveness of individual inpatient cognitive-behavioral therapy in early psychosis. *Social Psychiatry and Psychiatric Epidemiology, 34,* 254–258.

Hadjipavlou, G., Hiram, M. G., & Yatham, L. N. (2004). Pharmacotherapy of bipolar II disorder: A critical review of current evidence. *Bipolar Disorders, 6*(1), 14–26.

Hafner, H. (2000). Onset and early course as determinants of the further course of schizophrenia. *Acta Psychiatrica Scandinavica, 102*(407), 44–48.

Hales, D. R., & Hales, R. E. (1995). *Caring for the mind: The comprehensive guide to mental health.* New York: Bantam.

Haley, J. (1976). *Problem-solving therapy.* San Francisco: Jossey-Bass.

Haley, J. (1987). *Problem-solving therapy* (2nd ed.). San Francisco: Jossey-Bass.

Hall, J. A., Schlesinger, D. J., & Dineen, J. P. (1997). Social skills training in groups with developmentally disabled adults. *Research on Social Work Practice, 7*(2), 187–201.

Hall, J. M. (2003). Dissociative experiences of women child abuse survivors. *Trauma, Violence and Abuse, 4*(4), 283–309.

Hall, S. M., Muñoz, R. F., & Reus, V. I. (1996). Mood management and nicotine gum in smoking treatment: A therapeutic contact and placebo-controlled study. *Journal of Consulting and Clinical Psychology, 64,* 1003–1009.

Halligan, P.W., Athwal, B. S., Oakley, D. A., & Frackowiak, R. S. J. (2000). The functional anatomy of a hypnotic paralysis: Implications for conversion hysteria. *Lancet, 355,* 986–987.

Hanna, S. M., & Brown, J. H. (1995). *The practice of family therapy: Key elements across models.* Pacific Grove, CA: Brooks/Cole.

Hanson, M. (2001). Alcoholism and other drug addictions. In A. Gitterman (Ed.), *Handbook of social work practice with vulnerable and resilient populations* (2nd ed., pp. 64–96). New York: Columbia University Press.

Harper, K. V., & Lantz, J. (1996). *Cross-cultural practice social work with diverse populations.* Chicago: Lyceum Books.

Harris, D. J., & Kuba, S. A. (1997). Ethnocultural identity and eating disorders in women of color. *Professional Psychology: Research and Practice, 26,* 341–347.

Harris, M., & Bergman, H. C. (1986). Case management with the chronically mentally ill: A clinical perspective. *American Journal of Orthopsychiatry, 56,* 296–302.

Harris, P. L. (1999). Individual differences in understanding emotion: The role of attachment status and psychological discourse. *Attachment and Human Development, 1*(3), 307–324.

Harsch, H. H., Pankiewicz, J., Bloom, A. S., Rainey, C., & Cho, J. K. (2000). Hepatitis C virus infection in cocaine users: A silent epidemic. *Community Mental Health Journal, 36*(30), 225–233.

Hartman, A. (1995). Family therapy. In *Encyclopedia of social work* (19th ed., Vol. 2, pp. 983–991). Washington, DC: NASW Press.

Hartvig, P., & Sterner, G. (1985). Childhood psychological environmental exposure in women diagnosed with somatoform disorder. *Scandinavian Journal of Social Medicine, 13,* 153–157.

Harvey, P. D. (2001). Cognitive and functional impairments in elderly patients with schizophrenia: A review of the recent literature. *Harvard Review of Psychiatry, 9*(2), 59–68.

Hatfield, A. B. (1990). *Family education in mental illness.* New York: Guilford.

Hatfield, A. R., & Lefley, H. P. (1993). *Surviving mental illness: Stress, coping and adaptation.* New York: Guilford.

Hawkins, J. D., Catalano, R. F., & Associates. (1992). *Communities that care: Action for drug abuse prevention.* San Francisco: Jossey Bass.

Hawley, D. R., & de Haan, L. (1996). Toward a definition of family resilience: Integrating life span and family perspectives. *Family Process, 35,* 283–298.

Hayashida, M. (1998). An overview of outpatient and inpatient detoxification. *Alcohol Health & Research World, 22*(1), 44–46.

Hayes, L. L. (1997). Comprehensive services required when helping pregnant women overcome addiction. *Counseling Today, 1,* 20.

Health Insurance Association of America. (1996). *Sourcebook of health insurance data, 1995.* Washington, DC: Author.

Healy, D. (2002). *The creation of psychopharmacology.* Cambridge, MA: Harvard University.

Heard, H., & Linehan, M. (1994). Dialectical behavior therapy: An integrative approach to the treatment of the borderline personality disorder. *Journal of Psychotherapy Integration, 4,* 55–82.

Heath, A. W., & Stanton, M. D. (1998). Family-based treatment. In R. J. Frances & S. J. Miller (Eds.), *Clinical textbook of addictive disorders* (2nd ed.). New York: Guilford.

Hebert, L. E., Wilson, R. S., Gilley, D. W. K., Beckett, L. A., & Scherr, P. A. (2000). Decline of language among women and men with Alzheimer's disease. *The Journals of Gerontology Series B: Psychological Sciences and Social Services, 55,* P354–P361.

Heila, H., Isometsa, E. T., Henriksson, M. M., & Marttunen, M. J. (1997). Suicide and schizophrenia: A nationwide psychological autopsy study on age- and sex-specific clinical characteristics of 92 suicide victims with schizophrenia. *American Journal of Psychiatry, 154,* 1235–1242.

Heller, N. R. (2002). Eating disorders and treatment planning. In A. R. Roberts & G. J. Greene (Eds.), *Social workers' desk reference* (pp. 328–333). New York: Oxford University Press.

Heller, N. R., & Johnson, H. C. (2001). Borderline personality. In A. Gitterman (Ed.), *Handbook of social work practice with vulnerable and resilient populations* (2nd ed., pp. 97–123). New York: Columbia University Press.

Heller, T., Roccoforte, J. A., Hsieh, K., Cook, J. A., & Pickett, S. A. (1997). Benefits of support groups for families of adults with severe mental illness. *American Journal of Orthopsychiatry, 67*(2), 187–198.

Henderson, J. N. (1996). Cultural dynamics of dementia in a Cuban and Puerto Rican population in the United States.

In G. Yeo and D. Gallagher-Thompson (Eds.), *Ethnicity and the dementias* (pp. 153–166). Washington, DC: Taylor and Francis.

Hendrickson, E. L., Schmal, M. S., & Ekleberry, S. C. (2004). *Treating co-occurring disorders: A handbook for mental health and substance abuse professionals.* Binghamton, NY: Haworth.

Henry, J. A., Jeffreys, J. A., & Dawling, S. (1992). Toxicity and deaths from 3, 4-methylenedioxymethamphetamine ("ecstasy"). *Lancet, 340,* 384–387.

Henry, S. (1992). *Group skills in social work: A four-dimensional approach* (2nd ed.). Pacific Grove, CA: Brooks/Cole.

Hepworth, D., Rooney, R., & Larsen, J. (2002). *Direct social work practice: Theory and skills* (6th ed.). Belmont, CA: Brooks/Cole.

Herman, J., Perry, J., & Van der Kolk, B. (1989). Childhood trauma in borderline personality disorders. *American Journal of Psychiatry, 146,* 490–495.

Herz, A. (1997). Endogenous opioid systems and alcohol addiction. *Psychopharmacology, 129,* 99–111.

Herz, M. J. (1996). Psychosocial treatment. *Psychiatric Annals, 26*(8), 531–535.

Hess, S. (1999). *Interns' critical incidents of nondisclosure and reluctant disclosure in supervision: A qualitative analysis.* Unpublished doctoral dissertation, University of Maryland at College Park.

Hewitt, H. (1996). Facilitating an effective process in treatment groups with persons having serious mental illness. *Social Work with Groups, 19*(1), 5–18.

Hewitt, P. L., & Flett, G. L. (1993). Dimensions of perfectionism, daily stress, and depression: A test of the specific vulnerability hypothesis. *Journal of Abnormal Psychology, 192,* 58–65.

Hilarski, C., & Wodarski, J. S. (2001). Comorbid substance abuse and mental illness: Diagnosis and treatment. *Journal of Social Work Practice in Addictions, 1*(1), 105–120.

Hill, R. (1949). *Families under stress.* New York: Harper and Brothers.

Hipplus, H. (1999). A historical perspective of clozapine. *Journal of Clinical Psychiatry, 60*(Suppl. 12), 22–23.

Hirayama, H., & Hirayama, K. K. (1998). Fostering resiliency in children through group work: Instilling hope, courage, and life skills. Presentation at XX Annual Symposium, Association for the Advancement of Social Work with Groups, in Miami, Florida.

Hirsch, S. R., Kissling, W., Baumi, J., & Power, A. (2002). A 28-week comparison of Ziprasidone and haloperidol in outpatients with stable schizophrenia. *Journal of Clinical Psychiatry, 63*(6), 516–523.

Ho, M. K. (1987). *Family therapy with ethnic minorities.* Newbury Park, CA: Sage.

Hollander, E., & Stein, D. (Eds.). (1997). *OCD: Diagnosis, etiology, treatment.* New York: Marcel Dekker.

Hollis, F. (1970). *The psychosocial approach to casework.* In R. Roberts and R. Nee (Eds.), *Theories of social casework,* pp. 33–75. Chicago: University of Chicago Press.

Hollon, S. D., & K. L. Haman (2002). Cognitive-behavioral treatment of depression. In I. H. Gotlib (Ed.), *Handbook of depression* (pp. 383–403). New York: Guilford.

Holzman, P. (2003). Less is truly more: Psychopathology research in the twenty-first century. In M. F. Lenzenweger & J. M. Hooley (Eds.), *Principles of experimental psychopathology: Essays in honor of Brendan A. Maher* (pp. 175–193). Washington, DC: American Psychology Association.

Homrich, A. M., & Horne, A. M. (2000). Brief family therapy. In A. M. Horne (Ed.), *Family counseling and therapy* (3rd ed., pp. 243–271). Itasca, IL: F. E. Peacock.

Hooyman, N. R., & Kiyak, H. A. (1996). *Social gerontology* (4th ed.). Boston: Allyn & Bacon.

Horne, A. M. (2000). *Family counseling and therapy* (3rd ed.). Itasca, IL: F. E. Peacock.

Horne, A. M., & Passmore, J. L. (1991). *Family counseling and therapy.* Itasca, IL: F. E. Peacock.

Horney, K. (1950). *Neurosis and human growth: The struggle toward self-realization.* New York: Norton.

Howard, D. L., & McCaughrin, W. C. (1996). The treatment effectiveness of outpatient substance misuse treatment organizations between court-mandated and voluntary clients. *Substance Use and Misuse, 31,* 895–925.

Hoyt, M. F. (1995). Brief psychotherapies. In A. S. Gurman & S. B. Messer (Eds.), *Essential psychotherapies: Theory and practice* (pp. 441–487). New York: Guilford.

Hubble, M. A., Duncan, B. L., & Miller, S. D. (Eds.). (1999). *The heart and soul of change: What works in therapy.* Washington, DC: American Psychological Association.

Hudson, C. G. (2001). Changing patterns of acute psychiatric hospitalization under a public managed care program. *Journal of Sociology and Social Welfare, 28*(2), 141–176.

Hughes, J. R. (1993). Pharmacotherapy for smoking cessation: Unvalidated assumptions, anomalies, and suggestions for future research. *Journal of Consulting and Clinical Psychology, 61,* 751–760.

Hughes, J. R., Goldstein, M. G., Hurt, R. D., & Shiffman, S. (1999). Recent advances in the pharmacotherapy of smoking. *Journal of the American Medical Association, 281*(1), 72–76.

Hughes, J. R., Gust, S. W., Skoog, K., Keenan, R. M., & Fenwick, J. W. (1991). Symptoms of tobacco withdrawal: A replication and extension. *Archives of General Psychiatry, 48*(1), 52–59.

Humphries, K. (1999). Professional interventions that facilitate 12-step self-help group involvement. *Alcohol Research & Health, 23*(2), 93–98.

Humphries, L. L., & Stern, S. (1988). Object relations and the family system in bulimia: A theoretical integration. *Journal of Marital and Family Therapy, 14,* 337–350.

Hunter, E. C. M., Phillips, M. L., Chalder, T., Sierra, M., & David, A. S. (2003). Depersonalization disorder: A cognitive-behavioural conceptualisation. *Behaviour Research and Therapy, 41*(12), 1451–1468.

Hurcom, C., Copello, A., & Oxford, J. (2000). The family and alcohol: Effects of excessive drinking and conceptualizations of spouses over recent decades. *Substance Use and Misuse, 35*(4), 473–502.

Hurdle, D. (2001). Less is best: A group-based treatment program for persons with personality disorders. *Social Work with Groups, 23*(4), 71–80.

Hurt, R. D., & Robertson, C. R. (1998). Prying open the door to the tobacco industry's secrets about nicotine. *Journal of the American Medical Association, 280*, 1173–1181.

Husted, J., & Ender, E. (2001). Understanding successful community living by individuals with serious and persistent mental illness. *Psychological Reports, 89*(1), 135–141.

Hutchins, J. (1996). Managing managed care for families. *NAFBS News, 5*(2), 102–113.

Hwang, M. I. (1999). Do you have a drinking problem? *The American Journal of Medicine, 281*(14), 1352–1362.

Hyman, B., & Pedrick, C. (1999). *The OCD workbook.* Oakland, CA: New Harbinger.

Inaba, D. S., & Cohen, W. E. (1997). *Uppers, downers, all arounders: Physical and mental effects of drugs of abuse* (3rd ed.). Ashlanuma, OR: Cineme.

Inclan, J., & Hernandez, M. (1992). Cross-cultural perspectives and codependence: The case of poor Hispanics. *American Journal of Orthopsychiatry, 62*(2), 245–255.

Inouye, S. K., & Charpentier, P. A. (1996). Precipitating factors for delirium in hospitalized elderly persons: Predictive model and interrelationships with baseline vulnerability. *Journal of the American Medical Society, 275*, 852–857.

International Society for the Study of Dissociation (ISSD). (1997). *Guidelines for treatment.* Northbrook, IL: Author.

InterStudy. (2003). The inter-study competitive edge: HMO industry report 13.2. St. Paul, MN: Author.

Irvin, J. E., Bowers, C. A., Dunn, M. E., & Wang, M. C. (1999). Efficacy of relapse prevention: A meta-analytic review. *Journal of Consulting and Clinical Psychology, 67*(4), 563–570.

Ishikura, R., & Tashiro, N. (2002). Frustration and fulfillment of needs in dissociative and conversion disorders. *Psychiatry and Clinical Neurosciences, 56*, 381–390.

Ivanoff, A., & Fisher, P. (2001). Suicide and suicidal behavior. In A. Gitterman (Ed.), *Handbook of social work practice with vulnerable and resilient populations* (2nd ed., pp. 788–819). New York: Columbia University Press.

Ivey, A. E., & Ivey, M. B. (2003). *Intentional interviewing and counseling: Facilitating client development in a multicultural society* (5th ed.). Pacific Grove, CA: Brooks/Cole.

Ivey, A. E., Ivey, M. B., & Simek-Morgan, L. (1997). *Counseling and psychotherapy: A multicultural perspective* (4th ed.). Boston: Allyn & Bacon.

Jackson, C., & Birchwood, M. (1996). Early intervention in psychosis: Opportunities for secondary prevention. *British Journal of Clinical Psychology, 35*, 487–502.

Jacobs, E. E., Masson, R. L., & Harvill, R. L. (2002). *Group counseling: Strategies and skills* (2nd ed.). Pacific Grove, CA: Brooks/Cole.

Jacobs, T. J. (1999). Countertransference past and present: A review of the concept. *International Journal of Psychoanalysis, 80*, 575–594.

Jacobson, N. S., & Christensen, A. (1996). *Integrative couple therapy: Promoting acceptance and change.* New York: Norton.

Jacobson, S. F. (1998). A faculty case management practice: Integrating teaching, service and research. *Nursing and Health Care Perspectives, 19*(5), 220–223.

Jaffee, A. J., Rounsaville, B., Chang, G., Schottenfeld, R. S., Meyer, R. E., & O'Malley, S. S. (1996). Naltrexone, relapse prevention, and supportive therapy with alcoholics: An analysis of patient treatment matching. *Journal of Consulting & Clinical Psychology, 64*(5), 1044–1053.

Jagmin, M. G. (1998). Postoperative mental status in elderly hip surgery patients. *Orthopedic Nursing, 17*(6), 32–34.

James, R. K., & Gilliand, B. E. (2005). *Crisis intervention strategies* (5th ed.). Belmont, CA: Brooks/Cole.

Janzen, C., & Harris, O. (1997). *Family treatment in social work treatment.* Itasca, IL: F. E. Peacock.

Jarrett, P. G., Rockwood, K., & Mallery, L. (1995, May). Behavioral problems in nursing home residents. Safe ways to manage dementia. *Postgraduate Medicine, 97*(5), 189–191, 195–196.

Jayaratne, S., Croxton, T., & Mattison, D. (1997). Social work professional standards: An exploratory study. *Social Work, 42*, 187–199.

Jenkins, A. (1993). *Invitations to responsibility: The therapeutic engagement of men who are violent and abusive.* Adelaide, Australia: Dulwich Centre Publications.

Jessor, R., & Jessor, S. S. (1977). *Problem behavior and psychosocial development: A longitudinal study of youth.* New York: Academic Press.

Jibson, M. D., & Tandon, R. (1998). New atypical antipsychotic medications. *Journal of Psychiatric Research, 32*, 215–228.

Joffe, R. T. (2002). Increasing sophistication of the pharmacotherapy of mood disorders. *Journal of Psychiatry and Neuroscience, 27*(2), 89.

Joffe, R. T. (2003). Treating mood disorders. *Journal of Psychiatry and Neuroscience, 28*(1), 9–10.

Johannessen, E. (2001). Early recognition and intervention: The key to success in the treatment of schizophrenia? *Disease Management & Health Outcomes, 9*(6), 317–327.

Johnson, B. A., & Ait-Daoud, N. (1999). Medications to treat alcoholism. *Alcohol Research and Health, 23*(2), 99–106.

Johnson, B. A., Roache, J. D., Javors, M. A., Di Clemente, C. C., Cloninger, C. R., Prihoda, T. J., Bordnick, P. S., Ait-Daoud, N., & Hensler, J. (2000). Ondansetron for reduction of drinking among biologically predisposed alcoholic patients. *Journal of the American Medical Association, 284*, 963–970.

Johnson, E. D. (2000). Differences among families coping with serious mental illness: A qualitative analysis. *American Journal of Orthopsychiatry, 70*(1), 126–134.

Johnson, E. H., & Gant, L. M. (1996). The association of anger-hostility and hypertension. In H. W. Neighbors and J. S. Jackson (Eds.), *Mental health in black America* (pp. 95–116). Thousand Oaks, CA: Sage Publications.

Johnson, H. C. (1999). *Psyche, synapse, and substance: The role of neurobiology in emotions, behavior, thinking, and addiction for non-scientists.* Greenfield, MA: Deerfield Valley.

Johnson, H. C. (2001). Neuroscience in social work practice. *Journal of Social Work Practice and the Addictions, 1*(3), 81–102.

Johnson, L. C., & Yanca, S. J. (2001). *Social work practice: A generalist approach* (7th ed.). Boston: Allyn & Bacon.

Joiner, T. E., Pettit, J. W., & Rudd, M. D. (2004). Is there a window of heightened suicide risk if patients gain energy in the context of continued depressive symptoms? *Professional Psychology: Research and Practice, 35*(1), 84–89.

Joiner, T. E., & Rudd, M. D. (2000). Intensity and duration of suicidal crises vary as a function of previous suicide attempts and negative life events. *Journal of Counseling and Clinical Psychology, 68*(5), 909–916.

Jones-Webb, R. (1998). Drinking patterns and problems among African-Americans: Recent findings. *Alcohol Health & Research World, 22*(4), 260–264.

Jongsma, A. E., & Peterson, M. (1995). *The complete psychotherapy treatment planner.* New York: Wiley.

Joransson, D. E., Ryan, K. M., & Dahl, J. L. (2000). Trends in medical use and abuse of opioid analgesics. *Journal of the American Medical Association, 283*(13), 1710–1714.

Jordan, C., Barrett, M., Vandiver, V., & Lewellen, A. (1999). Psychoeducational family practice (pp. 175–197). In C. Franklin and C. Jordan (Eds.), *Family practice: Brief systems methods for social work.* Pacific Grove, CA: Brooks/Cole.

Jordan, C., & Franklin, C. (1995). *Clinical assessment for social workers.* Chicago: Lyceum Books.

Joyce, A. S., Duncan, S. C., Duncan, A., Kipnes, D., & Piper, W. E. (1996). Limiting time-unlimited group psychotherapy. *International Journal of Group Psychotherapy, 46*(1), 61–79.

Judd, L. L. (1997). The clinical course of unipolar major depressive disorders. *Archives of General Psychiatry, 54,* 989–991.

Judd, L. L. (2000). Course and chronicity of unipolar major depressive disorder: Commentary on Joiner. *Child Psychology Science and Practice, 7*(2), 219–223.

Judd, L. L., Paulus, M. P., Wells, K. B., & Rapaport, M. H. (1996). Socioeconomic burden of subsyndromal depressive symptoms and major depression in a sample of the general population. *American Journal of Psychiatry, 153,* 1411–1417.

Kadushin, G. (1996). Adaptations to the traditional interview to the brief-treatment context. *Families in Society: The Journal of Contemporary Human Services, 79*(4), 346–357.

Kagan, J. (1998). *Three seductive ideas.* Cambridge, MA: Harvard University Press.

Kahn, C., & Pike, K. M. (2001). In search of predictors of dropout from inpatient treatment for anorexia nervosa. *International Journal of Eating Disorders, 30,* 237.

Kalodner, C. R. (1998). Eating disorders. In S. Roth-Roemer & S. R. Kurpius (Eds.), *The emerging role of counseling psychology in health care* (pp. 253–278). New York: Norton.

Kandel, D. B., & Chen, K. (2000). Types of marijuana users by longitudinal course. *Journal of Studies on Alcohol, 61*(3), 367–378.

Kane, J. M. (2001). Extrapyramidal side effects are unacceptable. *European Neuropsychopharmacology, 11*(4) (Suppl. 4), S397–S403.

Kane, M. N. (2000). Ethnoculturally sensitive practice and Alzheimer's disease. *American Journal of Alzheimer's Disease, 15*(4), 80–86.

Kant, I. (1798). *The classification of mental disorders.* Konigsberg, Germany: Nicolovius.

Kanter, J. (1995). *Clinical issues in case management.* San Francisco: Jossey Bass.

Kaplan, H. I., & Sadock, B. J. (1996). *Pocket handbook of psychiatric drug treatment* (2nd ed.). Baltimore: Williams & Wilkins.

Kaplan, H. I., & Sadock, B. J. (1998). *Synopsis of psychiatry* (8th ed.). Baltimore: Williams & Wilkins.

Kapur, S., Zipursky, R. B., Remington, G., Jones, C., DaSilva, J., & Wilson, A. A. (1998). Serotonin-dopamine interaction and its relevance to schizophrenia. *American Journal of Psychiatry, 153,* 466–476.

Karger, H. J., & Stoesz, D. (2002). *American social welfare policy: A pluralist approach* (4th ed.). Boston: Allyn & Bacon.

Karls, J. M., & Wandrei, K. E. (1992). PIE: A new language for social work. *Social Work, 37,* 80–85.

Karroll, B. R., & Memmott, J. (2001). The order of alcohol-related life experiences: Gender difference. *Journal of Social Work Practice in the Addictions, 1*(2), 45–60.

Kart, C. S., & Kinney, J. M. (2001). *The realities of aging.* Boston: Allyn & Bacon.

Kashner, T. M., Rost, K., Cohen, B., Anderson, M., & Smith, G. R. Jr. (1995). Enhancing the health of somatization disorder patients. *Psychosomatics, 36*(5), 462–470.

Kaslow, N. J., Thompson, M. P., Okun, A., Price, A., & Young, S. (2002). Risk and protective factors in suicidal behavior in abused African American women. *Journal of Consulting and Clinical Psychology, 70*(2), 311–319.

Kaslyn, M. (1999). Telephone group work: Challenges for practice. *Social Work with Groups, 22*(1), 63–77.

Katon, W. (1993). Somatization disorder, hypochondriasis, and conversion disorder. In D. L. Dunner (Ed.), *Current psychiatric therapy* (pp. 314–320). Philadelphia: W. B. Saunders.

Kaye, W., Strober, M., Stein, D., & Gendall, K. (1999). New directions in treatment research of anorexia and bulimia nervosa. *Biological Psychiatry, 45,* 1285–1292.

Keane, T. M. (1998). Psychological effects of military combat. In B. P. Bohrenwend (Ed.), *Adversity, stress, and psychopathology* (pp. 52–65). New York: Oxford Press.

Keitel, M. A., & Kopala, M. (2000). *Counseling women with breast cancer: A guide for professionals.* Thousand Oaks, CA: SAGE Publications.

Keith, D. V. (2000). Symbolic experiential family therapy. In A. M. Horne (Ed.), *Family counseling and therapy* (3rd ed., pp. 102–139). Itasca, IL: F. E. Peacock.

Kelley, S. D. M., & Benshoff, J. J. (1997). Dual diagnosis of mental illness and substance abuse: Contemporary challenges for rehabilitation. *Journal of Applied Rehabilitation Counseling, 28*(3), 43–49.

Kellner, R. (1992). Diagnosis and treatments of hypochondriacal syndromes. *Psychosomatics, 33*(3), 278–279.

Kelly, G. (1955). *The psychology of personal constructs.* New York: Norton.

Kelly, T. B. (1999). Mutual aid groups with mentally ill older adults. *Social Work with Groups, 21*(4), 63–80.

Kelsey, B. L. (1998). The dynamics of multicultural groups. Ethnicity as a determinant of leadership. *Small Group Research, 29*(5), 602–623.

Kempa, M. L., & Thomas, A. J. (2000). Culturally sensitive assessment and treatment of eating disorders. *Eating Disorders, 8*(1), 17–30.

Kennedy, G. J. (2000). *Geriatric mental health care*. New York: Guilford.

Kenny, M. G. (1986). *The passion of Ansel Bourne: Multiple personality in American culture*. Washington, DC: Smithsonian Press.

Kent, D. A., Tomasson, K., & Coryell, W. (1995). Course and outcome of conversion and somatization disorders: A four-year follow-up. *Psychosomatics, 36*(2), 138–144.

Kernberg, O. (1984). *Severe personality disorders*. New Haven: Yale University Press.

Kerr, M. E., & Bowen, M. (1988). *Family evaluation: An approach based on Bowen's theory*. New York: Norton.

Kessler, R. J. (1996). Panic disorder and the retreat from meaning. *Journal of Clinical Psychoanalysis, 5,* 505–528.

Kihlstrom, J. (2001). Dissociative disorders. In P. B. Sutker & H. E. Adams (Eds.), *Comprehensive handbook of psychopathology* (3rd ed., pp. 259–276). New York: Plenum.

Kinder, B. N. (1997). Eating disorders. In S. M. Turner & M. Hersen (Eds.), *Adult psychopathology and diagnosis* (3rd ed., pp. 465–482). New York: Wiley.

King, S. A., & Strain, J. J. (1996). Somatoform pain disorder: A review. In T. A. Widiger, A. J. Frances, H. A. Pincus, M. R. Ross, & W. W. Davis (Eds.), *DSM-IV sourcebook* (Vol. 2). Washington, DC: American Psychiatric Press.

Kirby, L. D., & Fraser, M. W. (1997). Risk and resilience in childhood. In M. W. Fraser (Ed.), *Risk and resiliency in childhood: An ecological perspective* (pp. 10–33). Washington, DC: National Association of Social Workers Press.

Kirk, S. A., & Einbinder, S. D. (1994). *Controversial issues in mental health*. Boston: Allyn & Bacon.

Kirk, S. A., & Kutchins, H. (1992). *The selling of DSM: The rhetoric of science in psychiatry*. New York: Aldine de Gruyter.

Kirk, S. A., & Kutchins, H. (1994, June 20). Is bad writing a mental disorder? *New York Times,* A-17.

Kirk, S. A., Siporin, M., & Kutchins, H. (1989). The prognosis for social work diagnosis. *Social Casework, 70,* 295–304.

Kirst-Ashman, K. K., & Hull, G. H., Jr. (1999). *Understanding generalist practice* (2nd ed.). Chicago: Nelson-Hall.

Kirst-Ashman, K. K., & Hull, G. H., Jr. (2002). *Understanding generalist practice* (3rd ed.). Pacific Grove, CA: Brooks/Cole.

Kiser, D. J., Piercy, F. P., & Lipchik, E. (1993). The integration of emotion in solution-focused therapy. *Journal of Marital and Family Therapy, 19*(3), 233–242.

Kitano, H., & Nakaoka, S. (2001). Asian Americans in the twentieth century. In N. Choi (Ed.), *Psychosocial aspects of the Asian-American experience: Diversity within diversity* (pp. 7–17). New York: Haworth.

Klonoff, E. A., & Moore, D. J. (1986). "Conversion reactions" in adolescents: A biofeedback-based operant approach. *Journal of Behavioral Therapy and Experimental Psychiatry, 17,* 179–184.

Kluft, R. P. (1987). The simulation and dissimulation of multiple personality disorder. *American Journal of Clinical Hypnosis, 30,* 104–118.

Kluft, R. P. (1993). The initial stages of psychotherapy in the treatment of multiple personality disorder patients. *Dissociation, 6*(2/3), 145–161.

Kluft, R. P. (1996). Treating the traumatic memories of patients with dissociative identity disorder. *American Journal of Psychiatry, 153,* 103–110.

Kluft, R. P. (1999a). Current issues in dissociative identity disorder. *Journal of Practical Psychology and Behavioral Health, 5,* 3–19.

Kluft, R. P. (1999b). An overview of the psychotherapy of dissociative identity disorder. *American Journal of Psychotherapy, 53,* 289–319.

Kluft, R. P. (2000). The psychoanalytic psychotherapy of dissociative identity disorder in the context of trauma therapy. *Psychoanalytic Inquiry, 20*(2), 259–286.

Kluger, J. (2003). Real men get the blues. *Time, 162*(12), 48–50.

Knapp, M. (2000). Schizophrenia costs and treatment cost-effectiveness. *Acta Psychiatrica Scandinavica, 102*(407), 15–18.

Koerner, K., & Linehan, M. M. (2000). Research on dialectical behavior therapy for patients with borderline personality disorder. *Psychiatric Clinic of North America, 23*(1), 151–167.

Kohut, H. (1977). *The restoration of the self*. New York: International Universities Press.

Kok, C. J., & Leskela, J. (1996). Solution-focused therapy in a psychiatry hospital. *Journal of Marital and Family Therapy, 22*(3), 397–406.

Kolevson, M., & Green, R. (1985). *Family therapy models*. New York: Springer.

Kopelowicz, A., Wallace, C. J., & Zarate, R. (1998). Teaching psychiatric inpatients to re-enter the community: A brief method of improving the continuity of care. *Psychiatric Services, 49*(10), 1313–1316.

Kosloski, K., Young, R. F., & Montgomery, R. J. V. (1999). A new direction for intervention with depressed caregivers to Alzheimer's patients. *Family Relations, 48*(4), 373–379.

Krahn, L. E., Li, H, & O'Connor, M. K. (2003). Patients who strive to be ill: Factitious disorder with physical symptoms. *American Journal of Psychiatry, 160*(6), 1163–1168.

Kranzler, H. (2000). Medications for alcohol dependence—new vistas. *Journal of the American Medical Association, 284*(8), 1016–1017.

Krause, R., & Merten, J. (1999). Affects, regulation of relationship, transference and countertransference. *International Forum of Psychoanalysis, 8,* 103–114.

Kreisler, J. D., & Lieberman, A. A. (1986). Dorothea Lynde Dix. In W. I. Tattner (Ed.), *Biographical dictionary of social welfare in America* (pp. 241–244). New York: Greenwood.

Kroenke, K., & Swindle, R. (2000). Cognitive-behavioral therapy for somatization and symptom syndromes: A critical review of controlled clinical trials. *Psychotherapy and Psychosomatics, 69*(4), 205–215.

Kruczek, T., & Vitanza, S. (1999). Treatment effects with an adolescent abuse survivor's group. *Child Abuse and Neglect, 23,* 477–485.

Kruger, A. (2000). Empowerment in social work practice with the psychiatrically disabled: Model and method. *Smith College Studies in Social Work, 70,* 427–440.

Krupnick, J. L. (1996). The role of therapeutic alliance in psychotherapy and pharmacotherapy outcome: Findings in the National Institutes of Mental Health treatment of depression, collaborative research program. *Journal of Consulting and Clinical Psychology, 64*, 532–539.

Krusky, M. S. (2002). Women and Thinness: The watch on the eve of the feast. Therapy with families experiencing troubled eating. *Journal of Systemic Therapies, 21*(1), 58–76.

Kukleta, M., Dufek, J., & Rektor, I. (1997). Possible mechanism of functional dystonia of the hand induced by a psychological conflict. *Studia Psychologica, 39*(4), 325–327.

Kumanyika, S. K. (1997). Aging, diet, and nutrition in African Americans. In K. S. Markides & M. R. Miranda (Eds.), *Minorities, aging, and health* (pp. 205–234). Thousand Oaks, CA: Sage.

Kumet, R., & Freeman, M. P. (2002). Clozapine and tardive dyskinesia. *Journal of Clinical Psychiatry, 63*(2), 167–168.

Kurland, R., & Salmon, R. (1999). Education for the group worker's reality: The special qualities and world view of those drawn to work with groups. *Journal of Teaching in Social Work, 19*(1/2), 123–127.

Kutchins, H., & Kirk, S. A. (1987). DSM–III and social work malpractice. *Social Work, 32*, 205–211.

Kutchins, H., & Kirk, S. A. (1997). *Making us crazy: DSM: The psychiatric bible and the creation of mental disorders.* New York: Free Press.

La Fountain, R. M., & Garner, N. E. (1996). Solution-focused counseling groups: The results are in. *Journal for Specialists in Group Work, 21*(2), 128–143.

Laing, R. D. (1967). *The politics of experience.* New York: Ballantine.

Lam, D. (1991). Psychosocial family intervention in schizophrenia: A review of empirical studies. *Psychological Medicine, 21*, 423–441.

Lam, R. W., Goldner, E. M., Solyom, L., & Remick, R. A. (1994). A controlled study of light therapy for bulimia nervosa. *American Journal of Psychiatry, 151*(5), 744–750.

Latkin, C. A. (1998). Outreach in natural settings: The use of peer leaders for HIV prevention among injecting drug users' networks. *Public Health Reports, 113*(Suppl. 1), 151–159.

Lauer, R. H., & Lauer, J. C. (2002). *Social problems and the quality of life* (8th ed.). Boston: McGraw-Hill.

Lauriello, J. (2001). Medication treatments for schizophrenia: Translating research findings into better outcomes. *Journal of Psychiatric Practice, 7*(4), 260–265.

Laws, G. (1995). Understanding ageism: Lessons from feminism and postmodernism. *The Gerontologist, 35*, 112–118.

Lawton, M. P., Van Haitsma, K., & Klapper, J. (1996). Observed affect in nursing home residents with Alzheimer's disease. *Journal of Gerontology, 51B*, 3–14.

Lazarus, R. (1984). On the primacy of cognition. *American Psychologist, 39*, 124–129.

Leahy, M. (1997). Preparation of rehabilitation counselors for case management practice in health care settings. *Journal of Rehabilitation, 63*(3), 53–59.

Lebow, J. (1997, March). The integrative revolution in couple and family therapy. *Family Process, 36*(1), 1–17.

Lecomte, T., Cyr, M., Lesage, A. D., & Wilde, J. (1999). Efficacy of a self-esteem module in the empowerment of individuals with schizophrenia. *The Journal of Nervous and Mental Disease, 187*(7), 406–413.

LeCroy, C. W. (1999). *Case studies in social work practice* (2nd ed.). Pacific Grove, CA: Brooks/Cole.

Lee, C. C. (1997). The promise and pitfalls of multicultural counseling. In C. C. Lee (Ed.), *Multicultural issues in counseling: New approaches to diversity* (2nd ed., pp. 1–13). Alexandria, VA: American Counseling Association.

Lee, E. (Ed.). (1997). *Working with Asian Americans: A guide for clinicians.* New York: Guilford.

Lee, J. A. B. (1996). The empowerment approach to social work practice. In F. J. Turner (Ed.), *Social work treatment: Interlocking theoretical approaches* (4th ed., pp. 218–249). New York: Free Press.

Lee, J. A. B. (2001). *The empowerment approach to social work practice* (2nd ed.). New York: Columbia University Press.

Lee, M. Y., Greene, G. J., & Rheinscheld, J. (1999). A model of short-term solution-focused group treatment of male domestic violence offenders. *Journal of Family Social Work, 3*(2), 39–57.

Leff, J. (2000). Family work for schizophrenia: Practical application. *Acta Psychiatrica Scandinavica, 102*(407), 78–82.

Lefley, H. (1987). Impact of mental illness in families of mental health professionals. *Journal of Nervous and Mental Disease, 175*, 613–619.

Lefley, H. P. (1996). *Family caregiving in mental illness.* Thousand Oaks, CA: Sage.

Lehman, A. F., & Dixon, L. B. (Eds.). (1995). *Addictive disorders: Chronic mental illness and substance use disorder.* Langhorne, PA: Hardwood Academic.

Lehman, A. F., & Steinwachs, D. M. (1998). Patterns of usual care for schizophrenia: Initial results from the schizophrenia Patient Outcomes Research Team (PORT) client survey. *Schizophrenia Bulletin, 23*, 11–20.

Lehmann, P., & Coady, N. (Eds.). (2001). *Theoretical perspectives for direct social work practice.* New York: Springer.

Lemonick, M. D. (2003). How to heal a hypochondriac. *Time, 162*(14), 54–55.

Lerner, V., Miodownik, A., & Cohen, H. (2001). Vitamin B6 in the treatment of tardive dyskinesia: A double-blind, placebo-controlled, crossover study. *The American Journal of Psychiatry, 158*(9), 1551–1514.

Lesch, K., Bengel, D., Heils, A., Sabol, S. Z., Greenberg, B. D., Petri, S., Benjamin, J., Muller, C. R., Hamer, D. H., & Murphy, D. L. (1996). Association of anxiety-related traits with a polymorphism in the serotonin transporter gene regulatory region. *Science, 274*, 1527–1531.

Lesure-Lester, E. G. (2002). An application of cognitive-behavior principles in the reduction of aggression among abused African American adolescents. *Journal of Interpersonal Violence, 17*(4), 394–403.

Levin, S. M., & Kruger, J. (Eds.). (2000). *Substance abuse among older adults: A guide for social service providers.* Rockville, MD: Substance Abuse and Mental Health Services Administration.

Levine, M. P., & Smolak, L. (1996). Media as a context for the development of disordered eating. In L. Smolak, M. P. Levine, & R. Striegel-Moore (Eds.), *The development of psychopathology of eating disorders: Implications for research, prevention, and treatment* (pp. 235–257). Mahwah, NJ: Erlbaum.

Levitt, D. H. (2001). Anorexia nervosa: Treatment in the family context. *Family Journal, 9*(2), 159–163.

Lewis, D. O., Yeager, C. A., Swica, Y., Pincus, J. H., & Lewis, M. (1997). Objective documentation of child abuse and dissociation in 12 murders with dissociative identity disorder. *American Journal of Psychiatry, 154,* 1703–1710.

Lewis, I. D., & Ausberry, M. S. C. (1996). African American families: Management of demented elders. In G. Yeo & D. Gallagher-Thompson (Eds.), *Ethnicity and the dementias* (pp. 167–174). Washington, DC: Taylor and Francis.

Lewis, J. A., Dana, R. Q., & Blevins, G. A. (2002). *Substance abuse counseling* (3rd ed.). Pacific Grove, CA: Brooks/Cole.

Lewis, J. R., Boyle, D. P., Lewis, L. S., & Evans, M. (2000). Reducing AIDS and substance abuse risk factors among homeless HIV-infected, drug-using persons. *Research on Social Work Practice, 10*(1), 15–33.

Lewis-Fernandez, R. (1994). Culture and dissociation: A comparison of ataque de nervios among Puerto Ricans and possession syndrome in India. In D. Spiegel (Ed.), *Dissociation: Culture, mind, and body* (pp. 123–167). Washington, DC: American Psychiatric Press.

Library of Congress. (2004). *THOMAS: Legislative Information on the Internet.* Available at http://thomas.loc.gov. Accessed March 27, 2004.

Liddle, B. (1986). Resistance in supervision: A response to perceived threat. *Counselor Education and Supervision, 26,* 117–127.

Lidz, T., Cornelison, A., Fleck, S., & Terry, D. (1957). The intrafamilial environment of schizophrenic patients: II. Marital schism and marital skew. *American Journal of Psychiatry, 114,* 241–248.

Lieberman, J. A. (1996a). Atypical antipsychotic drugs as first-line treatment of schizophrenia: A rationale and hypothesis, *Journal of Clinical Psychiatry, 57*(Suppl. 11), 68–71.

Lieberman, J. A. (1996b). New developments in antipsychotic drug treatment. *Psychiatric Times, 13*(3), 41–43.

Lieberman, R. P., Wallace, C. J., Blackwell, G., & Kopelwicz, A. (1998). Skills training versus psychosocial occupational therapy for persons with persistent schizophrenia. *American Journal of Psychiatry, 155,* 1087–1091.

Liebschutz, J. M., Mulvey, K. P., & Samet, J. H. (1997). Victimization among substance-abusing women. *Archives of Internal Medicine, 157,* 1093–1097.

Liem, J. H., James, J. B., O'Toole, J. G., & Boudewyn, A. C. (1997). Assessing resilience in adults with histories of childhood sexual abuse. *American Journal of Orthopsychiatry, 67,* 594–606.

Lilienfeld, S. O. (1992). The association between antisocial personality and somatization disorders: A review and integration of theoretical models. *Clinical Psychology Review, 12,* 641–662.

Lin, K-M., Poland, R. E., & Chien, C. P. (1990). Ethnicity and psychopharmacology: Recent findings and future research directions. In E. Sorel (Ed.), *Family, culture, and psychobiology.* New York: Legas.

Linde, K., Ramirez, G., Mulros, C. D., Pauls, A., Weidenhammer, W., & Melchart, D. (1996). St. John's wort in major depression: A randomized control trial. *Journal of the American Medical Association, 285,* 1978–1986.

Lindemann, E. (1944). Symptomatology and management of acute grief. *American Journal of Psychiatry, 101,* 141–148.

Lindenmayer, J. P., Iskander, A., Park, M., Apergi, F. S., & Czobor, P. (1998). Clinical and neurocognitive effects of clozapine and Risperidone in treatment-refractory schizophrenic patients: A prospective study. *Journal of Clinical Psychiatry, 59,* 521–527.

Lindforss, L., & Magnusson, D. (1997). Solution-focused therapy in prison. *Contemporary Family Therapy, 19*(1), 89–103.

Lindsey, E. W. (2000). Social work with homeless mothers: A strength-based solution-focused model. *Journal of Family Social Work, 4*(1), 59–78.

Lindström, E., & Bingefors, K. (2000). Patient compliance with drug therapy in schizophrenia: Economic and clinical issues. *Pharmacoeconomics, 18*(2), 105–124.

Linehan, M. M. (1991). Asuicidal borderline patients. *Archives of General Psychiatry, 48,* 1060–1064.

Linehan, M. M. (1993). *Skills training manual for treating borderline personality disorder.* New York: Guilford.

Linehan, M. M. (2000). The empirical basis of dialectical behavior therapy: Development of new treatments versus evaluation of existing treatments. *Clinical Psychology: Science and Practice, 7*(1), 113–119.

Linehan, M. M., Armstrong, H. E., Suarez, A., Allmon, D., & Heard, H. (1991). Cognitive-behavioral treatment of chronically parasuicidal borderline patients. *Archives of General Psychiatry, 48,* 1060–1064.

Linhorst, D. M., Hamilton, G., Young, E., & Eckert, A. (2002). Opportunities and barriers to empowering people with severe mental illness through participation in treatment planning. *Social Work, 47*(4), 425–434.

Link, B., & Phelan, J. (1995). Social conditions as fundamental causes of disease. *Journal of Health and Social Behavior, 36*(Suppl.), 80–94.

Linzer, N. L. (1999). *Resolving ethical dilemmas in social work practice.* Boston: Allyn & Bacon.

Lipchik, E. (1994). The rush to be brief. *The Networker,* 35–39.

Littell, J. H., & Tajima, E. A. (2000). A multilevel model of client participation in intensive family preservation services. *Social Service Review, 74*(3), 405–435.

Litten, R., & Allen, J. (1998). Advances in the development of medications for alcoholism. *Psychopharmacology, 139*(1–2), 20–33.

Litten, R., Allen, J., & Fertig, J. (1996). Pharmacotherapies for alcohol problems: A review of research with focus on developments since 1991. *Alcoholism: Clinical and Experimental Research, 20*(5), 859–876.

Littrell, J. M. (2003). Obtaining informed consent when a profession labels itself as providing treatment for mental illness. *Social Work in Mental Health Care, (1)*4, 107–122.

Littrell, J. M., Malia, J. A., & Vanderwood, M. (1995). Single-session brief counseling in a high school. *Journal of Counseling and Development, 73,* 451–458.

Livesley, W. J. (2004). Introduction to the special feature on recent progress in the treatment of personality disorder. *Journal of Personality Disorders, 18*(1), 1–2.

Llorca, P., Chereau, I., Bayle, F., & Lancon, C. (2002). Tardive dyskinesias and antipsychotics: A review. *European Psychiatry, 17*(3), 129–138.

Lochman, J. E. (2000). Parent and family skills training in targeted prevention programs for at-risk youth. *Journal of Primary Prevention, 21*(2), 253–266.

Lock, J., & Giammona, A. (1999). Severe somatoform disorder in adolescence: A case series using a rehabilitation model for intervention. *Clinical Child Psychology and Psychiatry, 4*(3), 341–351.

Loft, S., Olesen, K. L., & Dossing, M. (1987). Increased susceptibility to liver disease in relation to alcohol consumption in women. *Scandinavian Journal of Gasteroenterology, 22,* 1251–1256.

Loftus, E. F. (1996). Memory distortion and false memory creation. *Bulletin of the American Academy of Psychiatry and the Law, 24,* 281–295.

Longhofer, J., Floersch, J., & Jenkins, J. H. (2003). The social grid of community medication management. *American Journal of Orthopsychiatry, 73*(1), 24–34.

Longo, L. P., & Johnson, B. (2000). Addiction: Part I. Benzodiazepines—side effects, abuse risk, and alternatives. *American Family Physician, 61,* 2121–2131.

LoPiccolo, C. J., Goodkin, K., & Baldewicz, T. T. (1999). Current issues in the diagnosis and management of malingering. *Annals of Medicine, 31*(3), 166–173.

Lovinger, D. M. (1997). Serotonin's role in alcohol's effects on the brain. *Alcohol Health & Research World, 21*(2), 114–120.

Lowe, R., & Guy, G. (1996). A reflecting team format for solution-oriented supervision: Practical guidelines and theoretical distinctions. *Journal of Systemic Therapies, 15*(4), 26–45.

Lowenberg, F. M., & Dolgoff, R. (1996). *Ethical dilemmas for social work practice* (5th ed.). Itasca, IL: F. E. Peacock.

Lowenberg, F. M., Dolgoff, R., & Harrington, D. (2000). *Ethical decisions for social work practice.* Itasca, IL: F. E. Peacock.

Lowenstein, R. J. (1996). Dissociative amnesia and dissociative fugue. In L. K. Michelson & W. J. Ray (Eds.), *Handbook of dissociation: Theoretical, empirical, and clinical perspectives* (pp. 307–336). New York: Plenum Press.

Lowenstein, R. J. (1997). Treatment of dissociative amnesia and dissociative fugue. In W. Reid (Ed.), *Treatment of DSM-IV psychiatric disorders* (pp. 283–292). New York: Brunner/Mazel.

Lown, A. E., & Vega, W. A. (2001). Alcohol or dependence among Mexican American women who report violence. *Alcoholism: Clinical & Experimental Research, 25*(10), 1479–1486.

Luhrmann, T. M. (2000). *Of two minds: The growing disorder in American psychiatry.* New York: Knopf.

Lukens, E. (2001). Schizophrenia. In A. Gitterman (Ed.), *Handbook of social work practice with vulnerable and resilient populations* (2nd ed., pp. 275–302). New York: Columbia University Press.

Lukens, E. P., & Thorning, H. (1998). Psychoeducation and severe mental illness: Implications for social work practice and research. In J. B. W. Williams & S. E. Hyman (Eds.), *Mental health research: Implications for practice* (pp. 343–364). Washington, DC: NASW Press.

Lum, D. (1999). *Culturally competent practice: A framework for growth and action.* Pacific Grove, CA: Brooks/Cole.

Lum, D. (2000). *Social work practice and people of color* (4th ed.). Pacific Grove, CA: Brooks/Cole.

Lum, D. (Ed.). (2003). *Culturally competent practice: A framework for understanding diverse groups and justice issues* (2nd ed.). Pacific Grove, CA: Brooks/Cole.

Lum, D. (2004). *Social work practice and people of color: A process-stage approach* (5th ed.). Belmont, CA: Brooks/Cole.

Lum, D. (Ed.). (2005). *Cultural competence, practice stages and client systems: A case study approach.* Belmont, CA: Brooks/Cole.

Lumpkin, P. W., Silverman, W. K., & Markham, M. R. (2002). Treating a heterogeneous set of anxiety disorders in youths with group cognitive-behavioral therapy: A partially non-concurrent multiple-baseline evaluation. *Behavior Therapy, 33*(1), 163–177.

Lundwall, R. (1996). How psychoeducational support groups can provide multidiscipline services to families of people with mental illness. *Psychiatric Rehabilitation Journal, 20*(2), 64–71.

Lutz, M. E., & Flory, M. J. (1993). Instruments and psychometrics: A response to Mattaini and Kirk. *Social Work, 38,* 229–230.

Lydiard, R. B. (2000). An overview of generalized anxiety disorder: Disease state-appropriate therapy. *Clinical Therapeutics: The International Journal of Drug Therapy, 22*(Suppl. A), A3–A9.

Lykouras, L., Agelopoulos, E., & Tzavellas, E. (2002). Improvement of tardive dyskinesia following switch from neuroleptics to olanzapine. *Progress in Neuro-Psychopharmacology & Biological Psychiatry, 26*(4), 815–817.

Lynch, K. (2000). The long road back. *Journal of Clinical Psychology: In Session, 56*(11), 1427–1432.

MacFarlane, M. M. (Ed.). (2004). *Family treatment of personality disorders: Advances in clinical practice.* New York: Haworth.

MacKenzie, K. R. (1996). Time-limited group psychotherapy. *International Journal of Group Psychotherapy, 46*(1), 41–60.

Macleod, A. D. (1999). Post-traumatic stress disorder, dissociative fugue and a locator beacon. *Australian and New Zealand Journal of Psychiatry, 33,* 102–104.

Madsen, W. C. (1999). *Collaborative therapy with multi-stressed families: From old problems to new futures.* New York: Guilford.

Magarinos, M., Zafar, U., Nissenson, K., & Blanco, C. (2002). Epidemiology and treatment of hypochondriasis. *CNS Drugs, 16*(1), 9–22.

Magni, G., Moreschi, C., Rigatti-Luchini, S., & Merskey, H. (1994). Prospective study between depressive symptoms and chronic musculoskeletal pain. *Pain, 56*(3), 289–297.

Maguire, L. (2002). *Clinical social work: Beyond generalist practice with individuals, groups, and families.* Pacific Grove, CA: Brooks/Cole.

Mahler, M. S. (1968). *On human symbiosis and the vicissitudes of individuation.* New York: International Universities Press.

Mahler, M. S., Pine, F., & Bergman, A. (1975). *The psychological birth of the human infant: Symbiosis and individuation.* New York: Basic Books.

Mahoney, D. M. (2000). Panic disorder and self states: Clinical and research illustrations. *Clinical Social Work Journal, 28*(2), 197–212.

Mahoney, M. J. (1974). *Cognition and behavior modification.* Cambridge, MA: Ballinger.

Mahoney, M. J., & Arnkoff, D. (1978). Cognitive and self-control therapies. In S. L. Garfield & E. A. Bergin (Eds.), *Handbook of psychotherapy and behavior change: An empirical analysis* (pp. 689–722). New York: Wiley.

Maldonado, J. R., Butler, L. D., & Spiegel, D. (2002). Treatments for dissociative disorders. In P. E. Nathan & J. M. Gorman (Eds.), *A guide to treatments that work* (2nd ed., pp. 463–496). London: Oxford University Press.

Malec, T. S., Malec, E. A., & Dongier, M. (1996). Efficacy of buspirone in alcohol dependence: A review. *Alcoholism: Clinical & Experimental Research, 20,* 853–858.

Malenbaum, R. D., Herzog, S. E., & Wysbak, G. (1988). Overeaters Anonymous: Impact on bulimia. *International Journal of Eating Disorders, 7,* 139–143.

Malhi, G. S., Moore, J., & McGuffin, P. (2000). The genetics of major depressive disorder. *Current Psychiatry Representation, 2*(2), 165–169.

Malla, A. K., Norman, R. M., McLean, T. S., & Cheng, S. (1998). An integrated medical and psychosocial treatment program for psychotic disorders: Patient characteristics and outcome. *Canadian Journal of Psychiatry, 43*(7), 698–705.

Mallinckrodt, B. (1996). Capturing the subjective and other challenges in measuring transference: Comment on Multon, Patton, and Kivlighan. *Journal of Counseling Psychology, 43,* 253–256.

Manji, H. K., Moore, G. J., Rajkowska, G., & Chen, G. (2000). Neuroplasticity and cellular resilience in mood disorders. *Molecular Psychiatry, 5,* 578–593.

Mann, J. J., Waternaux, C., Hass, G. L., & Malone, K. M. (1999). Toward a clinical model of suicidal behavior in psychiatric patients. *American Journal of Psychiatry, 156*(2), 181–189.

Manning, S. S. (1998). Empowerment in mental health programs: Listening to the voices. In L. M. Gutierrez, R. J. Cox, & E. O. Cox, *Empowerment in social work practice: A sourcebook* (pp. 89–109). Pacific Grove, CA: Brooks/Cole.

Mannion, E., Mueser, K., & Solomon, P. (1994). Designing psychoeducational services for spouses of persons with serious mental illness. *Community Mental Health Journal, 30*(2), 177–190.

Marcenko, M. O., Kemp, S. P., & Larson, N. C. (2000). Childhood experiences of abuse, later substance use, and parenting outcomes among low-income mothers. *American Journal of Orthopsychiatry, 70*(3), 316–326.

Marder, S. R. (2001). Integrating pharmacological and psychosocial treatments for schizophrenia. *Acta Psychiatrica Scandinavica, 102*(407), 87–90.

Mark, T. L., Dirani, R., Slade, E., & Russo, P. A. (2002). Access to new medications to treat schizophrenia. *The Journal of Behavioral Health Services & Research, 29*(1), 15–29.

Markarian, M., & Franklin, J. (1998). Substance abuse in minority populations. In R. J. Frances & S. I. Miller (Eds.), *Clinical textbook of addictive disorders* (2nd ed.). New York: Guilford.

Markowitz, J. S., Brown, C. S., & Moore, T. R. (1999). Atypical antipsychotics, Part 1: Pharmacology, pharmacokinetics, and efficacy. *Annals of Pharmacotherapy, 33,* 73–85.

Marks, A. (2002, March). Illicit drug use grows among the elderly. *Christian Science Monitor, 94*(85), 3.

Marks, J. (1983). The benzodiazepines—for good or evil. *Neuropsychobiology, 10,* 115–126.

Markward, M., Dozier, C., Hooks, K., & Markward, N. (2000). Culture and the intergenerational transmission of substance abuse, woman abuse, and child abuse: A diathesis-stress perspective. *Children and Youth Services Review, 22*(3/4), 237–250.

Marlatt, G., & Kristeller, J. (1999). Mindfulness and meditation. In W. Miller (Ed.), *Integrating spirituality into treatment: Resources for practitioners* (pp. 175–197). Reno, NV: Context Press.

Marsh, D. T. (2000). Personal accounts of consumer/survivors: Insights and implications. *Journal of Clinical Psychotherapy: In Session, 56*(11), 1447–1457.

Marsh, J. C. (2000). Theories of professions: Implications for social work. In S. Muller, H. Sunker, T. Olk, & K. Bollert (Eds.). *Sozial arbeit* (pp. 389–399). Neuwied, Kriftel: Luchterhand.

Marsh, J. C. (2002). Learning from clients. *Social Work, 47*(4), 341–343.

Marsh, J. C. (2003). To thine own ethics code be true. *Social Work, 48*(1), 5–7.

Marshall, H. (1973). *Dorothea Dix: Forgotten samaritan.* Chapel Hill, NC: University of North Carolina Press.

Martichuski, D. K., Knight, B. L., Karlin, N. J., & Bell, P. A. (1997). Correlates of Alzheimer's disease caregivers' support group attendance. *Activities, Adaptation and Aging, 21*(4), 27–40.

Martin, B. C., Miller, L. S., & Kotzan, J. A. (2001). Antipsychotic prescription use and costs for persons with schizophrenia in the 1990s: Current trends and five-year time series forecasts. *Schizophrenia Research, 47*(2–3), 281–292.

Martina, C. M., Thakore, R., & Thakore, J. H. (2002). Physical consequences of schizophrenia and its treatment: The metabolic syndrome. *Life Sciences, 71,* 239–257.

Masand, P. S., & Gupta, S. (2003). Long-acting injectable antipsychotics in the elderly. *Drugs and Aging, 20*(15), 1099–1111.

Mash, E. J., & Barkley, R. A. (1998). *Treatment of childhood disorders* (2nd ed.). New York: Guilford.

Mason, B. J., Salvato, F. R., Williams, L. D., Ritvo, E. C., & Cutler, R. B. (1999). A double-blind, placebo-controlled study of oral nalmefene for alcohol dependence. *Archives of General Psychiatry, 56,* 719–724.

Mathiesen, S. G. (2001). Family involvement and schizophrenia. *Journal of Family Social Work, 6*(1), 35–52.

Mathre, M. L. (2001). Cannabis series—the whole story. Part I: Overview. *The Drug and Alcohol Professional, 1*(1), 3–7.

Mattick, R. P., & Hall, W. (1996). Are detoxification programs effective? *The Lancet, 347,* 97–100.

Mavangell, L. B., Yudofsky, S. C., & Silver, J. M. (1999). Psychopharmacology and electroconvulsive therapy. In R. E. Hales, S. C. Yudofsky, & J. A. Talbott (Eds.). *The American Psychiatric Press textbook of psychiatry* (3rd ed., pp. 1025–1132). Washington, DC: American Psychiatric Press.

Mavissakalian, M. R., & Ryan, M. T. (1997). The role of medication. In W. T. Roth (Ed.), *Treating anxiety disorders* (pp. 175–204). San Francisco: Jossey Bass.

Max, M. B., Lynch, S. A., Muir, J., Shoaf, S. E., Smoller, B., & Dubner, R. (1992). Effects of desipramine, amitriptyline, and fluoxetine on pain in diabetic neuropathy. *New England Journal of Medicine, 326*(19), 1250–1256.

Maxmen, J. S., & Ward, N. G. (1995). *Essential psychopathology and its treatment* (2nd ed.). New York: W. W. Norton and Company.

Mayer, L. E., & Walsh, B. T. (1998). The use of selective serotonin reuptake inhibitors in eating disorders. *Journal of Clinical Psychiatry, 59*, 15.

Mayeux, R., Foster, N. L., Rossor, M., & Whitehouse, P. J. (1993). The clinical evaluation of patients with dementia. In P. J. Whitehouse (Ed.), *Dementia* (Vol. 40 of Contemporary Neurology series, pp. 92–129). Philadelphia: F. A. Davis.

McAleavey, K. M., Fiumara, M. C., & Zelvin, L. (2001). Eating disorders: Are they addictions? A dialogue. *Journal of Social Work Practice in the Addictions, 1*(2), 107–113.

McCahill, M. E. (1995). Somatoform and related disorders: Delivery of diagnosis as the first step. *American Family Physician, 52*(1), 193–204.

McCallion, P. M., & Toseland, R. W. (1995). Supportive group interventions with caregivers of frail older adults. *Social Work with Groups, 18*(1), 11–25.

McCallion, P. M., Toseland, R. W., Gerber, T., & Banks, S. (2002). Increasing the use of formal services by caregivers of people with dementia. *Social Work, 49*(3), 441–450.

McCrae, R. R., Costa, P. T., Jr., Ostendorf, F., Angelitner, A., Hrebickova, M., Avia, M. D., Sanz, J., Sanchez-Bernardos, M. L., Kusdil, M. E., Woodfield, R., Saunders, P. R., & Smith, P. B. (2000). Nature over nurture: Temperament, personality and life span development. *Journal of Personality and Social Psychology, 78*(1), 173–186.

McCubbin, H., & McCubbin, M. (1992). Research utilization in social work practice of family treatment. In A. J. Epstein (Ed.), *Research utilization in the social work services: Innovations for practice and administration* (pp. 149–192). New York: Haworth Press.

McCubbin, H. I., McCubbin, M. A., & Thompson, A. I. (1993). Resiliency in families: The role of family schema and appraisal in family adaptation to crises. In T. H. Brubaker (Ed.), *Family relations: challenges for the future.* Newbury Park, CA: Sage.

McDaniel, S. H., Hepworth, J., & Doherty, W. J. (1995). Medical family therapy with somatizing patients: The co-creation of therapeutic stories. In R. H. Mikesell, D. D. Lusterman, & S. H. McDaniel (Eds.), *Integrating family therapy: Handbook of family psychological and systems theory* (pp. 377–388). Washington, DC: American Psychological Association.

McFarlane, W. R. (1994). Multiple-family groups and psychoeducation in the treatment of schizophrenia. *New Directions for Mental Health Services, 62*, 13–22.

McFarlane, W. R. (1997). Family psychoeducation: Basic concepts and innovative applications. In S. W. Hengeller & A. B. Santos (Eds.), *Innovative approaches for hard-to-treat populations* (pp. 211–237). Washington, DC: American Psychiatric Press.

McFarlane, W. R. (2000). Psychoeducational multi-family groups: Adaptations and outcomes. In B. Martindale, A. Bateman, M. Crowe, & F. Margison (Eds.), *Psychosis: Psychological approaches and their effectiveness* (pp. 68–95). London, England: Gaskell/Royal College of Psychiatrists.

McFarlane, W., Lukens, E., Link, B., & Zuccato, C. (1995). Multiple-family groups and psychoeducation in the treatment of schizophrenia. *Archives of General Psychiatry, 52*, 679–687.

McGaffigan, D., & Bliwise, D. L. (1997). The treatment of sun downing. A selective review of pharmacological and nonpharmacological studies. *Drugs Aging, 10*(1), 10–17.

McGoldrick, M., & Gerson, R. (1985). *Genograms in family assessment.* New York: Norton.

McGoldrick, M., Gerson, R., & Shellenberger, S. (1999). *Genograms: Assessment and intervention* (2nd ed.). New York: Norton.

McGoldrick, M., Giordano, J., & Pearce, J. K. (1996). *Ethnicity and family therapy* (2nd ed.). New York: Guilford.

McGuffin, P., Marusic, A., & Farmer, A. (2001). What can psychiatric genetics offer suicidology? *Crisis: The Journal of Crisis Intervention and Suicide Prevention, 22*(2), 61–65.

McGurk, S. R. (1999). The effects of clozapine on cognitive functioning in schizophrenia. *Journal of Clinical Psychiatry, 60*(Supp. 12), 23–29.

McIntyre, R. S. (2001). Lithium revisited. *Canadian Journal of Psychiatry, 46*(4), 322–328.

McKisack, C., & Waller, G. (1997). Factors influencing the outcome of group psychotherapy for bulimia nervosa. *International Journal of Eating Disorders, 22*(1), 1–13.

McNair, L. K., & Roberts, G. W. (1997). Pervasive and persistent risk: Factors influencing African American women's HIV/AIDS vulnerability. *Journal of Black Psychology, 27*, 180–192.

McNally, R. J. (2003). *Remembering trauma.* Cambridge, MA: Harvard University Press.

McQuaid, J. R., Granholm, E., McClure, F. S., & Pedrelli, P. (2000). Development of an integrative cognitive-behavioral and social skills training intervention for older patients with schizophrenia. *Journal of Psychotherapy Practice, 9*(3), 149–156.

McQuaide, S. (1999). A social worker's use of the diagnostic and statistical manual. *Families in Society, 80*(4), 410–416.

Medrano, M. A., Hatch, J. P., Zule, W. A., & Desmond, D. P. (2002). Psychological distress in childhood trauma survivors who abuse drugs. *American Journal of Drug and Alcohol Abuse, 28*(1), 1–13.

Meeks, S., & Hammond, C. T. (2001). Social network characteristics among older outpatients with long-term mental illness. *Journal of Mental Health and Aging, 7*(4), 445–464.

Meezan, W., O'Keefe, M., & Zariani, M. (1997). A model of multi-family group therapy for abusive and neglectful parents and their children. *Social Work with Groups, 20*(2), 71–88.

Meichenbaum, D. (1977). *Cognitive-behavior modification: An integrative approach*. New York: Plenum.

Menninger, J. A. (2002). Assessment and treatment of alcoholism and substance-related disorders in the elderly. *Bulletin of the Menninger Clinic, 66,* 166–184.

Merinder, L. B. (2000). Patient education in schizophrenia: A review. *Acta Psychiatrica Scandinavica, 102*(2), 98–106.

Mermier, M. B. (1993). *Coping with severe mental illness: Families speak out.* Lewiston, NY: Edwin Mellen.

Merriam, B. W., & Murray, M. K. (1997). Eating disorders: Identification, prevention, and treatment. In T. N. Fairchild (Ed.), *Crisis intervention strategies for school-based helpers* (2nd ed., pp. 323–369). Springfield, IL: Charles C. Thomas.

Merskey, H. (1992). The manufacture of personalities: The production of MPD. *British Journal of Psychiatry, 160,* 327–340.

Merskey, H. (1995). The manufacture of personalities: The production of MPD. In L. M. Cohen, J. N. Berzoff, & M. R. Elin (Eds.), *Dissociative identity disorder: Theoretical and treatment controversies*. Northvale, NJ: Aronson.

Messman-Moore, M., & Long, P. J. (2002). Alcohol and substance use disorders as predictors of child to adult sexual revictimization in a sample of community women. *Violence and Victims, 17*(3), 319–340.

Meyer, C. (1993). The eco-systems perspective. In R. Dorfman (Ed.), *Paradigms of clinical social work*. New York: Brunner/Mazel.

Meyer, C. (1993a). *Assessment in social work practice.* New York: Columbia University Press.

Meza, E., & Kranzler, H. R. (1996). Closing the gap between alcoholism research and practice: The case for pharmacotherapy. *Psychiatric Services, 47,* 917–920.

Middleton, W., & Butler, J. (1998). Dissociative identity disorder: An Australian series. *Australian and New Zealand Journal of Psychiatry, 32,* 794–804.

Miklowitz, D. J., Richards, J. A., George, E. L., Suddath, R., & Wendel, J. S. (2000, November). Family-focused psychoeducation for bipolar disorder. Paper presented at 34th meetings of the Association for the Advancement of Behavior Therapy, New Orleans, LA (November 16–19).

Miley, K. K., O'Melia, M., & DuBois, B. (2001). *Generalist social work practice: An empowering approach* (3rd ed.). Boston: Allyn & Bacon.

Miller, D. D., Andreasen, N. C., O'Leary, D. S., Watkins, G. L., Boles Ponto, L. L., & Hichwa, R. D. (2001). Comparison of the effects of risperidone and haloperidol on regional cerebral blood flow in schizophrenia. *Biological Psychiatry, 49*(8), 704–715.

Miller, D. K., Malmstrom, M. S., Joshi, S., Andresen, E. M., Morley, J. E., & Wolinsky, F. D. (2004). Clinically relevant levels of depressive symptoms in community-dwelling middle-aged African Americans. *Journal of the American Geriatrics Society, 52,* 741–748.

Miller, G. A. (1999). *Learning the language of addiction counseling*. Boston: Allyn & Bacon.

Miller, J. (2001). September 11, 2001: Implications for social work practice and education. *Professional Development, 4*(2), 5–14.

Miller, J. (2002). Social workers as diagnosticians. In K. J. Bentley (Ed.), *Social work practice in mental health: Contemporary roles, tasks and techniques* (pp. 43–72). Pacific Grove, CA: Brooks/Cole.

Miller, J. B., & Stiver, I. P. (1997). *The healing connection*. Boston: Beacon Press.

Miller, R., & Mason, S. E. (1998). Group work with first-episode schizophrenia clients. *Social Work with Groups, 21*(1/2), 19–33.

Miller, R., & Mason, S. E. (1999). Phase-specific psychosocial interventions for first-episode schizophrenia. *Bulletin of the Menninger Clinic, 63*(4), 499–511.

Miller, R., & Mason, S. E. (2001). Using group therapy to enhance treatment compliance in first-episode schizophrenia. *Social Work with Groups, 24*(1), 37–52.

Miller, S. P., Hubble, M. A., & Duncan, B. L. (1996). *Handbook of solution-focused brief therapy*. San Francisco, CA: Jossey-Bass Publishers.

Miller, S., de Shazer, S., Berg, I. K., & Hopwood, L. (1993). *From problem to solution: The solution-focused brief therapy approach*. New York: Norton.

Miller, W. R., & Rollnick, S. (2002). *Motivational interviewing: Preparing people for change* (2nd ed.). New York: Guilford.

Miller, W. R., Westerberg, V. S., & Waldron, H. B. (1995). Evaluating alcohol problems in adults and adolescents. In R. K. Hester & W. R. Miller (Eds.), *Handbook of alcoholism treatment approaches* (2nd ed.). New York: Allyn & Bacon.

Millon, T., & Davis, R. (2000). *Personality disorders in modern life*. New York: Wiley.

Milner, B. (1959). The memory defect in bilateral hippocampal lesions. *Psychiatric Research Reports, 11,* 43–52.

Milner, B., Corkin, S., & Teuber, H. L. (1968). Further analyses of the hippocampal amnesic syndrome: 14-year follow-up study of H.M. *Neuropsychologia, 6,* 215–234.

Milstein, G., & Argiles, N. (1992). Si dios quiere: Hispanic families' experience of caring for a seriously mentally ill family member. *Culture, Medicine, Psychiatry, 16,* 187–215.

Minino, A. M., Arias, E., Kochanek, K. D., Murphy, S. L., & Smith, B. L. (2002). Deaths: Final data for 2000. *National Vital Statistics Reports, 50*(15). Hyattsville, MD: National Center for Health Statistics.

Minkoff, K. (2001). Best practices: Developing standards of care for individuals with co-occurring psychiatric and substance use disorders. *Psychiatric Services, 52,* 597–599.

Minuchin, S. (1974). *Families and family therapy*. Cambridge, MA: Harvard University Press.

Minuchin, S., & Fishman, H. C. (1981). *Family therapy techniques*. Cambridge, MA: Harvard University Press.

Minuchin, S., Montalvo, B., Guerney, B. G., Jr., Rosman, B. L., & Schumer, F. (1967). *Families of the slums: An exploration of their structure and treatment*. New York: Basic Books.

Minuchin, S., Rosman, B., & Baker, L. (1978). *Psychosomatic families*. Cambridge, MA: Harvard University Press.

Mitchell, C. G. (1998). Perceptions of empathy and client satisfaction with managed behavioral health care. *Social Work, 43*(5), 404–411.

Mittelman, M. S., Ferris, S. H., & Shulman, E. (1995). A comprehensive support program: Effect on depression in spouse-caregivers of AD patients. *Gerontologist, 35,* 413–418.

Mittelman, M. S., Ferris, S. H., & Shulman, E. (1996). A family intervention to delay nursing home placement of patients with Alzheimer's disease. *Journal of the American Medical Association, 276,* 1725–1731.

Mizes, J. S., & Palermo, T. M. (1997). Eating disorders. In R. F. Catalano, M. Arthur, R. T. Ammerman, & M. Hersen (Eds.), *Handbook of prevention and treatment with children and adolescents: Intervention in the real world context* (pp. 572–603). New York: Wiley.

Modesto-Lowe, V., & Kranzler, H. R. (1999). Diagnosis and treatment of alcohol-dependent patients with comorbid psychiatric disorders. *Alcohol Research and Health, 23*(2), 144–149.

Mohan, R. (2002). Treatments for borderline personality disorder: Integrating evidence into practice. *International Review of Psychiatry, 14*(1), 42–52.

Moncrieff, J. (2001). Are antidepressants overrated: A review of methodological problems in antidepressant trials. *Journal of Nervous and Mental Disease, 189,* 288–295.

Mondros, J. B., & Wilson, S. M. (1994). Organizing for power and empowerment. New York: Columbia University Press.

Moore, A. R., & O'Keeffe, S. T. (1999). Drug-induced cognitive impairment in the elderly. *Drugs and Aging, 15*(1), 15–28.

Moore, S. E. (2002). Substance abuse treatment with adolescent African American males: Reality therapy with an Afrocentric approach. *Journal of Social Work Practice in the Addictions, 1*(2), 21–32.

Moorehead, D. J. (2001). Early risk factors and current functioning of young adult women with full or partial eating disorders. *Dissertation Abstracts International, A: The Humanities and Social Sciences, 62*(1), 332-A.

Moreno, F. A., Delgado, P. L. (2000). Living with anxiety disorders: As good as it gets . . . ? *Bulletin of the Menninger Clinic, 64*(3, Suppl. A), A4–A21.

Moreno, J. K., Selby, M. J., Aved, K., & Besse, C. (2000). Differences in family dynamics among anorexic, bulimic, obese and normal women. *Journal of Psychotherapy in Independent Practice, 1*(1), 75–87.

Morgan, M. (1981). The ceremony of healing. *Journal of the American Medical Association, 9,* 32–47.

Morley, K. I., & Hall, W. D. (2004). Using pharmacogenetics and pharmacogenomics in the treatment of psychiatric disorders: Some ethical and economic considerations. *Journal of Molecular Medicine, 82*(1), 21–31.

Morrison, J. (1995). *DSM-IV made easy.* New York: Guilford.

Morse, R. M., & Flavin, D. K. (1992). The definition of alcoholism. *Journal of the American Medical Association, 268,* 1012–1014.

Morton, A. (1992). *Diana: Her true story.* New York: Pocket Books.

Moseley, P. G., & Deweaver, K. L. (1998). Empirical approaches to case management. In J. S. Wodarski &

B. A. Thyer (Eds.), *Handbook of empirical social work practice: Vol. 2: Social problems and practice issues* (pp. 393–412). New York: Wiley.

Mueller, T. I., Leon, A. C., Keller, M. B., Solomon, D. A., Endicott, J., Coryell, W., Warshaw, M., & Maser, J. D. (1999). Recurrence after recovery from major depressive disorder during 15 years of observational follow-up. *American Journal of Psychiatry, 156*(7), 1000–1006.

Mueser, K., & Gingerich, S. (1994). *Coping with schizophrenia: A guide for families.* Oakland, CA: New Harbinger.

Mueser, K., Sengupta, A., Schooler, N. R., Bellack, A. S., Xie, H., & Glick, I. D. (2001). Family treatment and medication dosage reduction in schizophrenia: Effect on patient functioning, family attitudes, and burden. *Journal of Consulting and Clinical Psychology, 69*(1), 3–12.

Munson, C. E. (1994). Cognitive family therapy. In D. K. Granvold (Ed.), *Cognitive and behavioral treatment: Methods and applications* (pp. 202–220). Pacific Grove, CA: Brooks/Cole.

Munson, C. E. (2001). *The mental health diagnostic desk reference* (2nd ed.). New York: Haworth.

Murphy, B. A. (2000). Delirium. *Emergency Medical Clinic of North America, 18*(2), 243–252.

Murphy, J. M., Laird, N. M., Monson, R. R., Sobel, A. M., & Leighton, A. H. (2000). A 40-year perspective on the prevalence of depression: The Stirling county study. *Archives of General Psychiatry, 57,* 209–215.

Murray, A. M., & Levkoff, S. E. (1993). Acute delirium and functional decline in the hospitalized elderly patient. *Journal of Gerontology, 48*(5), 181–187.

Murray, T. (2003). Wait not, want not: Factors contributing to the development of anorexia nervosa and bulimia nervosa. *The Family Journal: Counseling and Therapy for Couples and Families, 11*(3), 276–280.

Musselman, E. S., Evans, D. L., & Nemeroff, C. B. (1998). The relationship of depression to cardiovascular disease. *Archives of General Psychiatry, 55,* 580–592.

Myer, R. A., & James, R. K. (2005). *CD-ROM and workbook for crisis intervention.* Belmont, CA: Brooks/Cole.

Myers, P. L. (2002). Pain, poverty, and hope: The charter issue of Journal of Ethnicity in Substance Abuse. *Journal of Ethnicity in Substance Abuse, 1*(1), 1–5.

Najavits, L. M. (2001). *Seeking safety: A treatment manual for PTSD and substance abuse.* New York: Guilford.

Najavits, L. M., Crits-Christoph, P., & Dierberger, A. (2000). Clinicians' impact on the quality of substance use disorder treatment. *Substance Use and Misuse, 35*(12–14), 2161–2190.

Napier, A., & Whitaker, C. (1978). *The family crucible.* New York: Bantam Books.

Narendran, R., Young, C. M., Valenti, A. M., Pristach, C. A., Pato, M. T., & Grace, J. J. (2001). Olanzapine therapy in treatment-resistant psychotic mood disorders: A long-term follow-up study. *Journal of Clinical Psychiatry, 62*(7), 509–516.

Nash, M. (2000, May 15). The new science of Alzheimer's. *Time,* 51–57.

Nathan, D. (1994). Dividing to conquer? Women, men, and the making of multiple personality disorder. *Social Text, 40,* 77–114.

Nathan, P. E. (1993). Alcoholism: Psychopathology, etiology and treatment. In P. B. Sutker & H. E. Adams (Eds.), *Comprehensive handbook of psychopathology* (pp. 151–476). New York: Plenum Press.

National Alliance for the Mentally Ill (NAMI). (1999, November 8). *Brief notes on mental health.* Retrieved November 10, 2002, from http://www.nimh.nih.gov/publicat/childnotes.cfm.

National Alliance for the Mentally Ill. (2001). *State Parity Legislation 2001,* Tracking Report (August 2001). Available at http://www.nami.org. Accessed March 25, 2004.

National Association of Social Workers. (1997). NASW Code of Ethics, Approved by the 1996 Delegate Assembly. In R. L. Edwards (Ed.), *Encyclopedia of social work, 19th ed., 1997 supplement,* Appendix 1 (pp. 371–385). Washington, DC: NASW Press.

National Collaborating Centre for Mental Health (NCCMH). (2004). *Eating disorders: Core interventions in the treatment and management of anorexia nervosa, bulimia nervosa, and related eating disorders.* Great Britain: Stanley L. Hunt (Printers) Ltd.

National Family Caregivers Association. (1997). *Member survey 1997: A profile of caregivers.* Retrieved August 12, 2003, from http://www.nfcacares.org/survey.html.

National Institute of Mental Health. (2001). *The numbers count: Mental disorders in America.* Bethesdsa, MD: Author.

National Institute on Alcohol Abuse and Alcoholism. (1997). *Ninth Special Report to the U.S. Congress on Alcohol and Health.* Washington, DC: U.S. Department of Health and Human Services.

National Institute on Alcohol Abuse and Alcoholism. (2004). Alcohol's damaging effects on the brain. *Alcohol Alert, 63,* 1–5.

National Institute on Drug Abuse (NIDA). (1999). *Principles of drug addiction treatment: A research-based guide* (NCADI publication BKD347), *14*(5), 15.

National Institute on Drug Abuse (NIDA). (2000). *Anabolic steroid abuse.* Rockville, MD: National Clearinghouse on Alcohol and Drug Information.

National Institutes of Health (1992). *Progress report on Alzheimer's disease, 1992.* (NIH Publication No 92-3409). Washington, DC: U.S. Government Printing Office.

Needle, R. H. (1998). HIV prevention with drug-using populations—Current status and future prospects: Introduction and overview. *Public Health Reports, 113*(Suppl. 1), 4–18.

Neligh, G. L. (1996). Somatoform and associated disorders. In J. H. Scully (Ed.), *Psychiatry* (pp. 167–189). Baltimore: Williams & Wilkins.

Nemeroff, C. B., & Owens, M. J. (2002). Treatment of mood disorders. *Nature Neuroscience Supplement, 5,* 1068–1070.

Neufeld, K. J., Swartz, K. L., Bienvenu, O. J., Eaton, W. W., & Cai, G. (1999). Incidence of DSI/DSM-IV social phobia in adults. *Acta Psychiatrica Scandinavica, 100,* 186–192.

Nichols, M. P. (1984). *Family therapy: Concepts and methods.* New York: Gardner Press.

Nichols, M. P., & Schwartz, R. C. (1995). *Family therapy: Concepts and methods* (3rd ed.). Needham Heights, MA: Allyn & Bacon.

Nickerson, P. R. (1995). Solution-focused therapy. *Social Work, 40*(1), 132–133.

Nietzel, M. T., Speltz, M. L., McCauley, E. A., & Bernstein, D. A. (1998). *Abnormal psychology.* Boston: Allyn & Bacon.

Nixon, S. J., Phillips, M., & Tivis, R. (2000). Characteristics of American Indian clients seeking inpatient treatment for substance abuse. *Journal of Studies on Alcohol, 61*(4), 541–547.

Norcross, J. C., & Goldfried, M. R. (Eds.). (1992). *Handbook of psychotherapy integration.* New York: Basic Books.

Norman, E. (2000). *Resiliency enhancement: Putting the strengths perspective into social work practice.* New York: Columbia University Press.

Norman, R., & Townsend, L. A. (1999). Cognitive-behavioral therapy for psychosis: A status report. *Canadian Journal of Psychiatry, 44*(3), 245–253.

North, C. S. (2002). Somatization in survivors of catastrophic trauma: A methodological review. *Environmental Health Perspectives, 110*(4), 637–640.

North, C. S., & Guze, S. B. (1997). Somatoform disorders. In S. B. Guze (Ed.), *Adult psychiatry* (pp. 269–283). St. Louis: Mosby.

Nugent, W. R., & Williams, M. (2001). The relationship between the comorbidity of depression with problems in psychosocial functioning and the severity of suicidal ideation. *Social Service Review, 75*(4), 581–604.

Nunes, E. V., Weissman, M. M., Goldstein, R. B., McAvay, G., Seracini, A. M., Verdeli, H., & Wickramaratne, P. (1998). Psychopathology in children of parents with opiate dependence and/or major depression. *Journal of the American Academy of Child and Adolescent Psychiatry, 37,* 1142–1151.

Nylund, D. (2002). Poetic means to anti-anorexic ends. *Journal of Systemic Therapies, 21*(4), 19–34.

O'Brien, C. P. (1996). Recent developments in the pharmacotherapy of substance abuse. *Journal of Consulting and Clinical Psychology, 64*(4), 677–686.

O'Connor, P. G. (2000). Treating opioid dependence: New data and new opportunities. *New England Journal of Medicine, 343,* 1332–1333.

O'Dell, K. J., Turner, N. H., & Weaver, G. F. (1998). Women in recovery from drug misuse: An exploratory study of their social networks and social support. *Substance Use and Misuse, 33,* 1721–1734.

O'Gorman, P. (2004). The anatomy of resilience: What makes some clients bounce back better than others? *Counselor: The Magazine for Addiction Professionals, 5*(1), 14–17.

O'Hanlon, B. (1996). *Do one thing different.* New York: William Morrow.

O'Hanlon, B., & Bertolino, B. (1998a). *Even from a broken web: Brief, respectful solution-oriented treatment of sexual abuse and trauma.* New York: Wiley.

O'Hanlon, B., & Bertolino, B. (1998b). *Evolving possibilities: Bill O'Hanlon's selected papers.* Philadelphia: Brunner/Mazel.

O'Hanlon, S., & O'Hanlon, B. (2002). Solution-oriented therapy with families. In J. Carlson & D. Kjos (Eds.), *Theories and strategies of family therapy* (pp. 190–215). Boston: Allyn & Bacon.

O'Hanlon, W. H. (1990). A grand unified theory for brief therapy: Putting problems in context. In J. K. Zeig & S. L.

Gilligan (Eds.), *Brief therapy: Myths, methods, and metaphors*. New York: Brunner/Mazel.

O'Hanlon, W. H., & Weiner-Davis, M. (1989). *In search of solutions: A new direction in psychotherapy*. New York: Norton.

O'Keeffe, S. T. (1999, September). Delirium in the elderly. *British Geriatrics Society, 28*, 5–8.

O'Malley, S. S., Jaffee, A. J., Rode, S., & Rounsaville, B. J. (1996). Experience of a "slip" among alcoholics treated with naltrexone or placebo. *American Journal of Psychiatry, 153*, 281–283.

O'Neill, J. V. (2000). Practice-research sync 'crucial for survival.' *NASW News, 45*(6), 3.

Odell, S. M., & Commander, M. J. (2000). Risk factors for homelessness among people with psychotic disorders. *Social Psychiatry Psychiatric Epidemiology, 35*(9), 396–401.

Oehl, M., Hummer, M., & Fleischhacker, W. W. (2000). Compliance with antipsychotic treatment. *Acta Psychiatrica Scandinavica, 102*(407), 83–86.

Oei, T. P. S., & Jackson, P. R. (1980). Long-term effects of group and individual social skills training with alcoholics. *Addictive Behaviors, 5*, 129–136.

Office of Applied Studies (2000). *Summary of findings from the National Household Survey on Drug Abuse*. DHHS Pub. NO. (SMA) 00-3466. SAMHSA.

Okun, B. F. (1997). *Effective helping: Interviewing and counseling techniques* (5th ed.). Pacific Grove, CA: Brooks/Cole.

Okundaye, J. N., Smith, P., Lawrence-Webb, C. (2001). Incorporating spirituality and the strengths perspective into social work practice with addicted individuals. *Journal of Social Work Practice in Addictions, 1*(1), 65–82.

Olfson, M., & Guardino, M. (2000). Barriers to the treatment of social anxiety. *The American Journal of Psychiatry, 157*(4), 521–527.

Opler, L. A. (1999). *Primary care psychiatry and behavioral medicine: Brief office treatment and management pathways* (pp. 230–255). New York: Springer.

Oquendo, M. A. (1995). Differential diagnosis of ataque de nervios. *American Journal of Orthopsychiatry, 65*(1), 60–65.

Orbach, I. (1997). A taxonomy of factors related to suicidal behavior. *Clinical Psychology: Science and Practice, 4*, 205–224.

Oren, M. L., Carella, M., & Helma, T. (1996). Diabetes support group—Study results and implications. *Employee Assistance Quarterly, 11*(3), 1–20.

Osborn, C. J. (1999). Solution-focused strategies with "involuntary" clients: Practical applications for the school and clinical settings. *Journal of Humanistic Education and Development, 37*, 169–181.

Ost, L. G. (1992). Blood and injection phobia: Background and cognitive, physiological and behavioral variables. *Journal of Abnormal Psychology, 10*(1), 68–74.

Ouimette, P. C., Finney, J. W., & Moos, R. H. (1997). Twelve-step and cognitive-behavioral treatment for substance abuse: A comparison of treatment effectiveness. *Journal of Consulting and Clinical Psychology, 65*, 230–240.

Overholser, J. C. (1990). Differential diagnosis of malingering and factitious disorder with physical symptoms. *Behavioral Sciences and the Law, 8*, 55–65.

Owings-West, M., & Prinz, R. J. (1987). Parental alcoholism and child psychopathology. *Psychological Bulletin, 102*(2), 204–281.

Parad, H. J. (1971). Crisis intervention. In R. Morris (Ed.), *Encyclopedia of social work* (16th ed., Vol. 1). New York: National Association of Social Workers.

Parad, H. J., & Parad, L. G. (Eds.). (1990). *Crisis intervention* (Book 2). Milwaukee, WI: Family Service America.

Parad, H. J., & Parad, L. G. (Eds.). (1999). *Crisis intervention* (Book 2, 2nd ed.). Milwaukee, WI: Family Service America.

Paris, J. (1997). Childhood trauma as an etiological factor in the personality disorders. *Journal of Personality Disorders, 11*(1), 34–49.

Parnetti, L. (2000). Therapeutic options in dementia. *Journal of Neurology, 247*(3), 163–168.

Parrott, III, L. (2003). *Counseling and Psychotherapy* (2nd ed.). Pacific Grove, CA: Brooks/Cole.

Paul, R. W., & Elder, L. (2002). *Critical thinking: Tools for taking charge of your professional and personal life*. Upper Saddle River, NJ: Financial Times/Prentice Hall.

Pearson, Q. M. (2000). Opportunities and challenges in the supervisory relationship: Implications for counselor supervision. *Journal of Mental Health Counseling, 22*(4), 283–295.

Pecoraro, C. (2000). Understanding gay, lesbian, and bisexual issues in treatment. *Counselor: The Magazine for Addiction Professionals, 1*, 23–32.

Pendergrast, M. (1995). *Victims of memory* (2nd ed.). Hinesburg, VT: Upper Access Press.

Pendleton, V. R., Goodrick, G. K., & Reeves, R. S. (2002). Exercise augments the effects of cognitive-behavioral therapy in the treatment of binge eating. *International Journal of Eating Disorders, 31*(2), 172–184.

Pennington, H., Butler, R., & Eagger, S. (2000). The assessment of patients with alcohol disorders by an old age psychiatric service. *Aging and Mental Health, 4*, 182–185.

Perlman, H. H. (1957). *Social casework: A problem-solving process*. Chicago: University of Chicago Press.

Perlman, H. H. (1970). The problem-solving model in social casework. In R. Roberts & R. Nee (Eds.), *Theories of social casework* (pp. 130–179). Chicago: University of Chicago Press.

Perlman, H. H. (1979). *Relationship: the heart of helping people*. Chicago: University of Chicago Press.

Perloff, J. D. (1998). Medicaid managed care and urban poor people: Implications for social work. In G. Shamess & A. Lightburn (Eds.), *Humane managed care?* (pp. 65–74). Washington, DC: NASW Press.

Pernell, R. (1986). Old themes for a new world. In P. Glasser & N. Mayadas (Eds.), *Group workers at work: Theory and practice in the '80s* (pp. 11–21). Totowa, NJ: Rowman and Littlefield.

Perris, C., & McGorry, P. D. (Eds.). (1998). *Cognitive psychotherapy of psychotic and personality disorders: Handbook of theory and practice* (pp. 37–62). Chichester, England: Wiley.

Persons, J. B. (1997). Dissemination of effective methods: Behavior therapy's next challenge. *Behavior Therapy, 28*, 465–471.

Perugi, G., Akiskal, H. S., Lattanzi, L., Cecconi, P., Mastrocinque, C., Patronelli, A., Vigonli, S., & Bemi, E. (1998). The high prevalence of "soft" bipolar features in atypical depression. *Comparative Psychiatry, 39*(2), 63–71.

Pescosolido, B., Wright, E., & Sullivan, W. (1995). Communities of care: A theoretical perspective on case management models in mental health. *Advances in Medical Sociology, 6,* 37–79.

Peterson, C. B., & Mitchell, J. E. (1999). Psychosocial and pharmacological treatment of eating disorders: A review of research findings. *Journal of Clinical Psychology, 55,* 685–697.

Pfammatter, M., Garst, F., & Teschner, C. (2000). Effects of a coping-oriented group therapy for schizophrenia and schizoaffective patients: A pilot study. *Acta Psychiatrica Scandinavica, 101,* 318–322.

Phillips, H. U. (1954). What is group work skill? *The Group, 5,* 3–10.

Phillips, K. A. (1991). Body dysmorphic disorder: The distress of imagined ugliness. *American Journal of Psychiatry, 150,* 302–308.

Phillips, K. A. (2000). Quality of life for patients with body dysmorphic disorder. *Journal of Nervous and Mental Disease, 188,* 170–175.

Phillips, K. A. (Ed.). (2001). *Somatoform and factitious disorders.* Washington, DC: American Psychiatric Publishing.

Phillips, K. A. (2002). Body dysmorphic disorder: Diagnostic controversies and treatment challenges. *Bulletin of the Menninger Clinic, 64*(1), 18–35.

Phillips, K. A., Albertini, R. S., Siniscalchi, J. M., Khan, A., & Robinson, M. (2001). Effectiveness of pharmacotherapy for body dysmorphic disorder: A chart-review study. *Journal of Clinical Psychiatry, 62*(9), 721–727.

Phillips, K. A., Dufresne, R. G., Wilkel, C. S., & Vittorio, C. C. (2000). Rate of body dysmorphic disorder in dermatology patients. *Journal of the American Academy of Dermatology, 42,* 436–441.

Phillips, M. R. (1993). Strategies used by Chinese families coping with schizophrenia. In D. Davis & S. Harrell (Eds.), *Chinese families in the post-Mao era* (pp. 277–306). Berkeley: University of California Press.

Piccinelli, M., & Simon, G. (1997). Gender and cross-cultural differences in somatic symptoms associated with emotional distress. An international study in primary care. *Psychology Medicine, 27*(2), 433–444.

Pidlubny, S. R. (2002). Group cognitive behaviour therapy for residual depression: Effectiveness and predictors of response. *Cognitive Behaviour Therapy, 31*(1), 31–41.

Pies, R. (1998a). Progress in psychoses: Safety and efficacy of atypical antipsychotics in schizophrenia and demented patients. *Psychiatric Times, 15*(1), 22–27.

Pies, R. (1998b). The horsemen of the atypicals. *Psychiatric Times, 15*(1), 28–30.

Pinderhughes, E. (1989). *Understanding race, ethnicity, and power: The key to efficacy in clinical practice.* New York: Free Press.

Pinderhughes, E. (1995). Empowering diverse populations: Family practice in the 21st century. *Families in Society, 76*(3), 131–140.

Pinel, J. P. J., Assanand, S., & Lehman, D. R. (2000). Hunger, eating, and ill health. *American Psychologist, 55,* 1105–1116.

Pinikahana, J., Happell, B., Taylor, M., & Keks, N. A. (2002). Exploring the complexity of compliance in schizophrenia. *Issues in Mental Health Nursing, 23*(5), 513–528.

Pinsof, W. M. (1983). Integrative problem-centered therapy: Toward the synthesis of family and individual psychotherapies. *Journal of Marital and Family Therapy, 9,* 19–35.

Pinsof, W. M. (1995). *Integrative problem-centered therapy: A synthesis of family, individual, and biological therapies.* New York: Basic Books.

Pittenger, S. (1998). Family therapy and family psycho-educational approaches for schizophrenia: An integrated model. *The Sciences and Engineering, 59*(5-B), 2429.

Pizer, A. G. (2002). The relationship between general parental controllingness and eating disorder symptomatology in mothers. *Dissertation Abstracts International, A: The Humanities and Social Sciences, 63*(2), 758-A.

Plasse, B. R. (2000). Components of engagement: Women in a psychoeducational parenting skills group in substance abuse treatment. *Social Work with Groups, 22*(4), 33–50.

Plomin, R., DeFries, J. C., McClearn, G. E., & McGuffin, P. (2001). *Behavioral genetics.* New York: Worth.

Polcin, D. L. (1992). Issues in the treatment of dual diagnosis clients who have chronic mental illness. *Professional Psychology: Research and practice, 23,* 30–37.

Polivy, J. M., & Herman, C. P. (1993). Etiology of binge eating: Psychological mechanism. In C. G. Fairbain & G. T. Wilson (Eds.), *Binge eating: Nature, assessment, and treatment.* New York: Guilford.

Pomeroy, E. C., Kiam, R., & Green, D. L. (2000). Reducing depression, anxiety, and trauma of male inmates: An HIV/AIDS psychoeducational group intervention. *Social Work Research, 24*(3), 156–167.

Pomeroy, E., & Wambach, K. (2003). *The clinical assessment workbook: Balancing strengths and differential diagnosis.* Pacific Grove, CA: Brooks/Cole.

Pope, H. G., Jr., Phillips, K. A., & Olivardia, R. (2000). *The Adonis complex: The secret crisis of male body obsession.* New York: Free Press.

Pope, K. S., & Vasquez, M. J. (1998). *Ethics in psychotherapy and counseling* (2nd ed.). San Francisco: Jossey-Bass.

Popli, A. P., Masand, P. S., & Dewan, M. J. (1992). Factitious disorders with psychological symptoms. *Journal of Clinical Psychiatry, 53,* 315–318.

Porcerelli, J. H., & Sandler, B. A. (1998). Anabolic-androgenic steroid abuse and psychopathology. *The Psychiatric Clinics of North America, 21,* 829–833.

Posavac, H. D., Posavac, S., & Weigel, R. G. (2001). Reducing the impact of media images on women at risk for body image disturbance: Three targeted interventions. *Journal of Social and Clinical Psychology, 20*(3), 324–340.

Potash, J. B., & De Paulo, J. R., Jr. (2000). Searching high and low: A review of the genetics of bipolar disorder. *Bipolar Disorders, 2*(1), 8–26.

Potter, J. D. (1997). Hazards and benefits of alcohol. *The New England Journal of Medicine, 337,* 1763–1764.

Power, M. J., & Holmes, J. (2002). Integrative therapy from a cognitive-behavioural perspective. In J. Holmes & A. Bateman (Eds.), *Integration in psychotherapy: Models and methods* (pp. 27–47). Oxford: Oxford University Press.

Prater, C. D., Miller, K. E., & Zylstra, R. G. (1999). Outpatient detoxification of the addicted or alcoholic patient. *American Family Physician, 60,* 1175–1183.

Preston, J., & Johnson, J. (2001). *Clinical psychopharmacology made ridiculously simple.* Miami: MedMaster, Inc.

Pribor, E. F., Yutzy, S. H., Dean, J. T., & Wetzel, R. D. (1993). Briquet's syndrome, dissociation, and abuse. *American Journal of Psychiatry, 150,* 1507–1511.

Prochaska, J. O. (1999). How do people change and how can we change to help more people? In M. A. Hubble, B. L. Duncan, & S. D. Miller (Eds.), *The heart and soul of change: What works in therapy* (pp. 227–255). Washington, DC: American Psychological Association.

Prochaska, J. O., & Norcross, J. C. (1999). *Systems of psychotherapy* (4th ed.). Pacific Grove, CA: Brooks/Cole.

Procyshyn, R. M., Thompson, D., & Tse, G. (2000). Pharmacoeconomics of clozapine, risperidone and olanzapine: A review of the literature. *CNS-Drugs 13*(1), 47–76.

Putnam, F. W., & Lowenstein, R. J. (1993). Treatment of multiple personality disorder: A survey of current practices. *American Journal of Psychiatry, 150,* 1048–1052.

Pyne, J. M., Bean, D., & Sullivan, G. (2001). Characteristics of patients with schizophrenia who do not believe they are mentally ill. *Journal of Nervous Mental Disorders, 189*(3), 146–153.

Quick, E. K. (1996). *Doing what works in brief therapy: A strategic solution-focused approach.* New York: Academic Press.

Quick, E. K. (1998). Strategic solution-focused therapy: Doing what works in crisis intervention. *Crisis Intervention and Time Limited Treatment, 4*(2/3), 197–214.

Rabinowitz, J., & Marjefsky, S. (1998). Predictors of being expelled from dropping out of alcohol treatment. *Psychiatric Services, 49,* 187–189.

RachBeisel, J., Scott, J., & Dixon, L. (1999). Co-occurring severe mental illness and substance use disorders: A review of recent research. *Psychiatric Services, 49,* 187–189.

Radke-Yarrow, M., & Sherman, T. (1990). Hard-growing: Children who survive. In J. E. Rolf & A. S. Masten (Eds.), *Risk and protective factors in the development of psychopathology* (pp. 97–109). New York: Cambridge University Press.

Rafanelli, C., Park, S. K., & Fava, G. A. (1999). New psychotherapeutic approaches to residual symptoms and relapse prevention in bipolar depression. *Clinical Psychology and Psychotherapy, 6,* 194–201.

Ramana, R., Paykel, E. S., Cooper, Z., Hayhurst, H., Saxty, M., & Surtees, P. G. (1995). Remission and relapse in major depression. *Psychological Medicine, 25,* 1161–1170.

Ramlow, B. E., White, A. L., Watson, D. D., & Leukefied, C. G. (1997). The needs of women with substance use problems: An expanded vision for treatment. *Substance Use and Misuse, 32,* 1395–1404.

Randall, E. (2001). Existential therapy of panic disorder: A single system study. *Clinical Social Work Journal, 29*(3), 259–267.

Randolph, W. M., Stroup-Benham, C., Black, S. A., & Markides, K. S. (1998). Alcohol use among Cuban-Americans, Mexican-Americans, and Puerto Ricans. *Alcohol Health and Research World, 22,* 265–269.

A rapid move to diversity. (2001, March 13). *Sacramento Bee,* p. A.

Rapp, C. A. (1998). *The strengths model: Case management with people suffering from severe and persistent mental illness.* New York: Oxford University Press.

Rapp, R. (2002). Strengths-based case management: Enhancing treatment for persons with substance abuse problems. In D. Saleebey (Ed.), *The strengths perspective in social work practice* (3rd ed.). New York: Longman.

Rappaport, J. (1987). Terms of empowerment/exemplars of prevention: Toward a theory for community psychology. *American Journal of Community Psychology, 15,* 121–128.

Ravona-Springer, R., Dolberg, O. T., Hirschmann, S., & Grunhaus, L. Delirium in elderly patents treated with risperidone: A report of three cases. *Journal of Clinical Psychopharmacology, 18,* 171–172.

Ray, O. S., & Ksir, C. (1993). *Drugs, society and human behavior* (6th ed.). St. Louis: C.V. Mosby.

Razali, S. M., Hasanah, C. I., & Khan, A. (2000). Psychosocial interventions for schizophrenia. *Journal of Mental Health, 9*(3), 283–289.

Read, J., Agar, K., Barker-Collo, S., Davies, E., & Moskowitz, A. (2001). Assessing suicidality in adults: Integrating childhood trauma as a major risk factor. *Professional Psychology: Research and Practice, 32*(4), 367–372.

Read, J., Kahler, C. W., & Stevenson, J. F. (2001). Bridging the gap between alcoholism and practice: Identifying what works and why. *Professional Psychology, 32*(3), 47–57.

Reamer, F. G. (1998). The evolution of social work ethics. *Social Work, 43*(6), 488–500.

Reamer, F. G. (1999). *Social work values and ethics* (2nd ed.). New York: Columbia University Press.

Reamer, F. G. (2000). The social work ethics audit: A risk management strategy. *Social Work, 45*(4), 355–366.

Reamer, F. G. (2001). *Ethics education in social work.* Alexandria, VA: Council on Social Work Education.

Reamer, F. G. (2002). Ethical issues in social work. In A. R. Roberts & G. J. Greene (Eds.), *Social workers' desk reference* (pp. 65–69). New York: Oxford University Press.

Rector, N. A., & Beck, A. T. (2001). Cognitive behavioral therapy for schizophrenia: An empirical review. *Journal of Nervous Mental Disorders, 189*(5), 278–287.

Redpath, R., & Harker, M. (1999). Becoming solution-focused in practice. *Educational Psychology in Practice, 15*(2), 116–121.

Reich, J. (2000). The relationship of social phobia to the personality disorders. *European Psychiatry, 15,* 151–159.

Reich, J. (2002). Drug treatment of personality disorder traits. *Psychiatric Annals, 32*(10), 590–600.

Reid, W. H., Balis, G. U., & Sutton, B. J. (1997). *Treatment of psychiatric disorders* (3rd ed., revised for DSM-IV). Bristol, PA: Brunner/Mazel.

Reinecke, M. (1994). Suicide and depression. In F. M. Dattilio & A. Freeman (Eds.), *Cognitive-behavioral strategies in* crisis intervention (pp. 67–103). New York: Guilford Press.

Reinstein, M. J., Sonnenberg, J. G., Hedberg, T. G., Jones, L. E., & Reyngold, P. (2003). Oxcarbazepine versus divalproex sodium for the continuing treatment of mania. *Clinical Drug Investigation, 23*(10), 671–677.

Reisch, M., & Gorin, S. (2001). Nature of work and the future of the social work profession. *Social Work, 46*(1), 9–19.

Reiss, D. (1981). *The family's constriction of reality.* Cambridge, MA: Harvard University Press.

Remick, R. A. (2002). Diagnosis and management of depression in primary care: A clinical update and review. *Canadian Medical Association Journal, 167*(11), 1253–1261.

Reuss, N. H. (1997). The nightmare question: Problem talk in solution-focused brief therapy with alcoholics and their families. *Journal of Family Psychotherapy, 8*(4), 3–17.

Rey, J. M. (1996). Antecedents of personality disorders in young adults. *Psychiatric times 13*(2). Retrieved May 16, 2005 from http://www.psychiatrictimes.com.html.

Rhodes, R. (1995). A group intervention for young children in addictive families. *Social Work with Groups, 18*(2/3), 123–133.

Ribner, D. S., & Knei-Paz, C. (2002). Client's view of a successful helping relationship. *Social Work, 47*(4), 379–387.

Richards, P. S., Baldwin, B. M., Frost, H. A., Hardman, R., Berrett, M., & Clark, J. (2000). What works for treating eating disorders: A synthesis of 28 outcome reviews. *Eating Disorders: Journal of Treatment and Prevention, 8,* 189–206.

Richardson, V. (2002). Psychotherapy with older adults. In A. R. Roberts and G. J. Greene (Eds.), *Social workers' desk reference* (pp. 624–627). Oxford: Oxford University Press.

Richmond, M. (1899). *Friendly visiting among the poor: A handbook for charity workers.* New York: Macmillan.

Richmond, M. (1917). *Social diagnosis.* New York: Russell Sage Foundation.

Richmond, M. (1922). *What is social casework?* New York: Russell Sage Foundation.

Richmond, M. (1930). *The long view.* New York: Russell Sage Foundation.

Riess, H. (2002). Integrative time-limited group therapy for bulimia nervosa. *International Journal of Group Psychotherapy, 52*(1), 1–17.

Riess, H., & Dockray-Miller, M. F. (2001). *Integrative group treatment for bulimia nervosa.* New York: Columbia University Press.

Riffe, H. A., & Kondrat, M. E. (1997). Social worker alienation and disempowerment in a managed care setting. *Journal of Progressive Human Services, 8*(1), 41–56.

Rigler, S. K. (2000). Alcoholism in the elderly. *American Family Physician, 61,* 1710–1716.

Ripich, D., Vertes, D., Whitehouse, P. J., & Fulton, S. (1991). Turn-taking and speech act patterns in the discourse of senile dementia of the Alzheimer's type patients. *Brain Language, 40,* 330–343.

Rittner, B., & Dozier, C. D. (2000). Effects of court-ordered substance abuse treatment in child protective services cases. *Social Work, 45*(2), 131–140.

Rivas-Vazquez, R. A., Blais, M. A., Rey, G. J., & Rivas-Vazquez, A. (2000). Atypical antipsychotic medications: Pharmacological profiles and psychological implications. *Research and Practice, 31*(6), 735–740.

Robbins, C. J. (2002). Dialectical behavior therapy for borderline personality disorder. *Psychiatric Annals, 32*(10), 608–616.

Robbins, C. J. (2004). Dialectical behavior therapy: Current status, recent developments, and future directions. *Journal of Personality Disorders, 18*(1), 73–89.

Robbins, S. P., Chatterjee, P., & Canda, E. R. (1998). *Contemporary human behavior theory: A critical perspective for social work.* Boston: Allyn & Bacon.

Robbins, S. P., Chatterjee, P., & Canda, E. R. (1999). Ideology, scientific theory, and social work practice. *Families in Society: The Journal of Contemporary Human Services, 80*(4), 374–384.

Roberts, A., & Dziegielewski, S. F. (1995). Foundation skills and applications of crisis intervention and cognitive therapy. In A. Roberts (Ed.), *Crisis intervention and time-limited cognitive treatment* (pp. 3–27). Thousand Oaks, CA: Sage.

Robinson, D., Woerner, M., Alvir, M. J., Bilder, R., & Goldman, R. (1999). Predictors of relapse following response from a first episode of schizophrenia or schizoaffective disorder. *Archives of General Psychiatry, 56,* 241–247.

Robinson, D., Woerner, M., & Schooler, N. (2000). Intervention research in psychosis: Issues related to clinical assessment. *Schizophrenia Bulletin, 26*(3), 551–556.

Robinson, T. N. (1999). Reducing children's television to prevent obesity: A randomized controlled trial. *Journal of the American Medical Association, 383,* 1561–1567.

Robinson, V. (1930). *A changing psychology in social case work.* Chapel Hill, NC: University of North Carolina Press.

Rock, B. (2001). Social work under managed care: Will we survive or can we prevail? In R. Perez-Koening & B. Rock (Eds.), *Social work in the era of devolution: Toward a just practice* (pp. 69–85). New York: Fordham University Press.

Rock, B., & Congress, E. (1999). The new confidentiality for the twenty-first century in a managed care environment. *Social Work, 44*(3), 253–262.

Rodell, D. E., Benda, B. B., & Rodell, L. (2001). Effects of alcohol problems on depression among homeless. *Alcoholism Treatment Quarterly, 19*(3), 65–81.

Rodnitzky, R. L. (2002). Drug-induced movement disorders. *Clinical Neuropharmacology, 25*(3), 142–152.

Rodriguez, N., Ryan, S., Vande Kemp, H., & Foy, D. (1997). Post-traumatic stress disorder in adult female survivors of childhood sexual abuse: A comparison study. *Journal of Consulting and Clinical Psychology, 65,* 53–59.

Ronel, N. (1998). Twelve-step self-help groups: The spontaneous emergence of "grace communities." *Social Development Issues, 20*(3), 53–72.

Ronel, N., & Libman, G. (2003). Eating disorders and recovery: Lessons from Overeaters Anonymous. *Clinical Social Work Journal, 31*(2), 155–171.

Room, R. (1993). Alcoholics Anonymous as a social movement. In B. S. McCrady & W. R. Miller (Eds.), *Research on Alcoholics Anonymous: Opportunities and alternatives* (pp. 167–187). New Brunswick, NJ: Rutgers Center of Alcohol Studies.

Rose, S. (1990). Advocacy/empowerment: An approach to clinical practice for social work. *Journal of Sociology and Social Welfare, 17,* 41–51.

Rose, S. M., & Moore, V. L. (1995). Case management. In *Encyclopedia of social work* (Vol. 1, pp. 335–340). Washington, DC: NASW Press.

Rosen, A. L., & Zlotnik, J. L. (2001). Demographics and reality: The "disconnect" in social work education. *Journal of Gerontological Social Work, 36*(3/4), 81–97.

Rosen, J. C. (1995). The nature of body dysmorphic disorder and treatment with cognitive behavior therapy. *Cognitive and Behavioral Practice, 2*(1), 143–166.

Rosen, J. C., & Reiter, J. (1996). Development of the body dysmorphic disorder examination. *Behavior Research and Therapy, 34*(9), 755–766.

Rosenquist, K. J., Walker, S. S., & Ghaemi, S. N. (2002). Tardive dyskinesia and Ziprasidone. *American Journal of Psychiatry, 159*(8), 1436–1442.

Roses, A. D., Saunders, A. M., Charness, M. E., & Rubinstein, M. (1996). Evaluation of suspected dementia. *New England Journal of Medicine, 335,* 1996–1998.

Rosik, C. H. (2003). Critical issues in the dissociative disorders field: Six perspectives from religiously sensitive practitioners. *Journal of Psychology and Theology, 31*(2), 113–128.

Ross, C. A. (1997). *Dissociative identity disorder, clinical features, and treatment of multiple personality* (2nd ed.). New York: Wiley.

Ross, C. A., & Pam, A. (1995). *Pseudoscience in biological psychiatry: Blaming the body.* New York: Wiley.

Rossau, C. D., & Mortensen, P. B. (1997). Risk factors for suicide in patients with schizophrenia: Nested case-control study. *British Journal of Psychiatry, 171,* 355–359.

Rotgers, F., Morgenstern, J., & Walters, S. T. (2003). *Treating substance abuse: Theory and technique* (2nd ed.). New York: Guilford.

Roth, B. L., Sheffler, D. J., & Kroeze, W. K. (2004). Opinion: Magic shotguns versus magic bullets: Selectively non-selective drugs for mood disorders and schizophrenia. *Nature Reviews Drug Discovery, 3*(4), 353–360.

Rothbart, M. K., Ahadi, S. A., & Evans, D. E. (2000). Temperament and personality: Origins and outcomes. *Journal of Personality and Social Psychology, 78,* 122–135.

Rothbaum, B. O. (2002). Exposure therapy for posttraumatic stress disorder. *American Journal of Psychotherapy, 56*(1), 59–75.

Rotheram-Borus, M. J., Murphy, D. A., Kennedy, M., & Kuklinski, M. (2001). Health and risk behaviors over time among youth living with HIV. *Journal of Adolescence, 24*(6), 791–802.

Rothman, D. J. (1971). *The discovery of the asylum: Social order and disorder in the new republic.* Boston: Little, Brown.

Rowan, T., & O'Hanlon, B. (1999). *Solution-oriented therapy for chronic and severe mental illness.* New York: Wiley.

Rubin, E. H. (1997). Psychopathology. In S. B. Guze (Ed.), *Adult psychiatry.* St. Louis: Mosby-Year Book.

Rubin, J. (2001). Countertransference factors on the psychology of psychopharmacology. *Journal of the American Academy of Psychoanalysis, 29*(4), 565–573.

Rudnick, A. (2001). The impact of coping in relation between symptoms and quality of life in schizophrenia. *Interpersonal and Biological Processes, 64*(4), 304–308.

Rudnick, A., & Kravetz, S. (2001). The relation of social support-seeking to quality of life in schizophrenia. *Journal of Nervous Mental Disorders, 189*(4), 258–262.

Rush, C. R., & Pazzaglia, P. J. (1998). Pretreatment with isradipine, a calcium-channel blocker does not attenuate the acute behavioral effects of ethanol in humans. *Alcoholism: Clinical & Experimental Research, 22,* 539–547.

Rutan, J. S., & Rice, C. A. (1999). Personality disorders: Group psychotherapy as a treatment of choice. *Journal of Psychotherapy in Independent Practice, 1*(1), 3–11.

Rutter, M. (1985). Resilience in the face of adversity: Protective factors and resistance to psychiatric disorder. *British Journal of Psychiatry, 147,* 598–611.

Rutter, M. (1987). Psychosocial resilience and protective mechanisms. *American Journal of Orthopsychiatry, 57,* 316–331.

Rutter, M. (1988). *Studies of psychosocial risk: The power of longitudinal data.* New York: Cambridge University Press.

Rutter, M., & Casaer, P. (1991). *Biological risk factors for psychosocial disorders.* New York: Cambridge University Press.

Rutter, M., Pickles, A., Murray, R., & Eaves, L. (2001). Testing hypotheses on specific environmental causal effects on behavior. *Psychological Bulletin, 127,* 291–324.

Ryan, S., Delva, J., & Gruber, S. J. (2001). A study of family fighting and illegal drug use among adults who completed substance abuse treatment. *Journal of Family Social Work, 6*(1), 69–78.

Ryff, C. D., Singer, B., Love, G. D., & Essex, M. J. (1998). Resilience in adulthood and later life. In J. Lomranz, (Ed.), *Handbook of aging and mental health: An integrative approach* (pp. 69–96). New York: Plenum.

Ryle, A. (2004). The contribution of cognitive analytic therapy to the treatment of borderline personality disorder. *Journal of Personality Disorders, 18*(1), 3–35.

Sable, J. A., & Jeste, D. V. (2002). Antipsychotic treatment for late-life schizophrenia. *Current Psychiatry Reports, 4*(4), 299–306.

Sachdev, P. (2002). Citalopram-clonazepam combination for primary depersonalization disorder: A case report. *Australian and New Zealand Journal of Psychiatry, 36*(2), 424–425.

Sacks, S. (2000). Co-occurring mental and substance use disorders: Promising approaches and research issues. *Substance Use and Misuse, 35*(12–14), 2061–2093.

Sacristan, J. A., Gomez, J-C., Montejo, A-L., Vieta, E., & Gregor, K. J. (2000). Doses of olanzapine, risperidone, and haloperidol used in clinical practice: Results of a prospective pharmacoepidemiologic study. *Clinical Therapeutics: The International Peer-Reviewed Journal of Drug Therapy, 22*(5), 583–599.

Safer, D. J. (2002). Design and reporting modifications in industry-sponsored comparative psychopharmacology trials. *Journal of Nervous and Mental Disease, 190,* 583–592.

Safran, J., & Muran, J. (Eds.). (1998). *The therapeutic alliance in brief psychotherapy.* Washington, DC: American Psychological Association.

Sagor, R. (1993). *At-risk students: Reaching and teaching them.* Swampscott, MA: Watersun Press.

Sagor, R. (2002). Lessons from skateboarders. *Educational Leadership,* 34–38.

Saitz, R. (1998). Introduction to alcohol withdrawal. *Alcohol Health and Research World* 22(1), 5–12.

Sajatovic, M., Madhusoodanan, S., & Buckley, P. (2000). Schizophrenia in the elderly: Guidelines for management. *CNS-Drugs, 13*(2), 103–115.

Saleebey, D. (1992). *The strengths perspective in social work practice.* White Plains, NY: Longman Press.

Saleebey, D. (1994). Culture, theory, and narrative: The intersection of meanings in practice. *Social Work, 39,* 351–359.

Saleebey, D. (1996). The strengths perspective in social work practice: Extensions and cautions. *Social Work, 41,* 296–305.

Saleebey, D. (Ed.) (1997). *The strengths perspective in social work practice* (2nd ed.). New York: Longman.

Saleebey, D. (2001). The diagnostic strengths manual. *Social Work, 46*(2), 183–187.

Saltz, B. L., Woerner, M. G., Kane, J. M., Lieberman, J. A., Alvir, J. M., Bergmann, K. J., Blank, K., Koblenzer, J., & Kahner, K. (1991). Prospective study of tardive dyskinesia incidence in the elderly. *Journal of the American Medical Association, 266*(17), 2402–2406.

Salzman, C., & Tune, L. (2001). Neuroleptic treatment of late-life schizophrenia. *Harvard Review of Psychiatry, 9*(2), 77–83.

SAMHSA. (2000). *Club Drugs: The DAWN report, drug abuse warning network.* Office of Applied Studies, Substance Abuse and Mental Health Services Administration, Washington, DC: SAMHSA.

Sanchez-Craig, M. (1995). *Saying when: How to quit drinking or cut down* (2nd ed.). Toronto, Ontario, Canada: Addiction Research Foundation.

Sanchez-Craig, M., Davila, R., & Cooper, G. (1996). A self-help approach for high-risk drinking: Effect of an initial assessment. *Journal of Consulting and Clinical Psychology, 64*(4), 694–700.

Sander, F. M. (1979). *Individual and family therapy: Toward an integration.* New York: Jason Aronson Publishers.

Sanderson, W. C. (Spring, 1997). Cognitive behavior therapy. *American Journal of Psychotherapy, 51*(2), 289–292.

Sands, R. G. (2001). *Clinical social work practice in behavioral mental health: A postmodern approach to practice with adults* (2nd ed.). Boston: Allyn & Bacon.

Sandstrom, K. L. (1996). Searching for information, understanding, and self-value: The utilization of peer support groups by gay men with HIV/AIDS. *Social Work in Health Care, 23*(4), 51–74.

Sansone, R. A., & Shaffer, B. (1997). An introduction to psychotropic medications. In J. R. Matthews & C. E. Walker (Eds.), *Basic skills and professional issues in clinician psychology* (pp. 195–224). Boston: Allyn & Bacon.

Santisteban, D., Coatsworth, J. D., & Perez-Vidal, A. (1997). Brief structural/strategic family therapy with African American and Hispanic high-risk youth. *Journal of Community Psychology, 25,* 453–471.

Sapia, J. L. (2001). Using groups for the prevention of eating disorders among college women. *Journal for Specialists in Group Work, 26*(3), 256–266.

Saporito, J. W. (2001). Group work for heterosexual couples of mixed HIV status. In T. B. Kelly, T. Berman-Rossi, & S. Palombo (Eds.), *Group work: Strategies for strengthening resiliency* (pp. 181–201). New York: Haworth.

Sarbin, T., & Mancuso, J. (1980). *Schizophrenia: Medical diagnosis or moral verdict?* Elmsford, NY: Pergamon.

Sasich, L. D., Torrey, E. F., & Wolfe, S. M. (1997). Report on the international comparison of prices of antidepressant and antipsychotic drugs. *The Health Research Group Publication # 1446.* Washington, DC: Public Citizen's Health Research Group.

Sass, H., Soyka, M., Mann, K., & Zieglgänsberger, W. (1996). Relapse prevention by Acamprosate. Results from a placebo-controlled study on alcohol dependence. *Archives of General Psychiatry, 49*(11), 876–880.

Satir, V. (1967). *Conjoint family therapy.* Palo Alto, CA: Science and Behavior Books.

Satir, V. (1972). *Peoplemaking.* Palo Alto, CA: Science and Behavior Books.

Satir, V., & Baldwin, M. (1983). *Satir step by step: A guide to creative change in families.* Palo Alto, CA: Science and Behavior Books.

Satir, V., Banmen, J., Gerber, J., & Gomori, M. (1991). *The Satir model: Family therapy and beyond.* Palo Alto, CA: Science and Behavior Books.

Sayre, S. L., Schmitz, J. M., Stotts, A. L., & Averill, P. M. (2002). Determining predictors of attrition in an outpatient substance abuse program. *American Journal of Drug and Alcohol Abuse, 28*(1), 55–72.

Scarinci, I. C., Beech, B. M., Naumann, W., et al. (2002). Depression, socioeconomic status, age, and marital status in black women: A national study. *Ethnic Discourse, 12,* 421–428.

Scaturo, D. J. (2002). Technical skill and the therapeutic relationship: A fundamental dilemma in cognitive-behavioral and insight-oriented therapy. *Family Therapy, 29*(1), 1–22.

Schamess, G., & Lightburn, A. (Eds.). (1998). *Humane managed care?* Washington, DC: NASW Press.

Scharff, D. E., & Scharff, J. S. (1987). *Object relations family therapy.* Northvale, NJ: Jason Aronson.

Scharff, J. S., & Scharff, D. E. (2002). Objection relations therapy. In K. Carlson & D. Kjos (Eds.), *Theories and strategies of family therapy* (pp. 251–274). Boston: Allyn & Bacon.

Scheel, K. R. (2000). The empirical basis of dialectical behavior therapy: Summary, critique, and implications. *Clinical Psychology: Science and Practice, 7*(1), 68–86.

Scheff, T. (1966). *Being mentally ill.* Chicago: Aldine Atherton.

Scherz, F. H. (1953). What is family-centered casework? *Social Casework, 34,* 343–349.

Schilling, R. F., & El-Bassel, N. (1998). Substance abuse interventions. In J. B.W. Williams & K. Ell (Eds.), *Advances in mental health research: Implications for practice* (pp. 437–481). Washington, DC: NASW Press.

Schindehette, S., Sandler, B., Nelson, M., & Seaman, D. (2003). Recipe for life. *People, 60*(24), 135–139.

Schmidt, N. B., Wollaway-Bickel, K., & Trakowski, J. H. (2002). Antidepressant discontinuation in the context of cognitive-behavioral treatment for panic disorder. *Behaviour Research and Therapy, 40*(1), 67–73.

Schoenwolf, G. (1993). *Counterresistance: The therapist's interference with the therapeutic process.* Northvale, NJ: Jason Aronson.

Schopler, J. H., & Galinsky, M. J. (1996). Expanding our view of support groups as open systems. *Social Work with Groups, 18*(1), 3–10.

Schopler, J. H., Galinsky, M. J., & Abell, M. (1997). Creating community through telephone and computer groups: Theoretical and practice perspectives. *Social Work with Groups, 20*(4), 19–34.

Schor, J. D., & Levkoff, S. E. (1992). Risk factors for delirium in hospitalized elderly. *Journal of the American Medical Association, 267*(6), 827–832.

Schuckit, M. A. (1996). Alcohol, anxiety and depressive disorders. *Alcohol Health & Research World, 20,* 81–86.

Schuepbach, D., Keshavan, M. S., Kmiec, J. A., & Sweeney, J. A. (2002). Negative symptom resolution and improvements in specific cognitive deficits after acute treatment in first-episode schizophrenia. *Schizophrenia Research, 53*(3), 249–261.

Schulman, K. A., Seils, D. M., Timbie, J. W., Sugarman, J., Dame, L. A., Weinfurt, K. P., Mark, D. B., & Califf, R. M. (2002). A national survey of provisions in clinical-trial agreements between medical schools and industry sponsors. *New England Journal of Medicine, 347,* 1335–1341.

Schulz, S. C. (2000). New antipsychotic medications: More than old wine and new bottles. *Bulletin of the Menninger Clinic, 64*(1), 60–75.

Schwartz, J., Stoessel, P. W., Baxter, L. R., Martin, K. M., & Phelps, M. E. (1996). Systematic changes in cerebral glucose metabolic rate after successful behavior modification treatment of obsessive-compulsive disorder. *Archives of General Psychiatry, 53,* 109–113.

Schwartz, R. C., Petersen, S., & Skaggs, J. (2001). Predictors of homicidal ideation and intent in schizophrenia: An empirical study. *American Journal of Orthopsychiatry, 71*(3), 379–384.

Schwartz, W. (1971). On the use of groups. In W. Schwartz & S. Zalba (Eds.), *The practice of group work* (pp. 3–24). New York: Columbia University Press.

Schwartz, W. (1974). The social worker in the group. In R. Klenk & R. Ryan (Eds.), *The practice of social work* (pp. 257–276). Pacific Grove, CA: Wadsworth.

Schwitzer, A. M., Bergholz, K., Dore, T., & Salimi, L. (1998). Eating disorders among college women: Prevention, education, and treatment responses. *Journal of American College Health, 46*(5), 199–207.

Scully, J. H. (1996). *Psychiatry.* Baltimore: Williams & Wilkins.

Seagram, B. C. (1997). *The efficacy of solution-focused therapy with young offenders.* Unpublished doctoral dissertation. York University, North York, Ontario.

Searles, L. M. (2001). Clinical and cultural knowledge of multiple personality disorder as a social site of perplexity. Minneapolis: University of Minnesota, unpublished dissertation.

Segal, S. P., Akutsu, P. D., & Watson, M. A. (1998). Factors associated with involuntary return to a psychiatric emergency service within 12 months. *Psychiatric Services, 49*(9), 1212–1217.

Segal, S., Silverman, C., & Temkin, T. (1993). Empowerment and self-help agency practice for people with mental disabilities. *Social Work, 38*(6), 705–712.

Selekman, M. D. (1993). *Pathways to change.* New York: Guilford.

Selvini-Palazzoli, M. S., Boscolo, L., Cecchin, G., & Prata, G. (1980). Hypothesizing-circularity-neutrality: Three guidelines for the conductor of the session. *Family Process, 19*(1), 3–12.

Selvini-Palazzoli, M., Boscolo, L., Cecchin, G. F., & Prata, G. (1978). *Paradox and counterparadox: A new model in the therapy of the family schizophrenic transaction.* New York: Jason Aronson.

Selye, H. (1956). *The stress of life.* New York: McGraw-Hill.

Sensky, T., Turkington, D., Kingdon, D., Scott, J. L., & Scott, J. (2000). A randomized controlled trial of cognitive-behavioral therapy for persistent symptoms in schizophrenia resistant to medication. *Archives of General Psychiatry, 57*(2), 165–172.

Severson, M. A., Smith, E. G., & Tangalos, E. G. (1994). Patterns and predictors of institutionalization in community-based dementia patients. *Journal of American Geriatric Society, 4,* 181–185.

Shaner, R. (1997). *Psychiatry.* Baltimore: Williams & Wilkins.

Sharf, R. S. (2001). *Life's choices: Problems and solutions.* Pacific Grove, CA: Brooks/Cole.

Sharry, J., Madden, B., & Darmody, M. (2003). *Becoming a solution detective: Identifying your clients' strengths in practical brief therapy.* New York: Haworth Press.

Shaw, B. A., & Krause, N. (2001). Exploring race variations in aging and personal control. *Journal of Gerontology Series B: Psychological Sciences and Social Sciences, 56,* 119–124.

Shay, J. (1995). *Achilles in Vietnam: Combat trauma and the undoing of character.* New York: Simon and Schuster.

Sheafor, B. W., & Horejsi, C. R. (2003). *Techniques and guidelines for social work practice* (6th ed.). Boston: Allyn & Bacon.

Sheafor, B. W., Horejsi, C. R., & Horejsi, G. A. (2000). *Techniques and guidelines for social work practice* (5th ed.). Boston: Allyn & Bacon.

Shearin, E. N., & Linehan, M. M. (1994). Dialectical behavioral therapy for borderline personality disorder: Theoretical and empirical foundations. *Acta Psychiatrica Scandinavica, 89* (Suppl. 379), 61–68.

Shelton, R. C., Keller, M. B., Gelenberg, A., Dunner, D. L., Hirschfeld, R., Thase, M. E., et al. (2001). Effectiveness of St. John's wort in major depression: A randomized controlled trial. *Journal of the American Medical Association, 285,* 1978–1986.

Sher, K. J. (1991). *Children of alcoholics.* Chicago: University of Chicago Press.

Sher, K. J. (1997). Psychological characteristics of children of alcoholics. *Alcohol Health and Research World, 21*(3), 247–254.

Sher, K. J., Walitzer, K. S., Wood, P. K., & Brent, E. E. (1991). Characteristics of children of alcoholics: Putative risk factors, substance use and abuse and psychopathology. *Journal of Abnormal Psychology, 100,* 427–448.

Sherman, C. (2000). Acamprosate proven effective for alcohol treatment. *Clinical Psychiatry News, 28*(7), 14.

Sherman, S. N. (1959). Joint interviews in casework practice. *Social Work, 4,* 20–28.

Sherr, J. D., Thanker, G., & Tamminga, C. (2002). The prevention and management of tardive dyskinesia in the elderly. *Psychiatric Annals, 32*(4), 237–243.

Shorley, C. T. (1994). Use of behavioral methods with adults recovering from substance dependence. In D. K. Granvold (Ed.), *Cognitive and behavioral treatment: Methods and applications* (pp. 135–156). Pacific Grove, CA: Brooks/Cole.

Shorter, E. (1997). *A history of psychiatry: From the era of the asylum to the age of Prozac.* New York: Wiley.

Shulman, L. (1999). *The skills of helping individuals, families, groups, and communities* (4th ed.). Itasca, IL: F. E. Peacock.

Sidell, E. R. (1997). Easing transitions: Solution-focused principles and the nursing home resident's family. *Clinical Gerontologist, 18*(2), 21–41.

Siegel, D. (1999). *The developing mind.* New York: Guilford.

Silverman, M. M. (1989). Children of psychiatrically ill parents: A prevention perspective. *Hospital and Community Psychiatry, 40,* 1257–1265.

Silverstein, J. L. (1994). Power and sexuality: Influence of early object relations. *Psychoanalytic Psychology, 11,* 33–46.

Simeon, D., Guralnik, O., Gross, S., Stein, D. J., Schmeidler, J., & Hollander, E. (1998). The detection and measurement of depersonalization disorder. *Journal of Nervous and Mental Diseases, 186*(9), 536–542.

Simeon, D., Guralnik, O., & Schmeidler, J. (2001). Development of a depersonalization severity scale. *Journal of Traumatic Stress, 14*(2), 341–349.

Simeon, D., Knutelska, M., Nelson, D., & Guralnik, O. (2003). A depersonalization disorder update of 117 cases. *Journal of Clinical Psychiatry, 64*(9), 990–997.

Simon, C. E., McNeil, J. S., Franklin, C., & Cooperman, A. (1991). The family and schizophrenia: Toward a psychoeducational approach. *Families in Society, 72*(6), 323–334.

Simon, G. E. (2003). Social and economic burden of mood disorders. *Biological Psychiatry, 54*(3), 208–216.

Simpson, T. L. (2002). Women's treatment utilization and its relationship to childhood sexual abuse history and lifetime PTSD. *Substance Abuse, 23*(1), 17–30.

Singleton, S. (2002). Personal communication. Miami Shores, FL.

Sinha, R., & O'Malley, S. S. (2000). Alcohol and eating disorders: Implications for alcohol treatment and health services research. *Alcoholism: Clinical and Experimental Research, 24*(8), 1312–1319.

Sipahimalani, A., & Masand, P. S. (1997). Use of risperidone in delirium: Case reports. *Annals of Clinical Psychiatry, 9,* 105–107.

Siporin, M. (1956). Family centered casework in a psychiatric setting. *Social Casework, 37,* 167–174.

Sirey, J. A., Bruce, M. L., Alexopoulos, G. S., Perlick, D. A., Friedman, S. J., & Meyers, B. S. (2001). Stigma as a barrier to recovery. Perceived stigma and patient-rated severity of illness as predictors of antidepressant drug adherence. *Psychiatric Services, 52,* 1615–1620.

Siris, S. G. (2001). Suicide and schizophrenia. *Journal of Psychopharmacology, 15*(2), 127–135.

Sirota, P., Mosheva, T., Shabtai, H., & Korczyn, A. D. (2001). Treating tardive dyskinesia with ondansetron. *Journal of Clinical Psychopharmacology, 21*(3), 355–356.

Skodol, A. E., Oldham, J. M., & Gallaher, P. E. (1999). Axis II comorbidity of substance use disorders among patients referred for treatment of personality disorders. *American Journal of Psychiatry, 156*(5), 733–738.

Slaiku, K. A. (1990). *Crisis intervention* (2nd ed.). Boston: Allyn & Bacon.

Slattery, J. M. (2004). *Counseling diverse clients: Bringing context into therapy.* Pacific Grove, CA: Brooks/Cole.

Slavin, P. (2004). Teamwork key in managing medication. *NASW News, 49*(6), 4.

Slavney, P. R. (1994). Pseudoseizures, sexual abuse, and hermeneutic reasoning. *Comprehensive Psychiatry, 35*(6), 471–477.

Small, J., Hirsch, S., & Arvanitis, L. (1997). Quetiapine in patients with schizophrenia: A high- and low-dose double blind comparison with placebo. *Archives of General Psychiatry, 54,* 549–557.

Smalley, R. E. (1967). *Theory for social work practice.* New York: Columbia University Press.

Smith, C., & Carlson, B. E. (1997). Stress, coping and resilience in children and youth. *Social Service Review, 7,* 231–236.

Smith, G. R. Jr., Monson, R. A., & Ray, D. C. (1986). Patients with multiple unexplained symptoms: Their characteristics, functional health, and health care utilization. *Archives of Internal Medicine, 146,* 69–72.

Smith, J., & Birchwood, M. (1987). Specific and non-specific effects of educational intervention with families living with a schizophrenic relative. *British Journal of Psychiatry, 150,* 645–652.

Smith, J., & Meyers, R. (2004). *Motivating substance abusers to enter treatment: working with family members.* New York: Guilford.

Smith, N. (2002). Reunifying families affected by maternal substance abuse: Consumer and service provider perspectives on the obstacles and the need for change. *Journal of Social Work Practice in the Addictions, 2*(1), 33–53.

Smolak, L., & Levine, M. P. (1996). Adolescent transitions and the development of eating problems. In L. Smolak, M. P. Levine, & R. Striegel-Moore (Eds.), *The developmental psychopathology of eating disorders: Implications for research, prevention, and treatment* (pp. 207–233). Mahwah, NJ: Erlbaum.

Snow, K. (2002). Experiential family therapy. In J. Carlson & D. Kjos (Eds.), *Theories and strategies of family therapy* (pp. 296–316). Boston: Allyn & Bacon.

Sohn, E. (2002). The hunger artists. *U.S. News and World Report, 132*(20), 45–50.

Solomon, B. B. (1976). *Black empowerment: Social work in oppressed communities.* New York: Columbia University Press.

Solomon, D. A., Keller, M. B., Leon, A. C., Mueller, T. I., Lavori, P. W., Sea, T., Coryell, W., Warshaw, M., Turvey, C., Maser, J. D., & Endicott, J. (2000). Multiple recurrences of major depressive disorder. *American Journal of Psychiatry, 157*(2), 229–233.

Solomon, H. M. (1997). The not-so-silent couple in the individual. *Journal of Analytical Psychology, 42*(3), 383–404.

Solomon, P. (1996). Moving from psychoeducation to family education for families of adults with serious mental illness. *Psychiatric Services, 47,* 1346–1370.

Solomon, P., Draine, J., Mannion, E., & Cohen, L. G. (1997). Effectiveness of two models of brief family education: Retention of gains by family members of adults with serious mental illness. *American Journal of Orthopsychiatry, 67,* 177–186.

Solowij, N., Stephens, R. S., Roffman, R. A., Babor, T., Kadden, R., Miller, M., Christiansen, K., McRee, B., & Vendetti, J. (2002). Cognitive functioning of long-term heavy cannabis users seeking treatment. *JAMA, 287*(9), 1123–1131.

Solyom, C., & Solyom, L. (1990). A treatment program for functional paraplegia/Munchausen syndrome. *Journal of Behavioral Therapy and Experimental Psychiatry, 21,* 225–230.

Sosin, M., & Bruni, M. (2000). Personal and situational perspectives on rejection of homelessness and substance abuse program. *Social Work Research, 24*(1), 16–27.

Spanagel, R., & Zieglgänsberger, W. (1997). Anti-craving compounds for ethanol: New pharmacological tools to study addictive processes. *Trends in Pharmacological Sciences, 18,* 54–58.

Spangler, D. L. (1999). Cognitive-behavioral therapy for bulimia nervosa: An illustration. *Journal of Clinical Psychology, 55,* 699–713.

Spanos, N. P. (1996). *Multiple identities and false memories: A socio-cognitive perspective.* Washington, DC: American Psychological Association.

Spence, S. (1999). Hysterical paralyses as disorders of action. In P. W. Halligan & A. S. David (Eds.), *Conversion hysteria: Towards a cognitive neuropsychological account* (pp. 203–226). Hove, United Kingdom: Psychology Press.

Sperry, L. (1995). *Psychopharmacology and psychotherapy: Strategies for maximizing treatment outcomes.* New York: Brunner/Mazel.

Sperry, L. (Ed.). (1995a). *Handbook of diagnosis and treatment of the DSM–IV personality disorders.* Levittown, PA: Brunner/Mazel.

Sperry, L. (1999). *Cognitive therapy of DSM–IV personality disorders.* Philadelphia: Brunner/Mazel.

Sperry, L., Gudeman, J., Blackwell, B., & Faulkner, L. (1992). *Psychiatric formulation.* Washington, DC: American Psychiatric Press.

Stalker, C. A., Levene, J. E., & Coady, N. F. (1999). Solution-focused brief therapy—One model fits all? *Families in Society, 80*(5), 468–477.

Stallard, P. (2002). Cognitive behaviour therapy with children and young people: A selective review of key issues. *Behavioural and Cognitive Psychotherapy, 30*(3), 297–309.

Staples, L. (1999). Consumer empowerment in a mental health system: Stakeholder roles and responsibilities. In W. Shera & L. M. Wells (Eds.), *Empowerment in social work: Developing richer conceptual foundations* (pp. 119–141). Toronto: Canadian Scholars' Press.

Stein, D. J., Frenkel, M., Islam, M. N., & Hollander, E. (1995). An open trial of valproate in borderline personality disorder. *Journal of Clinical Psychiatry, 56*(11), 506–510.

Steinberg, M. (1994). *Structured clinical interview for DSM-IV dissociative disorders-revised* (2nd ed). Washington, DC: American Psychiatric Press.

Steinberg, M. (2000). Advances in the clinical assessment of dissociation: The SCID-D-R. *Bulletin of the Menninger Clinic, 64*(2), 146–164.

Steinberg, M., & Hall, P. (1997). The SCID-D diagnostic interview and treatment planning in dissociative disorders. *Bulletin of the Menninger Clinic, 61*(1), 108–121.

Steketee, G. (1999). *Overcoming OCD: A behavioral and cognitive protocol for the treatment of OCD.* Oakland, CA: New Harbinger.

Stevens, L. M. (2002). Cocaine addiction. *Journal of the American Medical Association, 287*(1), 146–152.

Stevenson, H. C., Reed, J., Bodison, P., & Bishop, A. (1997). Racism stress management: Racial socialization beliefs and the experience of depression and anger in African American youth. *Youth and Society, 29,* 197–222.

Stevenson, J. L., & Wright, P. S. (1999). Group dynamics. *Activities, Adaptation and Aging, 23*(3), 139–173.

Stewart, C. (2002). Family factors of low-income African-American youth associated with substance use: An exploratory analysis. *Journal of Ethnicity in Substance Abuse, 1*(1), 97–111.

Stice, E. (1999). Clinical implications of psychosocial research on bulimia nervosa and binge-eating disorder. *JCLP/In Session: Psychotherapy in Practice, 55*(6), 675–683.

Stone, G. (1999). *Suicide and attempted suicide: Methods and consequences.* New York: Carroll and Graf.

Stone, M. (1993). *Abnormalities of personality: Within and beyond the realm of treatment.* New York: Norton.

Stone, M. (1997). *Healing the mind: A history of psychiatry from antiquity to the present.* New York: Norton.

Stoudemire, A. (Ed.). (1994). *Clinical psychiatry for medical students* (2nd ed.). Philadelphia: J. B. Lippincott.

Strain, E. C., Bigelow, G. E., Liebson, I. A., & Stitzer, M. L. (1999). Moderate- vs. high-dose methadone in the treatment of opioid dependence: A randomized trial. *Journal of the American Medical Association, 281*(11), 1000–1005.

Strain, E. C., Stitzer, M. L., & Liebson, I. A. (1993). Dose-response effects of methadone in the treatment of opioid dependence. *Annals of Internal Medicine, 119*(1), 23–27.

Straussner, S. L. A. (1993). Assessment and treatment of clients with alcohol and other drug abuse problems: An overview. In S. L. A. Straussner (Ed.), *Clinical social work with substance-abusing clients* (pp. 3–32). New York: Guilford.

Straussner, S. L. A. (2004). *Clinical work with substance-abusing clients* (2nd ed.). New York: Guilford.

Streeck, U. (1999). Acting out: Interpretation and unconscious communication. *International Forum of Psychoanalysis, 8,* 135–143.

Strickland, T. L., Lin, K-M., Fu, P., Anderson, D., & Zheng, Y. (1995). Comparison of lithium ratio between African-American and Caucasian bipolar patients. *Biological Psychiatry, 37,* 325–330.

Strickland, T. L., Ranganath, V., Lin, K-M., Poland, R. E., Mendoza, R., & Smith, M. W. (1991). Psycho-pharmacological considerations in the treatment of black American populations. *Psychopharmacology Bulletin, 27,* 441–448.

Strittmatter, W. J., Saunders, A. M., Schmechel, D., Pericak-Vance, M., & Enghild, J. (1993). Apolipoprotein E: High-avidity binding to beta-amyloid and increased frequency of type 4 allele in late-onset familial Alzheimer's disease. *Proceedings of the National Academy of Sciences USA, 90*(5), 1977–1981.

Strom-Gottfried, K. (1997). The implications of managed care for social work education. *Journal of Social Work Education, 33,* 7–18.

Strom-Gottfried, K. (2002). Enacting the educator role: Principles for practice. In A. R. Roberts & G. J. Greene (Eds.), *Social workers' desk reference* (pp. 437–446). New York: Oxford Press.

Stromwall, L. K. (2002). Is social work's door open to people recovering from psychiatric disabilities? *Social Work, 47*(1), 75–83.

Stromwall, L. K., & Hurdle, D. (2003). Psychiatric rehabilitation: An empowerment-based approach to mental health services. *Health and Social Work, 28*(3), 206–214.

Stuart, G., & Laraia, M. (2001). *Principles and practice of psychiatric nursing* (7th ed.). St. Louis: Mosby.

Stuart, H., & Arboleda-Florez, J. (2001). Community attitudes toward people with schizophrenia. *Canadian Journal of Psychiatry, 46*(3), 245–252.

Stunkard, A. J. (1980). *Obesity.* Philadelphia: W. B. Saunders.

Substance Abuse and Mental Health Services Administration. (1999). *Mental health, United States, 1998.* Rockville, MD: Author.

Sue, D. W., & Sue, D. (1999). *Counseling the culturally different: Theory and practice* (3rd ed.). New York: Wiley.

Sue, D., Sue, D. W., & Sue, S. (2000). *Understanding abnormal behavior* (6th ed.). Boston: Houghton Mifflin.

Sue, S. (1999). Science, ethnicity, and bias: Where have we gone wrong? *American Psychologist, 54,* 1070–1077.

Sue, S. W., & Sue, D. (1990). *Counseling the culturally different: Theory and practice* (2nd ed.). New York: Wiley.

Sue, S. W., & Sue, D. (1999). *Counseling the culturally different: Theory and practice* (3rd ed.). New York: Wiley.

Sullivan, G., Burnam, A., & Koegel, P. (2000). Pathways to homelessness among the mentally ill. *Social Psychiatry and Psychiatric Epidemiology, 35*(10), 444–451.

Sullivan, H. S. (1953). *The interpersonal theory of psychiatry.* New York: Norton.

Sullivan, W. P. (1996). Beyond the twenty-eighth day: Case management in alcohol and drug treatment. In C. Austin & R. McClelland (Eds.), *Perspectives on case management practice* (pp. 125–144). Milwaukee: Families International, Inc.

Sullivan, W. P. (2002). Case management with substance-abusing clients. In A. R. Roberts & G. J. Greene (Eds.), *Social workers' desk reference* (pp. 492–496). New York: Oxford University Press.

Sullivan, W. P., Hartmann, D. J., Dillon, D., & Wolk, J. L. (1994). Implementing case management in alcohol and drug treatment. *Families in Society, 75,* 67–73.

Sumerall, S. W., Barke, C. R., Timmons, P. L., Oehlert, M. E., Lopez, S. J., & Trent, D. D. (1998). The adaptive counseling and therapy model and supervision of mental health care. *The Clinical Supervisor, 17,* 171–176.

Sumerel, M. B., & Borders, L. D. (1996). Addressing personal issues in supervision: Impact of counselors' experience level on various aspects of the supervisory relationship. *Counselor Education and Supervision, 35,* 268–286.

Summers, N. (2001). *Fundamentals of case management.* Pacific Grove, CA: Brooks/Cole.

Summers, N. (2003). *Fundamentals for practice with high-risk populations.* Pacific Grove, CA: Brooks/Cole.

Suominen, K., Isometsa, E., & Lonnqvist, J. (2004). Elderly suicide attempters with depression are often diagnosed only after the attempt. *International Journal of Geriatric Psychiatry, 19*(1), 35–41.

Sussal, C. M. (1992). Object relations family therapy as a model for practice. *Clinical Social Work Journal, 20,* 313–321.

Sussman, L. K., Robbins, L. N., & Earls, F. (1987). Treatment-seeking for depression by African-American and white Americans. *Social Science Medicine, 24,* 187–196.

Sutton, C. E. T., & Broken Nose, M. A. (1996). American Indian families: An overview. In M. McGoldrick, J. Giordan, & J. K. Pearce (Eds.), *Ethnicity and family therapy* (pp. 31–44). New York: Guilford.

Swan, S., & Andrews, B. (2003). The relationship between shame, eating disorders and disclosure in treatment. *British Journal of Clinical Psychology, 42,* 367–378.

Swann, A. C., Johnson, B. S., Cloninger, C. R., & Chen, Y. R. (1999). Relationships of plasma tryptophan availability to course of illness and clinical features of alcoholism: A preliminary study. *Psychopharmacology, 143,* 380–383.

Swartz, M., Blazer, D., George, L., & Landerman, R. (1988). Somatization disorder in a community population. *American Journal of Psychiatry, 143,* 1403–1408.

Swenson, C. R. (1997). *Psychology and the law* (2nd ed.). Pacific Grove, CA: Brooks/Cole.

Swenson, C. R. (1998). Clinical social work's contribution to a social justice perspective. *Social Work, 43*(6), 527–537.

Swenson, C. R. (2004). Dementia diary: A personal and professional journal. *Social Work, 49*(3), 451–460.

Swift, R. M. (1999). Drug therapy for alcohol dependence. *New England Journal of Medicine, 340*(19), 1482–1490.

Szasz, T. (2001). *Pharmacracy: Medicine and politics in America.* Westport, CT: Praeger.

Szasz, T. (2003). Psychiatry and the control of dangerousness: On the apotropaic function of the term "mental illness." *Journal of Social Work Education 39*(3), 375–381.

Szybek, K., Gard, G., & Linden, J. (2000). The physiotherapist-patient relationship: Applying a psychotherapy model. *Physiotherapy Theory and Practice, 16,* 181–193.

Takhar, J. (1999). Pimozine augmentation in a patient with drug-resistant psychosis previously treated with olanzapine. *Journal of Psychiatry and Neuroscience, 24*(3), 248–249.

Tang, M. X., Stern, Y., Marder, K., Bell, K., & Gurland, B. (1998). The APOE-epsilon 4 allele and the risk of Alzheimer's disease among African American, whites, and Hispanics. *Journal of American Medical Association, 279*(10), 751–755.

Tanofsky, M. B., Wilfley, D. E., Spurrell, E. B., Welch, R., & Brownell, K. D. (1997). Comparison of men and women with binge eating disorder. *International Journal of Eating Disorders, 21*(1), 49–54.

Tantillo, M. (1998). A relational approach to group therapy for women with bulimia nervosa: Moving from understanding to action. *International Journal of Group Psychotherapy, 48*, 477–498.

Tarsy, D., Baldessarini, R. J., & Tarasi, F. I. (2002). Effects of newer antipsychotics on extrapyramidal function. *CNS Drugs, 16*(1), 23–45.

Taubes, G. (1998). As obesity rates rise, experts struggle to explain why. *Science, 280,* 1367–1368.

Taubes, T. (1998). Healthy avenues of the mind: Psychological theory building and the influence of religion during the era of moral treatment. *American Journal of Psychiatry, 155*(8), 1001–1007.

Tavris, C. (1992). *The mismeasure of woman.* New York: Simon & Schuster.

Taylor, M. J. (2000). The influence of self-efficacy on alcohol use among American Indians. *Cultural Diversity and Ethnic Minority Psychology, 6*(2), 152–167.

Taylor, S. E. (1999). *Health psychology* (4th ed.). Boston: McGraw-Hill.

Teall, B. (2000). Using solution-oriented interventions in an ecological frame: A case illustration. *Social Work in Education, 22,* 54–61.

Teyber, E. (2000). *Interpersonal process in psychotherapy: A relational approach* (4th ed.). Pacific Grove, CA: Brooks/Cole.

Thaker, G. K., & Carpenter, W. T. (2001). Advances in schizophrenia. *Nature Medicine, 7*(6), 667–671.

Thiels, C., Schmidt, U., Treasure, J., & Garthe, R. (1998). Guided self-change for bulimia nervosa incorporating use of a self-care manual. *American Journal of Psychiatry, 155,* 947–953.

Thomas, C. L. (Ed.). (1997). *Taber's cyclopedic medical dictionary* (18th ed.). Philadelphia: F. A. Davis.

Thompson, L. W., & Gallagher-Thompson, D. (1996). Practical issues related to maintenance of mental health and positive well-being in family caregivers. In L. L. Carstensen, B. A. Edelstein, and L. Dornbrands (Eds.), *The practical handbook of clinical gerontology* (pp. 129–150). Thousand Oaks, CA: Sage.

Thorning, H., & Lukens, E. (1999). Clinical social work in psychiatry. In B. Fallon & J. Gorman (Eds.), *New York State Psychiatric Institute—American psychiatry at the centennial, 1896–1996.* New York: New York State Psychiatric Institute.

Thyer, B., & Birsinger, P. (1994). Treatment of clients with anxiety disorders. In D. K. Granvold (Ed.), *Cognitive and behavioral treatment: Methods and application* (pp. 272–282). Pacific Grove, CA: Brooks/Cole.

Tice, C. J., & Perkins, K. (1996). *Mental health issues and aging: Building on the strengths of older persons.* Pacific Grove, CA: Brooks/Cole.

Todd, R. D. (2002). Genetics of early onset bipolar affective disorder. *Current Psychiatry Reports 4*(2), 141–145.

Todd, R. D., & Botteron, K. N. (2001). Family, genetic, and imaging studies of early-onset depression. *Child and Adolescent Psychiatric Clinic of North America, 10*(2), 375–390.

Todd, R. D., & Botteron, K. N. (2002). Etiology and genetics of early-onset mood disorders. *Child and Adolescent Psychiatric Clinic of North America, 11*(3), 499–518.

Tollefson, G. D., Beasley, C. M., Tran, P. V., Street, J. S., & Krueger, J. A. (1997). Olanzapine versus haloperidol in the treatment of schizophrenia and schizophreniform disorders: Results of an international collaborative trial. *American Journal of Psychiatry, 154,* 457–465.

Torres-Gil, F., & Moga, K. B. (2001). Multiculturalism, social policy and the new aging. *The Journal of Gerontological Social Work, 36*(3/4), 13–32.

Torres-Rivera, E. (1999). Group work with Latino clients: A psychoeducational model. *Journal of Specialists in Group Work, 24,* 383–396.

Torrey, E. F. (1995). *Surviving schizophrenia* (3rd ed.). New York: Harper Perennial.

Toseland, R. W., & Rivas, R. F. (1984). *An introduction to group work practice.* New York: Macmillan.

Toseland, R. W., & Rivas, R. F. (1998). *An introduction to group work practice* (3rd ed.). Boston: Allyn & Bacon.

Toseland, R., & McCallion, P. (1997). Trends in caregiving intervention research. *Social Work Research, Special Issue, Social work Intervention Research, 21*(3), 154–164.

Toseland, R., Smith, G., & McCallion, P. (2001). Family caregivers of the frail elderly. In A. Gitterman (Ed.), *Handbook of social work practice with vulnerable and resilient populations* (pp. 548–581). New York: Columbia University Press.

Triantafillou, N. (1997). A solution-focused approach to mental health supervision. *Journal of Systemic Therapies, 16,* 305–328.

Tuckman, B. W., & Jensen, M. A. (1977). Stages of small group development revisited. *Group and Organizational Studies, 2,* 419–427.

Turner, F. (2002). Psychosocial therapy. In A. R. Roberts & G. J. Greene (Eds.), *Social workers' desk reference* (pp. 109–116). New York: Oxford Press.

Turner, S. (1997). Building on strengths: Risks and resiliency in the family, school, and community. In E. Norman (Ed.), *Drug-free youth* (pp. 95–112). New York: Garland.

Tyhurst, J. S. (1958). The role of transitional states—including disaster—in mental illness. In Walter Reed Army Institute of Research, *Symposium on Preventive and Social Psychiatry.* Washington, DC: U.S. Government Printing Office.

Tyson, K. (1999). An empowering approach to crisis intervention and brief treatment for preschool children. *Families in Society, 80*(1), 64–77.

U.S. Bureau of the Census. (1996). *Current population reports. Special studies, p. 23–190. 65+ in the United States.* Washington, DC: U.S. Government Printing Office.

Ungvarski, P. J., & Grossman, A. H. (1999). Health problems of gay and bisexual men. *Nursing Clinics of North America, 34,* 313–326.

United States Department of Health and Human Services. (2003). *Suicide in the United States.* Atlanta, GA: Centers for Disease Control and Prevention.

Valenti, A. M., & Pristach, C. A. (2001). Olanzapine therapy in treatment-resistant psychotic mood disorders: A long-term follow-up study. *The Journal of Clinical Psychiatry, 62*(7), 509–520.

Valentine, L., & Feinauer, L. L. (1993). Resilience factors associated with female survivors of childhood sexual abuse. *American Journal of Family Therapy, 21,* 216–224.

van Dalen, A. (2001). Juvenile violence and addiction: Tangled roots in childhood trauma. *Journal of Social Work Practice in the Addictions, 1*(1), 25–40.

Van der Hart, O., van der Kolk, B., & Boon, S. (1998). The treatment of dissociative disorders. In J. D. Bremner & C. R. Marmar (Eds.), *Trauma, memory, and dissociation* (pp. 3–20). Washington, DC: American Psychiatric Press.

Van Voorhis, R. M. (1998). Culturally relevant practice: A framework for teaching the psychosocial dynamics of oppression. *Journal of Social Work Education, 34*(2), 121–133.

Van Den Berg, C. M., Kazmi, Y., & Jann, M. W. (2000). Cholineterase inhibitors for the treatment of Alzheimer's disease in the elderly. *Drugs and Aging, 16*(2), 123–138.

Vandereycken, W., & Beumont, P. J. V. (Eds.). (1998). *Treating eating disorders: Ethical, legal and personal issues.* New York: New York University Press.

Vanderlin, J., Van Dyck, R., Vandereycken, W., Vertommen, H., & Verkes, R. J. (1993). The dissociation questionnaire (DIS-Q): Development and characteristics of a new self-report questionnaire. *Clinical Psychology and Psychotherapy, 1,* 21–27.

Veale, D. (2002). Cognitive behaviour therapy of body dysmorphic disorder. In D. J. Castle (Ed.), *Disorders of body image* (pp. 121–138). Petersfield, England: Wrightson Biomedical Publishing, Ltd.

Veeder, N., & Peebles-Wilkins, W. (2000). *Managed care services.* New York: Oxford University Press.

Verheul, R., Van Den Bosch, L. M., Koeter, M. W., De Ridder, M. A., Stinjen, T., & Van Den Brink, W. (2003). Dialectical behavior therapy for women with borderline personality disorder: 12-month, randomized clinical trial in The Netherlands. *British Journal of Psychiatry, 182,* 135–140.

Verma, S., & Gallagher, R. M. (2000). Evaluating and treating co-morbid pain and depression. *International Review of Psychiatry, 12*(2), 103–114.

Vermetten, E., & Bremner, J. D. (2000). Dissociative amnesia: Re-remembering traumatic memories. In G. E. Berrios & J. R. Hodges (Eds.), *Memory disorders in psychiatric practice* (pp. 400–431). New York: Cambridge University Press.

Volpicelli, J. R., Alterman, A. I., Hayasgida, M., & O'Brien, C. P. (1992). Naltrexone in the treatment of alcohol dependence. *Archives of General Psychiatry, 49,* 876–880.

Volpicelli, J. R., Rhines, K. C., Rhines, J. S., Volpicelli, L. A., Alterman, A. I., & O'Brien, C. P. (1997). Naltrexone and alcohol dependence. Role of subject compliance. *Archives of General Psychiatry, 54*(8), 737–742.

Volpicelli, J. R., Watson, N. T., King, A. C., Sherman, C. E., & O'Brien, C. P. (1995). Effects of naltrexone on alcohol "high" in alcoholics. *American Journal of Psychiatry, 152*(4), 613–615.

von Bertalanffy, L. (1968). General systems theory: A critical review. In W. Buckley (Ed.), *Modern systems research for the behavioral scientist* (pp. 11–30). Chicago: Aldine.

von Bertalanffy, L. (1968a). *General systems theory: Foundation, development, applications.* New York: George Braziller.

von Bulow, B., & Braiman, S. (2001). Eating problems. In A. Gitterman (Ed.), *Handbook of social work practice with vulnerable and resilient populations* (2nd ed., pp. 224–248). New York: Columbia University Press.

Vourlekis, B. S., Edinburg, G., & Knee, R. (1998). The rise of social work in public mental health through aftercare of people with serious mental illness. *Social Work, 43,* 567–575.

Wachtel, P. L. (2002). Psychoanalysis and the disenfranchised: From therapy to justice. *Psychoanalytic Psychology, 19,* 199–215.

Wade, C., & Tavris, C. (2003). *Psychology* (7th ed.). Upper Saddle River, NJ: Prentice Hall.

Wagnild, G. M., & Young, H. M. (1993). Development and psychometric evaluation of the resilience scale. *Journal of Nursing Measurement, 1,* 165–178.

Wahlbeck, K., Cheine, M., Essali, A., & Adams, C. (1999). Evidence of clozapine effectiveness in schizophrenia: A systematic review and meta-analysis of randomized trials. *American Journal of Psychiatry, 15,* 156, 990–999.

Wahlund, L., & Bjorlin, G. A. (1999). Delirium in clinical practice: Experiences from a specialized delirium ward. *Dementia, Geriatrics and Cognitive Disorders, 10*(5), 389–392.

Wakefield, J. C. (1992). Disorder as harmful dysfunction: A conceptual critique of DSM III-R's definition of mental disorders. *Psychological Review, 90,* 238.

Wakeman, S. (2002). Working with the center: Psychiatric rehabilitation with people who dissociate. *Psychiatric Rehabilitation Journal, 26*(2), 115–122.

Walitzer, K. S., & Connors, G. J. (1999). Treating problem drinking. *Alcohol Research & Health, 23*(2), 138–143.

Walker, J. R., & Kjernisted, K. D. (2000). Fear: The impact and treatment of social phobia. *Journal of Psychopharmacology, 14*(Suppl. 11), S13–S23.

Walker, L. E. A. (1994). Are personality disorders gender biased? Yes. In S. A. Kirk & S. D. Einbender (Eds.), *Controversial issues in mental health* (pp. 21–30). Boston: Allyn & Bacon.

Waller, N., & Ross, C. A. (1997). The prevalence and biometric structure of pathological dissociation in the general population: Taxometric and behavior genetic findings. *Journal of Abnormal Psychology, 106,* 499–510.

Walsh, B. B., Gillespie, C. K., Greer, J. M., & Eanes, B. E. (2002). Influence of dyadic mutuality on counselor trainee willingness to self-disclose clinical mistakes to supervisors. *The Clinical Supervisor, 21*(2), 83–98.

Walsh, B. T., & Devlin, M. J. (1998). Eating disorders: Progress and problems. *Science, 280,* 1387–1390.

Walsh, B. T., & Kahn, C. B. (1997). Diagnostic criteria for eating disorders: Current concerns and future directions. *Psychopharmacology Bulletin, 33*(3), 369–372.

Walsh, B. T., Stewart, J. W., Roose, S. P., Gladis, M., & Glassman, A. H. (1984). Treatment of bulimia with phenelzine: A double-blind, placebo-controlled study. *Archives of General Psychiatry, 41*(11), 1105–1109.

Walsh, B. T., Steward, J. W., Wright, W., Harrison, W., Roose, S. P., & Glassman, A. (1982). Treatment of bulimia with monoamine-oxidase inhibitors. *American Journal of Psychiatry, 139,* 1629–1630.

Walsh, F. (1995). From family damage to family challenge. In R. H. Mikesell, D. D. Lusterman, & S. H. McDaniel (Eds.), *Integrating family therapy: Handbook of family psychology and system theory.* Washington, DC: American Psychological Association.

Walsh, F. (1996). The concept of family resilience: Crisis and challenge. *Family Process, 35,* 261–281.

Walsh, F. (1998). *Strengthening family resilience.* New York: Guilford.

Walsh, F. (Ed.). (1999). *Spiritual resources in family therapy.* New York: Guilford.

Walsh, J. (1998). Psychopharmacological treatment of bipolar disorder. *Research on Social Work Practice, 8*(4), 406–425.

Walsh, J. (2000). *Clinical case management with persons having mental illness: A relationship-based perspective.* Pacific Grove, CA: Brooks/Cole.

Walsh, J. (2002). Social workers as therapists. In K. Bentley (Ed.), *Social work practice in mental health: Contemporary roles, tasks and techniques* (pp. 73–99). Pacific Grove, CA: Brooks/Cole.

Walsh, J. (2002a). Supervising the countertransference reactions of case managers. *The Clinical Supervisor, 21*(2), 129–144.

Walsh, J., & Bentley, K. J. (2002). Psychopharmacology basics. In A. R. Roberts & G. J. Greene (Eds.), *Social workers' desk reference* (pp. 646–651). New York: Oxford University Press.

Walsh, J., & Hewitt, H. (1996). Facilitating an effective process in treatment groups with persons having serious mental illness. *Social Work with Groups, 19*(1), 5–18.

Walsh, J., Walsh, W. M., & McGraw, J. A. (1996). *Essentials of family therapy: A therapist's guide to eight approaches.* New York: McGraw-Hill.

Walter, J. L., & Peller, J. E. (1992). *Becoming solution-focused in brief therapy.* New York: Brunner/Mazel.

Walters, G. D. (1994). The drug lifestyle: One pattern or several? *Psychology of Addictive Behaviors, 8,* 8–13.

Walters, K. L. (1999). Urban American Indian identity attitudes and acculturation styles. *Journal of Human Behavior in the Social Environment, 2*(1/2), 163–178.

Warn, D. J. (1997). Recovery issues of substance-abusing gay men. In S. L. A. Straussner & E. Zelvin (Eds.), *Gender and addictions.* Northvale, NJ: Jason-Aronson.

Warner, J. (2001). Divining dementia. *Journal of Neurology, Neurosurgery, and Psychiatry, 71*(3), 289–299.

Warwick, H. M. C., & Salkovskis, P. M. (1990). Hypochondriasis. *Behavior Research and Therapy, 28,* 105–107.

Waters, R. (2003). The wounds of war: Treating combat stress on the modern battlefield. *Psychotherapy Networker, 27*(4), 13–14.

Watzlawick, P., Beavin-Barelas, J., & Jackson, D. D. (1967). *Pragmatics of human communication: A study of interactional patterns, pathologies and paradoxes.* New York: Norton.

Watzlawick, P., Weakland, J., & Fisch, R. (1974). *Change: Problem formation and problem resolution.* New York: Norton.

Weaver, H. N. (1999). Indigenous people and the social work profession: Defining culturally competent services. *Social Work, 44*(3), 217–225.

Weaver, H. N. (2000). Activism and American Indian issues: Opportunities and roles for social workers. *Journal of Progressive Human Services, 11*(1), 3–22.

Weaver, H. N. (2005). First nations peoples: Ethnic-specific communities of people. In K. L. Guadalupe and D. Lum (Eds.), *Multidimensional contextual practice: Diversity and transcendence* (pp. 287–307). Belmont, CA: Brooks/Cole.

Webb, W. (1999). *Solutioning.* (pp. 219–319). Philadelphia: Taylor and Francis Group.

Webster, D. C., Vaughn, K., & Martinez, R. (1994). Introducing solution-focused approaches to staff in inpatient psychiatric settings. *Archives of Psychiatric Nursing, 8,* 254–261.

Weekes, C. (1990). *Peace from nervous suffering.* New York: Penguin / G. P. Putnam.

Weekes, C. (1999). *Pass through panic.* New York: Penguin / G. P. Putnam.

Weick, A. (1983). Issues in overturning a medical model of social work practice. *Social Work, 28,* 467–471.

Weick, A., & Chamberlain, R. (1997). Putting problems in their place: Further explorations in the strengths perspective. In D. Saleebey (Ed.), *The strengths perspective in social work practice* (2nd ed., pp. 39–48). White Plains, NY: Longman.

Weiner-Davis, M. (1987). Building on pre-treatment change to construct a therapeutic solution. *Journal of Marital and Family Therapy, 13*(4), 359–363.

Weintraub, M. I. (1995). Chronic pain in litigation: What is the relationship? *Neurology Clinics, 13*(2), 341–349.

Weiss, M. G. (1995). Eating disorders and disordered eating in different cultures. *Psychiatric Clinics of North America, 18,* 537–553.

Weissman, M. M., Myers, J. K., & Ross, C. E. (Eds.). (1986). *Community surveys of psychiatric disorders.* New Brunswick, NJ: Rutgers University Press.

Weissman, M. M., Warner, V., Wickramaratne, P., Moreau, D., & Olfson, M. (1997). Offspring of depressed parents: 10 years later. *Archives of General Psychiatry, 54,* 932–940.

Welch, I. D. (1998). *The path of psychotherapy: Matters of the heart.* Pacific Grove, CA: Brooks/Cole.

Wells, R., & Giannetti, V. (Eds.). (1993). *Handbook of the brief psychotherapies.* New York: Plenum.

Wernet, S. (1999). *Managed care in the human services.* Chicago: Lyceum Books.

West, C. G., Reed, D. M., & Gildengorin, G. L. (1998). Can money buy happiness? Depressive symptoms in an affluent older population. *Journal of the American Geriatric Society, 46,* 49–57.

Wetchler, J. L. (1990). Solution-focused supervision. *Family Therapy, 17*(2), 129–138.

Whitaker, C. A. (1965). Countertransference in the family treatment of schizophrenia. In I. Boszormenyi-Nagy & J. L. Framo (Eds.), *Intensive family therapy.* (pp. 323–341). New York: Harper and Row.

Whitaker, C. A., & Bumberry, W. M. (1988). *Dancing with a family: A symbolic-experiential approach.* New York: Brunner/Mazel.

Whitaker, J. K. (1974). *Social treatment.* New York: Aldine.

White, J. R., & Freeman, A. S. (Eds.). (2000). *Cognitive-behavioral group therapy for specific problems and populations.* Washington, DC: American Psychological Association.

White, M. (1995). *Re-authoring lives: Interviews and essays.* Adelaide, South Australia: Dulwich Centre Publications.

Whitlatch, C. J., Feinberg, L. F., & Stevens, E. J. (1999). Predictors of institutionalization for persons with Alzheimer's disease and the impact of family caregivers. *Journal of Mental Health and Aging, 5*(3), 275–288.

Whittal, M. L., & McLean, P. (2002). Group cognitive-behavioral therapy for obsessive compulsive disorder. In R. O. Frost & G. Steketee (Eds.), *Cognitive approaches to obsessions and compulsions: Theory, assessment, and treatment.* (pp. 417–433). Amsterdam, Netherlands: Pergamon/Elsevier Science.

Widom, C. S. (1999). Posttraumatic stress disorder in abused and neglected children grown up. *American Journal of Psychiatry, 156*(8), 1223–1229.

Wild, T. C., Cunningham, J., & Hobdon, K. (1998). When do people believe that alcohol treatment is effective? The importance of perceived client and therapist motivation. *Psychology of Addictive Behaviors, 12*, 93–100.

Wilhelm, S., Otto, M. W., Lohr, B., & Deckersbach, T. (1999). Cognitive behavior group therapy for body dysmorphic disorder: A case series. *Behavior and Research Therapy, 37*(1), 71–75.

Wilker, H. I., Gray, S. W., & Zide, M. R. (1998). A solution-orientated model for bereavement groups in rural areas: Advantages and more advantages. Paper presented at the Association for Death Education and Counseling (ADEC), Twentieth Annual Conference. Chicago, Illinois.

Willie, C. V., Rieker, P. P., Kramer, B. M., & Brown, B. S. (Eds.). (1995). *Mental health, racism, and sexism* (Rev. Ed.). Pittsburgh: University of Pittsburgh Press.

Wilson, G. T., Agras, W. S., Kraemer, H., Fairburn, C. C., & Walsh, B. T. (2002). Cognitive-behavioral therapy for bulimia nervosa: time course and mechanisms of change. *Journal of Consulting and Clinical Psychology, 70*(2), 267–275.

Wilson, G. T., Loeb, K. L., Walsh, B. T., Labouvie, E., Petkova, E., Liu, S., & Waternaux, C. (1999). Psychological versus pharmacological treatments of bulimia nervosa: Predictors and processes of change. *Journal of Counseling and Clinical Psychology, 67*, 451–459.

Wilson, J. J., Rojas, N., Haapanen, R., & Duxbury, E. (2000). Substance abuse and criminal recidivism: A prospective study of adolescents. *Child Psychiatry and Human Development, 21*(4), 297–312.

Wilson, S., & Stevens, B. (1999). Introduction to groups. *Activities, Adaptation and Aging, 23*(3), 135–137.

Wineburgh, M. (1998). Ethics, managed care, and outpatient psychotherapy. *Clinical Social Work Journal, 26*(4), 433–443.

Winger, G., Hofmann, F. G., & Woods, J. H. (1992). *A handbook on drug and alcohol abuse: The biomedical aspects* (3rd ed.). New York: Oxford University Press.

Winslow, R. (1998, January 20). Health-care inflation kept in check last year. *The Wall Street Journal,* pp. B1, B4.

Wirz-Justice, A., Graw, P., Krauchi, K., et al. (1993). Light therapy in seasonal affective disorder is independent of time of day or circadian phase. *Archives of General Psychiatry, 50*(12), 929–937.

Witkin, S. L. (2000). Ethics-r-us. *Social Work, 45*(3), 197–201.

Wiztum, E. B., Maragalit, H., & van der Hart, O. (2002). Combat-induced dissociative amnesia: Review and case example of generalized dissociative amnesia. *Journal of Trauma and Dissociation, 3*(2), 35–55.

Wolfe, J., Erickson, D. J., & Sharkansky, E. J. (1999). Course and predictors of posttraumatic stress disorder among Gulf War veterans: A prospective analysis. *Journal of Consulting and Clinical Psychology 67*(4), 520–528.

Wolfe, K. B. (2003). Treatment transitions: Improving patient recovery through effective collaboration. *Eating Disorders Review, 14*(5), 1–3.

Wolin, S. J., & Wolin, S. (1993). *The resilient self: How survivors of troubled families rise above adversity.* New York: Villard.

Woodruff-Borden, J. (2002). Anxious parents, anxious kids. *Journal of Clinical Child and Adolescent Psychology, 31*(3), 364–374.

Woods, M., & Hollis, F. (2000). *Casework: Psychosocial therapy* (5th ed.). New York: McGraw-Hill.

Woodside, M., & McClam, T. (1998). *Generalist case management: A method of human services delivery.* Pacific Grove, CA: Brooks/Cole.

Woodstock, J. (2001). Being, noticing, knowing: The emergence of resilience in group work. In T. Kelly, T. Berman-Rossi, & S. Palombo (Eds.), *Group Work: Strategies for strengthening resiliency.* (pp. 5–17). New York: Haworth Press.

Wright, K. (2000). The secret and all-consuming obsessions: Eating disorders. In D. Capuzzi & D. R. Gross (Eds.), *Youth at risk: A prevention resource for counselors, teachers and parents* (3rd ed., pp. 197–242). Alexandria, VA: American Counseling Association.

Wyatt, R. J., Damiani, L., Henter-Ioline, D. (1998). First-episode schizophrenia: Early intervention and medication discontinuation in the context of course and treatment. *British Journal of Psychiatry, 172* (Suppl. 33), 77–83.

Wykes, T., Tarrier, N., & Lewis, S. (Eds.). *Outcome and innovation in psychological treatment of schizophrenia.* Chichester, England: Wiley.

Yager, J. (1994). Eating disorders. In A. Stoudemire (Ed.), *Clinical psychiatry for medical students* (pp. 355–371). Philadelphia: J. B. Lippincott.

Yalom, I. (1995). *The theory and practice of group psychotherapy* (4th ed.). New York: Basic Books.

Yehuda, R. (1998). Psychoneuroendocrinology of post-traumatic stress disorder. *Psychiatric Clinics of North America, 21*(2), 359–379.

Yellow Horse Brave Heart, M. (1998). The return to the sacred path: Healing the historical trauma and historical unresolved grief response among the Lakota through a psychoeducational group intervention. *Smith College Studies in Social Work, 68*(3), 287–305.

Yeo, G., Gallagher-Thompson, D., & Lieberman, M. (1996). Variations in dementia characteristics by ethnic category. In G. Yeo & D. Gallagher-Thompson (Eds.), *Ethnicity and the dementias* (pp. 21–30). Washington, DC: Taylor and Francis.

Young, A. S., Forquer, S. L., Tran, A., Starzynski, M., & Shatkin, J. (2000). Identifying clinical competencies that support rehabilitation and empowerment in individuals with severe mental illness. *Journal of Behavioral Health Services and Research, 27*(3), 321–333.

Young, S. L., & Ensing, D. S. (1999). Exploring recovery from the perspective of people with psychiatric disabilities. *Psychiatric Rehabilitation Journal, 22*(3), 219–231.

Zanarini, M. C. (1997). Evolving perspectives on the etiology of borderline personality disorder. In M. C. Zanarini (Ed.), *Progress in psychiatry: Role of sexual abuse in the etiology of borderline personality disorder* (vol. 49, pp. 1–14). Washington, DC: American Psychiatry Press.

Zanarini, M. C., & Frankenburg, F. R. (1997). Pathways to the development of borderline personality disorder. *Journal of Personality Disorders, 11*(1), 93–104.

Zanarini, M.C., Frankenburg, F. R., Reich, D. B., Marino, M. F., Lewis, R. E., Williams, A. A., & Khera, G. S. (2000). Biparental failure in the childhood experience of borderline patients. *Journal of Personality Disorders, 14*(3), 264–273.

Zapka, J. G., McCusker, J., Stoddard, A. M., & Morrison, C. (1990). Psychosocial factors and AIDS-related behavior of homosexual men: Measurement and associations. *Evaluation and the Health Professions, 13,* 283–297.

Zarate, R., & Agras, W. S. (1994, May). Psychosocial treatment of phobia and panic disorders. *Psychiatry: Interpersonal and Biological Processes, 57*(2), 133–141.

Zarit, S. H., & Edwards, A. B. (1996). Family caregiving: Research and clinical intervention. In R. T. Woods, (Ed.), *Handbook of the clinical psychology of aging* (pp. 331–368). New York: Wiley.

Zastrow, C. (1999). *The practice of social work* (6th ed.). Pacific Grove, CA: Brooks/Cole.

Zelvin, E. (1997). Codependency issues of substance-abusing women. In Straussner, S. L. A., & Zelvin, E. (Eds.). *Gender and addictions*. Northvale, NJ: Jason-Aronson.

Zide, M. R., & Cherry, A. L. (1992). A typology of runaway youth: An empirically based definition. *Child and Adolescent Social Work Journal, 9*(2), 155–168.

Zide, M. R., & Gray, S. W. (1999). *Bereavement groups: Exploring the possibilities of solution-focused grief therapy.* Barry University, School of Social Work. Association for the Advancement of Social Work with Groups (AASWG), 16th Annual Fall Conference, Miami Shores, Florida.

Zide, M. R., & Gray, S. W. (2000). The solutioning process: Merging the genogram and the solution-focused model of practice. *Journal of Family Social Work, 4*(1), 3–19.

Zide, M. R., & Gray, S. W. (2001). *Psychopathology: A competency-based assessment model for social workers.* Pacific Grove, CA: Brooks/Cole.

Zide, N. (2002). Personal communication. October 12, 2002. Ft. Lauderdale, FL.

Ziedonis, D., & Brady, K. (1997). Dual diagnosis in primary care. *Medical Clinics of North America, 81,* 1017–1036.

Zimmerman, M. (1994). *Interview guide for evaluating DSM-IV psychiatric disorders and the mental status examination*. Philadelphia: Psych Press Products.

Zimmerman, M. A., & Arunkumar, R. (1994). Resiliency research: Implications for schools and policy. *Social Policy Report*. Ann Arbor, MI: Society for Research in Child Development.

Zuercher-White, E. (1999). *Overcoming panic disorder and agoraphobia: A cognitive-restructuring and exposure-based protocol for the treatment of panic and agoraphobia.* Oakland, CA: New Harbinger Press.

Zygmunt, A., Olfson, M., Boyer, C. A., & Mechanic, D. (2002). Interventions to improve medication adherence in schizophrenia. *American Journal of Psychiatry 159*(10), 1653–1664.

Name Index

Subject Index